London's West End

London's West End

Creating the Pleasure District, 1800–1914

ROHAN McWILLIAM

OXFORD
UNIVERSITY PRESS

OXFORD

UNIVERSITY PRESS

Great Clarendon Street, Oxford, OX2 6DP,
United Kingdom

Oxford University Press is a department of the University of Oxford.
It furthers the University's objective of excellence in research, scholarship,
and education by publishing worldwide. Oxford is a registered trade mark of
Oxford University Press in the UK and in certain other countries

© Rohan McWilliam 2020

The moral rights of the author have been asserted

First Edition published in 2020

Impression: 1

Published in the United States of America by Oxford University Press
198 Madison Avenue, New York, NY 10016, United States of America

British Library Cataloguing in Publication Data

Data available

Library of Congress Control Number: 2020931645

ISBN 978-0-19-882341-4

Printed and bound by
CPI Group (UK) Ltd, Croydon, CR0 4YY

Links to third party websites are provided by Oxford in good faith and
for information only. Oxford disclaims any responsibility for the materials
contained in any third party website referenced in this work.

For Kelly Boyd

'always *the* woman'

Acknowledgements

London's West End really commenced at the age of twelve when I was allowed by my parents to travel up to town by myself. Walking up the Charing Cross Road (then a lot dingier than it is now) bound for Foyle's bookshop, I was taken over by the feeling that the city was a huge adventure and the West End the essential place to be. I already knew that the Odeon Leicester Square was the greatest of all cinemas and would come to love the theatres, where, in my teenage years, I could only afford to watch plays from the back of the balcony. Another point of origin for the book was the interval during West End shows where I would walk round the auditorium and wander at the sumptuous curtain, the boxes, and the elaborate use of red velvet. Whilst I hope this book shows that I have learned to think more critically about the pleasure district, I have never entirely lost these feelings of awe.

All books constitute a journey and I have been sustained on my path by friends, colleagues, and family. My only regret is that my mother, Charmian, did not live to see this volume. She often asked about it and wondered why it was taking so long. Mum hailed from the country that used to be called (when she was born) Ceylon, yet had a huge love of her adopted nation. She touched a large number of people because she always looked for the best in others and spoke to them as though they were their best selves. Any achievements in life, she taught, are less important than trying to be a good person. My father, the artist Allan McWilliam, showed his son that we can only be complete through living in the imagination. We all need arrows of desire. My aunt Fay (my other mother) gave me my love of books, the greatest of gifts. My sister Tara, her husband Steven Bagley, and their much-loved children, Alex and Saskia, have made a huge difference.

There are so many people to thank that I will not be able to list everyone. From lunch at the Ivy to cocktails at the Duke's Hotel, Rachel 'Tink' Acland prowled every inch of the West End with me whilst teaching me more than she knew. Historian, actor, and jazz musician, Peter Bailey has been the best of mentors—an inspiration to anyone working on popular culture. Tracy Davis and Jerry White both shared their prodigious expertise on, respectively, theatre and London history right at the start of the project. Michael Diamond kindly showed me his magnificent collection of theatre ephemera and allowed me to use images from it. His enthusiasm for the project and for nineteenth-century popular literature and theatre meant a great deal. Chris Law (with whom I have written and performed shows) will be surprised to read about how great an influence he has been on these pages. Paul Maloney has been an admired friend since our days at university; his pioneering work on Scottish music hall is a counterpart to what I have attempted here. Jim Obelkevich shared generously his astonishing knowledge but, even better, his time. Gillian Piggott and her husband, the actor Andrew Jarvis, have been true friends and champions. Days spent at their remarkable home in Clenchwarton are treasured memories. Susie Steinbach and Tony Taylor remain my lodestars in this profession, combining brilliant scholarship with personal generosity and a dedication to the right causes.

I was hugely privileged during my presidency of the British Association for Victorian Studies (BAVS) to work with a group of gifted scholars brought together by the warm, interdisciplinary atmosphere we strived to create. Serving on the BAVS executive with them is one of the great honours of my life. The same would be true of the editorial board at the *Journal of Victorian Culture*. I could not hope for better colleagues than the ones I possess at Anglia Ruskin University. Every day we work together to challenge and inspire our students, placing them at the centre of everything we do. I would particularly like to thank Alison Ainley, Lucy Bland, Paul Bloomfield, Liz Bradbury, Marlene Buick, Clarissa Campbell Orr, Richard Carr, Jonathan Davis, Susan Flavin, Martin Hewitt, Sean Lang (a force of nature), and Will Tullett.

The following have provided guidance, references, support, or friendship (or all of these): Grace Allen, Judith Allen, Sarah Allen, Brenda Assael, Belinda Beaton, Fabrice Bensimon, Helen Berry, Helen Blier, Wendy Bracewell, Dympna Callaghan, Christina Casley, George Casley, the late Malcolm Chase, Sonia Constantinou, James W. Cook, Rachel Bryant Davis, Richard Dennis, Michael Diamond, Jonathan Drori, David Drummond, Heidi Egginton, Kathryn Ferry, Margot Finn, Barbara Franses, Simon Franses, John Gardner, Jill Garrow, Wendy George ('the Wendy Lady'), Anne Goldgar, Vicky Greenaway, Simon Gunn, Peter Gurney, Sasha Hamlin, Mark Hampton, Ian Haywood, Clare Head, Patrick Higgins, Tim Hitchcock, Robert Hodge, Eilidh Innes, Louis James, Dom Christopher Jamison OSB, Stephen Jarvis, David Kathman, Bernadette Kiernan, Helen Kingstone, Marius Kwint, Sarah Louise Lill, Ring Mei-Han Low, Elizabeth Ludlow, Toireasa McCann, Paul McDermott, Peter Mandler, Lucinda Mathews-Jones, Thelma May, David Mayer, Clare Midgley, the late Sir Jonathan Miller, Rosemary Mitchell, the late Jane Moody, Kemille Moore, Frank Mort, Paul Myers, Katrina Navickas, Lynda Nead, Kate Newey, Polly North, Mary O'Dowd, Robert O'Kell, Neal Pye, Stephen Ridgwell, Krisztina Robert, Helen Rogers, Tom Ruffles, Deborah Sugg Ryan, Rachel Ryder, Mary Shannon, Bob Shoemaker, Andy Simpson, Michael Slater, Daniel Snowman, Catherine Turner, Peter Tyldesley, Carolyn Williams, Sue Wiseman, Anne Witchard, Peter Yeandle and Sarah J. Young. I would also like to thank Cathryn Steele, Katie Bishop, Christine Ranft, Jayashree Thirumaran, and the team at Oxford University Press.

This book has been researched in a wide range of libraries and archives. I would particularly like to thank Athene Bain and the University of Bristol Theatre Collection, the British Library, the Courtauld Library, the London Library, the

London Metropolitan Archives, the National Archives, the Royal Opera House Archives (Jane Fowler and Julia Creed), the Savoy Hotel Archive (Susan Scott), the National Art Library and the Theatre Collection (both Victoria and Albert Museum), the Westminster City Archives (Adrian Autton, Gillian Butler, and Alison Kenney) and the Westminster Reference Library. A special mention should be made of Matthew Lloyd and the Arthur Lloyd webpage (http://www. arthurlloyd.co.uk/), which has proved an invaluable reference work. Martin Hewitt, Lee Jackson, and Tim Wales read individual chapters. None is responsible for any errors and failings in the book.

Kelly Boyd read and edited the manuscript numerous times. This was the least of her contribution. As historian, as cinema lover, and, most of all, as my wife, Kelly is everything to me. A long time ago I learned that she was always the smartest person in the room. Any room with Kelly in it is where I want to be.

Contents

List of Illustrations and Maps   xiii

List of Abbreviations   xv

Introduction   1

PART ONE   THE ARISTOCRATIC WEST END, 1800–50

1. Drury Lane, 1800   13

2. Arcadia   21

3. The Beau Monde   41

4. The Histrionic Art   63

5. Curiosity   84

PART TWO   THE BOURGEOIS WEST END, 1850–1914

6. The Making of the West End, 1850–1914   107

7. Capital of Pleasure   119

8. Capital of Culture   137

PART THREE   SHOWBIZ

9. The Age of Boucicault, 1843–80   153

10. Theatreland, 1880–1914   173

11. The Populist Palatial   199

12. Gaiety Nights   219

PART FOUR   OUR HOSPITALITY

13. Eating Out   249

14. Grand Hotel   264

15. Shopocracy   279

PART FIVE HEART OF EMPIRE

16. The Other West End   301

Appendix: List of West End Theatres and some Music Venues, 1800–1914   317
Bibliography   319
Index   353

List of Illustrations and Maps

Illustrations

1.1 Map of the West End in 1801	19
2.1 1818 plan for the New Street (Regent Street)	27
2.2 Regent Street Quadrant	29
2.3 The Burlington Arcade	31
3.1 King's Theatre/Her Majesty's Theatre in the early nineteenth century	45
3.2 Tom and Jerry in the saloon at Covent Garden	49
3.3 The Cider Cellars	56
3.4a and b The *Nobby Songster*	58–9
4.1 The Sans Pareil Theatre	73
5.1 Robert Barker's panorama in Leicester Square	89
5.2 Madame Warton in the role of 'Innocence' at the Walhalla, Leicester Square	95
5.3 Wyld's Great Globe in Leicester Square	97
5.4 Egyptian Hall, *c*.1816	99
6.1 Piccadilly Circus	108
7.1 Frederick Godfrey, *The Electric Galop* (1878)	126
7.2 Alhambra stage door, 1890s	129
7.3 Marie Studholme	131
8.1 St. James's Hall	142
9.1 The Princess's Theatre, Oxford Street	155
9.2 The rebuilt Adelphi Theatre, 1858	162
10.1 The Haymarket Polka	186
10.2 Her Majesty's Theatre, London	195
11.1 Oxford Music Hall programme, 1874	201
11.2 The back of an 1890s Empire Variety programme	203
11.3 The London Pavilion 1904	207
11.4a and b London Pavilion programme	209–10
12.1 The London Coliseum by night	220
12.2 Gaiety Theatre programme	225
12.3 Gabrielle Ray *carte de visite*	228
12.4 Marie Studholme *carte de visite*	229

12.5 The Alhambra, Leicester Square   232

12.6 Alhambra programme   233

12.7 The London Coliseum   240

13.1 The Gaiety Theatre restaurant, early twentieth century   252

13.2 Royal Adelaide Gallery   261

14.1 Morley's Hotel   269

14.2 The original courtyard at the Savoy: *Souvenir of Savoy Hotel*   271

14.3 A private sitting room at the Savoy: *Souvenir of Savoy Hotel*   273

14.4 Café à la Turque: *Souvenir of Savoy Hotel*   274

14.5 Hotel Cecil   275

14.6 Palm Court, Hotel Cecil   277

15.1 Arthur Liberty choosing a new design   292

15.2 Liberty's Japanese furniture   293

Maps

4.1   West End theatres and some key music venues in 1800   66

9.1   West End Theatres and some key music venues in 1860   158

10.1 West End theatres in 1914   174

10.2 West End music venues in 1914   175

List of Abbreviations

BL   British Library
HO   Home Office Papers (The National Archives)
ODNB   The Oxford Dictionary of National Biography
PP   Parliamentary Papers
TNA   The National Archives

Introduction

The Pleasure District

'When a man is tired of London, he is tired of life.' So said that great Londoner Doctor Johnson. Even today, when many want to see the thing called 'life', they head for London's West End. The names in lights, the grandeur of Regent Street, Eros in Piccadilly Circus, premieres at one of Leicester Square's majestic cinemas, the street performers in Covent Garden, the dazzle of Shaftesbury Avenue show-business, a dinner at the Savoy, the dark pleasures of Soho, the retail therapy of Oxford Street department stores; these are what most people think of when they imagine the West End. Together, they comprise the greatest of all pleasure districts.

This is the first of a projected two-volume work that explores how the West End came to be. It analyses the period from 1800–1914 (the second volume will bring the story up to the present). Although scholars have addressed some aspects of West End life (especially its theatres), this is the first ever history of the district which was a substantial force for cultural change in the nineteenth century.[1] What follows is both a free-standing history of the West End but also an analysis of its multiple meanings and experiences. I argue the pleasure district provides for visitors an education in the nature of metropolitan culture. It is a network of sophisticated business enterprises but also offers a way of understanding popular and material culture, the lives of both sexes, social class, and the identities created by buildings and spaces. My purpose is to explain why the West End became more than just an area in the centre of the metropolis but, rather, one that helped

---

[1] For key recent cultural histories that include the West End, see Christopher Breward, *The Hidden Consumer: Masculinities, Fashion and City Life, 1860-1914* (Manchester: Manchester University Press, 1999); Lynda Nead, *Victorian Babylon: People, Streets and Images in Nineteenth Century London* (London: Yale University Press, 2000); Erika Diane Rappaport, *Shopping for Pleasure: Women in the Making of London's West End* (Princeton, NJ: Princeton University Press, 2000); Jim Davis and Victor Emeljanow, *Reflecting the Audience: London Theatregoing, 1840-1880* (Hatfield: University of Hertfordshire Press, 2001); Matt Cook, *London and the Culture of Homosexuality, 1885-1914* (Cambridge: Cambridge University Press, 2003); Matt Houlbrook, *Queer London: Perils and Pleasures in the Sexual Metropolis, 1918-1957* (Chicago: University of Chicago Press, 2005); Frank Mort, *Capital Affairs: London and the Making of the Permissive Society* (London: Yale University Press, 2010); Jacky Bratton, *The Making of the West End Stage: Marriage, Management and the Mapping of Gender in London, 1830-1870* (Cambridge: Cambridge University Press, 2011); Julia Laite, *Common Prostitutes and Ordinary Citizens: Commercial Sex in London, 1885-1960* (Basingstoke: Palgrave Macmillan, 2012); Judith R. Walkowitz, *Nights Out: Life in Cosmopolitan London* (London: Yale University Press, 2012).

London's West End: Creating the Pleasure District, 1800–1914. Rohan McWilliam, Oxford University Press (2020).
© Rohan McWilliam.
DOI: 10.1093/oso/9780198823414.001.0001

shape the modern imagination. But what do I understand by the 'West End'? The term has considerable slippage and is a very different term from 'West London'. When many people in the nineteenth century used it, it meant the luxury world of Mayfair and St James's. When I employ the term, however, I mean the pleasure district: essentially, the area bordered by Bond Street on the west, Oxford Street on the north, (what is now) Kingsway on the east, and the river or the Strand on the south. This area had (and has) a distinct character. By 1914 there were forty-three major theatre or music venues in what was roughly a square mile (and this does not count, for example, pubs that were licensed for music).[2] Between 1906 and 1914, thirty-five cinemas were established in the West End. There were also large numbers of restaurants, galleries, hotels, and department stores. This clustering of cultural locations set the West End apart from every other district in London. Whatever else the West End was, it was not suburban.

The 'West End' is, in many ways, a construction: a form of imaginative mapping. Should we shift our gaze a few blocks over in any direction (say, over to Green Park or Holborn), we would see the area in a slightly different way. Much of what we associate with the West End can be found elsewhere. The City of London, for example, developed restaurants for a mass clientele at least as much as the West End did.[3] Nor has the West End ever enjoyed a monopoly on theatre. The playhouses south of the river in the nineteenth century were vibrant places that, in many ways, met the needs of working-class audiences more effectively than West End venues. Yet the centre of London has its own particular atmosphere and dynamic that this book seeks to trace and explain.

The meaning of a 'pleasure district' is not as straightforward as it might appear. Towns devoted to leisure, such as seaside resorts and spas, can reasonably be described as pleasure districts. A Google search for the term throws up references to 'red light districts'. This is different from the way I am using the expression but the latter connection illuminates the linkages to the conspicuous sexuality and eroticism that characterize such areas (as we will see in the discussion of the numerous prostitutes who thronged the Haymarket and the music halls of the West End). When I use the term, I am drawing attention to areas within the interstices of cities where recreation, rather than production, administration, or domesticity, became dominant. These areas created networks of culture, entertainment, fashion, and retail, and developed a creative energy through bringing different forms of enterprise together. In Britain, they were the product of the eighteenth-century urban renaissance which produced the demand for what Peter Borsay terms 'high status leisure'.[4] In some towns, the pleasure district was

---

[2] See Appendix.

[3] Brenda Assael, *The London Restaurant, 1840–1914* (Oxford: Oxford University Press, 2018).

[4] Peter Borsay, *The English Urban Renaissance: Culture and Society in the Provincial Town, 1660–1770* (Oxford: Clarendon Press, 1989), p. 117. See also Neil McKendrick, John Brewer, and

the high street which had shops and entertainment centres. Whatever the form, they had a magnetic attraction which made people gravitate there and were vital for the development of fashion, style, and taste. Modern cities tended to produce such areas from Times Square in New York to La Rambla in Barcelona, and Shinjuku in Tokyo. Pleasure districts enjoyed considerable imaginative space as emblems of the modern city but they need to be more strongly integrated into urban history in future.

How did they work (both by day and by night)? Remarkably, few historians have addressed this issue.[5] Yet the creation of theatres, restaurants, and hotels were integral to urbanization itself. What we find in pleasure districts is a way of life based on perpetual stimulation: the juxtaposition of shops, art, performance spaces, traffic, people, posters, advertisements, food, alcohol, exoticism of all kinds. This captures the impact of a stroll up Shaftesbury Avenue. Pleasure districts confer alternative forms of identity upon spectators. These are spaces where people feel they can behave differently, where it is possible to be respectable and unrespectable at the same time. Dr Jekyll could saunter past the smart shops of Piccadilly but Mr Hyde knew the fleshpots of the Haymarket and Soho were not far away.

I argue that pleasure districts have a dynamic effect on the culture at large. In shop window displays, luxurious theatre interiors, hotel lobbies, arcades, romantic melodramas, music hall songs, sexualized images, and the display of glamorous clothing we find the construction of modern ways of urban living. They represent lifestyles driven by consumption rather than production: proclamations of the new. They usher in a different kind of mental life conferring identities that break with tradition. In addition, they offer their own versions of bodily theatre: the elegant toff, the energetic bargain hunter, the opinionated critic, the inquisitive tourist, the rule-breaking lesbian, the deferential shopworker, the suburban couple dressed up for their night out. In this sense, pleasure districts are utopian; they are places for the manipulation but also celebration of desire and aspiration.

Most cities in Britain have a centre characterized by entertainment and culture industries. What makes the West End different is that it helped serve the function of making London a capital city; a place that constructed a version of the national culture (a point I return to in the final chapter). The West End proved to be a creative space where new forms of entertainment could be developed and exported to other pleasure districts. It was also a place where international forms of culture

J.H. Plumb, *The Birth of a Consumer Society: The Commercialisation of Eighteenth Century England* (London: Europa, 1982).

[5] See, however, William R. Taylor (ed.), *Inventing Times Square: Commerce and Culture at the Crossroads of the World* (Baltimore: Johns Hopkins University Press, 1996 [1991]); João Silva, 'Porosity and Modernity: Lisbon's Auditory Landscape from 1864 to 1908' in Ian Biddle and Kirsten Gibson (eds), *Cultural Histories of Noise, Sound and Listening in Europe, 1300–1918* (London: Routledge, 2017), pp. 235–51.

could enter Britain, giving it a cosmopolitan dimension. The West End made London a world city, tied into an international network based on finance, fashion, and culture. This is one reason why one often compares London with New York, Paris, or Tokyo rather than other British cities.[6] London shaped the global imagination in the nineteenth century much as New York did after 1945 and the West End was key to this wave of cultural imperialism.

My focus on pleasure districts allows me to write a history of nineteenth-century nightlife and the way it was opened up to more and more people. Night life always courted the possibility of being unrespectable because it was pursued outside the home. It stood for the feeling that ties of family, church, or status could be relinquished, if only for a short while, and hedonism, rather than duty, could dominate. Nightlife involves spaces whose artificiality (as opposed to the alleged authenticity of the domestic) is part of their appeal. It takes on the feeling of a dream which is all the more powerful because dreams are usually meant to take place at night. In the West End, metropolitan life was imagined as Vanity Fair: a grand theatre where titled people performed and played multiple roles. But in the nineteenth century the cast was expanded to include middle-class men and women as mass entertainment moved from pubs and cellars to grand venues such as the London Coliseum.

At one level, mine is an argument about the rise of the bourgeoisie, who laid claim to the area. Yet the West End continued to be dominated in some respects by the world of the elite (by which I mean the aristocracy as well as, later, the international plutocracy). The monumental style adopted by both theatres and department stores was an expression of what I term the 'populist palatial'. The allure of the West End was based on the feeling of working- and middle-class visitors that they too could get access (if briefly) to the kind of luxury that the elite was used to. The peculiarity of the populist palatial as a cultural style in architecture and performance is that it flattered the people, rather than simply making them feel deferential to their so-called social superiors. It was thus linked to forms of conspicuous consumption.

The West End, as I make clear throughout, was a strongly conservative space. Yet we will also see that its conservatism did not mean resistance to novelty. The pleasure district's default setting may have been the worship of hierarchy but it remained open to changes in morality and culture. The West End offered a home to a kind of Tory modernism, part of the cultural bricolage that informs the discourse of the West End. We find its imprint today in various West End spaces: in the theatre bar, in the ornaments in Rule's restaurant in Covent Garden, in the foyer of the Ritz. The paradox of the West End was that it was conservative but also modern, fashionable, up-to-date. I argue that the West End demonstrates the

---

[6] Christopher Breward and David Gilbert (eds), *Fashion's World Cities* (Oxford: Berg, 2006).

ways in which conservatism could be strongly theatrical and based on performance. This would include not just the worship of all things royal and aristocratic but the ways in which the West End was shaped around the performance of being a gentleman and a lady. Men and women from the suburbs and elsewhere would dress up for a night out to take on those roles in their most theatrical versions. This is why the dress code in various West End theatres and restaurants was important (and why theatres have a 'dress circle').

The built environment of the pleasure district matters. Buildings have meanings; they help spectators feel things and confer notions of taste and sophistication. This is why they possess what I call a psychic charge. Churches, to take the obvious example, encourage reverence. West End theatres and restaurants, by contrast, hail viewers by telling them that they are potential consumers, pleasure-seekers, honoured guests, discriminating patrons, bon viveurs. Department stores seek to impress through their monumental scale. Regent Street accomplishes different things from Old Compton Street in Soho which is only a few minutes walk away, even though they are both streets with shops. The West End was made up of urban icons that were 'visually noisy': 'attention grabbers, addressed to a distracted public'.[7] Buildings such as the Alhambra on Leicester Square were important in the development of larger structures of feeling because shops and entertainment industries shaped the imagination and presented themselves as a common possession for the multitude.

A History of Glitz

Any discussion of pleasure districts inevitably borrows from the interwar German critic Walter Benjamin who recognized that the Parisian arcades represented vivid elemental forces that were transforming the culture but also argued that modern history must be understood in terms of consumption as well as production.[8] The impact of Benjamin is such that urban historians now explore the city in terms of its appeal to the senses; as something to be seen, felt, and experienced. Critical of consumer capitalism, Benjamin nevertheless understood its dazzling and liberating qualities as well as the way physical space moulded identity. For Benjamin, glitz was not a trivial matter. Although I have not attempted a Benjaminian analysis, his emphasis on material culture, kitsch, exhibitions, iconology, the politics of light, and the importance of display in a Parisian context stimulated my curiosity about the equivalent in the West End. Benjamin captured

---

[7] Philip J. Ethington and Vanessa R. Schwartz, 'Introduction: An Atlas of the Urban Icons Project', *Urban History*, 33 (2006): p. 13.

[8] Walter Benjamin, *The Arcades Project* (Cambridge, MA: Harvard University Press, 1999); see also Vanessa R. Schwartz, 'Walter Benjamin for Historians', *American Historical Review*, 106 (2001): pp. 1721–43.

the utopian dimensions to metropolitan life: the way they could produce hypnotic experiences with panoramas, arcades, casinos, and railway stations all being considered as 'dream houses of the collective'.[9] Above all, Benjamin introduced the category of the *flâneur* (by way of Baudelaire) into modern critical thinking. In the pages that follow, there is much evidence for the West End as a place designed to service the needs of masculine upper-class lounge lizards idly strolling their way through local attractions (at least up to 1850). Yet even before mid-century, the West End was drawing in female viewers and servicing the needs of a middle-class public including men and women from the new suburbs. The concept of the *flâneur* thus explains something, but not everything, about urban spectatorship in the area.

London's West End is influenced by American cultural historians who have identified the ways in which spectacle was integral to the development of modern consciousness and mass culture.[10] Modernity in this view thrives on what Vanessa Schwartz (strongly influenced by Walter Benjamin) calls 'spectacular realities'.[11] The new consumer culture generated glitzy forms of crowd pleasing including popular newspapers, macabre waxworks, and urban spectatorship evident on the boulevards of Paris. Nineteenth-century cities therefore showed people quite simply how to have a good time. This educative function, I argue here, was part of the mission of pleasure districts. The historian Jean-Christophe Agnew has established that American pleasure districts were 'bounded yet free, exploitative yet liberating, familiar yet exotic'. For Agnew, such zones 'offered their customers the scenery, props, and idiom with which to translate the potentially explosive tensions of class, race, gender, and ethnicity into energy and that energy, in turn, into spectacle'.[12] This use of theatrical metaphor (scenery, props) contains the insight that theatre has a major role in identity construction. The 'modern' in the nineteenth century involved new forms of urban spectacle that led to forms of hyper-stimulation such as the cinema.[13] These developments need to be placed alongside

[9] Benjamin, *Arcades Project*, p. 405.

[10] John F. Kasson, *Amusing the Million: Coney Island at the Turn of the Century* (New York: Hill and Wang, 1978); Michael B. Miller, *The Bon Marché: Bourgeois Culture and the Department Store, 1869–1920* (London: George Allen and Unwin, 1981); Lewis A. Erenberg, *Steppin' Out: New York Nightlife and the Transformation of American Culture, 1890–1930* (Westport, CT: Greenwood Press, 1981); William R. Taylor, *In Pursuit of Gotham: Culture and Commerce in New York* (New York: Oxford University Press, 1992); David Nasaw, *Going Out: The Rise and Fall of Public Amusements* (Cambridge, MA: Harvard University Press, 1993); H. Hazel Hahn, *Scenes of Parisian Modernity: Culture and Consumption in the Nineteenth Century* (Basingstoke: Palgrave Macmillan, 2009); Cindy R. Lobel, *Urban Appetites: Food and Culture in Nineteenth-Century New York* (Chicago: University of Chicago Press, 2014).

[11] Vanessa R. Schwartz, *Spectacular Realities: Early Mass Culture in fin-de-siècle Paris* (Berkeley: University of California Press, 1998).

[12] Jean-Christophe Agnew, 'Times Square: Secularization and Sacralization' in Taylor (ed.), *Inventing Times Square*, pp. 2–3.

[13] Alexander Nicholas Vardac, *Stage to Screen: Theatrical Method from Garrick to Griffin* (Cambridge, MA: Harvard University Press, 1949); Leo Charney and Vanessa R. Schwarz (eds), *Cinema and the Invention of Modern Life* (Berkeley, CA: University of California Press, 1995).

other changes such as the growth of industry and democracy. Popular culture was in part a device through which urban society tried to understand itself.

This focus on spectacular pleasure districts explains why aspects of the West End's history have drifted to the fore in recent historical inquiry. The historical context has been the emergence of increasingly consumer-driven forms of politics since the 1980s, where the focus has been on individual satisfaction rather than producer interests. Judith Walkowitz has produced a dazzling set of studies principally of Soho from 1890 to 1945, revealing how the area was shaped by a cosmopolitan approach to culture and to sexuality. The cultural and racial mix in the area made it feel different from elsewhere and thus could be constructed as exotic or even as dangerous. Frank Mort's comparable work on the 1950s showed how Soho, both as a real and an imagined space, anticipated the sexual revolution of the 1960s.[14] These works relate to just one part of the West End though their implications for understanding modern culture are much wider. My own perspective, as I range across the whole of the West End, produces a slightly different reading. I emphasize the ways in which the West End made middle-class audiences feel safe rather than challenged (by the avant-garde). We need to be aware of the wholesome and the conformist as well as the disruptive elements in the culture. If the West End had its bohemian dimensions, it was also characterized by distinctly conservative forms of bohemianism. Devoting extensive attention to the theatre, I find an area that is concerned with what a later generation would define as 'middle-brow' fare.

Erika Rappaport argues that gender was central to the construction of pleasure in the metropolis. She has shown how the West End department store was a vital feature in the construction of female identity in the later nineteenth century. It is instructive to compare her work with cultural historian Jacky Bratton who has similarly argued that the female audience was central to the emergence of the West End theatre in the mid-Victorian period and observes that this is one reason why such theatre-going is often discussed in hostile and patronizing ways.[15] My book provides further evidence of the feminization of the West End whilst also allowing for its masculine dimensions which shaped shows and shops. As Christopher Breward shows, the apparent lack of interest by men in clothes covered up an underlying interest in style, neatness, texture, and sartorial effect. The West End addressed this need. Breward rightly argues that 'One might justifiably read retail space in the late nineteenth- and early twentieth-century city as a theatre in which modern forms of masculinity were acted out'; an appropriate metaphor for thinking about pleasure districts.[16] For both men and women,

[14] Walkowitz, *Nights Out*; Mort, *Capital Affairs*.
[15] Bratton, *Making of the West End Stage*, p. 3.
[16] Breward, *The Hidden Consumer*, p. 147.

clothing purchased in the West End became a way to pursue and proclaim one's social status.

Theatre historians now insist that they are creating new forms of social history by studying performance in all its aspects, including ordinary life.[17] In this sense, they are following in the wake of the novelist Henry James who noted that theatre-going offered important evidence of the 'customs of the people' and that the audience and even the attendants in a theatre 'testify to the civilization' around the social observer.[18] Theatre history and discussions of performance often lack the most important frame through which people experience plays: the built environment of the pleasure district. Mine is an attempt to rectify this. As will be obvious, my form of theatre history is not confined to what happens on the stage (though I explore some key theatrical events). I am interested in audiences before the lights begin to dim in the auditorium (and the fact that auditoriums were often undimmed in the nineteenth century). The material culture of theatre-going needs to be analysed (in a way that is not normally done) right down to the counterfoil on a printed ticket. This is a rare work of theatre history in that it is interested in front of house staff. We also need to think about the experience of getting to the theatre, the meal before or after, the playbill or poster, the programme, the drink in the interval. These are all the rituals of theatre-going and they have a history which needs to be written.

My approach is to consider the forces that shaped the West End and then focus in depth on particular spaces, people, and institutions including the Burlington Arcade, Her Majesty's Theatre, the bawdy world of Maiden Lane, the Egyptian Hall, the music hall artiste Jenny Hill, the producer George Edwardes, and Liberty's department store. What unites them is that they were part of 'culture industries'. The assumption behind the interwar Frankfurt School of theorists (who put this term on the scholarly map and who included Walter Benjamin) is that modern mass culture, with its roots in the nineteenth century, is a form of deception which is intended to keep the masses compliant by buying them off with cheap commodities and forms of entertainment. Entertainment, in this view, is never politically innocent as it allows for the manipulation of the masses and prevents profound thinking about the inequalities of modern capitalism. It also transforms art into a standardized commodity which eschews originality and promotes passivity.[19]

This study, however, opts for a less reductive approach. West End audiences and shoppers were sophisticated actors, opting for shows and products they liked

---

[17] Peter Yeandle, Katherine Newey, and Jeffrey Richards (eds), *Politics, Performance and Popular Culture: Theatre and Society in Nineteenth-Century Britain* (Manchester: Manchester University Press, 2016).

[18] Henry James, *The Scenic Art: Notes on Acting and the Drama, 1872–1901* (London: Rupert Hart-Davis, 1949), p. 93.

[19] Theodor Adorno and Max Horkheimer, *Dialectic of Enlightenment* (London: Verso, 1979 [1944]), pp. 120–67.

and resisting others. As the final chapter makes clear, the West End could become a space for radicalism and resistance. There was in any case a perpetual series of negotiations between artists and their audiences who had agency, including the right not to attend a show they did not anticipate liking. George Edwardes, who helped invent the modern musical, would often have to rework his shows when he found that they did not take with an audience. In addition, although the West End was undoubtedly driven by commerce, there was always an element of artistry that elevated the proceedings, as shown by the approach of figures like the conductor Michael Costa who demanded a more serious approach to the musical score, respecting the work of the composer (see Chapter 8). The West End is therefore best viewed as a cultural resource for visitors which helped them to understand the possibilities of modern life through fashion, music, story telling, and images of glamour.

The more difficult issue is establishing what people did with what they found in the West End. The question of reception is always an elusive quarry for the cultural historian and certainly one that is difficult to deal with in a scientific way. Clearly, the various forms of entertainment described here reached an appreciative public even if individual events, styles, and fashions could flop. This confirms that the West End shaped the people who visited: but how? Did men and women react differently to the varied sites of entertainment? How did they appropriate what the pleasure district had to offer in their mental lives? I have dealt with this by using, at various points, diary entries (and indeed have tried to recover the well-known diarist Arthur Munby as a man of the West End which has not been a notable feature of the discussion of his extraordinary life). Diaries, however, are useful but complex sources, which sometimes need to be read against the grain. So, too, are the comments of social observers and investigators such as Henry Mayhew and James Grant as well as the numerous press accounts that I have used. We now see how literary devices and forms of self-presentation govern how information is shaped in both diaries and reportage. Another source I have employed are the autobiographies of people in showbusiness but such volumes often count as the most unreliable of memoirs. Some theatrical anecdotes are (soft whisper) not true or, at least, exaggerated. Of course showbiz memoirs should be consulted but they should not always be interpreted on their own terms. Instead, they should be seen as forms of performance which created a mythology of the West End; part of a larger process in which the pleasure district was turned into an urban spectacle.

Above all, this is a study of cultural style. I argue that the West End possesses a discourse or, at least, a form of rhetoric which shapes the popular imagination.[20]

---

[20] For an important discussion of the discourses of mass entertainment, see Peter Bailey, 'Entertainmentality: Liberalizing Modern Pleasure in the Victorian Leisure Industry' in Simon Gunn and James Vernon (eds), *The Peculiarities of Liberal Modernity in Imperial Britain* (Berkeley, CA: University of California Press, 2011), pp. 119–33.

It was a discourse that disdained the work ethic. Self help becomes about helping yourself to have some fun. The West End discourse is the language of the customer always being right. It is also, as we have seen, the language of monumentalism and the exotic. Listen to the names of some West End buildings: Hippodrome, Empire, Coliseum, Palladium, Alhambra. The West End hails spectators with its message that a bit of lust, fun, and gluttony all enjoyed in a smart location are fine in their place. Its discourse is that of the great lie of the Enlightenment: that happiness is the same thing as pleasure.

The status of the West End today is not uncontested. Many artists and bohemians have come to despise it. Some of the best restaurants and most innovative sites of artistic endeavour can be found outside the area. The former director of the National Theatre, Nicholas Hytner, confesses that he remains immune to the theatres of the West End which are constrained by being built for the kind of plays that were written one hundred years ago: 'my heart beats faster at the National, at the Manchester Royal Exchange or in a disused warehouse than it does on Shaftesbury Avenue'.[21] This book is written at a time when the urban nexus of department stores and high street retailing is in crisis because of the rise of online shopping. It may well be that the world, whose origins are described here, is coming to an end or, more likely, will be subject to considerable reinvention in the future.

The first section of the book looks at the embryonic pleasure district in the period 1800–50, exploring the ways in which it became characterized by leading shops and places of entertainment aimed mainly at the elite. The book then argues in Part Two that the modern West End really emerged after 1850 when it started to appeal to a broader public, especially the middle classes. In the post-1850 period, the West End generated new popular forms including music hall and light entertainment. This wave of mid to late Victorian popular culture is dealt with in Part Three ('Showbiz') which considers, in particular, the ways in which the West End became theatreland. Well before the Great War, the multitude was able to access the West End in search of larger than life stars, prestigious venues, and (from the late 1890s) cinema treats. Part Four examines the wave of hospitality industries that developed in the later Victorian and Edwardian era: restaurants, hotels, and new forms of retail. These were all forms of education in metropolitan style. The book ends (in Part Five) by considering the West End as the heart of empire. At the same time, it reveals the ways in which a space that was meant to shape a conservative consensus ended up creating resentment and discord.

---

[21] Nicholas Hytner, *Balancing Acts: Behind the Scenes at the National Theatre* (London: Vintage, 2018), p. 284.

PART ONE
THE ARISTOCRATIC
WEST END, 1800–50

1

Drury Lane, 1800

Royal Box

15 May 1800. The show at the Theatre Royal Drury Lane is a double bill of Colley Cibber's *She Woud and She Woud Not* and James Cobb's farce *The Humourist*. As the evening's entertainment is about to commence, the national anthem is played. Attention in the auditorium turns towards the boxes. When the owner of a box enters to take his seat, he is the target of a gun fired from the pit. Fortunately, the person sitting next to the assassin quickly realizes what is happening and pushes the shooter's arm up so that the bullet from the horse pistol terminates in the roof above the box.

The object of the assassin's attention is King George III. He immediately signals to the Queen, the Princesses, and the attendants following him not to enter the box. Princess Augusta faints. The king stands and bows to the audience to prove that he is unharmed. The assassin, meantime, is grabbed by musicians from the orchestra who haul him across the palisades and down to the music room. A solicitor called Wright later discovers the pistol under the assassin's seat, dropped in the melee. The assassin is questioned by the owner of Drury Lane, the playwright and MP Richard Brinsley Sheridan. He is searched but has no further weapons or papers on him. He does, however, sport a military waistcoat with buttons of the Fifteenth Light Dragoons. The assassin says 'he has no objection to tell who he is—it is not over yet—there is a great deal more and worse to be done'. He is asked if he belongs to the Corresponding Society (the London Corresponding Society being the radical organization demanding universal manhood suffrage and supporting the French Revolution), but replies he is only a member of a club called the Odd Fellows and of a benefit society. He rambles on about mysterious dreams that he has experienced, suggesting that he would one day be a martyr. Much of what he says is incoherent. His name is James Hadfield and he is directly dispatched to Coldbath Fields prison.

Back in the theatre the royal display of sangfroid and coolness literally under fire impresses the audience. 'God Save the King' is twice sung. When the royal party leaves, a shoemaker on the corner of Southampton Street follows their carriage, shouting abuse. He has waited there for the opportunity to do this and

London's West End: Creating the Pleasure District, 1800–1914. Rohan McWilliam, Oxford University Press (2020).
© Rohan McWilliam.
DOI: 10.1093/oso/9780198823414.001.0001

proves a nuisance. Hadfield is later judged insane. Tried for high treason, he ends up incarcerated in Bedlam for the rest of his life.[1]

In 1800, it was not unusual to see the monarch at Drury Lane. Indeed, there had been an attempt to kill the future George II in the same venue back in 1716. The theatre was not just about entertainment; it was central to the visibility of power. The aristocracy spent large sums of money purchasing boxes for the season not only to see the shows but also to view each other. This is why auditoriums were designed so that boxes could face each other rather than being directed at the stage. The audience was as much the star of the show as the actors. Better still for the toffs was the fact that they could literally look down on the people congregating in the pit. The theatre was the place to discover who was in and who was out, showing how society was designed for the benefit of the landowning classes. The Georgian elite paraded in splendour whilst performances during the Napoleonic Wars frequently offered dazzling patriotic spectacles. On stage the virtues of the nation's army and navy were hymned whilst soldiers could often be found in the pit showing off their uniforms. How one dressed determined where one sat.[2] The monarchy, the aristocracy, the military: they were all made visible at Drury Lane and the other major London theatres.

The Theatre Royal was (and is) the oldest in London with a continuous record of performance. Built originally in 1663, this was the third theatre on the site. The architect Henry Holland had produced an enlarged version of the theatre in 1794 which was so vast it could hold 3600 spectators. It was the largest theatre in Europe and all classes (with the exception of the very poor) went, aided by cheaper prices in the galleries. Drury Lane was therefore a national theatre in embryo but imagined in its most conservative form. And yet the atmosphere in the theatre was anything but deferential, with orange peel regularly being thrown, abuse of anything French, rowdiness, and the odd fight. The vastness of the stage and auditorium produced a declamatory style of acting as performers struggled to make an impact. Audiences had to be courted by actors or their derision would be made clear.

Outside Drury Lane, the atmosphere was even less conservative. Covent Garden heaved with coffee houses, brothels, and taverns together with the lively Grub Street world of scurrilous journalists and artists. The affairs of the Georgian *gliteratti* became the talk of the town. Their manners and foibles were satirized on the stage and became the subject of newspapers and devastating caricatures that enlivened the windows of print shops throughout the city and beyond. Cartoonists removed that most precious asset of High Society,

---

[1] *Gentleman's Magazine*, 70 (1800): pp. 478–81; 'A Constant Observer', *Sketches in Bedlam; Or, Characteristic Traits of Insanity* (London: Sherwood, Jones and Co., 1823), pp. 14–18.
[2] Gillian Russell, *The Theatres of War: Performance, Politics and Society, 1793–1815* (Oxford: Clarendon Press, 1995), pp. 152–3.

its dignity, and exposed the people who rented the boxes at Drury Lane in all their plumed and steatopygous corporeality.

Here, then, was a pleasure district in embryo but on a limited scale. It extended only as far as the Strand a few yards away and over to the Haymarket with its opera house and another Theatre Royal. In the century that followed, the pleasure district would expand and reach Oxford Street, adding theatres, hotels, and restaurants as well as other places of entertainment and creating the idea of the night out. But how had this embryonic pleasure district come into being?

Building Quality Street

In 1612 (or thereabouts), a tailor called Robert Baker purchased land for a grand house in what were open fields located at the top of what is now the Haymarket. Baker had made his pile selling stiff collars called 'picadils' to the court. When he built a mansion, locals mockingly dubbed it 'Piccadilly Hall', a joke which, in retrospect, acknowledges the force of the new money emerging from trade and commerce. By the 1620s, the name 'Pickadillie' was being applied to the locality as a whole.[3] Baker's shop was on the Strand, the site of grand palaces for the nobility but also the seedbed of the West End. At that time, London was a tale of two cities: the City of London and the City of Westminster. They were linked by the Strand. Here the Stuart aristocracy shopped for fancy goods, patronizing the New Exchange (a predecessor to the department store), acquiring the latest fashions from France or curios from far-away lands. Inigo Jones laid out Covent Garden just to the north of the Strand in the 1630s, providing more homes for the well-to-do.

The transformatory moment was the Restoration. The return of Charles II in 1660 kicked off the relentless pivot of London towards the west. London was remade in a twenty-year period as the elite launched a building boom that reshaped the built environment. As architectural historian Elizabeth McKellar argues, the Restoration 'released a revitalization of the city and an explosion of the economy, which had been arrested by the turmoil and strife of the 1640s and 1650s'.[4] Another factor propelled the growth of the city: people. Between 1550 and 1700, London's population more than quadrupled. By the later seventeenth century, London began to surpass Paris as Europe's largest city; a magnet sucking in people and demanding housing of all kinds.[5]

[3] Charles Lethbridge Kingsford, *The Early History of Piccadilly, Leicester Square, Soho & Their Neighbourhood* (Cambridge: Cambridge University Press, 1925), pp. 71–8.
[4] Elizabeth McKellar, *The Birth of Modern London: The Development and Design of the City, 1660–1720* (Manchester: Manchester University Press, 1999), p. 3.
[5] E.A. Wrigley, 'A Simple Model of London's Importance in Changing English Society and Economy, 1650–1750', *Past and Present*, 37 (1967): pp. 44–70.

In the 1660s, two events contrived to change the geography of high society. The first was the Plague of 1665, which mainly struck the slummier parts of the City, and the second was the Great Fire of 1666. The Quality had lived around the Strand and Westminster although their primary loyalty was to their estates in the countryside. It made sense for the toffs to get further and further away from the noxious airs of the City. Winds generally blew from west to east so the air in the west proved a more pleasant experience than the vaporous stink downriver. Parliament began to legislate more frequently (particularly after the Glorious Revolution of 1688). Noblemen could no longer remain on their country estates with occasional forays to the capital. They needed grand town houses, preferably close to the monarchy in St James's Palace and within reasonable distance of the Palace of Westminster. Mayfair and St James's fitted the bill and mansions linked by squares started to emerge from the late seventeenth century onwards.

The built environment of the area was then shaped by the world of the Georgians: the clear lines of the Palladian style hymning the rationalistic mind of the Whigs, who established their ascendancy with the coming of the Hanoverians. This concentration of one class into a relatively small area helped give the elite definition. People in the eighteenth century would refer to the 'west end of the town'; London, at the time, extended only over to Hyde Park. The West End (as defined in the Introduction to this book) took in (mainly) the parishes of St Anne (Soho), St. Paul (Covent Garden), St Mary le Strand, St Martin-in-the-Fields, the precinct of the Savoy, and parts of St Clement Danes (though the constituency of Westminster, of which it was a part, extended over to Kensington).

The aristocracy profoundly shaped the West End, creating spaces that basked in opulence. Wealth was matched by the deployment of ostentatious taste with the classical style in architecture becoming the emblem of landed but also commercial society. Spaciousness banished the cramped buildings and shadows of Shakespeare's London. A new city built of brick, not wood, emerged. Red brick offered bold splashes of colour. These vistas created the dynamic for a new urban culture in which Mayfair led the way and was emulated by towns and cities all over the country. Aristocratic London was characterized by civility, politeness, and good manners with the expectation of deference from service workers, servants, and shopkeepers.[6]

The West End aristocracy needed a range of goods and services. They could find some of these on the Strand but St James's Street, and then Old and New Bond Street, emerged off Piccadilly to provide fashionable and luxurious consumer products. West End shops began to offer the latest fashions from Paris. These emporia were aimed at the Quality, the people of fashion, the bon ton, or, the beau monde: in other words, the movers and shakers who determined what

[6] Peter Borsay, *The English Urban Renaissance: Culture and Society in the Provincial Town, 1660–1770* (Oxford: Clarendon Press, 1989).

counted as fashionable.[7] Flouncing around Vauxhall Gardens, they had no interest in mingling with the hoi polloi. They were there to impress and to be seen. It was not enough to possess a title or money to be part of the beau monde; manners and style also counted. They showed up in London for the Season and could be observed at concerts, operas, and pleasure gardens. This was a world of conspicuous consumption in which the fashionable set out to dazzle, showing off their refined taste by decorating gorgeous homes.

The West End became the emblem of a new consumer revolution. Its shops displayed silver plates, luxurious teapots, chandeliers, precious gems, and Wedgwood creamware. Chinese porcelain, Japanese lacquerware, and Indian muslins tied the West End into a global network of production and consumption.[8] Shops in the eighteenth century also still manufactured products on their premises. The pewter purchased at Richard Poole's shop on Jermyn Street was made in the shop itself. Thomas Chippendale on St Martin's Lane supplied the aristocracy with the best cabinets and furniture.[9] The district became synonymous with the promotion of luxury both for the landed elite and the middle classes. But the district stood for more than luxury: it stood for style. Here were the trends and designs that people could adopt, emulate, gaze at; objects to be transported to suburb or country estate and artworks to create awe at a dinner party. Ostentatious ornamentation was important but so was the deployment of authentic designer brands such as Wedgwood. The best shops presented themselves as galleries, implying that they too offered fine art and things to delight the eye.

Mayfair and St James's were attractive not only because the elite could separate themselves from the lower orders but because of their pavements, piped water, and links to sewers. They therefore stood for hygiene and expressed what was seen as a more civilized way of living. Another way of putting this is that they enjoyed high quality local government. It was based on the parish vestry (so-called as the parish officers would often meet in church vestries) which supervised the relief of the poor, oversaw street lighting, paving, road maintenance, and public health. It also kept an eye on public morals and provided what little policing existed before the nineteenth century. After 1722, the vestry was responsible for workhouses. Local householders were often charged with paving the street outside their home and maintaining street lighting. The separateness of aristocracy was such that, when it developed in the nineteenth century, public transport in

[7] Hannah Greig, *The Beau Monde: Fashionable Society in Georgian London* (Oxford: Oxford University Press, 2013).

[8] Maxine Berg, *Luxury and Pleasure in Eighteenth-Century Britain* (Oxford: Oxford University Press, 2005).

[9] Jerry White, *London in the Eighteenth Century: A Great and Monstrous Thing* (London: Vintage, 2013 [2012]), pp. 214, 216.

the form of the horse-drawn omnibus system was banned from much of Mayfair and St James's. There were street barriers to keep passers-by out.[10]

The elite also needed to be entertained. Court life in Britain was relatively weak which meant that the Quality (including the monarch) would frequently go out. Charles II's court was theatre-mad. It included the courtiers Sir William Davenant and Thomas Killigrew. Davenant had established himself as a poet and play-wright in the 1630s. He had particularly good credentials in this respect, being Shakespeare's godson (even if we might want to dismiss the rumour that he was his son). Killigrew was also a playwright who requested permission from the new king in 1660 to open a theatre. Davenant, however, already possessed a patent and so they were both issued with legal documents to form theatre companies. Similar patents were extended to theatres outside London. Davenant's Company (the Duke's Men) commenced performances at the tennis court theatre in Lincoln's Inn Fields whilst Killigrew's troupe (the Kings Men) had its own theatre built in 1663: the Theatre Royal Drury Lane. The granting of patents to Killigrew and Davenant had deeper consequences. These documents carried the royal imprima-tur which meant their holders (who could sell them on) enjoyed a monopoly on the right to perform plays. Anyone else who sought to perform the spoken word in the metropolis was therefore engaged in an act that was illegal, a view that the patent holders enforced (backed up by the Lord Chamberlain). The Davenant patent eventually led to an alternative theatre to Drury Lane: the Theatre Royal in Covent Garden (now the Royal Opera House). It opened on 7 December 1732 with Congreve's *The Way of the World*.

There was an explosion of high culture based on the cultivation of professional artists, writers, and musicians. As John Brewer puts it, 'In the late seventeenth century high culture moved out of the narrow confines of the court and into diverse places in London. It slipped out of palaces and into coffee houses, reading societies, debating clubs, assembly rooms, galleries, and concert halls; ceasing to be the handmaiden of royal politics, it became the partner of commerce.'[11] The young Mozart, aged only nine, played in a concert at Hickford's Rooms in Brewer Street, Soho, in 1765. Covent Garden in the 1760s could boast ten artists, but there were also clusters in St Martins Lane and, from the 1770s, in the area just north of Oxford Street, particularly on Newman Street.[12] The elite became increasingly defined by the cultivation of refinement and the West End became a stage where the delights of high culture could be sampled (Fig. 1.1).

---

[10] P.J. Atkins, 'The Spatial Configuration of Class Solidarity in London's West End, 1792–1939', *Urban History Year Book*, 17 (1990): pp. 36–65; P.J. Atkins, 'How the West End was Won: The Struggle to Remove Street Barriers in Victorian London', *Journal of Historical Geography*, 19 (1993): pp. 265–77.
[11] John Brewer, *The Pleasures of the Imagination: English Culture in the Eighteenth Century* (London: Harper Collins, 1997), p. 3.
[12] White, *London in the Eighteenth Century*, pp. 281–2.

Fig. 1.1 Map of the West End in 1801 (Westminster City Archives)

The West End, as it came to be in the nineteenth century, was the centre of gravity in London. Most parts of the metropolis could access it. It connected the world of Mayfair to Fleet Street and the City on the east, and the corridors of power further south in Westminster. West End addresses and entertainments thus enjoyed prestige but also the feeling of inbetweenness: an intermediary between the patricians and the people down the social scale. This shaped the character of West End theatre (as we will discover in Chapter 4) and other entertainments. London's increasing population (around a million in 1800) allowed it to sustain an elaborate entertainment quarter. The presence of theatres, galleries, restaurants, and high status shops in close proximity became an essential part of metropolitan identity.

By the later eighteenth century, areas that had been the site of upmarket addresses, such as the Strand and Leicester Square, were places of crime and disorder, no longer providing smart homes for the elite. Change was on the way. Leicester House, formerly the residence of the Prince of Wales, was bought by the naturalist Ashton Lever who turned it into a museum in the 1770s for the display of his natural history collection (the house was demolished in 1792). Savile House (where the Empire cinema, Leicester Square, now stands) was badly damaged in 1780 during the Gordon Riots as its owner, Sir George Savile, had been a sponsor of the 1778 Catholic Relief Act. It evolved into a pleasure palace offering concerts, a shooting gallery, billiards, and a museum of embroidery (see Chapter 5). Bonham's fine art auctioneers opened in Leicester Square in 1793 and the following year Robert Barker launched his panorama close by. In 1796, the San Souci Theatre opened on the square as a base for the singer and dramatist Charles Dibdin (see Chapter 4). Two years later, Rules, London's first restaurant, opened in Covent Garden. Here were the beginnings of the pleasure district.

2

Arcadia

Shopping

In the early nineteenth century a young woman would come up to London from her Hampshire home to take in the shops and see the shows. On different visits, she caught a version of Moliere's *Tartuffe* at the Lyceum ('and was well entertained'), viewed some watercolours at a gallery, watched Indian jugglers, marvelled at Edmund Kean's acting, and visited Grafton House in New Bond Street where she could purchase the best muslins and other fabrics. She also loved to patronize Bedford House in Covent Garden and buy poplin from Layton & Shears in nearby Henrietta Street. In a letter to her sister, she announced that she had purchased twenty yards for her.[1]

The intrepid theatre-goer and shopper was Jane Austen. The novelist was typical of the rural gentry and middle classes who would descend on the West End in search of the new fashions, quality fabrics, and the latest in entertainment. London was a storehouse where it was possible to purchase the kind of elegant items that would be a talking point when she returned home.

This chapter explores the under-studied world of consumption and retail in the first half of the nineteenth century. It argues that the shops of the West End were transformative, developing new forms of selling that built on the consumer revolution of the eighteenth century. Many of the features of London retail, once thought to commence in the nineteenth century, were evident as early as the later seventeenth century; for example, the use of elaborate window displays and fixed prices rather than barter.[2] The early nineteenth-century West End, however, produced new kinds of spectacular shopping spaces. The coming of Regent Street was a statement of what the modern might become, influencing, among other things, Baron Haussmann's reconstruction of Paris in the mid-nineteenth century. Even if only a small number of people had access to the West End and could afford to shop there, it helped shape the culture of conspicuous

---

[1] Alison Adburgham, *Shops and Shopping, 1800–1914: Where, and in what Manner the Well-dressed Englishwoman Bought her Clothes* (London: Barrie and Jenkins, 1989 [1964]), p. 4; R.W. Chapman (ed.), *Jane Austen's Letters to her Sister Cassandra and Others* (Oxford: Oxford University Press, 1979 [1932]), pp. 275, 319, 324, 325, 326, 327.

[2] Claire Walsh, 'Shop Design and the Display of Goods in Eighteenth Century London', *Journal of Design History*, 8 (1995): pp. 157–76; See also Hoh-Cheung Mui and Lorna H. Mui, *Shops and Shopkeeping in Eighteenth-Century England* (Kingston, ON: McGill-Queen's University Press, 1989).

London's West End: Creating the Pleasure District, 1800–1914. Rohan McWilliam, Oxford University Press (2020).
© Rohan McWilliam.
DOI: 10.1093/oso/9780198823414.001.0001

consumption. When Elizabeth Sander leased nos 46–7 in the Burlington Arcade to hairdresser Thomas Sisson, the legal document stated that he could not use the premises for such activities as establishing a tavern or a cheesemonger's (which were beneath the dignity of the location).[3] Status was essential in West End shopping. It proclaimed the coming of a consumer-based society, in which life was about the aspiration to own goods. The increasing use of plate glass for shop windows, which rendered goods transparent from street level, was one of the most significant urban developments of the nineteenth century. To wander through pleasure districts was to participate in an urban dreamscape. One of the great insights of the inter-war critic Walter Benjamin was that he recognized the way commodities on display provided a secular alternative to religion and magic in the modern world. Pondering the Parisian arcades, he caught the way in which each was a 'nave with side chapels'.[4] We see something similar in the West End.

The display and sale of fashionable goods was a major driver of historical change. The pleasure district was associated with goods that could only be acquired there and with the fashions that it developed from ladies' hairdressers to gentleman's waistcoats. It shaped the sartorial image of the dandy, the man of affairs, the fashionable lady; but also the sex worker whose clothing parodied the aristocratic finery on display in the West End.[5] Such figures helped turn the streets of the metropolis into a glamorous performance space where people could amble, peacock, and parade. It did not just matter what you wore; it was how you wore it and where.

The district emphasized distraction, flux, and transient experiences. Its commitment to fashion meant that it was a space that emphasized change and novelty. The fluidity of the West End was the point; it dealt with the ephemeral. Fashions changed almost as rapidly as theatrical attractions. This meant that the West End played a role in constructing forms of popular identity based upon consumption and openness to change that would prove vital to the development of modern society. The consumer's eye could wander amongst the emporia, wanting more and more products if he or she could afford to buy.[6]

This chapter examines three new spaces of exclusive retail: Regent Street, the Burlington Arcade, and the Pantheon Bazaar on Oxford Street. The Mayfair aristocracy were eager customers in these places but the middle classes could find their way in as well.A central preoccupation in this volume is that the West End is full of public spaces on private property. People are invited to enter buildings on

[3] Indenture of Elizabeth Sander and Thomas Sisson, 19 November 1853: 0085/071 (Westminster City Archives).

[4] Walter Benjamin, *The Arcades Project* (Cambridge, MA: Harvard University Press, 1999), p. 37.

[5] Mariana Valverde, 'The Love of Finery: Fashion and the Fallen Woman in Nineteenth Century Social Discourse', *Victorian Studies*, 32 (1989): pp. 168–88.

[6] Lise Shapiro Sanders, *Consuming Fantasies: Labor, Leisure and the London Shopgirl, 1880–1920* (Columbus, OH: Ohio State University Press, 2006), p. 4.

very particular terms. They are constructed as private individuals and not a larger entity; they are 'customers', 'patrons', or 'audiences', not 'crowds' or 'communities'. They are endowed with identities such as the 'gentleman' or the 'lady' but not the 'citizen' or (unless in Church) the 'Christian'. Pleasure districts promise individual happiness rather than collective fulfilment.

The New World of West End Retail

In the early modern period, there were two major shopping arteries running through London. The first started at Mile End and extended over to Fleet Street and then on to the Strand and Charing Cross, The other commenced in Shoreditch and weaved its way through to Oxford Street.[7] The pleasure district was built around the western end of these two shopping zones.

Where did the elite shop in the early nineteenth century and what services were there? Bond Street was associated with male tailoring and fashion needs (though most gentlemen expected tailors to come to them for fittings rather than the other way around). John Weston at no. 34 Old Bond Street was tailor to the Prince Regent and, equally importantly, Beau Brummell.[8] On New Bond Street, the jewellers Hunt and Roskell was a shop that only the wealthy dared enter. It was the largest dealer in precious stones in Europe. When the social investigator Henry Mayhew visited in 1865, he was shown an £8000 diamond.[9] Bond Street provided the wealthy with other services. Theatre tickets could be obtained from its circulating libraries. John Ebbers's role in booking opera tickets from his shop at 27 Old Bond Street eventually led to his role as manager of the Kings Theatre (which performed opera) from 1820 to 1827.

Publishing and the book trade were well established in Piccadilly. John Murray, who published Byron, was in Albermarle Street. Bookshops were important for the construction of the networks that made a British intelligentsia possible. Wright and Ridgway at no.169 Piccadilly issued the *Anti-Jacobin* and included Burke, Pitt, Fox, Sheridan, and a range of bluestockings amongst its customers.[10] In 1797, John Hatchard established his bookshop at no. 173 Piccadilly (it later moved to its present address at no. 187). Hatchard was an evangelical whose edition of John Bowdler's *Reform or Ruin: Take your Choice* (which attacked universal suffrage as mob rule in 1797) helped make his fortune. In contrast to the Whiggism

---

[7] Adburgham, *Shops and Shopping*, p. 5.

[8] Christopher Breward, Edwina Ehrman, and Caroline Evans, *The London Look: Fashion from Street to Catwalk* (London: Yale University Press, 2004), p. 21.

[9] Henry Mayhew (ed.), *The Shops and Companies of London and the Trades and Manufactories of Great Britain* (London: Strand, 1865), pp. 31–3.

[10] Arthur L. Humphreys, *Piccadilly Bookmen: Memorials of the House of Hatchard* (London: Hatchards, 1893), p. 23.

of Debrett's bookshop close by, Hatchard's was a Tory house. George Canning (later a Tory prime minister) bought pamphlets by Edmund Burke from there. Other customers included William Wilberforce and Queen Charlotte. Like many West End shops, links with the aristocracy, the royal family, and the middle classes worked to make shopping at Hatchard's a sign of prestige.[11] The Strand, however, was also known for its book and print shops, notably Rudolph Ackerman's Repository of Arts, which offered lectures on painting and design.

The German traveller Sophie von La Roche was enchanted by Oxford Street, which she visited in 1786. By then, it had become home to shops serving the west London public. Her description captures the phantasmatic quality of West End shopping:

> We strolled up and down lovely Oxford Street this evening, for some goods look more attractive by artificial light. Just imagine, dear children, a street taking half an hour to cover from end to end, with double rows of brightly shining lamps, in the middle of which stands an equally long row of beautifully lacquered coaches, and on each side of these there is room for two coaches to pass one another; and the pavement, inlaid with flag stones, can stand six people deep and allows one to gaze at the splendidly lit shop fronts in comfort. First one passes a watchmaker's, then a silk or fan store, now a silversmith's, a china or glass shop...Just as alluring are the confectioners and fruiterers, where, behind the handsome glass windows, pyramids of pineapples, figs, grapes, oranges and all manner of fruits are on show.[12]

The wide pavements that La Roche notices here were important. They show that a space was constructed for shoppers who could wonder and gaze without fear of being run over by traffic. Light was also being employed to show goods off to their best effect.

Savile Row developed as a major space for male tailoring in the early Victorian years. Its focus on men's fashions complemented the female fashions that became the stock in trade of Regent Street which ran parallel to it. James Dean, for example, developed a gentleman's tailor business at no. 23 Savile Row. From his 1839–40 workbook, we find him supplying mohair waistcoats, velvet collars, buckles, black plush breeches, and blue frock coats.[13] Henry Poole moved his family tailoring business into Savile Row in 1848 (it is still there). The firm built its reputation on military uniforms, women's riding habits, and on court dress (the founder of the firm had redesigned formal dress at Queen Victoria's court

[11] James Laver, *Hatchards of Piccadilly, 1797–1947* (London: Hatchards, 1947).
[12] Sophie von la Roche, *Sophie in London, 1786: Being the Diary of Sophie v. la Roche* (ed. Clare Williams) (London: Jonathan Cape, 1933), pp. 141–3.
[13] Workbook of James Dean, draper, 23 Savile Row, 1839–40: 1197 (Westminster City Archives).

giving him immense prestige). Poole helped develop what became the dinner jacket. Customers included the future Napoleon III, the Rothschilds, and the Prince of Wales.[14] The quality of Poole's livery for servants, with its bright colours, enhanced the reputation of their masters.[15] Savile Row was not only a significant street for tailors; it also was an address for doctors and surgeons, complementing the rise of Harley Street and Wimpole Street, and a further form of service for the Mayfair elite.[16]

Over on Charing Cross, Francis Place, the radical tailor, formed a business in 1799 catering presumably to people in the West End and the City. Within a year he found himself employing thirty-two tailors and three or four leather breeches makers because there was so much demand. He later noted, 'At that time there was no shop at the West-end of the Town which exposed first rate fashionable articles of dress for men in the windows, and we sold a considerable number of waistcoats at a high price.'[17] After falling out with his business partner, Place established a new shop at no. 16 Charing Cross (a former 'house of ill fame'). He installed large plate glass windows (then an expensive novelty) but 'sold from the windows more goods for about three years than paid journeymen's wages.'[18] Place later sardonically recalled the way he focussed on dealing with customers: 'the most profitable part for me to follow was dancing attendance on silly people, to make myself acceptable to coxcombs, to please their whims, to have no opinion of my own, but to take especial care that my customers should be pleased with theirs.'[19] Fashionable dress was a force in the making of the West End but it was also built on deference to the elite. Even a radical like Francis Place had to fit in with a conservative way of life: a theme we will return to.

The Genius of Mr Nash

Regent Street allowed the pleasure district to expand northwards from the Strand and connect up with Oxford Street. It was the first street in London to be deliberately designed as a shopping street. Regent Street was an idea, a vision, and a state of mind which transformed a confusion of roads into a graceful and elegant avenue. London had mostly developed in a piecemeal way. Regent Street was, however, one of the rare attempts before the twentieth century at a controlled,

[14] Stephen Howarth, *Henry Poole: Founders of Savile Row: The Making of a Legend* (Honiton: Bene Factum Publishing, 2003).
[15] Richard Walker, *Savile Row: An Illustrated History* (New York: Rizzoli, 1989), p. 51.
[16] Zuzanna Schonfield, *The Precariously Privileged: A Professional Family in Victorian London* (Oxford: Oxford University Press, 1987), p. 1.
[17] Mary Thale (ed.), *The Autobiography of Francis Place* (Cambridge: Cambridge University Press, 1972), pp. 201–2.
[18] Thale (ed.), *Autobiography of Francis Place*, p. 215.
[19] Thale (ed.), *Autobiography of Francis Place*, p. 217.

planned environment, though we can link it to the architectural harmony in the squares of Mayfair and Bloomsbury. It represented a new period of state involvement in public architecture and drew its inspiration from the Rue de Rivoli which Napoleon Bonaparte created in Paris as a site for elegant shopping.[20] If it was Napoleonic in inspiration, it reflected the personality of the Prince Regent (later George IV) who employed it to leave his mark on London.

The Prince Regent wanted a major thoroughfare that would link Regent's Park (then Marylebone Park) in the north with his residence, Carlton House (which he later abandoned for Buckingham Palace). In 1811, the ownership of much of the Marylebone estate reverted back to the crown after having been in private hands. There was a need for greater revenue and so it made sense to develop this property and exploit its commercial possibilities but the prospect of improving the city centre was a major opportunity.

The man behind Regent Street was the master builder John Nash.[21] Few architects have left as great a mark not just on London but on Britain. Well connected, he moved with ease amongst the Whig elite, building in a variety of styles, including the Gothic and the Palladian, with an eclectic eye for both the lavish and the picturesque. Nash became the Prince Regent's favourite architect and the most significant force in developing the Royal Pavilion in Brighton (1815–23) as well as the reconstruction of Buckingham Palace in the 1820s. It was always likely that he would be drawn upon for Regent Street. The actual Regency began in 1811 and the Prince Regent was enthusiastic about what Nash had in mind for New Street (as it was originally called).

Regent Street was conceived in three sections (see Fig. 2.1). Lower Regent Street was imagined as a site for hotels and gentleman's clubs. The long section running from Oxford Street up to Regent's Park (where it becomes Portland Place) was intended to be residential but also to draw city dwellers up to the rustic harmony of the parkland. Between the two was a central stretch intended for shops. Nash observed that Swallow Street separated the rich from the poor and so this supplied the essential line that he pursued with Regent Street (a small section of Swallow Street survives). He conceived an elegant semi-circular curve, which became known as the Quadrant and avoided the squalor of Soho. The architect claimed that his purpose was to provide 'a boundary and complete separation between the Streets and Squares occupied by the Nobility and gentry, and the narrow streets and meaner Houses occupied by mechanics and the trading parts of the community'.[22] It is not true to say that Regent Street represented an act of social cleansing. The adjacent neighbourhoods had already acquired their

---

[20] Geoffrey Tyack, 'Reshaping the West End' in Geoffrey Tyack (ed.), *John Nash: Architect of the Picturesque* (Swindon: English Heritage, 2013), pp. 102–3.

[21] The standard work on John Nash is John Summerson, *The Life and Work of John Nash, Architect* (London: George Allen and Unwin, 1980). See also Tyack (ed.), *John Nash*.

[22] Summerson, *The Life and Work of John Nash*, p. 77.

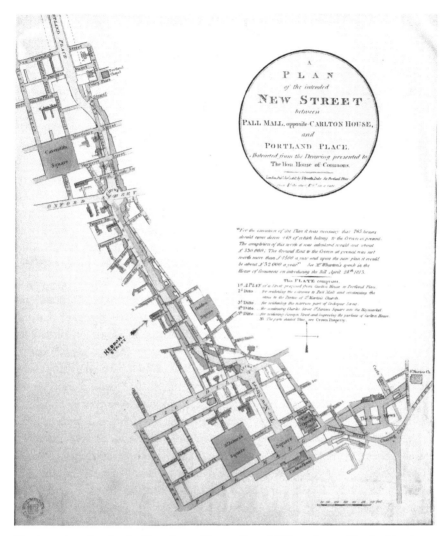

Fig. 2.1 1818 plan for the New Street (Regent Street) (Westminster City Archives)

essential characters before its construction but it did represent a frontier, creating a wedge between aristocratic London and the rest. Thus one of its most important characteristics was its width.

The street was built by 1823. This was in spite of objections from local tradesmen who objected to the loss of their premises and trade networks, but the prospect of creating shops which could afford high rents was too strong a temptation for the Crown.[23] Whilst Nash designed the overall layout of the street and

---

[23] Laurel Flinn, 'Elegant Buildings and Pestilential Alleys: Space, Society, and Politics in London's West End, 1753–1873', Johns Hopkins University, PhD thesis, 2014, ch. 3.

sought a consistent use of elegant stucco as part of the visual impact, he did not design all the buildings. A number of different architects, including John Soane, came up with houses for the wealthy customers likely to purchase them from the developers who supervised construction.

One by-product of the building of Regent Street was the construction of Oxford Circus which linked Regent Street with Oxford Street, making both thoroughfares a magnet for shoppers. Regent (Piccadilly) Circus, meanwhile, emerged from the demolition of most of Swallow Street to become a significant London landmark. It was known as the terminal location for coaches arriving from Bath, Bristol, and the West of England.

The central section between Piccadilly Circus and Oxford Circus was designed as a shopping district but not for any old shop (Fig. 2.2). Butchers and greengrocers were not allowed leases. Regent Street was London's quality street; it was meant for luxury and high fashion. Leases for shops, such as the tailors Poole and Company (later of Savile Row) at no.171, show how important the look of the street was. Poole, as leaseholder, was expected to maintain the appearance of the shop, including repainting the exterior in August every fifth year 'in good and proper oil colours' and maintaining the outside stucco.[24] The Quadrant was distinguished by the colonnades that were erected outside its shops, enabling customers to shop even when raining.

Advertisements liberally employed the information that particular shops supplied the royal family in various ways. In the 1850s, J. Medwin at no. 86, for example, made the most of being Prince Albert's bootmaker whilst Johnson and Co. at no. 113 were hatters to the Queen. There was a strongly female dimension to Regent Street (in contrast to the very masculine Savile Row). J.T Piver at no.160 was a French perfumer with a shop on the Boulevard de Strasbourg in Paris.[25] Regent Street therefore seemed like a conduit to the best of French fashion and taste. The jewellers Howell, James, and Co. could count on the patronage of the aristocracy during the Season. Founded in 1819, their shop on Regent Street constantly had a line of carriages outside as well as, according to Henry Mayhew, 'tall, be-powdered, large-calved footmen who lounge on or about the seats at the doorway'. Unusually, the shop specialized both in jewellery and in silk. Not surprisingly, the establishment was known for the courteous way it treated its customers. Shoppers could purchase terracotta clocks, crystal lockets with double horseshoes of gold and coral, *cartes de visite* albums, and other items which made excellent presents.[26] Customers developed personal bonds with Regent Street shops which stood for quality and prestige. And yet, the street also became

[24] Howarth, *Henry Poole*, p. 18.
[25] [H.J. and D. Nicoll], *A Visit to Regent Street, London* (London: Henry Vizetelley, 1856?), pp. 9, 20, 34.
[26] Mayhew (ed.), *Shops*, pp. 19–21.

Fig. 2.2 Regent Street Quadrant (no date) (Westminster City Archives)

notorious for the large number of prostitutes, plying their trade (drawn by the prospect of wealthy customers). They congregated under the colonnades of the Quadrant, which eventually had to be removed in 1848.

Nash did not conceive of this part of Regent Street simply in retail terms. Early in the project, he agreed with the newly formed-Philharmonic Society (established in 1813) to build it a concert hall. The result was the Argyll Rooms, just south of Oxford Circus. It could be entered from Regent Street or Little Argyll Street. The venue became a major site for the development of instrumental music, housing the Royal Harmonic Institution. One of the first buildings to employ interior gas lighting, the venue felt up-to-date when it opened in 1820. It included a concert room, a ballroom, a drawing room, and an ante-room. Leanne Langley argues that, in its short life, the Argyll Rooms lifted the status of modern instrumental music in British culture.[27] Liszt gave a concert there in 1824 (aged merely twelve) and Mendelssohn made his first London appearance in 1829. The fire of

[27] Leanne Langley, 'A Place for Music: John Nash, Regent Street and the Philharmonic Society of London', *Electronic British Library Journal* (2013) article 12 pp. 1–48 (quotation from p. 42): https://www.bl.uk/eblj/2013articles/article12.html (accessed 31 July 2018). This paragraph relies heavily on Dr Langley's excellent research.

February 1830 that burned it down represented a huge blow to musical life in the capital. The Philharmonic Society transferred to the nearby Hanover Square Rooms, which had been established in 1774 and remained London's major concert venue until the mid-nineteenth century.

As part of the development of Regent Street, Nash had his eye on the two theatres at the bottom of the Haymarket which were brought into his plans to develop the Pall Mall and Charing Cross area. He wanted to make them connect architecturally with Regent Street. The Theatre Royal in the Haymarket dated back to 1720. John Nash demolished the original building and opened its successor on the site next door in 1821. The classical portico of the Theatre Royal Haymarket was thus made visible from aristocratic St James's Square, a picturesque effect that is still there. Similarly, Nash reconstructed the King's Theatre (now Her Majesty's Theatre) almost opposite with a new exterior and the creation of the Royal Opera Arcade round the back (the first arcade in Britain). Nash also widened Pall Mall and extended Charles II Street so that it reached the Haymarket. It was possible to move from the stately worlds of St James's through to the theatre and opera house without any unfortunate encounters with lower class neighbourhoods.

The Burlington Arcade

Arcades were not entirely new (Fig. 2.3). They were a development of the 'exchanges' (early shopping malls) from the late sixteenth century onwards and the craze for 'bazaars' which started with the one in Soho Square, launched in 1816.[28] They also have their roots in spaces for elite entertainment and promenades such as Vauxhall Gardens. Their nineteenth-century form was inspired by the Parisian *passages*, memorably described by Walter Benjamin as radiating France's capital city 'like grottoes' from the late eighteenth century onwards.[29] They helped, in his view, to make Paris the 'capital of the nineteenth century'. The arcades should be seen as part of a wider Anglo-French conversation in which new technology and cultural forms criss-crossed the channel in the age of revolution: panoramas, fashionable dress, restaurants, the gothic, melodrama, the serialized novel. The West End arcades were a cosmopolitan space that exemplified sophistication by replicating the best that Paris had to offer.[30]

What is an arcade? It is a slippery term (a translation of the French word 'passage') and, in the nineteenth century, terms such as 'piazza', 'exchange', and 'bazaar'

---

[28] See Rohan McWilliam, 'The Bazaars of London's West End', in Helen Kingstone and Kate Lister (eds), *Paraphernalia!: Victorian Objects* (London: Routledge, 2018), pp. 17–36.

[29] Benjamin, *The Arcades Project*, p. 874.

[30] For further discussion of arcades, see Rohan McWilliam, 'Fancy Repositories: The Arcades of London's West End in the Nineteenth Century', *London Journal*, vol. 44 no. 2 (2019):pp. 93–112.

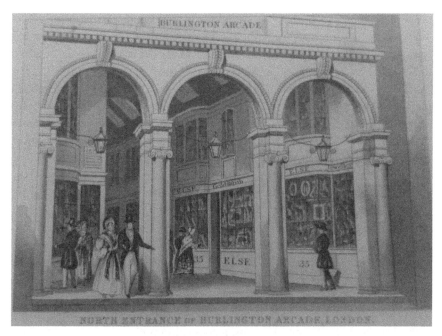

Fig. 2.3 The Burlington Arcade (Westminster City Archives)

could also be employed to describe these spaces. The most useful definition comes in architectural historian Johann Geist's magisterial work on the subject: 'a glass-covered passageway which connects two busy streets and is lined on both sides with shops'.[31] The glass roof offered the benefits of natural light for the display of goods. Artificial light could also be employed to make goods look more attractive or even seductive. The glass in the shop windows allowed for a clear viewing experience but also reflected the image of consumers in pursuit of goods, or just loitering and enjoying the spectacle. The purpose of arcades was straightforward, allowing consumers relief from poor weather and the inevitable mud of London streets together with a space where it was possible to enjoy a range of goods and services that were beyond the capacity of any one shop. They were respectable but, as we will find, might contain elements of unrespectable behaviour.

Arcades proved to be amongst the first major buildings created on a monumental scale for the purpose of shopping. For that reason, Walter Benjamin saw them as building blocks of modernity.[32] He was echoing Charles Baudelaire who defined 'modernity' as 'the transient, the fleeting, the contingent'.[33] Arcades were

---

[31] Johann Friedrich Geist, *Arcades: The History of a Building Type* (Cambridge, MA: The MIT Press, 1983), p. 4.
[32] Benjamin, *The Arcades Project*.
[33] Charles Baudelaire, *The Painter of Modern Life* (London: Penguin, 2010 [1863]), p. 17.

threshold spaces, crystallizing the cultural work of pleasure districts as a whole. The gent, the *flâneur*, the voyeur, the middle-class hostess, and shopper: all these types could find something in the arcades. Social observers Charles Dickens, Henry Mayhew, and George Augustus Sala described them as 'arcadian'.[34] They were being ironic. The bustle and noise of arcades was the antithesis of rural simplicity and contentment. However, the image of the 'arcadian' captures something of their charm. Arcades were (and are) easy to miss, yet offered an escape from the bustle of the metropolis. They therefore flattered a metropolitan notion of being 'in the know' (recognizing that all sort of delights lie hidden away down an obscure passage). Their shops offered the feeling of privacy.

Arcades had the appeal of the doll's house. They contained the utopian promise of a city in miniature (we will discover a similar appeal in the grand hotel and the department store).[35] The shops felt provisional and were often described as 'bays', not buildings. One can link this focus on the miniature to a particular stimulation of desire through creating the simulacrum of a shop. They seemed to reference the fact that shops were usually larger. At the same time, they may also have had a nostalgic feel, containing a folk memory of the early modern shop which was often very small. They managed to combine this sense of privacy and intimacy with what should be its opposite: conspicuous consumption.

But it would be a mistake to describe the arcades as static buildings. Their existence was predicated on the rapid flow of people going in and out: shopping, window shopping, loitering.[36] Shops themselves did not stand still; their displays constantly being reassembled, the seasons bringing new kinds of goods, the shop assistants sometimes changing. If the arcades were emblems of modernity, as Benjamin held them to be, it was partly because of this fluidity and their kaleidoscopic appeal. They were paradigms of the new market economy; invitations to perpetually consume, to glance, and to gaze at what was new over and over again.

The Burlington Arcade, launched in 1819, reflected, like Regent Street, the need for amenities to benefit the bon ton. Lord George Cavendish, owner of Burlington House on Piccadilly, was annoyed that an avenue on the western side of his property was being used by passers-by to throw oyster shells and rubbish into his garden.[37] He therefore decided to enclose the space and commissioned the architect Samuel Ware to turn it into an arcade with shops on the Parisian model.

---

[34] Charles Dickens, 'Arcadian London' in Charles Dickens, *Reprinted Pieces: The Uncommercial Traveller and other Stories* (London: The Nonesuch Press, 1938), pp. 444–52; Mayhew (ed.), *Shops*, pp. 100–2; [George Augustus Sala], 'Arcadia', *Household Words*, 7 (1853): pp. 376–82.

[35] Susan Stewart, *On Longing: Narratives of the Miniature, the Gigantic, the Souvenir, the Collection* (Baltimore: Johns Hopkins University Press, 1984).

[36] See Katharina Boehm and Josephine McDonagh (eds), 'New Agenda: Urban Mobility: New Maps of Victorian London', *Journal of Victorian Culture*, 15 (2010): pp. 194–267.

[37] 'Domestic Occurrences', *Gentleman's Magazine*, 87 (1817): p. 272.

At 585 feet, the Burlington Arcade remains the longest arcade in Britain with entrances on Piccadilly and Burlington Gardens. It also became the prototype of the double-sided passageway and employed transverse arches, large skylights, and flattened bow windows for the shop fronts, a style that was in vogue during the Regency period.[38] The narrowness of the passage meant that customers could easily view the goods on display and take everything in. It was an instant success and the seventy-two units offered for rent were immediately taken up. The small-ness of the bays meant that they offered an intimate, even domestic, atmosphere while the beadles on the gates proclaimed that this was a place of safety.[39] With its prime location on Piccadilly, it proved a commercial success and inspired the building of refined arcades throughout Britain. Such was its impact that within two years it featured in the show *Tom and Jerry* at the Adelphi (which included a song with the line 'arcades are all the go') whilst Eliza Vestris recreated it on stage in 1832 for the play, *The Conquering Game*, further evidence that it had become a landmark.[40] In 1838, it was the subject of a comedy by the playwright Charles Dance called *Burlington Arcade* at the Olympic Theatre. It featured a barber and a tailor vying for the affections of an artificial-flowermaker in the arcade. The *Era* commented 'there is nothing so taking as a locality with which everybody is acquainted—a place everybody visits'. It considered the arcade to be the location of 'nearly all the assignations at the West End of the Town'.[41]

Like Regent Street, the Burlington Arcade was intended for luxury. For example, in 1861 it boasted four jewellery shops. In 1849, Perry the hairdresser was paying £175 a year in rent for his two shops.[42] Not everyone could therefore afford to set up a shop there.

George Augustus Sala noted that its shops 'sold no articles of positive neces-sity: the useful arts were repellent to Burlingtonian notions of industry: and luxury was almost exclusively purveyed for. Burlington...was intensely aristo-cratic.' He resorted to list form to convey the impact of shopping in the arcade:

The staple manufactures of this Arcade have been in turns jewellery, fans, fea-thers, French novels, pictorial albums, annuals, scrap-books, caricatures, harps, accordians, quadrille music, illuminated polkas, toys, scents, hair-brushes, odor-iferous vinegar, Rowlands' Macassar Oil, zephyr paletots, snuff-boxes, jewelled

[38] Kathryn A. Morrison, *English Shops and Shopping: An Architectural History* (New Haven and London: Yale University Press, 2003), p. 43.

[39] Jane Rendell, 'Gendered Space: Encountering Anthropology, Architecture and Feminism in the Burlington Arcade', *Architectural Design*, 66, no. 11/12 (1996): pp. 60–3.

[40] William T. Moncrieff, *Tom and Jerry: Or, Life in London* (London: W.T. Moncrieff, 1826), pp. 17, 19–21; Sybil Rosenfeld, *A Short History of Scene Design in Great Britain* (Oxford: Basil Blackwell, 1973), pp. 112–13.

[41] *Era*, 23 December 1838, p. 153.

[42] Peter Cunningham, *A Handbook for London, Past and Present* (London: John Murray, 1849), Vol. 1, p. 153.

whips, clouded canes, lemon-coloured gloves, and false whiskers. Scarcely a fashionable vice, an aristocratic frivolity, or a Belgravian caprice, but had (and has) a representative in the Burlington Arcade.[43]

Mayhew described 'shops for every description of expensive knick knacks' in the Burlington Arcade.[44] This was not entirely true. If we examine the shops that existed, many of these offered clothing and hairdressing, which, whilst no doubt high end, went beyond mere knick knacks. What is true is that the clothing sold always went beyond the merely functional. Sala acknowledged that 'Boots and shoes and gloves were certainly sold; but they fitted only the most Byronically small and symmetrical hands and feet; none but the finest and most odoriferous leathers were employed in their confection, and none but the highest prices charged for them'.[45] Such items possessed an aura which made the arcade a place of aspiration but also one structured around the male gaze. Some of the visual impact of the arcade was provided by the print shops which offered forms of diversion: 'photographs of celebrities, the highly-coloured prints, the caricatures, and those unaccountable little sketches of *ballet* girls on tinted paper, which are principally distinguished for intense impudence of face, brevity of petticoat, and development of leg'.[46] The West End traded on offering commodities for women but also deploying images of the female form as a source of fantasy.

William Jeffs's bookshop at no. 15 specialized in the sale of French literature in the mid-Victorian years (so did Frederick Horocastle at no. 50). His shop became a meeting place for French émigrés, often attracted by the supply of books from Paris but also by the anti-Napoleon III propaganda that could be found in the shop. The distinctive yellow covers of French novels made an impression: Jeffs sold Balzac, Dumas, Sand, and Hugo at a time when popular and literary taste was heavily shaped by France. Lounge lizards from clubland and the London intelligentsia all bought from Jeffs. It was in Jeffs's shop in 1851 that George Eliot first met her partner George Henry Lewes.[47]

Post Office directories reveal that roughly one-third of shops were listed under a female name. For example, in 1841, of the fifty-three shops listed, thirty-three gave male names, fifteen gave female names (and five give an initial so that the gender of the owner is unclear). In 1881, of the firms where we can identify the owner's gender, twenty-six gave male names and ten gave women's names. There was, however, a decline by the end of the century. In 1901, twenty-five firms were in male names and just three were female (though eight shops are difficult to identify). Many of the shops were clearly catering to female customers. In 1841,

[43] [Sala], 'Arcadia', pp. 376–7. [44] Mayhew (ed.), *Shops*, p. 101.
[45] [Sala], 'Arcadia', p. 376. [46] Mayhew, *Shops*, p. 101.
[47] Juliette Atkinson, 'William Jeffs, Victorian Bookseller and Publisher of French Literature', *The Library*, seventh series, 13 (2012): pp. 258–78.

William Mintram at no. 7 specialized not only in hairdressing but head-dresses. Paul Hase at nos. 40–1 sold ladies shoes and there were a range of milliners, florists, hosiers, and specialists in baby linen.[48]

The arcade was a controlled space, policed by beadles who enforced regulations. Smoking was forbidden; so was whistling, singing, playing musical instruments, and, more surprisingly, the carrying of parcels. Perambulators were not allowed partly because they were pushed by servants who often became the target of soldiers wanting to chat them up.

At another level, the Arcade was an uncontrolled space, which catered to the requirements of the beau monde in less respectable ways. Some French novels and prints sold in its shops were considered pornographic or, at least, not fit for polite society.[49] The heroine of Mary Elizabeth Braddon's novel *Lady Audley's Secret* (1862) purchases French novels from the arcade, a sign that she would prove to be a femme fatale. Notoriously, the Burlington Arcade became a location for prostitution, particularly in the later afternoon. Mayhew's assistant Bracebridge Hemyng found that 'cyprians [prostitutes] of the better sort' would frequent the arcade and employ a 'friendly bonnet shop' to meet men. Hemyng referred to their feet as '*bien chaussée*'; their elegant footwear blending in with the arcade and possibly purchased from there. Sex workers relied upon the 'Paphian intricacies' of the arcades and employed a series of signals to solicit custom. Respectable men often avoided the arcade in the later afternoon for fear that it might be thought they were looking for prostitutes.[50] The connection with prostitution emerged almost as soon as the arcade came into being. In 1846, the *New Swell's Night Guide to the Bowers of Venus* noted that higher class prostitutes would meet there in a circumspect way with the bucks of the town.[51] Shopgirls were often ogled by men fresh from their clubs and allegedly were considered as potential sex workers as well.[52] The heroes of *Tom and Jerry* exhibit predatory interest in the bonnet makers on the Arcade.[53] By virtue of their sex, shopgirls became in effect a commodity to be traded. Fashion, performance, courtship, and spectacle were the

---

[48] *The Post Office London Directory* (London: Frederick Kelly, 1841), pp. 37–8; *The Post Office London Directory* (London: Frederick Kelly, 1851), p. 154; *The Post Office London Directory* (London: Frederick Kelly, 1861), p. 186; *The Post Office London Directory* (London: Frederick Kelly, 1871), p. 204; *The Post Office London Directory* (London: Frederick Kelly, 1881), pp. 210–11; *The Post Office London Directory* (London: Frederick Kelly, 1891), p. 218; *The Post Office London Directory* (London: Frederick Kelly, 1901), p. 264.

[49] Juliette Atkinson, *French Novels and the Victorians* (Oxford: Oxford University Press, 2017).

[50] Henry Mayhew, *London Labour and the London Poor* (New York: Dover, 1968 [1861–2]) Vol. 4, pp. 217, 222.

[51] *The New Swell's Night Guide to the Bowers of Venus* (London: J. Paul, 1846), p. 27.

[52] Jane Rendell, '"Industrious Females" & "Professional Beauties", or, Fine Articles for Sale in the Burlington Arcade' in Iain Borden et al. (eds), *Strangely Familiar: Narratives of Architecture in the City* (London: Routledge, 1996), pp. 32–6; Jane Rendell, 'Thresholds, Passage and Surfaces: Touching, Passing and Seeing in the Burlington Arcade' in Alex Coles (ed.) *The Optics of Walter Benjamin* (London: Black Dog, 1999), pp. 168–91.

[53] Moncrieff, *Tom and Jerry*, pp. 20–1.

stock in trade of such West End locations. At the same time, conspicuous sexuality found ways of intersecting with conspicuous consumption.

This combination of respectable and unrespectable elements meant that the Arcade exemplified the peculiar atmosphere that the West End came to make its own. At one level, it expressed the values of both luxury and decorum. At another level, it stood for the continuation of an eighteenth-century world of aristocratic vice and frivolity, untainted by the rise of Victorianism.

Before the Department Store

Department stores were the logical consequence of the desire for spectacular retail which characterized pleasure districts all over the world. As a form of retail they developed with urbanization and are usually associated with the post-1850 period (see Chapter 15). A glance at the West End suggests that they were prefigured by the arcades. At the same time, they clearly grew out of draper's shops, such as Swan and Edgar on Piccadilly, which were beginning to expand in size in the early nineteenth century. Harding, Howell, and Co., established at 89 Pall Mall in 1796, was aimed at female shoppers and divided into a variety of departments selling different kinds of items including furs, haberdashery, jewellery, and fancy goods (complicating our view of the department store as a post-1850 phenomenon).[54] It even used the word 'department' in its self-description. When the partnership was dissolved in 1812, the firm informed Ladies that 'their very extensive and valuable Stock, with which every department of their warehouse is complete', was going cheap.[55] The West End was not alone. High streets elsewhere began to boast emporia with multiple forms of goods and purposes. In 1830, Bainbridge's in Newcastle and Kendal, Milne, and Faulkener in Manchester opened as drapery shops which expanded beyond their traditional stock.[56] With its arcades, bazaars, and early forms of department store, the West End played an important role in creating modern retail.

The Pantheon, which opened on Oxford Street in 1834, most clearly anticipated the department store. It did not have separate departments or window displays but marked a shift away from speciality shops which had been the norm in retail up to that point. It was, instead, shaped by visual spectacle and offered a space for sociability. The Pantheon experience was about more than the purchase of goods. It illustrates some of the juxtapositions between mass entertainments, exhibitions, and retail that made the West End distinctive.

---

[54] *The Repository of Arts, Literature, Commerce, Manufactures, Fashions and Politics*, no. 3, March 1809: p. 107.

[55] *The Courier*, 15 June 1812, p. 1.

[56] Tammy C. Whitlock, *Crime, Gender and Consumer Culture*, p. 32; Bill Lancaster, *The Department Store: A Social History* (Lancaster: Lancaster University Press, 1995), pp. 7, 9.

It was a building that had never quite worked. It had originally opened on Oxford Street in 1772 with a design by the architect James Wyatt: its grand rotunda and dome evoked Hagia Sofia in Istanbul (an orientalist trope) and was meant to provide entertainment for the elite. There were balls, masquerades, and concerts. Entrance was initially dependent on knowing the right people. It failed to pay its way and in 1789 the Italian Opera Company moved there when its home in the Kings Theatre on the Haymarket burned down. The Company had barely completed a season when the Pantheon itself burned down in 1792. Rebuilt shortly afterwards, it returned to its role of providing miscellaneous entertainments for the Georgian elite, but closed in 1814.

In 1833–4 the Pantheon was reopened as what was called a 'bazaar'. There was a huge refit by the architect Sidney Smirke which cost between £25,000 and £60,000 (accounts vary).[57] John Timbs described the sight once a visitor ascended a staircase decorated with Haydon's painting *Death of Lazarus*:

> the great Basilical Hall or Bazaar...is 116 feet long, 88 feet wide, and 60 feet high; it is mostly lighted from curved windows in the roof, which is richly decorated, as are the piers of the arcades, with arabesque scrolls of flowers, fruit and birds; the ornaments of *papier-maché* by Bielefeld. The style of decoration is from the loggias of the Vatican. The galleries and the floor are laid out with counters, and promenades between. From the southern end of the hall is the entrance to an elegant conservatory, and aviary, mostly of glass, ornamented in Saracenic style.[58]

Isobel Armstrong interprets the Pantheon as 'a glass fantasia, a fecund romanticized space'. The glass roof, the conservatory, and the fish swimming behind glass created hypnotic forms of transparency.[59] The conservatory also had its own fountain.[60] This feeling of transparency made for a perfect shopping area: everything could be seen with clarity. The customer was less likely to be sold shoddy goods which made it a comforting space.

The galleries upstairs were a great opportunity for contemporary artists to display their work. The Pantheon did not have the feel of an exclusive art gallery. Paintings were displayed to be sold with the gallery taking a 10 per cent commission on sales. It provided a way for paintings to filter down to a middle-class public. The number of painters living in London had increased by a remarkable

---

[57] *Morning Post*, 26 October, 1833, p. 3; 9 December, 1833, p. 3.

[58] John Timbs, *Curiosities of London; Exhibiting the Most Rare and Remarkable Objects of Interest in the Metropolis* (London: J.S. Virtue, 1867 [1855]), p. 41. The detail about Haydon's painting is from *Morning Post*, 21 December 1867, p. 3.

[59] Isobel Armstrong, *Victorian Glassworlds: Glass Culture and the Imagination, 1830–1880* (Oxford: Oxford University Press, 2008), p. 140.

[60] George Augustus Sala, *Twice Around the Clock; Or the Hours of the Day and Night in London* (Leicester: Leicester University Press, 1971 [1858]), p. 182.

70 per cent between 1840 and 1845, evidence of an increasing art market that went beyond the elite.[61] Sala treated its art works with disdain, holding that it featured 'twentieth-rate masters'.[62]

The Pantheon was the place to buy a parrot. Birds as pets were an important adornment to the home. Other goods for sale were various: fancy glass, wax figures, pencil cases, china, silverware, music.[63] Toys included indiarubber balls, drums, hares-and-tabors, and Noah's arks.[64] Sala found their price at the Pantheon 'ruinously expensive', which suggests that the bazaar focussed its attention on the well-off, middle-class consumer. It was not cheap and nasty. Shopgirls at the Pantheon dealt differently with customers on the basis of gender. Women were treated 'with great affability' whilst men were treated 'with condescension that mingled with a reserved dignity that awes the boldest spirit'.[65] Men clearly made purchases but the Pantheon (like later department stores) was constructed as a space where women had agency.

The Pantheon established its patriotic credentials on its opening day when it placed on top of its portico a huge pyramid to celebrate William IV's birthday. The pyramid was over fifty feet high and on the base were the king's initials with a crown sporting a laurel leaf and stars around. It was lit in such a way that it could be seen from miles away.[66] Queen Adelaide visited the Pantheon the following year and was much impressed by the experience.[67] These episodes fit with a pattern of royal patronage but they also suggest something of the conservative cultural politics of the Pantheon: royal approval (as on Regent Street) became an important part of the West End shopping experience.

The store became a distinctive London landmark. It included a refreshment counter which sold arrowroot cakes and thus was a place to meet people. Young people were also known to meet and flirt in the conservatory. In evoking this world of young people at the Pantheon, Sala expressed their sociability largely thorough the objects that could be found in the store:

> The world is as yet a delightful Pantheon, full of flowers—real, wax, and artificial, and all pleasant—sandal-wood fans, petticoats with worked edges, silk stockings, satin shoes, white kid gloves, varnished broughams, pet dogs, vanilla ices, boxes at the opera, tickets for the Crystal Palace, tortoise-shell card-cases, enamelled visiting-cards, and scented pink invitation notes, with 'On dansera' in the left-hand bottom corners, muslin slips, bandoline, perfumes, ballads and

[61] Thomas M. Bayer and John R. Page, *The Development of the Art Market in England* (London: Pickering and Chatto, 2011), p. 153.

[62] Sala, *Twice Around the Clock*, p. 175.

[63] *Morning Post*, 16 July, 1842, p. 7; 12 February, 1844, p. 7; *Morning Chronicle*, 7 August, 1844, p. 8; 18 October, 1865, p. 7.

[64] Sala, *Twice Around the Clock*, p. 180.   [65] Sala, *Twice Around the Clock*, p. 181.

[66] *Morning Chronicle*, 29 May, 1834, p. 2.   [67] *Morning Post*, 14 October 1835, p. 3.

polkas with chromolithographed frontispieces, and the dear delightful new novels from Mudie's with uncut leaves, and mother-o'-pearl paper knives with coral spring handles to cut them withal.[68]

The Pantheon provided a network and set of objects to provide items of entertainment and courtship for the sons and daughters of the well off. Many of these objects were gendered female and could become associated with romance and sentimentality. The Pantheon lasted until 1867 when it was turned into a depot by the wine merchants W. and A. Gilbey. The site is now the 'Oxford Street Pantheon' branch of Marks and Spencer.

The spectacle of West End shops was part of a process where central London became increasingly monumental. Grand buildings were intended as a statement of the national story. They proclaimed the power of commercial interests cheek by jowl with worship of patrician society. John Nash's impact on London was not confined to Regent Street. As early as 1812, he developed plans for what would become Trafalgar Square. Nash, however, died in 1835 before seeing his schemes come to fruition. Trafalgar Square ended up being laid out by architect Charles Barry in 1842 (with Nelson's Column finally erected in November 1843). The National Gallery preceded it, having been completed in 1838. Whitehall was heavily developed with its grand ministries whilst, following the fire of 1834, Charles Barry's new Palace of Westminster slowly emerged out of the London fog. The centre of London therefore acquired a cohesive role as a place for government, national celebration, retail, entertainment, and imperial splendour. John Nash proved to be a prime mover in turning London into a true capital city.

The West End was a place for the performance of status for both men and women. We catch some of this in an 1833 letter of Thomas Babington Macaulay where he mused that he was becoming so conceited about his appearance that he found himself 'meditating on the expediency of having my hair cut in the Burlington Arcade, rather than in Lamb's Conduit Street'.[69] Place and location gave the elite confidence that they were acquiring perfection in manicured self-presentation. Yet if the West End was about aristocratic style, it was also subject to change. As early as 1831, when the Lowther Arcade emerged on the Strand, what counted were shops aimed securely at middle-class consumers. In 1840, the new arcade offered a tailor, two milliners, a hosier, a perfumier, and a hairdresser, and was particularly known as a place to purchase toys.[70] It became a landmark in the geography of the middle-class child, a key place to visit at Christmas but also throughout the year. It was known for shops that styled themselves as 'fancy

[68] Sala, *Twice Around the* Clock, p. 182.
[69] George Otto Trevelyan (ed.), *The Life and Letters of Lord Macaulay* (London: Longman, 1908), p. 229.
[70] *Robson's London Directory* (London: William Robson, 1840), p. 201.

repositories', specializing in a variety of knick-knacks and other goods including embroidery, pincushions, paper flower-making kits, and a variety of goods to satisfy people with hobbies.[71] These were objects that stoked the material culture of middle-class domesticity.

This chapter has pointed to an atmosphere based, on the one hand, around knick-knacks and small luxury items and, on the other, the spectacle of West End emporia which impressed by their size. This promised an experience that much of the country could not reproduce (although town centres increasingly imitated the West End). It made sense for Jane Austen and others to travel up to town. If the West End became a much more feminized space after 1850, it is clear that the development of attractive and increasingly grand shops in the early nineteenth century played a part in this process. The West End built on the urban renaissance of the eighteenth century, proclaiming that pleasure came from conspicuous consumption. It reinforced the notion of the cultural superiority of the elite but also provided a spatial point of connection between fashion, literature, and creative industries, all of which needed to be in the centre of town to operate. We often think of the West End in terms of theatres but the most characteristic building in the area was, and is, the shop. Consumerism played an important role in shaping the West End as an area of exclusivity and prestige. Increasingly, its customers were those of the middle classes.

---

[71] The Lowther Arcade and the fancy repository are discussed at greater length in McWilliam, 'Fancy Repositories'.

3

The Beau Monde

Night Life

Pleasure districts are lively places by day but they make a point of offering particular pleasures after dark. This chapter is about the different forms of night-life which the man about town enjoyed in the first half of the nineteenth century. Definitions of 'nightlife' vary but the term suggests spaces of entertainment and exoticism outside the domestic sphere.[1] In theory, everyone can have some kind of nightlife but clearly in the nineteenth century people accessed it in very different ways. It was shaped by money but also expectations about gender and age (night-life was essentially for adults). Men owned nightlife whereas codes of respectability dictated that women out after dark were, in a significant phrase, 'ladies of the night' (unless clearly chaperoned by gentlemen). Workers had much shorter time available for relaxation. Partakers were often those who did not have to worry about getting up early for work the next morning.

The early nineteenth-century West End existed to fulfil the desires of the man about town and provide him with an identity. Yet elite and popular culture were never sealed off from each other. This chapter is based around a contrast between high and low worlds: St James's and Covent Garden. Aristocratic men developed forms of associational life though clubs and the enjoyment of high culture, includ-ing opera and ballet. The chapter contrasts this with the forms of lowlife that the West End threw up, evident in the taverns of the Covent Garden area, which are explored here in detail.

The Italian opera singer performing a Donizetti aria at the King's Theatre may appear to be in a totally different world from W.G. Ross singing the ballad 'Sam Hall' in the grubby surroundings of the Cider Cellars on Maiden Lane. Thinking about the West End as a multi-use pleasure district alerts us to the ways they were part of the same musical eco-system. Privileged men (though not women) could frequent both spaces. This allowed for the construction of the idea of the

---

[1] There is now an emerging literature on nightlife and the social significance of the night. See Wolfgang Schivelbusch, *Disenchanted Night: The Industrialization of Light in the Nineteenth Century* (Oxford: Berg, 1988); David Nasaw, 'Cities of Light, Landscapes of Pleasure' in David Ward and Oliver Zunz (eds), *The Landscape of Modernity: New York City, 1900–1940* (Baltimore: Johns Hopkins University Press, 1992), pp. 273–86; Joachim Schlör, *Nights in the Big City: Paris, Berlin, London, 1840–1930* (London: Reaktion, 1998); Peter C. Baldwin, *In the Watches of the Night: Life in the Nocturnal City, 1820–1930* (Chicago: University of Chicago Press, 2012); Matthew Beaumont, *Nightwalking: A Nocturnal History of London* (London: Verso, 2015).

London's West End: Creating the Pleasure District, 1800–1914. Rohan McWilliam, Oxford University Press (2020).
© Rohan McWilliam.
DOI: 10.1093/oso/9780198823414.001.0001

bohemian with its transgressive enjoyment of crossing boundaries. As Vic Gatrell puts it, 'It was in London that high-mindedness co-existed with low-mindedness most nakedly'.[2] The contrast explains why the cultural style of the West End proved to be a curious combination of ostentation and vulgarity. Gentlemen (patricians or members of the middle class) could find spaces in the West End for bawdy songs, drunkenness, and sex. Male pleasure set the pattern for West End entertainments in the first half of the nineteenth century.

The heart of the gentleman's world was St James's, but men and women of the elite would ride in Hyde Park and enjoy opera on the Haymarket and theatre at Drury Lane and Covent Garden. This was the world that became embodied in the silver fork novels of the 1820s and 1830s at which the young Disraeli excelled. Major Alan Chambre recalled how it was the fashion for young idlers to take in the Bedford and Piazza coffee-houses in Covent Garden, which appealed because of their proximity to the theatres.[3] The idlers were comparable to the figures who Baudelaire in Paris, and (later) the critic Walter Benjamin, would describe as *flâneurs*: loungers buoyed up by private incomes whose days were taken up in dressing well and absorbing the street scene but rarely in doing any work.[4] The West End was a superb location for well-off bachelors. This was the masculine world that (for a brief moment) Beau Brummell surveyed from the bow window of White's at the top of St James's Street, determining what was, and was not, in fashion and who was wearing the right kind of cravat. Many *flâneurs* lived in Mayfair but, in 1803, the Albany opened on Piccadilly, offering apartments for gentleman. Its occupants came to include Byron, the future prime minister George Canning, and Thackeray, whilst Macaulay would write much of his great history in his rooms there.

The poise and style of the dandy was a riposte to the age of revolution. With hierarchies challenged, it made sense to keep up appearances.[5] The dandy parading up and down St James's Street revealed how street life was a form of theatre. His was a performance that resisted the rise of middle-class manners. With his flamboyant assumption of superiority, the dandy was disliked but came to haunt nineteenth- century literature and culture, providing a model for figures such as Oscar Wilde.

St James's was notable for the way it was warrened by gentleman's clubs whose exclusivity made them a source of desire: the ultimate sign of having made it.[6]

[2] Vic Gatrell, *City of Laughter: Sex and Satire in Eighteenth-Century London* (London: Atlantic, 2006), p. 9.

[3] Major (Alan) Chambre, *Recollections of West-End Life; with Sketches of Society in Paris, India etc. etc.* (London: Hurst and Blackett, 1858), p. 23; see also *Illustrated London News*, 14 January 1843, p. 41.

[4] Walter Benjamin, *The Arcades Project* (Cambridge, MA: Harvard University Press, 1999), pp. 416–55.

[5] Ellen Moers, *The Dandy: Brummell to Beerbohm* (London: Secker and Warburg, 1960), p. 12.

[6] Amy Milne-Smith, *London Clubland: A Cultural History of Gender and Class in Late Victorian Britain* (London: Palgrave Macmillan, 2011).

Clubs like White's offered a masculine fraternity to aristocrats but also to sporting gentlemen, military officers, and others who wanted to stay as close to the elite as possible. These became masculine republics in which the process of election to a club was a major rite of passage: aristocratic pedigree usually counted for a lot whilst men in trade knew not to apply. To be black-balled was to risk social ignominy. The consolation was a world of privacy in which the stern gaze of the porter kept out undesirables.

Gentlemen's clubs gave St James's, and especially Pall Mall, a distinct character because club members helped bankroll the construction of luxurious buildings and hire leading architects. The Traveller's Club was established in 1814 and the United Service Club, aimed at army officers, came along the following year, later moving into a building designed by John Nash. At the latter, according to commentator James Grant, 'the never-failing topics of conversation are, the army and navy lists, promotions half-pay, full-pay, and so forth'.[7] The Athenaeum was created for men in the arts and sciences (but really the intellectual elite), moving into its clubhouse, with Decimus Burton's classical design, in 1830. The Carlton Club was established on Pall Mall in the turbulent year of 1832 as a bastion of Toryism. Four years later, the Reform was founded to support the principles of the Great Reform Act. Charles Barry (architect of the rebuilt Houses of Parliament) was hired to design its clubhouse in the Italian Renaissance style with a grand hall whose galleries were guaranteed to inspire awe in spectators. The Reform's first chef was Alexis Soyer, one of the great cooks of the period, helping make the club a centre for fine dining and gastronomic marvels. The Reform and the Carlton Clubs became the nerve centres of the Liberal and Conservative Parties. Their function was only usurped by the construction of mass party machines with professional forms of organization in the later Victorian years. The clubland side of the West End was therefore the centre of the British political establishment.

The Reform and the Athenaeum were also distinguished by their superb libraries although these were supplemented by the creation of the London Library round the corner in St James's Square in 1845 (it was originally founded in 1841) through the influence of Thomas Carlyle who found it impossible to get a seat at the British Library and wanted to be able to borrow books. The gentleman's club, I argue, had a wider cultural influence on the West End's development, despite its exclusivity. As we will see, both theatres and elite hotels aspired to create a club-like atmosphere.

Aristocratic women did have some access to this world. From the later eighteenth century, the London elite would gather at Almack's assembly rooms on King Street, just off St James's Square, for musical entertainments, balls, suppers, and gambling. Debutantes would make their mark there and often find a husband,

[7] James Grant, *The Great Metropolis* (New York: Saunders and Otley, 1837), Vol.1, p. 148.

making it a major elite marriage market. Other locations for aristocratic recreation were outside the West End. Vauxhall Gardens on the south side of the Thames was well known for its fireworks, concerts, and spectacular acts, including balloon ascents which captured the nineteenth-century imagination. Cremorne Gardens in Chelsea was not so exclusive. It originally opened in 1832 as a sporting venue but became a pleasure garden, featuring a theatre, a circus, and a bowling alley. There were also daytime pleasures that ran alongside the night side of London, including prize fights and the race track. Jackson's Rooms on Bond Street was the place to watch boxing in the 1820s whilst it was possible in the 1850s, for example, to get instruction in boxing 'taught every Monday by well known professors' at the Queen's Head pub, close to the Haymarket.[8] The St James's side of the West End created a network of leisure and sociability for the upper classes.

Music for the Elite

Music was one of the things that defined the beau monde. Musicians might play in private homes for the aristocracy, but the great musical form that enthralled the aristocracy was opera which became a grand social occasion. Hence, opera, rightly or wrongly, has always had a reputation for exclusivity. Of all the arts it was the most expensive to mount in the nineteenth century and thus felt like an event. West End opera developed from the early eighteenth century through royal and aristocratic patronage but never received government money. Its aesthetic was rooted in the world of the court but delivered through the commercial sphere. The nobility could thus claim their way of life involved the cultivation of the beautiful.

Let us look at the world of the King's Theatre (after 1837 Her Majesty's) which was the main London opera house. The theatre on the Haymarket was a majestic building. It was built around five tiers of boxes in a horseshoe shape, with a gallery above and a pit below (and from 1815 onwards eight rows of stalls in front of the pit). This meant that the elite literally faced each other and would glance sideways at the stage. Often known as the Italian Opera House, it was the perfect space to ascertain who was sporting the latest fashions and who was intriguing with whom. Opera glasses were as important for looking at other members of the audience as what was happening on the stage. James Grant recorded that the interior of each box 'is covered with crimson cloth; while the wooden division which separates the different tiers, and also the different boxes, is beautifully painted and gilded'.[9] The ceiling was decorated with handsome figures and devices. The

---

[8] *London by Night: Or, the Bachelor's Facetious Guide to all the Ins and Outs of the Nightly Doings of the Metropolis* (London: William Ward, 1859?), p. 58.
[9] Grant, *The Great Metropolis*, Vol.1, p. 32.

PROSCENIUM *OF THE* OPERA HOUSE.

Fig. 3.1 King's Theatre/Her Majesty's Theatre in the early nineteenth century (no date) (author collection)

entire house could hold an audience of up to 2000 people. The pit (which in the early nineteenth century might cost half a guinea) could include middle-class people but they were expected to be well dressed. Grant noted that audience members 'must all go in full dress. Any disregard of this regulation will be inevitably attended by the exclusion of the party, no matter what his rank'.[10] The gallery cost five shillings but it was mainly intended for the servants of the aristocracy attending the opera. There were also seats between the pit and the orchestra which cost twelve shillings and sixpence. In addition to the boxes for the aristocracy there were also general boxes where 700–800 people could find themselves crammed in (Fig. 3.1).

The theatre was financed by a subscription list (that included Queen Victoria) for the boxes and stalls.[11] As the leading opera historian Jennifer Hall-Witt observes, the boxes were the preserve of female patronesses whilst the pit was dominated by

---

[10] Grant, *The Great Metropolis*, Vol. 1, p. 36.

[11] Benjamin Lumley, *Reminiscences of the Opera* (London: Hurst and Blackett, 1864), p. 28.

men who engaged in what she calls 'social peacocking'. The pit enjoyed wide aisles on each side which allowed men to mingle and parade; it came to be known as 'Fop's Alley'.[12] The Marquis de Vermont was appalled by the sight of men who, after fraternizing with prostitutes in the pit, were then received by women of rank up in the boxes.[13] Opera was so vital to elite social life that aristocrats would pay large sums of money to purchase a box for an entire season (and then hire it out on the nights they did not wish to attend). The Duke of Gloucester paid 300 guineas for his box every season.[14] In 1843, subscriptions for all the boxes ran to more than £20,000.[15]

The season at the opera house usually lasted from the end of February to the end of August. Drawing on creative talent from across Europe was part of its attraction (and one reason why it cost as much as it did). Attention was particularly focussed on the stage when a star singer (often brought in from Italy) was on the stage. There was much interest in 1847, for example, when the tenor Italo Gardoni, blessed with a remarkable vocal range, debuted at Her Majesty's in Donizetti's *La Favorita*. He went on to enjoy a major international career.[16]

Opera became more serious. The work of the composer had been far from sacrosanct in the eighteenth century. Scores were rearranged with arias from other operas often interpolated if they were crowd-pleasers. The form began to evolve. There was the rise of the silent listener. Audiences were encouraged to demonstrate cultivation by not talking and following the music.[17] This in turn became a mark of class distinction as working-class audiences were notable for their boisterousness. Critics and music directors such as William Ayrton began to support the cause of the composer. It became unacceptable to cut up scores; they had to be performed complete. The repertoire also began to widen with Ayrton and others championing German opera in the form of Mozart. Ayrton was music director at the King's Theatre in 1817, 1821, and 1825. He was later succeeded by Michael Costa, between 1833 and 1845, who similarly insisted on respecting the artistic endeavour of the composer. The post of music director therefore became integral to a new approach to opera.

The production of Mozart's *Don Giovanni* at the opera house in 1817 was a turning point. From then on, the middle classes started to become more attracted

[12] Jennifer Hall-Witt, *Fashionable Acts: Opera and Elite Culture in London, 1780–1880* (Durham, NH: University of New Hampshire Press, 2007), pp. 4, 116.

[13] Marquis de Vermont and Sir Charles Darnley, *London and Paris; Or, Comparative Sketches* (London: Longman, Hurt, Rees, Orme, Brown and Green, 1823), pp. 170–1.

[14] Grant, *The Great Metropolis*, Vol. 1, p. 33.

[15] *Illustrated London News*, 22 July 1843, p. 56.

[16] *Illustrated London News*, 20 February 1847, p. 121; 27 February 1847, p. 135.

[17] Peter Gay, *The Naked Heart: The Bourgeois Experience Victoria to Freud*, Vol. 4 (London: Fontana, 1998), pp. 11–35; James H. Johnson, *Listening in Paris: A Cultural History* (Berkeley, CA: University of California Press, 1995).

to opera as a form.[18] By 1863, George Henry Lewes could argue that opera had lost its aristocratic connotations and was enjoyed by a wider public.[19] Opera could be found elsewhere in the West End, reaching a more diverse audience. Covent Garden, the Lyceum, and Drury Lane would perform opera, sometimes in English (in contrast to the Haymarket opera house where it was a considered a mark of breeding to be able to understand what was sung on stage). When Donizetti's opera, *Anna Bolena*, was performed at the Princess's in 1847, it was judged a creditable effort even though it could not be expected to measure up to the standards set on the Haymarket.[20]

Ballet was also a great draw. Like opera, it appealed because it seemed a total form of art, appealing to the eye and the ear. In London, it tended to be of foreign origin: the reliance on foreign dancers and dance masters made it difficult to develop an indigenous tradition of ballet performance. The King's Theatre was, however, sufficiently invested in ballet to establish its own dancing academy in 1810. Ballet expressed the full impact of Romanticism as dance could often be more expressive of feeling or the emotions than mere words. The Romantic ballet, which flourished in Paris in the 1830s, quickly came over to London. The spectacle of Marie Taglioni dancing in *La Sylphide* at Covent Garden in 1832 created the modern image of the tutu-clad ballerina in which dance had dream-like dimensions that made the imagination soar. The classic ballet *Giselle* was first performed in Paris in 1841 with the great ballerina Carlotta Grisi and arrived in London a year later.

The Romantic ballet strongly focussed on ballerinas, relegating male dancers thereafter to supporting roles.[21] It was also distinguished by the increasing use of the *pointe* with ballerinas going on their toes supported by special dancing shoes. Marie Taglioni and her great rival Fanny Elssler were part of the international dance circuit. This wave of Romantic ballet arguably climaxed in July 1845 when four of the greatest dancers of the age, Taglioni, Grisi, Fanny Cerito, and Lucile Grahn, danced together at Her Majesty's in *Pas de Quatre*. The stage was showered with bouquets after each performed. When a wreath was thrown on stage in homage of Taglioni, Cerito used it to crown her as queen of ballet.[22] The thrill of the West End partly consists of the possibility of seeing nights like this.

[18] Rachel Cowgill, '"Wise Men from the East": Mozart's Operas and their Advocates in Early Nineteenth Century London', in Christina Bashford and Leanne Langley (eds), *Music and British Culture, 1785–1914: Essays in Honour of Cyril Ehrlich* (Oxford: Oxford University Press, 2000), pp. 61–4.

[19] George Henry Lewis, 'The Opera in 1833–63', *Cornhill Magazine*, 8 (1863): p. 295.

[20] *Illustrated London News*, 16 January 1847, p. 42.

[21] Ivor Guest, *The Romantic Ballet in England: Its Development, Fulfilment and Decline* (London: Pitman, 1972 [1954]).

[22] *Illustrated London News*, 19 July 1845, pp. 33–4.

Dance, however, represented a challenge to Victorian notions of decorum which is why ballet was not necessarily respectable. James Grant captured this unease:

> when the dancers are females, it is not the best means which could be employed to inspire notions of delicacy in the minds of those ladies who are among the spectators. How they can, not only witness it without a blush mantling their cheeks, but talk of it in terms of unqualified admiration to their acquaintances of the other sex, must appear passing strange to those who have not mixed in the society of the metropolis.[23]

It was assumed that only the aristocracy had the sophistication to handle the near nudity of silk tights. There was an understanding that some of the revealing costumes and poses that ballerinas struck would not do outside the Haymarket. No wonder male aristocrats often took an interest in the careers of ballerinas and tried to consort with them in the green room. Marie Taglioni enjoyed star status partly because she appeared respectable: a perfect emblem for an increasingly bourgeois age. Yet in the wake of her success in the 1840s, Romantic ballet began to decline in Britain. The great dancers and choreographers, such as Perrot, moved on and their replacements did not have the same impact. Instead, as we will see, ballet was rediscovered in music hall.

Although opera and ballet were exclusive, it is striking how West End performances were followed in publications such as the *Illustrated London News* (from 1842 onwards), meaning that its middle-class readers would find out about what was performed and enjoy illustrations of leading singers, dancers, and musicians. The West End was therefore part of a process where high culture moved out towards a wider public. The Victorian media helped shape the perception that what happened in London should set the aesthetic standard for the rest of the country.

Flash

In 1821, Pierce Egan published what was in many ways one of the most influential novels of the nineteenth century. *Life in London* traced the adventures of three young roisterers: Corinthian Tom, Jerry Hawthorn, and Bob Logic. They set out to sample the pleasures of the city from high to low, from West End to East End. The author constructs a metropolis based on sites of pleasure for men about town. There are visits to theatres, operas, and Almack's. Egan's London was a place of spectacle and opportunity where the great sport was 'seeing life'. Covent Garden

---

[23] Grant, *The Great Metropolis*, Vol. 1, p. 37.

I.R. & G. Cruikshank.

TOM & JERRY, IN THE SALOON AT COVENT GARDEN.

Fig. 3.2 Tom and Jerry in the saloon at Covent Garden: Pierce Egan, *Life in London* (author collection)

at midnight was a place for 'dissipated ramblers touched with the potent juice of Bacchus', and 'hoarse Cyprians in the last stage of their existence'.[24] In the saloon at Covent Garden theatre or at a tavern near the Olympic close by, they carouse with 'Cyprians' of all descriptions (see Fig. 3.2). They also receive boxing lessons in Bond Street and take in the pictures at the Royal Academy but then plunge into the underworld. The promise of the pleasure district is the breaching of high and low. Their money opens doors wherever they go and they happily acknowledge the likelihood of getting into a fight when slumming it. Theirs is the way of the 'cockney' (at that time a term used to describe a metropolitan type rather than someone born within a mile of Bow Bells). Acquiring knowledge about what was happening in the town and picking up some underworld slang was a sign of hard-won sophistication.

The cultural style of men about town (such as Egan's characters) was described at the time as 'flash': well off but open to all the pleasures the metropolis could provide.[25] Pierce Egan, known for his journalism about prize fights, based his novel on his own experiences (carousing with the Cruikshank brothers who illustrated his text) and those like him. His novel fed into a wave of novels that explored adventures in the underworld including G.W.M. Reynolds's *The Mysteries of London* (1844–8) and Dickens's fiction (for its dramatization, see next chapter). Gregory Dart captures the social indeterminacy of Egan's men about

[24] Pierce Egan, *Life in London* (London: Sherwood, 1821), pp. 13, 24.
[25] Gatrell, *City of Laughter*, especially ch. 4.

town. What makes their exploits pleasurable, he argues, is the way that they were playing a role, one that others could take up or at least enjoy reading about.[26]

The 'flash', their haunts, and their alpha male qualities were the subject of contemporary guides. *The Every Night Book* describes Mrs H's establishment opposite the Theatre Royal in Drury Lane:

> At the close of the performance its rooms are frequently thronged with young blades, having some money in their pockets and few brains in their heads, who come here to treat themselves and 'Cynthia of the minute' to a shell-fish supper. It is one of those places to which those who are desirous of seeing 'whatever may be seen' in the metropolis after nightfall, once a year or so, pay a brief visit in the course of their rounds. Our reader...will find little to delight and much to disgust him...[27]

Such accounts have the tone of self-regarding gossip which informs many of these guides to the city; deploring unrespectable activity while describing it with semi-pornographic relish (we will return to West End prostitution in Chapter 7). The flash patronized West End pubs such as Tom Cribb's on Panton Street, named after its former publican, the Regency boxer, and a notorious haunt of pugilists as well as 'Flash tradesmen, professional betters, a swell amateur or two...and pugilistic reporters.'[28] The man about town would develop into the figure of the sporting gentleman, notorious for his familiarity with clubland, the turf, the billiard hall, the pub, and the boxing ring. The sporting gentleman was the epitome of the *flâneur* and thus decisive in making the West End.

The identity of the swell or the masher became one that was conferred by the West End. It was a pose that could be adopted by men further down the social scale. The performer and rake Renton Nicholson (who will feature below) recalled that 'It was the custom then, as it still is, for the young men of the suburbs not to content themselves with the resources of amusement found in their own neighbourhood, but to go, as it is termed, "down town", to seek diversion; and this predilection led me often to the popular haunts of nightly debauchery at the West-end of London, among flats and sharps of all sorts'.[29]

One of the characteristics of the man about town was his addiction to gambling. This was partly catered for at gentleman's clubs as well as in lowlife gambling dens. The most elite gambling house was Crockford's on St James's Street, which took over from Brook's and Watier's as a centre for hazard and other card

[26] Gregory Dart, *Metropolitan Art and Literature, 1810–1840: Cockney Adventures.* (Cambridge: Cambridge University Press, 2012), pp. 107–36.

[27] *Every Night Book: Or, Life after Dark* (London: T. Richardson, 1827), p. 155.

[28] *Every Night Book*, p. 83.

[29] Renton Nicholson, *Rogue's Progress: The Autobiography of 'Lord Chief Baron' Nicholson* (ed. John L. Bradley), (London: Longmans, 1965 [1860]), p. 70.

games. Its actual name was the St James's Club and it was founded by William Crockford in 1823. Crockford was one of the most remarkable of the entrepreneurs who built the West End. He was the son of a fishmonger in Temple Bar. Despite his working-class upbringing, his mathematical talent allowed him to make money from gambling which he used as a passport to the elite. In 1823 he acquired a bridgehead on St James's Street, offering high stakes gambling. He made so much money that that he was able to demolish four houses at the top of St James's Street and hire the leading architects Benjamin and Philip Wyatt to create a luxurious casino. Crockford made money from each bet placed. His club was seductive because only the best circles were allowed in. To entice them, Crockford hired the best chefs: Louis Eustache Ude and Charles Elmé Francatelli. According to Alan Chambre:

> The suppers were on so grand a scale, and so excellent, that the Club became the refuge of all the undinnered members and *gourmets*, who flocked in after midnight from White's, Brooke's, and the Opera, to partake of the good cheer, and try their fortunes at the hazard-table afterwards. The wines were of first-rate quality, and champagne and hock of the best growths peeped out of ice-pails, to cool the agitated nerves of those who had lost their money.[30]

Great fortunes were frequently lost at the Crockford tables.

Crockford's and other gentleman's clubs represented the upscale end of the gambling market, but the West End was increasingly taken over by unrespectable locations for less well off people. There were five minor gambling houses in Regent Street whilst Leicester Square, in particular, became known for its 'hells'. According to James Grant, 'Among those who frequent the second class of gaming-houses, are a very great number of city merchants, and city clerks in situations of confidence. They are called Cits by the "Greeks" and hellites, and are looked on as prime game'. He also identified a third class of gambling den frequented by 'noblemen's and gentleman's servants, and shopmen with small salaries'. Grant noted (in an example of the anti-Semitism not uncommon in the period) that such hells were run by Jews.[31]

In 1842, the police broke up a well-known working-class gambling den in Castle Street, Leicester Square. Inspector Beresford, in plain clothes, kept the house under observation and noted how one of the porters, Abraham Levey, would only allow men in with a special pass key. The police made a dramatic entrance by seizing Levey's key and taking possession of the casino's bank. According to the *Illustrated London News*, this bank 'as may be expected from the wretched class of players and the poverty-stricken proprietors did not amount to more than a few

[30] Chambre, *Recollections of West-End Life*, pp. 250–1, 253.
[31] Grant, *The Great Metropolis*, Vol. 1, pp. 207, 208, 214.

shillings. As soon as the alarm of the police was given a scene that beggars description ensued. Each tried to make his escape by either jumping out of the windows or overpowering the constables by a sudden rush down stairs'. Cards, dice, and the bank were taken away and Levey was among the men fined for running the establishment.[32] A similar incident in Castle Street followed in 1848 when a group of men was found in a gambling den by police who confiscated two cups used to make the coins come out heads or tails as desired. In the same year, the gaming house at 17 Castle Street was found to employ a device where a roulette table could be transformed (presumably by being raised) into a chandelier if the police showed up.[33]

The existence of this lower class level of gambling reveals how pleasure in the West End was starting to become democratized. Gambling was, and is, one of the pursuits that united the classes, especially patricians and the working class. It was this cultural connection that helped give the West End its character, uniting high and low. The addictive qualities of gambling were also important, drawing men back to the gaming tables over and over again. Aristocratic gaming tables acted as a form of policing, establishing who were men of honour (and could thus pay their debts) and who were not. The image of the gentleman gambler (not quite respectable but indubitably part of High Society) helped give the West End a reputation for risk in all forms.

Low Life

We can find in the Strand and Covent Garden area new types of pleasure that transformed popular culture, especially in its pubs which provided entertainment and ballads, sometimes with amateur singers and performers. This was the world of the back room in saloons and taverns from which music hall would emerge. It was a world that stressed the values of conviviality. Elite men, possibly modelling themselves on Pierce Egan's characters, could flatter themselves they were entering the underworld.

Here was a world of jobbing writers and artists struggling with little money. William Blake lived the last few years of his life in penury on Fountain Court off the Strand. The Crown and Anchor Tavern on Arundel Street, just off the Strand, was notorious for its radical discussions. The London Corresponding Society met there in 1793–4, championing the French Revolution, and the Hampden Club, chaired by Sir Francis Burdett, used it to demand parliamentary reform. The pub thus enjoyed a reputation for political dissent and the construction of radical

---

[32] *Illustrated London News*, 6 August 1842, p. 206.
[33] Newspaper clippings in St Martin's Scrapbook Series: Leicester Square Vol. 1 part 1, pp. 46, 48 (Westminster City Archives).

networks. It was at the Crown and Anchor that the young Lancashire radical Samuel Bamford met 'Orator' Henry Hunt ('always beating against a tempest of his own or of others' creating') who would go on to address the crowd at St Peter's Field in Manchester in 1819.[34] The pub was vast and a good place for societies and social organizations to hold meetings, benefiting from its central location, close to the West End, the law courts and the City. The Society of Antiquaries regularly dined there which shows how a respectable middle-class organization could find its way into pub life.[35] The Glee Club of England used the Crown and Anchor for its meetings in 1815.[36]

The Coal Hole pub on Fountain Court, just off the Strand, was famous for its music and theatrical associations (the actor Edmund Kean created the Wolf Club there for drinking). Edmund Yates recalled that in the early Victorian years, 'The landlord was one John Rhodes, a burly fellow with a bass voice, who sat at the head of the singers' table and joined in the glees, which were sung without musical accompaniment'.[37] A former singer at Drury Lane, he allegedly inspired the character of Mr Hoskins, landlord of the Cave of Harmony, in Thackeray's *The Newcomes*, which evoked this new world of pleasure around the Strand.

The Coal Hole also included Renton Nicholson's Judge and Jury shows at one point. This entertainment moved round the Covent Garden area fetching up, among various locations, at the Garrick's Head Hotel on Bow Street and at the 'Hall of Justice', no. 404 Strand. These were evenings featuring mock trials, sending up the world of legal London and the corridors of power. The Inns of Court, the Old Bailey, and the Houses of Parliament were not far away and provided an audience who were prepared to laugh at themselves or at people they were familiar with. The Judge and Jury Society would employ obscenity to satirize people in authority and bring them down to earth. On one occasion, a Strand prostitute complained that she was being made fun of in one of Nicholson's shows.[38] According to a witness, the performers included a man dressed in women's clothing.[39] Advertising made clear that the shows were for men only.[40]

Renton Nicholson had become known in the 1830s for frequenting gambling establishments and then editing *The Town* (1837–40), a semi-pornographic paper which exposed scandals in high society. He also penned a plagiarism of Dickens, *Dombey and Daughter*, and a number of works on boxing.[41] Nicholson performed the role of the judge (the 'Lord Chief Baron') and the evenings included food,

[34] Samuel Bamford, *Passages in the Life of a Radical* (Oxford: Oxford University Press, 1984 [1884]), pp. 19–20.

[35] *Morning Chronicle*, 24 April 1816, p. 2.

[36] *Morning Post*, 6 February 1815, p. 3.

[37] Edmund Yates, *Recollections and Experiences* (London: Richard Bentley, 1884), Vol.1, pp. 165–6.

[38] *Morning Chronicle*, 5 May 1858, p. 8.

[39] James Greenwood, *The Wilds of London* (London: Chatto and Windus, 1874), pp. 103–4.

[40] Advertisement in *London Low Life* (Adam Matthew Digital Collection).

[41] ODNB (Renton Nicholson); Nicholson, *Rogue's Progress*.

bottled stout, and 'tableaux vivants' to add sexuality to the mix. He would enter with mock gravity in a judicial wig, call for silence, expect everyone to rise and, having taken his place, would order a brandy and water. Figures such as the leading barrister Serjeant Ballantine were impersonated by a comedian playing 'Serjeant Valantine'.[42] Publicity for the Judge and Jury included a statement attributed to Henry Brougham, the leading jurist: 'The Judge and Jury is the speaking *Punch* of London; what *Punch* is in literature, the Judge and Jury is orally'. The connection to the magazine *Punch*, with its satire of contemporary pretensions, is revealing. Its offices were close by and both suggest that one function of the West End was to act as a place where a form of conservative anarchism was possible. The mighty could be mocked but no attempt to create an alternative political structure would be proposed. This was linked to a Bacchanalian evening of alcohol, sex, and banter.

Divorce and prostitution were frequent subjects, deflating the claims of respectability. An example of a Judge and Jury case concerned Sir Robert Peel who had for many years had an affair with a 'Miss Protection' but had now been seen entering a 'House of Ill-Fame, known as the Lower House, Westminster' and embracing a 'Mrs League' who had previously been 'Miss Free Trade'.[43] The Judge and Jury club was a continuation of the scurrilous radicalism of Regency satirists and activists who would employ satire and even pornography to attack the powerful.[44] In 1846, Nicholson gave lectures on art, using male and female models in simulations of undress to 'illustrate Masculine Symmetry and Feminine Loveliness'.[45]

A similar song and supper location was Offley's on Henrietta Street, noted for its chops (cooked by Offley himself) which was bustling after the curtains came down at the theatres.[46] Simpson's in the Strand commenced in 1828 as a cigar divan: a place with sofas for smoking and chess. Smoking was not uncommon among all classes of men but these sites made it a source of glamour. Gliddon's cigar divan on King Street, Covent Garden was decorated like a Grecian Temple. Its mocha coffee was allegedly 'so powerful and aromatic as to satisfy even the fastidious taste of a Turk'.[47] Also in King Street, the tobacconist Thomas Kilpack

---

[42] Clipping ('Man About Town') in St Martin's Scrapbook Series: Covent Garden Vol. 2 part 2 p. 31 (Westminster City Archives).

[43] Advertisements in St Martin's Scrapbook Series: Covent Garden Vol. 2 part 2 p. 26 (Westminster City Archives).

[44] Iain McCalman, *Radical Underworld: Prophets, Revolutionaries and Pornographers in London, 1795–1840* (Cambridge: Cambridge University Press, 1988).

[45] Advertisement in St Martin's Scrapbook Series: Covent Garden Vol. 2 part 2 p. 28 (Westminster City Archives).

[46] *Every Night Book*, p. 156; John Timbs, *Clubs and Club Life in London* (London: Chatto and Windus, 1908), pp. 437–38.

[47] Clipping in St Martin's Scrapbook Series: Covent Garden Vol. 2 part 2 p. 55 (Westminster City Archives).

introduced a bowling alley, reminding patrons that bowls had been a part of merrie England 'to which old Chaucer would resort'.[48]

Maiden Lane, which runs parallel to the Strand, proved a place of cultural innovation. The street dated back to the development of Covent Garden and was allegedly named after a statue of the Virgin Mary, which once adorned it. The painter J.M.W. Turner was born there in 1775. Previous residents included Andrew Marvell and (briefly) Voltaire who lodged at the house of a French peruquier. It was formerly a cul-de-sac (a footpath connected it to Southampton Street) but was made more accessible when a way was cut through so that Queen Victoria's carriage did not have to turn round when leaving her at the Adelphi Theatre on the Strand. The houses were dirty and the pavements uneven with a variety of shops. Not quite a back street, it was nevertheless not a major thoroughfare which may have given it some allure as a site for lowlife pleasures. It was the site of Rules restaurant. Established by Thomas Rule in 1798, it quickly developed a reputation for pies and oysters. The latter in particular was seen as an important accompaniment to a night out on the town in the nineteenth century, often celebrated for their aphrodisiac qualities.

Across the road at no. 21 Maiden Lane were the Cider Cellars (sometimes spelt 'Cyder Cellars'). They dated back to 1730 and became a site for concerts that were notable for celebrating criminality and obscenity. Their song and supper evenings were marked by considerable male camaraderie, bonhomie, and good cigars (see Fig. 3.3).[49] The Cellars could be accessed from the Strand. The entrance was two doors west of the Adelphi Theatre by Mr Page's shell-fish warehouse and customers were told to look out for a lamp with 'Cider Cellars' painted on it. This circuitous form of entrance (through a notoriously dirty court) made it an ideal place for those in the know; the Cider Cellars needed seeking out. It was literally underground which would have shaped the atmosphere. Its proprietors emphasized that there would be entertainment after the theatres had finished and that it was possible to get a bed for the night.[50] Entrance in 1837 cost two shillings and sixpence, which excluded the working classes.[51] That same year, Charles Dickens in *The Pickwick Papers* gave a taste of its clientele. Satirizing the gradations of clerks in the Temple, he wrote of the salaried clerk who 'repairs half-price to the Adelphi, dissipates majestically at the cider cellars afterwards, and is a dirty caricature of the fashion, which expired six months ago'.[52] Yet it is also clear that the Cider Cellars attracted more upscale people including luminaries such as the chef Alexis

---

[48] Advertisement in St Martin's Scrapbook Series: Covent Garden Vol. 2 part 2 p. 60 (Westminster City Archives).

[49] *Era*, 21 September 1856, p. 10.

[50] Advertisements in St Martin's Scrapbook Series: Covent Garden Vol. 2 part 2 p. 28 (Westminster City Archives).

[51] Advertisement in *London Low Life* (Adam Matthew Digital Collection).

[52] Charles Dickens, *The Pickwick Papers* (Oxford: Clarendon Press, 1986 [1836]), p. 459.

Fig. 3.3 The Cider Cellars (Westminster City Archives)

Soyer who used it on at least one occasion as a place to discuss business.[53] Blanchard Jerrold recalled that the Cellars were patronized by MPs, 'the pick of the Universities and the bucks of the Row' because it permitted the singing of indecent songs.[54]

Among the vocalists who could be heard at both the Coal Hole and the Cider Cellars was Thomas Hudson. His songs such as 'Jack Robinson' found their way into street slang. Herr Von Joel's yodelling was popular as was Tom Penniket who sang a song about a raw recruit, 'Soldier Bill'.[55] Here W.G. Ross sang his blasphemous song 'Sam Hall' about a murderous chimney sweep; it became a staple of the popular tradition because of its refusal of shame in the face of a public

[53] Annabel to Eliza, 12 July 1851: LMA/4467/A/03/001 (London Metropolitan Archives).

[54] Gustave Doré and Blanchard Jerrold, *London: A Pilgrimage* (London: n.p. 1872), p. 168.

[55] *Morning Post*, 25 July 1865, p. 2; Charles Douglas Stuart and A.J. Park, *The Variety Stage: A History of the Music Halls from the Earliest Period to the Present Time* (London: T. Fisher Unwin, 1895), pp. 25–31.

hanging (there is even a version by Johnny Cash).[56] Edmund Yates recalled 'for months and months, at the hour when it was known that "Sam Hall" would be sung, there was no standing-place in the Cider Cellars'.[57] John Evans, who managed the venue, thought it declined when the song 'Sam Hall' lost its popularity.[58] Renton Nicolson also brought his Judge and Jury evenings to the Cellars in 1858 with *poses plastiques* and a concert at midnight.[59]

This was a world rooted in obscenity. One guide noted its deployment of 'flash inuendos'.[60] We gain an insight from a book of obscene songs sung at the Cider Cellars and other similar venues. Titled *The Nobby Songster*, it was published from an address on Wych Street, a few blocks away and associated with the pornographic book trade. The louche content of the songs can be deduced from some of their titles: 'Wanted A Woman!!! (a curious and rummy chaunt)', 'Miss Bounce of Cock Lane', and 'A Young Flash Whore and an old Jack Daw'. The one illustration in the songbook is mildly pornographic with a Jack Tar gaining access to a woman's bedroom (see Figs 3.4a and 3.4b). A number of songs referenced actors in the West End. 'The Bill Sticker' tells of Shiney Sam who put up posters around Charing Cross and excels in double entendre:

> I've hung Macready twelve feet high,
> And though it may seem funny,
> Day after day against the wall I've
> stuck up Mrs. Honey
> There's Ellen Tree, I'm proud to say,
> the stage's great adorner,
> I've had the honour of sticking her in
> every hole and corner
> And Helen Fawcett, bless her eyes, she
> takes the paste quite freely,
> And leaves enough to plaster Hall on
> the top of Mrs Keeley.[61]

A contributor to *Lloyd's Weekly Newspaper* complained that the Cider Cellars and the pornography of Holywell Street was ruining the elite. It was worrying that 'indecent songs are sung that are known to select circles of men in every part of

---

[56] David Masson, *Memories of London in the 'Forties* (Edinburgh: Blackwood, 1908), pp. 153–56.

[57] Yates, *Recollections and Experiences*, Vol.1, pp. 167–68.

[58] Report from the Select Committee on Theatrical Licenses and Regulations (1866), pp. 203–4.

[59] Newspaper clipping in St Martin's Scrapbook Series: Leicester Square Vol. 1 part 1 p. 48 (Westminster City Archives).

[60] *The New Swell's Night Guide to the Bowers of Venus* (London: J. Paul, 1846 [?]), p. 11.

[61] *The Nobby Songster: A Prime Selection as now Singing at Offleys, Cider Cellars: Coal Hole etc* (London: W. West, 1842?).

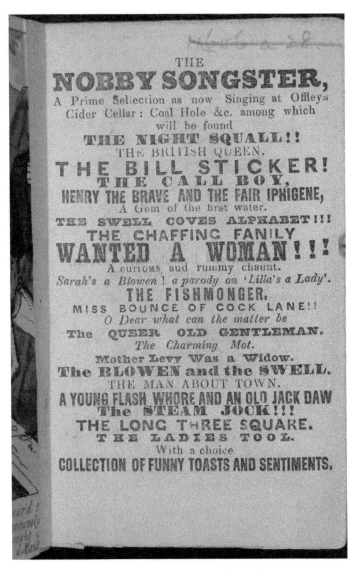

Fig. 3.4a The *Nobby Songster*: © British Library Board (shelfmark c.116 a 13)

the country'.[62] In 1853, there was an attempt to prevent renewal of the music licence of the Cider Cellars on the grounds that obscene songs were sung there. The manager insisted the songs were not indecent but admitted that different constructions could be put on the lyrics. The licence was renewed but in 1862 a similar application failed.[63]

---

[62] *Lloyd's Weekly Newspaper*, 8 January 1854, p. 6.
[63] *Daily News*, 7 October 1853, p. 6; 11 October 1862, p. 6.

It near'd the time when a Cove with smiles.
Was cautiously stealing along the tiles.
He thought of the joys his visit had led.
To see a Maid fast asleep in Bed.

Fig. 3.4b The *Nobby Songster*

A more working-class version of this kind of venue were the free-and-easies, which took place in pubs, such as the Hope on Drury Lane, with song and drink. These evenings were notoriously boisterous but there were also more respectable tavern concert rooms which appealed to a lower middle-class audience. They fostered a network of professional and semi-professional entertainers. Over at the Horse and Dolphin on Macclesfield Street, Soho, in 1840, singers entertained a room that could take 160 people and cost a penny for admittance.[64]

This rich underground culture of bawdiness, song, and food was then taken a stage further with the emergence in the 1840s of Evans's on King Street, Covent Garden, just a block to the north of the Cider Cellars. More than a spatial move, it took the low forms familiar from Maiden Lane and made them more respectable. Its owner William Carpenter Evans had formerly run the Cider Cellars so there was some continuity, but Evans's was far grander. It became a supper room and hotel with the unusual name of Evans's late Joy's (the previous owner, who ran a club for the nobility, had been called Joy). Bed and breakfast was available and it was aimed at the select, including men who might not have patronized the Cider Cellars.

---

[64] Laurence Senelick (ed.), *Tavern Singing in Early Victorian London: The Diaries of Charles Rice for 1840 and 1850* (London: Society for Theatre Research, 1997), pp. 4–7.

This shift towards the genteel and away from the world of Maiden Lane rakes suggests a moment of transition in the West End: the creation of respectable entertainments that drew from popular culture but in a more refined setting. This would become the hallmark of West End music hall. Evans's became the site of popular singers who would deliver musical numbers with a few laughs and became a fashionable site for men about town. Women were only allowed to watch from behind a screen so as not to disrupt the masculine atmosphere (though another contemporary source suggests it was for men only). They also reportedly had to give their names and addresses which was presumably intended to keep out prostitutes.[65] The audience in the early Victorian years included authors like Thackeray, George Augusts Sala, Douglas Jerrold, and Albert Smith as well as barristers such as Serjeant Ballantine.[66] In its origins, it was known for obscene songs but it became more respectable and was rebuilt as a concert hall by Evans's successor, John 'Paddy' Greenmore (who had sung there), and featured drink and dining. It is usually thought of as one of the points of origin of music hall and indeed became a middle-class alternative to the halls.

One of the stars of Evans's (circa 1850) was 'Jack Sharp' who also sang comic songs at Cremorne Gardens and the Mogul Saloon in Drury Lane.[67] By the 1850s it was offering 'Aethiopian Serenaders' (white men in black face) who were regularly encored.[68] John Timbs in 1855 captured the feel of Evans's:

> It is in a bold, handsome style, with a coved ceiling, richly ornamented. It is divided by fluted columns into nave and aisles, and embellished with works of Poetry, the Drama, Music etc, and it is brilliantly lighted by gas in ten richly-cut lutes. Here are sung glees, madrigals, and other fine old melodies; besides pieces from foreign operas, and songs and ballads by living composers.[69]

Evans's in its advertising promoted itself as situated in an historic mansion which appealed to gentlemen. The menu included steaks, chops, and toasted cheese whilst the provision of cigars shaped the character of the evening.[70] A bed for the night cost two shillings and it was possible to hire a servant for a shilling.[71] Here

---

[65] Walter Thornbury and Edward Walford, *Old and New London* (London: Cassell, Petter, and Galpin, 1879–85), Vol. 3, p. 254; *Era*, 8 June 1873, p. 14; Stuart and Park, *The Variety Stage*, p. 17.

[66] Yates, *Recollections and Experiences*, Vol. 1, p. 171.

[67] Warwick Wroth, *Cremorne and the Later London Gardens* (London: Elliot Stock, 1907), p, 10; Stuart and Park, *The Variety Stage*, p. 20.

[68] Clipping in St Martin's Scrapbook Series: Covent Garden, Vol. 2 part 1 p. 20 (Westminster City Archives).

[69] John Timbs, *Curiosities of London; Exhibiting the most Rare and Remarkable Objects of Interest in the Metropolis* (London: J.S. Virtue, 1867 [1855]), p. 608.

[70] Clipping in St Martin's Scrapbook Series: Covent Garden, Vol. 2 part 1 p. 20 (Westminster City Archives).

[71] Programme in St Martin's Scrapbook Series: Covent Garden, Vol. 2 part 1 p. 19 (Westminster City Archives).

were the foundations of the cultural style that will be described in Chapter 11 as the populist palatial.

This form of lowlife enjoyed by the men of the beau monde was part of a new kind of identity. The 1830s was the moment when bohemianism emerged to describe a way of living and a location on the outside of polite society.[72] The term was first employed in Paris to describe artists living in penury for their art. Bohemianism stood for the idea of the artist as a kind of outlaw, holding established values in contempt. Vic Gatrell has described the Covent Garden area as creating the first Bohemians in the eighteenth century but argues it changed with the onset of Victorianism, when the codes of respectability undermined the louche world of masculine pleasures that were the district's stock in trade.[73] Gatrell senses that these artistic networks began to move northwards in the late eighteenth century. And yet if we look at the early Victorian years, there was still a remarkable atmosphere of song and creativity around Covent Garden sustained by the proximity of theatres and literary circles.

In one sense there was nothing, strictly speaking, bohemian about the toffs who patronized the West End. They did create, I argue, a conservative version of bohemianism, enjoyed by those who did not feel the need to slum it or live in a garret and which flourished in the later Victorian period. Richard Burton, for example, established his Cannibal Club (lasting from the 1860s to the 1880s) at Bertolini's restaurant in St Martin's Lane by Leicester Square; its orientalist name proclaimed its disdain for puritanism. The club, whose members included Sala and Algernon Swinburne, collected pornography and discussed flagellation with schoolboyish obsession.[74] There were other bohemian enclaves. In the 1870s, the Carlisle Arms pub in Carlisle Street, Soho, was a familiar space for poorer bohemians, attracted by the diverse ethnic mix in Soho.[75] The Unity Club on Holywell Street in the Strand was the haunt of actors and journalists.[76] The bohemian life could draw in artists and writers such as Wilkie Collins. Dickens feared that his protegé, George Augustus Sala, had been ruined by his immersion in bohemia. Sala wrote for the *Daily Telegraph* and moved in the best circles but was never quite a gentleman because he was too familiar with the dark shadows.[77] The West End offered spaces where bohemianism could emerge in bars and cafés although

[72] Christopher A. Kent, 'The Idea of Bohemia in Mid-Victorian England', *Queen's Quarterly* 80 (1973): pp. 360–9; Jacky Bratton, *The Making of the West End Stage: Marriage, Management and the Mapping of Gender in London, 1830–1870* (Cambridge: Cambridge University Press, 2011), ch. 3.

[73] Vic Gatrell, *The First Bohemians: Life and Art in London's Golden Age* (London: Allen Lane, 2013).

[74] Deborah Lutz, *Pleasure Bound: Victorian Sex Rebels and the New Eroticism* (New York: W.W.Norton, 2010), pp. 75–6.

[75] Daniel Kirwan, *Palace and Hovel; Or, Phases of London Life* (London: Aberlard-Schuman, 1963 [1870]), p. 57.

[76] George R. Sims, *My Life: Sixty Years' Recollections of Bohemian London* (London: Eveleigh Nash, 1917), p. 41.

[77] Peter Blake, *George Augustus Sala and the Nineteenth-Century Periodical Press: The Personal Style of a Public Writer* (Farnham: Ashgate, 215), pp. 1, 131.

by 1900 bohemians were expressing contempt for the West End and beginning to discover themselves in other parts of London such as Bloomsbury and Chelsea.[78]

What are we to make of the world described here? The King's Theatre/Her Majesty's Theatre was a female space both in terms of the aristocratic ladies in the boxes but also in the ballerinas who sidelined male dancers. It offered the elite a stage for its performance of aesthetic superiority and was characterized by its cultivation of politeness. Opera and ballet were thus vital in constructing the worldview of the elite with their sense of artistic and social hierarchy. The Covent Garden area, however, was effectively the backstage of the aristocracy; a world of male libertines who mixed easily with the lower orders in pursuit of bawdiness, alcohol, and wenches. Yet from this encounter we see the foundations of music hall and the articulation of new bohemian identities. The West End acted as an intermediary between high and low culture, interpreting one to the other. Bohemianism was one of the dynamic forces in Victorian culture, creating spaces outside the elite where new identities could be constructed. Within the West End, we can locate this spatially in the gap between St James's and Maiden Lane. Patrician males could go between both worlds, especially if they were bachelors. This passion for lowlife in one sense was transgressive but was also relatively conservative in that hierarchies were never truly questioned.

---

[78] Rohan McWilliam, 'Elsa Lanchester and Bohemian London in the Early Twentieth Century', *Women's History Review*, 23 (2014): pp. 171–87.

4

The Histrionic Art

The people of London are a theatre-going people.

James Grant[1]

Theatre in the Age of Romanticism

It was not just the beau monde who were at play. London's population was expanding rapidly and there was a need to provide new spaces of entertainment. There were fairs, pleasure gardens, circuses, and sites of curiosity and conviviality. Above all, there was the stage. The proximity of a large number of theatres confirmed the West End as a place given to different kinds of performance. If we agree that describing the West End as a pleasure district involves a form of mental mapping (see Introduction), it follows that the sites of playhouses and other sites of entertainment were, and are, crucial to seeing the area as distinct in atmosphere from elsewhere. Theatre was the great popular form of the nineteenth century, drawing in audiences from across the classes.

James Grant (with a little exaggeration) argued that theatres 'may be said to be the principal source of amusement to all classes of the inhabitants. The highest and the lowest, the most intellectual and most illiterate, evince an equal partiality to them.' This posed a problem: 'Persons from the country, unacquainted with plays and players, often feel themselves very uncomfortably situated in company, owing to the large share of the conversation which is assigned to matters pertaining to the histrionic art.'[2] The stage clearly had an integrative function allowing urban society to understand itself. London itself was a common subject on stage as were the manners and characteristics of city folk. Theatres inscribed themselves into the metropolis not just through what they presented but also through posters and playbills pasted to walls, hoardings, and any available space. Large, block typefaces, dramatic images, and elaborate numbers of exclamation marks were employed in a battle to grab the attention of spectators away from counter-attractions.

---

[1] James Grant, *The Great Metropolis* (London: Saunders and Otley, 1837), Vol. 1, p. 24.
[2] Grant, *The Great Metropolis*, Vol. 1, pp. 23, 27.

London's West End: Creating the Pleasure District, 1800–1914. Rohan McWilliam, Oxford University Press (2020).
© Rohan McWilliam.
DOI: 10.1093/oso/9780198823414.001.0001

There has been a convention in the history of the drama that there was a long silence between the plays of Sheridan in the later eighteenth century and the revival of the dramatic art through the influence of Ibsen, Shaw, and Wilde in the later nineteenth century. No significant play (of any literary merit) was written between these two high points. This ignores the fact that the stage in the nine-teenth century was a more popular form than it ever would be again and that audiences mostly loved what they saw. The nineteenth-century stage adopted new theatrical forms such as melodrama to tell stories that addressed at least some of the preoccupations of the era.

What existed on West End stages in the early nineteenth century was a theatre for the age of Romanticism. This was the era when readers thrilled to Byron's poems and devoured the swashbuckling Toryism of Walter Scott with his evocations of Scottish history and the flowering of chivalry in the middle ages. Romanticism stood for a deeper interiority and focus on the nature of the self, whilst also acknowledging the possibility of sometimes uncontrollable emotions: passions, sadness, fear, joy. William Hazlitt claimed that the actress Sarah Siddons 'raised Tragedy to the skies or brought it down from thence'. To have seen her perform 'was an event in everyone's life', thus capturing the mythology of the West End: it does not merely present plays but 'events' that make it the essential place to be.[3] Playhouses also featured Romantic tales of the orient and the exotic. We can find the themes of Romanticism in the passionate performances of Edmund Kean and the burlesques of Jane Scott (see below).

The stage had a deeper social meaning. The increasing concentration of theatres in the West End began to give it a distinct 'liminoid' character. For anthropologists, liminality involves a threshold space which is neither one thing nor another, which trades in ambiguity, where identity is not definite but subject to role playing. Theatreologist Marvin Carlson catches the essence of pleasure districts: 'an arena of entertainment and recreation where citizens go for a variety of experiences set apart from the concerns of everyday life. This liminoid quality gives to districts of this sort a special excitement, often with a distinctly raffish or risqué element.'[4] This risqué element to the West End theatre world can be identi-fied through their spatial connections to brothels (see Chapter 7) but also to pubs and the sites of gambling described in the previous chapter. I argue below that this explains the success of the play *Tom and Jerry* (1821) which is a depiction of the pleasure district itself. Theatres became key to the urban experience; import-ant landmarks and (in terms of the argument made in this book) icons that signified the existence of the pleasure district.

[3] William Hazlitt, 'Mrs. Siddons' (1816) in Geoffrey Keynes (ed.), *Hazlitt: Selected Essays* (London: Nonesuch Press, 1948), pp. 683, 684.
[4] Marvin Carlson, *Places of Performance: The Semiotics of Theatre Architecture* (Ithaca, NY: Cornell University Press, 1989), p. 110.

Yet Londoners in the early nineteenth century would not have talked in terms of a distinct West End theatre. They would instead have thought about the small number of patent theatres licensed to perform drama. This chapter explores this world and the reasons why it fell apart, leading to the West End theatrical network that we know today. It argues that there was a struggle between the patrician forces controlling the patent theatres and middle-class money coming into the West End creating new venues which challenged the old order. Links between Court and stage were weakened. The patent theatres considered themselves custodians of quality theatre; it followed that everything else was inferior. What followed was a battle over status and what counted as legitimate drama.

The Patent Theatres

In 1836, there were twenty-one theatres in operation (and another six in occasional use) in London as a whole.[5] And yet, theatre in London was meant to be confined to the four stages that enjoyed the royal patent to perform. Drury Lane, Covent Garden, and the Theatre Royal, Haymarket, could stage the written word whilst the King's Theatre was devoted to opera (Map 4.1). This monopoly, dating back to the Restoration, shaped theatrical culture in London (see Chapter 1).

The theatrical monopoly was an integral part of the confessional state where power in Britain was dominated by the needs of the monarchy, the House of Lords, and the Church of England.[6] In the early nineteenth century the assumptions of patrician society were profoundly challenged with agitations for social reform and the widening of the franchise to non-Anglicans and even to working-class men. Demands for change in the theatre were therefore part of the wider conflict over power and authority being fought over by the protestors at Peterloo in 1819 and the Chartists in the 1840s. The conservatism of the West End can profitably be seen as produced by a location where the confessional state still held sway; one in which the *ancien régime* continued to dominate British society. Britain remained a monarchy and the landed classes to some extent maintained their control of the political system up to at least the mid-Victorian period. But the confessional nature of the theatre was apparent in other ways. The patent theatres did not perform on Wednesdays and Fridays in Lent and in Easter Week.[7] Whilst formal religion was kept off the stage, the West End submitted to the obligations of the Christian calendar.

---

[5] Leman Thomas Rede, *The Road to the Stage* (London: J. Onwhyn, 1836), pp. 12–13.
[6] J.C.D. Clark, *English Society, 1688–1832: Ideology, Social Structure and Political Practice During the Ancient Regime* (Cambridge: Cambridge University Press, 1985).
[7] Report from the Select Committee on Dramatic Literature (1832), p. 17.

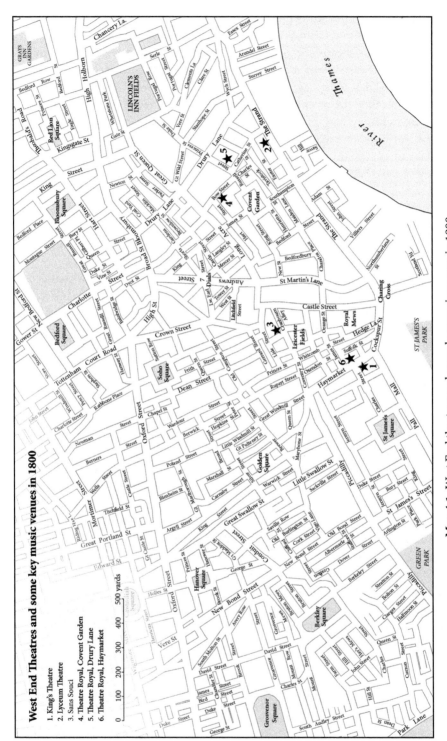

West End Theatres and some key music venues in 1800

1. King's Theatre
2. Lyceum Theatre
3. Sans Souci
4. Theatre Royal, Covent Garden
5. Theatre Royal, Drury Lane
6. Theatre Royal, Haymarket

Map 4.1 West End theatres and some key music venues in 1800

The patent theatres (especially Drury Lane and Covent Garden) insisted that by law they had a monopoly on the legitimate stage. Not only did they have a royal seal to that effect, they also argued that this served the national interest as they built up companies of the best quality actors who could be trusted to do justice to works by the best writers. Allowing other theatres to perform meant cheapening the drama; hence the plays performed at these 'minor' theatres were, by definition, 'illegitimate'.[8]

Theatre was policed by the Lord Chamberlain, an office that was the product of the confessional state. All plays had to be submitted to him two weeks in advance of performance (at a cost of two guineas) and he had the power to strike out profane, immoral, or political references. Irregularities could lead to a fifty pound fine.[9] All scripture references were removed, even the use of the word 'angels'. Expressions such as 'damme' and 'hang me' were not allowed. The playwright William Thomas Moncrieff was even forced to remove the word 'thighs' from his play, *The Bashful Man*, as it was considered indecent.[10]

The Theatres Royal in Drury Lane and Covent Garden were titans that dated back to the seventeenth century and were a few minutes' walk from each other. As noted in Chapter 1, their origins were intertwined and actors would often go from one to the other. Both were easily accessible from the Strand (see Map 4.1). Both commanded the attention of the best circles but also drew in a heterogeneous audience, playing a season that lasted for nine months of the year; usually from October through to July. Yet by the early nineteenth century Drury Lane and Covent Garden had become bloated monsters. In order to survive financially and to justify their patents, they had to offer not only all forms of drama but also ballet and opera as well. This required an enormous number of players, many of whom would not be employed on any particular evening. The theatres's financial affairs declined rapidly.[11]

The monopoly on legitimate drama enjoyed by the patents included the playing of Shakespeare as well as comedies such as Sheridan's *The School for Scandal* which had entered the canon. Shakespeare was the national bard and enjoyed a following throughout society. Even working-class radicals would invoke his name in support of their activities and insist that his words should be the property of everyone and not just the elite.[12] There were, however, concerns that Shakespeare was not always a paying proposition and required the drawing power of a Kean or a Macready. The rest of the dramatic canon was drawn upon selectively. In 1832,

---

[8] Jane Moody, *Illegitimate Theatre in London, 1770–1840* (Cambridge: Cambridge University Press, 2000).

[9] Report from the Select Committee on Dramatic Literature (1832), pp. 29, 34.

[10] Report from the Select Committee on Dramatic Literature (1832), pp. 60, 178.

[11] Dewey Ganzel, 'Patent Wrongs and Patent Theatres: Drama and the Law in the Early Nineteenth Century', *Proceedings of the Modern Language Association*, 76 (1961), p. 390.

[12] Antony Taylor, 'Shakespeare and Radicalism: The Uses and Abuses of Shakespeare in Nineteenth-Century Popular Politics', *Historical Journal*, 45 (2002), pp. 357–79.

it was observed that the Restoration playwright William Wycherley, author of *The Country Wife* (1675), could no longer be performed as his work was not moral.[13]

Covent Garden and Drury Lane had to be rebuilt in the early nineteenth century, following fires. Drury Lane burnt down in 1809 and was succeeded by the present building (the fourth built on the spot) in 1812. The architect was Benjamin Wyatt and it could hold about 3000 people.[14] In the early nineteenth century, Drury Lane was associated with the actor Edmund Kean who took over two years after it was rebuilt, saving the theatre from bankruptcy. The idea of the patent theatres was that they were to be open to all but their vast size meant that it was difficult for much of the audience to hear what was said on stage. There was a strict dress code in the boxes and dress circle, which were hence restricted to the elite. Prices for the gallery and the pit (frequently made up of benches in front of the stage) were much cheaper. Prostitutes could frequently be found in these spaces.[15]

Originally built in 1732, the Theatre Royal in Covent Garden burnt down in 1808 and was replaced at a cost of £240,000 by a new building designed by Robert Smirke the following year.[16] It was, in the early nineteenth century, still a house mainly for the performance of drama. The rich had a separate entrance from the rest and enjoyed private boxes. An index of how wealthy the clientele could be is illustrated by an incident in 1842 when an audience member had £9000 worth of diamonds stolen from him while at the theatre.[17] The gallery, the pit, and the dress boxes were for middling groups and better paid workers. Performances would start at six-thirty or seven and continue up to midnight. Half way through the evening programme, people would be allowed in for half price (usually 6d). For many workers, this was the earliest point in the evening when they could attend, given their hours of work, so the policy was not just about providing cheap seats. It was thus possible for people in all classes (except the very poorest) to get access to West End theatre in some form. The gallery and pit had a demotic character. The vast theatre could hold 2500 people in the auditorium. At any one time, 1000 people were employed by the theatre but at various times it could employ up to 2000 people.[18]

The reopening of the theatre in 1809 led to trouble. The actor manager John Philip Kemble decided to raise prices as the rebuilding (which involved purchasing adjoining property) had proved expensive. The interior of the theatre had also changed with an additional row of dress boxes and the prices of the pit, gallery, and regular boxes increased. There was also disquiet because the Italian soprano

---

[13] Report from the Select Committee on Dramatic Literature (1832), p. 28.
[14] Benjamin Wyatt, *Observations on the Design for the Theatre Royal, Drury Lane* (London: J. Taylor, 1813).
[15] Grant, *The Great Metropolis*, Vol. 1, p. 48.
[16] Report from the Select Committee on Dramatic Literature (1832), p. 50.
[17] *Illustrated London News*, 15 October 1842, p. 359.
[18] Report from the Select Committee on Dramatic Literature (1832), pp. 114, 131.

Angelina Catalani had been hired at the cost of £75 a night. On 18 September 1809, Kemble decided to open with *Macbeth*. The performance was disrupted by the audience, complaining about the new ticket prices and Kemble found it impossible to perform. What became known as the Old Price (or OP) riots had begun. On the following evening there were shouts of 'God save the King—No Foreigners—No Catalani—no Kemble.'[19] The actors could not get a hearing. The next night Kemble tried to reason with the crowd that the prices had not risen for many years but the crowd clung to the idea that there was such a thing as a 'just price'. *Bell's Weekly Messenger* had some insight when it disapprovingly described the rioters as 'resembling more the frequenters of Bartholomew Fair than the rational audience of a Theatre Royal'.[20] There was a strong carnivalesque dimension to the OP riots in which the world seemed to be turned upside down. The audience commanded the theatre rather than the actors. The disorder continued through to December with fruit thrown at performers (though the stage was never invaded). The audience created its own committee to negotiate with the management, engaged in rough music, and even developed an OP Dance, whilst some sported OP medals. The doorkeeper of Covent Garden tried to arrest one of the ringleaders, the radical barrister Henry Clifford. This led to more disorder in which the windows of Kemble's house were broken. Kemble hired boxers to try and subdue the crowd but this made things worse. Theatre riots were not unknown but this disruption was distinctive because of the way it reflected a contest between commercial society and the right of the people to cheap entertainment. By December 1809, Kemble was forced to give in. The price of the private boxes was reduced and the old charges for the pit restored (although increased prices for the elite boxes were retained).

The OP riots were caused in part because of the ambiguities of the spatial economy of the West End. Like shops, theatres were public spaces on private property. The rioters felt they had a stake or form of ownership in the theatres they were visiting; hence their employment of rhetoric about the English constitution which they felt had been violated by Kemble's actions. In his major study of the riots, Marc Baer found that most of the arrested rioters came from within walking distance of Covent Garden.[21] Thus the protests were shaped by a defence of locality. The occupations of the arrested also provide evidence about the heterogeneous audience for the patent theatres: a government clerk, a Pimlico labourer, a warehouseman of Lower Thames Street, a Shoreditch cabinet maker. At the same time, two dozen of the arrested were recorded as 'gentlemen'. Women were also active in the protest though few were arrested.[22] This was a trans-class form of protest. It did, however, mark a moment of resistance as West End

---

[19] Marc Baer, *Theatre and Disorder in Late Georgian London* (Oxford: Clarendon Press, 1992), p. 27.
[20] *Bell's Weekly Messenger*, 24 September 1809, p. 1.
[21] Baer, *Theatre and Disorder*, p. 135.   [22] Baer, *Theatre and Disorder*, pp. 139, 141.

entertainments began to exclude people by price, a process that went on through the nineteenth century.

There were concerns that the upper classes were deserting theatre for opera. George IV and William IV did not prove to be great patrons of theatre. The disorder of the OP riots may have been a factor in the shift in aristocratic taste but it was probably minor. Given that the elite lived in Mayfair and were moving further and further west (including Marylebone), the patent theatres were situated in the wrong place. They were at least a mile away from many aristocratic homes. The whole basis of the patent theatres needed reform. In the early nineteenth century, their status was powerfully challenged.

The Minor Theatres

If the patent theatres had the monopoly on playing drama, it followed that no one else could do so. Yet around 1800 new stages began to emerge in London and even in the West End. How was this possible?

The Lord Chamberlain had jurisdiction over the content of plays throughout the kingdom but also had the authority to license theatres within Westminster (the area covered by the West End).[23] In 1807, the Licensing Act was reinterpreted by the Lord Chamberlain to allow the licensing of minor theatres (which had started to emerge in the late eighteenth century). These so-called 'minor' theatres claimed they were not performing drama but offering a different kind of entertainment.

The great theatrical form of the nineteenth century was melodrama which was taken up by the minor theatres (although what was arguably the first melodrama in English, Thomas Holcroft's *A Tale of Mystery*, appeared at Covent Garden in 1803). The strict definition of melodrama was a drama with music (or a melodious drama). In practice, melodrama meant a stirring narrative that pitted good against evil and featured scenes of peril, hysteria, and coincidences. The stage abounded with evil aristocrats bent on seduction, patriotic Jack Tars, comic yokels, scheming lawyers, talented dogs, and dainty maids. There were gothic tales of terror and adaptations of popular novels such as *Frankenstein* and *The String of Pearls* (Sweeney Todd). Founded in an age of Romanticism and revolution, melodrama often took the side of the poor against the rich, offering to teach virtue and Christian morality in a changing and secularizing society. Melodrama also suited large theatres because its tales of hysteria required grand gestures as well as dramatic music. It was not always necessary to hear what was being said to follow the plot. Melodrama was deliberately meant to stimulate the emotions.

---

[23] Report from the Select Committee on Dramatic Literature (1832), pp. 9–10.

Tears (whether of sadness or laughter) were an integral part of melodrama's appeal. Its not infrequent storm scenes signalled not only spectacle but deep passions and the relationship between humanity and the elements.[24] The melodramatic imagination shaped fiction, music, and the arts throughout the nineteenth century. When melodrama was adopted by the minors, they claimed that theirs was an alternative to the legitimate stage and that they were not doing the same thing.[25] They were helped by the fact that the law was complex and magistrates would often turn a blind eye. Even when a case was successfully brought by a patent theatre against a minor, it was very difficult to make a conviction stick.[26]

Had the minors really offered something very different, the situation would not have needed reform. Yet the Surrey (Blackfriars Road), the Royal Coburg (now the Old Vic), and Sadler's Wells all began to perform Shakespeare. Elite audiences were quite happy to make a trip to these theatres because the content of their plays was similar to the fare at the patent theatres. This also suggests that the allure of West End theatre did not exist in the early nineteenth century. Sadler's Wells or the Surrey were not seen necessarily as inferior to Drury Lane. At the same time, the patent theatres offered melodramas for commercial reasons. They were thus not so different from the minors in practice.

The patent theatres were then challenged by the coming of minor theatres within the West End itself which reconfigured the theatrical economy. The embryonic pleasure district of the Strand began to sprout playhouses: the Lyceum, the Adelphi, and the Olympic. They represented middle-class money creating new forms of entertainment whilst hoping to appeal to the aristocracy. The Lyceum began life in 1772 on a site adjacent to where it is now on Wellington Street and with an entrance on the Strand. Crucially, it was not built as a theatre which would have flouted the law. Instead, it was intended as the exhibition room of the Royal Incorporated Society of Artists of Great Britain, although the building was rented out for a variety of entertainments including boxing matches, panoramas, a circus, and a zoo. In 1794, there was an attempt to turn it into a theatre but the patent theatres objected and a licence was refused. For a while (in 1802), it was taken over by Madame Tussaud for her waxworks. Ironically, the Lyceum only became a theatre because, when the Theatre Royal Drury Lane burnt down in 1809, its company needed a replacement venue quickly. It occupied the Lyceum from 1809 to 1812 thereafter, confirming that the venue was suitable for theatrical entertainments. The Duke and Duchess of Gloucester took in *The Maid and the Magpie* in 1816, endowing royal patronage on a non-patent theatre.[27] A fire in

---

[24] Carolyn Williams (ed.), *The Cambridge Companion to English Melodrama* (Cambridge: Cambridge University Press, 2018).

[25] Moody, *Illegitimate Theatre in London, 1770–1840.*

[26] Ganzel, 'Patent Laws and Patent Theatres', pp. 387–8; Report from the Select Committee on Dramatic Literature (1832), p. 194.

[27] *Bell's Weekly Messenger*, 11 August 1816, p. 1.

1830 led to the theatre being rebuilt on the site next door. It was taken over by the English Opera Company in 1841 and three years later was providing equestrian performances. The house was not to acquire a settled management regime until the coming of Henry Irving in the 1860s.

The Olympic on Wych Street (later torn down for the Aldwych development) commenced in 1806 as the New Olympic Pavilion. It was managed by the circus owner Philip Astley and was intended for equestrian entertainments. The venue was not a success and in 1813 was sold to the actor manager Robert Elliston who turned it into a theatre intended for fashionable society. The theatre went through a variety of managements and was not a huge success until it was taken over by Eliza Vestris in 1830.

Vestris had the Olympic refitted and turned into a house specializing in bur-lesques for an upscale audience. This was surprising as the Olympic was not in a polite location. Wych Street was the centre of the radical booktrade. As James Grant concluded, 'Notwithstanding its being in one of the dirtiest and most disreputable neighbourhoods in London, the Olympic is most fashionably attended.'[28] What pulled people in was the star power of Madame Vestris herself; just one example of how women were driving forces in theatre management in the nineteenth century, operating more or less on the same terms as men.[29] The theatre could take about a thousand people and the boxes cost four shillings, the pit two shillings, and the gallery one shilling. An evening at the Olympic involved light fare and the show always ended at eleven.

The Adelphi opened on the Strand in 1806, the same year as the Olympic. It was called the *Sans Pareil* for the first fifteen years of its existence and was built by John Scott, a merchant who sold a blue dye for stockings (Scott's 'Old True Blue'). He told the Lord Chamberlain that his purpose was to show off 'the genius and Pen of my Daughter Miss Jane Scott who from childhood professed extra-ordinary Musical Talents and was peculiarly gifted as an actress and dramatic writer.'[30] He transformed his warehouse (the term used for a shop in the early nineteenth century) on the Strand into a theatre for Jane to sing. Having established the importance of shops in constructing the pleasure district, we can see that the transformation of a shop into a theatre was appropriate. Scott's venture cost him £10, 000. He defined the heterogeneous, but non-elite, audience that found its way into his auditorium (and into the West End more generally):

The frequenters of the *Sans Pareil* are the better sort of the Middling Orders, persons of small income, young students and others, who come from all parts of

[28] Grant, *The Great Metropolis*, Vol. 1, p. 71.

[29] Jacky Bratton, *The Making of the West End Stage: Marriage, Management and the Mapping of Gender in London, 1830–1870* (Cambridge: Cambridge University Press, 2011), ch. 5.

[30] John Scott to Marquis of Hertford, 24 April 1818: HO 119/4, f. 8 (TNA).

INTERIOR *OF THE* SANS PAREIL THEATRE,

Fig. 4.1 The Sans Pareil Theatre (Westminster City Archives)

London to prosecute their studies in the different arts, sciences and liberal professions and persons of retired habits and those mostly at half-price, to whom the moderate prices and early hours are particularly adapted, who wish a rational entertainment at a small expense, our prices of admission being little more than half that of the great theatres.[31]

By contrast to the grand entrances of the patent theatres, the Adelphi was approached by a narrow entrance on the Strand flanked by Doric pillars and its auditorium was in the Grecian style with two galleries. There was room for 1800 at a performance. When she visited in 1822, the Tory hostess Harriet Arbuthnot found it 'crowded to overflow' with people 'hollowing & talking to each other from the pit to the gallery, & fighting & throwing oranges at each other'.[32] Figure 4.1 shows how such a theatre could nevertheless offer an intimate form of playing.

Like Eliza Vestris, Jane Scott proved a major innovator. She was open to the kinds of cross-fertilization that made the West End possible, offering both variety and illusion. The first evening contained songs written by her followed by phantasmagoria (a light show called 'Tempest Terrific'), and then a shadow play called 'The

[31] John Scott to Marquis of Hertford, 24 April 1818: HO 119/4, f. 15 (TNA).

[32] Francis Bamford and the Duke of Wellington (eds), *The Journal of Mrs Arbuthnot, 1820–1832* (London: Macmillan, 1950), vol. 1, p. 144.

Vision in the Holy Land; or, Godfrey of Bouillon's dream'.[33] It was an evening of song, light, and shadow, the phantasmagoria providing an anticipation of the cinema. Jane Scott wrote and managed her shows at the *Sans Pareil*/Adelphi, with a diet of melodramas, burlettas, pantomimes, and light operas. Her *The Old Oak Chest*, a 'melo-romantic Burletta of Interest' in 1816, made the elite into figures of fun; itself a recognition that the *Sans Pareil* was a middle-class rather than aristocratic space.[34] She retired in 1819 but established her theatre as an important West End venue.

In 1821, the Adelphi presented a dramatization by William Thomas Moncrieff of Pierce Egan's *Life in London*; a 'realization' of Egan's original, creating a dramatic commentary on the world explored in the last chapter. Titled *Tom and Jerry*, the dramatization ran for one hundred evenings at a time when most plays were only performed for two or three nights. It pointed to a future where the West End would become associated with the long-running hit show. The success of *Tom and Jerry* is understandable as it would have appealed to the 'flash' who were dealt with in the previous chapter. Moncrieff claimed that 'Dukes and Dustmen were equally interested in its performance' and this may not have been far off the mark. The author produced his own de luxe edition of the playtext (with a glossary of the fashionable slang) aimed presumably at the dukes rather than the dustmen.[35] Harriet Arbuthnot was appalled by the show's vulgarity ('a sort of very low Beggar's Opera') but noted how the performance at the Adelphi connected with the audience because it seemed to represent their experiences of low life.[36] As we saw in Chapter 2, one scene in the play takes place in the Burlington Arcade, which had only recently opened and is the subject of a knowing song. The character Bob Logic (a 'professor of the flash') lives in the Albany on Piccadilly and the characters depend on Dicky Primefit, a Regent Street tailor, to (as they put it), 'fig' them out in the best clothes. There are also scenes at Almack's and 'a fashionable Hell, at the west end of the town': a statement of up-to-dateness.[37] The West End was self-referential, one form of entertainment and location connecting with another. A characteristic of pleasure districts is that they develop these kind of informal networks of information which flatter audiences, allowing them to draw on books they have read (like Egan's) and their awareness of locations nearby such as gaming houses. The West End made these locations seem squalid but also alluring and larger than life.

[33] Adelphi Theatre Project: http://www.umass.edu/AdelphiTheatreCalendar/m06d.htm#Label003 [accessed 26 September 2014].

[34] Jacky Bratton, 'Introduction', *Nineteenth Century Theatre & Film*, 29 (2002), pp. 3–4.

[35] William T. Moncrieff, *Tom and Jerry: Or, Life in London* (London: W.T. Moncrieff, 1826), p. v.

[36] Bamford and the Duke of Wellington (eds), *The Journal of Mrs Arbuthnot*, Vol. 1, p. 144.

[37] Moncrieff, *Tom and Jerry*, pp. 10, 17, 19, 55.

Given the new theatre's success, it was unsurprising that Covent Garden believed that the *Sans Pareil*/Adelphi in particular was a major threat; it allegedly reduced Covent Garden's annual income by £2000. In 1818 an attempt was made by the patent theatres to have the licences of the Olympic and *Sans Pareil* removed on the grounds that they damaged their means of 'supporting the dignity of the national drama'. John Scott would not have this, pointing out that his takings were usually £46 a night (and he believed the Olympic made even less) and so they could not be all that damaging to the patent theatres. As for the 'dignity of the national drama', the latter were putting on shows involving horses, elephants, monkeys, and dogs. He also noted the patent theatre audience included prostitutes; hardly evidence of great dignity.[38] The attempt to crush the West End minors failed.

The Strand was also the site of the *Sans Souci* Theatre, established in 1793 by Charles Dibdin (he later moved the theatre in 1796 to Leicester Place, off Leicester Square, where he performed up to 1804). Both versions of the *Sans Souci* were small, intimate venues. Dibdin was at various times (and frequently at the same time), a song writer, an actor, a novelist, a comedian, a singer, a theatre manager, a speculator, a journalist, a music tutor, a pamphleteer, and a publisher.[39] At the *Sans Souci*, he was an early architect of the one-man show, singing patriotic numbers that helped create a more positive image of the Royal Navy during the struggle with Napoleon. He developed a persona that was defined by its authenticity, manliness, and patriotism. What we see here is the creation of a conservative cultural style that was not unusual in the West End (and elsewhere). The *Sans Souci* had a troubled history after Dibdin sold it, occasionally used as a theatre but more often as an hotel or even a warehouse. For a while it became the German Theatre and, in 1832, hosted amateur performances.[40] The West End also included a number of private theatres which could be hired by stage-struck people who wanted the opportunity to try out acting and invite their friends.

The minor theatres of the West End were sources of innovation, developing new theatrical forms whilst also reproducing much of what the patent theatres were already doing. For that reason, they had a populist style which was prepared to simply ignore the law. They represented the larger forces of commerce that were creating a market economy and turning entertainment into a paying business enterprise. If we had gone to a playhouse, what would we have seen?

---

[38] John Scott to Marquis of Hertford, 24 April 1818: HO 119/4, ff. 9–10 (TNA).

[39] Oskar Cox Jensen, David Kennerley, and Ian Newman (eds), *Charles Dibdin and Late Georgian Culture* (Oxford: Oxford University Press, 2018).

[40] Newspaper clipping from 1806 in St Martin's Scrapbook Series: Leicester Square Vol. 1 part 2 p. 8 (Westminster City Archives); A Collection of Handbills and programmes of exhibitions and entertainments in Leicester Square, together with admission tickets; and of advertisements of tradesmen in Leicester Square. 1800–1870? (British Library: 1880.b.25), p. 24.

Playbill

A visit to the theatre in the early nineteenth century was a different experience to what it is now. If we examine a playbill from the period, we would find that that an evening did not offer one single play but a number of dramas including (possibly) a pantomime, an afterpiece, as well as a farce. The playbill might be two feet long, its physical length creating a sense of promise. As Jacky Bratton argues, an evening's entertainment would have been made up of contrasting elements. To think of this period in terms of single works by playwrights does not capture the dynamism of the event as experienced by the audience. Part of the propulsion of an evening at the theatre was the contrast between different plays which could often be the antithesis of one another; a tragedy followed by a farce, for example.[41] Audiences were familiar with the nature of repertoire and genre. What mattered was variety. The closest equivalent today would be to think of an evening's schedule on television. The playbill therefore offered a kind of contract between theatre and audience that the evening would offer different but inter-related pleasures. Thus, if we had gone to the Theatre Royal Haymarket in April 1836, we could not only have seen John Vandenhoff play Hamlet but also a farce called *My Husband's Ghost*. The evening then concluded with a ballet called *Zulema*.[42]

To a large extent, nineteenth-century theatre was dominated by melodrama but pantomime was also integral to theatrical fare.[43] Intended for all ages, it differed from what the form became in the later nineteenth century. Pantomime emerged from the harlequinade, a stock feature of early modern theatre. This was a short episode, often derived from fairy tales, which focussed on slapstick. It was dialogue-free, the word 'mime' in 'pantomime' being significant, and drew on the continental *commedia dell'arte* tradition (hence pantomime was a way round the laws restricting the spoken word to the patent theatres). The stage erupted with actors playing Harlequin, Columbine, Pantaloon, and the comic servant, Scaramouche. A production of *Mother Goose* established Joseph Grimaldi as the greatest comic performer of the century. Pantomime was usually the opener to an evening's entertainment on stage. It was only in the 1840s that it began to be identified with children.

The burletta was a comic opera. The form had developed in eighteenth-century Italy. Increasingly, the use of the term 'burletta' was deployed as a way of getting round the law. It was possible for a few musical numbers to be added to a straight play in order to make the claim that it was not covered by the law about the spoken word on stage. Burletta had affinities with another popular form: burlesque. The

[41] Jacky Bratton, *New Readings in Theatre History* (Cambridge: Cambridge University Press, 2003), pp. 37–9.

[42] Poster in St Martin's Scrapbook Series: Leicester Square Vol. 2 part 2 p. 16 (Westminster City Archives).

[43] Jeffrey Richards, *The Golden Age of Pantomime: Slapstick, Spectacle and Subversion in Victorian England* (London: I.B. Tauris, 2014).

performance of burlesque benefited from the proximity to other theatres and cultural forms that the West End provided. Indeed, shows would often send up other shows that were being performed in other theatres. The West End therefore allowed theatres to enter into conversation with one another, one of the distinctive features of the pleasure district. Burlesque was often not subversive or satirical but offered an alternative lens through which nineteenth-century life could be interpreted.

The distinction between the theatre and the circus was not clear-cut.[44] Animals proved a huge draw on the stage. One of the major founders of the circus, Philip Astley, began to develop equestrian entertainments south of Westminster Bridge from the 1770s onwards. Astley's Amphitheatre of Equestrian Arts survived him (it came to offer the horsemanship of Andrew Ducrow) and lasted up to 1893. The circus bled into the stage as Ducrow provided talented animals for shows. In this sense, animals helped make the West End just as much as human beings; for example, the dog dramas at the Adelphi. In 1838, the production of *Charlemagne* at Drury Lane was hugely admired for its spectacle but also for its talented animals. *The Era* noted:

> Horses, lions and tigers played their parts admirably. One of Mr Ducrow's horses not only allows himself to be turned into a horse-hair sofa and a mahogany dining table, but during the transformation actually turns round his head and dines with his company.[45]

The stage dealt with issues of race though often in ways suffused by contemporary attitudes, shaped by the existence of slavery. John Fawcett's pantomime, *Obi; Or, Three Finger'd Jack*, first appeared at the Haymarket Theatre in 1800. It featured a black man (played by a white actor in blackface) in Jamaica who frightens people into believing he can employ forms of magic (a skill sometimes attributed to the enslaved). In 1833, Ira Aldridge became the first black actor to actually play Othello in the West End (he had played it elsewhere). The Covent Garden audience reaction was fairly positive but some reviews were condescending to Aldridge due to his race and it only played for two out of the scheduled nine performances (although this was partly because many actors were affected by the flu epidemic causing the shows to be cancelled). Aldridge, however, did carve out a career as a tragedian in London and around Europe. This was particularly remarkable because, when he performed, slavery was only just coming to an end in the British colonies and of course still existed in the United States.[46]

[44] Marius Kwint, 'The Legitimization of the Circus in Late Georgian England', *Past and Present*, 174 (2002), pp. 72–115; Brenda Assael, *The Circus and Victorian Society* (Charlottesville, VA: University of Virginia Press, 2005).

[45] *The Era*, 28 October 1838, p. 57.

[46] Bernth Lindfors, *Ira Aldridge: The Early Years, 1807–1833* (Rochester, NY: University of Rochester Press, 2011), ch. 19.

More typical of stage depictions involving race was the minstrel show. In the 1830s the American performer Thomas 'Daddy' Rice would enjoy success on both sides of the Atlantic with his blackface routines and 'Jim Crow' dances which became a huge craze. Following the visit of the American Ethiopian Serenaders in 1848 (who played at the Adelphi), minstrel shows became a popular attraction.[47] Such acts became an acceptable form of musical entertainment for refined audiences.

Who wrote for the stage? The selling point for a play was that it was being performed at a particular theatre; not that it was by a particular writer. Playwrights were often considered producers of a lower form of literature; something that would not count as art. The most respected authors did not feel theatre was the best location for their work. It reeked of vulgarity (too many performing animals) and quite simply did not pay. For all his love of the stage, Dickens mainly reserved his playwriting and acting for the amateur theatre. The people who wrote for playhouses may have been hacks but they knew their audience. Playwriting also proved to be an area in which women could find a voice with a significant number of female dramatists penning dramas.[48] The best known of these was the Scottish dramatist Joanna Baillie whose plays included *De Montfort* which Edmund Kean performed at Drury Lane in 1821.

Authors were paid for the initial performances but received nothing after that; a major reason why dramatists were often in a state of penury at the end of their lives. Thomas Serle wrote *The Merchant of London* for Drury Lane in 1832. It was performed for nine nights with ten pounds coming to him for each performance (ninety pounds in total). After that, he ceased to earn money from the play.[49] In order to survive, playwrights had to knock out script after script. A case in point was William Thomas Moncrieff, author of *Tom and Jerry*, who wrote well over two hundred plays both for the patent theatres and the minor houses. He was engaged by Drury Lane for ten pounds a week and was sometimes given twenty-four hours' notice to knock out a drama. His *The Cataract of the Ganges* ran for almost 100 nights at Drury Lane in 1823.[50] It featured real horses and a waterfall on stage. Yet Moncrieff ended his life as a pauper, needing help from the Royal Literary Fund.

Nineteenth-century theatre turned writing into a commodity. Writers survived by their ability to deliver on time. At first glance, this was not a writing medium that favoured originality. It certainly involved writing plays with the different acting strengths of a company in mind. But it did require an understanding of

---

[47] Jessica H. Legnini, 'Identity, Class and Emulation: American Blackface Minstrelsy and its British Audiences', University of Warwick, PhD thesis 2011.

[48] Katherine Newey, *Women's Theatre Writing in Victorian Britain* (Basingstoke: Palgrave Macmillan, 2005).

[49] Report from the Select Committee on Dramatic Literature (1832), p. 116.

[50] Report from the Select Committee on Dramatic Literature (1832), pp. 175–6.

narrative tension and the ability to create satisfying dramatic climaxes. Even hacks have to deploy craft and skill.

Subsequent Performances

By the 1830s it was common to talk about theatre employing a 'star' system.[51] Audiences were fascinated by charismatic performances but critics helped create stars through their reviews. Yet, in the early nineteenth century, actors were still often considered unrespectable. Actresses, in particular, were often viewed as in effect prostitutes.[52] The decision to become an actor could mean being ostracized by family. It was thus not unusual for actors to come from theatrical families and continue the tradition of their parents.

Acting in an early nineteenth-century play was a different proposition from what it subsequently became. There was no director. Instead, this was the age of the actor manager. Figures like John Philip Kemble and Edmund Kean dominated the stage, determining what plays were performed and how they should be acted. Actors were usually part of a repertory company with each person specializing in a particular kind of part. Acting technique, moreover, was not intended necessarily to provide naturalism or reality. Instead, it offered a deliberately stylized reality with a complex set of manual gestures and forms of delivery that would have been comprehensible to the audience of the day.

The early nineteenth century saw a shift in acting style. The neoclassical performances of Sarah Siddons and John Philip Kemble no longer seemed appropriate although they were capable of portraying great feeling. The age called for acting that suited the values of Romanticism. Edmund Kean fascinated because he lacked acting technique; instead, he had raw passion. He also had the good fortune to be observed by one of the greatest of all theatre writers, William Hazlitt, who was awestruck by Kean's ability to render the interplay of emotions. This was apparent in Kean's Shylock in *The Merchant of Venice* at Drury Lane in 1814, in some ways his breakthrough role, which Hazlitt witnessed. Instead of a one-dimensional villain, Kean opted to show a figure of complexity and many-sidedness, a man equipped with an inescapable, if damaged, humanity. Hazlitt marvelled at his ability to give 'effect to the conflict of passions arising out of the contrast of situation' and 'the rapidity of his transitions from one tone or feeling to another'.[53] The effect on the audience seems to have been electric. George Henry Lewes, who saw Kean perform when he was young, considered him the greatest actor he had

---

[51] Report from the Select Committee on Dramatic Literature (1832), p. 30.
[52] Tracy C. Davis, *Actresses as Working Women: Their Social Identity in Victorian Culture* (London: Routledge, 1991).
[53] William Hazlitt, 'Kean' in Jon Cook (ed.), *William Hazlitt: Selected Writings* (Oxford: Oxford University Press, 1998), p. 248.

ever seen: 'a stormy spirit uttering itself in tones of irresistible power'. He recalled that 'Byron was not so worshipped as Kean'.[54] This feeling of adulation for heroic acting was what drew people to the West End.

Kean's successor was William Macready who established himself as the great innovator in poetic and heroic drama. Macready was somewhat embarrassed by his success as he was never persuaded that acting was something that a gentleman did. He triumphed in many of the great Shakespeare roles and established new works as part of the popular repertoire such as Bulwer Lytton's *Lady of Lyons* and *Richelieu*. His diaries reveal how much time he devoted to thinking about the meaning of a part in psychological terms.

Eliza Vestris (who, as we have seen, made the Olympic a major venue) was one of the entrepreneurs who made the West End. Lucia Elizabeth Vestris was born in 1797 and was a leading actress and opera singer. Her surname was derived from a brief marriage at the age of sixteen to the French ballet dancer Auguste Vestris. She triumphed in opera both in London and Paris, including enjoying a major hit in Moncrieff's burlesque opera *Giovanni in London* at Drury Lane (1820). This gave her a reputation for succeeding in breeches roles. Amongst other songs, she popularized 'Cherry Ripe' whilst possessing a slightly scandalous reputation. After building the reputation of the Olympic, she went on to manage Covent Garden and later the Lyceum. She enjoyed a strong association with the playwright James Robinson Planché and married the actor Charles James Matthews with whom she performed a new kind of refined light comedy on the stage. We catch some of her stage magnetism in a description of the Olympic audience when she returned in 1839 after a tour of the United States:

> such a reception—such a welcome—such cheers—we never heard in any the-atre, on any occasion whatsoever. Cheer followed cheer, mingled with loud cries of welcome, and accompanied by waving of handkerchiefs, while bunches and wreaths of flowers were showered on the stage…Madame Vestris was com-pletely overpowered; she clasped her hands upon her heart, seeming to say it was too full for the expression of its feelings, and then pressed them on her eyes to stop the unbidden tears that burst from them, in token of the sense of the kindness with which she was greeted.[55]

This study will show that the West End became a more feminized and middle-class space in the later nineteenth century. Such a shift was made possible by figures such as Vestris in the early Victorian period.

But what of actors beyond the great stars? Theatres had sprouted in major town centres with the development of urbanization in the eighteenth and nineteenth

---

[54] George Henry Lewes, *On Actors and the Art of Acting* (Leipzig: Tauchnitz, 1875), pp. 15, 60.
[55] *The Era*, 6 January 1839, p. 175.

centuries but the West End was the place many actors would head for. Actors would aim to be engaged by one of the patent theatres or, failing that, one of the stock companies in the metropolis. They were expected to specialize in a particular kind of role: juvenile lead, comic yokel, evil seducer. Theatres also required actors to provide their own make up, costumes, and even props.[56]

Actors generally associated with other actors. In the 1830s, the centre of the acting community was the Harp pub in Little Russell Street, Drury Lane, although players would also patronize the Albion nearby and the Kean's Head, which was on a passage leading from Brydges Street to Drury Lane. The Harp served as a place where actors could make contact with provincial stage managers and arrange out-of-London appearances. A Mr Sims acted as an early form of theatrical agent from his base there.[57] It was also a place for stage-struck young men hoping for a way into the profession. Actors' conversations and bonhomie were legendary: at the Harp, actors would 'cut up the best performers of the day, rail against fate and fashion, tell strange stories of bad benefits in towns, and love-feats among the pretty Cowslips during their rural campaigns....'.[58] The Harp and the Kean's Head developed stage networks but flourished as locations for gossip.

The need to assist actors in illness and old age helped reinforce an associational culture amongst actors. In 1838, the Theatrical Benevolent Society was formed at the Haymarket Theatre in order to help 'aged and decaying performers'. Drury Lane and Covent Garden had both already established similar organizations to help their actors. No one was allowed to benefit from the scheme unless they had paid into it.[59] Perhaps the most celebrated form of associational culture was the Garrick Club. Founded in 1831, its purpose was to support artists and actors and its early members included figures such as Macready. It was first housed in King Street, Covent Garden, but in 1864 moved to its present building on Garrick Street and gained a reputation for developing a remarkable collection of paintings about the theatre. Its location in Covent Garden always gave it a different reputation from the clubs of St James's discussed in the previous chapter.

Reform

In the 1830s, West End theatre was still shaped by a set of arrangements that went back to 1660s. The system based on patent and minor theatres was increasingly difficult to defend especially in an age of social reform. The great political idea of the day was liberalism with its championing of free trade. Drury Lane and Covent

---

[56] Michael Baker, *The Rise of the Victorian Actor* (London: Croom Helm, 1978), p. 121.
[57] Rede, *The Road to the Stage*, p. 3.
[58] *Every Night Book: Or, Life after Dark* (London: T. Richardson, 1827), pp. 122–3; 142.
[59] *Era*, 11 November 1838, p. 74.

Garden were examples of vested interests, institutions that could not continue unchanged in the age of laissez faire. Owners of minor theatres no longer took the monopoly of the patent theatres over drama seriously. The great reformer Francis Place studied the patent system and argued it had been an 'injurious monopoly', run for private gain rather than public benefit.[60] Free trade in theatre therefore made sense. The system was rife with restrictive practices, an example of what was being termed 'Old Corruption'. The power bloc that made up the confessional state was fundamentally challenged in the years between 1828 and 1832 when Catholics and nonconformists were admitted to the franchise which was also extended and made more uniform.

The Coburg was fined in 1820 when it produced *Richard III* but this did not deter the minor theatres who just carried on putting on plays with the spoken word.[61] In 1830, following a complaint by Kemble at Covent Garden, the courts forced the closure of the Tottenham Street theatre after it performed spoken word drama. When Benjamin Rayner was prevented by the patent theatres from performing in 1831 at the New Strand Subscription Theatre, there were public meetings demanding reform.[62] The result was the 1832 Select Committee on Dramatic Literature chaired by the novelist and MP Edward Bulwer-Lytton who had adopted the poor state of the stage as a cause. The committee was concerned that the theatre was now in decline and should be reformed. For that reason, it recommended that the minor theatres should have the right to perform legitimate drama and the privileges of the patent theatres should be abolished. Allowing theatres to expand would cater effectively for the rise in population. It argued that the Lord Chamberlain should have the right to suppress unlicensed theatres and supported the rights of authors so that plays could not be not performed without permission.

The Select Committee led to the Dramatic Literary Property Act of 1833, which extended copyright: authors gained reproduction and public performance rights and unauthorized performances were prevented (though this proved difficult to enforce). However, no further change happened in the short term. The parliamentary bill that contained the anti-monopoly proposals of the 1832 committee passed through the Commons but was then resisted in the House of Lords as it was considered to undermine the Royal Prerogative and the issue of compensating the patent holders was divisive.

In 1843, the issue of theatre control was revisited under challenge from Chartists who demanded 'Freedom for the People's Amusements'. The minor theatres catered for working-class audiences and so their restriction was an example of class

---

[60] Francis Place, *A Brief Examination of the Dramatic Patents* (London: Baylis and Leighton, 1834), p. 12.

[61] Tracy C. Davis, *The Economics of the British Stage, 1800–1914* (Cambridge: Cambridge University Press, 2000), p. 31.

[62] Bratton, *New Readings*, p. 71.

monopoly.[63] Robert Peel's Tory government was also amenable to arguments about free trade whilst Whigs usually supported the abolition of protectionism whether in the economy or in the theatre.[64] The 1843 Theatre Regulation Act broke the monopoly of the patent theatres allowing other theatres to perform the spoken word without fear of being taken to court. It also confirmed the authority of the Lord Chamberlain, who could censor all plays (including those in some provincial theatres). The main function of the Lord Chamberlain's role was to police the stage for reason of moral regulation, protecting it from obscenity and blasphemy as well as overt political commentary.

The early nineteenth-century West End enjoyed a vigorous theatrical culture but it was continually restrained by the actions of the patent theatres and the reach of the confessional state. All of this changed in 1843 with the passage of the Theatre Regulation Act, a landmark in performance history. Up to 1843, the main distinction was the difference between the patent and minor theatres. During the mid-Victorian years, the distinction would be the difference between West End theatres and the rest.

Yet there is a deeper issue here. If we look at the Old Price riots, what is clear is that theatres could be spaces that seemed to belong to the community. The disturbances in 1809 were about price but also space and territory. The audiences were outraged about a place that in a symbolic way belonged to them. West End theatre lost that quality shortly thereafter. The playhouses became places to visit; they were no longer sites of community.

The proximity of theatres suggested that the West End was a place apart. The Olympic, the Lyceum, the Adelphi, as well as the Theatres Royal in Covent Garden and Drury Lane were within a short walk of each other. Theatres created distinct kinds of spaces not just in their auditoriums but also in the surrounding area. They provided an incentive for people to come to town and made the creation of taverns, restaurants, and hotels a better economic proposition. This was an area of fantasy, song, laughter, satire, and sexuality. Theatres were thus creative forces in the urban landscape, shaping its networks but also its atmosphere of excitement, possibility and, sometimes, transgressive danger.

---

[63] Clive Barker, 'The Chartists, Theatre, Reform, and Research', *Theatre Quarterly*, 1 (1971), p. 9.
[64] Davis, *Economics of the British Stage*, pp. 35–7.

5

Curiosity

Exhibition-Mania

Consider the story of Sara Baartman, exhibited in 1810 as the 'Hottentot Venus'. Baartman was born in the Camdeboo valley in Cape Colony in Africa and spoke Khoekhoe. She was brought to London and placed on exhibition at no. 225 Piccadilly, where she was the object of fascination both because of her blackness and her large buttocks, emphasizing racial and sexual difference. The use of the name 'Venus' required customers to view her in sexual terms and she wore a brief garment which exposed much of her body. Spectators were even invited to feel her posterior although she was, in some respects, imagined in an anti-erotic way (as subject of an ethnological approach) and so comforted respectable society.[1] Later, the suggestion of nudity meant that Baartman had to be covered up to make the show more respectable. The actor Charles Mathews, a connoisseur of these kinds of spectacle, went to see Baartman:

> He found her surrounded by many persons, some females! One pinched her, another walked round her; one gentleman *poked* her with his cane; and one *lady* employed her parasol to ascertain that all was, as she called it, 'nattral'. This inhuman baiting the poor creature bore with sullen indifference, except upon some great provocation, when she seemed inclined to resent brutality, which even a Hottentot can understand. On these occasions it required all the authority of the keeper to subdue her resentment.[2]

The exhibition outraged the leading abolitionist Zachary Macaulay, who insisted that Baartman was being treated like a slave, despite the abolition of the slave trade in 1807 and (more relevant) the 1772 Mansfield judgement that slavery was forbidden on English soil. This led to a court case in which a contract was produced to show that Baartman was not doing anything against her will. She later moved to Paris where she died in 1815.[3]

---

[1] Z.S. Strother, 'Display of the Body Hottentot' in Bernth Lindfors (ed.), *Africans on Stage: Studies in Ethnological Show Business* (Bloomington, IN: Indiana University Press, 1999), pp. 2, 27.
[2] Mrs Anne Mathews (ed.), *Memoirs of Charles Mathews, Comedian* (London: Richard Bentley, 1839), Vol. 4, p. 137.
[3] On Baartman see ODNB (Sara Baartman); Rachel Holmes, *The Hottentot Venus: The Life and Death of Saartjie Baartman: Born 1789–Buried 2002* (London: Bloomsbury, 2007); Clifton Crais and

London's West End: Creating the Pleasure District, 1800–1914. Rohan McWilliam, Oxford University Press (2020). © Rohan McWilliam.
DOI: 10.1093/oso/9780198823414.001.0001

Popular exhibitions of this kind acted as a form of reassurance for an Anglo-Saxon audience about their racial superiority. The West End assisted in constructing the idea of 'Western' culture by staging encounters with phenomena that were imagined as 'the other', as in the case of Baartman. She was by no means an isolated example. In 1859, a black family, allegedly from the island of Madagascar, were put on display in Leicester Square so that people could observe the transparent quality of their skin, their long white hair, and their 'fiery eyeballs'.[4] This habit of placing mainly non-white peoples on exhibition is rightly troubling to the modern mind but was clearly integral to the nineteenth-century metropolitan world; feeding on racial and imperial views of hierarchy but also satisfying the desire to understand other cultures.[5] Pleasure districts are thus always mirrors of their times. They serve to embrace a normative view through offering forms of difference based particularly on non-whiteness or on disability. The body in the West End was unstable as it came in different forms. Thus from the mid-century we see the increasing use of the word 'freak' to describe these kinds of exhibit.[6]

The West End abounded with exhibitions not just of foreign peoples and freak shows but of panoramas, cosmoramas, dioramas, and other forms of visual entertainment. Why did these prove so popular? As India, Africa, and other parts of the world were opened up in terms of trade routes, exploration, and colonization, there was a desire to know more about natural phenomena and foreign peoples. Up to the 1840s, this was a pre-photography world where even illustrations were not ubiquitous. Although much was written about other peoples, places, flora, and fauna, visual examples were scarce. Panoramas helped people situate themselves in global terms whilst live specimens revealed what they looked like and how they lived. The fact that figures such as Baartman could be brought from other countries further substantiated the importance of London—and hence the West End—as a major global and imperial centre, further flattering the visitors to its entertainments.

Entrepreneurs found ways of turning real life and the natural world into entertainment. When an area comes to enjoy a convergence of spectacles, it develops the atmosphere of the fairground: colourful, ever-changing, built to stimulate but also to inform, delighting in the uncanny and the grotesque. It constructs its audience as individuals who are curious but also open to the charms of deception. The result was what we might call exhibition-mania, remaking life as spectacle. These

Pamela Scully, *Sara Baartman and the Hottentot Venus: A Ghost Story and a Biography* (Princeton, NJ: Princeton University Press, 2009).

[4] Poster in St Martin's Scrapbook Series: Leicester Square Vol. 1 part 2 p. 89 (Westminster City Archives).

[5] Sadiah Qureshi, *Peoples on Parade: Exhibitions, Empire, and Anthropology in Nineteenth-Century Britain* (Chicago: University of Chicago Press, 2011).

[6] Nadja Durbach, *Spectacle of Deformity: Freak Shows and Modern British Culture* (Berkeley, CA: University of California Press, 2010).

sites of curiosity could of course be found elsewhere as well but the West End attractions gain, I argue, from being interpreted within their immediate spatial context as they demonstrate some of the ways in which the pleasure district offered a mental mapping based on the macabre as well as an enhanced visual culture. Even Richard Altick's magisterial study of the attractions that pulled in Londoners does not employ this frame as his gaze is on the metropolis as a whole.[7] Leicester Square, in particular, but also the Egyptian Hall on Piccadilly, came to be associated with spectacle and distortions of nature and the gaze. An area that could offer panoramas, automata, and living statues made the rest of the city look humdrum and demonstrates the way in which Victorian structures of feeling prized the romantic, the grotesque, and the spectacular. It also shows the way that entrepreneurs saw the West End as a place of commercial possibilities because of the proximity to other forms of entertainment. Some of the acts below were authentic but others were clearly fraudulent. Were people really deceived? As P.T. Barnum found in the United States, some people could be taken in but there was also a pleasure in suspending disbelief in order to imagine that one was looking at a real mermaid. Could the fish displayed on Piccadilly in 1859 really talk? What mattered was the media spectacle it created and the pleasure in not knowing if it was real (it was a seal).[8]

Exhibition-mania had links to other cultural forms that were emerging in the same period. These included advertising, the press, and the novel; new modes which addressed and helped constitute the growing consumer world. We might view the pleasure district as resembling a newspaper with its informative exhibits and sensational approach to knowledge. There were certainly points of continuity between the panoramas of Leicester Square and the images that Victorians could find in the periodical press or in the *Illustrated London News*. For all the exuberant showmanship that went into these spectacles, there was frequently a seriousness about providing information. The press and street broadsides alerted readers to strange events and bizarre physical characteristics; West End exhibitions did the same thing. They were two sides of modern mass culture.

Spectators at exhibitions were slightly different from theatre audiences in that that they were mobile, wandering around panoramas, able to look at exhibits from different perspectives and even, in the case of Baartman above, actually touching the people being exhibited. Spectators were also not simply the aristocratic *flâneurs* we encountered in Chapter 2. Instead, they were often middle-class men (such as Charles Matthews above) and women who were not just loitering

[7] Richard D. Altick, *The Shows of London* (Cambridge, MA: Belknap Press/Harvard University Press, 1978).

[8] James W. Cook, *The Arts of Deception: Playing with Fraud in the Age of Barnum* (Cambridge, MA: Harvard University Press, 2001); Caroline Radcliffe, 'The Talking Fish: Performance and Delusion in the Victorian Exhibition' in Joe Kember, John Plunkett, and Jill A. Sullivan (eds), *Popular Exhibitions, Science and Showmanship, 1840–1910* (London: Pickering and Chatto, 2012), pp. 133–51.

on the way to the club. The concept of the *flâneur* therefore cannot entirely account for the way the West End was made. Instead, the pleasure district provided a democratization of knowledge and leisure.

The exhibitionary urge took new forms in the early nineteenth century. As Richard Altick shows, there was a shift away from the cabinet of curiosities approach that had characterized the eighteenth century towards more commercial and spectacular shows after 1800.[9] Not only were curiosities more effectively seen, but more people knew of them and were able to look at them. This display of curiosities became part of the urban fabric. Exhibits such as Sara Baartman or the freak shows that we will encounter might have been easy to dismiss had they taken place in fairgrounds or in marginal locations; the detritus of a vulgar and disorderly popular culture. Placing them in the West End meant they existed in a liminal state that was peculiar to pleasure districts; not wholly respectable but not so unrespectable that middle-class people would be embarrassed by going to see them. What was crucial to the Hottentot Venus event is that it took place on Piccadilly, a few blocks away from aristocratic residences. The location was therefore important to the meaning of exhibition-mania.

Exhibitions were not totally different from museums. Objects had to be established within their proper place in the natural world; this, as Tony Bennett suggests, was a particular approach to knowledge but also to power and government. Imposing neat categories on nature, art, and science, and making them available for inspection, mirrored the forms of liberal government in the nineteenth century, particularly with the growth of state inspectors delivering medical and moral regulation.[10] But this was also a world in which the distinctions between art and science were not fixed; they criss-crossed and worked through juxtaposition. Popular entertainment often reflected issues highlighted by the development of scientific knowledge, as well as history, geography, and archaeology. Different cultural forms, including visual and print media, intersected. Knowledge circulated in diverse ways, sometimes wearing fancy dress and taking malleable forms to embed itself into the culture at large.

Panoramas

One characteristic of nineteenth-century pleasure districts is that they offered new forms of visual culture which both gave pleasure to the eye but also trained it and directed it in new ways. Optical illusions offered both depth and size but also distortions so that images were never quite what they seemed.[11] The eye was

[9] Altick, *The Shows of London*, p. 288.

[10] Tony Bennett, *The Birth of the Museum* (London: Routledge, 1995).

[11] Oscar G. Brockett, Margaret Mitchell, and Linda Harberger, *Making the Scene: A History of Stage Design and Technology in Europe and the United States* (San Antonio, TX: University of Texas Press,

manipulated through the use of light and management of darkness, including the development of the theatre blackout. There was nothing new about exhibitions but their deployment of novelty meant that they always felt up-to-date.

Panoramas were vast paintings on a cylindrical canvas. They were not just images on a large scale; they could be enhanced by lighting effects. The idea was to create an immersive effect so that the viewer felt he or she was in the picture, not just a distant spectator, generating a feeling of what a later generation would call 'virtual reality'. The scale of the paintings was part of their pleasure (equivalent to seeing a film on an IMAX screen today); the product of the age of balloon ascents in the later eighteenth century which made aerial views possible. They played a role in the development of landscape painting but can also be linked to the development of binoculars and microscopes which either broadened or focused the view.[12] Panoramas need to be viewed as part of the history of nineteenth-century realism in culture. Their claims to offer true, detailed pictorial accounts of places, landscapes, and buildings was part of the informal contract they established with viewers. To gain their effects, lighting was kept low so as to maintain the effect of looking at reality rather than a painting. The tragedy of panoramas as a form is that few survive (there is one in the Hague); they were too unwieldy to store.

The figure initially associated with panoramas was the artist Robert Barker who patented the idea in 1787 and initially exhibited in the Haymarket. In 1791 he put on a panorama of London in Castle Street, by Leicester Square.[13] Two years later, Barker moved to a specially-built rotunda, also on Leicester Square, by the corner of Cranbourn Street.[14] The latter venue had enough sense of its own grandeur that it would later style itself the Panorama Royal, offering vast historical canvases in a cylindrical building from ten till dusk (it was dependent on natural light). There were two panoramas, one on top of the other. Viewers had to ascend a series of walkways to view them (see Fig. 5.1). The cylindrical nature of the panorama meant that the viewer had nowhere else to look. George III attended in 1794 to view the panorama of the Grand Fleet at Spithead, a spectacle that allegedly left Queen Charlotte feeling seasick.[15] In 1799, the panorama of

2010), p. 185; see also Christopher Otter, *The Victorian Eye: A Political History of Light and Vision, 1800–1910* (Chicago: University of Chicago Press, 2008).

[12] On panoramas, see Ralph Hyde, *Panoramania! The Art and Entertainment of the 'All-Embracing' View* (London: Trefoil, 1988); Stephan Oettermann, *The Panorama: History of a Mass Medium* (New York: Zone Books, 1997); Bernard Comment, *The Panorama* (London: Reaktion, 1999); Erkki Huhtamo, *Illusions in Motion: Media Archaeology of the Moving Panorama and Related Spectacles* (Cambridge, MA: MIT Press, 2013); John Plunkett, 'Moving Panoramas, c. 1800 to 1840: The Spaces of Nineteenth-century Picture Going', *19* (online journal) no. 17 (2013): http://www.19.bbk.ac.uk/index.php/19/article/viewFile/674/934 (accessed 29 October 2014).

[13] *Morning Chronicle*, 17 October 1791, p. 1.

[14] On Barker's panorama, see Altick, *The Shows of London*, pp. 128–40.

[15] Oettermann, *The Panorama*, p. 105.

Fig. 5.1 Robert Barker's panorama in Leicester Square: © British Library Board (shelfmark 10349.T.15 (19))

Nelson's defeat of the French at the Battle of the Nile was a huge hit, showing that the form was effective at involving a sense of war and battle.

The panorama was nothing less than a new way of seeing. As a form, panoramas gave expression to a cultural mode that sought forms of visual representation that could signify an all-embracing vision. It embodied the conceit that the viewer had an all-seeing eye. The word 'panorama' was quickly adopted and influenced paintings, guidebooks, and popular illustration. Victorian novels in turn strove for a panoramic view of society.[16] There were strong links between panoramas and the theatres nearby (which adopted more realistic backcloths showing spectacular scenery). Both made claims about the importance of increasing verisimilitude; both featured scenes of war and imperial grandeur.[17] The panorama was thus a building block of modern culture but it also made the West End synonymous with panoramic forms of visual culture and hence spectacle.

Barker's building was taken over in 1823 by John and Robert Burford who ran it until it closed in 1861. Global landmarks found their counterparts on the massive canvases in Leicester Square, feeding the passion for nature that was fostered by Romanticism. John Ruskin acclaimed Burford's panorama as 'an educational

---

[16] Jonathan Potter, *Discourses of Vision in Nineteenth-Century Britain: Seeing, Thinking, Writing* (Basingstoke: Palgrave Macmillan, 2018), p. 30.

[17] Gillian Russell, *The Theatres of War: Performance, Politics and Society, 1793–1815* (Oxford: Clarendon Press, 1995), p. 76.

institution of the highest and purest value' and thought it ought to be supported by the government.[18] Panoramas also reflected the greater opportunities for travel in the nineteenth century. Global tourism had become a possibility (at least for some) as demonstrated by the rise of guide books and travel literature. The Burfords and other artists travelled all over Europe making sketches in actual locations which were then turned into dramatic canvases. There were panoramas of Versailles, Coblentz, Baden Baden, Athens, and Rome.

There was a strong continuum between Victorian landscape and historical painting, theatre backcloths, and panoramas. Take, for example, the 1847 panorama of Cairo, derived from drawings by the major Victorian painter, David Roberts. Roberts's career in turn epitomizes something of the cross-fertilization that the West End produced. A Royal Academician, noted for his remarkable drawings and paintings of the Middle East, he began his career as a scene painter at the Coburg (later the Old Vic) and Drury Lane theatres, before developing a reputation for painting scenes derived from his travels. His panorama of Cairo was taken from the view on a mound above the city. Cairo existed in the Victorian imagination as a gateway to the east but Egypt as a whole was viewed through the prism of the Book of Exodus and the discovery of antiquities. The guide book to the Cairo panorama praised 'the great number of fine Mosques, whose noble domes, cupolas, and beautiful minarets, are seen rising above the ordinary dwellings' and announced that the city 'has been made the theatre of many romantic and surprising occurrences in Arabian fable'. Cairo was described as a place of former glory having been, up to the fifteenth century, 'the emporium of at least two quarters of the world'.[19] A visit to Leicester Square thus provided an immersion in exotic, orientalist rhetoric which owed a lot to the Arabian Nights.

Panoramas influenced the development of set design. The Grieve family of set designers in 1820 introduced the panorama into a theatre in *Harlequin and Cinderella*. To create a marine scene, they wound a back canvas across the stage from one cylinder to another. Three years later they introduced an aeronautic panorama.[20] David Roberts and Clarkson Stanfield also devised similar panoramas at Drury Lane and later Covent Garden. The West End was the place to see moving pictures and scenes that impressed because of their size.

A variation of the panorama was the diorama developed by Louis Daguerre (later to become a key figure in the development of photography) in Paris. A room was specially constructed to house a painting. Special lighting effects would then illuminate the painting which would seem to change in front of the audience. A static image was made not to seem static. The sense of movement generated a

---

[18] Oettermann, *The Panorama*, p. 114.

[19] Robert Burford, *Description of a View of the City of Cairo* (London: T. Brettell, 1847) pp. 3, 4: in Burford, *The Panorama Leicester Square. Tracts 1812–53* (British Library call mark 10349.T.15).

[20] Sybil Rosenfeld, *A Short History of Scene Design in Great Britain* (Oxford: Basil Blackwell, 1973), p. 107.

demand for moving pictures that would eventually be satisfied with the cinema. The Queen's Bazaar on Oxford Street employed a diorama with paintings on rollers to pull in customers. In 1832, it offered representations of the recent French Revolution (two years before) with scenes such as the taking of the Louvre, claiming that it was based on sketches taken at the time by 'eminent artists who were present'.[21] This meant that it had the function of a living newspaper, allowing spectators to experience real events.

The cosmorama developed out of the peep show that opened in St James's Street in 1820 and later moved to Regent Street. In it, paintings were exhibited but enhanced through the use of lenses and lighting so that the images could be magnified or contorted.[22] The cosmorama distinguished itself from peep shows by the quality of the oil paintings that it employed. The Lowther Bazaar on the Strand, for example, drew people in with its Magic Cave; a gallery of cosmoramic pictures.

Panoramas and optical entertainments turned visitors to West End entertainments not only into tourists but also people equipped with the tourist's gaze; an eye for landscape, the picturesque, and the exotic. At the same time they generated particular forms of identity: the liberal seeker after knowledge and experience, the believer in the march of progress, the orientalist seeker after exotic experiences. The West End helped create a new kind of visual culture, equipped literally with a panoramic vision. Pleasure districts therefore functioned through distortions of vision and, as we will see, the body.

Leicester Square

In the mid-nineteenth century it was possible to walk round the National Gallery (completed in 1838) and gaze at the Old Masters. One could then stroll round the corner into Leicester Square where paintings were literally coming to life. *Tableaux vivants* drew in the crowds with models re-enacting famous pictures. Official and unofficial art was juxtaposed. *Tableaux vivants* presented themselves as representing high art in a different way but few were likely really fooled. The simulation of nudity was likely another source of their attraction. The pleasure district was a place where stillness (the original art work) could be turned into movement, two dimensions could become three. Alternatively, if one looked elsewhere in Leicester Square, one would find famous paintings rendered through the medium of needlework. Formal systems of aesthetic thought would hold that the paintings in the National Gallery were superior; the other cultural works were cheap imitations, lacking authenticity and legitimacy. Hence they were confined

---

[21] 'French Revolution': Dioramas 3 (56), in *The John Johnson Collection: An Archive of Printed Ephemera*, http://johnjohnson.chadwyck.com (accessed 2 October 2019).

[22] Altick, *The Shows of London*, p. 211.

to a cultural zone defined in the twentieth century as the kitsch and the tacky. Yet they were clearly an integral part of popular culture: doppelgängers or impostors who managed to render art more accessible.

In the later eighteenth century Leicester Square came into its own as a site for spectacle, although it also housed a wide variety of shops including (if we pick the year 1817) an artificial-flower manufacturer, a silk merchant, and an ostrich feather warehouse.[23] The presence of such shops is not an incidental detail or just a matter of contrast. Exhibition sites in the West End were one form of retail among many. Horne's Public Library was at no. 19 whilst the Parisian Concert Hall at no. 5 boasted music by Rossini as well as Chinese jugglers.[24] In the 1830s the Museum of National Manufactures and of the Mechanical Arts (housed at no. 28) showed off a solar stove, fusible cement, a Jacquard loom for Figure silk weaving, and a new specimen of Damask table-linen manufactured in Belfast for the King.[25] We have seen how Robert Barker's panorama in Leicester Square proved a draw. No wonder Prince Albert originally considered Leicester Square as a location for the Great Exhibition before deciding on Hyde Park; it was associated with exhibitions and sites of curiosity.[26]

Savile House, the former stately home built in 1683 (the site of the current Empire cinema), became a major location for both retail and entertainment. As we saw in Chapter 1, it was turned into a space that offered diversions such as billiards and a concert hall (as well as a carpet manufacturer, a draper, and a bookseller).[27] At any time Savile House contained exhilarating juxtapositions of poetry, painting, sculpture, concerts, ventriloquists, billiards, waxworks, athletic demonstrations, and Professor Krosso, the 'Modern Hercules', who was allegedly the strongest man in the world.[28] In one room, where it was claimed (inaccurately) that George III was born, could be seen Don Santiago de los Santos, the smallest man in existence and King of all dwarfs. For a shilling guests would also receive refreshments including a cigar (evidence of the masculine nature of the audience) though a muffin could be substituted for this.[29] In the year of the Great Exhibition, Savile House exhibited Joseph Gatano, the Italian Giant who

---

[23] *Johnstone's London Commercial Guide and Street Directory* (London: Barnard and Farley, 1817), p. 293.

[24] Newspaper clippings in St Martin's Scrapbook Series: Leicester Square Vol. 1 part 1 p. 38 (Westminster City Archives).

[25] Newspaper clippings in St Martin's Scrapbook Series: Leicester Square Vol. 1 part 2 p. 31 (Westminster City Archives).

[26] Altick, *The Shows of London*, p. 229.

[27] Walter Thornbury and Edward Walford, *Old and New London* (London: Cassell, Petter, and Galpin, 1879–85), Vol. 3, p. 166.

[28] Newspaper clippings in St Martin's Scrapbook Series: Leicester Square Vol. 1 part 2 p. 42 (Westminster City Archives).

[29] Newspaper clippings in St Martin's Scrapbook Series: Leicester Square Vol. 1 part 2 p. 53 (Westminster City Archives).

measured seven feet seven inches.[30] Exhibits included people who defied human categories either though being miniature or enormous or who had some form of deformity.

In one wing could be found the Linwood Gallery, a longstanding feature of the square from 1787 to 1846. This was an exhibition of Miss Linwood's needlework. She copied paintings by Old Masters representing their exact colouring in a finely detailed form. Miss Linwood effectively democratized tapestry (an art form of the rich) making it available to more people. Her gallery also included spectacular attractions which were continually changed to bring in the crowds. In the 1850s the Gallery offered Atkins's Great Pictorial Entertainment of Creation, Science, and Civilization which promised to show spectators the Earth from Pole to Pole. The programme featured astronomy and geology including the antediluvian era. At the same time, the programme promised a 'new view of emigration' and a model of a steam war battery which had the potential to 'put an end to War, and establish the Basis of Peace and Progress'. The pit and the gallery cost one shilling and two shillings respectively, which suggests the event was aimed at a middle-class audience. There were stalls seats at just three pence, which would have allowed in a wider range of people.[31] Cheaper was the panorama of the Crimean War which offered scenes from Sebastapol, Balaclava, and Alma. It made great claims for its authenticity, suggesting it could do better than battle reports (presumably those in newspapers):

> the Painter steps in and supplies to the eye those scenic details which words can only suggest; the plain or the mountain...the city and the camp...the heights crowned with the enemy, and the gallant troops marching to the attack...the fleets in sail and at rest. All these phases and scenes of war stand before us, through the medium of art, as clearly and distinctly as though we were gazing at the very places and the very men etc.[32]

The Crimean War was therefore refought in Leicester Square. Visitors grasped something of the conflict through the ways it was represented in battle art and in panoramas. Spectators also got to listen to music produced by the celebrated Crystal-Ophonic, a novel instrument capable of producing powerful harmony. Admission was only one penny, suggesting this was widely accessible.

The reference to emigration shows how the West End responded to preoccupations of the moment with a strong focus on movement to the colonies as a

---

[30] Newspaper clippings in St Martin's Scrapbook Series: Leicester Square Vol. 1 part 2 p. 54 (Westminster City Archives).

[31] A Collection of Handbills and programmes of exhibitions and entertainments in Leicester Square, together with admission tickets; and of advertisements of tradesmen in Leicester Square. 1800–1870? (British Library callmark 1880.b.25), p. 3.

[32] A Collection of Handbills, p. 5.

solution to poverty at home. In 1849, no. 6 Leicester Square offered a panorama of New Zealand, painted by Samuel Charles Brees, formerly principal engineer to the New Zealand Company. Brees provided a commentary on the panorama along with musical accompaniment and a closing song which urged viewers to come to New Zealand and discover independence and serenity. It clearly had a promotional dimension. The publicity included an endorsement from the *Morning Post*: 'We beheld the savages, and listened to tales of "life in the bush".' The *Ladies Companion*, we are told, enjoyed the verisimilitude of the panorama: 'We found New Zealand at home, on the first floor of Savile House.'[33]

An enduring draw were the Aztec Lilliputians in 1853:

> The Aztec Lilliputians, the reputed gods of Iximaya and the Earthmen, or Erdmanniges, people who burrow under the Earth, subsisting on insects; the first of either Race, ever discovered and altogether unlike other inhabitants of the earth; so remarkable indeed that no one would believe such people did exist were they not to be seen in living form.

When they were first exhibited in Hanover Square, 100,000 people paid to see them.[34] Scientists, anatomists, and Queen Victoria were also fascinated to observe these alleged last descendants of an ancient race. Another draw in the 1850s was Herr Lidusdroph's 'Industrious and Learned Russian Fleas'.[35] There was also much that appealed to the ghoulish. Waxworks of the body snatchers Bishop and Williams (allegedly modelled from the dissection rooms after their executions) were exhibited on the grounds that it was a 'good idea for morals'.[36]

Madame Warton's Walhalla on Leicester Square offered 'living statues': 'personations' of Venus, Sappho, Innocence, Diana, and Ariadne and a *tableau vivant* of Lady Godiva, based on Edwin Landseer's new painting at the Royal Academy. Given the prevalence of nudity in painting, models wore flesh-coloured stockings to simulate nakedness (see Fig. 5.2). This was inevitably controversial but counts as the Victorian equivalent of striptease. Madame Warton emphasized the high art dimension of her presentations but the Walhalla would have appealed to well-heeled men about town. Her cheapest ticket was the promenade at one shilling whilst stalls cost three shillings so this was not affordable for all.[37] There was a similar establishment in the Haymarket run by a Madame Duval who would perform scenes from paintings such as Venus Rising from the Sea.[38] *Poses*

---

[33] A Collection of Handbills, p. 8.   [34] A Collection of Handbills, p. 12.
[35] Advertisement in St Martin's Scrapbook Series: Leicester Square Vol. 1 part 2 p. 27 (Westminster City Archives).
[36] Advertisement in St Martin's Scrapbook Series: Leicester Square Vol. 1 part 2 p. 28 (Westminster City Archives).
[37] A Collection of Handbills, p. 15.
[38] Poster in St Martin's Scrapbook Series: Leicester Square Vol. 2 part 2 p. 42 (Westminster City Archives).

Fig. 5.2 Madame Warton in the role of 'Innocence' at the Walhalla, Leicester Square (Westminster City Archives)

plastiques were not uncommon and respectable opinion often did not consider them to be indecent.[39] They exploited the notoriously thin line between art and obscenity, as usages of the nude tend to do.

They had a peculiar appeal, referencing famous paintings and sculptures but then bringing them to life, Pygmalion-style. The moment of transformation becomes hypnotic because the convention that inanimate objects do not move had been disrupted. They were (like panoramas) the logical consequence of the nineteenth century desire for realism.[40] We do not know the names of most *tableau vivant* models but they still need to be reclaimed as performers engaged in a distinctive form of performance comparable to what was happening in Drury Lane. An actor brings an author's words to life; the *pose plastique* does the same with a painter.

The West End, we will keep discovering, traded on these ambiguities between the respectable and the unrespectable. The carefully draped *poses plastiques* were para-sexual, that zone defined by Peter Bailey as 'sexuality that is deployed but

[39] Report from the Select Committee on Theatrical Licenses and Regulations (1866), p. 50.
[40] Aura Satz, 'Tableaux Vivants: Inside the Statue' in Aura Satz and Jon Wood (eds), *Articulate Objects: Voice, Sculpture and Performance* (Oxford: Peter Lang, 2009), pp. 157–81.

contained, carefully channelled rather than fully discharged; in vulgar terms it might be represented as "everything but".[41] This kind of contained sexuality (which Bailey associates with images of Victorian barmaids) co-existed with the more overt displays of sexuality offered on the streets by prostitutes (see Chapter 7). There was always an erotic dimension to the forms of display in the West End.

Leicester Square contained two other sites of popular science and the march of mind. The Western Literary and Scientific Institution was at no. 47 providing lectures on, amongst other subjects, galvanism and magnetism as well as a diorama about the Arctic regions which capitalized on the interest in the Franklin expedition.[42] In 1851, the same year as the Great Exhibition, the Liberal MP James Wyld launched his Great Globe in Leicester Square. For visitors, it offered a journey to the centre of the earth. They could wander round the interior of a sixty-foot globe. Its staircases allowed visitors to ponder the wonders of the world in a manner that resembled the panoramas nearby. They found representations of different civilizations but also confirmation that the centre of London was the centre of the 'civilized' world. The entrance fee was initially high (at five shillings) but was later reduced to just one shilling. Wyld was a member of the Royal Geographical Society and the Great Globe provided a way of teaching the wonders of the world in an entertaining way. In 1854, Wyld included a model of the Crimea during the Crimean War with the position of British and Russian troops clearly marked and moved as the conflict developed (this would have complemented the Crimean panorama offered at the Linwood Gallery). In 1859 an Oriental Museum was introduced, which provided models and waxworks of life in Turkey, Armenia, and Albania.[43] The Globe became such a London landmark that James Robinson Planché wrote a comedy at the Haymarket about it in 1854: *Mr Buckstone's Visit round the Globe*, another example of the way in which different kinds of West End entertainment could interact with one another. The Globe proved the biggest draw in London after the Great Exhibition itself although Wyld decided not to renew the lease when it expired in 1861 and the attraction was demolished (Fig. 5.3).[44]

When the Royal Panopticon of Science and Art opened in 1854. it insisted that it was of a higher class than other Leicester Square entertainments. The venue was intended for improving scientific exhibitions and lectures, an example of the Victorian belief in 'rational recreation' where people were expected to improve their minds through self-education. The building included a luminous fountain

[41]   Peter Bailey (ed.), *Popular Performance and Culture in the Victorian City* (Cambridge: Cambridge University Press, 1998), p. 151.

[42]   Newspaper clipping in St Martin's Scrapbook Series: Leicester Square Vol. 1 part 1 p. 49 (Westminster City Archives).

[43]   Thornbury and Walford, *Old and New London*, Vol. 3, pp. 170–1.

[44]   Bernard Lightman, 'Spectacle in Leicester Square: James Wyld's Great Globe, 1851–1861' in Joe Kember, John Plunkett, and Jill A. Sullivan (eds), *Popular Exhibitions, Science and Showmanship, 1840–1910* (London: Pickering and Chatto, 2012), pp. 19–39.

Fig. 5.3 Wyld's Great Globe in Leicester Square (Westminster City Archives)

with water shooting ninety-seven feet in the air, an organ with bellows operated by steam power and a vast diorama overlooked by an enormous dome decorated in gold. The interior and exterior were built in the Islamic style with coloured tiles and minarets at the top. In the course of a week it was possible to catch lectures on chemistry, the use of the microscope, electro-magnetism, and Messrs Reinke's diving apparatus which had won a prize at the Great Exhibition.[45] It did not, however, pay its way and closed in two years flat and was eventually turned into the Alhambra music hall. Its organ was given to St Paul's Cathedral.

There were other significant spaces of popular science in the West End. In 1838, the Royal Polytechnic Institution was founded on Regent Street. This made a point of offering scientific demonstrations in the evenings for all who were busy during the day. The principal attractions included a diving bell and diver who showed how to work underwater. At the same time spectators could discover the wonders of the microscope and observe iron filings being rearranged by a magnet. It would also become known for its magic lantern shows and what we would now

---

[45] Newspaper clippings in St Martin's Scrapbook Series: Leicester Square Vol. 2 part 1 p. 2 (Westminster City Archives).

consider pre-cinema devices.[46] The Adelaide Gallery on the Strand (part of the Lowther Arcade) included the National Gallery of Practical Science. It claimed it was 'established for the practical illustration of general science, and for the reception of works of art, and specimens of the rare production of nature'.[47] Its lower gallery included fossil remains and John Adcock's condensing steam engine whilst the upper floor included works of art including John Martin's painting of the Fall of Nineveh.[48] Faraday's electric eel was exhibited there but it also included magic lantern shows with 'dissolving views', representing the increasing focus on optical science that characterized the Gallery.[49] This centre of culturally improving works was not a success and, following the bankruptcy of the owner, it became, in 1846, a dance hall called the Casino. The failure of the Gallery of Practical Science and Royal Panopticon indicated that this world of popular science could not find a place in the West End. From the 1850s, South Kensington's developing museum quarter started to become the more acceptable location for the display of science, technology, and natural history.

The Egyptian Hall

Napoleon's expedition to Egypt and Syria in 1798–1801 provoked a passion for all things Egyptian. This led to the creation in 1812 of the Egyptian Hall at nos. 171–2, Piccadilly, which became central to the exhibition world of the West End (see Fig. 5.4). Originally named the London Museum, its statues of Isis and Osiris, and details from the great temple of Tentyra meant that it was always known by its other title. Almost opposite the Burlington Arcade, it was built by William Bullock at a cost of £16,000 and was originally intended to house his collection of natural history; objects built up during his travels in central America. Bullock quickly sold his collection and turned the building into a huge exhibition hall. In its original form, there was a lecture room, a bazaar, and what became the Waterloo Gallery (a large central room).[50] The vast hall meant that it could accommodate large-scale paintings and panoramas. It housed high art and freak shows before becoming associated with stage magic in the later nineteenth century, making it an ideal haunt for the Victorian middle classes who saw it as an improving place to take children whilst also doing some shopping.

---

[46] *Era*, 25 November 1838, p. 102; Jeremy Brooker, *The Temple of Minerva: Magic and the Magic Lantern at the Royal Polytechnic Institution, London, 1837–1901* (London: Magic Lantern Society, 2013).

[47] *Examiner*, 25 May 1834, p. 329.

[48] *National Gallery of Practical Science, Blending Instruction with Amusement: Catalogue for 1833* (London: J. Homes, 1833).

[49] *Illustrated London News*, 28 October 1843, p. 284.

[50] John Timbs, *Curiosities of London; Exhibiting the most rare and remarkable Objects of interest in the Metropolis* (London: J.S. Virtue, 1867 [1855]), p. 320.

Fig. 5.4 Egyptian Hall, *c.*1816 (Westminster City Archives)

In 1816, Napoleon's carriage was exhibited there, having been captured at Waterloo. It proved a huge draw, presumably because it represented the man who had dominated British lives for almost two decades. Some 800,000 people saw it, marvelling at the way the carriage could serve as bedroom, kitchen, and dressing room. The carriage was later transferred to Madame Tussaud's. Popular culture delighted in the miniature and the gigantic. The venue raised £125 a day in ticket sales when it hosted 'General' Tom Thumb in 1846. Born in Connecticut, Tom Thumb's real name was Charles Sherwood Stratton and he barely grew after his infancy. He was taken up by his distant cousin P.T. Barnum and transformed into a global sensation. Tom Thumb was well known for his impersonation of Napoleon. The act contrasted his smallness with his grand military titles. In 1829 Siamese twins were put on exhibition, showing that the Egyptian Hall always relished a 'freakshow' in which disability was made into entertainment. In 1837, it purported to have a male child with four arms, four legs, four feet, and two bodies, who had been born at Stalybridge.[51] Even in 1880, it was still exhibiting conjoined twins: the Pygopagis. These two girls from Bohemia were fused at the back but were otherwise independent. They were roughly three years old but became a major spectacle.[52]

[51] John Timbs, *Curiosities of London*, p. 320.
[52] The Pygopagi twins: John Johnson Collection, in *The John Johnson Collection: An Archive of Printed Ephemera*, http://johnjohnson.chadwyck.com: London Play Places 10 (57), Egyptian Hall: Human Freaks (accessed 5 November 2018).

In 1852 the Egyptian Hall hosted a diorama of the Orient (defined as the Holy Land and Egypt). The spectacle was accompanied by a full choir who sang Hebrew, Arab, and English melodies. A ticket to the event has survived; it admitted three, which implies that it was aimed at a family audience, perhaps a mother and two children.[53]

In 1841, the American George Catlin brought a group of native Americans over and placed them on exhibition so that they could show off their clothing and customs. Catlin was known for his paintings of native Americans which shaped the way they were perceived in the nineteenth century.[54] He had travelled up the Mississippi river in 1830 and painted numerous pictures of native Americans, developing a formidable Indian Gallery. As we saw with Sara Baartman, this was part of a larger entertainment zone in which non-white people were put on exhibition for commercial gain. It was both a form of popular anthropology and a foundation for the emergence of scientific racism in the mid-nineteenth century. Although some of these people were from the empire, others were not, but they reflected Britain's development as a maritime power and its trade connections, transporting human beings from other countries to be sources of education, fascination, curiosity, and (sometimes) disgust. Such displays echoed the freak shows; an invitation to stare at living people with the notion of popular science and anthropology providing the event with a spurious legitimacy.[55] Needless to say, the people on display were not allowed to speak for themselves and not just because they often could not speak English. Showmen, lecturers, and curators controlled the narrative.

Not unusual was the exhibition of the Bosjemans (Bushmen) from South Africa at the Egyptian Hall. The *Illustrated London News* described their nomadic lifestyle as a branch of the Hottentot race who have taken to wandering: 'They are now beginning to be surrounded by civilization; and consequently, they must either become civilised themselves or become extinct. The latter seems more probable; and, on this account, the present Exhibition is important, especially in the illustration of the study of Ethnology, which is every year advancing in popularity.'[56] The Egyptian Hall was thus a key venue for the emergence of allegedly scientific forms of race theory.

Automata and speaking machines were another stock in trade of the Egyptian Hall. John Hollingshead recalled seeing Professor Faber in 1846, who invented an automaton called Euphonia. It repays a long quotation:

---

[53] Egyptian Hall ticket: D137 Egyptian Hall (8–11) (Westminster City Archives).
[54] Kate Flint, *The Transatlantic Indian, 1776–1930* (Princeton, NJ: Princeton University Press, 2009), ch. 3; Qureshi, *Peoples on Parade*, ch. 3.
[55] Qureshi, *Peoples on Parade*.   [56] *Illustrated London News*, 12 June 1847, p. 381.

I paid my shilling and was shown into a large room, half filled and lighted with lamps. In the centre was a box on a table, looking like a rough piano without legs and having two key-boards. This was surmounted by a half-length weird figure, rather bigger than a full-grown man, with an automaton head and face looking more mysteriously vacant than such faces usually look. Its mouth was large and opened like the jaws of Gorgibuster in the pantomime, disclosing artificial gums, teeth, and all the organs of speech. There was no lecturer, no lecture, no music— none of the usual adjuncts of a show. The exhibitor, Professor Faber, was a sad-faced man, dressed in respectable well-worn clothes that were soiled by contact with tools, wood, and machinery. The room looked like a laboratory and work-shop, which it was. The Professor was not too clean, and his hair and beard sadly wanted the attention of a barber. I have no doubt that he slept in the same room as his figure—his scientific Frankenstein monster—and I felt the secret influence of an idea that they too were destined to live and die together. The Professor, with a slight German accent, put his wonderful toy in motion. He explained its action; it was not necessary to prove the absence of deception. One keyboard, touched by the Professor, produced words, which, slowly and deliberately in a hoarse sepulchral voice came from the mouth of the figure, as if from the depths of a tomb.[57]

Hollingshead's description captures the gothic elements of the scene (the reference to Frankenstein and pantomime but also the voice coming 'from the depths of a tomb'). The Euphonia is described here as a 'toy' but it was also a significant technical achievement. Note how Hollinghead talks of an 'absence of deception': the voice is rendered remotely, the scientific equivalent of ventriloquism. Indeed, the Euphonia seems to have been an influence on Alexander Graham Bell in inventing the telephone. Faber developed a line of thought that led to the electrical reproduction of speech. The idea of a virtual body that operated through being acted upon fascinated because of the way it drew attention to the body as a machine in a very stark way.[58] In retrospect, it prefigured the modern fascination with robots and cyborgs.

The Egyptian Hall was also linked to the illustrated lecture or the comic monologue. The great exponent of this form was Albert Smith and his great one-man show, 'The Ascent of Mont Blanc' in 1852 at the Egyptian Hall in Piccadilly. Briefly a doctor, he opted for the life of the *litterateur*, penning plays, and publishing articles in comic periodicals. After a disastrous attempt at ballooning, Smith made an ascent on Mont Blanc and then gave a popular lecture about it (which

---

[57] John Hollingshead, *My Lifetime* (London: Sampson Low, Marston, and Co., 1895), Vol. 1, pp. 68–9.

[58] Steven Connor, 'Incidents of the Breath: In Pneumatic and Electric Ventriloquisms', in Satz and Wood (eds), *Articulate Objects*, pp. 64, 73.

helped popularize mountaineering). The set at the Egyptian Hall (by theatre designer William Beverley) was a Swiss chalet with a moving panorama of the mountain. Edmund Yates recalled, 'the comfort of the audience had been thoroughly attended to. They sat on good chairs in a room well carpeted and curtained, charmingly decorated, and properly ventilated'.[59] In other words, it became a perfect location for the middle-class audience in the wake of the Great Exhibition. The show was comic but improving. It ran for six years and Smith became wealthy from sales of his books and merchandise as well as tickets.

The Egyptian Hall, having been a site of curiosity on Piccadilly, was later associated with conjurors and magicians. In 1873 the magicians John Nevil Maskelyne and George Alfred Cooke leased the main hall and stayed until 1904. The location of the Egyptian Hall on Piccadilly meant that it could appeal to the best circles but also employ the techniques of show business to bring people in.

As I write, the former London Pavilion building on Piccadilly Circus is home to Gunther von Hagen's Body Worlds exhibition in which real bodies of deceased people are put on display. Whilst von Hagen claims novelty for his use of real people, this chapter confirms that the West End has long been home to disruptive presentations of the human body. Even the disgust occasioned by von Hagen's use of real bodies echoes the disgust and awe occasioned by exhibits in Leicester Square and Piccadilly in the nineteenth century.

This world of popular art and science that the West End generated began to change in the mid-Victorian years. Savile House, centre of much of this world of populist entertainment, burned down in 1865 whilst *poses plastiques* migrated to music hall. In the 1870s, a commentator dolefully reflected on the change 'The moral of Leicester-square is that the British public have no hungering and thirsting after knowledge, that they love to drink and smoke, to listen to singing men and singing women; and that to make money you must pander to the lust of the flesh, to the lust of the eye and the pride of life'.[60] The West End became much more about undiluted entertainment.

In the first half of the nineteenth century, this world of curiosity did, however, draw middle-class people into the West End (including their children). It created a space of visual spectacle but also linked it to themes about science, geography, and racial hierarchy. The pleasure district was therefore built around notions of difference, encouraging spectators to see the rest of the world as 'the other': exotic, colourful, sometimes primitive and frequently ripe for conquest. It confirmed the 'civilized' identity of spectators and built a connection between the West End and empire that would last well into the twentieth century.

[59] Edmund Yates, *Recollections and Experiences* (London: Richard Bentley, 1884), Vol. 1, p. 243.
[60] Newspaper clipping in St Martin's Scrapbook Series: Leicester Square Vol. 1 part 1 p. 30 (Westminster City Archives).

Panoramas were part of a larger world of entertainment that employed optical devices, peep shows, stereoscopes, and magic lantern slides to produce new ways of seeing. Light was employed in dazzling new ways. Cinema was the product of the rich visual culture developed in pleasure districts. In looking at the Euphonia in the Egyptian Hall we saw how it combined scientific and gothic elements. There is also a sense in which Sara Baartman, the automata, and the *tableaux vivants* suggest that the appeal of pleasure districts consisted of the way they drew attention to the body as a symbol. The West End was shaped by the age of Romanticism which made it the home of the exotic and the strange. In this sense, they complemented the novel and the gothic melodramas (including versions of *Frankenstein*) adopted by the stage. West End theatres, curiosities, and exhibitions were suffused with Romantic values.

The fairground atmosphere of the district emerged in part because of the way inanimate objects could come to life but also the way in which living people like Baartman could be reduced to the status of an object. Pleasure districts satisfied the desire for the fantastic and the real. In Hollingshead's account, the Euphonia looked like a real body and yet was also a creature rendered in the gothic mode. Pleasure districts abounded with what were seen as distorted bodies. They had the quality of what Michel Foucault called 'heterotopias': 'a kind of effectively enacted utopia in which...all the other real sites that can be found within the culture, are simultaneously represented, contested, and inverted'.[61] Heterotopic spaces draw upon, but disturb, the culture at large. The pleasure district was thus based on ways of seeing in which vision and the imagination were stretched. Pleasure districts possess this utopian capacity to enchant and transform. The shift of the Egyptian Hall into a theatre for magicians, conjurers, and escapologists in the Maskelyne and Cooke era of the later nineteenth century played on the delight in deception and misdirection that characterized the area. Theatre and spectacular curiosities allowed the West End to become a space which could turn mass consumerism into a dreamworld for the many. This became clearer after 1850.

---

[61] Michel Foucault, 'Of Other Spaces', *Diacritics*, 16 (1986), p. 24.

PART TWO

THE BOURGEOIS WEST END, 1850–1914

6

The Making of the West End, 1850–1914

Metropolis

Let us take the quintessential West End experience: meeting a friend in Piccadilly Circus by Eros. The Circus is a study in confusion as it not a circus. There is none of the smooth harmony we associate with continental street planning. The streets that flow into it do so awkwardly. Yet it hums with traffic, proclaiming that it is the heart of London and source of its pulsating energy. People cavort through Piccadilly Circus twenty-four hours a day. There is the elegant geometry of the London Pavilion, a Greek temple that proclaims the lofty ambitions of the West End and confronts the smaller Criterion Theatre opposite. Look round and you will see the stately curve of Regent Street. Another glance will give you Shaftesbury Avenue, a synonym for West End theatre. You will then need to re-orient yourself to look over to the Haymarket and, along Coventry Street, to Leicester Square. These sights only took shape in their entirety at the end of the nineteenth century (Fig. 6.1).

A new West End emerged gradually during the later Victorian years. After 1850, the West End acquired many of its present-day characteristics: a constellation of theatres, restaurants, billboard hoardings, music halls, concert venues, pubs, bars, galleries, and grand hotels. It was described in 1896 as 'undoubtedly the centre of pleasure-seeking London'.[1] Symptomatic of this change was the employment of the term 'West End' to specifically mean the pleasure district. Previously, it had been used in an inexact way. Up to the mid-nineteenth century, it meant Mayfair and St James's and signified 'High Society'. But after 1850 there is evidence of a real shift in its usage. In 1866, for example, the playwright Dion Boucicault commented: 'it seems to me that the number of theatres...is small in comparison to the number of persons who come to the centre of amusement in London, which is generally the West-End'.[2] The area from the Strand up to Oxford Street became a 'centre of amusement'. How did this happen?

Simon Gunn argues that 'Space is an active element in the constitution of social identities'.[3] The new West End was a space that played a role in the making of the Victorian middle classes and was built upon inequalities. To view this in action,

---

[1] *Caterer and Hotel-Keeper's Gazette*, 15 October 1896, p. 491.
[2] Report from the Select Committee on Theatrical Licenses and Regulations (1866), p. 150.
[3] Simon Gunn, 'The Spatial Turn: Changing Histories of Space and Place', in Simon Gunn and R.J. Morris (eds), *Identities in Space: Contested Terrains in the Western City since 1850* (Aldershot: Ashgate, 2001), pp. 5, 9.

London's West End: Creating the Pleasure District, 1800–1914. Rohan McWilliam, Oxford University Press (2020).
© Rohan McWilliam.
DOI: 10.1093/oso/9780198823414.001.0001

Fig. 6.1 Piccadilly Circus (author collection)

we need to consider changes in the built environment and circulation in the forms of streets and alleys. The poor (as we will see) were pushed out of the pleasure district. The rebuilding of the later nineteenth century transformed the district and made it more accessible, shaped by the demands of middle-class life (similar patterns can be found in other nineteenth-century cities).[4] The West End was subject to the impulses of Victorian social and municipal reform though there were no schemes quite on the scale of John Nash's Regent Street. The change from an aristocratic to a bourgeois West End reflected not only the political transformations of the age but also a shift in social and cultural authority.

The period after 1850 was the age of the masses, characterized by cultural production aimed at a heterogeneous public defined in trans-class terms. This suited a period based on mass production of goods and the growth of consumerism but it also explains the language of the developing mass media, including the press. The rhetoric and forms of address in the West End sought the attention of a public undifferentiated by class. Underpinning this was the increased prosperity of the economy and the improvement in living standards. The focus on a mass public accounts for the spectacular size of theatres such as the Alhambra and of the new department stores. Yet, in practice, the area became a statement about the desirability of middle-class life. Its shops were notable for their abundance of goods which could fill the domestic interior. Even if many people could not afford to visit, let alone shop there, they would see advertisements in newspapers with

---

[4] Simon Gunn, *The Public Culture of the Victorian Middle Class: Ritual and Authority in the English Industrial City, 1840–1914* (Manchester: Manchester University Press, 2008).

West End addresses prominent. The appeal of the area was that it made the middle class feel safe and respected at the same time. The pleasure district was made possible by a culture that had less investment in the idea of deferred gratification, formerly a feature of the more puritanical end of the middle class.

Additionally, as we will see in succeeding chapters, the West End was increasingly opened up to middle-class women. As Lynne Walker has shown, women after c.1850 could walk the streets without chaperones and enjoy some of the pleasures of the West End such as galleries, teashops, and matinees. There were, however, obstacles to their mobility. Local vestries refused to play to provide lavatories for women. Even in 1887, proposals for a female public lavatory in Regent Street were turned down.[5] Feminization was a connecting thread in the new matinee performances, department stores, hotels, restaurants (all of which provided lavatories), and the development of couture and new styles in fashion. Significantly, the Langham Place group of feminists, who demanded the vote in the mid-Victorian years, met in a location just above Oxford Street, a small signal that the West End offered a space to rethink gender identity. The period also saw the development of a female counterpart to clubland London with the emergence of clubs around Mayfair for women where they could dine and socialize.[6]

Whilst the built environment was the work of speculators, the new West End was also the conscious creation of local government. The Metropolitan Board of Works was established in 1855 as an attempt to bring order to the chaos of London administration. It was succeeded by the London County Council in 1889, initially governed by a majority of progressives—essentially reform-minded Liberals—bent on municipal reform to improve housing and transport. These two organizations oversaw the redevelopment of the West End (for example, the construction of Shaftesbury Avenue) along with local vestries.

This chapter examines the way the physical environment of the West End changed so that it became an elaborate stage set in which people could pursue pleasure. Yet if the West End was frontstage, Soho was its backstage area, a different world which is juxtaposed here with the pleasure district. The changes in the built environment 1850–1914 provide a context for the analysis of the way the West End became a space for cultural transformation in the chapters that follow.

West End Streets

By the early 1850s, the turmoil of the early Victorian decades (when Chartism threatened revolution) was being left behind. London itself was changing,

[5] Lynne Walker, 'Vistas of Pleasure: Women Consumers of Urban Space in the West End of London, 1850–1900' in Clarissa Campbell Orr (ed.), *Women in the Victorian Art World* (Manchester: Manchester University Press, 1995), p. 81.

[6] Erika Diane Rappaport, *Shopping for Pleasure: Women in the Making of London's West End* (Princeton, NJ: Princeton University Press, 2000), pp. 85–107.

usurping the claims of Paris to be the capital of the nineteenth century. The new West End was the product of deeper structural changes in the metropolis: the growth of London suburbs from the 1830s onwards, combined with the development of the railway network. The London to Croydon line, for example, was opened in 1839. New forms of transport transformed cities, allowing for social segregation. The suburbs were the home of the middle classes, including the new lower-middle-class world of clerks. This permitted the development of the West End as a different kind of pleasure district, one that did not simply aim to service aristocrats and others who lived nearby. The residential population of the West End declined but the numbers of people drawn to its attractions increased. Indeed, one factor behind the expansion of West End entertainment was that it was required to keep pace with the fact that there were simply many more Londoners. A city which had about one million inhabitants in 1800 housed some 6.7 million inhabitants in 1900.

Paddington Station first opened in 1838, Kings Cross in 1850–1, Victoria in 1860, Charing Cross in 1864, St Pancras in 1868, and Liverpool Street in 1874. Victoria, in particular, was built because the owners of the London, Brighton, and South Coast Railway (which originally terminated at Battersea) felt they needed a final stop closer to the West End. The railway age led to a period of hotel construction (frequently on a grand scale) so that visitors to London would have a place to stay. The emergence of omnibuses from the late 1820s assisted (although it was not until the mid-Victorian period that good access to the West End was established). The development of bridges across the Thames opened up the district to South London. The modern version of Westminster Bridge (which dated back to 1750) was completed in 1862. Hungerford railway bridge (integral to Charing Cross Station) was constructed two years later and Waterloo Bridge (originally built in 1817) was freed from tolls in 1877. In 1906 Piccadilly Circus and Leicester Square underground stations began serving the public. Many stores close by (including Swan and Edgar) immediately reported increased business. The Criterion on Piccadilly played to its fullest houses, noting that its audiences could now get to the theatre 'without leaving cover' and could get home afterwards more easily.[7]

Yet traffic in London seemed to impede progress; the streets so clogged up with vehicles that movement frequently came to a standstill. The district appeared impervious to modernization. Attempts to revamp Regent Street produced hostility which prevented rebuilding until the interwar period.[8] St Martin's Vestry, however, pushed on in the 1890s with the widening and repaving of the western end of the Strand, the provision of new sewers for the Adelphi area and a house-to-house

---

[7] *Evening News*, 7 May 1907, p. 3.
[8] Erika Rappaport, 'Art, Commerce, or Empire?: The Rebuilding of Regent Street, 1880–1927', *History Workshop Journal*, 53 (2002): pp. 95–117.

sanitary inspection led by its medical officer.[9] The centres of Victorian low life started to disappear and a renovated district took its place.

There was a desperate need for new thoroughfares. Northumberland House was demolished to make way for Northumberland Avenue, which linked Charing Cross with the Victoria Embankment. In 1877, Parliament gave the Metropolitan Board of Works powers to create what became Shaftesbury Avenue and the Charing Cross Road. These were cut through areas of poverty and thus acted as slum clearance while also cleaning up the West End. Shaftesbury Avenue was named after the seventh earl of Shaftesbury, the distinguished philanthropist who had championed the rights of the poor. The two thoroughfares created spaces both for shopping and for new theatres, thus enhancing the character of the pleasure district. Shaftesbury Avenue was completed in 1886. By 1907 six theatres had been built on what was a prime site: the Lyric, the Apollo, the Globe (now the Gielgud), the Shaftesbury, the Queen's, and the Palace. The Charing Cross Road was opened in February 1887 by the Duke of Cambridge who gave his name to Cambridge Circus where the thoroughfare met Shaftesbury Avenue. It became known for its bookshops in the early twentieth century.

A by-product of the building of Shaftesbury Avenue was the creation of Piccadilly Circus in its modern form. Previously Regent Circus, it opened in 1885 and was three times the size of the original. It became a great meeting place especially after the erection of the statue known as Eros in 1893. Eros was intended by the designer Alfred Gilbert as a further celebration of Shaftesbury's legacy and was titled 'The Age of Christian Charity'. Flower sellers congregated underneath it, allowing men about town the opportunity to purchase a carnation for their button holes. Eros became a London landmark, partly because Piccadilly Circus was a frontier after 1900; the respectable world of Piccadilly and Regent Street confronting the darker pleasures of Soho.[10]

Leicester Square was transformed in the later nineteenth century as private residents moved out. It was instead increasingly dominated by hotels, theatres, and exhibitions: a hodgepodge of shops, the Alhambra music hall, and the Dental Hospital of London. The garden in Leicester Square itself was shabby and used as a garbage dump, full of dead cats, with the statue of George I on a horse in the middle (it ended up disfigured with polka dots by pranksters). In 1874 it was purchased and cleaned up through the generosity of financier and MP Baron Albert Grant (whose title was conferred on him by the Italian monarchy). Grant then donated the gardens to the Metropolitan Board of Works. Grant also had a fountain and a statue of Shakespeare placed at the centre, dignifying the area as a

[9] *London*, 27 July 1893, p. 406.
[10] Alex Potts, '*Eros* in Piccadilly Circus: Monument and Anti-Monument', in David J. Getsy (ed.), *Sculpture and the Pursuit of a Modern Ideal in Britain, c.1880–1930* (Aldershot: Ashgate, 2004), pp. 105–39.

centre for artistic works and establishing the square as the site of middle-class promenading. It became such a manicured space that the owner of a local pub was charged in 1883 when his goat wandered into the square and began to eat the plants.[11]

Yet the West End continued to retain some areas of substantial poverty, especially around Drury Lane and St Giles. The St Giles area, notorious for its rookeries and places associated with crime, was transformed when New Oxford Street was pushed through it in the later 1840s so that it linked up with Holborn. Neal Street above Covent Garden, however, was considered by Charles Booth's investigators in 1889 to be getting worse rather than better. Further east, the population of Clare Market (now the site of the London School of Economics) was seen as 'violent and drunken, but not criminal' by the police though the local priest insisted that he found examples of good neighbourliness. Shelton Street was so narrow that a vehicle could barely pass through it and pedestrians would prefer to walk on the roadway rather than on what existed of the curb because of the nails sticking out from the buildings. Its forty houses contained two hundred families: 'In little rooms no more than 8 ft. square, would be found living father, mother and several children'.[12] No rooms were free from vermin and Booth was revolted by accounts of dirt, violence, and bad language. Most inhabitants made a living as market porters (presumably in Covent Garden) or selling food on the streets.[13]

The slums of Drury Lane, which appalled Charles Booth, were subject to demolition, mainly to assist with the continuing problem of traffic congestion. Many were destroyed by the London County Council with the creation of Kingsway and the Aldwych in 1905. This wave of slum clearance really pushed the poor out of the West End.[14] Kingsway was named after Edward VII and has always had the reputation for being rather soulless. It became the eastern side of the West End with the Inns of Court and Fleet Street on the other side, going on to St Paul's and the City.[15] The semi-circular Aldwych (an old English term meaning 'old settlement') required the destruction of Wych Street as well as the Gaiety Theatre which had to be relocated nearby. The Waldorf Hotel was built between the two great theatres of W.G. Sprague: the Strand and the Aldwych.

These slum clearance schemes were performed in the name of modernization and securing the flow of traffic. The poor had been in the way of the bourgeois

---

[11] Newspaper clipping in St Martin's Scrapbook Series: Leicester Square Vol. 1 part 1 p. 50 (Westminster City Archives).

[12] Charles Booth, *Life and Labour of the People in London* (London: Macmillan, 1889–1903) First Series, Vol. 2, p. 47.

[13] Booth, *Life and Labour*, Third Series Vol. 2, p. 178.

[14] Francis Boormann (with Jonathan Comber and Mark Latham), *St Clement Danes, 1660–1900* (London: Victoria County History, 2018), p. 6.

[15] On the construction of Kingsway, see Jonathan Schneer, *London 1900: The Imperial Metropolis* (New Haven, CT: Yale University Press, 1999), pp. 19–28.

pleasure district. By the beginning of the twentieth century the main thoroughfares of the West End were in place.

Soho

From its very beginnings in the seventeenth century, Soho had been a place apart. The site of many aristocratic residences, it lost its cachet under the Hanoverians. Instead, it became dominated by a multitude of nationalities, especially French and Greeks. On one side of Regent Street was Serious Money; on the other, there were tradesmen, artisans, small shopkeepers, and the poor. Even the construction of Shaftesbury Avenue in the 1880s, which bisected Soho (and removed some bad slum housing), did not prevent the area from the north side of Leicester Square up to Oxford Street from acquiring a dark reputation. Charles Booth noted that Shaftesbury Avenue (along with the other big West End thoroughfares) did not belong to its immediate locality: 'step but fifteen paces, and you will find yourself in another world, with another people—other habits, other thoughts, and other manners seem to prevail'.[16]

Soho was 'another world' but, I argue, complex. It was associated with poverty but there were many successful businesses. It was urban but there were some two hundred cows kept at various places in the neighbourhood at mid-century to produce milk.[17] It was also a centre of industrial production. Crosse and Blackwell ran their sauces and pickles business from a factory in Soho Square.[18] Brothels could be found there but the Haymarket was more often identified with sex workers than Soho for much of the nineteenth century (see Chapter 7). Its reputation as a red light district was ultimately something that gathered pace in the twentieth century but it did gain a reputation for criminality.

If we cast our eye over Charles Booth's poverty map from 1889, we find that none of Soho was coloured black (which denoted the lowest class who were considered 'vicious, semi-criminal' in the social investigator's typology). There were only a few streets coloured blue which meant 'very poor'. Rather, the dominant colour was mauve which meant mixed ('some comfortable, others poor').[19] Few streets were consistently poor. In an important insight, Booth argued that 'Poverty in these streets usually goes by floors; the poorest people, often extremely poor, are to be found at the top of the houses, and as you descend floor by floor the

---

[16] Booth, *Life and Labour*, First Series, Vol. 1, p. 182.

[17] John Hollingshead, *Ragged London in 1861* (London: Smith, Elder, 1861), p. 123.

[18] Nigel Jeffries with Lynn Blackmore and David Sorapure, *Crosse and Blackwell, 1830–1921: A British Food Manufacturer in London's West End* (London: Museum of London/Crossrail, 2016), pp. 3, 36.

[19] https://booth.lse.ac.uk/ (accessed 27 July 2018).

position mends.'[20] This produced a varied neighbourhood, though the central location made for high rents. Around Soho Square, however, Booth found that nearly half the population was below the poverty line.[21] There certainly was poverty though it was not as bad in 1889 as it still was in the St Giles area.

Soho was cosmopolitan with different languages spoken, different ways of life evident on the streets and, above all, different forms of cuisine and food cultures juxtaposed in its cafés, restaurants, and food shops. Soho had a history of taking in immigrants from abroad which made it feel different. It helped give the West End a feeling of being in London but not entirely English. Unlike the rest of the West End, it was more obviously residential.

With the exception of the Shaftesbury Avenue theatres, the area did not have strong theatre connections. Soho pleasures were those of food and alcohol rather than the stage. There was, however, the theatre on Dean Street that was established in 1840 as Miss Kelly's Theatre and Dramatic School but which, for much of its history, was the Royalty. Frequently dark, it went through multiple ownerships, but enjoyed only the odd hit show; for example, Sarah Bernhardt performed there in 1907 with her company.

Wardour Street established itself as a central location for the purchase of pictures and curiosities with some upmarket dealers and customers. Berwick Street market dated from the eighteenth century. It bustled with traders selling food, shouting about their wares, and offering unexpected bargains. Household goods, knick-knacks, and children's toys could be found there. As Charles Booth noted, Soho streets were often impervious to traffic as they were crowded with street traders and costers.[22]

The cosmopolitanism of Soho shaped its character and also made it a force for cultural change, suggesting alternative ways of living that attracted radicals and bohemians.[23] The neighbourhood had distinct communities that provided sources of innovation in eating and display. It had long been associated with French immigrants but also with political refugees.[24] Mayhew noted that the area was full of French, Germans, Swiss, Spaniards, and Portuguese. This meant that there were different styles of dress evident on the street: 'here are to be seen those peculiar...hooded cloaks, and those tumescent peg-top-shaped trousers and hats which foreign gentlemen generally rejoice in, as well as the high-heeled bronze boots and blush-coloured silk stockings of which the French ladies of this neighbourhood are so strikingly proud'.[25] Soho restaurants were decidedly cheap both

[20] Booth, *Life and Labour*, First Series, Vol. 1, p. 185.
[21] Booth, *Life and Labour*, First Series, Vol. 2, appendix, p. 2.
[22] Booth, *Life and Labour*, First Series, Vol. 1, pp. 182–3.
[23] Judith R. Walkowitz, *Nights Out: Life in Cosmopolitan London* (London: Yale University Press, 2012).
[24] *Once a Week*, 30 May 1868, pp. 480–2.
[25] Henry Mayhew (ed.), *The Shops and Companies of London and the Trades and Manufactories of Great Britain* (London: Strand, 1865), p. 174.

in what they charged for food but also in appearance. One description records that they had barely any decoration apart from bright wallpaper; the chairs were often rickety, the tables narrow, and there was sand on the floor. Balzac was invoked to describe them: 'You may see the Père Goriot and Vautrin any day in Soho.'[26] The bon viveur Nathaniel Newnham Davis was familiar with the world of Soho (as many men about town prided themselves on being). Here he captures Old Compton Street, one of the main thoroughfares through the district:

> Old Compton Street is not aristocratic. Its inhabitants live much in the street, and talk all European languages except that of England. Gas jets, untrammelled by globes, flare in front of many of the shops. Fish bars, French laundries, French butchers' shops, and cheap haberdashers' are the principal characteristics of the street; and the names above the shop windows are mostly foreign.[27]

The restaurants of Soho were often considered second rate. After it was founded in 1867, however, Kettner's on Romilly Street caused a stir because a letter appeared in the *Times* by jurist and gastronome E.S. Dallas claiming it offered the best meals in London outside of gentlemen's clubs. Up to this point, it mainly served non-English people, particularly refugees from the European revolutions of 1848 and those who had gone on to fight with Garibaldi. After the Dallas letter High Society moved in and the cheap prices were no more.[28] Oscar Wilde became a devotee. It was noted for its nooks and corners where it was possible to achieve privacy and made a point of advertising that it offered 'Suppers after the Theatres', drawing on its proximity to Shaftesbury Avenue.[29]

Increasingly, Soho was notable for Jewish immigration (though not to the same extent as areas like Bethnal Green in the East End), especially after 1880 when eastern European Jews had to flee from anti-Semitic pogroms. Berwick Street in particular was notable for the large number of Jewish tailors by the turn of the century, However, Jews had been a presence in Soho before this. The Westminster Jews Free School moved to Greek Street in 1843. A girls' school was opened in Dean Street in 1846 and the two schools were amalgamated in Greek Street in 1853. By 1883, the building was not big enough, given the increase in Jewish families, and the school was moved to Hanway Place, just north of Oxford Street.[30] The area also included the West Central Jewish Girls' Club in Dean Street

---

[26] *Caterer and Hotel Proprietor's Gazette*, 1 November 1879, pp. 156–7.
[27] Nathaniel Newnham-Davis, *Dinners and Dining: Where and How to Dine in London* (London: Grant Richards, 1901 [1899]), p. 129.
[28] *Caterer and Hotel Proprietor's Gazette*, 14 May 1881 p. 86; 15 February 1898 pp. 64–6.
[29] *Caterer and Hotel Proprietor's Gazette*, 15 January 1896, p. lix.
[30] http://discovery.nationalarchives.gov.uk/details/r/5664a734-ee57-4af5-bdd5-c51920b99a37 (accessed 28 July 2018).

which was founded in 1893.[31] There was thus a substantial increase in the religious and associational life for Jewish people in the area.

Soho became notable also as the home not just of immigrants but also of political refugees. The failed revolutions of the nineteenth century added to the local population. In retrospect, the most famous of these was Karl Marx. Following the collapse of the 1848 French revolution and his authorship of the manifesto of the Communist Party, Marx was compelled to move his family to London. They eventually settled in Dean Street, Soho (from 1850–6), where his daughter Eleanor was born and where three of his children died. Marx earned some money as the London correspondent for the *New York Daily Tribune* and lived in Soho because it was so cheap. The family and their servant made do in just three rooms, though Marx would daily leave for the British Museum to conduct the studies destined to become *Das Kapital*. Marx was part of the radical network in the West End, speaking to the German Workers' Education Society, which met in Great Windmill Street, and was active in the International Working Men's Association which rented rooms in Greek Street.[32] Financial assistance from his associate Friedrich Engels later allowed Marx to move his family to Kentish Town.

Soho was notorious for dirt. It was not connected to the sewer system and refuse was not cleared away. John Hollingshead was appalled by the overcrowding he discovered in his social investigations in 1861. It was not unusual to find a family of six living in one room. Entering a house in Pulteney Court, not far from Regent Street, he thought he was in Bethnal Green in the East End:

> The small yard seemed rooting with damp and dirt. The narrow window of the lower back room was too caked with mud to be seen through…The stench throughout the house, although the front and back doors were wide open, was almost sickening.

Such conditions made for ill health. In one room Hollingshead found a tailor working for one of the West End fashion houses who was bent double with consumption but had to keep working in order to live. Elsewhere, he encountered an unemployed French-polisher who had sold off most of his possessions to passers-by but who refused to ask for poor-relief because it would suggest he had a bad character. This, observed Hollingshead, was 'a very common feeling, especially amongst poor ratepayers.'[33]

In 1854, Soho was badly affected by an outbreak of cholera. There were repeated eruptions of the miserable disease during the nineteenth century which brought with it fears not only of death but also the breakdown of the social order;

---

[31] http://www.sohomemories.org.uk/page_id__41.aspx (accessed 28 July 2018).
[32] Asa Briggs and John Callow, *Marx in London* (London: Lawrence and Wishart, 2008).
[33] Hollingshead, *Ragged London*, pp. 119, 121, 123.

616 people died in the area. Locals had to flee. At the time, physicians were divided over what spread disease: bad air (the miasma theory) or germs? Dr John Snow tracked the source of the cholera to a contaminated pump on Broad Street (now Broadwick Street). The authorities put the pump out of use although Snow himself considered that the spread of disease had already started to decline. The flight of people may have itself brought the wave of cholera to an end. Snow's discovery led to the broader acceptance of the germ theory, a major factor in the development of social reform.[34]

Even without cholera, wealthier people were leaving. The housing left behind was usually cheap, making it suitable for the poor (and especially immigrants). More and more people were packed into fewer and fewer houses. This in turn produced an increase in rents as housing was scarce, leading to a perfect storm of poverty in the later nineteenth century. In the winter of 1895, conditions in Soho were so bad that soup kitchens were common and some families had to pawn all their furniture. In one street visited by the reformer Arthur Sherwell, 115 adults were out of work though he noted this was a time of exceptional distress. The average number of persons to a house in St Anne's parish, Soho was 13.1 (compared to 7.0 in St George's, Hanover Square). The housing stock in the area tended to be smaller, making overcrowding even worse.[35] It was not uncommon to see advertisements with the phrase 'part of a room to let'. Sherwell found one house occupied by five different families.[36] The infant mortality level was one of the highest in London.

A persistent problem was that many casual workers were involved in dressmaking, sewing clothing for the Mayfair elite. This work was, however, seasonal. When the aristocracy was away in the country, there was little work to tide such people over which meant they experienced bitter poverty. The coming of the sewing machine meant that it remained a sweated trade, where workers had to work long hours for low pay. Given the number of women who were involved in dressmaking, many could only survive by turning to prostitution. It explains why attempts were made to provide local facilities for working-class women. Thus the Soho Working Girls Club on Greek Street offered music, dance, and some dramatic performances.[37] Soho provided a lively cosmopolitan atmosphere which contrasted with the self-conscious Englishness of much of the West End.

There were therefore different kinds of West End. It could combine riches but also the prospect of serious poverty. Ordinary people continued to live in the

---

[34] John Snow, *On the Mode of Communication of Cholera* (London: John Snow, 1855). On Cholera and social reform, see Pamela K. Gilbert, *Cholera and Nation: Doctoring the Social Body in Victorian England* (New York: State University of New York, 2008).

[35] Arthur Sherwell, *Life in West London: A Study and a Contrast* (London: Methuen, 1901 [third edition]), pp. 9–10, 15.

[36] Sherwell, *Life in West London*, pp. 35, 42.

[37] LCC Theatre and Music Halls Committee Minutes, 1 October 1890, p. 342: LCC/MIN/10, 713 (London Metropolitan Archive).

West End but the nature of the district rendered community life invisible. Despite the existence of numerous skilled trades and even factories, it was not viewed as a centre of production. The spatial nature of the West End was therefore crucial in creating a pleasure district, making it feel different from elsewhere.

In fact, the West End as a whole had many features common to most urban areas, including being a place of faith, healthcare, and education. The West End was blessed with its churches which included St Martin's-in-the Fields and St Paul's in Covent Garden (known as the actor's church). The Salvation Army took over Regent's Hall (a former skating rink) on Oxford Street in 1882, making it a basis of operations in the West End. In 1880, the West End Synagogue (West End Talmud Torah) was founded in Green's Court, off Brewer Street. Charing Cross Hospital was on Agar Street, close to the Strand. The St Giles's Boys School on Endell Street, off Covent Garden, in the later nineteenth century, provided education for boys from the tough neighbourhoods of St Giles and Drury Lane.[38] Leicester Square housed (from 1895 to 1928) Archbishop Tenison's School, a mark of its increasing respectability.

The West End in the later nineteenth century was imagined in contrast to the East End which was increasingly viewed as 'Outcast London': a site of poverty and unrest that needed to be reformed. If this study seeks to emphasize the distinctive qualities of the West End, it is as well to put this in some perspective. When we look up close some of these polarities between East and West are not so clear-cut. There was poverty in Soho just as much as in Bethnal Green. The lavish wealth of the West End co-existed with exploited seamstresses, soup kitchens, and families packed into single rooms.

---

[38] Cutting in St Martin's Scrapbook Series: General Vol. 1 p. 48 (Westminster City Archives).

7

Capital of Pleasure

Big Bang

In 1900, it was possible to shop at Liberty's on Regent Street, dawdle on the Burlington Arcade, dine at the Criterion in Piccadilly, catch Henry Irving's revival of the great melodrama, *The Bells*, at the Lyceum, and stay the night at the Savoy Hotel. Eight years later, the first illuminated advertisements were erected in Piccadilly Circus, giving it an identity that dazzled passers-by with its bright lights announcing the pleasure and energy of urban living. The imperial metropolis was increasingly an electric city where diverse forms of image, music, sound, and mass media celebrated modernity.

The West End represented a cultural Big Bang. It was a rococo commotion of ideas and splashes of colour. Art, music, theatre, and literature felt the effects of this concentration of talent into a small area of London. Of a morning, artists and chorus girls would pass businessmen, sporting journalists, French chefs, and skilled artisans engaged in the luxury trades. This generated the cosmopolitanism that shaped the West End cultural style. Here was a pleasure district produced by the turbo-capitalism of the mid-nineteenth century in which living standards improved (though not for all) and a certain amount of disposable income made it possible for even working-class people to purchase goods beyond the simple necessities of life. The West End was a location for new cultural styles, fashions, and experiences that shaped modern metropolitan culture. Money gave the West End its rhythm and its swagger.

This chapter explores the cultural work of the pleasure district. To accomplish this, we have to unpack what was so pleasurable about pleasure districts and think, quite simply, about how the West End made people feel. This decoding will employ a succession of different frames, incorporating the senses, glamour, and sexuality. Taken together, these frames shaped the way people interacted with the pleasure district and help explain why it resonated with the popular imagination.

In the Realm of the Senses

The West End had (and has) a self-mythologizing quality, where theatrical first nights acquire symbolic importance and buildings promise the latest in luxury. Its constant stream of novelty helped create new needs and desires. This appeal to the

London's West End: Creating the Pleasure District, 1800–1914. Rohan McWilliam, Oxford University Press (2020).
© Rohan McWilliam.
DOI: 10.1093/oso/9780198823414.001.0001

senses explains why pleasure districts had the feeling of being dream-worlds, a characteristic recognized by the German critic Walter Benjamin in his study of the Parisian arcades.[1] Pleasure districts trade on forms of hyper-stimulation. The act of window shopping has a trance-like quality. In this view, objects on display have a charisma of their own, because they describe a lifestyle. The pleasure district offers a form of unwritten contract: that it will satisfy every desire—at a price.

We cannot describe the West End's impact on the senses with precision but we can conjure some of it through the use of collage. What follows is a sketch but, hopefully, a suggestive one. By putting sensory impacts together, we gain an awareness of the drawing power of the West End and its addictive qualities, weaving its fantasies into our unconscious.

Sound tells us something of the appeal of the pleasure district, based as it was on a desirable sonic culture ranging from the coloratura of the operatic aria to the music hall ballad and on to the refined precision of the actor's voice in classical theatre. Another distinctive sound was that of two hands clapping, sometimes with shouts of 'bravo!' and 'encore!' Sound mattered. It embodied the emergence of the nineteenth-century city and its new ways and manners, its bustling energy and momentum. A comedy that did not provoke laughter would have worried the performers on stage. Actors in a melodrama might have hoped for the low whine of crying at moments of pathos. Pleasure in the pleasure district was partly defined in auditory terms, although, as we will discover in Chapter 9, the West End began to cultivate the silent listener. Music with its capacity to transform the emotional self was something that was worth paying for and travelling a long way to hear. The West End created spaces for music appreciation at all levels of taste. The musical press in the later nineteenth century featured articles about the art of applause; how and when to clap. Concert purists would get angry with applause at the wrong moments.[2] Attending a musical event also required the self-discipline to listen well. Such cultural capital was integral to the making of middle-class culture but could also be about aspiration. It meshed with Victorian attitudes to the importance of character, affirming a person's quality by their sense of cultivation. Pleasure districts thus contrasted with the quietness which was often a characteristic of the middle-class home where the raised voice was disliked and children were expected to be seen and not heard. The pleasures of the district were aural as well as visual though the incoherent hubbub, roar, and commotion of the streets provided unwelcome forms of noise as well.[3] There was also the clatter of restaurants

[1]   Walter Benjamin, *The Arcades Project* (Cambridge, MA: Harvard University Press, 1999).
[2]   Sven Oliver Müller, 'Audience Behaviour in the Nineteenth Century', in Daniel Morat (ed.), *Sounds of Modern History: Auditory Cultures in 19th and 20th Century Europe* (New York: Berghahn, 2014), pp. 163–4.
[3]   Peter Bailey, 'Breaking the Sound Barrier', in Peter Bailey (ed.), *Popular Culture and Performance in the Victorian City* (Cambridge: Cambridge University Press, 1998), pp. 194–211; John Picker, *Victorian Soundscapes* (Oxford: Oxford University Press, 2003).

as diners ate at the same time or the growl of conversation by men in pubs. Sound could be disruptive; the negative side of urban change. Modern life was noisy. Yet silence could also find a place: the deliberate hush of the art gallery, for example, assisted the contemplative gaze of the sophisticated viewer who knew her Ruskin.

The West End developed the restaurant as a major attraction after 1850 (see Chapter 13). Thus part of the appeal of the West End was to the taste sensations that satisfied different kinds of appetite. Food at high-end restaurants became a form of spectacle, helping to create the figure of the gourmet. We should, however, put this in some perspective. Henry James developed a liking in Paris for consuming a slice of gateau in the 'coquettish' pastry shops on the boulevards. Alas, in London, he lamented 'there were no *gateaux* to consume'. He had to make do with royal digestives and oat cakes in shops that lacked the Parisian style.[4] This is perhaps evidence of more subdued English tastes; foreigners often loathed the quality of food on offer, especially in the middle- and low-range establishments. Nevertheless, hotels and restaurants offered to satisfy a variety of appetites. Pleasure districts trade in gluttony (even while some were doomed by poverty to be perpetually hungry). Middle-class suburbanites cherished the prospect of a meal in town, turning locations like Gatti's restaurant into important urban landmarks.

We have some anecdotal evidence of the smells of the West End, though many are the aromas of most urban areas at the time (horse dung on the streets, for example). The management of smell, however, was important for the kind of upscale people the West End attracted; they bathed more frequently than working-class people and would partly define their gentility through avoiding bad odours.[5] The relative cleanliness of public sites in the West End is easy to miss but important. Covent Garden (whose food market acquired its permanent building in 1830) was, however, notorious for its stench. The agents of the Duke of Bedford were responsible for its cleaning but the market was never properly washed down. In summer the smell of decayed vegetation was particularly noticeable.[6] Worse, the proximity to the Thames, the destination of much of London's sewage (up to the 1860s), meant that the West End frequently stank.

What of touch? We might approach this through the fabrics of nightlife: satin and velvet. When John Hollingshead was consulted about the coverings for the stalls and balcony seats at the Gaiety Theatre for its opening in 1868, he said that 'he thought the dress-coats of men and the "society gowns" of ladies could not be

---

[4] Henry James, *The Scenic Art: Notes on Acting and the Drama, 1872–1901* (London: Rupert Hart-Davis, 1949), pp. 97–8.

[5] On the history of smell, see William Tullett, *Smell in Eighteenth-Century England: A Social Sense* (Oxford: Oxford University Press, 2019).

[6] Charles Booth, *Life and Labour of the People in London* (London: Macmillan, 1889–1903), First Series, Vol. 1, pp. 194–5.

improved upon', meaning a commitment to luxury.[7] Soft fabrics helped construct the pleasure district.

The visual impact of the West End was crucial to its impression on the senses. We can say something of the particular colour palette that became the stock in trade of the West End: scarlet, rose, ruby, and crimson. These are warm, passionate colours that draw attention to themselves. Most London theatres opted for red velvet, giving their interiors a 'heavy' look.[8] The table lamps at the Café Monico on Shaftesbury Avenue were 'curtained with crimson' whilst the mirrors in the dining rooms of the Grand Hotel, Northumberland Avenue, were 'set in a frame of deep-coloured velvets'.[9] The West Room of the Criterion on Piccadilly was a 'symphony in shades of rose colour'.[10] The royal box in the New Theatre (built in 1903) enjoyed a crimson pile carpet (also found in its adjacent lavatory).[11] The main colour of luxury was, of course, gold; thus the royal box in theatres was often 'smothered with gingerbread gold'.[12]

The ravishing look of the auditorium was the product of an increasingly rich West End visual culture that produced buildings intended to impress. The exteriors of the London Pavilion, the Alhambra, and Her Majesty's Theatre (all treated later in this study) were grandiloquent architectural statements. They looked different from each other but shared a similar visual vocabulary: a feeling of monumentalism and scale. Restaurants were meant to offer an ambience that was at least as attractive as the food. One quality of pleasure districts is that they are places where the eye is guided and ravished with images of the beautiful: the shop, the theatre foyer, the poster. The visual culture of the West End is about what I call the 'licensed stare'. The obsessive or fixed gaze is something that can feel uncomfortable in normal society. But the whole point of West End entertainments is an invitation to stare; the attraction in theatres was increasingly what was on the stage with the auditoriums darkened so that spectator had nowhere else to look.[13] Posters and billboard advertising (often with female figures) offered the opportunity of unlimited staring. The West End was about scopic obsession.

Pleasure districts were distinctive because they were spaces with painted faces. Actors slapped on greasepaint and sometimes more elaborate forms of makeup, which illuminated their skin. Light bounced off it making actors seem different from mere mortals. But elaborate make-up could be found off the stage as well.

---

[7] John Hollingshead, *My Lifetime* (London: Sampson Low, Marston and Co., 1895), Vol. 2, p. 2.

[8] Daniel Joseph Kirwan, *Palace and Hovel; or, Phases of London Life* (London: Abelard-Schuman, 1963 [1870]), p. 155.

[9] Nathaniel Newnham-Davis, *Dinners and Dining: Where and How to Dine in London* (London: Grant Richards, 1901 [1899]), pp. 290, 301.

[10] Newnham-Davis, *Dinners and Dining*, p. 316.

[11] Wendy Trewin, *All on Stage: Charles Wyndham and the Alberys* (London: Harrap, 1980), p. 183.

[12] Hollingshead, *My Lifetime*, Vol. 2, p. 16.

[13] Rohan McWilliam, 'The Licensed Stare: Melodrama and the Culture of Spectacle', *Nineteenth Century Studies*, 13 (1999), pp. 153–75.

Shopping with his wife at Swan and Edgar on Piccadilly Circus, Oscar Wilde was struck by the painted boys on the pavement outside offering sexual services.[14] Female prostitutes also employed elaborate forms of make-up to signify they were different from other women. Sex workers at the Argyll Rooms (see below) could be detected by their blackened eyebrows and eyelashes.[15] Thus if we want to understand the mental world induced by pleasure districts we should view it as one made up of performance but also the deployment of masks and masquerade. Performances took place off the stage as well as on, through dress, make-up, and behaviour.

Integral to visual culture was the development of sheet glass after 1850 which allowed shop window displays to become an established part of the area's landscape. If one can get past his condescension about female shoppers, Mayhew may not have been wrong in noting how the displays in Oxford Street windows were 'so enormous that the emotions peculiar to the amiable sex are constantly aroused'. Women would form groups for 'enraptured' gazing at the displays in the windows of drapers's shops, an example of the licensed stare.[16] As Isobel Armstrong argues, 'glass creates an aura of glamour and duplicity—a "double lustre"'—through the act of gazing out and gazing in. Glassworlds shaped the modern experience of shopping—creating a 'fantasmatic vicarious ownership' of the contents in shop displays.[17]

Above all, the West End was a world created by artificial light. The West End allowed for the night to be reclaimed for leisure and thus helped create modern nightlife.[18] Pleasure districts thrive on bright lights that draw people in, creating a sense of safety, difference, and luxury. As early as 1786, the German traveller Sophie von la Roche was attracted by the 'splendidly lit shop fronts' on Oxford Street.[19] London was one of the first cities to employ gas lighting in the early nineteenth century. Pall Mall, Oxford Street, Regent Street, and Piccadilly were predictably quick to take advantage of this new technology which meant that the West End (at least in the early nineteenth century) felt like a place apart.

The coming of gas transformed theatres. Previously, they had been candle lit. Improved illumination allowed scenery and indeed actors' faces to be properly seen. The coming of limelight after 1837 allowed for even more focussed lighting

[14]   Richard Ellmann, *Oscar Wilde* (New York: Knopf, 1988), p. 275.

[15]   *Reynolds's Newspaper*, 13 October 1878, p. 5.

[16]   Henry Mayhew (ed.), *The Shops and Companies of London and the Trades and Manufactories of Great Britain* (London: Strand, 1865), p. 86.

[17]   Isobel Armstrong, *Victorian Glassworlds: Glass Culture and the Imagination, 1830–1880* (Oxford: Oxford University Press, 2008), p. 7.

[18]   Wolfgang Schivelbusch, *Disenchanted Night: The Industrialization of Light in the Nineteenth Century* (Oxford: Berg, 1988); Lynda Nead, *Victorian Babylon: People, Streets and Images in Nineteenth Century London* (London: Yale University Press, 2000), pp. 83–146.

[19]   Sophie von la Roche, *Sophie in London, 1786: Being the Diary of Sophie v. la Roche* (ed. Clare Williams) (London: Jonathan Cape, 1933), p. 226.

effects.[20] Lighting was in every sense dramatic and could be used in new ways to affect the senses. Throughout the nineteenth century, theatres employed shows of light and shadow including phantasmagoria. The magic lantern made possible colourful forms of enchantment and directed lighting allowed all forms of drama to possess a brilliant allure.

There was a sensuous quality to artificial light as it sought to restrain the darkness of night. It made the West End theatrical by turning the district into one big theatre. Late Victorian shops, restaurants, and playhouses were made dramatic by the use of gas and, later, electricity. The Grosvenor Gallery which opened on New Bond Street in 1877, was one of the first to have electric light. The restaurant in Challis's Hotel on Rupert Street blazed with electric light, according to Nathaniel Newnham-Davis: 'a starry constellation in the ceiling, lights shaded with blue and pink and old-gold shades in brackets on the wall, and on the table candle-lamps crowned with deep red shades'.[21] César Ritz experimented with concealed lighting at the Savoy hotel restaurant to avoid the glare of naked light bulbs. He also went through a range of lampshades until he settled on apricot pink as the one that would prove most attractive and 'kinder to his dowagers'. His wife acted as a model 'for endless experiments until he was completely satisfied with angles and watts'.[22]

Liberty's (established on Regent Street in 1875) originally had a basement offering Japanese knick-knacks that was notable for its electric lights.[23] Selfridge's, which opened on Oxford Street in 1909, would keep its window displays lit till midnight so that it remained a source of vicarious pleasure even when the store was closed.[24] A slight shift away from the main part of the West End involved a change in lighting in the late Victorian period. The lights on Fleet Street were relatively dim at the end of the nineteenth century whilst those of the Strand were brilliant.[25] Similarly, Old Compton Street in Soho was full of shops that were lit by gas jets but no globes to shape the light, imparting a rough quality which signalled that they were more downmarket. The Café D'Italie on the street employed electric lights hung from the ceiling. This in turn illuminated the coloured glass in

[20] Michael R. Booth, *Theatre in the Victorian Age* (Cambridge: Cambridge University Press, 1991), pp. 83–7; Terence Rees, *Theatre Lighting in the Age of Gas* (Cambridge: Entertainment Technology Press, 1978), pp. 42–64.

[21] Newnham-Davis, *Dinners and Dining*, pp. 362–3.

[22] Stanley Jackson, *The Savoy: A Century of Taste* (London: Muller, 1989 [1964]) p. 27; Derek Taylor and David Bush, *The Golden Age of British Hotels* (London: Northwood, 1974), p. 128.

[23] Alison Adburgham, *Liberty's: A Biography of a Shop* (London: George Allen and Unwin, 1975), p. 43.

[24] Alison Adburgham, *Shops and Shopping, 1800–1914: Where, and in what Manner the Well-dressed Englishwoman Bought her Clothes* (London: Barrie and Jenkins, 1989 [1964]), p. 275.

[25] Frederick Willis, *A Book of London Yesterdays* (London: Phoenix House, 1960), p. 232.

the window which shielded diners from the street outside and created a bright effect inside that was also enhanced by the mirrors.[26]

Electricity shone a brighter light on stage and the theatre interior, revealing imperfections that could be hidden in the age of gaslight. Stage scenery and make-up had to evolve to deal with the more searching focus of light. Electricity was such a novelty that it extended to the wardrobe department. In F.C. Burnand's *Ariel* (1883) at the Gaiety, electric lights were employed as part of Nellie Farren's costume, creating a poetic effect on stage.[27] By the beginning of the new century, electricity was helping move stage machinery as well, using motor power. Most importantly, dimmers allowed for a full blackout in the auditorium.

The Gaiety Theatre on the Strand promoted itself through an electric search-light on its roof, powered by an enormous battery.[28] John Hollingshead, the manager, went to Paris to examine innovations in lighting and came back with the Lontin light system. He kept six arc lights beaming into the night sky to publicize the Gaiety. Though Hollinghead brought the experiment to an end after nine months for reasons of expense, it demonstrated the importance of illumination to sell the products of the West End.[29] During its use, it inspired a song, 'The Electric Galop', whose sheet music shows a diabolical figure clothed in bright red shining a bright lamp on the Gaiety (see Fig. 7.1).

The Savoy theatre (which opened in 1881) was not only the first theatre, but the first building in the world, to be lit entirely by electric light. It offered 1200 lights attached to a 120 horse-power generator nearby. It was considered an experiment and gas was available in case the electricity failed.[30] When the curtain fell on the first night, D'Oyly Carte came on stage with an electric lamp in his hand and delivered a short lecture about electricity in theatres to an audience who he feared were sceptical about its safety.[31]

The lights of the West End reflected a perception that major urban centres should be distinctive for their illuminated qualities. In this sense the West End was part of a conversation with the brightly lit boulevards of Paris and the dazzle of Broadway and Times Square in New York.Light was part of an appeal to the different senses. It allowed buildings to be visually noisy. This sensory dimension is one reason why pleasure districts tend to feel different from suburbs or other urban locations. The West End hails its visitors by saying: look, listen, taste, smell, feel, *imagine*.

---

[26] Newnham-Davis, *Dinners and Dining*, pp. 129, 130.
[27] Hollingshead, *My Lifetime*, Vol. 2, p. 154.   [28] Hollingshead, *My Lifetime*, Vol. 2, p. 19.
[29] See also John Hollingshead, *Gaiety Chronicles* (London: Constable, 1898), pp. 381–91.
[30] *Times*, 3 October 1881, p. 7.
[31] Cutting in D'Oyly Carte Archive: THM/73/8/3 (Victoria and Albert Museum Theatre and Performance Archives).

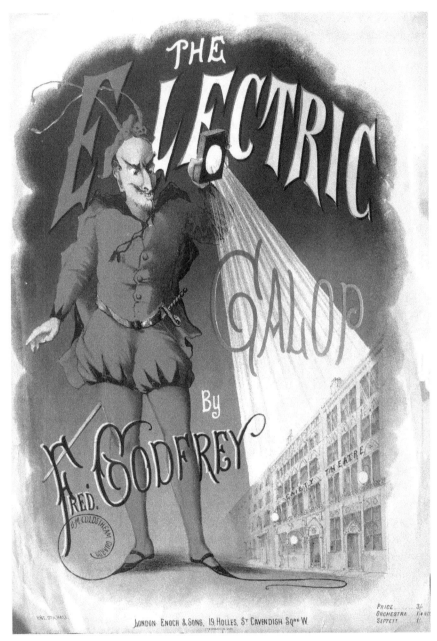

Fig. 7.1 Frederick Godfrey, *The Electric Galop* (1878) (Michael Diamond Collection)

Glamour and Sexuality

Nell Bacon, a waitress at the Lyons tea shops, recalled that her only recreation in the 1890s was sitting 'in the gods' at the theatre where she came to idolize Sir John Martin Harvey, whom she allegedly saw forty times in *The Only Way*. When Bacon served Harvey in a tea room, she was so star-struck that she substituted the coins he gave her for her own when paying in so that she could retain those he had actually touched.[32] The West End was about the appeal of stardom. Henry Irving, for example, received reverential adulation from fans who would besiege him at the Lyceum stage door and, in some cases, try to bestow presents on him. The most bizarre gift was a kangaroo which had to be donated to a zoo.[33] When Irving died, five years later in 1905, London cabmen put black bows on their whips.[34]

Juxtaposing glamour and sexuality with a discussion of the senses points to the sensual and erotic feelings that pleasure districts constructed and which made them alluring and troubling. This section examines the sexual appeal of the West End star and contrasts it with the explicit sexuality of prostitution.

As we have seen, there was nothing new about the figure of the 'star' but the mass culture of the later nineteenth century provided enhanced opportunities for access through photographs and a range of advertisements, posters, and magazines which fixed the star as an object of wish-fulfilment. Stars were admired for their skills in performance, but were also possessed of a magical quality. It was not merely their beauty; it was also their ability to evoke a way of living that was different from ordinary mortals. Glamour involves a larger-than-life quality. The very word 'glamour' was connected to magic in the nineteenth century (though the word only really became part of common parlance in the late Victorian period). Stars may have been sorcerers but they were also educators, teaching audiences about metropolitan life, fashion, clothing, and even smell. Carol Dyhouse argues, for example, that glamour 'includes a dimension of sensuality and magic through touch, texture and scent'.[35] The West End fashioned notions of good taste, joy, and aspiration.

Glamour was closely related to the development of consumerism and, in the view of Stephen Gundle, was a 'fabrication' by middle-class entrepreneurs who employed images derived from High Society to make the everyday seem magnificent through style, fashion, and goods.[36] It also thrived on an increasingly visual culture fostered by the increasing availability of pictorial images. The world of the

---

[32] Memories of Nell Bacon (Lyons archive): ACC/3527/231 (London Metropolitan Archive).
[33] Michael Holroyd, *A Strange, Eventful History: The Dramatic Lives of Ellen Terry, Henry Irving and Their Remarkable Families* (London: Chatto and Windus, 2008), p. 108.
[34] Jeffrey Richards, *Sir Henry Irving: A Victorian Actor and his World* (London: Hambledon, 2005), p. 1.
[35] Carol Dyhouse, *Glamour: Women, History, Feminism* (London: Zed Books, 2011), pp. 1, 8.
[36] Stephen Gundle, *Glamour: A History* (Oxford: Oxford University Press, 2008), pp. 5–7, 19.

West End with its spectacular shops and aristocratic customers (as we have seen in Chapter 2) was ideally placed to both employ images of glamour and make people feel glamorous. So too were theatres with their deployment of images of beauty and the construction of stars (a marked feature of the post-1850 stage though it had always been there). Glamour thrived on performance and artifice. Spectacular shops offered enticement, acknowledging that selling could not be separated from forms of theatricality.[37] This is why the conjunction of theatres, shops, and nodes of fashion and display made the West End not only a distinctive space but one that could ripple outwards into the wider culture.

The roots of the West End in servicing the elite were also important. The aristocracy in popular culture was associated not only with power but also with total freedom. This may explain why some of the cultural effects of the West End felt like liberation: they followed a template about behaving like the toffs who could do whatever they liked. In Lottie Collins's hit song 'Ta-ra-ra Boom-de-ay' (introduced at the Tivoli in 1891), she described herself as 'A queen of swell society / Fond of fun as fond can be'. Glamour meant identification with the well-off ('swell society') because they were the only truly free people. Hence the music hall was full of Champagne Charlies and Burlington Berties. Stars and glamour itself represent a disavowal of moves towards equality. They dispute the view that everyone is equal.

A vital part of West End life thus was the poster, evident in this photograph of the stage door at the Alhambra in the 1890s (see Fig. 7.2). The playbill had given way in the later nineteenth century to colourful images providing theatre with a form of exotic promise. Posters with dramatic images (a contrast with the old theatre bill) were a consequence of the shift to long runs for plays. Walter Smith's firm in Bloomsbury, for example, produced elaborate three-colour posters for the Alhambra among other venues.[38] The Magazine of Art accepted in 1881 that the pictorial advertisement (for consumer goods or plays) had become a form of street art; it enlivened the lives of people who did not have access to art galleries and needed to be taken seriously.[39] The poster had turned the street into a gallery, giving neighbourhoods a character. Reformers complained that posters outside the Palace Theatre had a 'suggestive and demoralizing' effect on young men, advertising as they did the nude poses plastiques within.[40] Posters hailed spectators by informing them that they were the kind of people who would enjoy the sensual and colourful world of the theatre and the music hall. They were not

---

[37] Stephen Gundle and Clino T.Castelli, The Glamour System (Basingstoke: Palgrave Macmillan, 2006), p. 9.

[38] Michael R. Booth (ed.), Victorian Theatrical Trades: Articles from 'The Stage', 1883–1884 (London: Society for Theatre Research, 1981), pp. 38–41.

[39] 'The Street as Art-Galleries', Magazine of Art, 4 (1881), p. 299.

[40] Tracy C. Davis, 'Indecency and Vigilance in the Music Halls', in Richard Foulkes (ed.), British Theatre in the 1890s: Essays on Drama and the Stage (Cambridge: Cambridge University Press, 1992), p. 117.

Fig. 7.2 Alhambra stage door, 1890s (University of Bristol/ArenaPAL)

limited to the West End but they did reinforce the identity of the district as a place worth travelling to in search of glamour.

Stars are clues about the mentality of an age. The image of the actor and actress was important even when they were not on stage. When Lilly Langtry was interviewed by *The Sketch* while rehearsing *A Society Butterfly* at the Opera Comique, readers were told she was wearing the 'latest Parisian creation' and accompanied by a Russian poodle. Her lifestyle included a love of yachting and horse racing. She performed the role of the big star at all times.[41] Langtry denied that an actress's success was dependent on the clothes she wore yet publications like the *Sketch* devoted extensive space to actresses's costumes and apparel.[42] When the *Standard* reviewed *The Chalk Line* at the Queen's in 1912, it included a section describing Maud Beerbohm Tree's gowns and the coat she wore in the second act.[43] Theatre and theatrical journalism became vehicles for the worship of male and female beauty, an integral part of the attraction of the West End. Mrs E.T. Cook claimed to 'know of many well-to-do girls who never think of buying their season's hats and gowns till they have seen them on Mrs Patrick Campbell, Mrs. Tree, or Miss Winifred Emery'. For her, 'Millinery and costume are the most important factors in the modern theatre.'[44] Pleasure districts thrived on imitation which was part of their appeal; people could learn about the new styles and adorn themselves (or hope to) in the new fashions.

[41] *Sketch*, 16 May 1894, p. 116.   [42] *Sketch*, 8 February 1893, pp. 68–9.
[43] *Standard*, 4 March 1912, p. 4.
[44] (Mrs) E.T. Cook, *Highways and Byways in London* (London: Macmillan 1911), p. 283.

Periodicals such as *The Theatre* and *Play Pictorial* fed this passion. By 1900 there were about fifty illustrated theatrical periodicals for the consumer to enjoy. This wave of print media underlines how the reach of the West End extended beyond central London. Such periodicals could be read anywhere and kept people around the world aware of West End stars. The image of the actor or actress proved ubiquitous, even featuring on articles of china. Stars would agree to autograph *cartes de visite* and then postcards, visible signs of their emergence as icons. Photographs served as souvenirs—a part of West End life that could be carried in a wallet, placed upon a mantelpiece, or included in a scrapbook.[45]

There were also spatial linkages when it came to photography. Charles Kean's company at the Princess's Theatre were photographed by 'Martin Laroche' (William Henry Sylvester) whose photographic studio was close by on Oxford Street.[46] It became possible to purchase photographs of actors in newsagents. The photographic image of the actor or actress provided further mystery. They posed often with their gaze directed to the middle distance, inviting the viewer to uncover their inner life: men with firm chins and even firmer posture, women exuding poise and grace (see the picture of Gaiety Girl Marie Studholme in Fig. 7.3). Women would model their hair on stars whilst actresses could make additional money through advertising a variety of products. Constance Collier, when at the Gaiety, would provide advice in newspapers about how to stay beautiful.[47] Theatre became part of a glamour industry, comparable to what cinema and television achieved in the twentieth century.

There was another form of sexualized visual culture in the pleasure district but it was hidden away. In 1880 the Leicester Square newsagent, Caroline Thoviste, was found by police to have been selling obscene photographs. A detective called in and asked if she had any pictures 'more from nature'. Thoviste said she was expecting a shipment from Vienna shortly. The detective called back and was sold two obscene pictures. He returned with a number of other detectives who raided Thoviste's parlour and found it full of obscene photographs received from a firm in Paris as well as correspondence in French with people who wanted to purchase the pictures. She was remanded for a week.[48] Arthur Munby visited a photographer (he does not record where but he lived close to the West End) who attempted to sell him photographs of naked women. Munby was shocked and wondered about women who would allow themselves to be shown in that manner. The

---

[45] David Mayer, '"Quote the Words to Prompt the Attitudes": The Victorian Performer, the Photographer and the Photograph', *Theatre Survey*, 43 (2002), pp. 223–51.

[46] David Mayer, 'The Actress as Photographic Icon: From Early Photography to Early Film', in Maggie B. Gale and John Stokes (eds), *The Cambridge Companion to the Actress* (Cambridge: Cambridge University Press, 2007), p. 79.

[47] Constance Collier, *Harlequinade: The Story of my Life* (London: John Lane, 1929), pp. 60–1.

[48] Newspaper clipping in St Martin's Scrapbook Series: Leicester Square Vol. 1 p. 48 (Westminster City Archives).

PHILCO SERIES 3229 A   MISS MARIE STUDHOLME

Fig. 7.3 Marie Studholme (author collection)

photographer insisted that he had taken the pictures and claimed that one of the models had been a governess.[49]

Juxtaposing obscene photographs with late Victorian glamour suggests that the West End contained respectable and unrespectable elements. There was a sensual quality that ran through West End entertainments. It became a site for courtship. On Valentine's Day, for example, the Gaiety theatre would give away Gaiety valentines.[50] Music hall and theatre produced images that were delicately sexualized, touching the senses in a subtle way.

Alongside this were the explicit forms of sexuality in the form of street prostitution. The Haymarket had been associated with prostitution ever since the seventeenth century.[51] The same was true of the night houses (nightclubs) such as Kate Hamilton's that clustered around the Haymarket and Panton Street areas. When Inspector Webb entered Kate Hamilton's in 1862, he discovered fifty-five

---

[49] Derek Hudson (ed.), *Munby: Man of Two Worlds* (London: Abacus, 1974), p. 84.

[50] Hollingshead, *My Lifetime*, Vol. 2, p. 16.

[51] The world of the Haymarket, dance halls, and night houses is dealt with at length in Rohan McWilliam, 'Man about Town: Victorian Night Life and the Haymarket Saturnalia, 1840–1880', *History*, 103 (2018), pp. 758–76.

women, most of whom were 'well known prostitutes'.[52] Kate Hamilton also seems to have run a brothel at no. 4 Jermyn Street under the name Kate Franks.[53] Panton Street was reportedly packed all night with broughams and cabs: 'frequently prostitutes are taken away in them drunk'.[54] Some café owners even encouraged the more attractive prostitutes to enter because they brought in customers. The *Yokel's Preceptor* in 1855 listed some of the notorious prostitutes who made a living on the street and documented how they often came to a tragic end.[55] In 1864, Sarah Williams was indicted for running a disorderly house at 32 Oxenden Street, Haymarket, that had formerly been let out to 'ladies who frequented the Argyll Rooms' (see below) but was now filled with child prostitutes whilst the customers were old men.[56]

A letter to the *Times* in 1846 complained about the lack of policing which made it difficult to secure a passage through the Haymarket.[57] A local protested about the Café Regence on the corner of Windmill Street and the Haymarket because 'a friend of his had been nearly ruined there, and…the local police would not interfere'.[58] Arthur Munby described the Haymarket at four in the morning as 'Hogarthian', identifying 'two gentlemen in evening dress, a few unwashed foreigners, several half-drunken prostitutes, one of whom, reeling away, drops her splendid white bonnet in the gutter, & another dances across the street, showing her legs above the knee'.[59] Similarly, Albert Smith in 1857 complained that a visit to the Haymarket involved negotiating one's way through 'sparring snobs, and flashing satins, and sporting gents, and painted cheeks, and brandy-sparkling eyes, and bad tobacco, and hoarse-horse laughs, and loud indecency'.[60] In other words, the area offered a rich assault on the senses both in terms of the visual spectacle as well as in terms of morality.

The Argyll Rooms dance hall (not to be confused with the concert hall on Regent Street) at the top of the Haymarket was frequented by prostitutes. Established in 1849 to offer gambling and dancing, it drew in High Society but always enjoyed a louche reputation. *Reynolds's Newspaper* reported that Haymarket prostitutes would gather in the gallery of the Argyll between eleven and midnight, 'magnificently dressed in silks, satins and seal-skins'.[61] The spectacle of aristocrats consorting openly with sex workers was a troubling sight for the local middle classes who repeatedly tried to have the establishment closed down. Amongst fashionable Victorians known to frequent it were Rossetti, Dickens, and Wilkie

[52] *Morning Chronicle*, 15 March 1862, p. 6.
[53] *Pall Mall Gazette*, 30 January 1869, p. 9; *Era*, 25 April 1869, p. 7.
[54] Metropolitan police report, 8 December 1869: HO 45/9511/17216 (TNA).
[55] *Yokel's Preceptor: Or, More Sprees in London!* (London: H. Smith, 1855), pp. 7–10.
[56] *Morning Post*, 5 October 1864, p. 7.   [57] *Times*, 21 October 1846, p. 5.
[58] Commissioner of Metropolitan Police Report, 5 October 1870: HO 45/9511/17216 (TNA).
[59] Hudson (ed.), *Munby*, p. 35.
[60] [Albert Smith], 'Rogue's Walk', *Household Words*, 12 September 1857 p. 264.
[61] *Reynolds's Newspaper*, 20 October 1872, p. 5.

Collins.[62] The Argyll's owner was Robert Bignell, a wine merchant and owner of the cigar shop and saloon next door; he had a reputation as a sporting gentlemen and provided a location that would be enjoyed by that set.[63] The basic entrance fee was a shilling, which kept out the lower orders. Admission to the sumptuous galleries was even more exclusive at two shillings. On the dance floor (in front of the fifty-instrument orchestra), a railing separated the clerks, tradesmen, and other hoi polloi from the privileged.[64] When it opened, the *Era* admired its décor and the band of M. Laurent.[65]

J. Ewing Ritchie complained about 'painted and bedizened females...driving up in broughams from St. John's Wood or Chelsea or Belgravia, with their gallants, or "protectors", to the well-known rendezvous, at a late hour, to leave a little later for the various oyster-rooms in the district, through a dense crowd of lookers-on, drunk or sober, poor or rich, old or young, as the case may be.'[66] He feared that such examples made prostitution attractive to young women. Another commentator highlighted the prostitutes' use of blackened eyebrows and eyelashes as well as their 'fast looking hats'.[67] There is no evidence of sexual congress at the Argyll Rooms itself (two paid constables were retained to ensure order) but contemporaries noted that men would go away with prostitutes to 'houses of ill fame'.[68] *Reynolds's Newspaper* noted how Haymarket prostitutes would collect at the Argyll between eleven and midnight, 'magnificently dressed in silks, satins and seal-skins'. They never bothered to dance but would congregate in the gallery.[69] The Argyll Rooms was a place based on impulse (to gamble, to dance, to flirt) and a feeling of opportunity. It was thus a favourite with medical students, often renowned for wild and rowdy behaviour.[70]

Prostitutes were a familiar sight on many West End highways including the Strand and Regent Street. Their presence requires some decoding. They ruptured conventions about sexual respectability that permeated Victorian society but also offered a form of illegitimate retail that contrasted with the commerce in the shops. We can imagine that they elicited different kinds of male gaze: the man about town eyeing up each woman and the respectable man directing his gaze

[62] For Rossetti and the Argyll Rooms, see Deborah Lutz, *Pleasure Bound: Victorian Sex Rebels and the New Eroticism* (New York: W.W. Norton, 2010), p. 85; for Dickens and Collins, see Dickens to Collins, 22 April 1856: Jenny Hartley (ed.), *The Selected Letters of Charles Dickens* (Oxford: Oxford University Press, 2012), p. 306.

[63] *Era*, 8 June 1851, p. 7.

[64] Daniel Kirwan, *Palace and Hovel; Or, Phases of London Life* (London: Aberlard-Schuman, 1963 [1870]), p. 148.

[65] *Era*, 25 November 1849, p. 11; 29 December 1850, p. 13.

[66] J. Ewing Ritchie, *Days and Nights in London: Or, Studies in Black and Gray* (London: Tinsley Brothers, 1880), pp. 26–7.

[67] *Reynolds's Newspaper*, 13 October 1878, p. 5.

[68] *Reynolds's Newspaper*, 1 February 1863, p. 5. Detail about constables from *Reynolds's Newspaper*, 20 October 1872, p. 5.

[69] *Reynolds's Newspaper*, 20 October 1872, p. 5.

[70] *Lloyd's Weekly Newspaper*, 27 July 1856, p. 8.

forward so as not to establish eye contact (and the respectable woman with her gaze modestly directed to the pavement to avoid the sight?). The streetwalkers's performance of visible sexuality meant that the opulence of the West End always co-existed with vulgarity and the satisfaction of bodily desires.

In the early 1870s, over one hundred prostitutes were reported to work from rooms in Gerrard Street in Soho, not far from the Haymarket. Some landlords in the street gave their houses entirely over to prostitutes from whom they extracted high rents. A 'foreign prostitute', complaining about a landlord who had assaulted her, stated that she was paying two guineas a week for lodging and one guinea for food.[71] Police were surprised when a respectable man, 'holding a situation in Regent Street', turned up to offer bail for a prostitute who lodged in his Gerrard Street address. When the sergeant objected that the house was mainly occupied by prostitutes, the gentleman replied:

'Yes, yes, but I am myself a respectable man. I cannot get anyone else to take the rooms and cannot afford to let them lie empty. And the girls pay well and conduct themselves quietly.'[72]

Dostoevsky claimed that he was approached by girls as young as twelve on the Haymarket urging him to come with them. He entered a casino nearby (probably the Argyll Rooms but we cannot know for sure) and was struck by the contrast between the grandeur of the surroundings and the sadness of the faces, even when dancing, as if they were locked in a gloomy ritual.[73] This may say more about Dostoevsky but it offers an insight into the tragic element in an entertainment world based on forced merriment and masculine pleasure. There was a concerted attempt by police to stamp out Haymarket prostitution in the 1870s and 1880s. The Argyll Rooms and most night houses ended up being closed down. However, prostitution remained a common feature of both street life and of music halls, as we will see.

The West End became increasingly the site of queer encounter in its theatres and pubs as well as Hyde Park. The presence of soldiers at West End entertainments made it particularly attractive whilst Piccadilly Circus was known as a place for gay cruising.[74] Ernest Boulton and Frederick Park (or 'Fanny' and 'Stella') frequented West End spaces such as the Burlington Arcade and the Alhambra music hall in women's clothing.[75] They were arrested at the Royal Strand Theatre

[71] Metropolitan Police Report, 15 March 1870: HO 45/9511/17216 (TNA).

[72] Metropolitan Police Report, 15 March 1870: HO 45/9511/17216 (TNA).

[73] Fyodor Dostoevsky, *Winter Notes on Summer Impressions* (London: OneWorld Classics, 2008 [1863]), p. 56.

[74] *Star*, 19 July 1902, p. 3; See also Matt Cook, *London and the Culture of Homosexuality, 1885–1914* (Cambridge: Cambridge University Press, 2003).

[75] Neil McKenna, *Fanny and Stella: The Young Men who shocked Victorian England* (London: Faber and Faber 2014).

and put on trial in 1871 but acquitted as the prosecution was unable to prove that anal sex had occurred although the trial linked homosexuality with effeminacy. Boulton and Park's promenades in women's clothes round the West End reflected the way that it was a place for theatricality and the destablilization of conventions; gender itself had its performative dimensions. In pantomimes and music halls men would dress as women. Its theatres relished the thrill of dressing up in costume and putting on make-up. This was a world of fancy dress. In 1871, a woman called Rose Brown was charged with wearing men's clothes when attempting to get into the Argyll Rooms (she was thrown out but apprehended by a policeman), evidence that the site had transgressive associations.[76] In 1897, a German called William Julius was arrested at ten in the evening on Piccadilly, wearing women's clothing 'supposed for an unlawful purpose'.[77] One function of pleasure districts then is to suggest that even gender is not a totally stable category.

The West End allowed a queer sub-culture to develop, feeding off its theatres, restaurants, and hotels. Here was a heavily sexualized space that could resist Victorian norms in the most flamboyant way. A symbol of this was the first night of *Lady Windermere's Fan* at the St James's Theatre. Oscar Wilde attended with a group of young men who all sported green carnations; the flower that in Paris was linked to homosexual desire.[78]

Why do the sensory or sexual dimensions of the West End matter? At some level they change the people who go there (though they can also produce resistance and opposition). Walter Benjamin understood this, grasping that the built environment of the pleasure district and the entertainments and ephemera that it spawned had a psychic charge. The more difficult question is: a psychic charge for whom? This book argues that the pleasure district was intended for a heterogeneous but broadly middle-class public. Clearly, the sensory dimensions of the West End would have varied depending on gender. Pleasure was defined overwhelmingly in masculine terms although there was an increasingly female dimension to the pleasure district. What about age? All ages seem to have found their way in but the appeal of the West End was different for families, for children, for courting couples, and for intellectuals and aesthetes of both sexes.

Spectacle and glamour became part of a larger mass culture that shaped everyday life in the second half of the nineteenth century, expressing new forms of consumer culture. The pleasure district proved a site of hyper stimulation, based on sites of display and fantasy. What defined a pleasure district in one sense was its ability to construct glamour through a conjunction of fashion and theatre but also through the employment of visual media and sound. We have noted the prevalence of the colour red in its various spaces with its connotations of passion, luxury, and danger; a history of the West End is, of necessity, a study in scarlet.

---

[76] *Pall Mall Gazette*, 30 August 1871, p. 6.   [77] *Echo*, 14 April 1897, p. 3.
[78] Cook, *London and the Culture of Homosexuality*, p. 29.

Mass culture took different forms: mass eating, mass shopping, mass music. This meant that it was at odds with the thrift and self-help ethic of other parts of Victorian culture. The Liberal, pro-temperance social reformer Arthur Sherwell registered some of this when he complained about 'a mad, and irresistible craving for excitement, stimulated by the excitements and vicious luxury of West End life: a serious and wilful revolt against the monotony of commonplace ideals, and the uninspired drudgery of every-day life'.[79] This is why pleasure districts are different from other urban locations. They produce a different kind of mindset.

We can thus understand the West End in terms of what it was not: the suburbs. In the later nineteenth century, it became common for the suburbs to be treated by intellectuals in terms of disdain. The monotony of houses which all looked the same and where people lived allegedly monotonous lives contrasted with the pleasure district where each building looked different and offered a variety of delights and experiences. The cultural work of the West End can be understood as a contribution to suburban anxiety. The suburban middle classes were put in their place. What mattered were the bright lights and the big city.

---

[79] Arthur Sherwell, *Life in West London: A Study and a Contrast* (London: Methuen, 1901 [third edition]), p. 147.

8

Capital of Culture

Habitus

If the West End was associated with vulgarity, it still retained a role as a space for high culture. Since its origins in the later seventeenth century, it had been characterized by a commercial approach to the arts and to literature.[1] The art exhibition and the concert were crucial to the making of high art, whilst Covent Garden and the Strand boasted a literary bohemia.[2] The West End functioned as a place to distinguish which cultural goods should enjoy high status and which should be labelled inferior.

The West End was what the sociologist Pierre Bourdieu calls a 'habitus': a place where people who defined themselves as sophisticated could find forms of art that enhanced their sense of hierarchy and status. It was a place for the formation of cultural capital.[3] West End pleasures always functioned at a symbolic level. They allowed the elite to define itself as separate, using the distinctions of rank, taste, and education. Mayfair and Pall Mall were threaded with art galleries which were essentially exclusive. Like theatre, art was a business (although it often pretended not to be). As a space for high culture, the West End created areas for connoisseurship, close to elite residences, offering opportunities for up-and-coming artists and musicians to make an impact. Even in Science, the area had considerable impact. Albermarle Street boasted the Royal Institution where Humphrey Davy and Michael Faraday in the early nineteenth century promoted work on electricity among other forms of scientific research. The Royal Society, which had been in Somerset House since 1780, moved to Burlington House on Piccadilly in 1857. It was joined there in 1874 by the Geological Society, the Royal Astronomical Society, and the Society of Antiquaries. The West End made the march of scientific progress visible.

This is a chapter about the way the West End provided spaces for creativity and innovation. I will look briefly at painting, music, and the literary and journalistic worlds. Each in its different way demonstrated how the city could employ art and

[1] John Brewer, *The Pleasures of the Imagination: English Culture in the Eighteenth Century* (London: Harper Collins, 1997).
[2] Vic Gatrell, *The First Bohemians: Life and Art in London's Golden Age* (London: Allen Lane, 2013).
[3] Pierre Bourdieu, *Distinction: A Social Critique of the Judgement of Taste* (London: Routledge and Kegan Paul, 2010 [1984]).

London's West End: Creating the Pleasure District, 1800–1914. Rohan McWilliam, Oxford University Press (2020).
© Rohan McWilliam.
DOI: 10.1093/oso/9780198823414.001.0001

intellectual work to propel the economy.[4] The West End created spaces for high art, separate from the brashness of other entertainments. The Royal Academy (and its all-important summer exhibition) relocated to Burlington House in 1869, joining the Royal Society. Spatially, the art world tended to cluster around the area from Regent Street over to Bond Street (though the National Gallery was a major exception); likewise, concert music could be found in the same area, but opera and operetta increasingly gravitated toward the eastern side of the West End: Covent Garden and the Savoy Theatre. These same areas around the Strand saw the development of a journalistic bohemia.

This spatial segregation was, however, never complete. High and low culture remained porous, feeding off one another and creating intriguing juxtapositions. Thus, for example, the St James's Hall offered Monday 'pop' concerts. At the Egyptian Hall it was possible to view paintings by Louise Jopling in its gallery and then go upstairs and take in the magic show of John Nevil Maskelyne and George Alfred Cooke in which Mrs Maskelyne was made to float through the air. The fact that department stores such as Selfridge's and Marshall and Snelgrove contained their own galleries meant that the art market was available to a wider middle-class public than was possible on Bond Street. The cultural eruption in the West End developed identities such as the connoisseur, the aficionado, the aesthete, and the snob. This is a social function of pleasure districts.

The Art Market

In 1893, a Mrs Hawkins opened the Artists Models Agency on South Moulton Street, off Bond Street. Whilst Mrs Hawkins provided men and women who came from Clapham Common and Wimbledon, she refused to accept people from the East End as they did not provide 'high class models', a form of class exclusion but also an example of the art profession's pretension to gentility.[5]

London became central to the development of the international art market in the nineteenth century and established a system based on commercial galleries and global connections that has persisted up to the present.[6] Art had been central to aristocratic homes but it also played an important role in the conspicuous consumption of the upper middle class.[7] As we saw in Chapter 1, artists found themselves gravitating to the West End from the eighteenth century onwards. The

---

[4] Martina Hessler and Clemens Zimmermann (eds), *Creative Urban Milieus: Historical Perspectives on Culture, Economy and the City* (Frankfurt: Campus Verlag, 2008).

[5] *Sketch*, 15 March 1893, p. 404.

[6] Pamela Fletcher and Anne Helmreich (eds), *The Rise of the Modern Art Market in London, 1850–1939* (Manchester: Manchester University Press, 2011).

[7] See, for example, John Seed, '"Commerce and the Liberal Arts": The Political Economy of Art in Manchester, 1775–1860', in Janet Woolf and John Seed (eds), *The Culture of Capital: Art, Power and the Nineteenth-Century Middle Class* (Manchester: Manchester University Press, 1988), pp. 45–81.

streets immediately north of Oxford Street such as Charlotte Street and Newman Street were notable for the number of artists who lived and worked there, giving what became known as Fitzrovia in the twentieth century the feeling of a creative bohemia with cheap housing and good access to patrons and exhibition spaces, as well as a cross-class feeling. The Society of Female Artists was established on Oxford Street in 1856 and Louise Jopling rented a studio in Newman Street in the 1870s: the area thus provided a space in which some women could develop their creativity.[8]

The West End dominated the art world, not only through its galleries but also through shops that sold artists' materials and provided framing services. There was a shift away from a model of selling based on the artist and the patron. The commercial art dealer rose in importance; so did the auction houses Sotheby's and Christie's which had originated in the eighteenth century.[9] Art was a commodity that could command large sales. In 1911 alone, Christie's was responsible for £1,300,000 in art sales.[10] Dealers satisfied the demands of the upper classes (providing decorations for their mansions) but also the discerning middle-class purchaser of art as well as the American plutocrat. They cultivated an atmosphere of specialist intellectual authority and developed international networks of art and taste. Dealers also mounted exhibitions with elaborate catalogues and links to the growing art press such as the *Burlington Magazine*, founded in 1903. Alongside this were firms that specialized in restoration, antiques or *objets d'art*.

Old and New Bond Street offered at various times the Goupil, Doré, Hanover, and Grosvenor galleries whilst the Fine Art Society (which commenced at 148 New Bond Street in 1876) lasted in its West End location till 2018. The concentration of galleries was such that *Truth* claimed Bond Street was 'one elongated picture gallery tempered by tea shops'.[11] Art was a luxurious commodity, comparable to the jewels sold in Bond Street. The Grosvenor Gallery (1877–90) became a centre of the Aesthetic Movement in the later nineteenth century and was hailed as an alternative to the Royal Academy. Among the artists exhibited there were Lawrence Alma-Tadema, John Everett Millais, and Louise Jopling. The Grafton Galleries opened in 1893 on Grafton Street in Mayfair. Its magnificence included a series of connecting rooms: the Octagon Room, Music Room, Long Gallery,

[8] Jesús Pedro Lorente and Clare Targett, 'Comparative Growth and Urban Distribution of the Population of Artists in Victorian London', in Peter Borsay, Gunther Hirschfelder, and Ruth-E. Mohrmann (eds), *New Directions in Urban History: Aspects of European Art, Health, Tourism and Leisure since the Enlightenment* (Berlin: Waxmann, 2000), pp. 65–86; Deborah Cherry, 'Going Places: Women Artists in Central London in the Mid-19th Century', *London Journal*, 28 (2003), p. 78.

[9] Fletcher and Helmreich (eds), *The Rise of the Modern Art Market*; Anne Helmreich, 'The Art Market and the Spaces of Sociability in Victorian London', *Victorian Studies*, 59 (2017), pp. 436–49.

[10] Pamela Fletch and Anne Helmreich, 'Introduction', in Fletcher and Helmreich (eds), *The Rise of the Modern Art Market in London*, p. 5.

[11] Quoted in Kemille Moore, 'Feminisation and the Luxury of Visual Art in London's West End, 1860–1890', in Deborah Simonton, Marjo Kaartinen, and Anne Montenach (eds), *Luxury and Gender in European Towns, 1700–1914* (London: Routledge, 2014), p. 91.

Vestibule, End Gallery. Amongst the paintings at the opening exhibition were Whistler's portrait of Lady Meaux and Degas's 'L'Absinthe' (now in the Musée d'Orsay).[12] The gallery went on to host some of the key exhibitions in the creation of artistic modernism when Roger Fry became an advisor; this included 'Manet and the Post-Impressionists' in 1910–11. Like theatres, galleries were intended to flatter potential customers and hail them as figures of taste and discernment. For that reason, they projected a strong sense of exclusivity.

The Society of Painters in Water Colours regularly mounted exhibitions in Pall Mall whilst the Suffolk Street Gallery exhibited round the corner. The former had been founded in 1831 to compete with the Watercolour Society and evolved into the Royal Institute of Painters in Watercolours. The aim of both organizations was to establish watercolours as a vital sphere of visual art. The Pall Mall location meant that artists could cultivate wealthy customers, though the focus of the art world remained the Royal Academy. The St Martin's School of Art was established in Castle Street, off Long Acre, in 1854. Later on, the New Gallery on Regent Street (founded in 1888) was associated with the Pre-Raphaelites and the Arts and Crafts movement. William Morris, for example, gave a lecture there in 1889 in which he praised the gothic and complained that workmen were not allowed to think.[13]

But if this assumes that the West End was simply concerned with high art, we can contrast it with other forms of paintings that were on display. Oxford Street in the nineteenth century was known for its 'correct likeness' artists who would rapidly produce portraits on the street of particularly vain passers-by.[14] This was a form of popular art that merits little discussion in academic literature and yet has remained an important part of West End street life. Aesthetes despised it as it is a form of art that is purely commercial. These street painters offered an accessible form of art that was relatively cheap and which could be purchased even by the lower-middle-classes. They should be understood as a part of the West End art world and one of the ways in which the pleasure district threw up strange juxta-positions that challenged the forms of artistic hierarchy it also struggled to create.

Music

In the mid-Victorian years, the musical world was in flux. There was what music historian William Weber calls the 'new capitalism of sheet music and the move-ment of musical idealism that both opposed it and joined it'.[15] This meant the

[12] *Sketch*, 1 March 1893, p. 276.

[13] Zuzanna Shonfield, *The Precariously Privileged: A Professional Family in Victorian London* (Oxford: Oxford University Press, 1987), pp. 163–4.

[14] Henry Mayhew (ed.), *The Shops and Companies of London and the Trades and Manufactories of Great Britain* (London: Strand, 1865), p. 86.

[15] William Weber, *Music and the Middle Class: The Social Structure of Concert Life in London, Paris and Vienna between 1830 and 1848* (Aldershot: Ashgate, 2004 [1975]), pp. xx–xxi.

construction of a stronger version of the classical music canon that was distinct from popular music and an opposition to attempts to water it down through medleys. There was an attempt to create distinctions that reflected notions of professionalism and expertise. By 1890, it was more common to talk of 'popular' and 'classical' music with 'popular music' viewed by critics as lacking the complexity of 'art music' and hence having a lower value.[16] Concerts were an important part of middle-class life, described by publications such as the *Musical World*, which commenced in 1836. Music reflected the emergence of the class system but it must be emphasized that there was never a clear aesthetic division. In a West End setting, popular music had its adherents amongst the higher classes (see Chapter 11). Similarly, we can find lovers of the classical repertoire among the lower classes, evident in the performances of opera as part of the music hall programme. Like the 'correct likeness' artists described above, they show how pleasure districts produced cultural transformations, diffusing art and music so that they become more accessible.

The Victorian middle classes developed important sites for classical music outside the West End, including the Albert Hall and the Crystal Palace. Locations inside the West End included the Queen's Hall on Upper Regent Street (established in 1893), the new home of the Philharmonic Society.[17] Here Robert Newman put on promenade concerts on a regular basis and Henry Wood acquired a national reputation as a conductor. In 1901, the Bechstein Hall was opened in nearby Marylebone by the German piano firm who operated next door. The German name later necessitated a change and it subsequently became the Wigmore Hall, notable for chamber music and its perfect acoustics.

Concert music was democratized even though there was a stronger emphasis on musical seriousness. German musical culture inculcated the notion of music as something holy that needed to be revered.[18] Like the art gallery, the concert hall had a contemplative dimension. The Sacred Harmonic Society organized concerts at the Exeter Hall, enhancing the connections between music as a spiritual and religious force in Victorian Britain, whilst Louis Jullien's promenade concerts at Covent Garden in the mid-1850s created a greater appetite for orchestral music amongst a middle-class public. Tickets were only 1s 6d. Jullien's theatricality as a conductor proved a draw as did the music of Beethoven and Mendelssohn.

The great West End contribution to the performance of music proved to be the St James's Hall, which had entrances on Piccadilly and Regent Street (see Fig. 8.1). It was financed by Chappell, the music publishers, designed by architect Owen Jones, and opened in 1858. It also hosted balls where large numbers of people

---

[16] Weber, *Music and the Middle Class*, p. xxiii.
[17] Robert Elkin, *Queen's Hall, 1893–1941* (London: Rider, 1941).
[18] Sven Oliver Müller, 'Audience Behaviour in the Nineteenth Century', in Daniel Morat (ed.), *Sounds of Modern History: Auditory Cultures in 19th and 20th Century Europe* (New York: Berghahn, 2014), p. 164.

Fig. 8.1 St. James's Hall (author collection)

danced and in 1869 became the home of the Philharmonic Society. Its restaurant seems to have been the first in London to become a limited company (in 1887).[19] The venue could seat over 2000 people in its main hall (it had two smaller halls), its huge size reflecting the expanding audience for chamber music in the mid-Victorian years. Attending a concert given by the Moravian violinist Wilma Norman-Neruda in 1869, Munby reflected on the audience at the St James's Hall. In his view they were 'cultivated folk, studying the music from score, and earnestly sympathetic, yet quite simple in dress and unpretending in manner.'[20] Amongst its pleasures was the 'Monday Pops' evenings which only cost a shilling. It also became the home of the Christy Minstrels (later the Moore and Burgess Minstrels), a blackface troupe who played in a small hall downstairs all the way from 1862 to 1904. An evening would include songs, sketches, and comic monologues. The St James's Hall therefore embodied the West End's combination of high culture side by side with minstrel shows, the Victorian rock n' roll. This was

---

[19] Brenda Assael, *The London Restaurant, 1840–1914* (Oxford: Oxford University Press, 2018), p. 58.
[20] Hudson (ed.), *Munby*, p. 277.

another way in which pleasure districts made the boundaries between high and low culture porous.

Opera ceased to be mainly an entertainment put on solely for the Mayfair aristocracy, who subscribed to boxes for a season; instead, it began to appeal to a wider middle-class public. Managers felt it worth their while to place advertisements in provincial newspapers and, as early as 1840, Bellini's opera *I Puritani* could be referred to as 'the idolized of railroad travellers to London'.[21] In the mid-nineteenth century, however, a transformation took place that started to make Covent Garden the centre of opera-going in London. Previously, as we saw in Chapter 3, the operatic world was centred on Her Majesty's Theatre in the Haymarket, although Covent Garden and Drury Lane had put on opera seasons as well. The regime at Her Majesty's, however, ran into trouble.

In 1846, Benjamin Lumley took over as manager at Her Majesty's and immediately embarked upon a programme of redecoration whilst enjoying the services of the great singing sensation of the nineteenth century, Jenny Lind. Despite this, there were complaints that the quality of music was declining, leading to the resignation of Lumley's musical director, Michael Costa, who was developing the role of what John Goulden calls the 'conductor-manager' as a key figure within the music industry.[22]

The same year, however, a new management took over Covent Garden and turned it into the Royal Italian Opera. This was a huge threat to Her Majesty's as it was believed there was only room for one major opera house in London. Covent Garden was rebuilt and re-opened on 6 April 1847. Audiences marvelled at the excellence of the decoration, including the elaborate white, blue, and gold fronts of the boxes and the caryatides on the grand tier.[23] Moreover, the theatre acquired Costa as resident conductor (as well as much of his former orchestra) which promised musical excellence. This new regime was uneven in its early years and the management quickly went bankrupt. A crucial decision was made, however, to appoint Frederick Gye as artistic director. He leased the theatre for thirty years and turned Covent Garden into a major rival to Her Majesty's.

Gye was one of the great impresarios of the nineteenth century.[24] He was born into a family that provided entertainment. Gye helped his father in managing Vauxhall Gardens and organized concerts for the conductor Louis Jullien at Covent Garden and Drury Lane. Determined to make Covent Garden a centre of excellence, Gye went looking for the best musical talent throughout Europe. His

---

[21] Jennifer Hall-Witt, *Fashionable Acts: Opera and Elite Culture in London, 1780–1880* (Durham, NH: University of New Hampshire Press, 2007), p. 167.

[22] John Goulden, *Michael Costa: England's First Conductor: The Revolution in Musical Performance in England, 1830–1880* (Aldershot: Ashgate, 2015).

[23] *Illustrated London News*, 10 April 1847, pp. 233–4; 24 April 1847, p. 268.

[24] Gabriella Dideriksen and Matthew Ringel, 'Frederick Gye and "The Dreadful Business of Opera Management"', *19th Century Music*, 19 (1995), pp. 3–30.

1854 diary, for example, shows him making visits to Brussels, Cologne, Dresden, Berlin, and other locations, building the crucial networks on which a world-class opera house depended. To take one example, when he saw Rosina Penco, who created the role of Leonora in *Il Travatore*, he felt firmly that, though her voice was agreeable, she was 'certainly not worth 45000 francs for 4 months which she asks'.[25] He also went on the look-out for operas. Taking in Weber's *Euryanthe* in Berlin, he found it 'much too heavy & devoid of melody'.[26] Gye was therefore instrumental in helping create an operatic canon based on the musical culture of major European cities. He focussed on through-sung *grand opéra* (in productions overseen by the elder Augustus Harris), so that Covent Garden would rival the great continental opera houses. Gye's relationship with Costa could be testy. The conductor claimed that he was 'too much in the theatre', despite the fact that he was often on the road.[27]

In 1856, disaster struck. Whilst Gye was in Paris, he received news that his theatre had burned down. A fire had commenced during a masked ball, gutting the building. Gye made it back to London the next day. Barely had he turned up to survey the wreckage than he was joined by Queen Victoria who demonstrated great sympathy.[28] Most people would have been destroyed by what had happened; not Gye. He may have lacked an opera house but he still had people: musicians, and singers. He looked around for another location and found it close by at the Lyceum which became the company's home for the next two years. He also used the company to put on concerts at the Crystal Palace. In the meantime he commissioned Edward Barry to build a new opera house which cost £112,000 (including the floral hall beside the theatre, whose elaborate use of glass echoed the Great Exhibition).[29] It opened on 15 May 1858 with a gala performance of Meyerbeer's *Les Huguenots*. Gye enjoyed great artistic success, introducing stars like Adelina Patti. Verdi's *Rigoletto* and Wagner's *Lohengrin* both had their English premieres at Covent Garden, part of a policy of only performing new operas that had gained success on the continent.[30] It was, however, still difficult to make money with two major opera houses in the West End competing for the same audience.

A fire destroyed Her Majesty's in 1867 leading to its reconstruction. It went on to stage the first London performance of Bizet's *Carmen* in 1878 and Wagner's Ring cycle in 1882, aided at points by the swashbuckling management of James Henry Mapleson and appearances by the Carl Rosa company. Covent Garden and Her Majesty's were like sirens drawing the best circles from Mayfair and St James' for music and rapture. However, it was Covent Garden that started to dominate,

---

[25] Frederick Gye diary, 9 February 1856: SC 1/2/06 (Royal Opera House Archive).
[26] Frederick Gye diary, 12 March 1854: SC 1/1/15(Royal Opera House Archive).
[27] Frederick Gye diary, 16 November 1854: SC 1/1/15(Royal Opera House Archive).
[28] Frederick Gye diary, 5 March 1856: SC 1/2/06 (Royal Opera House Archive).
[29] Dideriksen and Ringel, 'Frederick Gye', p. 7.
[30] Dideriksen and Ringel, 'Frederick Gye', p. 12.

especially when Augustus Harris (the younger) took over in 1888 and moved to a policy of presenting operas in their original language rather than Italian. He also introduced Nellie Melba to audiences whilst the Polish tenor Jean de Reszke and his brother Edouard became enormous stars. The Royal Opera House (as it was now known) became a major location for international singers and developed its reputation for prestige and excellence.

Light opera also found new talents and venues. A shift in musical taste can be detected with the first performance of Offenbach's operettas. *Les Bouffes* was first presented at the St James's Theatre in 1857, making the composer a major force creating shows that large numbers would pay to see. Opera was combined with farce and frivolity. Offenbach's popularity laid the basis not only for comic opera but for the genre of musical comedy that developed at the end of the century (see Chapter 12).

The dynamic figures in British light opera were W.S. Gilbert and Arthur Sullivan. Gilbert had become known as a comic writer whilst Sullivan had developed a strong reputation composing music for churches and for High Society. They were brought together by John Hollingshead at the Gaiety for the show *Thespis* in 1871, which did not do well and the two went their separate ways. *Thespis* was, however, admired by a figure who wanted to become an impresario. Richard D'Oyly Carte had formerly been part of his family firm which manufactured woodwind instruments but left to become that vital new figure in the life of the West End: an agent.[31] He set up his own business in Craig's Court, Charing Cross, managing over two hundred musicians and finding them bookings. D'Oyly Carte wanted to develop English operettas which could rival what was happening in Paris. In 1875, it was D'Oyly Carte who suggested Gilbert work with Sullivan on *Trial by Jury* at the Royalty Theatre in Soho. The show's satire of the legal profession and of the conventions of opera itself proved a huge success. D'Oyly Carte created a syndicate for Gilbert and Sullivan and soon became managing director. With *HMS Pinafore* in 1878, a remarkable run of success in comic opera followed. Gilbert proceeded to make his way through British institutions such as the law (in *Iolanthe*), subjecting them to gentle satire at just the moment when these institutions were subject to reform. Their operas exported effectively around the world and could be performed by amateurs. Gilbert and Sullivan were such a phenomenon that D'Oyly Carte was able to finance the building of a theatre to present their work: the Savoy.

The musical world in the West End changed, both in the places where it could be accessed and the fare that people could enjoy. It was less exclusive and more open to anyone with the money to pay for a ticket. By the late nineteenth century, the number of musicians in London as a whole increased dramatically and

---

[31] Paul Seeley, *Richard D'Oyly Carte* (London: Routledge, 2019).

many would have found work at West End venues.[32] There was a new feeling of seriousness in the musical world, exemplified by figures such as the conductor Michael Costa. The emergence of Gilbert and Sullivan underscored how the district could be a place of innovation, creating new forms of both music and comedy. Yet music was also a business and was equally the product of entrepreneurial figures like Frederick Gye who had an eye for the best talent but also insisted on appealing to High Society, creating an air of prestige at Covent Garden.

Literary London

From its origins, the West End had proved to be the intellectual capital of Britain. It became a centre of the publishing industry but also a major site of literary production. Novels, journals, periodicals, newspapers were all issued from West End addresses. It was therefore a major location in the development of mass media. Popular newspapers were a vital force in the development of mass culture and the consumer economy.

Although Fleet Street was becoming associated with the press, the editorial offices of some twenty newspapers and periodicals could be found on the Strand in the early Victorian years, which proved a place of innovation. One reason for this concentration was that the Strand was also a major centre of literary and intellectual life, assisted by its proximity to the theatrical West End whilst enjoying connections to the law courts nearby and the corridors of power in Westminster. Newspapers and periodicals at one level created the 'West End' providing its places, styles, fashions, and entertainments with glamour and glitz.

The *Morning Chronicle* was at no. 332 Strand (opposite Somerset House) whilst the *Illustrated London News* was at no. 198 and the *Economist* could be found at no. 340. Each shaped the print culture of the Victorians. The *Morning Chronicle* (founded in 1770) was London's daily paper and a leading vehicle for the Whigs. Charles Dickens served an apprenticeship as parliamentary correspondent for the paper before becoming a novelist. Eliza Lynn Linton became the first female correspondent for a daily paper in 1848. It was the *Morning Chronicle* that published Henry Mayhew's interviews with street people in London that subsequently became *London Labour and the London Poor*. Mayhew's depiction of the poor proved a sensation because he treated his interviewees without condescension and allowed them to speak in their own voice. The paper was absorbed into the *Daily Telegraph* in 1862.

The initial appeal of the *Illustrated London News*, when it was launched in 1842, was its pictorial content. Illustrated news in this form represented a

[32] Cyril Ehrlich, *The Music Profession in Britain since the Eighteenth Century* (Oxford: Clarendon Press, 1985), p. 52.

revolution in print media. Readers (or perhaps, it would be as accurate to say, viewers) got realistic images of events shortly after they occurred. For its finely detailed woodcuts, it drew on some of the leading illustrators of the day such as Sir John Gilbert, Henry Anelay, and the French artist Gavarni. The paper dramatized the world of London and its affairs for the middle-class drawing room. Royal ceremonials and other national events were recorded in engravings that could be framed or retained in family scrapbooks. The *Economist* was founded in 1843 to champion free trade, three years before the repeal of the Corn Laws. It thereafter became the key periodical monitoring politics, statistics, and business, making it integral to economic development. Its editors included Walter Bagehot (author of the *English Constitution*) who developed its reputation for clear-eyed political observation.

In addition to newspapers, there were also booksellers and publishers. For example, John Chapman established a publishing and bookselling business at 142 Strand (formerly a coffee house called the Turk's Head).[33] He began to publish Ralph Waldo Emerson's essays in Britain, evidence of a commitment to free thinking and dissenting literature (Emerson actually employed 142 Strand as a base when he visited Britain). In 1852 Chapman bought the *Westminster Review*, which had originally been founded by Jeremy Bentham and James Mill in 1826, drawing on content from leading liberal luminaries such as George Henry Lewes and the historian J.A. Froude. His editorial assistant was Mary Ann Evans (George Eliot) and the periodical was notable for disseminating early feminist viewpoints. If we take establishments like Chapman's shop or the *Economist*, it is clear that the West End had an input into the intellectual development of Victorian liberalism, even though this study argues that there was a strong Tory dimension to the area.

Two other streets off the Strand were locations for newspaper and periodical offices. Catherine Street (which included the front entrance to the Theatre Royal Drury Lane) contained the offices of *The Era* which became in the 1850s the great newspaper of the theatrical community. Although it covered the whole country, the paper was a vital force in creating the idea of the West End as a distinctive pleasure district, containing news of first nights as well as show business events.[34] It also housed the office of *The Echo*, the first halfpenny newspaper in London, and the *Racing Times* as well as *The Court Gazette*.[35] Wellington Street, off the Strand, was an important location for literary production high and low. As Mary Shannon has shown, in the early Victorian period there were twenty newspapers and periodicals represented on the street. Charles Dickens edited *Household*

[33] Rosemary Ashton, *142 Strand: A Radical Address in Victorian London* (London: Chatto and Windus, 2006).

[34] Jacky Bratton, *The Making of the West End Stage: Marriage, Management and the Mapping of Gender in London, 1830–1870* (Cambridge: Cambridge University Press, 2011), ch. 2.

[35] Walter Thornbury and Edward Walford, *Old and New London* (London: Cassell, Petter, and Galpin, 1879–85), Vol. 3, p. 110.

Words from no. 17 Wellington Street and later launched *All the Year Round* from no. 11. Henry Mayhew's offices were at no. 16 (from where he issued *London Labour and the London Poor* in 1851–2). One of the leading intellectual periodicals, the *Athenaeum*, was issued from no. 14. Across the road, George W.M. Reynolds issued *Reynolds's Newspaper*.[36] Arguably the most popular novelist of the nineteenth century with his best-seller, *The Mysteries of London*, Reynolds became a leading Chartist in 1848, denouncing the aristocracy and supporting the rights of labour. *Reynolds's Newspaper* (1850–1967) was one of the best-selling newspapers aimed at the working-class. It pioneered Sunday journalism, offering its readers a diet of radical politics, smut, true crime, and sensation. On the south side of Wellington Street could be found the offices of *Punch* (up to 1844) which was founded by Henry Mayhew and Mark Lemon and quickly became the leading satirical journal of the age. Almost opposite, across the road was the literary periodical, *The Examiner*, enjoying a renaissance in the early Victorian period with Dickens, Thackeray, John Forster, and John Stuart Mill among the illustrious contributors.

Another thoroughfare just off the Strand was Holywell Street. Later demolished to make way for the Aldwych, it was notorious for its booksellers offering scurrilous radical and often irreligious publications and for pornography. One of a series of dark alleyways, it linked poverty, dirt, squalor, and obscenity.[37] Holywell Street made sexuality visible amongst the second-hand clothes shops that also filled the street. There had long been connections between radicals and pornographers, using vulgarity as a way of attacking the social order.[38] The presence of prostitution and pornography meant that the West End was often the site of moral regulation (as we saw in Chapter 7). In 1857, the new Obscene Publications Act was particularly targeted at Holywell Street, allowing the police to make raids on a number of shops, removing books and prints and prosecuting the owners. The street continued as the centre of obscene publications until the trade moved into Soho in the twentieth century.

The Strand area played a vital role in the intellectual culture of Victorian Britain and hence the world. The books and newspapers that issued from it were written in many different locales but the West End proved a place for the construction of networks of talent, intelligence, and ideas. During the later Victorian period, the world of journalism began to shift over to Fleet Street which became known for its newspapers. What existed in the Strand and Covent Garden area was a creative bohemia, an alternative to the clubland of St James's. The West End

[36] Mary Shannon, *Dickens, Reynolds, and Mayhew on Wellington Street: The Print Culture of a Victorian Street* (Farnham: Ashgate, 2015), p. 28.

[37] Lynda Nead, *Victorian Babylon: People, Streets and Images in Nineteenth Century London* (London: Yale University Press, 2000), pp. 161–203.

[38] Iain McCalman, *Radical Underworld: Prophets, Revolutionaries and Pornographers in London, 1795–1840* (Oxford: Clarendon Press, 1993).

became the centre of a national conversation about social reform, art, morality, and culture.

Well before the Bloomsbury Group, Bloomsbury had been the centre of intellectual London, encouraged by the British Museum and the dissenting role of the medical schools.[39] The West End had something of the same function, creating spaces for intellectual and artistic production in a very visible way. After 1900, the world of the artistic avant-garde would turn away from the West End, seeking other spaces in London, including Chelsea and Fitzrovia, which were not tainted by commercialism. Avant-garde opinion (following Matthew Arnold) increasingly began to link the word 'bourgeois' with 'philistinism'. The unabashedly bourgeois world of the West End by 1900 felt like a place whose pretensions needed to be resisted. This was not the case in the nineteenth century. With its juxtapositions of art, commerce, and information, the West End was the capital of culture.

We can put the West End in perspective by comparing it with world of South Kensington which developed in the mid to late Victorian years. The Albert Hall and the grand museums that characterized the area represented a different view of culture, shorn of the brashness and vulgarity of the West End. South Kensington never entirely replaced the West End which continued to offer spaces of high culture but it was based on a different approach to knowledge, one that prized accessibility but also what Matthew Arnold termed 'sweetness and light'. Here the arts and sciences were joined together. Significantly, it lacked theatres or anything that could subvert the tone of aesthetic seriousness.

The West End cultural project included exclusivity on the one hand and openness to popular culture on the other. The hothouse atmosphere of artists, pubs, theatres, and journalists created the category of the bohemian (as we have seen) which allowed for new forms of thinking to emerge. At the same time, concerts and art exhibitions were locations where the middle classes could gather. The literary spaces we have documented were more difficult to access but the results percolated through the middle-class drawing room in the form of the newspaper and the popular novel. The overlays, contrasts, and juxtapositions between art, music, and journalism were what gave the West End its character. Artistic status mattered in the West End which functioned as a marketplace in which aesthetic value could be discerned and championed. Was it a coincidence that all these culture industries were in the same place? This chapter suggests it clearly was not. Commercial art, music, and literature emerged to serve an increasingly middle-class world which defined itself by its sense of taste and sophistication.

[39] Rosemary Ashton, *Victorian Bloomsbury* (London: Yale University Press, 2012).

PART THREE
SHOWBIZ

9

The Age of Boucicault, 1843–80

The Corsican Trap

It is 1852. At the end of the first act of *The Corsican Brothers* at the Princess's Theatre, the character Fabien dei Franchi in Corsica feels a pain in his side. He immediately recognizes that its cause is some violence that has occurred to his brother Louis studying in far-off Paris. The two have shared a telepathic bond since childhood. Fabien sits down to write to Louis asking if all is well. As he folds the letter, a blue light fills the stage and an apparition slowly emerges from the floor. It is Louis in a blood-stained shirt. He touches his brother on the shoulder. As he does so, Fabien looks up and shouts 'My Brother! Dead!' The ghost of Louis waves his arm and the walls of the house disappear to reveal the glade of a forest in Fontainbleau. There we see Louis having just been run through in a duel by the villainous Château-Renaud. The duellists' supporters look on. A surgeon is attending to Louis but he is dead. Seeing this apparition, Fabien in Corsica knows he will have to avenge the death of his brother. The curtain falls.

In this scene, Louis and Fabien were both played by the actor Charles Kean. How could the two characters be on stage together? The answer was the Corsican trap—one of the most famous stage effects in the nineteenth century. At the end of the scene, where Kean had been playing Fabien, he walked off stage briefly and was replaced by a double. The audience believed they were still seeing Kean as Fabien. Meanwhile, Kean dashed below the stage and did a quick change into Louis's blood-stained shirt. Employing a complex system of pulleys drawn by a number of strong stage hands, Kean stood on a platform that was then drawn on a 45-degree incline up through a trap door onto the stage so that he gradually emerged from the floor as a spectral image. The orchestra conveyed an air of ghostly mystery. When the Corsican set was raised into the flies to reveal the scene in Fontainbleau, the dead Louis was also played by another double on the ground. Queen Victoria was so taken with the scene that she saw the show four times and even drew her own sketch of the scene.[1]

This chapter commences with *The Corsican Brothers* by Dion Boucicault (based on Alexandre Dumas's novella) as a way of understanding the changes in

---

[1] Dion Boucicault, *The Corsican Brothers* (1852) in George Taylor (ed.), *Trilby and other Plays* (Oxford: Oxford University Press, 1996), pp. 105, 281–2; Richard W. Schoch, *Queen Victoria and the Theatre of her Age* (Basingstoke: Palgrave Macmillan, 2004), pp. 154–5.

London's West End: Creating the Pleasure District, 1800–1914. Rohan McWilliam, Oxford University Press (2020).
© Rohan McWilliam.
DOI: 10.1093/oso/9780198823414.001.0001

West End theatre in the mid-Victorian years, when it took on something of its modern form. I argue that it became much more explicitly a theatre for the middle classes, in line with other developments in the West End that we have seen. Boucicault's spectacular plays suited this audience. Previously, West End dramas were as likely to be attended by aristocrats and workers with many middle-class people considering theatres as immoral (too many prostitutes hanging around). We can see the shift to a bourgeois theatre in the emergence of fixed ticketing, in the coming of matinee performances, in the long run, and in the way theatres became more comfortable. The great symbol of this was the way the stalls elbowed out the pit and became the most desirable seats in the house. John Baldwin Buckstone at the Haymarket argued in 1866 that his audience had become the new middle classes of the suburbs. He noticed lots of people in the auditorium leaving at the same time, no doubt with an eye on the train (last trains from stations such as Charing Cross and Victoria were just after midnight).[2] The spectacle of *The Corsican Brothers* was accompanied by a shift to what a later generation would call 'well-made plays' and new forms of realism on stage.

Let us start with the theatre that staged *The Corsican Brothers*. The location of the Princess's Theatre was significant: Oxford Street, not far from the intersection with Regent Street (on the eastern side of Oxford Circus), and thus close to a range of upmarket shops (see Fig. 9.1). Previously a bazaar, the site was transformed into a theatre in 1840 that could attract affluent shoppers. In the West End the built environment of the theatre mattered as it promised prestige and spectacle. The sumptuous auditorium was in the Louis Quatorze style with a magnificent chandelier and four tiers of boxes. Gold mouldings and crimson paint were combined with Arabesque ornaments and gilt Cupids.[3] In 1843, it was described by the *Illustrated London News* as 'this *bijou* of a theatre'.[4] Such a setting meant that drama was always interpreted within a frame based on notions of the select, the refined, and the exotic. The location of the Princess's meant that it was the closest theatre to the Great Exhibition in 1851 which may also have enhanced its profitability.

It was at the Princess's that Charles Kean in the 1850s launched a series of Shakespeare productions noted for the historical accuracy of their settings. *The Corsican Brothers* was followed in the same month by a production of *King John*. Kean prided himself on the level of his research so that the elaborate scenery and costumes were allegedly completely accurate. His programmes listed the authorities he had consulted in order to ensure total authenticity. In 1859 his *Henry V* was, according to the diarist Arthur Munby, 'a series of brilliant spectacles, strung

---

[2] Report from the Select Committee on Theatrical Licenses and Regulations (1866), pp. 123–5.

[3] Raymond Mander and Joe Mitchenson, *Lost Theatres of London* (London: New English Library, 1976 [1968]), p. 135.

[4] *Illustrated London News*, 25 November 1843, p. 348.

Fig. 9.1 The Princess's Theatre, Oxford Street (author collection)

together by "appropriate Shakespearian readings": scenes & speeches being left out by whole sale'. The evening abounded in flights of arrows, cannonballs, and cannon which enhanced the realism. Munby was more impressed by Kean's ability to put on a spectacle than by his acting skills.[5] The West End therefore took on the role of constructing popular versions of the nation's past, complementing the novels of Sir Walter Scott and Macaulay's histories and presenting the national epic in romantic terms.[6]

Kean was an innovator in another sense. He dimmed the lights in the auditorium so that attention was totally focused on the stage. The result was a greater disciplining of the audience which was there to watch a play rather than each other. This was an important change in the theatre-going experience. The disorderly audience of the early nineteenth century was forced to be quiet, a shift that suited the move to a more stable middle-class following. Respectability and refinement became important. Lewd comments on the action were quashed. It was important to only applaud at the appropriate moments (and to develop an understanding of when those appropriate moments were). Nelson Lee, the manager of the City of London Theatre, noted how the West End audience was increasingly silent

---

[5] Derek Hudson (ed.), *Munby: Man of Two Worlds* (London: Abacus, 1974), p. 29.
[6] Rosemary Mitchell, *Picturing the Past: English History in Text and Image* (Oxford: Oxford University Press, 2000).

and attentive to the action and the performance. He claimed in 1866: 'if you go the Adelphi and see "Rip Van Winkle" you can hear a pin drop; or go the Olympic and see the refined acting of Kate Terry, if anybody sitting next to you was even to speak a word, everybody would look round and say "silence".'[7] Henry James described the West End audience as 'well dressed, tranquil, motionless; it suggests domestic virtues and comfortable homes'. The key word here is 'motionless'. The West End stalls were aware of the codes of politeness that ruled its behaviour. James noted how this contrasted with the 'deep-lunged jollity and individual guffaws' of the gallery and pit.[8] The segregated audience differed not only in their location in the theatre but in their conduct.

The Corsican Brothers was the first of a series of Dion Boucicault plays that combined spectacle, realism, and sensation, remaking what a night at a West End show was all about. The Corsican Trap was more than a fancy stage device. Part magic act, it rendered the stage a place of enchantment. It was also expensive to install (though widely imitated) but the effect promised to draw people in. The formula worked. *The Corsican Brothers* ran for sixty six nights initially. In so doing it commenced the shift from the repertory system (that dated back to the seventeenth century) towards the long run.

Scenery in the age of the Corsican Trap became more elaborate. When the Shakespearian actor Charles Fechter played at the Lyceum between 1863 and 1867, he abolished the grooves on stage which allowed flats to be simply moved into place. Instead, the set was increasingly flown in from a gridiron above which allowed it to be preset. [9] The scenery in a production of Victorien Sardou's *Peril* at the Prince of Wales's in 1876 was so intricate that it could not be moved, requiring a boudoir set to be placed inside it.[10] The long run therefore reshaped the West End theatre experience in fundamental ways, allowing for greater exuberance in stage design.

Another feature of *The Corsican Brothers* is easy to miss. It was one of many West End productions subsequently reproduced in the form of toy theatres. The toy theatre was both a souvenir but also a way into the theatre for children. It introduced them to the proscenium arch and turned theatre into a utopian space, a place of fantasy and role playing. When some adults entered theatres, they found spaces that were realized versions of the spaces that they played with as children.

[7] Report from the Select Committee on Theatrical Licenses and Regulations (1866), p. 180.

[8] Henry James, *The Scenic Art: Notes on Acting and the Drama, 1872–1901* (London: Rupert Hart-Davis, 1949), p. 101.

[9] Sybil Rosenfeld, *A Short History of Scene Design in Great Britain* (Oxford: Basil Blackwell, 1973), pp. 127–8.

[10] Rosenfeld, *Short History*, pp. 114–15.

The West End Theatre

In the mid-Victorian years, West End theatres acquired a new aura. Boucicault observed in 1866 that 'There is a great desire on the part of actors to come to the west-end theatres, to be seen by a higher and better class of people; it is those theatres that particularly enjoy the monopoly of good acting.'[11] The West End stage (despite the end of the patent theatre monopoly) was therefore seen as something special, although the links to the aristocracy still imbued it with a peculiar quality of prestige. Boucicault identified the particular characteristics of the West End when accounting for the problems encountered by the St James's Theatre (on King Street) which focused too much on attracting the aristocracy to the exclusion of everyone else:

> In the first place, no 'first-class' theatre has ever been known to pay; but the St James's Theatre has attempted to give itself a character for elegant performances, and such a theatre does not pay, because the class that it appeals to does not support in sufficient number. Besides, you must not take a theatre too far west; it must be in the centre of the pleasure-seeking population, a certain portion of London which may be almost bounded on different sides by Drury-Lane, the Quadrant, Oxford-Street, and the Strand. One theatre feeds the other; the Lyceum I have known feed on the overspill of the Adelphi, and *vice versa*.[12]

By being situated where it was, the pleasure district had established itself as a hub of entertainment that could appeal to a wider public than simply the toffs of Mayfair (although Boucicault was wrong about the St James's Theatre which lasted until 1957) (Map 9.1).

The years from 1840 to 1880 were still influenced by actors and actor-managers who shaped what audiences saw. William Macready dominated classical theatre up to his retirement in 1851 with a series of titanic performances in Shakespeare and other roles. He was replaced by figures such as Charles Fechter and the romantic Italian player Tomasso Salvini. The era sported the performances of Helen Faucit, Ellen Farnon, Charles Mathews the younger, E.A. Sothern, the Bancrofts, and Charles Kean. John Baldwin Buckstone was a brilliant low comedian as well as a playwright. Among the performers starting out were Henry Irving and Ellen Terry. The plays of Boucicault, Tom Taylor, and Tom Robertson (as we will see) defined the theatre of their times. The period did, however, see the emergence of a group who were not actors but were instead specialists in management, including John Hollingshead at the Gaiety.

---

[11] Report from the Select Committee on Theatrical Licenses and Regulations (1866), p. 154.
[12] Report from the Select Committee on Theatrical Licenses and Regulations (1866), p. 157.

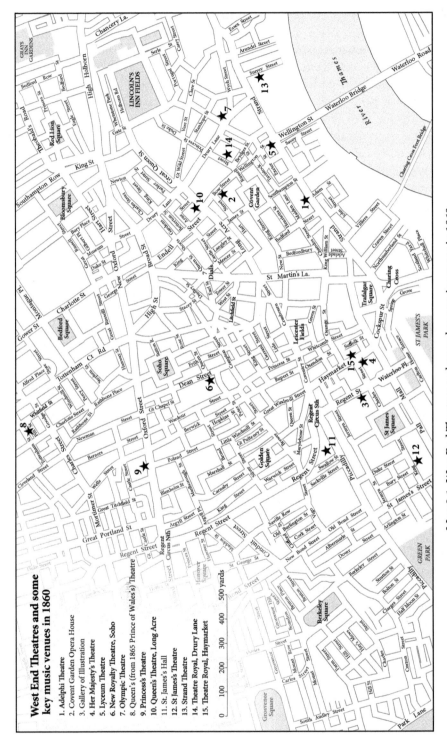

West End Theatres and some key music venues in 1860

1. Adelphi Theatre
2. Covent Garden Opera House
3. Gallery of Illustration
4. Her Majesty's Theatre
5. Lyceum Theatre
6. New Royalty Theatre, Soho
7. Olympic Theatre
8. Queen's (from 1865 Prince of Wales's) Theatre
9. Princess's Theatre
10. Queen's Theatre, Long Acre
11. St. James's Hall
12. St James's Theatre
13. Strand Theatre
14. Theatre Royal, Drury Lane
15. Theatre Royal, Haymarket

Map 9.1 West End Theatres and some key music venues in 1860

Whilst the artistic reputation of the stage was lower than that of music, painting, or the novel, it is striking that literary and intellectual figures venerated the stage. Dickens was a regular at London theatres, sometimes in company with Wilkie Collins. John Ruskin and William Gladstone were both enthusiasts for the stage.[13] The audience for *Leah the Forsaken* at the Adelphi one evening in 1864 included George Eliot, George Henry Lewes, and Anthony Trollope.[14]

Amongst the audience members at first nights were the critics. Victorian theatre managers usually issued seventy to one hundred tickets to critics, often including a second seat which the critic could use for a friend.[15] There were complaints at the time that theatre criticism had declined since the days of Hazlitt at the beginning of the century.[16] The critics at various times during this period included John Oxenford of the *Times*, Shirley Brooks (later editor of *Punch*) at the *Morning Chronicle*, Howard Glover at the *Morning Post*, Edward Dutton Cook at the *Pall Mall Gazette* and later *The World*, and Edmund Yates at the *Daily News*. When Yates resigned the latter position, John Hollingshead replaced him. Hollingshead said his main qualification for becoming a critic was having seen Macready perform. He did, however, innovate by always filing his review the night of the performance so that it could appear the next morning (which was not common practice at the time).[17] Whilst the theatre criticism of George Henry Lewes (George Eliot's partner) is often cited today, reviewers were essentially upmarket hacks.[18] They were also often playwrights themselves and thus not keen to produce bad reviews that would upset managers who might go on to purchase their next work. The major critical voice proved to be Clement Scott, theatre critic for the *Daily Telegraph* (1871–98), who had a strong sense of what was suitable for a West End audience (Scott is discussed in the next chapter). Though not hugely distinguished, the achievement of the mid-Victorian critics was that they helped draw the middle-classes back into the theatre and make a first night feel important.

Whilst there was a middle-class takeover of West End theatre, it is worth putting this in some perspective. Henry Hibbert later noted: 'every theatrical manager will tell you that the play which appeals to every class of the community has yet to be written. The stalls are often packed while the less expensive seats drag; or pit, circles, and gallery will, in their thousands, gaze across an empty stretch of stalls'.[19]

---

[13] Katherine Newey and Jeffrey Richards, *John Ruskin and the Victorian Theatre* (Basingstoke: Palgrave Macmillan, 2010).

[14] Jim Davis and Victor Emeljanow, *Reflecting the Audience: London Theatregoing, 1840–1880* (Hatfield: University of Hertfordshire Press, 2001), pp. 188–9.

[15] Henry George Hibbert, *Fifty Years of a Londoner's Life* (London: Grant Richards, 1916), pp. 129–30.

[16] Report from the Select Committee on Theatrical Licenses and Regulations (1866), p. 160.

[17] John Hollingshead, *My Lifetime* (London: Sampson Low, Marston, and Co., 1895), Vol. 1, pp. 179–80.

[18] George Henry Lewes, *On Actors and the Art of Acting* (Leipzig: Tauchnitz, 1875).

[19] Hibbert, *Fifty Years*, p. 129.

This was why the management would often have complimentary seats at their disposal. Not all plays managed to have a cross-class appeal: the drawing room comedies, favoured by the middle-classes, excluded poorer theatre-goers (though it is striking that workers, as far as we can judge, did not object to patronizing portrayals of proletarians on stage). We should, however, be cautious in discussing the audience. Jim Davis and Victor Emaljanow rightly argue that our evidence base, when it comes to West End audiences, is thin (ironically, East End audiences were more heavily described). The West End audience was treated as the norm and therefore few felt the need to describe it.[20]

The 1843 Theatre Regulation Act introduced free trade to theatre; the monopoly that the patent theatres enjoyed over spoken word was broken. The distinction ceased to be between patent theatres and the rest as it was before 1843; now it became the difference between a theatre and a music hall. The role of the Lord Chamberlain as censor of plays continued, making the theatre a heavily regulated space. Censored subjects included anything with biblical or political references or 'plays in which highwaymen or immorality are exalted'.[21] William Bodham Donne, examiner of plays for the Lord Chamberlain, came to worry less about political references on the stage and more about the tide of immorality associated with the performance of plays based on French originals. *La Dame aux Camélias* (the story of the tragic courtesan written by Alexandre Dumas *fils*) was originally banned, having been performed at the Parisian Theatre de Vaudeville in 1852. Donne complained that it was a 'glorification of harlotry'.[22] On the other hand, the Lord Chamberlain was often reluctant to interfere too much and in 1899 had to deal with a lawyer's plea to ban comic portrayals of policemen in pantomimes on the grounds that they encouraged disrespect for authority. The request was turned down.[23]

The Theatre Experience

If the years after 1843 witnessed a more distinctive West End theatre emerge, it was done without extensive construction of new theatres. In 1843, there were eleven theatres in the district. In 1865, the number was reduced to ten as the Theatre Royal Covent Garden had become an opera house (though the 1860s saw an increase in theatre construction in London as a whole).[24] The difficult

---

[20] Davis and Emeljanow, *Reflecting the Audience*, pp. 168–9.
[21] Report from the Select Committee on Theatrical Licenses and Regulations (1866), pp. 6–7. See Tracy C. Davis, *The Economics of the British Stage, 1800–1914* (Cambridge: Cambridge University Press, 2000), ch. 3.
[22] William Bodham Donne to Spenser Ponsonby, 26 March 1859: LC 1/70 (TNA).
[23] Davis, *Economics of the British Stage*, p. 142.
[24] I include in these figures the Queen's Theatre (later the Prince of Wales's) on Charlotte Street, just a few minutes north of Oxford Street, and Miss Kelly's Theatre in Dean Street, Soho (which later became the New Royalty). My figures are extrapolated from the Appendix to this book and from Report from the Select Committee on Theatrical Licenses and Regulations (1866), p. 293.

economic situation of the 1840s accounts for at least some of this. West End theatre managers resisted the construction of more theatres for fear that it would damage their business. The number of theatres, however, could not keep up with the rising population, though some theatres were vast in terms of the numbers they could hold. Covent Garden could take 3000 whilst Drury Lane could seat an enormous 3800. Even the Adelphi, close by, took 1560 in 1866.[25]

Theatres were straining. Rather than construct more buildings and stages, West End theatres began to specialize. The Adelphi continued to be known as a melo-drama house whilst the Prince of Wales's became known for refinement and drawing-room drama, and the Gaiety to be celebrated for its musical burlesques. The Vaudeville on the Strand, one of the few new theatres, was built in 1870 to house comedy and farce.

West End theatres made clear that they were after a select audience. In 1850 the Theatre Royal Haymarket created the most elaborate royal box in the capital with its own ante room and separate royal entrance in Suffolk Street.[26] Alongside the Adelphi, the Haymarket remained associated with royalty, which meant that the aristocracy would often be seen there. The Queen's patronage was also a reassuring sign for middle-class patrons who otherwise might have considered playgoing disreputable. Queen Victoria ceased to attend theatre after the death of Prince Albert. Thereafter, West End theatre was driven partly by appealing to the taste of the Prince of Wales.[27]

In 1852, Edward Smith, the former publican and owner of the Coal Hole Tavern on the Strand, took over the management of Drury Lane and transformed its auditorium. No longer was it simply divided as it had been into pit, gallery, and boxes. Instead, he introduced stalls (four shillings), the dress circle (two shillings and sixpence), a second circle and pit (each one shilling), and galleries (sixpence). Smith recognized that the stalls in front of the pit were really the best seats in the house and treated them as such in terms of pricing, thus reshaping the geography of the modern theatre. People in the stalls were treated to chairs rather than benches and a process began whereby the pit would ultimately disappear from theatres (its last remnant would be the provision for standing room when a show sold out).[28]

The years after 1840 saw dramatic change in the theatre-going experience. The actor-manager Frederick Yates, when he managed the Adelphi between 1825 and 1842, claimed the audience did not mind discomfort. His theatre was notoriously cramped and possessed terrible sightlines for the majority of spectators. Benjamin

[25] Figures from Report from the Select Committee on Theatrical Licenses and Regulations (1866), p. 293.

[26] *Era*, 20 October 1850, p. 10.

[27] Hugh Maguire, 'The Victorian Theatre as a Home from Home', *Journal of Design History*, 13 (2000), p. 113.

[28] Robert Whelan, *The Other National Theatre: 350 Years of Shows in Drury Lane* (London: Jacob Tonson, 2013), pp. 395–6.

Webster's tenure as actor manager at the same address was based on the recognition that this would no longer do. The Adelphi was completely rebuilt in 1858, setting new standards of comfort and sightline with ample room to show off ladies' dresses (see Fig. 9.2).[29] Queen Victoria had her own entrance on Maiden Lane. Webster abandoned half-time tickets whilst the size of seats were also increased: two feet wide in the orchestra stalls so that women sporting the new fashion for crinoline could be at ease. Ladies' cloakrooms seem to have been ample and the fees for using them were abandoned. This was a female-friendly space; indeed the ticket checkers and attendants were all women. The *Illustrated Times* noted that West End theatres had built their appeal on the conceit that they were mainly designed for the aristocracy. It saw Webster's new Adelphi as appealing to the middle class and claimed that the actor-manager had 'placed the middle-class within the theatre on a footing of complete equality with the highest and wealthiest in the land'.[30] The *Era* would later say that 'The style of most theatres is based on the idea of a drawing-room' (presumably minus all the clutter we associate with the middle-class home).[31]

This presaged the rebuilding that was to come. Webster went on to redesign the Haymarket, removing pit benches for stalls seats. There was a comfort revolution that swept through mid-Victorian theatres such that they created an atmosphere not entirely distinct from the nearby clubs of St James's (including facilities for

Fig. 9.2 The rebuilt Adelphi Theatre, 1858 (author collection)

---

[29] *Builder*, 11 December 1858, p. 833; 25 December 1858, p. 870.
[30] *Illustrated Times*, 1 January 1859, pp. 11–12.
[31] *Era*, 1 July 1893, p. 3.

smoking and drinking).[32] The Gaiety on the Strand had 'retiring rooms' for ladies on every floor as well as gentleman's lavatories. Evening papers could be found in the balcony of the lobby whilst telegrams from Parliament were obtained every half hour. The Gaiety manager John Hollingshead said explicitly that his theatre would offer 'some of the comforts of a club'.[33] The gentlemens' clubs we examined in Chapter 3 thus had a wide cultural impact despite their exclusivity. Clubs not only provided models of luxury but also an education in desirable metropolitan living that theatres picked up on in their design.

This comfort revolution was also evident at the Prince of Wales's Theatre where Marie Wilton introduced carpet into the stalls and a light blue colour scheme for the seats.[34] Her aim was to draw in a middle-class family audience to what had formerly been the Queen's Theatre, located in a relatively working-class area (Charlotte Street, close to the Tottenham Court Road). Light blue satin was employed throughout the house in the redecoration she introduced when she took over in 1865.[35] Workers could still be found in the gallery but it increasingly drew in a middle-class public. The shift of the Queen's Theatre upmarket needs, however, to be seen in terms of the changes of the area around it. Tottenham Court Road came to include major emporia of the furniture trade. Charlotte Street also enjoyed some fashionable restaurants such as Bertorelli's. This was an area with a bohemian feel as high culture rubbed shoulders with low life. It therefore made for a cultural dynamism.

Marie Wilton and the actor Squire Bancroft (whom she married) championed the long run. Increasingly, the theatre bill would feature just one play rather than the multiple contrasting plays and after-pieces that had dominated the stage previously. It also meant that audience members could see the same production multiple times if they enjoyed it. Word of mouth as well as reviews could establish the success of a play. From 1868, the Bancrofts began to introduce matinees for people visiting town. This was not totally new. Edward Smith introduced morning juvenile performances at Drury Lane in January 1853 and the Alhambra had put on Saturday matinees from 1865.[36] Pantomimes also often had matinees. John Hollingshead provided them at the Gaiety in the 1870s. The matinee form opened up the West End to female audiences and became a mark of sophistication. A visit to the theatre could be combined with shopping at a department store and a lunch in town. The actress Aida Jenoure observed that matinee audiences tended to be female. She found such spectators frustrating as 'they considered it *infra dig* to

---

[32] T.H.S. Escott, *England, its People, Polity and Pursuits* (London: Cassell, 1879), Vol. 2, p. 543.

[33] John Hollingshead, *Gaiety Chronicles* (London: Constable, 1898), p. 247.

[34] Squire Bancroft and Marie Wilton, *On and Off the Stage* (London: Richard Bentley, 1888), Vol. 1, pp. 185–6.

[35] Bancroft and Wilton, *On and Off the Stage*, Vol. 1, p. 284, 295.

[36] John Pick, *The West End: Mismanagement and Snobbery* (London: Offord/City Arts, 1983), p. 75; Davis and Emeljanow, *Reflecting the Audience*, p. 203; Report from the Select Committee on Theatrical Licenses and Regulations (1866), p. 55.

applaud'.[37] This was an audience that prided itself on restraint; on polite applause and dignified behaviour in the auditorium.

The mid-Victorian West End began a process of exclusion of the working-class audience through the mechanism of price. Stalls (as at the Prince of Wales's Theatre) moved from an average price of six or seven shillings in the 1860s up to ten shillings. The dress circle went from five shillings up to seven shillings and sixpence. The gallery cost sixpence, which thus provided access to less well-off people. The Bancrofts insisted that this did not deter audiences and that attendances increased at the higher prices.[38] Hollingshead's Gaiety at first asked a shilling price for the gallery but then reduced it to sixpence. The experiment was abandoned 'as it was found, that the low price attracted an audience a little too demonstrative for the general comfort of the house'.[39]

Another way in which the working class was excluded was through the process of advance booking. Up to the 1870s the ticketing system was haphazard. It was possible to book in advance for the stalls, boxes, and dress circle. At the same time designated agents and commercial libraries were also sites where tickets could be obtained. Theatres would send information about which seats were available on a particular evening on a card. Agents would take money and fill in the card by hand. This frequently led to confusion and discrepancy. The same seat could end up being sold twice. It could also lead to corruption with payment not making it back to the management. Charles Hawtrey found he was being defrauded by his own box office when playing *The Private Secretary* at the Prince's Theatre in 1883. He therefore introduced the system of printed tickets with a counterfoil stating the date and the seat number (though Benjamin Webster seems to have employed printed tickets at the Adelphi in 1858). This made it impossible for the seat to be sold twice as there was only one ticket. It also assisted with the accounting so that it was difficult for money to be creamed off. The coming of printed tickets made it possible to book tickets further and further in advance, though the Haymarket had been booking up to a month in advance from 1866. Working people in practice found it difficult to book in advance; their only option was to turn up on the evening to get a seat in the gallery. This was not a theatre designed for mass participation.[40] Another form of exclusion was through clothing (see Chapter 10). Dressing up for the theatre (with the exception of the balcony or gallery) was an expectation. The formality of the night out defined it strongly in class terms. This extended to the seats. Marion Sambourne (wife of the artist Linley Sambourne)

[37] *Sketch*, 8 March 1893, p. 331.
[38] Bancroft and Wilton, *On and Off the Stage*, Vol. 1, pp. 261, 305–7; George Taylor, *Players and Performances in the Victorian Theatre* (Manchester: Manchester University Press, 1989), p. 101; Report from the Select Committee on Theatrical Licenses and Regulations (1866), p. 55.
[39] John Hollingshead, *'Good Old Gaiety': An Historiette and Remembrance* (London: Gaiety Theatre Company, 1903), p. 21.
[40] Charles Hawtrey, *The Truth at Last* (London: Butterworth, 1924), pp. 142–4; Report from the Select Committee on Theatrical Licenses and Regulations (1866), p. 189; Pick, *West End*, pp. 79–81.

was a keen play-goer but in her diaries she often felt it more important to record where she sat ('Had Stage Box') than the name of the play she saw.[41]

One of the best observers of the West End was the diarist Arthur Munby. A minor poet and barrister, he fell in love with the servant Hannah Cullwick and later secretly married her.[42] In 1860, during the early years of their courtship, they arranged to meet at the Haymarket to see Tom Taylor's *The Overland Route*. The class system was such that she could not join him in the seats normally occupied by a gentleman. Even outside the theatre, they could not show that they knew each other. Instead, he joined her up in the gallery but was incapable (as he admitted to himself) of shaking the preoccupations of social status: 'As for me, to stand in the mob at the gallery door in the Haymarket, to sit in the gallery among the "roughs" by the side of a maid of all work, & drink with her out of the same bottle between the acts--is this not the very nadir of vulgarity & degradation?' He clearly regarded himself as slumming it and recorded the event with a disgust that was also the source of fascination. At the same time, he found himself interrogating the nature of class, 'looking over the rail, down upon my equals in the stalls and boxes' and imagining how they might view his relationship with contempt. He claimed to be indifferent to this but was clearly troubled.[43] The gallery in West End theatres remained essentially working class. In 1873, after she had secretly married Munby, Cullwick wanted to see *Arkwright's Wife* at the Globe Theatre as it featured working women like herself among the characters. She sat in the gallery because it did not occur to her to get any other seat. Munby joined her and found it a poor melodrama but recorded Cullwick's experience of watching the play: 'she was no languid or self-conscious listener; she was intent on the scene, her whole face was alive with emotion, and then, in rustic wise, she dashed away her tears with the back of her hand'. She clearly identified with the story and Munby thought that Helen Barry as the peasant wife looked similar to Cullwick.[44] Munby did take her to Drury Lane to hear *Fidelio*, where she dressed up in a silk dress and looked as ladylike as any of the high society women (though Cullwick disliked doing this).[45]

Another feature of the audience experience was the programme which evolved from the playbill. The Olympic seems to have been the first to introduce these in the 1850s and other theatres quickly imitated it, though John Hollingshead recalled that the programmes at Drury Lane were so badly printed with damp ink that it came off on the hands of audience members.[46] The Victorian theatre

[41] Shirley Nicholson (ed.), *A Victorian Household: Based on the Diaries of Marion Sambourne* (London: Barrie and Jenkins, 1988), p. 63.

[42] Leonore Davidoff, 'Class and Gender in Victorian England: The Case of Hannah Cullwick and A.J. Munby', in Davidoff, *Worlds Between: Historical Perspectives on Gender & Class* (London: Polity, 1995), pp. 103–50.

[43] Hudson, *Munby*, pp. 54–5.   [44] Hudson, *Munby*, pp. 349–50.

[45] Hudson, *Munby*, pp. 366–7.   [46] Hollingshead, *Gaiety Chronicles*, pp. 6–7.

programme was usually just one page but later developed into a booklet. It featured a cast list and sometimes the location of each scene. The ritual was that all male players were listed first followed by women. Otherwise, the bulk of it was for advertising which brought in revenue for the theatre. They were sometimes published in association with local catering firms which is why they contained advertisements for local restaurants. The nature of the audience can also be deduced from the advertisements for luxury household goods. There were some variations. In the 1860s the perfumier Eugene Rimmel offered scented programmes, which created an atmosphere of luxury and discrimination but also advertised his scents.[47] Rimmel had a strong link with the Adelphi theatre from the mid-1850s onwards so that the theatre's programmes would alert audiences to Rimmel's perfumed valentines, among other products.[48] When Edwin Booth played Hamlet at the Royal Princess's Theatre in 1880, an advertisement carried the information that, at Verrey's restaurant on Regent Street, 'The Luncheons at Moderate Prices are made a *specialité* for Ladies shopping in the neighbourhood', a statement about the kind of people who might be attending the show.[49] After about 1900, advertising in programmes became more extensive with multiple products being promoted.

Programmes of course were souvenirs and could be taken home and even collected. They thus built up the profiles of individual theatres. They could also involve social distinctions. At the Haymarket in the 1880s, programmes in the stalls were printed on cardboard whereas customers who paid less upstairs were given programmes on thinner paper. When audiences flocked to the Gilbert and Sullivan operas at the Savoy, they could purchase gilt-edged programmes adorned with sketches of Gilbert's characters.[50] The programme was a means to flatter the audience and make them feel they were something special.

Henry James considered the 'keynote' to West End theatre-going was the 'white-cravated young man' who led him to his stalls seat and sold him his programme. His 'grandeur', in the view of the novelist, set the tone of the evening.[51] Front of house was thus crucial in the middle-class theatre. Interval refreshments also became part of the West End theatre experience. In the 1850s, girls selling oranges still stood outside the entrances to Drury Lane and other theatres.[52] The Criterion Theatre in the 1870s was the first to sell coffee and strong liquor in the intermission. Ice cream and boxes of chocolates also became common from the

---

[47] Joseph Donohue, 'The Theatre from 1800 to 1895', in Donohue (ed.), *The Cambridge History of British Theatre* (Cambridge: Cambridge University Press, 2004) Vol. 2, p. 239.
[48] See programme for Boucicault's *Formosa* (1879) in Adelphi Programmes Box 1855–1919: TC/1/1/1879/2 (Westminster City Archives).
[49] Programme in THM/154/7/1 (Henry Arthur Jones collection): Victoria and Albert Museum Theatre Collection.
[50] Pick, *West End*, p. 84.   [51] James, *Scenic Art*, p. 101.
[52] Alfred Rosling Bennett, *London and Londoners in the Eighteen Fifties and Sixties* (London: T. Fisher Unwin, 1924), p. 342.

late 1870s.[53] Many of the rituals of a visit to a West End theatre therefore emerged in the mid-Victorian era.

Plays and Playwrights

In the early nineteenth century, the dramatist was frequently lowly in status. Hacks abounded and critics complained about the decline of the drama from the days of Sheridan. Yet in the mid-Victorian years, West End theatre started to become more obviously a writer's medium and its plays anticipated the drama of realism and naturalism in the later nineteenth century.

If the West End developed as a conservative space, it nevertheless had its quiet revolutionaries. Among these was the adaptor of *The Corsican Brothers*. Dion Boucicault may not have been an artistic innovator but he transformed the nature of popular theatre, adapting the themes of both melodrama and eighteenth-century comedy whilst refashioning them for the Age of Equipoise.

Boucicault hailed from a literary family in Dublin. It is likely that that he was the illegitimate son of Dionysus Lardner, the polymathic editor of the 133-volume *Cabinet Cyclopeadia*. He came to London to seek his fortune as an actor but turned quickly to writing. In 1841, his second play, *London Assurance* (written when the author was only twenty), proved a smash hit and remains one of the few nineteenth-century plays that can stand regular revival today. The play, with its leads, the foppish Sir Harcourt Courtley and the redoubtable Lady Gay Spanker, pastiched the comedies of town life that had flourished in the West End from the Restoration to Sheridan's *School for Scandal*. *London Assurance* was the first production to employ a box set in its modern form: a room placed on stage with one wall missing so that the audience could see. It made possible, amongst other things, the drawing-room comedy which became a West End staple.[54]

Boucicault became a recognizable brand on the popular stage, assisted by the fact that he sometimes acted (he played the title role in his 1854 play *The Vampire*). He left the nostalgic mode of *London Assurance* behind for topical plays that addressed key issues of the moment. Between 1854 and 1860 he was based in New York and transformed controversial issues into melodramas for the stage, including *The Octoroon* (1859) which dramatized the slavery question. They were, in some respects, the theatrical equivalent of the sensation novels of Wilkie Collins and Mary Elizabeth Braddon. In 1857, Boucicault staged *The Poor of New York*, a play that then became *The Poor of Liverpool*, *The Streets of London*,

---

[53] George Rowell, 'Wyndham of Wyndham's', in Joseph W. Donohue (ed.), *The Theatrical Manager in England and America: Player of a Perilous Game* (Princeton, NJ: Princeton University Press, 1971), p. 202; Pick, *West End*, p. 78.

[54] Michael Coveney and Peter Dazeley, *London Theatres* (London: Frances Lincoln, 2017), p. 19.

and *The Streets of Manchester* when it was staged in those respective cities in Britain. These were shows that could travel with multiple productions staged simultaneously. They were, in modern parlance, a franchise. *The Streets of London* was so ubiquitous on the touring circuit that actors found that audiences knew the lines better than they did and could prompt them.[55]

The experiment with the Corsican Trap at the Princess's signalled a move by Boucicault towards offering audiences ever greater spectacle. Boucicault recognized that a show that enjoyed a long run could afford elaborate scenery and more spectacular effects. The promise of spectacle would in turn draw in an audience. This became evident in Boucicault's *The Colleen Bawn* which premiered at New York in 1860 and later the same year at the Adelphi in London. The second act featured a scene in a cavern including a rescue from drowning, which reportedly provoked rounds of applause from the audience.[56] It created the vogue for 'sensation drama'. People loved its combination of spectacle, laughs, and dramatic tension.

In 1868, Boucicault presented *After Dark*, whose great scene was one where a character was tied to a railroad track before an oncoming train; the train actually burst onto the stage. Realistic effects gave the audience the feeling that they were in the action. What is Boucicault's legacy today? It is the chandelier crashing to the floor in *The Phantom of the Opera*; it is the helicopter landing in *Miss Saigon*; it is the high emotion of *Les Miserables*. All of these could have been written by Boucicault.

Playing for 230 nights at the Adelphi, *The Colleen Bawn* solidified the shift towards plays that enjoyed a long run, which allowed successful playwrights and managers to get rich. Boucicault's *Colleen Bawn* and *The Streets of London* were joined by other long-running hits such as Tom Taylor's *The Ticket of Leave Man* (1863). Contemporaries in the 1860s realized that there had never been a time when there were so many long-running shows in London.[57] Boucicault himself boasted that he could supply all of London's theatre with hit plays. There were worries that he might become a monopoly, preventing other authors from mounting their work.[58] This marked a change in the West End. Increasingly, the area came to be made of hit shows that were almost monuments in themselves. The show started to become bigger and more important than the theatre itself.

The long run also transformed the repertory system in acting and hence the life of the actor. Previously, actors were hired for the season and expected to play many parts. Now they were contracted to play a part in a particular play and their

---

[55] Jevan Brandon-Thomas, *Charley's Aunt's Father: A Life of Brandon Thomas* (London: Douglas Saunders, 1955), p. 65.

[56] Henry Morley, *The Journal of a London Playgoer* (Leicester: Leicester University Press, 1974 [1886]), p. 214.

[57] Report from the Select Committee on Theatrical Licenses and Regulations (1866), p. 137.

[58] Report from the Select Committee on Theatrical Licenses and Regulations (1866), p. 146.

fortunes depended on whether the play proved a hit. Rehearsals became longer, allowing them to grow into their parts and to feel them, allowing for a new approach to performance based on naturalism.

Boucicault was appalled that playwrights received so little from their own plays. Instead of a flat fee, he began to seek royalties and entered into a partnership with the manager of the Adelphi, Benjamin Webster. Boucicault arranged for payment by each performance, receiving one half of net profits.[59] When *The Streets of London* played at the Princess's, a profit of £32,000 was made, whilst his *Arrah-na-Pogue* made a similar sum.[60]

But if the effects were becoming more realistic, so to some extent was the content. Tom Robertson in the 1860s began to pen a series of comedies at the Prince of Wales's Theatre which appealed to a middle-class audience partly by sending up the foibles of high society. He delighted in the struggle between the nouveau riche and the aristocracy. *Society* had been rejected by London managers as it dared to make fun of journalists and of the bohemian set. Marie Wilton dared to mount it in 1865 at the Prince of Wales's and it became (in her words at least) the 'talk of the town'.[61] It was followed by *Caste* in 1867. These plays marked a shift away from melodrama and anticipated the comedies of Oscar Wilde. The theatre of realism that we associate with Ibsen and Shaw was in the future but Robertson's plays were prophetic. Robertson took time over rehearsals (whereas previous actors just focussed on the stock role that they usually played). Emotional restraint was promoted as opposed to the hysteria of melodrama (the smallness of the theatre allowed for a more intimate style of playing). Robertson's characters were meant to be drawn from life and not stereotypes. Even the scenery and props were more realistic. Henry James noted that 'This was the very pedantry of perfection, and makes the scenery somewhat better than the actors'.[62]

Robertson specialized in the kind of sophisticated comedy that became the stock in trade of the West End, but comedy of any kind was a draw. In 1847, John Baldwin Buckstone turned John Madison Morton's *Box and Cox* into a comedy sensation at the Lyceum. As so often, it was based on a French original. A one-act farce, it depicts a lodging-house keeper who rents a room to one man (Box) by day and to another (Cox) by night. The conceit of the play is that neither is aware of the other's existence. It was regularly revived and even turned into an operetta by Arthur Sullivan in 1866. Another successful comedy that shaped the era was Tom Taylor's *Our American Cousin*. A trans-Atlantic hit, it became notorious as the play that Abraham Lincoln was watching in Washington DC when he was assassinated in 1865. Originally premiered in New York in 1858, it came to the

[59] Report from the Select Committee on Theatrical Licenses and Regulations (1866), p. 147.
[60] Report from the Select Committee on Theatrical Licenses and Regulations (1866), pp. 193–4.
[61] Bancroft and Wilton, *On and Off the Stage*, Vol. 1, p. 202.
[62] James, *Scenic Art*, p. 107.

Haymarket in 1861. The play made a star of E.A. Sothern, who stole the show with his performance as the foppish bewhiskered aristocrat, Lord Dundreary. An Andrew Aguecheek figure, he allowed middle-class audiences to laugh at the vanity of the aristocracy. Sothern ended up being paid between £220 and £250 a week for playing the role.[63]

West End theatre thus proved a major force in the making of the middle classes, a space that could draw them away from their attachment to the home. Playhouses provided an unthreatening atmosphere that could be gently subversive but always ended up supporting conservative, patrician values. Even the sensationalist plays of Boucicault which took on topical questions did not fundamentally challenge the world of the middle class. Theatre was a form of social glue that could appeal to suburbanites.

The Actor's Life

The mid-Victorian years saw a transformation in the acting profession. Before that time, acting was not wholly respectable and being an actress certainly was not. The daughter of Samuel Phelps was actually dismissed from a school when her father was found to be an actor.[64] As West End theatre was remade in a respectable middle-class mould, the image of the actor changed and the number of performers increased. The amount of money that star actors could demand also went up.

Yet conditions backstage at theatres (essential to the actor's life) remained cramped and smelly. Performers at Covent Garden existed in primitive surroundings; the reverse of its plush auditorium. Even in the 1890s, its backstage was badly lit and ventilated. Worse, there were only nine dressing rooms and just one lavatory for the entire 100-person ballet.[65] Lavatories were close to eating spaces and dressing rooms; the air from backstage toilets sometimes carried out into the auditorium leading to talk about 'theatre headaches' and even 'theatre diarrhea'. Actors frequently complained of sore throats and rheumatism. Some theatres were notorious in the acting profession for spreading illness.[66] The Lord Chamberlain's Examiner of Plays was revolted when he carried out theatre inspections. He wrote in a letter in 1865: 'The heat, dirt, dust, smells, horrible. We took in the dressing-rooms this year. Talk of Ireland and pigsties...I have been sick and dizzy half-a-dozen times a day.'[67] Lack of toilet facilities and a poor sewage

[63]   Report from the Select Committee on Theatrical Licenses and Regulations (1866), p. 126.
[64]   Jeffrey Richards, *Sir Henry Irving: A Victorian Actor and his World* (London: Hambledon, 20005), p. 66.
[65]   Report from the Select Committee on Theatres and Places of Entertainment (1892), p. 181.
[66]   Report from the Select Committee on Theatres and Places of Entertainment (1892), p. 10.
[67]   Catharine B. Johnson (ed.), *William Bodham Donne and his Friends* (London: Methuen, 1905), p. 268.

system is one explanation why cholera, diptheria, and typhoid were not unknown in the West End.

The coming of the long run transformed the life of the actor in other ways than we have looked at. The repertory system had required actors to perform at night while devoting their day to learning lines for the following day's performance. Now actors were increasingly employed for a production and for a particular part rather than to be part of a company. The challenge was to keep a performance fresh when it had to be done over and over again. Actors earned a salary rather than a weekly wage. Suddenly they had time on their hands during the day (once the initial rehearsal period was over), which suited the lifestyle of many performers.[68] Actors had always cultivated a bohemian air in their manner and dress. George Arliss noticed that some actors (like Irving) wore their hair long so that they would look like romantic artists.[69] They relished their feeling of difference.

The long run also brought anxiety. Just as Charles Darwin and his followers were introducing contemporaries to the idea of the 'survival of the fittest', theatre found itself governed by a Darwinian logic. A hit meant work whereas a failure meant unemployment and the need to scour advertisements in the new stage press (such as the *Era*), looking for auditions or other openings. The long run helped create a new figure who became part of show business: the agent.[70] Agencies in the later nineteenth century would get actors to make a down payment (which could range from five shillings to a guinea) and then require 5 per cent of the actor's salary for the first fortnight of work.[71]

The most successful actors began to emulate the lifestyle of the middle-class audiences they served. Holidays would be in the south of France or genteel locations. Previously, performers lived in the West End so that they could be close to their theatres. Frederick Yates actually brought up his family in a suite in the Adelphi theatre. After mid-century, houses in fashionable areas were purchased; so were carriages. Charles Kean and T.P. Cooke lived in Woburn Square. Brompton Square in Knightsbridge claimed a large number of theatrical figures including John Baldwin Buckstone, James Vining, the Farrens, and the Keeleys.[72] John Reeve could be found in Brompton Row while Eliza Vestris lived in Gore Lodge, Fulham. Edmund Yates claimed, 'The omnibuses were filled with actors, and footlight celebrities were common as blackberries.'[73] Star actors thus resembled the bourgeois members of the stalls.

---

[68] Michael Baker, *The Rise of the Victorian Actor* (London: Croom Helm, 1978), p. 91.

[69] G.B. Soane-Roby, 'My First Experience of Hamlet', *Stage Stories: Actors and Actresses* (1895) no. 1, p. 7.

[70] Joseph Donohue, 'The Theatre from 1800 to 1895', p. 259.

[71] C.H. d'E. Leppington, 'The Gibeonites of the Stage: Work and Wages Behind the Scenes', *National Review*, 17 (1891), p. 255.

[72] Baker, *Victorian Actor*, pp. 68–9.

[73] Edmund Yates, *Recollections and Experiences* (London: Richard Bentley, 1884), Vol. I, p. 233; see also Hudson, *Munby*, p. 238.

This chapter has shown how theatre became an essential part of middle-class life, one that was increasingly respectable and a source of sophistication. The disciplined audience of the 1860s contrasted with the boisterous audience of the early nineteenth century. Much of the latter moved over to the music hall which proved much more attractive to the working classes. Yet, even if there was a shift towards a more bourgeois theatre, it is important to stress that the mid-Victorian audience was still heterogeneous. Theatre was a genuinely popular form even if servants like Hannah Cullwick felt their place was in the gallery.

The West End was, however, defined by more than class. It also represented a new form of visual culture. Let us return to *The Corsican Brothers*. In many ways it was a drama that reflected the themes of romanticism in the early nineteenth century: the wildness of Corsica was meant to contrast with Parisian refinement, the telepathic connection between the title characters had a gothic feel. And yet Charles Kean's production reflected a move towards realism and naturalism in its presentation. with its use of special effects (ghosts really seemed to walk on the stage). Theatre was part of an explosion in visuality that was evident, as we have seen, in the West End and elsewhere. The spoken and written word had to share space with increasingly elaborate forms of pictorial presentation with an emphasis on the reality effect. This pictorial culture could be found both in the development of illustrated periodicals and novels, in the epic paintings of John Martin and others, in the flamboyant set designs of the stage where actual locations (such as the Burlington Arcade, as we saw in Chapter 2) could be reproduced on stage.[74] But this culture of spectacle was also registered in the development of theatres which offered spectacle and sophistication. These included the Princess's where *The Corsican Brothers* was staged. Theatre architecture was part of a move towards providing theatre with a sumptuous frame. There was a connection, then, between *The Corsican Brothers*, the panoramas of Leicester Square, the conjurers and curiosities at the Egyptian Hall, and the magic lantern shows and 'dissolving views' offered at the Royal Polytechnic Institution. The eye was trained to enjoy spectacle in new colourful ways. As we saw in Chapter 7, the pleasure district was built on ravishing the senses. The West End was the home of the licensed stare.

[74] Martin Meisel, *Realizations: Narratives, Pictorial, and Theatrical Arts in Nineteenth-Century England* (Princeton, NJ: Princeton University Press, 1983).

10

Theatreland, 1880–1914

A Total Form of Art

By the late nineteenth century, the West End was theatreland. London's concentration of theatres in a relatively small area was unrivalled (except by New York). The West End had cohered as a cultural project, feeding off the way the arts came together in central London. It was a place where novels, poetry, plays, journalism, painting, and music all interpenetrated. The stage was a total form of art employing music and the visual arts.[1] Thus Henry Irving at the Lyceum could employ leading artists Sir Lawrence Alma-Tadema and Sir Edward Burne-Jones as designers whilst his musical scores were provided by (among other people) Sir Arthur Sullivan. Theatre borrowed liberally from Victorian culture more generally: the romance, the imperial adventure, the comedy of manners, the dilemmas of the shabby genteel (Maps 10.1 and 10.2).

This was the last moment when individual theatres were brands; when they were more important than the actual shows. If you wanted farce, you headed for Toole's Theatre and, if sensational drama was to your taste, you went to Drury Lane or the Adelphi. The Lyceum and (after 1897) Her Majesty's both offered the classical repertoire, especially Shakespeare. The Savoy was particularly associated with Gilbert and Sullivan. The pleasure district was so distinctive a space that the Society of West End Theatre Managers (now the Society of London Theatre) was formed in 1908 as a body to foster common interests and promote theatregoing.

The history of late Victorian drama is too often written up in terms of Ibsen, Wilde, Shaw, and perhaps Arthur Wing Pinero. But this ignores the plays that most theatre-goers actually saw. The long-running play is important because it indicates something about popular taste at this time. Increasingly, audiences were drawn to particular plays rather than whatever happened to be on at a theatre like the Adelphi.

Brandon Thomas's farce, *Aunt* (1892), for example, managed to knock up 1492 performances at the Globe Theatre, off the Strand, and was regularly revived in the West End at Christmas all the way up to 1930. It remains the great

---

[1] Jeffrey Richards, *Sir Henry Irving: A Victorian Actor and his World* (London: Hambledon, 2005), p. 443.

London's West End: Creating the Pleasure District, 1800–1914. Rohan McWilliam, Oxford University Press (2020).
© Rohan McWilliam.
DOI: 10.1093/oso/9780198823414.001.0001

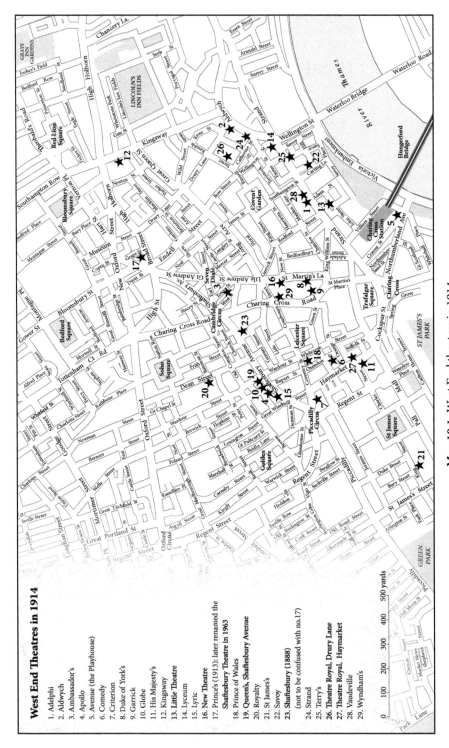

Map 10.1 West End theatres in 1914

West End Theatres in 1914

1. Adelphi
2. Aldwych
3. Ambassador's
4. Apollo
5. Avenue (the Playhouse)
6. Comedy
7. Criterion
8. Duke of York's
9. Garrick
10. Globe
11. His Majesty's
12. Kingsway
13. Little Theatre
14. Lyceum
15. Lyric
16. New Theatre
17. Prince's (1913): later renamed the
    Shaftesbury Theatre in 1963
18. Prince of Wales
19. Queen's, Shaftesbury Avenue
20. Royalty
21. St James's
22. Savoy
23. Shaftesbury (1888)
    (not to be confused with no.17)
24. Strand
25. Terry's
26. Theatre Royal, Drury Lane
27. Theatre Royal, Haymarket
28. Vaudeville
29. Wyndham's

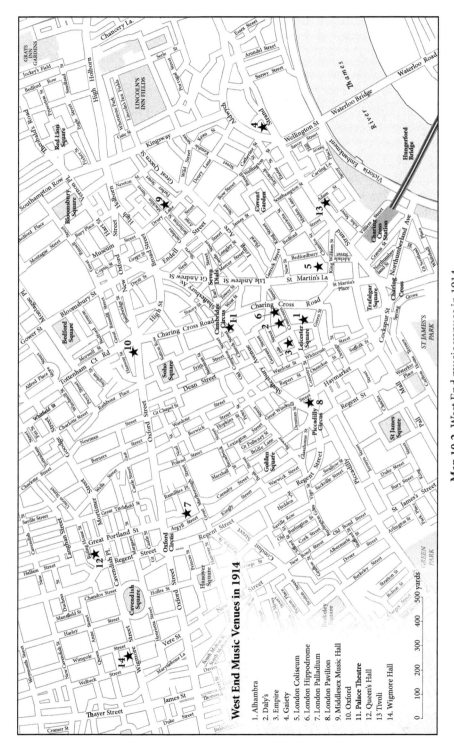

Map 10.2 West End music venues in 1914

West End Music Venues in 1914

1. Alhambra
2. Daly's
3. Empire
4. Gaiety
5. London Coliseum
6. London Hippodrome
7. London Palladium
8. London Pavilion
9. Middlesex Music Hall
10. Oxford
11. Palace Theatre
12. Queen's Hall
13. Tivoli
14. Wigmore Hall

0   100   200   300   400   500 yards

comedy about cross-dressing but rendered in a way that sustained Victorian proprieties. Audiences were thrilled by Herbert Beerbohm Tree's performance as Svengali in *Trilby* in 1895. He became one of the great stage villains of the age whilst the play became a mania generating parodies and burlesques; even a hat worn by a character became known as a 'trilby' thereafter. For those who cherished spectacle, there was the adaptation of *Ben Hur* at Drury Lane in 1902, part of a cycle of 'toga plays': stories with biblical or classical themes.[2] The play actually put both the galley scene (including its sinking) and the chariot race on stage with real chariots and horses. George Alexander at the St James's struck gold with Oscar Wilde's *Importance of Being Earnest* but also with his production of *The Prisoner of Zenda* in 1896 in which Alexander played both King Rudolf and his double Rudof Rassendyll (a reminder of Charles Kean's triumph in *The Corsican Brothers* in the previous generation).

The West End dominated theatre culture more than ever in the late nineteenth century. Its productions increasingly went on tour. There was nothing new about touring. London actors had previously taken plays around and performed with a local cast in each venue. Now, however, the whole production started to tour; the London cast with its costumes and scenery. Touring established the notion that a quality product in the theatre needed to have the imprimatur of a London appearance. A major calling card in the provinces was the notion that a production had come straight from the West End, a term that became suffused with glamour.[3] This was even more true as London productions went to Broadway in New York or toured the United States and parts of the British Empire. West End theatre thus served as a reminder to the rest of the world that Britain ruled.

Given its wider impact, we should note that West End theatre did not, however, always reflect the ways in which Britain was changing with the rise of labour, women demanding the vote, and fears about Britain's ability to dominate the world. 'What do we find depicted upon the English stage?' asked the critic Mario Borsa. His answer was: 'The squabbles of provincial life, conventionalized members of the aristocracy, romantic melodrama, drawing-room intrigues...and a nauseous mash-up of mis-represented history and exaggerated sentimentality, which is as false to art as it is false to life and history.'[4]

The West End stage reflected some of the values of Lord Salisbury's Britain. Whilst the Lord Chamberlain sought to keep politics off the stage, West End theatre remained a location for a kind of non-ideological, status-driven conservatism. It developed a cultural style that could offer the seriousness of high culture

[2] David Mayer (ed.), *Playing out the Empire: 'Ben Hur' and other Toga Plays and Films, 1883–1908* (Oxford: Clarendon Press, 1994); Jeffrey Richards, *The Ancient World on the Victorian and Edwardian Stage* (Basingstoke: Palgrave Macmillan, 2009).

[3] Tracy C. Davis, *The Economics of the British Stage, 1800–1914* (Cambridge: Cambridge University Press, 2000), p. 342.

[4] Mario Borsa, *The English Stage of To-Day* (London: John Lane, 1908), pp. 54–5.

(Henry Irving excelled in the plays of both Shakespeare and Tennyson) but also developed the middle-brow sensibility that had been evident in the plays of Tom Robertson. Yet theatre also offered pantomime, fantasy, and spaces where alternative selves could be imagined. The later nineteenth century was the moment when the modern pantomime canon really emerged, leaving behind its roots in the harlequinade. Old stories such as *Cinderella* and *Babes in the Wood* were re-told for children. The West End fed off children's literature, much as Walt Disney would in the twentieth century. Lewis Carroll (Charles Dodgson) was involved with the first adaptation of *Alice in Wonderland*. More profoundly, the West End added to the world of childhood with J.M. Barrie's *Peter Pan* which was first performed at the Duke of York's in 1904 and became a fixture after that.

This chapter considers the West End theatre business in its different forms (including the world of the West End audience) and builds to a case study of the rebuilt Her Majesty's Theatre which exemplified many of the trends discussed here. The built environment of theatre was intended to instil awe and a conservative version of selfhood. The construction of new theatres (many of which still exist) had huge consequences for the West End in the twentieth century.

Conservative or Modern?

When Gladstone asked the actor Herbert Beerbohm Tree about the political views of the theatre world, he replied 'Conservative, on the whole' but went on to say 'the scene shifters are Radical almost to a man'. Beerbohm Tree would later spend a weekend at Hatfield with the Conservative premier Lord Salisbury (for whom Tree's wife Maud professed a 'deep hero worship').[5] Different spaces had different cultural politics. At the beginning of the twentieth century, the Savoy would play the national anthem at performances and people were expected to stand up; the experimental and bohemian Court Theatre over on Sloane Square (and hence outside the West End) did not do this.[6] Theatre was undoubtedly conservative (which explains the shock of George Bernard Shaw's early plays).

The increased focus on sumptuous decoration in theatres also expressed an age which focussed increasingly on pageantry, ceremonial, and invented traditions. It went hand in hand with a popular view of history that emphasized the romantic and picturesque whilst feeding into a conservative construction of national identity.[7] Fred Terry's star turn in 1905 at the New Theatre in *The Scarlet Pimpernel*

[5] Max Beerbohm (ed.), *Herbert Beerbohm Tree: Some Memories of Him and of His Art* (London: Hutchinson, 1920), pp. 48, 86.

[6] Michael Holroyd, *Bernard Shaw* (London: Chatto and Windus, 1989), Vol. 2, p. 177.

[7] Eric Hobsbawm and Terence Ranger (eds), *The Invention of Tradition* (Cambridge: Cambridge University Press, 1983); Rosemary Mitchell, *Picturing the Past: English History in Text and Image* (Oxford: Oxford University Press, 2000); Billie Melman, *The Culture of History: English Uses of the Past, 1800-1953* (Oxford: Oxford University Press, 2006).

(subsequently much revived) produced positive images of monarchy and aristocracy with an emphasis on duty and sacrifice balancing out the democratizing tendencies of the later nineteenth century and establishing a continuing role for these groups in modern Britain. This cultural Toryism was not only played out on stage but was inscribed into the built environment of theatres themselves, as we will see below.

The West End's conservatism did not, however, prevent theatre from engaging with issues of morality or from taking on board some of the themes of modernism. The sexual politics of the West End (for example, farce at the Criterion) reflected end- of-century concerns with decadence. Despite the indirect policing by the state in the form of the Lord Chamberlain, West End conservatism was largely market-driven. These were plays that would not offend the villa Toryism of the suburbs or the populist Toryism that was a feature of East End politics.[8] This was not a conservatism that sank to ideological statements but worked through identity reinforcement. It was expressed through a broader commitment to values, decency, respect for marriage, and good humour whilst also insisting that the categories of 'lady' and 'gentleman' were founded in nature and were not the exclusive preserve of the elite. It helped maintain a society that was concerned with status and deference to the wealthy and powerful. Mrs E.T. Cook expressed it thus:

> The great middle-class supports Shakespeare and the 'legitimate' drama; shop girls, and dressmakers' apprentices like the 'society' plays of the St James's and kindred theatres, because they offer some opportunity for seeing the ways of that 'high life' from which they are themselves excluded.[9]

This statement should not be taken at face value as it assumes a deferential public (the St James's had less of a working-class following than other theatres). Attitudes to any performance would have been complex even if they are difficult to reconstruct. Did the audience get what it liked or did it learn to like what it got? People appropriate works of art in their own terms. It is reasonable to assume that different parts of a theatre 'read' a play in different ways because of their life experiences.

The West End expressed an essentially middle-class view of the world because managers and the leading cultural figures were either middle class or had bourgeois aspirations. There was in any case a tendency to play safe. Documentary realism did not seem like a paying proposition. The Ibsen revolution in drama was slow to make it into the West End. Lillie Langtry, for example, pronounced herself against his plays, emphasizing there were good playwrights at home such

---

[8]   Alex Windscheffel, *Popular Conservatism in Imperial London, 1868–1906* (Woodbridge: Boydell Press/Royal Historical Society, 2007).

[9]   (Mrs) E.T. Cook, *Highways and Byways in London* (London: Macmillan 1911), p. 283.

as Pinero and Henry Arthur Jones.[10] Pinero himself claimed the audience for Ibsen was limited to 'cranks'.[11] Edward Smyth Pigott, the Lord Chamberlain, considered Ibsen's characters to be 'morally deranged' with married female characters who were 'against all the duties and obligations of mothers and wives'.[12] Ibsen's plays were often written off as dealing with the psychologically abnormal or were merely dismissed as a boring night in the theatre.

At the same time, West End theatre could be subversive. Plays often celebrated cosmopolitanism and bohemianism. Henry Arthur Jones was a notoriously conservative playwright but his play *Saints and Sinners* (1884) dared to explore the place of religion in middle-class provincial life, causing a raft of complaints which failed to hurt it at the box office.[13] Theatre reflected the impact of more visible forms of sexuality and debates about marriage. On 15 May 1900, Samuel Smith, Liberal MP for Flintshire, moved a resolution in Parliament deploring the depravity of comedies and calling for restrictions on plays like *The Gay Lord Quex* (by Pinero) which deals with a reformed philanderer. For him this was a subject affecting the 'moral well-being of the Empire'. He claimed such plays had a 'demoralising character'; in other words, they caused the moral self of audiences to implode. Modest women were made to 'play the part of harlots'. Smith feared for young people being introduced to the 'fast life' and claimed that drama had become 'decadent'. He quoted a letter he received from a colonist from South Africa who, on his first visit to London, visited a theatre where 'he saw such orgies of vice that his loyalty to the mother country was greatly shaken'. Smith was in turn attacked by Gibson Bowles for not having set foot in a theatre.[14] In 1880, the *Times* commented, 'A literal and faithful transcript of real life would make but a dull play.'[15] Reality was not the stock in trade of the West End.

The conservatism of the theatre meant that it was ill at ease with the social, economic, and political ruptures of the late nineteenth century. Life was represented in patrician terms. As Borsa made clear, it was not dealing with the realities of the lives of its audience, let alone the people who did not come. This meant that in the twentieth century alternative plays and stages had to emerge outside the West End.

Building and Managing Theatres

West End theatre-going changed in fundamental ways, creating experiences that would not be unfamiliar to people today. For one thing, there were far more

---

[10] *Sketch*, 1 February 1893, p. 69.   [11] *Sketch*, 15 March 1893, p. 413.
[12] Report from the Select Committee on Theatres and Places of Entertainment (1892), p. 334.
[13] Henry Arthur Jones, 'Religion and the Stage', *The Nineteenth Century*, 17 (1885), pp. 154–69.
[14] Hansard, 4th series, vol. 83 (15 May 1900), cols. 276–307. Quotations from col. 276, 279, 283.
[15] *Times*, 2 February 1880, p. 8.

theatres to choose from. They were also designed to be more comfortable and hospitable in line with comparable developments in restaurants and hotels as we will see. What caused the wave of theatre building that commenced in the later Victorian period and went on into the Edwardian period? It was a delayed response to the abolition of the monopoly that the patent theatres had enjoyed before 1843 but was also the product of London's increasing population and the prosperity that was becoming clear.

Between 1880 and 1900 twelve new theatres were built in the West End. They were the Comedy (1881), the Savoy (1881), the Avenue (now the Playhouse on Northumberland Avenue) (1882), the Novelty (1882), the new Prince of Wales's on Coventry Street (1883), Terry's (1887), the Shaftesbury Theatre (1888), the Lyric (1889), the Garrick (1889), The Duke of York's (originally the Trafalgar Square Theatre) (1892), Daly's (1893), and the Wyndham's in 1899. In addition, some theatres like Her Majesty's were entirely rebuilt. If we take the existing thirteen theatres (I am excluding music halls, opera houses, and variety theatres like the Gaiety), this means that in 1900 there were twenty-five theatres in the West End.

Theatre management represented a considerable financial risk. Henry Irving compared it to Monte Carlo.[16] Much of the working-class audience had been lost to music hall. Nevertheless, there were many who were ready to invest. Theatres were usually owned by speculators, entrepreneurs like Richard D'Oyly Carte at the Savoy, or by actor-managers. Speculators spent a lot of money but the returns on leasing a theatre to a manager (who would then put on shows) were considerable.[17] The financier and newspaperman Lionel Lawson built the Gaiety and then leased it to John Hollingshead to manage. John Lancaster, who built the Shaftesbury Theatre in 1888, was the owner of the Harpurhey dye works in Manchester. The theatre was built to provide his wife Ellen Wallis (who performed Shakespeare in the provinces) with a London base but this ambition did not live up its promise.[18]

The West End enjoyed long periods of management which helped theatres to establish both a distinctive house style but also to shape the theatrical diet that people associated with the West End.[19] George Alexander at the St James's between 1891 and 1899 made it a centre for plays about high society. Charles Wyndham at the Criterion between 1879 and 1898 turned it into a centre for light comedy (introducing the full-length farce to London audiences). Henry Irving's tenure of the Lyceum lasted from the moment when he took over from the

---

[16] Report from the Select Committee on Theatres and Places of Entertainment (1892), p. 70.

[17] Hugh Francis Bernard Maguire, 'C.J. Phipps (1835–97) and Nineteenth Century Theatre Architecture (1863-97)' (University of London (Courtauld Institute of Art) PhD, 1990), p. 86.

[18] Maguire, 'C.J. Phipps', p. 94.

[19] John Pick, The West End: Mismanagement and Snobbery (London: Offord/City Arts, 1983), p. 103.

Bateman management in 1878 until his death in 1905 (though the theatre was managed by a syndicate by that time). Beerbohm Tree ran the Haymarket from 1888 to 1896 and then, having rebuilt Her Majesty's in 1897, ran it till he died in 1917. Charles Hawtrey had two substantial periods of management at the Comedy Theatre (1887–93 and 1896–1903). Augustus Harris ran Drury Lane from 1879 to 1897 and combined it with running Covent Garden from 1888 to 1896. This was a very masculine group; a far cry from the days of Eliza Vestris and other women who helped shape the West End. These men had a strong sense of the public taste, but also of their own taste. As most of them were actors they were able to fashion a strong public identity which involved clothing West End performances with the trappings of prestige. They also became more organized, forming in 1889 a committee of theatre managers and hiring a solicitor to represent them.[20]

Theatre management had to work with changing political parameters. Apart from the Lord Chamberlain, theatres were also answerable to the Metropolitan Board of Works. Fire was a persistent problem. When fire broke out at the Alhambra in 1882, two firemen were killed. In 1878, the Board was given formal powers by the Metropolitan Management and Building Act to inspect theatres for reasons of health and safety (though full authority to undertake inspections did not come till 1882). The Board was particularly concerned with issues of fire safety, exits, and door fastenings.[21] Its impact was such that the Prince of Wales's Theatre, off the Tottenham Court Road, was actually forced to shut down in 1882 as major reconstruction was required by the Board.

In 1888 the new London County Council created its own Theatres and Music Hall Committee to regulate London entertainment. Much of its work remained overseeing the structure of buildings in the interests of safety which it rigorously policed. Thus it insisted that the flap seats in the pit at Drury Lane be made secure.[22]

The Council quickly developed progressive tendencies and was resented by theatre managers who complained about its busybody tendencies (not least because these included questions about the moral tone of performances).

As the number of theatres expanded, their seating capacity began to diminish. There was no longer a need for the cavernous spaces that the West End had created earlier. Drury Lane could still seat 2500 people in 1892 but the Comedy Theatre on Panton Street was a more intimate space, seating 910, whilst Terry's Theatre on the Strand could take just 531.[23] As theatres became smaller, actors were able to develop a new, more naturalistic style of acting which offered greater

---

[20] Report from the Select Committee on Theatres and Places of Entertainment (1892), p. 55.
[21] Report from the Select Committee on Theatres and Places of Entertainment, (1892), pp. 3, 26.
[22] London County Council Theatre and Music Halls Committee: Agenda Papers 19 May 1890, p. 3: LCC/MIN/10, 705 (London Metropolitan Archives).
[23] Report from the Select Committee on Theatres and Places of Entertainment (1892), p. 451.

realism. They did not need to engage in the kind of grand gestures and manual semaphore that had characterized melodramatic acting.

Theatres also began to manage their audiences in other ways. The Savoy Theatre opened on 10 October 1881 and was from the start a site for innovation. As we saw in Chapter 7, it was the first building to rely fully on electric light. There was a cloakroom for hats and coats, which was free of charge (as were the programmes). The manager D'Oyly Carte controlled the bars himself rather than sub-letting to an outside contractor (reasoning that it increased costs and hence the price of refreshment to the public). The theatre queue was also invented outside the Savoy, putting an end to the unseemly scrum to gain cheap seats that had previously characterized London theatres. D'Oyly Carte was therefore a theatrical moderniser. The profits from his theatre were so large that he was able to use them to build the Savoy Hotel on the site with the entrance to the theatre moved to the hotel courtyard in 1903.

At an aesthetic level, theatre design meant that audiences would have a succession of experiences as they moved from the front of the building into the auditorium, encouraging receptiveness to what they would encounter on the stage. The smart theatre lobby performed important work in shaping audience experience. It reassured visitors about their status, although the box office was often forbidding; an enclosed space with which the theatre-goer communicated through a small glass aperture. Then there was the move into the auditorium. As theatres began at the end of the century to truly darken the house, the accompanying hush as the lights went down was a cue for audience focus and concentration.

The dress code remained important. Evening dress at the Aldwych was compulsory in the front three rows of the dress circle and optional for the rest.[24] When a visitor to the Adelphi wanted seats that did not require evening dress, he was told that the balcony stalls offered seating where dress was optional although ladies had to leave their hats in the cloakroom.[25] Refreshments played a part in the evening's entertainment. Apart from the Savoy, most theatres used outside companies and many were notorious for poor catering at inflated prices. In 1881, the newly-built Royal Comedy Theatre (now the Harold Pinter) in Panton Street awarded its contract to the New York catering firm Belle and Boid, hoping to improve quality with a fixed tariff.[26]

The auditoriums of West End theatres had begun to change and by 1914 they were often made up of the following. There was the stalls with a pit at the back (characterized by cheap seats), usually with a barrier between the two. Above was the dress circle and, above that, the upper circle (though the latter could

[24] Victor Glasstone, *Victorian and Edwardian Theatres: An Architectural and Social Survey* (London: Thames and Hudson, 1975), pp. 107, 111.

[25] W. Curry to Theatre Committee of the LCC, 14 October 1892: LCC Theatre Committee Papers: Adelphi Theatre 1898–1906: LCC/MIN/10, 768 (London Metropolitan Archives).

[26] *The Caterer and Hotel Proprietor's Gazette*, 15 November 1881, p. 222.

sometimes be simply the back of the dress circle). In a separate tier above was the gallery or balcony (the first few rows of this was described as the 'amphitheatre' in some houses). Then there were the boxes on either side of the stage for high society and royalty.[27] The stalls, however, increasingly encroached upon the pit as managers realized these were the best seats and could charge more for them. When Squire Bancroft revamped the Theatre Royal Haymarket in 1880 by abolishing the pit (offering a second circle as an alternative), there was a near-riot in the theatre on the first night and he was forced to come out on stage, dressed up to perform in Bulwer Lytton's *Money*, to placate the crowd.[28] It echoed the 1809 Old Price riots at Covent Garden. The pit continued to be a feature of West End theatres into the early twentieth century.

Theatre architecture was a specialized task. It required understanding the functional needs of actors and audience. Thus sightlines and spaces for refreshment and circulation were important. With the rise of new forms of drama, such as the plays of Oscar Wilde which relied upon sharp dialogue, acoustics really mattered. Wood-lined interiors were found to work best for the transmission of sound.[29] At the same time theatre architects had to deal with restrictions on the amount of space available to them (a particular problem in the West End) and the requirements of safety in case of fire. Rapid scene changes and the need to drop additional backcloths introduced the need for a fly tower in most theatres. These were all major considerations in theatre construction.

The wave of new West End theatres and opera houses was the work of a remarkably small group of architects. They included Charles Phipps, Thomas Verity, Walter Emden, Frank Matcham, Bertie Crewe, and W.G. Sprague. The most important of these were Phipps and Sprague who, between them, shaped much of what we associate with West End theatre. In the West End, Phipps designed the Queen's (Long Acre), the Gaiety, the Vaudeville, the Savoy, the Princess's, the Prince of Wales's, the Lyric, the Shaftesbury, and supervised the rebuilding of the Haymarket and the Lyceum. Sprague designed the Wyndham's, the New (now the Noel Coward), the Strand, the Aldwych, the Hicks (now the Gielgud Theatre), the Queen's (Shaftesbury Avenue), the Ambassadors, and the St Martin's. Sprague's theatres worked in pairs: the Wyndham's and the New bookending each other (one on the Charing Cross Road and one behind it on Saint Martin's Lane), the Hicks and the Queen's twinned on Shaftesbury Avenue, the Strand and the Aldwych complementing each other as part of the reconstruction that became Kingsway.

Having been contracted to design the theatre, it was usually the architect who put the building work out to tender, receiving some 5 per cent of the cost of

[27] Maguire, 'C.J. Phipps', p. 199.   [28] *Times*, 2 February 1880, p. 8.
[29] Maguire, 'C.J. Phipps', pp. 213–14.

building (plus expenses) as their commission.[30] It is worth dwelling briefly on their designs as they determined a great deal of the West End experience. At the Aldwych (opened in 1905), Sprague mixed Georgian and French Baroque-Classicism in the design. The interiors were crimson, cream, and gold, with rose du Barry upholstery and draperies. They were lit by electric candles with silk shades. At the Queen's on Shaftesbury Avenue (opened in 1907), Sprague went for a baroque design on the ceiling whilst the putti on the fronts of the balcony were a paraphrase of Donatello. There was also liberal use of Art Nouveau *bachanantes*. At the same time the exterior design of theatres was often lost because of the need for advertising billboards to publicize the latest production.

Charles Phipps was the great theatre master-builder because he built up a strong record of erecting theatres quickly, thus granting speculators a quick return on their investment.[31] Phipps's work dominated the West End but his signature can be found on theatres throughout Britain as well as Ireland. His speed was assisted by his ongoing association with firms such as the building contractors Simpsons on the Tottenham Court Road who built both the Queen's on Long Acre in 1867 and then the Gaiety in 1868. His designs were eclectic so that there was no discernable Phipps style, just elements of classical, gothic, and Romanesque details. Like a lot of theatre architects, he was influenced by Parisian theatre designs. In designing the Carlton Hotel and Her Majesty's Theatre complex, he actually visited Paris to study the Grand Hotel.[32] Phipps remained busy as the London County Council often demanded alterations in the buildings for which he was responsible.[33]

A signature of Phipps's approach was that there should be different entrances for the different parts of the auditorium and that they should be kept far apart. This way there would be no danger of the classes intermixing in the circulation areas. There were separate pay boxes for the gallery from where to purchase tickets.[34] Phipps and his fellow architects made social class visible. Their buildings were founded on notions of hierarchy. The endless stairs made access to theatre-goers with disabilities a trial or simply excluded them (though this was rarely a consideration in the nineteenth century).

The relationship between the architect and the decorators of the interior of the auditorium is less clear. Did the architect approve the interior design? Practice seems to have varied but it does mean that the architect was not the single 'author' of a theatre.[35] Artists were brought in to assist. Albert Moore, for example, painted

[30] Maguire, 'C.J. Phipps', pp. 120–1.
[31] Görel Garlick, *Charles John Phipps F.S.A.: Architect to the Victorian Theatre* (Cambridge: Entertainment Technology Press, 2016).
[32] Maguire, 'C.J. Phipps', p. 73.
[33] See Theatre and Music Halls Committee Agenda Papers 1893–98: 19 July 1893, pp. 2–4: LCC/MIN/706 (London Metropolitan Archives).
[34] Maguire, 'C.J. Phipps', pp. 122–5, 175, 178 186.
[35] Maguire, 'C.J. Phipps', pp. 274–6.

a scene of figures watching *Antigone* for the proscenium panel at the Queen's Theatre.[36] For the Haymarket, the scenic artist T. Ballard painted figurative panels above the proscenium representing the muses Terpsichore, Euterpe, Thalia, Erato, and Melpomene (see Fig. 10.1). The front of the Haymarket second circle was enlivened by small panels representing themes of dancing, poetry, music, comedy, and going to the play. After its redecoration in 1885, the ceiling of the Lyceum featured panels devoted to literary figures of the classical world such as Homer, Sophocles, and Aeschylus.[37] Theatre ceilings and act drops (curtains) were awash with images from antiquity or all things Venetian. The built environment of theatres therefore involved a performance of their own: a demonstration of good taste, the sublime, and a set of codes elaborated through colour and painting which prepared the audience for the events on the stage. They became an integral part of a visit to a West End theatre.

Toilet facilities, on the other hand, remained restricted. When the Vaudeville was built by Phipps in 1870, there were no toilets for ladies in either the pit or the gallery. This assumed a masculine audience in those parts of the house. Improvements in cleanliness were a factor in the middle-class takeover of West End theatre. Toilet facilities for both sexes improved in the later nineteenth century though they had to be tucked into existing corridors, leading to cramped facilities.[38] The lack of an adequate number of toilets means that, even today, intervals in West End theatres are characterized by long queues outside ladies' lavatories.

The stage itself was heavily remade. The major innovation came in the form of Squire and Marie Bancroft's rebuilding of the Haymarket. In 1880, the forestage was abolished and the proscenium was surrounded by a gilded frame so that it resembled a painting (see the sheet music cover in Fig. 10.1 which shows the drop curtain at the Haymarket).[39] It was a deliberate attempt to distance the actors from the audience to create a sense of illusion. This was another example of the way in which the arts in the West End referenced one another. It created a more restrained setting with actors and audience cut off from each other. The proscenium was an expression of respectable society. The Bancrofts also made other innovations;. they even paid for ladies' costumes, a major shift given that actors had previously often had to provide their own wardrobe. The Haymarket was meant to reek of prestige which is why they raised the salaries of actors.[40] The use

---

[36] *Building News*, 18 October 1867, p. 719.   [37] Maguire, 'C.J. Phipps', pp. 308, 310.

[38] Maguire, 'C.J. Phipps', p. 188; see Tracy C. Davis, 'Filthy-Nay-Pestilential: Sanitation and Victorian Theaters', in Della Pollock (ed.), *Exceptional Spaces: Essays in Performance and History* (Chapel Hill, NC: University of North Carolina Press, 1998), pp. 161–86.

[39] *Times*, 2 February 1880, p. 8; Squire Bancroft and Marie Wilton, *On and Off the Stage* (London: Richard Bentley, 1888), Vol. 2, pp. 196–7; Richard Southern, 'The Picture Frame Proscenium of 1880', *Theatre Notebook*, 5 (1951), pp. 59–61.

[40] Marie Tempest, 'Foreword' in W.H. Leverton (with J. B. Booth), *Through the Box-office Window: Memories of Fifty Years at the Haymarket Theatre* (London: T. Werner Laurie, 1932), p. 17.

Fig. 10.1 The Haymarket Polka (Michael Diamond Collection)

of the picture frame device also gained from the proximity of the Haymarket to the National Gallery and, as we saw in Chapter 8, to important centres of the Victorian art world.

Productions like *Ben Hur* required an industrial approach to stage production. They could only exist because of the plentiful supply of cheap labour. This took the form of hundreds of supernumeraries (or 'supers') for the large crowd scenes and an army of stagehands who were needed both to manage the stage machinery and to effect scene changes. Theatres were like factories. The Lyceum employed about 650 people in total to put on some of its productions.[41] Managing this required intense levels of organization. Bram Stoker recalled that running the Lyceum for Henry Irving involved him having to write fifty letters a day; the correspondence was endless.[42]

The main permanent roles backstage were the stage carpenter, property master, super-master, and wardrobe mistress (as well as some scene painters and a gas man). The stage carpenter was well paid because he also had to attend rehearsals and acted as a foreman, assembling different forms of labour to create a product. He made the scenery that would then be worked on by scene painters. He would also devise the ways in which the scenery would be moved on and off the stage, employing jobbing carpenters. The property master had to find and make the props. Many commenced their careers as shoemakers or engineers. The super-master was in charge of recruiting supernumeraries and drilling them in what was needed in the play. The gas man ensured that the stage was properly lit. The wardrobe mistress not only looked after costumes but oversaw an army of needle-women who were needed to create and maintain them. All these functions required a level of expertise which made them essential to the running of the theatre.[43] Their importance can be determined by their level of pay. A stage carpenter could expect four to five pounds a week whilst ordinary journeymen carpenters received twenty-five to thirty shillings. The property master received about two pounds a week whilst his assistant got twenty shillings. The wardrobe mistress received between thirty shillings and two pounds whilst seamstresses (classic examples of Victorian cheap labour) only got twelve shillings.[44] Figures, however, vary. We know that Arnott, the property master at the Lyceum, in 1881, received five pounds a week.[45]

---

[41] Alan Hughes, 'The Lyceum Staff: A Victorian Theatrical Organization', *Theatre Notebook*, 28 (1974), pp. 11–17.

[42] Bram Stoker, *Personal Reminiscences of Henry Irving* (London: William Heinemann, 1907 [1906]), p. 39.

[43] C.H. d'E. Leppington, 'The Gibeonites of the Stage: Work and Wages Behind the Scenes', *National Review*, 17 (1891), pp. 245–61.

[44] All figures derived from Leppington, 'The Gibeonites of the Stage', p. 261.

[45] Alan Hughes, 'The Lyceum Staff', p. 16.

Many, however, were employed on a temporary basis. Scene painters were employed for a particular production though, when leading artists took on this role, they expected a higher salary. Front of house was often staffed by people supplementing their income from a daytime job. The same was true of call boys backstage. Supernumeraries, the chorus, and the corps de ballet sometimes had daytime jobs. The Brigade of Guards provided supernumeraries for many London theatres. The work provided soldiers with some additional beer money and officers considered it good for discipline as it kept men out of mischief. Other supers worked during the day as porters and gas men. Bram Stoker did not want to employ people if this was their sole source of income as he considered them loafers (though supers also included some stage-struck young men and women desperate to tread the boards even if fleetingly). For the production of *The Lady of Lyons* at the Lyceum in 1879 a scene which required an army to march past at the back used real soldiers who would march across the stage and then run backstage and come on again at the same place to give the impression of constant movement.[46]

Children in plays often had parents who were actors. However, it was not unusual in London for the children of clerks and shopkeepers to be used. There was a clear class difference here. Cheaper theatres outside central London would employ working-class children whereas better off children would become actors in the West End.[47]

The key figure in the backstage world was the stage-door keeper. Of all the personnel in the theatre, it was his job to know everybody who worked there if only for reasons of security. Even big stars usually had to acknowledge his brief authority as they passed by. Mr Holloway at the Globe was one of the longest serving in the role. He virtually lived in the theatre, working from nine in the morning to eleven thirty at night with his family having to come and see him. He frequently had to use his huge size to see off stage-door Johnnies (including the use of violence) whilst employing his fierceness to see off aspiring actresses who wanted an interview with the manager.[48] James Jupp at the Gaiety was recruited from an army background which may have served him well. There was thus an enduring (and sometimes permanent) backstage and front of house staff at many theatres. The Gaiety was able to create its own football and cricket teams for social activities on Sundays when there was no performance.[49] Henry Irving adopted a paternalist approach to all staff. At Christmas, the cast as well as front of house and backstage workers each received a goose with all the trimmings and a bottle

[46] Stoker, *Personal Reminiscences*, p. 101.
[47] Leppington, 'The Gibeonites of the Stage', p. 254.
[48] *Sketch*, 8 August 1894, p. 96.
[49] James Jupp, *The Gaiety Stage Door: Thirty Years' Reminiscences of the Theatre* (London: Jonathan Cape, 1923), pp. 13, 268.

of gin (this was substituted with cake for the child performers).[50] Theatres were small communities.

Audiences

The Italian critic Mario Borsa in 1908 noted the common sight in the early evening at the main terminus station of trains disgorging well-dressed men and women bound for the theatre:

> through the foul, smoky, suffocating atmosphere of the station they thread their way—delicate visions of white, pale blue, or pink, in hoods or wraps of Japanese silk, embroidered slippers and fleecy boas, wrapped in their brocaded opera cloaks beneath which stray glimpses are caught of the lace and chiffon of evening bodices—on they flit, with a fantastic shimmer of pearls and diamonds, with a soft rustle of silks, satins, and tuile.

> These are the patrons of the stalls and the boxes, on their way to the theatre to see and be seen, who will finish up the evening gaily with champagne in the warm, brilliantly lighted, gilded saloons of the 'Cecil' and the 'Savoy'.[51]

The audience was clearly part of the West End spectacle; there was dressing up on the stage and in the auditorium. First nights became grand occasions. The social and cultural glitterati would attend and it was customary for supper to be served to invited guests afterwards often on the stage itself. Beerbohm Tree invited people to a room in the Carlton Hotel after first nights at Her Majesty's. Royalty would often be present; the royal box replete with white silk programmes.[52] When the young Molly Hughes (well known for her autobiographies featuring her Victorian childhood) was taken to see the farce *Betsy* at the Criterion, her middle-class mother put her in her 'nearest approach to an evening dress'. She was subsequently taken by her brothers to the grill room (probably the Criterion restaurant) which she recalled as being like 'something in the *Arabian Nights*' which conjures up the feel of a West End night out.[53]

Borsa noted how, on performance days, every London theatre featured a long queue waiting outside in all weathers for cheap tickets in the pit and the gallery. Who were these people? Borsa (not totally free of condescension) suspected they were 'shopmen, clerks, and spinsters in pince-nez; but more numerous still are the shopgirls, milliners, dressmakers, typists, stenographers, cashiers of large and

---

[50] Stoker, *Personal Reminiscences*, p. 202.   [51] Borsa, *The English Stage*, pp. 3–4.

[52] Cook, *Highways and Byways*, pp. 278–80.

[53] Molly Hughes, *A London Girl of the 1880s* (Oxford: Oxford University Press, 1978 [1946]), p. 16.

small houses of business, telegraph and telephone girls...'.[54] Theatre was still a way of life for all classes (except the poor). A. St John Adcock in 1902 depicted the spectacle of West End audiences at the end of the show as one of 'aristocrats and plebeians' including 'opera-cloaked ladies waiting for a bus'.[55]

Whilst West End theatre was heavily aimed at the middle-class audience, it is clear that all classes found something in the theatre. A shilling could give people access to Irving, Beerbohm Tree, and Ellen Terry. Booking for the theatre remained exclusive. Although the coming of the telephone made it easier in theory, only the well-off had this amenity. Bill Leverton, who managed the box office at the Haymarket, remembered the exclusionary tactics of Lacon and Ollier of Bond Street who specialized in providing high society with theatre tickets:

> Lacon's had a very distinguished clientèle, and Charles Ollier would not sell or allow to be sold in his office any other seats than the highest priced ones—orchestra stalls or private boxes. If a stranger entered, and dared ask for dress circle or—worse still—upper circle tickets, the venerable Mr Ollier would lead him courteously to the door, hold it wide open for his exit, and say, with infinite suavity: 'You will be able to buy that class of ticket opposite, at Messrs Blanks'.
>
> And the delicate emphasis with which he stressed the words 'that class of ticket' would reduce the vulgar stranger to perspiring shame.[56]

By the early twentieth century, firms like Lacon and Ollier had begun to sell all prices of tickets. Henry James obtained tickets from one of these West End agencies, noting how customers often included old ladies with a large carriage waiting outside who asked sweetly if a particular play was good. The clerk (who James thought had stepped out of a novel by Dickens or Thackeray) would say ' "It is thought very good, my lady"... as if he were uttering a "response" in church.'[57]

The majority of tickets were purchased in advance, and clearly status was important in terms of where one sat. Bill Leverton recalled a provincial gentleman at the Haymarket saying: 'I don't mind *what* I pay... but I do want to sit among the right sort of people. I shall be in full evening dress, and I don't want to be surrounded by a lot of fellows in cloth caps and girls with shawls over their heads.'[58] Men in West End theatres were usually expected to wear dress suits in the stalls and boxes. At Her Majesty's Theatre, evening dress was compulsory everywhere except the gallery, 'frock-coats and coloured trousers and cravats not

---

[54] Borsa, *The English Stage*, pp. 4–5.
[55] A. St John Adcock, 'Leaving the London Theatres', in George R. Sims (ed.), *Living London* (London: Cassell, 1902–3), Vol. 2.1, p. 10.
[56] Leverton, *Through the Box-office Window*, p. 27.
[57] Henry James, *The Scenic Art: Notes on Acting and the Drama, 1872–1901* (London: Rupert Hart-Davis, 1949), p. 100.
[58] Leverton, *Through the Box-office Window*, p. 145.

being admissable'.[59] This extended to front of house workers. Box office managers would wear morning suits during the day and then change to evening suits later on before the audience arrived. This enhanced the theatricality of the evening.

Figures like Bill Leverton played a major role as gatekeepers to West End pleasures. Managing the Haymarket box office meant that he worked his way during the day through the postal, personal, and telephone bookings. The evening involved checking the tickets from agencies, going through advance booking, and making up complete returns of the night's takings, including a record of complimentary tickets given away to the press and others. Tickets also had to be counted in the manager's office and made to tally with the box office statement and payment.[60] The Haymarket, he noted, had a loyal following but this was not sufficient to see it through if a play was bad. Saturday nights were predictably the most popular night, especially for people seeking cheaper seats.[61]

There was always a queue at the Lyceum which ran out onto the Strand, especially when Irving or Ellen Terry were playing. The queue for the Haymarket or Her Majesty's could reach up to Piccadilly Circus. Some would come prepared with campstools. Given that theatre-goers queued from early morning for the chance of seeing them play, Irving and Terry would have assistants take out tea and bread and butter at about four, an example of largesse which reveals how the relationship between an actor and the audience could even commence before entry to the theatre.[62] Reports suggest that the mood of the crowd was stoic and good humoured, perhaps sustained by the belief that it was composed of true theatre lovers. Newsboys eager to sell the latest edition and Italian organ grinders often turned up.[63] Queuing gave theatre a stronger feeling of a communal event.

As we have seen, the West End audience was often polite and passive but trouble could break out. If curtain-up was late, the pit and gallery got restless, making a din.[64] At the first night of *The Chalk Line* in 1912, a play demanding war preparations against a country that was clearly Germany, the authors were booed by people in the gallery (the *Standard* called it an 'unmannerly scene').[65] *Husband and Wife* was booed at the Wyndham's in 1904, leading to a fight breaking out. The theatre's gallery was shut for a month.[66] The boos following the first night of *Guy Domville* at the St James's in 1895 ensured that Henry James never wrote another play. There was a real attempt to ensure the atmosphere of the theatre was different from that of music hall and people were expected to behave in a different way. Irving (like most theatre managers) insisted there should be no smoking or

[59] E.L. Blanchard, *Bradshaw's Guide through London and its Environs 1862* (London: W.J. Adams, 1861), p. 102.
[60] Leverton, *Through the Box-office Window*, p. 118.
[61] Leverton, *Through the Box-office Window*, p. 158.
[62] *Graphic*, 30 January 1897, p. 133; Bram Stoker, *Personal Reminiscences*, p. 80.
[63] Borsa, *The English Stage*, p. 4.   [64] Cook, *Highways and Byways*, p. 280.
[65] *Standard*, 4 March, 1912, p. 4.   [66] Borsa, *The English Stage*, pp. 12–13.

drinking in the auditorium (the very things that made music hall attractive to many), arguing that the ban 'was absolutely and vitally necessary for the safeguarding of the dramatic art'. He was also dismissive of the income drawn from the bar and the sale of opera glasses which only amounted to about a quarter of total receipts.[67] Most theatres had a separate smoking room for men to use in the interval as it was clear that ladies objected to the practice.[68]

A perennial problem was ladies' hats, especially as fashion ran to millinery that got ever grander, sometimes adorned with a plumed bird. Management in programmes asked women to remove their bonnets and hats for the enjoyment of people sitting behind them.[69] Ralph Blumenfeld was actually contacted by Beerbohm Tree for journalistic assistance in trying to get women to remove their picture hats in theatres. He would later encounter the problem when he went to see *A Woman of Kronstadt* at the Garrick in 1908:

> Mostyn Piggott, who was with me at the Garrick, got into a little difficulty with the escort of a lady in front of us. She was in evening dress, but wore a large picture hat, and appeared to be disinclined to remove it; so that first Mostyn could not see the stage. He leaned over and asked her to remove the hat, which she did only after considerable demur and some rather exaggerated exchange of compliments. The escort then took a hand, and, turning round, said 'You are very impolite, sir!' Mostyn answered sweetly: 'You are of course, a nice little gentleman.' The lady said, 'Shut up, 'Enry' and we had peace.[70]

Theatres were designed ostensibly to address high society and high fashion (including the importance of spaces for carriages outside). We might see them as a buffer zone which translated an aristocratic idiom to a wider public. It explains why the West End experience mixed populism and deference.

Critics and Playwrights

The relationship of an audience member with a play begins often with a review (or a poster) that draws him or her to the theatre. The shift towards realism and naturalism made reviewing something more than it had been. Figures like George Bernard Shaw were drawn into theatre criticism both to make money but also to conduct an argument about what theatre might be.

---

[67] Report from the Select Committee on Theatres and Places of Entertainment (1892), pp. 64, 65.
[68] Report from the Select Committee on Theatres and Places of Entertainment (1892), p. 58.
[69] See, for example, the 1908 programme for *Dolly Reforming Herself* at the Haymarket (Victoria and Albert Museum Theatre Collection).
[70] Ralph D. Blumenfeld, *R.D.B.'s Diary, 1887–1914* (London: Heinemann, 1930), pp. 69, 216.

The dominant critic of the later nineteenth century was Clement Scott of the *Daily Telegraph*. Scott's aesthetic conservatism was at odds with his deep love of the stage. He possessed the gift, as would Kenneth Tynan in the twentieth century, of making theatre seem important and thus was an important figure in the making of the West End. He believed that theatre had reached its perfection in the plays of Tom Robertson in the mid-Victorian period with their wit and sophistication. Scott commenced in satirical journalism and was originally the theatre critic for the *Sunday Times* where his savage reviews upset the theatre community. In 1878 he commenced a long period as reviewer for the *Daily Telegraph*. Here he championed the heroic acting style of Henry Irving. The two became good friends which no doubt raised questions about his independence. Similar questions might be raised about his relationship with the Bancrofts for whom he translated a number of plays. He became a notable West End figure with his fur coat, white waistcoat, flower in the buttonhole, and love of scent which was apparently quite overpowering. His relationship with Beerbohm Tree soured over the first night of *Trilby*. Scott was accustomed to a box but that night the demand for boxes was so high that two stalls tickets were sent over. The *Daily Telegraph* was the only paper not to feature a review the next day. Scott seems to have bought himself two seats for the next night and penned a positive notice for the day after but the breach between him and Tree was never healed.[71] Like Irving, he disliked Ibsen (who, he thought, brought sordid motives into the theatre) and indeed anything that foregrounded the woman question. Scott was thus in his own way as much a censor as the Lord Chamberlain.

Despite the objections of Scott, the stage was beginning to change. The first appearance of Ibsen in the West End was, surprisingly, in a matinee at the Gaiety. John Hollingshead employed the afternoons to try out serious plays in contrast to the burlesques and light entertainment in the evening. On 15 December 1880 he put on *Quicksands or the Pillars of Society* in a translation by the critic William Archer, one of Ibsen's great champions in Britain. The play did not make much impact. Henry Arthur Jones and Henry Herman penned an adaptation of *A Doll's House* at the Princess's in 1884 under the title, *Breaking a Butterfly*. The play's feminism was stripped out. The version performed had more in common with the socially conservative plays that Jones normally put out. Archer went on to translate and direct Ibsen's *A Doll's House* at the Novelty Theatre in 1889, *Ghosts* at the Royalty in 1891, and then *Hedda Gabler* at the Vaudeville which starred the actress Elizabeth Robins.

George Bernard Shaw's plays became part of his campaign to bring a new seriousness to the drama that was lacking in the West End and some were performed outside it; *Major Barbara* commenced in 1905 at the Royal Court. His great West

---

[71] Leverton, *Through the Box-office Window*, pp. 70–2.

End smash hit was *Pygmalion* in 1914 at Her Majesty's (though its first performance was in Vienna) but this was very much perceived as a comic vehicle for its stars, Mrs Patrick Campbell and Herbert Beerbohm Tree who played Eliza Doolittle and Henry Higgins.

During the later nineteenth century, Shaw, and others, began to argue for a National Theatre. The campaign would take another half a century to succeed but it represented a rejection of the kind of theatre that existed in the West End. There was a demand for realism and psychological complexity as well as a need to address the major social questions of the day. Attempts were made to create alternatives to the West End; for example, the New Century Theatre project which William Archer and Elizabeth Robins established in 1897. It was not successful. More serious theatre did begin to emerge outside the West End in the shape of Harley Granville Barker's plays such as *The Voysey Inheritance* (1905) at the Court Theatre. The Lord Chamberlain banned Barker's play *Waste* (1907), requiring that it be staged by the Stage Society. It was problematic because it dealt with an MP's affair with a married woman who dies after an abortion. The West End therefore resisted change. Theatre was both shaped by the Lord Chamberlain, the views of theatre owners, and the relatively conservative taste of theatre-goers of all classes. For that reason, it shines a light on British manners and culture.

Pleasure at Her Majesty's

Charles Phipps's last major project was to rebuild Her Majesty's Theatre on the Haymarket. Let us look more closely at the theatre as it expressed the dynamic of the new West End theatre. Opening in 1897, it was part of a larger complex with the Carlton Hotel (later destroyed by aerial bombardment in 1940). Phipps died during construction and the hotel was completed in July 1899 by the architects Lewis H. Isaacs and Henry L. Florence, maintaining Phipps's design. Formerly, the West End's major opera house, the new Her Majesty's Theatre was designed to express the vision of the great actor-manager Herbert Beerbohm Tree. The financing of the theatre remains slightly murky. Tree claimed to have been the proprietor and his theatre was intended to provide a home for the spectacular images in his imagination.

The visual impact of Her Majesty's expressed the new West End focus on cultivated style, luxury, and comfort (see Fig. 10.2). The building thus carried a substantial psychic charge. For some it was an opportunity to enter what felt like one of the grand houses of Mayfair a few minutes' walk away. The exterior, built in French Renaissance style, was executed in Portland stone and red granite. At the top was a huge dome covered in copper. Inside, the curtain featured a reproduction of the Gobelin tapestry of Dido receiving Aeneas. The proscenium was made

Fig. 10.2 Her Majesty's Theatre, London (Michael Diamond Collection)

up of *Brèche Violette* marble with ormolu mountings and the stage could move up and down in sections.

The auditorium, designed by Romaine Walker, the leading interior decorator, took its inspiration from Louis XIV, adopting a combination of red, gold, and blue in its colour scheme. There were hangings of cerise-coloured embroidered silk with wall paper of a similar colour. The carpet was blue. The use of the colour red varied. The curtain and drapery had a subdued rose colour whilst the red of the seats was much brighter.[72] Seating in the stalls, dress, and family circles took the form of armchairs. Even the pit at the back of the stalls had armrests. Overhead were velvet hangings and a large glass electrolier (chandelier). There were good sight lines for the entire house with no obscuring pillars as each tier was built on iron cantilevers. The galleries curved so that no part of the house was too far from the stage, creating a space that was both grand and intimate. In the front of house, there were footmen wearing breeches and stockings. A new ventilation system kept the entire house at sixty-two degrees through the year. The house used only electricity without a gas back-up which proclaimed its modernity, despite the architectural style.[73]

Her Majesty's represented a shift in theatre construction as it reduced the number of boxes; there were only three on either side of the stage. Beerbohm Tree told a reporter he did not believe in them and, anyway, they did not pay (he had also reduced the number of boxes at the Haymarket).[74] This was a theatre that looked aristocratic but was aimed at the middle classes. The seats ranged from £4 4 s 6d for the most expensive box to 10s 6d for the stalls and five shillings for the balcony. This could clearly only have been afforded by a middle-class theatre-goer. On the other hand, the pit cost 2s 6d, the upper circle had seats at 4s, 3s, and 2s and the gallery would only set one back 1s for a ticket, which allowed for the possibility of some working-class theatre-goers, though even a shilling would have been too much for the poorest in 1897. One theatre-goer we know about is Hesketh Pearson, later an actor and biographer. He first saw Beerbohm Tree in *Nero* at Her Majesty's in 1908 while he was a humble clerk in a shipping company in the City. He would thereafter often sit in the pit or upper circle, which suggests that people of limited means could find their way into Her Majesty's.[75]

The whole building was a statement about refinement. A large number of paintings on the walls featured the owner in his major roles.[76] Her Majesty's felt like a temple to Beerbohm Tree. At the same time, this use of paintings had a particular narrative effect. It offered a statement that a building has continuity with a larger tradition of theatre and encouraged regular theatre-goers to develop a narrative of their own life as one punctuated by being present at a succession of great stage moments and theatres. In some respects such paintings had an iconic effect not dissimilar to the use of pictures and statues in a church. Alternatively, the use of paintings, playbills, and photographs from previous productions in

[72] *Pall Mall Gazette*, 22 April 1897, p. 3.

[73] *Builder*, 13 March 1897, p. 251; *Building News*, 30 April 1897, p. 629; 14 May 1897, p. 703; *Morning Post*, 26 April 1897, p. 6; Michael R. Booth, *Victorian Spectacular Theatre, 1850–1910* (London: Routledge and Kegan Paul, 1981), p. 135.

[74] *Pall Mall Gazette*, 22 April 1897, p. 3.

[75] Hesketh Pearson, *Beerbohm Tree: His Life and Laughter* (London: Columbus Books, 1988 [1956]), p. 201.

[76] David Schulz, 'The Architecture of Conspicuous Consumption: Property, Class, and Display at Herbert Beerbohm Tree's Her Majesty's Theatre', *Theatre Journal*, 51 (1999), pp. 238–9.

West End theatres encouraged a view of them as haunted houses—haunted by the ghosts of generations of performers. This is part of the discourse of the West End.

The programmes at Her Majesty's were also particularly sumptuous, going beyond the bare cast list that one purchased at other theatres such as the Criterion. At other theatres, programmes contained lots of advertising for local firms. Beerbohm Tree clearly would not accept anything as vulgar as advertising in his programmes which featured elaborately staged photographs and essays on the play. In the cast list at Her Majesty's, the full names of the performers were given whereas the lead performer was always 'Mr Tree'.[77] Programmes were also issued for each specific day with the date prominent on each.

Even George Bernard Shaw was impressed: 'Nobody can say of Her Majesty's that it proclaims itself a place built by a snob for the entertainment of snobs with snobbish plays. It rises spaciously and brilliantly to the dignity of art…'[78] Yet class did shape the way people experienced the theatre. Shaw Desmond remembered the early years of Her Majesty's in this way:

The powdered flunkeys with the balustrade calves and, as I remember, in royal red. The oil paintings, like Tree himself, larger than life. The staircases. The carefully relegated grades and prices of seats. Her Majesty's had the taste of the real thing, and not one of us who paid our 4s., 3s., or 2s., the three degrees of the Upper Circle, but felt regal, or at least as 'select' as any stall-holder in any other theatre.

The upper circles had, each, their several degrees of flavour. Earnest young teachers; slightly impecunious virgins in their thirties and forties; city clerks with stage aspirations. The Fabian socialist, a young man with long dark hair and midnight oil in his face, frightfully earnest but nonchalant. Bevies of the first of the flappers, just beginning to 'flap' and secretly in love with Gerald Lawrence or Basil Gill—never with Tree, for no one ever dared to love *him*. 'Adore' him—yes; 'love' him—no.

Everything at 'Her Majesty's' was 'done decently and in order, as the prayer book has it. The free programmes were handed around like prayer books.[79]

The theatre flattered an audience drawn from diverse sections of society with its shows and with its design and architecture, offering itself as high art in commercial form. The building itself was intended to induce an emotional response. As the playwright Louis Parker argued, 'there was always an indefinable air of princely hospitality about (Her) Majesty's. The public felt that they were getting

---

[77] See, for example, the programme for *A Midsummer Night's Dream* performed on 10 January 1900, preserved in the British Library (call mark 1874.b.4).

[78] George Bernard Shaw, *Our Theatres in the Nineties* (London: Constable, 1932), Vol. 3, p. 118.

[79] Shaw Desmond, *London Nights of Long Ago* (London: Duckworth, 1927), pp. 194–5.

something beyond their money's worth, in the way of comfort, of consideration, of elegance.'[80] Beerbohm Tree's daughter Viola (also an actress) related that the size of Her Majesty's became a problem for her father after the relative compactness of the Haymarket. He had to maintain a large staff and to put on plays geared up for spectacle. He lost out on producing more intimate dramas.[81]

Critics frequently discuss plays without reference to the built environment that shapes the audience response. At Her Majesty's and other West End theatres, people experienced drama through very specific frames. Beerbohm Tree's building was a frame proclaiming itself a temple of high art; its footmen in livery giving it an *ancien régime* feeling. The marble proscenium was another frame. The theatre's claim to cultural authority was reinforced by its long history dating back to 1705 and its existence as London's home of opera and High Society. We should see buildings like Her Majesty's as having an active function, rather than simply one that is reflective of social values. Like the West End as a whole, it constructed an idea of what theatre should be; everything else was alien.

Shaw Desmond's claim that even the audience in the upper circle at Her Majesty's felt 'regal' and 'select' expresses the psychic charge of the environment Beerbohm Tree helped create. It explains the magic that drew suburban dwellers from their homes of an evening, turning theatre into an object of reverence and seriousness. At the same time it is evident that such West End theatres were controlled environments. Beerbohm Tree had a strong sense of what he wanted his audience to feel when they walked through the doors of his theatre. A night at the theatre is never just the play itself. The theatre itself does a lot of the work in structuring the audience experience as does the atmosphere of the pleasure district. West End playhouses acquired the status that had previously attached itself to the patent theatres in the early nineteenth century. Their obsession with hierarchy, prestige, and social class mapped onto the cultural requirements of an imperial metropolis.

---

[80] Beerbohm, *Herbert Beerbohm Tree*, p. 213.   [81] Beerbohm, *Herbert Beerbohm Tree*, p. 175.

11

The Populist Palatial

Otium cum Dignitate

In 1861, the Oxford Music Hall first opened its doors on the site of what had been the Boar and Castle Coaching Inn on Oxford Street. The brainchild of entrepreneur Charles Morton, it commenced as a simple stage with gas footlights and a small band. The audience entered through a Corinthian portico which drew it up towards a spectacular grand staircase. Within the auditorium, there was a roomy promenade and a picture gallery (from where the show could be seen) and a bar. A trapeze was thrown across the ceiling. The opera singer Charles Santley performed on the opening night and became a strong draw. The *Morning Chronicle* described it as a 'music hall for the million' and noted that it was aiming higher than similar venues, with its eye on a middle-class audience.[1] John Earl, the great scholar of theatre architecture, describes the Oxford as the 'first cathedral of the music halls', bringing pub and music hall together in one unit and outshining comparable venues.[2] Its stars included the dancers John and Emma D'Auban, Mr Eugen (who danced in female clothing), the cockney comedian Harry Liston, the Great Vance, and George Leybourne, who became known for his song 'Champagne Charlie'.[3] At the same time, its selections from Verdi operas such as *La Traviata* were also popular.[4]

The Oxford was visited the year after it opened by Arthur Munby who contrasted it with the halls he knew in Islington and elsewhere. The audience was of a higher social standing though it included businessmen and clerks 'of no very refined aspect':

One result of this was that the women present were whores, instead of respectable wives & sweethearts. Therefore, another result was, that there was nothing wholesome or genial in the folks' enjoyment: they drank their grog staring gloomily or lewdly grimacing.

---

[1] *Musician and Music-Hall Times*, 28 May 1862, p. 2; *Daily News*, 27 March 1861, p. 2; *Morning Chronicle*, 27 March 1861, p. 7.
[2] John Earl, 'Building the Halls', in Peter Bailey (ed.), *Music Hall: The Business of Pleasure* (Milton Keynes: Oxford University Press, 1986), p. 22.
[3] *Musician and Music-Hall Times*, 28 May 1862, p. 2; W.H. Morton and H. Chance Newton, *Sixty Years' Stage Service: Being a Record of the Life of Charles Morton, the Father of the Halls* (London: Gale and Polden, 1905), pp. 61–3.
[4] *Musician and Music-Hall Times*, 28 June 1862, p. 46.

London's West End: Creating the Pleasure District, 1800–1914. Rohan McWilliam, Oxford University Press (2020).
© Rohan McWilliam.
DOI: 10.1093/oso/9780198823414.001.0001

Munby thought the content of the Oxford was the same as at less elevated establishments. This, he concluded, was the point. The Oxford had the appeal of the free-and-easy but with 'a certain pretence of refinement and splendour' (see Fig. 11.1). In particular, the selections from opera placed the audience briefly on a level with their social superiors and thus appealed to their vanity.[5] Munby here expressed the condescension of his class. Different cultural forms were mixed in the pleasure district. Opera intersected with popular culture; many working-class listeners enjoyed selections from individual works.

The Oxford Music Hall claimed to be the 'only Grand Music Hall where the public can enjoy *Otium cum Dignitate* and can, without vexatious constraint, Sup, Drink and Smoke at Pleasure.'[6] *Otium cum Dignitate* is a phrase associated with Cicero and means 'leisure with dignity'. The rhetoric of comfort and hospitality was a characteristic of pleasure districts as a whole (as we will see when we examine hotels and restaurants).

We might call the cultural style that West End music hall developed the 'populist palatial'. This style united performer and audience: it was about atmosphere, fashion, and indulgence on a grand scale, the possibility of a night out in epic surroundings. Everyone could get to spend at least an evening in a palace. I argue that the populist palatial style was a major force shaping the West End. It contained forms of aspiration and justified the expense and frequent challenges of a journey into town (even though music halls in the suburbs could often be lavish as well). From the 1860s, we see the creation of spectacular music halls in the West End that flattered audiences by creating a sense of prestige and luxury. They followed the style etched by the grandeur of Drury Lane and Covent Garden, built to welcome large audiences. But the populist palatial was not just a matter of buildings. It represented an approach to entertainment and performance that was elevated but in tune with popular culture; respectable but prepared to push the boundaries of taste and morality with its acknowledgement of low-life pleasures. This did not prevent artists and intellectuals from frequenting music halls; Oscar Wilde and Walter Sickert counted as fans.[7] One function of the populist palatial (and indeed of pleasure districts as a whole) was to create these kind of cross-class encounters.

Significantly, the style coincided with the emergence of the term 'classy' in the later nineteenth century to mean 'sophisticated', 'stylish', and of a superior class. The Oxford English Dictionary finds that the first use of the term was in

[5] Derek Hudson (ed.), *Munby: Man of Two Worlds* (London: Abacus, 1974), pp. 119–20.

[6] Peter Bailey, 'Entertainmentality: Liberalizing Modern Pleasure in the Victorian Leisure Industry', in Simon Gunn and James Vernon (eds), *The Peculiarities of Liberal Modernity in Imperial Britain* (Berkeley, CA: University of California Press, 2011), p. 127.

[7] Barry J. Faulk, *Music Hall and Modernity: The Late Victorian Discovery of Popular Culture* (Athens, OH: Ohio University Press, 2004).

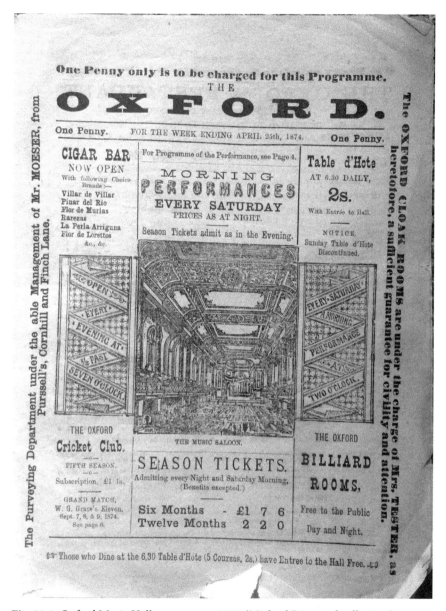

Fig. 11.1 Oxford Music Hall programme, 1874 (Michael Diamond collection)

H.J. Byron's play, *Cyril's Success* (1870), which was about a West End playwright.[8] West End entertainments were intended to reek of classiness. The populist palatial style was not confined to London but became a characteristic of pleasure districts elsewhere. The West End was, however, a template for the spectacularization

---

[8] H.J. Byron, *Cyril's Success* (London: Samuel French, 1870), p. iii.

of entertainment. The information that a performer or an act had played the West End was a mark of prestige and flattered audiences.

This chapter deals with the West End music hall, and focuses specifically on one location, the London Pavilion on Piccadilly Circus. The next chapter considers the broader world of light entertainment. Although there is clearly a major overlap, I describe upmarket venues such as the Alhambra and the Empire in Leicester Square as 'variety houses' rather than music halls and hence place them in the following chapter. Both chapters aim to take 'classiness' seriously and demonstrate its role in popular culture. They also further demonstrate how forms of conservatism were threaded through mass entertainment.

Patrick Joyce has described the popular understanding of what the city might have to offer as 'townology'.[9] This expresses something of the liberating set of emotions that urban mass culture released. Joyce finds townology in the press and in urban guides but music hall and the variety theatre were, we might say, 'townological entertainments'. The argument here is that West End music hall and light entertainment became spaces which audiences visited in order to try out different forms of identity. It was not just that they liked the songs; it was about the lifestyle that seemed to accompany it: carefree, clothes-conscious, suspicious of high-mindedness, avid for the gratification of desire, in love with the big city. As Peter Bailey says of music hall, 'Like the theatre it reduced the promiscuous social mix of city streets to some kind of territorial order while keeping open mutual contact of sight and sound among its different social elements. In this setting, the crowd were as much producers and consumers of a form of social drama, in which styles and identities were tried out and exchanged...'[10] The West End produced a form of mass entertainment that, it proclaimed, was truly national and integrative.

The libertarian spirit is captured by an image that featured on the back of the programmes at the Empire (discussed in the next chapter). In Fig. 11.2 , the dancing girl with the tambourine expresses the reverse of female passivity. Her crooked dancing posture, brief skirt, and raised feet proclaim a bacchanalian world; her backward glance is (one suspects) brief as she leaps forward and away from the viewer. The observer's eye pivots down the line of her leg.

The dancer was an image for male delectation but the West End also contained possibilities of female self-expression.[11] The presence of female performers speaking with humour and a sense of agency made these spaces transformative. If the West End was a conservative space in many ways, the representations it produced were often female, appealing to a female audience. Women were both sources of

---

[9]   Patrick Joyce, *The Rule of Freedom: Liberalism and the Modern City* (London: Verso, 2003), p. 204.

[10]   Peter Bailey, 'Introduction: Making Sense of the Music Hall', in Bailey, *Music Hall*, p. xvii.

[11]   Susan Glenn, *Female Spectacle: The Theatrical Roots of Modern Feminism* (Cambridge, MA: Harvard University Press, 2000).

Fig. 11.2 The back of an 1890s Empire Variety programme (London Metropolitan Archives)

glamour but also could also be shown to have the best jokes, not least because they offered comedy based on social observation in as acute a way as male performers. This was not peculiar to the area's world of fun but it was an important part of it and one that connected to the other ways women were entering the pleasure district. West End entertainments needed to be rooted in popular experience (so that audiences could recognize them) and yet to offer a transformation of those experiences as well into a fantasy realm. This became the idiom of music hall. The music hall artist Jenny Hill (as we will discover) made much of coming from the streets and yet performed street life in palatial settings.

The West End influenced the emergence of suburban and provincial music halls. Its own halls, however, differed from elsewhere. The poet Arthur Symons wrote to the *Star* in 1891 insisting that music halls were not all the same. He contrasted the boisterous scenes at the Metropolitan in Edgware with Gatti's in Charing Cross where 'high spirits have given place to something like sentimentality, with a more conventional kind of farce in the comic songs and dances'. Gatti's, in turn, was different from the London Pavilion whose audience, he claimed, rarely joined in the chorus. Symons counselled readers of the *Star* to see Katie

Lawrence not at Gatti's (where she was playing) but at the Metropolitan where 'her gaminerie was just in its element'.[12]

West End music hall was more respectable and a bit more tame than elsewhere. Marie Lloyd found that some songs went better in the West End than the East. Her satire of rational dress was not understood in Hoxton; what suited the audience was her song 'The Rich Girl and the Poor'. At the Pavilion, her burlesque of *Trilby* went down very well with an audience who had seen the original round the corner at the Haymarket. When she did it at Sadler's Wells, the audience did not get the jokes.[13] It is, however, not fruitful to see the West End music hall as a deviation from the allegedly more authentic working-class music hall of the East End and elsewhere. Few art forms are authentic, in the sense of emerging from 'the people' in any clearly defined or straightforward way. This chapter instead tracks some of the distinctive qualities of West End music hall and the populist palatial style.

The West End Music Hall

The West End contained some of the most successful music halls in London including the London Pavilion, the Tivoli on the Strand, Gatti's Charing Cross Music Hall (Gatti's Under the Arches), the Middlesex Music Hall in Drury Lane (on the site of the present day Gillian Lynne Theatre), the Trocadero, and the Oxford. The nature of these music halls differed and they had different audiences. They were, however, very lucrative. The London Pavilion in 1881 took £29,070 13s 9d at the doors with a further £11,777 2s 3d through its bars. This reveals how the income from drink was important to the halls (just over 28 per cent of the Pavilion's total £40, 847 16s). By 1891 the Pavilion took £51, 741 12s 5d on the doors with £13, 969 12s 3d from drink, making a total of £65, 711 4s 8d. Its total value as a business and building was estimated at £307,000 in 1892; its share capital was £180,000.[14]

West End music hall had some of the features of entertainment elsewhere but provided in an atmosphere of luxury. This meant that it could draw in all classes and ages, making a trip up to the West End an ideal occasion for a family outing or for courtship. The West End version of music hall grew out of Evans's in Covent Garden (see Chapter 3) although it is clear that music halls were already emerging in other British cities by that time. In 1847, the Mogul Saloon (originally a pub) opened on Drury Lane, setting up a model of popular entertainment that also reeked of prestige. Its interior was an optical sorbet of ornamentation, though it

---

[12] Karl Beckson and John M. Munro (eds), *Arthur Symons: Selected Letters, 1880–1935* (Basingstoke: Macmillan, 1989), p. 86: see also Arthur Symons, 'An Artist in Serio-comedy: Katie Lawrence', *Star*, 26 March 1892, p. 4.

[13] *Sketch*, 25 December 1895, p. 452.

[14] Report from the Select Committee on Theatres and Places of Entertainment (1892), pp. 252, 253.

was continually being rebuilt and enlarged. In 1851 it became the Middlesex Music Hall but remained colloquially known as the 'Old Mo', keeping its origins as a pub alive in popular memory. Dan Leno appeared there, singing 'Milk for the Twins' in 1872. The venue also proved the making of Marie Lloyd as a music hall star.[15]

The *Musical World* (champion of classical music) denounced the halls for their 'low vulgarities', noting that they were merely 'adjuncts to pot-houses' (pubs).[16] Music hall audiences seemed to differ from those in the theatre. People could stroll into a music hall whenever they wanted whilst by the late Victorian period the theatre audience was subject to time discipline, being expected to turn up at the correct time and spend the evening there. There were also different protocols including dress for the male audience member. As Mario Borsa noted, 'while for the theatre he must array himself in evening dress, he may attend the music-hall in the same garments in which he left the City'.[17] There was, however, some overlap in the audiences. James Graydon, manager of the Middlesex music hall, claimed that he would get customers coming in around eleven who had just been to the theatre.[18] Henry Irving argued that music hall ('which is really a tavern') lowered dramatic art. The Alhambra in his view was merely an extension of the drink interest.[19] At the same time, even legitimate theatres had their moments of vaudeville, particularly when it came to pantomime, which regularly employed music hall artistes.

The issue of obscenity separated the music hall from the theatre which was subject to the censorship of the Lord Chamberlain. Music halls argued that they acted as their own censors. Any artiste who sang an obscene song would be fined; Marie Lloyd (as we will see below) was often in trouble because of her use of the double entendre and the knowing wink. It was, however, very difficult for music hall managers to control their own performers.

Music halls fostered the emergence of the agent who would not only book acts but also talent spot. Hugh Jay Didcott's agency in Covent Garden was worth about £10,000 a year in 1890. According to Henry Hibbert, Didcott took 'performers from soldier sing-songs, from Margate sands, from East End music halls, from penny gaffs' and rehearsed, dressed and promoted them, turning some into stars. Didcott was a former actor and well-heeled man about town who would conduct a lot of business at Romano's restaurant on the Strand where he proved a connoisseur of cigars.[20] He could afford good cigars because he managed most of the leading music hall stars of the period and thus was as decisive a figure as any of the great entrepreneurs such as Charles Morton. There were also firms such as

[15] Henry George Hibbert, *Fifty Years of a Londoner's Life* (London: Grant Richards, 1916), p. 48.
[16] *Musical World*, 1 February 1862, p. 72.
[17] Mario Borsa, *The English Stage of To-Day* (London: John Lane, 1908), p. 19.
[18] Report from the Select Committee on Theatres and Places of Entertainment (1892), p. 197.
[19] Report from the Select Committee on Theatres and Places of Entertainment (1892), pp. 64–5.
[20] Hibbert, *Fifty Years*, pp. 143–5.

Warner and Co. (at one time on Wellington Street, Covent Garden), the Theatrical and Vaudeville Exchange on Panton Street, or the International Theatrical and Variety Agents on Cranbourn Street who handled international ballet stars.[21] Theatrical and music hall agents became a major part of the West End economy, although quite a few were headquartered across the river in Waterloo.[22]

West End music halls overlapped with, but differed from, entertainments elsewhere in the city and throughout the country. In working-class areas, music halls and melodrama houses often validated working-class life and gave expression to the ways in which society was becoming more diverse, with Irish and Jewish comedians, for example, becoming a feature of the Britannia Music Hall in Glasgow.[23] The West End certainly offered images of working-class life but served up for a middle-class audience. It stressed the fulfilment of individual aspirations rather than the collective.[24]

The London Pavilion

The London Pavilion (Piccadilly Circus) originally started as an extension of the Black Horse Inn on Tichbourne Street and was built in 1859. It covered the old court yard with a glass roof and included a rifle gallery and bowling alley along with its concert hall. The owners Ernst Loibl and Charles Sonnhammer were also the proprietors of the oyster emporium on Coventry Street that later became famous as Scott's. Music hall was therefore inseparable both from the pub and the restaurant. The Pavilion's strong central location made it a major draw and it was quickly expanded. Doors opened at seven but six American bowling alleys were open from noon. Amongst its early acts, audiences could hear selections from *Il Travatore* as well as catch 'ballets divertissements', black minstrels, Helena Stuart, the serio-comic, and Jolly John Nash.[25] The contract for Pavilion artistes included the clause that all performers must wear white kid gloves (unless doing character songs) and that anyone who turned up with a black eye was subject to dismissal.[26]

The site was taken over by the Metropolitan Board of Works in 1885 when Shaftesbury Avenue was constructed and the Pavilion was transformed into a

[21] Will Collins to Alfred Moul, 19 December 1912: THM/75/3/18; A. Braff to Alfred Moul, 23 March 1911: THM 75/4/4/12: Alhambra Moul Collection (Victoria and Albert Museum Theatre and Performance Archives).

[22] Charles Douglas Stuart and A.J. Park, *The Variety Stage: A History of the Music Halls from the Earliest Period to the Present Time* (London: T. Fisher Unwin, 1895), pp. 128–42.

[23] Paul Maloney, *The Britannia Panopticon Music Hall and Cosmopolitan Entertainment Culture* (Basingstoke: Palgrave Macmillan, 2016); see also Clare Robinson, 'Popular Theatre in Manchester', (University of Birmingham PhD thesis, 2015).

[24] Lawrence Senelick, 'Politics as Entertainment: Victorian Music Hall Songs', *Victorian Studies* 19 (1975), pp. 149–80.

[25] 1872 programme in MM/2/TH/LO/PAV/2 (University of Bristol Theatre Collection).

[26] *Sketch*, 15 November 1893, p. 136.

purpose-built, luxurious music hall on the rebuilt Piccadilly Circus (see Fig. 11.3). The classical exterior expressed the seriousness of high culture, elevating the tone of the more demotic entertainment within. It included a buffet on the ground floor, a public dining room on the first floor (paneled in walnut), and private dining rooms for the elite on the second floor.[27] There were bars on either side of

Fig. 11.3 The London Pavilion 1904 (author collection)

---

[27] *Builder*, 26 December 1885, p. 911.

the stage.[28] In other words, it offered a night out all in one: food, drink, and entertainment. The building was also fitted with lifts and electric light which made it feel modern.

The London Pavilion embodied the luxury associated with West End music hall. It shifted the emphasis away from the pub with its small tables and replaced it with a more conventional auditorium, tip-up seats (a novelty), and luxury. This included small shelves for glasses added to the backs of seats. Patter and inter-action with the audience was reduced and the role of the Chairman, who con-trolled the evening's entertainment, was abolished.[29] A further redevelopment in 1900 raked the auditorium (which had previously been flat) so as to improve sightlines and the bars were moved to the basement. The interior was decorated in the Louis XV style.[30]

The Pavilion came to dominate Piccadilly Circus and shape the West End more broadly. With the Criterion Theatre and restaurant opposite, the London Pavilion made the presence of the pleasure district visible on Piccadilly Circus, a proclam-ation of the populist palatial. The improved facilities seem to have made the Pavilion more attractive to women, who had been repelled by the pub-like atmos-phere of the original establishment. The owner of the new version of the Pavilion, Robert Edwin Villiers, immediately sold it to what became the basis of the first music hall syndicate (Syndicate Halls Limited).[31] As a company it had a large number of shareholders.[32] Edward Swanborough took over from Villiers and his flamboyance made the new Pavilion.

The intention was to pursue a more upscale audience. This is evident in the programmes which struck a romantic and arcadian feel with dancing figures and minstrels (see Figs 11.4a and 11.4b).[33] Such imagery (not unusual in music hall programmes) gave the Pavilion a utopian dimension as well as a form of preten-sion to high culture. In the imagery of the programme, the evening promised to be gentle and feminine.

In 1886, it was possible to get into the London Pavilion on the day for one shill-ing and 1/6d in the promenade (previously a cheap seat was 6d). This allowed skilled workers and the lower-middle-class to attend. Reserved seats were five shillings, aimed at a wealthier clientele, whilst private boxes ranged from a guinea to £3 3s, which meant that members of the aristocracy and the very rich would

---

[28] Charles B. Cochran, 'The Dear Old Pav', 1945 magazine cutting in MM/2/TH/LO/PAV (University of Bristol Theatre Collection).

[29] Archibald Haddon, *The Story of the Music Hall: From Cave of Harmony to Cabaret* (London: Fleetwood, 1935), pp. 66–7; Earl, 'Building the Halls', in Bailey, *Music Hall*, p. 27.

[30] MM/2/TH/LO/PAV (University of Bristol Theatre Collection).

[31] Haddon, *The Story of Music Hall*, p. 66.

[32] H.A. Graham, Lonsdale Chambers, to H. de La Hooke, LCC, 18 September 1889: LCC Theatres Committee London Pavilion, 1888–1903: LCC/MIN/10/10, 846 (London Metropolitan Archives).

[33] 1899 and 1901 London Pavilion programmes in MM/2/TH/LO/PAV/2 (University of Bristol Theatre Collection).

Fig. 11.4a London Pavilion programme (author collection)

also be present.[34] These boxes could be booked at Mitchell's Library, 33 Old Bond Street, which meant that they remained part of a system of elite theatre booking.[35] The effect was to create a heterogeneous audience with poorer people regarding a night out at the London Pavilion as a special occasion. This was a distinctive

---

[34] Information derived from 1886 London Pavilion poster in the Evanion Collection at the British Library: https://www.bl.uk/catalogues/evanion/Record.aspx?EvanID=024-000000671&ImageIndex=0 (accessed 3 December 2018).

[35] London Pavilion programme in MM/2/TH/LO/PAV/2 (University of Bristol Theatre Collection).

Fig. 11.4b London Pavilion programme (author collection)

cross-class audience which explains why the focus of West End music hall was on nation, empire, and the challenges of everyday life but not necessarily on class experience. The formula worked. By 1895, the London Pavilion was making a profit of £11, 150, 7s.[36]

If we take an evening's programme for the Pavilion in 1891, we will find that the show provided twenty-six acts. The evening started with Marie Collins, the

[36] *Financial News*, 5 February 1895, p. 6; LCC Theatres Committee London Pavilion, 1888–1903: LCC/MIN/10/10, 846 (London Metropolitan Archives).

serio-comic, and went on to include Lottie Collins, character vocalist and dancer, Jenny Hill, comedienne, Albert Chevalier, comedian, Prince Mignon, the smallest man in the world, Dan Leno, comedian, and the Zanettos (Japanese jugglers).[37] The stars who dominated the Pavilion included Arthur Lloyd, Marie Lloyd, Dan Leno, the Great MacDermott, and Jenny Hill, who made her name at the Pavilion. After 1885, the Pavilion tended (with exceptions) not to offer sketches. It did, however, include acts such as Arabella Allen's impersonation of Dickens characters (both male and female), Miss Lou Robinson's scientific demonstrations of iron making (a top hat turned into a crucible) and *poses plastiques*.[38] An evening at the Pavilion could start at 7.30 and not end till 11.30.

It is tempting to argue that figures like Villiers and Swanborough took a form of popular culture and transformed it into a commodity that could be bought and sold, shorn of any authentic or dissenting content. There is, of course, something in this view but it is simplistic. Rather than view music hall as the corruption of the popular voice, Peter Bailey argues powerfully that its 'particular mode of conceit, parody and innuendo constituted a second language for all classes, whose penetration had a powerful integrative force in English society'.[39] In some respects, we could extend this to the West End as a whole. Its pleasures offered a second language or identity which people could opt into and which they at least recognized. This was integral to townology. Light entertainment offered a world of bonhomie, though at a price.

The London Pavilion trumpeted its respectability, noting in 1870, when it successfully applied for renewal of its licence, that it had not had a police report made against it.[40] Respectability is a complex matter. Leading members of High Society could attend music halls without damaging their reputation. The Pavilion even claimed in some playbills to be 'under royal patronage'. Yet performances pushed at the boundaries of what was acceptable, making full use of innuendo and double entendre. There were, for example, complaints about a number that Marie Lloyd did at the Pavilion and the Oxford. She appeared on stage in her knickerbockers. The refrain of the song was 'So now you know the reason: it was a good thing I had these on'. In one verse she talks of going to the Continent where officials search all the women there (cue the refrain). In another she describes being out in a high wind with her clothes blowing up (cue the refrain). Needless to say, another verse relates her escape from a hotel conflagration down a fire escape (cue the refrain). It was mildly sexual in a contained way, cheeky rather than raunchy (underwear being a not uncommon subject of popular humour). The London County Council (LCC) found such content distasteful, also objecting

---

[37] Programme for 29 June 1891: LCC Theatres Committee London Pavilion, 1888–1903: LCC/MIN/10/10, 846 (London Metropolitan Archives).

[38] *Sketch*, 28 September 1894, p. 397; *Illustrated London News*, 22 February 1905, pp. 190–1; 1885 London Pavilion poster in MM/2/TH/LO/PAV/2 (University of Bristol Theatre Collection).

[39] Bailey, 'Introduction: Making Sense of the Music Hall', in Bailey, *Music Hall*, p. xviii.

[40] *Morning Post*, 18 October 1870, p. 7.

to a number in which Marie Duggan sang 'Give it a Wink', which was essentially about instructing young men on how to accost prostitutes. Jennie Valmore sang a song referring to the stripping and slapping of girls. Her refrain was 'It made a good impression on our—pause—Well, it made a great impression on our minds.' The Pavilion promised to take care with the contents of its acts, though it insisted the Marie Lloyd routine was not indecent.[41] The knickerbocker routine exploited the forms of 'knowingness' that Peter Bailey has defined as the heart of music hall routines.[42] It also showed the grand setting of the Pavilion did not prevent sauciness and low humour getting a hearing.

Reformers also complained about the amount of prostitution on the promenade of the Pavilion (a characteristic it shared with the Empire discussed in the next chapter). Charles Cory Reed, who worked for a City firm and was an ardent temperance advocate, claimed he was accosted by a prostitute:

> A woman came & knocked against me, apologising in an artificial way, & then borrowed my opera glasses, & wanted me to go downstairs with her; we should see better down there, she said. I said 'No, thank you, I can see better up here', whereupon she said 'I will come back in a minute or two'; & I saw her squeeze herself between two young fellows seated at a table behind, & proceed to drink with them.

Reed's wife, also investigating the promenade, saw a prostitute reject a man who offered her a pound and who then exclaimed: 'The idea of thinking I would go with him for a wretched quid...Besides, I know a man who comes here who always gives me a fiver if he comes.' She also overheard an obscene conversation amongst the staff: 'One of the waiters—I believe it was at the bar—had a small doll & he made a very objectionable remark to the waitress about this doll.' Later, a fight broke out between two men, one of whom was ejected leaving the other to brag about the episode. If the setting was palatial, this did not prevent lewd behaviour from existing on the part of both men and women. Edward Swanborough dismissed the Reeds' testimony at the LCC and claimed that Mrs Reed's 'mission in life is to make everybody miserable about her'. The Pavilion did not lose its licence.[43]

Both Jenny Hill and the Great MacDermott, who played in numerous different locations in London and the country, had to adapt to the particular audience they

---

[41] Licensing Committee minutes, 15 October 1896: LCC Theatres Committee London Pavilion, 1888–1903: LCC/MIN/10/10, 846 (London Metropolitan Archives).

[42] Peter Bailey, 'Music Hall and the Knowingness of Popular Culture', in his *Popular Performance and Culture in the Victorian City* (Cambridge: Cambridge University Press, 1998), pp. 128–50.

[43] LCC Theatres Committee London Pavilion, 1888–1903: LCC/MIN/10/10, 846 (London Metropolitan Archives). On the Reeds, see Susan Pennybacker, '"It was not what she said but the way in which she said it": The London County Council and the Music Halls', in Bailey, *Music Hall*, p. 131.

encountered in the West End and to the acoustics of the London Pavilion. Hill summed up the difference between playing in the West and the East End:

> What one likes another doesn't. Sometimes I have sung the same song at the East-end and at the West-end; but I have had to sing it in a perfectly different way. At the West they do not care for what we call a dramatic song. Take, for instance, 'Masks and Faces'. It was an enormous success at the East-end and in the provinces; but, thinking I knew my audience, I never even tried it at the Pavilion. Mr. Villiers heard about the song, and absolutely insisted on my sing-ing it, so I did, to please him. You never heard anything go so flat in all your life.

Hill, however, had to be careful about her coster songs. What enthralled the West End flopped in East End venues. Any suggestion of satire or exaggeration of working-class life irritated the latter. It had to be naturalistic or (presumably) it was guilty of patronizing the audience. This was less of a problem at the Pavilion where caricatures of working-class types were acceptable.[44]

Jenny Hill's career suggests the forms of transformation that the West End music hall brought about. [45] Her origins are obscure but she was clearly from a working-class background and was probably the daughter of a Paddington cab-driver. She became a child performer, commencing her career in pubs and pro-vincial music halls. Arriving at the Pavilion in 1871, she earned six pounds a week. A contract from 1874 originally stipulated that she could not sing elsewhere but this was crossed out and replaced by a statement that she could not perform at the Oxford music hall, presumably seen as a major competitor.

Hill performed a plebeian character for a middle-class audience, rejoicing in the authenticity this provided. She was, according to music hall commentator H. Chance Newton, 'the most humorous and most artistically "realistic" comic and pathetic singer on the music-hall boards'.[46] Louise Wingrove's research reveals that the subject material of her songs was dominated by the themes of working women and (a related category) coster girls as well as topical humour. She would often perform songs about servant girls, an occupation that large num-bers of her audience could identify with either because they employed servants or because they were servants.[47] Unlike East End music halls, her audiences did not necessarily share the experiences she described but they recognized the street

---

[44] *Era*, 17 June 1893, p. 14.

[45] ODNB (Jenny Hill); Jacky S. Bratton, 'Jenny Hill: Sex and Sexism in Victorian Music Hall', in Bratton (ed.), *Music Hall: Performance and Style* (Milton Keynes: Open University Press, 1986), pp. 92–110; Louise Wingrove, 'Reigniting the "Vital Spark": Reimagining and Reclaiming the Repertoires, Career Development and Image Cultivation of Serio-comediennes Jenny Hill and Bessie Bellwood from 1870–1896' (University of Bristol, D. Phil thesis, 2016).

[46] H. Chance Newton, *Idols of the 'Halls'; Being My Music Hall Memories* (Wakefield: EP Publishing, 1975 [1928]), p. 111.

[47] Wingrove, 'Reigniting the "Vital Spark"', pp. 70, 83.

types she embodied. On stage at the Pavilion and elsewhere, she rejoiced in the moniker, 'The Vital Spark', which captures some of her charm and appeal to audiences. Henry Hibbert recalled her in the following way:

> She was little, sharp-featured, and pretty on the stage, but terribly scarred by illness on inspection. She could sing a tawdry ballad, as *Sweet Violets*, with effect; and she made a brilliant pantomime boy. But she was at her best in Cockney impersonation, as of 'Arry, describing the joys of Southend, and particularly of 'The Coffee Shop Gal', a weary slut, with humorous impersonations of her customers, and skill in that unlearnable dance the 'Cellar Flap'.[48]

She expressed the vitality of street life but also what Peter Bailey calls the 'gregarious congeniality' that West End music hall retained from its roots in pubs and song and supper rooms.[49] Her innovation was to be one of the first to introduce female low comedy onto the music hall stage with an emphasis on strong female characters, though she would happily take on the role of pantomime boy at Christmas.

The role of the comedienne was vital in giving women a voice in Victorian society. Hill seems to have connected more with women in the audience than with men. She told a largely male audience in Johannesburg towards the end of her life that 'It's not a bit like at home where women always got to the music hall and seem to appreciate you more than men do.'[50] It may also be that her identity as working-class was less significant to West End audiences than her identity as a Londoner (or, at least, the ways in which a 'Londoner' could be constructed on stage). Jacky Bratton notes the way her act was based on a lot of spoken material which was delivered at speed.[51] We see here the development of a vernacular style based upon fast talking which was also apparent in vaudeville in New York and would translate into Hollywood screwball comedy.[52]

Jenny Hill dominated music hall from 1868 through to 1893 when she would often appear at several venues a night (including the Middlesex on Drury Lane). She could make £30 in the course of an evening. Audiences loved her personality as she could make them both laugh and cry. Ill health (as well as some unwise business decisions) ultimately caused her career to slow down. She was only forty-eight when she died from tuberculosis in 1896.

Jenny Hill's humorous persona needs to be mapped onto the stronger roles for women and the ways in which theatre signalled the arrival of the New Woman.

[48]   Hibbert, *Fifty Years*, p. 54.
[49]   Peter Bailey, *Leisure and Class in Victorian England: Rational Recreation and the Contest for Control* (London: Routledge and Kegan Paul, 1978), p. 152.
[50]   *Era*, 5 May 1894, p. 16.
[51]   Bratton, 'Jenny Hill', in Bratton, *Music Hall*, p. 92.
[52]   Maria DiBattista, *Fast-Talking Dames* (London: Yale University Press, 2001).

There was thus a continuum between Jenny Hill and Ibsen's plays but the latter played to a narrow audience. Jenny Hill was really a counterpart to figures like Ellen Terry or Sarah Bernhardt who came to have a magnetic attraction for their followers. Music hall was increasingly peopled by vivid female voices, creating a context in which modern feminism emerged. At the same time, popular entertainments also specialized in turning women into sources of glamour, spectacle, and sexuality. Modern popular culture was fissured by this tortuous dynamic.

'The Great MacDermott' (real name George Farrell), who was also an actor, first appeared at the London Pavilion in 1873 and became known as a *lion comique*, sending up the manners of the upper class. His reputation was made in 1877 with the song that introduced the word 'jingo' into the English vocabulary when Britain threatened to go to war with Turkey:

> We don't want to fight
> But by jingo if we do,
> We've got the ships, we've got the men,
> We've got the money too.

The song signalled music hall support for Disraeli's foreign policy and was an example of the pervasive Toryism of music hall.

MacDermott's Jingo song was composed by G.W. Hunt, former manager of the Canterbury Music Hall, who knocked it out after reading the morning papers.[53] Its impact may have rested not just on the words but on MacDermott's ability as a singer. Henry Hibbert noted that 'He had the rare gift of articulation, singing so clearly and sonorously that never a word escaped the most distantly located member of the audience.' The song doubled his salary from ten pounds a week at the Pavilion to twenty (and he would earn far more in the provinces).[54] It was so successful that it provoked a sequel written by Hunt called 'Waiting for the Signal', described in the sheet music as 'MacDermott's new War Song'. The song referred back to the original and its effectiveness in introducing the word 'jingo' into the English vocabulary:

> If it's 'jingo' to love honour then 'jingoes' sure we are.
> If it's 'jingo' to love England, then 'jingo's' we will be.
> There are 'jingoes' in our colonies who love the dear old land
> Who are ready too when wanted by the brave old flag to stand.[55]

---

[53] Hibbert, *Fifty Years*, pp. 95–6,100; ODNB (G. H. MacDermott).
[54] Hibbert, *Fifty Years*, p. 212.
[55] G.W. Hunt, *Waiting for the Signal* (London: Hopwood and Crew, 1878), p. 4.

The Hunt and MacDermott song 'True Blue for Ever!' mined a similar vein with its praise of the way the good ship Britannia has been brought 'safely into port' by the old commander Dizzy (Disraeli).[56] It promised to stand by him in the coming election battle. MacDermott felt that he had provided the state with some service by encouraging popular nationalism and complained that his input was never recognized. He certainly admired Disraeli and, following the latter's death in 1881, sang 'The Flower Our Hero Loved'. Its lyric by Felix McGlennon captures the sentimental side of Conservatism by focussing on Disraeli's alleged love of primroses (which also inspired the popular Tory organization, the Primrose League). It included the lines:

> We'll lavish our love on his favorite [*sic*] flower,
> The Primrose our emblem will be.
>
> 'Tis the flower our hero loved, the flower our hero loved,
> 'Tis cherished from the peasant to the Queen,
> And through each succeeding year, it will be a relic dear,
> In our hearts it will keep his memory green.[57]

The neo-feudal evocation of a flower 'cherished from the peasant to the Queen' expresses the belief in an organic form of Englishness. The sheet music featured a primrose wreath with the words, 'peace with honour', referring to Disraeli's description of the deal at the Congress of Berlin. This Tory approach to entertainment was not confined to MacDermott. In May 1894, the Pavilion restaged the battle of Balaclava. The *Sketch* observed that the scene involved 'British bulldogism, blood, and bombs'.[58] MacDermott at his height in the mid-1880s was making £60 a week but lost money through poor business advice and a love of the racecourse.

Music hall came into being at a time of invented traditions whereby institutions such as the monarchy found new ways of maintaining their status and employed a nostalgic version of the past to contain the pressures of a democratizing society and the emergence of the labour movement.[59] There was a royal presence in West End music hall, reinforcing its Tory dimensions. Edward VII, George V, and Queen Alexandra were all familiar with the Alhambra, the Empire, and the Pavilion. Dan Leno's appearance before the King at Sandringham in 1902

---

[56] G.W. Hunt, *True Blue for Ever!* (London: Hopwood and Crew, 1878?), p. 5.

[57] Felix McGlennon and T. Richards, *The Flower Our Hero Loved* (London: Hopwood and Crew, 1887), p. 5.

[58] Photograph in London Pavilion Box: THM/LON/LON (Victoria and Albert Museum Theatre Collection); *The Penny Illustrated Paper and Illustrated Times*, 26 May 1894, p. 333; *The Sketch*, 23 May 1894, pp. 171, 209.

[59] Eric Hobsbawm and Terence Ranger (eds), *The Invention of Tradition* (Cambridge: Cambridge University Press, 1983).

gave his performances a mark of prestige thereafter, linking royalty to music hall and further aiding the cult of monarchy. In 1912 the first Royal Variety Performance took place at the Palace Theatre, an event that connected monarchy to popular culture in iconic ways.[60] The 1912 London Pavilion programme showed the theatre flanked by Buckingham Palace and Windsor Castle, giving itself enhanced status.

This tide of bombastic nationalism is why the economist J.A. Hobson came to believe that music hall was behind the popular support for imperialism, describing it as 'a very serviceable engine for generating military passion'.[61] Music hall was held to stand for a cheap and sentimental form of patriotism. In 1889, the performer Charles Colette was prevented from singing a song that endorsed Gladstone and Irish Home Rule at the Trocadero music hall. The management feared a riot and prevented him from singing it, evidence that they knew their audience as the Conservative party did well in London elections (especially East London) in the later nineteenth century.[62] The role of sentimentality and nation combined with an affection for the foibles of toffs made Toryism a formidable political concoction.

Music halls throughout the country shared many of the features that defined the West End venues. In 1887, Ralph Blumenfeld visited the Trocadero music hall on Piccadilly and found 'Most of the artists appear to make their appeal with songs about "booze" or how they beat "the old woman", presumably the wife.'[63] Such a theme might be found in the East End or throughout the country. This chapter has, however, argued that the West End halls had certain peculiarities. There was an emphasis on respectability such that members of the royal family could attend. At the same time, the controversial role of prostitution, *double entendres*, sexualized imagery, and alcohol meant that there was always an unrespectable dimension which gave the halls a very particular identity. It was based upon a careful negotiation between audience taste, respectability and the deployment of capital.

Above all, these halls had the prestige of being in the pleasure district. Thus the West End featured in music hall songs, becoming, according to Keith Wilson, a 'common iconographic space' that reinforced the status quo and reminded all classes they lived in the most powerful city on Earth.[64] Songs suggested 'Let's all go down the Strand' (and maybe 'have a banana' depending on the version). The

---

[60] Hibbert, *Fifty Years*, pp. 135, 137–9.

[61] J.A. Hobson, *The Psychology of Jingoism* (London: Grant Richards, 1901), p. 2.

[62] Cutting from *Pall Mall Budget*, 21 March 1889: ACC/3527/456 (London Metropolitan Archives). See Alex Windscheffel, *Popular Conservatism in Imperial London, 1868–1906* (Woodbridge: Boydell Press/Royal Historical Society, 2007).

[63] Ralph D. Blumenfeld, *R.D.B.'s Diary, 1887–1914* (London: Heinemann, 1930), p. 10.

[64] Keith Wilson, 'Music-Hall London: The Topography of Class Sentiment', *Victorian Literature and Culture*, 23 (1996), p. 26.

Great MacDermott sang a song called 'I like a little Toddle Down Regent Street' in which he played his usual part of the blasé toff:

> Fields are very nice for cattle,
> I prefer a street up West.
> Where the stream of fashions flowing
> And of all I like the best.[65]

The chorus of Jack Judge's song 'It's a Long Way to Tipperary' in 1912 includes the words 'Goodbye Piccadilly, Farewell Leicester Square', though in this case the pleasure district is being rejected for the authenticity of Ireland. The song was first sung in a Stalybridge music hall suggesting that the pleasures of the West End had truly inscribed themselves into the consciousness of the nation as a whole.

The populist palatial as cultural style and as monumental built environment was central to the development of British national identity. It had close links to empire but was also a space for the construction of what it meant to be British. If there emerged a national culture in Britain (as opposed to one shaped by different regional cultures), the West End was a major site where this culture was produced.

---

[65] G.W. Hunt, *I Like a Little Toddle down Regent Street* (London: Hopwood and Crew, 1882), p. 5.

12

Gaiety Nights

Light Entertainment

The later nineteenth century abounded in grand theatres and opera houses. The Vienna State Opera, built in 1869, was a tribute to Habsburg magnificence, then entering its dying fall. In 1875, after fourteen years of construction, the Palais Garnier opera house opened in Paris, its architectural style trumpeting the eclecticism of the *beaux arts* and the imperial pretensions of the late Napoleon III. The following year, Richard Wagner launched the Bayreuth Festival Theatre, specially built to express the mythic vision of his operas and bankrolled by King Ludwig II of Bavaria. The Metropolitan Opera House opened in New York in 1883 and the Hungarian Royal Opera House opened in Budapest the following year.

The ripostes to these great theatres in London were the Royal English Opera House on Cambridge Circus and the London Coliseum on St Martin's Lane. The opera house was the project of Richard D'Oyly Carte who spent £150,000, building it as a rival to Covent Garden in 1891. It was noted for its terracotta exterior and could seat 2000 people. The first opera was the premiere of Arthur Sullivan's new work *Ivanhoe*. It initially did well but business dropped off dramatically after it had played one hundred performances. *Ivanhoe* failed so spectacularly that the building was quickly sold to a company run by Augustus Harris and turned into the Palace Theatre of Varieties. D'Oyly Carte's home for high culture was soon populated by vaudeville acts.

The London Coliseum emerged from the vision of Oswald Stoll who had built up a national music hall syndicate with Edward Moss (Moss Empires). Stoll decided to construct an enormous variety house on St Martin's Lane and commissioned architect Frank Matcham to design it in 1904. The aim was to outshine every theatre in London at that time, especially Drury Lane. The building was crowned by a globe which initially revolved (see Fig. 12.1). It could seat 2358 people and its stage was one of the largest in the world. All seats were bookable, including the balcony (previously, those who sought a ticket in the gods could only purchase it on the day). In other theatres, the balcony was made of hard wooden benches; at the Coliseum, visitors got tip-up seats so that their experience resembled the rest of the audience. The Coliseum may have been essentially a music hall but Stoll was determined to show that it was upmarket.

Whereas, on the continent, architectural grandiloquence was devoted to opera, in the West End it was usually associated with music hall and variety. The

London's West End: Creating the Pleasure District, 1800–1914. Rohan McWilliam, Oxford University Press (2020).
© Rohan McWilliam.
DOI: 10.1093/oso/9780198823414.001.0001

Fig. 12.1 The London Coliseum by night (Michael Diamond Collection)

architecture of conventional theatres tended to be restrained. Variety houses were happy to be grand, loud, and a bit vulgar. This chapter explores the emergence of what would later be called 'light entertainment'. It moves from musical comedy to variety, vaudeville, and the exotic ballets at the Alhambra. 'Variety' was of course a form of 'music hall' (the terms are often used interchangeably) but it is taken here to mean entertainments that offered sophistication but rarely pretended to be high culture. As we saw in the previous chapter, the London Pavilion offered a grand setting but could be cheerfully demotic. The deployment of major new ballets at the Alhambra (as opposed to the 'ballets divertissements' at the Pavilion) suggested a different kind of self-conscious artistry and cultural ambition even if the effect was also one of frivolity. I am using the slightly anachronistic term 'light entertainment' to group a set of genres and performances that became the preserve of the pleasure district. The term is not entirely satisfactory (the performances of Sarah Bernhardt at the Gaiety were hardly light entertainment) and the genres described here were not exactly the same. These spectacles were, however, expensive to mount and flamboyant in their execution. West End light entertainment was the work of a series of enterprising entrepreneurs and promoters: John Hollingshead, Oswald Stoll, and Augustus Harris. Their equivalents in the United States were figures like Florenz Ziegfield, George White, and perhaps P. T. Barnum. The figure who dominates this chapter is the impresario George Edwardes, who turned the Gaiety Girl into an icon of the age, but accomplished so much more as we will see. Moreover, the Gaiety Theatre proved to be a laboratory of light entertainment, making it a vital institution within the West End.

There has always been something we can class as light entertainment; shows that did not ask to be taken seriously and were presented as diversions which did not detract from standards of taste or refinement. We can find its roots in eighteenth-century *opera buffa*, which satirized serious opera, in the pantomime, the harlequinade, and in burlesque. The later Victorian West End took these forms and developed them in new ways.

Light entertainment has often not been taken seriously by scholars; its trivial qualities make it seem unworthy of analysis and yet in the later nineteenth century we see the emergence of popular forms that underpin much of modern popular culture, especially mainstream television.[1] Victorian light entertainment created a narrative in which the West End became a fantasy world with escapist dimensions. Here was a mode that dramatized the notion of capitalist abundance. Modern life was not to be taken too seriously but the satirical qualities of light entertainment never rocked the boat. The routine and everyday could become a source of enchantment in musical comedies such as *The Shop Girl*. These shows were the enemy of the drab, preferring the brash, the spectacular, the garish, and, what a later generation would call 'camp'.[2] This alternative reality is one reason why it could be reappropriated by gay men and women. The refinement of Victorian light entertainment meant that it had a delicious air of unreality, a place where other selves became possible.

Light entertainment provided a utopian alternative to the conformity of modern Britain. As the critic Richard Dyer argues, this form of utopia is different

---

[1] See, however, these studies of modern television and film: Richard Dyer, *Light Entertainment* (London: BFI, 1973); Richard Dyer, *Only Entertainment* (London: Routledge, 2002 [1992]).

[2] Susan Sontag, *Notes on Camp* (London: Penguin, 2018 [1966]).

from the worlds projected by Thomas More or William Morris: 'the utopianism is contained in the feelings it embodies. It presents, head-on as it were, what utopia would feel like rather than how it would be organized.'[3] This is why the experience of Victorian light entertainment was one of exhilaration and release. It is also the reason why light entertainment played a role in the construction of modernism, as we will discover at the end of this chapter.

Light entertainment made the claim that it was not there for the edification of critics or of the institutions of church and state. Instead, it merely sought to give pleasure to the public who were often addressed as its true masters (even though the producer determined what was programmed). Light entertainment was relaxing and deliberately intended to provide a contrast with the world of work. It was accessible and could appeal to a wide range of people from the aristocracy through to the working class. Yet Peter Bailey is correct when he writes (with reference to musical comedy) that its 'cultural centre of gravity, like so much else in the new world of manufactured pleasures and the invented self, lay in the lower middle classes'.[4] The latter were integral to the development of modern popular culture, essentially determining what was considered accessible and mainstream.

The Age of George Edwardes

One theatre proved to be a particularly innovative force in the development of light entertainment: the Gaiety. Its managers, John Hollingshead, and then George Edwardes, put it on the map for light entertainment that could appeal to a mass audience who also enjoyed its feeling of prestige. Many of the forms they deployed were not new but they created a package that was aspirational and accessible. Ultimately, this would fuse together in the new hybrid: musical comedy.[5]

The Gaiety was built in 1868 at what is now the Aldwych end of the Strand, on the site of the Strand Musick hall, with Wellington Street on one side and Catherine Street on the other. The finance came from Lionel Lawson, part-owner of the *Daily Telegraph*. Lawson commissioned Charles Phipps to build it and then hired the journalist John Hollingshead (who had been running the Alhambra) to run it.[6] The Gaiety offered operetta, serious drama, burlesque, pantomime, and light comedy. The entertainments constantly stressed novelty, flattering their audiences with an emphasis on their being 'in the know' about the latest trends

---

[3] Dyer, *Only Entertainment*, p. 20.

[4] Peter Bailey, 'Theatres of Entertainment/Spaces of Modernity: Rethinking the British Popular Stage, 1890–1914', *Nineteenth Century Theatre*, 26 (1998), p. 14.

[5] Len Platt, *Musical Comedy on the West End Stage, 1890–1939* (Basingstoke: Palgrave Macmillan, 2004).

[6] Eilidh Innes, 'The Many Lives of John Hollingshead' (PhD in progress, Anglia Ruskin University).

and fashions.[7] This proved attractive as a formula for both sexes in the audience and was more family-friendly. The Gaiety was therefore at odds with stuffiness and puritanism, making it a dynamic force in the culture.

To what extent did Hollingshead and Edwardes impose their formulas on the audience? Both clearly had strong instincts about what the audience would accept but were also alert to new initiatives and possibilities. Both respected the need to provide respectable entertainment for the middle class but were prepared to push at what could be done and were not constrained by tradition. Hollingshead claimed, 'My theory of management was that I had to provide the public with what they wanted, and not what I liked…I was a shop-keeper, not a thinker… I was governed by the nightly takings.'[8] Yet we should look on this critically. It is facile to say that Hollingshead and Edwardes merely gave the audience what it wanted and even more facile to view them as agents of social control. They helped move popular taste forward but this was always based on a notion of what an audience would accept. There was a process of negotiation between producer and audience. They knew that audiences could go elsewhere. No one had to watch their shows. Hollingshead and Edwardes were able to develop constructions of popular theatre that would prove durable, making them acceptable to an upscale public that feared anything that might diminish their status with lowlife entertainments.

Like the Criterion on Piccadilly, the Gaiety was both a theatre and a restaurant. It was meant to offer a night out all in one; people could dine and see a show on the same premises. The term 'gaiety' was an important one in West End discourse. The nineteenth century uses of the terms 'gay' and 'gaiety' had multiple meanings, standing for merry-making, brightness of apparel, and also prostitution. It can be linked back to theatre names like the *Sans Souci* (which effectively meant 'care-free'). This described the atmosphere the management wanted to create. The design was meant to have a Parisian feel. It was named after the theatre of the same name in Paris and based on the Théâtre Lyrique on the Place du Châtelet, employing the same projecting balcony with private boxes at the back. There were also no pillars to obstruct the view. At the same time, it stressed dignity and prestige. It had a grand entrance on the Strand but also a royal entrance in Exeter Street. The Prince of Wales visited six months after opening. The theatre was kept open all the year round. Maximizing the Gaiety's profitability yet further, Hollingshead arranged for matinees of different shows, an example of his innovative practice. Hollingshead was in effect the director of many of the shows at the

---

[7] On up-to-dateness, see Andrew Horrall, *Popular Culture in London, c. 1890–1918: The Transformation of Entertainment* (Manchester: Manchester University Press, 2001).

[8] John Hollingshead, *My Lifetime* (London: Sampson Low, Marston and Co., 1895), Vol. 2, p. 17.

Gaiety which proved so lucrative that the house made one and a quarter million pounds during his eighteen-year tenure as manager (Fig. 12.2).[9]

The Gaiety had a distinct house style. A performance was meant to feel like the 'pop' heard on opening a bottle of champagne (even though it was the only theatre in London without a bar). Hollingshead himself referred to 'our *soufflé* productions' which also captures some of the feeling of an evening at the Gaiety.[10] It developed a reputation for spectacular stage settings (designed by William Grieve) and frequently turned itself into an opera house, performing, for example, Donizetti's *Betley*, though the operettas of Offenbach better define the flavour of what was shown. At the same time there were light comedies and melodramas. The American actor Walter Montgomery played Hamlet whilst Hollingshead bowdlerized Congreve's *Love for Love* so that it would not offend Victorian audiences. Disraeli was even asked to write a play (though he declined).[11]

Although it presented a variety of different kinds of entertainment, the Gaiety became known as a burlesque house (particularly those featuring Nellie Farren). These were effectively musicals using a selection of popular airs and tunes. Burlesque also traded in actresses flaunting their legs and wearing tight fitting clothing that mocked Victorian ideas of decorum. Hollingshead had a very clear idea of what would draw people in:

> The choice of all the ladies on the stage, except a few of the chorus singers, where voice was an object, was openly and avowedly governed by a desire to put pleasing forms and faces before the public. My view of the stage was, that whatever it might be, judged from the lofty, not to say, stuck-up heights of Literature and Arts, it was not a platform for the display of grandmothers and maiden aunts. If physical beauty could be got in connection with brains and dramatic talent, so much the better, but my first duty seemed to me to get physical beauty, and I got it.[12]

For the pantomime season Hollingshead employed music hall performers such as Jenny Hill who took the principal boy roles. The Gaiety company was often sent on tour and thus enhanced the cultural reach of the theatre.

In 1885, Hollingshead formed a partnership to run the Gaiety with George Edwardes who became sole manager after the former lost money in a bad business speculation. It was Edwardes who would go on to invent musical comedy, a form that really emerged within the West End and dominated it from 1890 through to the Great War, ultimately creating the modern musical.[13] Significantly, Edwardes had previously been an assistant to D'Oyly Carte at the Savoy, helping with the management of Gilbert and Sullivan's operas. The move from the

---

[9] Hollingshead, *My Lifetime*, Vol. 2, p. 17.   [10] Hollingshead, *My Lifetime*, Vol. 2, p. 68.
[11] Hollingshead, *My Lifetime*, Vol. 2, p. 189.   [12] Hollingshead, *My Lifetime*, Vol. 2, p. 6.
[13] Thomas Postlewait, 'George Edwardes and Musical Comedy: The Transformation of London Theatre and Society, 1878–1914', in Tracy C. Davis and Peter Holland (eds), *The Performing Century: Nineteenth Century Theatre's History* (Basingstoke: Palgrave Macmillan, 2007), pp. 80–102.

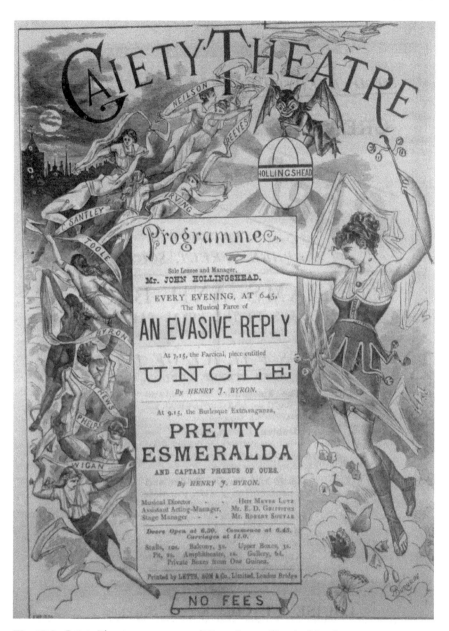

Fig. 12.2 Gaiety Theatre programme (Westminster City Archives)

Hollingshead management at the Gaiety to the Edwardes regime was a turning point in the history of light entertainment. Edwardes went on to construct a multi-theatre entertainment empire in the West End.

Musical comedy really began with Edwardes's show *In Town* at the Prince of Wales Theatre in 1892 followed by *A Gaiety Girl* (1893). *In Town* owed much to its lyricist Adrian Ross who developed musical comedy as an extension of the burlesque. The tone abandoned the satire of Gilbert and Sullivan for novelty, fashionable clothing, and good-natured comedy that never abandoned sexual propriety but employed the draw of female performers. There was romance but not raunch. In musical comedy the spoken elements were as important as the music, allowing it to appeal to a wide variety of people.

The Gaiety became associated with a string of hits, often with the word 'girl' in the title and always featuring the delights of chorus girls. *The Shop Girl* in 1894, which ran for 546 performances, reflected the rise of the department store, a significant feature of West End life (as we will see). It was followed by *The Circus Girl* (1896), and *A Runaway Girl* in 1898. Even in 1914 the Gaiety was putting on *After the Girl*. *The Shop Girl* significantly featured Ada Reeve who had originally appeared in music hall and now made the transition to more sophisticated entertainment, showing the way in which cultural forms fed off one another in the West End. The similarities of these shows meant that they became a form of standardized product, characteristic of mass culture which creates forms of art that look reassuringly familiar. This is not to deny differences between shows or to dispute the skill and artistry that went into making them, but it is to view the West End as a business whose purpose was to find ways of making money.[14] The Gaiety shows enjoyed scores from composers such as Ivan Caryll, Sidney Jones, and Lionel Monckton. Musical comedy proved more alluring and up-to-date than the shows of Gilbert and Sullivan who were by then in decline. Edwardes felt that his former collaborators at the Savoy had failed to experiment and now looked old-fashioned.[15]

The musical comedy form was particularly attractive to a female audience and was promoted through publications such as the *Play Pictorial* which featured photographs from the latest shows together with elaborate plot synopses. As Len Platt has shown, the periodical's advertisements were almost all aimed at women including one for 'Southalls' Towels...a boon to womankind'. This shift away from the masculine world of Hollingshead's Gaiety was another example of the way the West End had become a space whose rationale was to attract women. Platt argues that musical comedy 'transformed the Edwardian stage into a fantastic celebration of fashion, shopping, and general excess'. It was relentlessly consumerist and enjoyed close links with fashion designers and department stores, promoting early examples of product placement. *Our Miss Gibbs* at the Gaiety in 1909 was set in a department store that was clearly meant to be Harrods (or 'Garrods' in this version).[16]

[14] Gerben Bakker, *Entertainment Industrialised: The Emergence of the International Film Industry* (Cambridge: Cambridge University Press, 2008), ch. 2.

[15] *Sketch*, 12 September 1894, pp. 360–1.

[16] Platt, *Musical Comedy*, pp. ix–x, 4.

The Gaiety Girl became an iconic figure of the period. On stage, she was usually a working girl trying to make an honest living but with a cheerful sense of fun and a love for striking clothes. Convention, tradition, and religious piety did not constrain her but she made up for it by her good nature. The effect was one of Little Bo Peep as coquette with much comedy derived from flirtation. She was a female figure who was presented neither as a potential wife and mother nor as a femme fatale. In some respects, she had more in common with the presentation of knick-knacks in fancy repositories or, at the least, the dolls purchased on the Lowther Arcade on the Strand.

Edwardes knew how to spot girls who would stand out for their beauty. Gaiety Girls were embodiments of commodified femininity, a statement about woman as adornment that complemented the romances in which they appeared. Many of them were not required to sing or act but just to look pretty in a tableau. In one sense they anticipated the James Bond girls of the 1960s, standing for a particular lifestyle whilst also employed to advertise products. Women like Marie Studholme, Decima Moore, Hetty Hamer, Gabrielle Ray, and the Dare Sisters quickly figured on *cartes de visite* and postcards (see Figs 12.3 and 12.4). When Gabrielle Ray got married in 1912, it was front-page news.[17]

The stage door of the Gaiety was notorious for its crowd of young men trying to get access after the show. James Jupp, the stage-door keeper of the Gaiety, said he was always busy taking chocolates, bouquets, and other presents round to the stars and the chorus although he would not allow admirers into the dressing rooms unless he had the permission of the artiste visited. The stage door was festooned with flowers. According to Gaiety Girl Constance Collier, 'Night after night you would see the same people in the same stalls; they would book their seats for the whole season.'[18] Figures such as the Maharaja of Cooch Behar were eager to shower jewels on young actresses.[19] One of Winston Churchill's first contacts with the opposite sex during his Sandhurst years was when he gained access to the dressing room of an actress at the Gaiety and obtained a signed portrait. This is significant as it illustrates the appeal of this kind of light entertainment to soldiers and officers.[20]

In 1916 Henry Hibbert estimated that the presence of young aristocrats at the Gaiety stage door had led to twenty-three marriages to 'minor actresses' over the previous quarter century.[21] Constance Gilchrist, for example, married the Earl of Orkney. Gaiety Girls were frequently invited to parties at the Savoy and other similar locations. Dressmakers wanted to clothe them at fashionable gatherings

[17] *Evening News*, 1 March 1912, p. 1.
[18] Constance Collier, *Harlequinade: The Story of my Life* (London: John Lane, 1929), pp. 49–50.
[19] *Sketch*, 8 August 1894, p. 96; James Jupp, *The Gaiety Stage Door: Thirty Years' Reminiscences of the Theatre* (London: Jonathan Cape, 1923), pp. 13, 65.
[20] Henry Pelling, *Winston Churchill* (London: Pan, 1977), p. 66.
[21] Henry George Hibbert, *Fifty Years of a Londoner's Life* (London: Grant Richards, 1916), p. 195.

Fig. 12.3 Gabrielle Ray *carte de visite* (author collection)

so that their designs would be seen. Advertisers wanted to employ their image to advertise products. Collier found herself living such a glamorous life, when only sixteen, that she ran up huge debts that she could not repay. In model paternalist form, Edwardes took over the debt to save her from her creditors.[22] Gaiety Girls also provided the popular press with sources of scandal, such as the adultery trial of performer Mabel Duncan.[23] The cult of the Gaiety Girl was therefore part of a more public approach to sexuality.

Chorus lines were a distinctive development in late nineteenth-century popular theatre. Their aesthetic impact came from a group of young women dancing exactly the same steps with disciplined precision. Tiller girls commenced in Liverpool in 1890 and influenced popular dance thereafter in Europe and the United States. Siegfried Kracauer, the interwar cultural theorist, argued that they resembled a conveyor belt and expressed the shift to mass production of goods; hence they were the product of a particular stage of capitalism and the emergence of mass society. These dancers were 'no longer individual girls, but indissoluble

---

[22] Collier, *Harlequinade*, p. 60.   [23] *Evening News*, 7 May 1907, p. 1.

Fig. 12.4 Marie Studholme *carte de visite* (author collection)

girl clusters whose movements are demonstrations of mathematics'.[24] Mass society drained the individual of meaning. And yet the Gaiety Girl (even in the chorus) was about personality and charm. She was also defiantly modern. The Gaiety Girl was, in some respects, a conservative counter-blast to the New Woman of the 1890s and then the Suffragettes. Whilst some women fought for the vote, stood in local government, engaged in settlement house work, the message from the Gaiety was that girls just want to have fun.

Edwardes was not content with the Gaiety alone. From 1887 to 1908, he managed the Empire in Leicester Square (see below) and at various times had shows running at other theatres he leased whilst his productions also toured. Between 1885 and 1915 he was responsible for over sixty musical productions making him a major force in constructing popular taste and linking it to musical comedy. Edwardes's productions were tasteful but with a cheerfully vulgar undertone. The money spent on them could be seen on stage. Edwardes made so much money in turn that he was able to build a mansion near Ascot and devote himself to the turf.

---

[24] Siegfried Kracauer, *The Mass Ornament: Weimar Essays*, ed. Thomas Y. Levin (Cambridge, MA: Harvard University Press, 1995), p. 76.

In 1893 he teamed up with the American producer Augustin Daly to open Daly's Theatre on Cranbourn Street by Leicester Square (site of the present Vue cinema). It was deliberately intended by architects Spencer Chadwick and Charles Phipps to be a smaller theatre but, with its Italian Renaissance exterior, not lacking in grandeur. Daly's was intended for the presentation of sophisticated musical fare with an American influence. Shows such as *An Artist's Model, The Geisha, San Toy,* and, above all, Lehár's operetta *The Merry Widow* in 1907–9 proved enormous hits. These productions were intended to feel like events. The audience for the first anniversary of *The Geisha* on 26 April 1897 were presented with a sumptuous hardback George Edwardes Birthday Book full of photographs and quotations from his productions. Similar gifts awaited audiences at the first and second anniversaries *of The Merry Widow*.[25]

An Artist's Model made the most of its star power: Marie Tempest and Hayden Coffin. It ran for 405 performances which was just as well because one of its sets (a ballroom) had cost £2500 to build.[26] Discussing *An Artist's Model*, Owen Hall (one of its composers) said that he made 'every song and dance belong properly to the story and advance the action of the piece'. Nothing was done merely to introduce a 'variety number'.[27] The story of the show was slight but it was evidence of musical comedy becoming a form of sophisticated theatre. *The Geisha* (a post-*Mikado* Japanese musical with Marie Tempest) proved another draw in 1896, running for 760 performances.

Edwardes's entertainment empire was built on Daly's, the Empire, and the Gaiety. Other theatres began to offer similar entertainments. *The Arcadians*, with a score by Lionel Monckton and Howard Talbot, ran for 809 performances at the Shaftesbury in 1909. *Floradora* (1899) at the Lyric became the first West End production to transfer to New York where it proved an even bigger hit. When Daly's put on *The Count of Luxembourg* in 1911, West End libraries (which still acted as ticket agents) bought £50,000 worth of tickets in advance for the first six months of the run as they expected heavy demand. George V and Queen Mary attended the premiere.[28] In retrospect, the musical comedy set the stage for the emergence of the book musical in the twentieth century where Broadway in New York would prove the real innovator.

Leicester Square

The smaller West End music halls (treated in the previous chapter) were rather different from the spectacular variety halls that the district came to house: the

---

[25] Copies are in the University of Bristol Theatre Collection: TC/W/M/113; MM/REF/TH/LO/DAL/16.

[26] Platt, *Musical Comedy*, p. 33.   [27] *Sketch*, 30 January 1895, p. 4.

[28] D. Forbes-Winslow, *Daly's: The Biography of a Theatre* (London: W.H. Allen, 1944), p. 33.

Alhambra, the Empire, the Palace, the Coliseum, and the Hippodrome. These were very much the *grandes dames* of West End entertainment. They were (mostly) very profitable between 1890 and 1920, paying high dividends to share-holders, and attracted a higher class of clientele, who might otherwise have avoided music hall, by providing spectacular venues with an emphasis on taste and refinement but also the exotic and the cosmopolitan.[29] Thus they were ideal for a night out that included entertainment and fantasy but also a hint of sophisti-cation; further examples of the populist palatial.

The Alhambra and the Empire dominated Leicester Square. They offered a variety of acts but their centrepiece was ballet which flourished in this environ-ment. The Alhambra began life as the Royal Panopticon of Science and Art in 1854; it closed in two years flat (see Chapter 5). In 1858 it was turned into the Alhambra Palace, a form of circus and then a variety house which is essentially what it remained all the way through to 1936 when it was demolished. Its exotic design was Moorish with a minaret at the top, distancing it from the classical style often adopted in theatre architecture. It came to stand for spectacular entertain-ments including comic operas and ballet (see Fig. 12.5).

In 1870, the American commentator Daniel Kirwan was impressed by his visit. Inside, there was seating for families (costing two shillings) who wanted to see the show and who were railed off from the rest of the house. The respectable audience might include middle- and working-class people. Access to the promenade sim-ply cost a shilling and it was a space where upper-class men consorted with pros-titutes. There were a large number of bars on either side of the house. During Kirwan's visit:

> All these bars had splendid bottles, with various fluids in them, arranged with an eye to effect, making it look like a vast apothecary's window, and there were bright brass-pumps all in a row, and pewter and silver and metal pots and tank-ards, and oval glass frames with pies, sandwiches, and all kinds of lunches to satisfy the thirst and appetite of the audience. The promenade was choked with men and women, walking past each other, looking at the stage, drinking at the bars, chaffing each other in a rough way, and laughing loudly.[30]

What worked with the audience were comic songs, particularly numbers that mocked the swells that congregated in the West End.

Beneath the stage was a cafeteria where young men would compete to buy drinks for ballet girls. According to Kirwan, these included soldiers 'wearing the

---

[29] Andrew John Crowhurst, 'The Music Hall, 1885–1922: The Emergence of a National Entertainment Industry in Britain', University of Cambridge, D.Phil. thesis, 1991, pp. 185–8.

[30] Daniel Joseph Kirwan, *Palace and Hovel; or, Phases of London Life* (London: Abelard-Schuman, 1963 [1870]), pp. 139–40.

Fig. 12.5 The Alhambra, Leicester Square (Michael Diamond collection)

uniforms of different regiments, chiefly of the Household troops, with here and there a private'. The dancers were discriminating, preferring to drink with army officers.[31]

The allegation that the cancan had been danced led to the Alhambra losing its licence in 1870, forcing its closure. It reopened the following year as the Royal Alhambra Palace of Varieties and performed comic opera and ballet until the licence was renewed in 1884 (though dance continued to be a feature of the programme thereafter). The theatre burned down in 1882 and was rebuilt in a grand style which could seat 1800 people but could take 4000 in total in the promenades and bars. Admission in the 1880s could cost up to £2 12s 6d for the private boxes but it was possible to get into the Upper Balcony and Gallery for 6d whilst the pit stalls were a shilling, creating the possibility of a heterogeneous audience.[32] Let us take a typical week's programme in 1899. It included two new ballets (each lasting thirty to forty minutes), the Powers Brothers (cycle comedians), Turner's Piccaninnies (a black minstrel troupe who purported to offer 'realistic scenes of American Southern life'), Indian club juggling, and Mlle Leodiska's Performing Cockatoos and Paraqueets.[33] Apart from the ballet, the programme was not very different from other music halls but they were presented in a grander setting.

---

[31] Kirwan, *Palace and Hovel*, p. 144.
[32] 1887 Alhambra programme in University of Bristol Theatre Collection: PR/LALH/32.
[33] Alhambra Theatre programme: 21 August 1899 (British Library callmark 1562/2).

Fig. 12.6 Alhambra programme (Michael Diamond Collection)

The upscale variety house led to a revival of ballet which had declined since its brief heyday in the early Victorian years. Classical dance was redefined at the Alhambra in ways that could be understood and enjoyed by a mass public. The Alhambra could therefore claim to be a space for art, grace, and beauty. The times of the different Alhambra acts were included in the advertising so that people could, if they wished, arrive just to watch the ballet.[34] The Alhambra programme in Fig. 12.6 shows how the appeal of the Alhambra ballet had a sexually suggestive dimension (the exposed legs, the carefree posture) even if the proceedings were ostentatiously tasteful.

The corps de ballet was often untrained (though this improved as the Alhambra and Empire developed their own dancing schools) and badly paid. The focus was on the lead female dancer. Great dancers and ballet masters were brought in from all over Europe. Rita Sangalli, the Milanese Ballerina, danced in 1871 in *The Sylph of the Glen*—a version of *La Sylphide*. Erminia Pertoldi, however, emerged as the major Alhambra ballerina between 1874 and 1884. The theatre's musical director Georges Jacobi composed most of the music. These shows were rarely plot-driven though *Nana Shib* in 1872 was a ballet about the Indian Mutiny. The subjects of

---

[34] Ivor Guest, *Ballet in Leicester Square: The Alhambra and the Empire, 1860–1915* (London: Dance Books, 1992), p. 15.

Alhambra ballets were often about themes such as butterflies and birds (allowing for exciting movement) or simple stories set in Spain or the mysterious east. After the rebuilding of the Alhambra, grand narrative ballet became the great attraction with the variety and music hall elements very much subordinate. The theatre's stage was then dominated by three major ballerinas: Emma Palladino, Emma Bessone, and Pierina Legnani. Right up to the First World War, the Alhambra was importing major dancers such as Helena Adamowitz of the Imperial Opera House in Moscow.[35] *The Swans*, inspired by *Swan Lake* but with a score by Jacobi, ran for almost a year during 1884–5. The imperialist ballet, *Our Army and Navy* in 1889, also enjoyed a year-long run epitomizing the jingoistic feel of the theatre. By the 1890s Alhambra ballets received six weeks of rehearsal so that they showed off precision and technique. It was more spectacular than any other dance venue in London and had the best corps de ballet.

The Empire Theatre opened in 1884 and was destined to become the Alhambra's rival. It was designed by Thomas and Frank Verity. There were two major tiers, both of which had large promenades with bars (but no food). The first night was made up of Hervé's operetta *Chilpéric* and three ballets. A poster promised '50 Amazons'.[36] Within a year it offered the first performance in London of *Coppélia*, with sixty women in the corps de ballet. Later performances would also include variety acts and *poses plastiques*. The early shows did not work and the owner, Daniel de Nicola, brought in George Edwardes and Augustus Harris as joint managers. The theatre was also redesigned and reopened in 1887 under the name the Empire Theatre of Varieties, which proved far more successful. Its existence was an irritation to the Alhambra which attempted to get its music licence withdrawn in 1887 and claimed that, in the first six months of that year, it had received 27, 177 fewer visitors than in the previous year which it blamed on the new arrival.[37]

The Empire became another meeting place for swells and soldiers. Frederick Willis recalled:

Gilded youth coveted the honour of being chucked out of the Empire. The management of this beautiful theatre was always ready to oblige and used to engage a special force of ex-guardsmen, who would be dressed in the ordinary attendants' uniforms and concealed about the house when a rag was expected, as it always was on Boat Race and Henley regatta nights and other joyful occasions.[38]

---

[35] Agreement, 16 March 1911: THM/75.4/4/4: Alhambra Moul Collection (Victoria and Albert Museum Theatre and Performance Archives).

[36] Poster in St Martin's Scrapbook Series: Leicester Square Vol. 2 part 1 p. 73 (City of Westminster Archives).

[37] MR/L/MD/1403/03 (London Metropolitan Archives).

[38] Frederick Willis, *101 Jubilee Road: A Book of London Yesterdays* (London: Phoenix House, 1948), p. 32.

Like the Alhambra, the promenades at the Empire were associated with prostitution and with homosexual men. Oscar Wilde and Lord Alfred Douglas attended and, according to one witness, sat in an intimate embrace.[39] The theatre's front of house manager on one occasion punched and dragged off a man before going on to explain 'this man was a *sodomite*, & that more than half the audience in the shilling promenade were of that class & that he turned out half a dozen a night & gave them a good kicking'.[40]

The Empire ballets were shaped over many years by the choreographer Katti Lanner and the designer C. Wilhem. Lanner was born into a Viennese family associated with dance. She became ballet mistress at Drury Lane and then Her Majesty's before joining the Empire in 1887 and only retiring fully in 1906. Lanner was essential to the theatre's reputation for quality dancing whilst also serving as the directress of a dancing school on the Tottenham Court Road. Wilhelm designed for many theatres, including the Alhambra, but was especially associated with the look of the Empire shows, particularly through his dramatic use of colour. Despite his name, he was English (his real name was William Pitcher) and was a self-trained draughtsman who was initially taken up by Augustus Harris at Drury Lane to design ballets and pantomimes. Lanner and Wilhelm came together initially to create the Empire ballet *Dilara* in 1887 using a score by Hervé. Topics for ballets could involve classical themes or up-to-date stories, giving the theatre a modern feel. The Empire even cashed in on the popularity of Rider Haggard's *Cleopatra* by staging a ballet based on the novel as it was being serialized in 1889. Like the Alhambra, it also mounted imperial spectacles featuring chorus girls as British soldiers. The great ballerina at the Empire proved to be Adeline Genée who danced there from 1897 to 1907. When she started she earned £20 a week but this had become £70 by the time she retired.[41]

It was the costumes of the ballet dancers that partially antagonized the temperance reformer Frederick Charrington. In 1890 he attempted to deny the Empire the renewal of its licence on the grounds that the Katti Lanner ballet, 'A Dream of Wealth', was indecent and the Empire was a resort of prostitutes. Charrington argued before the London County Council (LCC) that the Empire was 'particularly dangerous to young men of the better class'. He was 'given to understand, on good authority, that there may be seen young fellows up from Oxford and Cambridge, and there they see prostitution and vice in its most attractive form'.[42]

---

[39] Matt Cook, *London and the Culture of Homosexuality, 1885–1914* (Cambridge: Cambridge University Press, 2003), pp. 28–9.

[40] Tracy C. Davis, 'Indecency and Vigilance in the Music Halls', in Richard Foulkes (ed.), *British Theatre in the 1890s: Essays on Drama and the Stage* (Cambridge: Cambridge University Press, 1992), p. 124.

[41] Alexandra Carter, *Dance and Dancers in the Victorian and Edwardian Music Hall Ballet* (Aldershot: Ashgate, 2005), p. 41.

[42] LCC Theatre Committee Papers: Empire Theatre of Varieties 1889–1904: LCC/MIN/10, 803 (London Metropolitan Archives).

His arguments echoed those used against the Argyll Rooms (see Chapter 7). The chairman of the licensing committee decided that the house was well conducted and there was no evidence that prostitutes were knowingly admitted.

A stronger case was made four years later by the social reformer Laura Ormiston Chant, who was active in the National Vigilance Association.[43] A supporter of women's suffrage and a leading figure in the Women's Liberal Federation, she visited the Empire in 1894 and was troubled by the way the ballet and music hall elements showed off women's bodies. Even worse was the presence of prostitutes in the promenade which were in full view of family members in the audience. She protested to the LCC that 'portions of the entertainment are most objectionable, obnoxious, and against the best interests and moral well being of the community at large'. The Empire, she found, attracted 'gaily dressed and painted women' because it was the best place to meet upscale gentlemen and practice their trade. She brought in a witness to complain about the ballet, 'La Frolique'. The witness stated 'there is a very indelicate scene indeed, concluding by one of the women putting her foot up on the man's hand &...he holds her foot up very disgustingly...'.[44]

In 1894, the Council voted to close down the promenades and insisted that alcohol not be sold in the auditorium. In the view of Chant's supporters at the *Vigilance Record*, 'The Battle of the Empire Music Hall has been fought and won'.[45] The *Daily Telegraph* responded by running a series of letters complaining about 'Prudes on the Prowl' whilst theatrical organizations like the Theatrical and Music Hall Operatives' Union passed motions against the decision, though the Tower Hamlets Mission wrote to the Council congratulating the committee on its decision. The paper received so many letters on the subject that it could not print them all but described Chant and her supporters as 'amateur inquisitors', judging that the LCC committee had made a decision it would regret.[46] Arthur Symons complained in the *Saturday Review* that it was a concession to the 'spirit of puritanism' and that the LCC had lost all credibility.[47] Chant, for her part, insisted that she was taking on the might of the aristocracy and attacking those who were merely interested in profit.[48]

---

[43] Joseph Donohue, *Fantasies of Empire: The Empire Theatre of Varieties and the Licensing Controversy of 1894* (Iowa City, IA: University of Iowa Press, 2005); Judith R. Walkowitz, *Nights Out: Life in Cosmopolitan London* (London: Yale University Press, 2012), ch. 2; Lucy Bland, *Banishing the Beast: English Feminism and Sexual Morality, 1885–1914* (London: Penguin, 1995), ch. 3.

[44] LCC Theatre Committee Papers: Empire Theatre of Varieties 1889–1904: LCC/MIN/10, 803 (London Metropolitan Archives).

[45] *Vigilance Record*, 15 November 1894, p. 25.

[46] *Daily Telegraph*, 13 October 1894, p. 5; 20 October 1894, p. 7; LCC Theatre Committee Papers: Empire Theatre of Varieties 1889–1904: LCC/MIN/10, 803 (London Metropolitan Archives).

[47] Arthur Symons, 'The Case of the Empire', *Saturday Review*, 10 November 1894, pp. 501–2.

[48] Laura Ormiston Chant, *Why We Attacked the Empire* (London: Horace, Marshall and Son, 1895), p. 3.

Edwardes eventually was forced to close down the Empire in order to erect a partition so that the bar could not be seen from the auditorium. This partition was seen as an attack on English liberties by a group of soldiers who included Winston Churchill. When the theatre reopened in November, they took a stand at the first performance and destroyed the partition, uttering groans for Laura Ormiston Chant and the LCC. At this performance, 'La Frolique' was presented once more.[49] In many ways, the Empire survived its fight with Laura Ormiston Chant and was not hugely changed although a number of the bars were removed.

The Empire licensing controversy was a battle over moral regulation. It represented a contest between the liberal reforming instincts of Chant versus what was effectively a cultural Tory approach (with its openness to fun and joy) represented by George Edwardes and Winston Churchill. The freeborn Englishman was entitled to his pleasures, even if they took some lowlife forms. Prudes should not be allowed to interfere with the pleasures of the common people. The Empire was not the only place that concerned the National Vigilance Association. Its gaze was also up on what was happening at Cambridge Circus.

Variety

After D'Oyly Carte's failure to make the English Opera House a centre of high culture on Cambridge Circus, Augustus Harris and Charles Morton were more successful. They turned it into the Palace Theatre of Varieties. It was in effect a music hall but it played, like the Alhambra and the Empire, to an upscale audience of both sexes and was a particular attraction for men about town. It included a skit on *Pagliacci*, a pantomime ballet titled 'Scaramouche', comedy with Dan Leno, and recitals by leading actors such as Lewis Waller.[50] It quickly developed 'Living Pictures': *tableaux vivants* which succeed the *poses plastiques* that had been a feature of Leicester Square in the early Victorian years. These simulated nudity in some instances. They were facilitated by the stage engineer, Walter P. Dando, who created a new revolve that could smoothly mount the tableaux without distracting noise and move them around.[51] Viewers could enjoy a series of tableaux: 'Diana', 'Venus of Milo', 'Psyche at the Well', 'Aphrodite'.[52] Dando also

---

[49] *Standard*, 5 November 1894, p. 2; Winston Churchill, *My Early Life: A Roving Commission* (London: Fontana, 1972 [1930]), ch. 4.

[50] W.H. Morton and H. Chance Newton, *Sixty Years' Stage Service: Being a Record of the Life of Charles Morton, the Father of the Halls* (London: Gale and Polden, 1905), pp. 181–3.

[51] Joseph Donohue, 'W.P. Dando's Improved Tableaux Vivants at the Palace Theatre of Varieties, London', *Theatre Notebook*, 63 (2009): pp. 151–79; Barry J. Faulk, *Music Hall and Modernity: The Late Victorian Discovery of Popular Culture* (Athens, OH: Ohio University Press, 2004), ch. 5; Brenda Assael, 'Art or Indecency? *Tableaux Vivants* on the London Stage and the Failure of Late Victorian Moral Reform', *Journal of British Studies* 45 (2006), pp. 744–58.

[52] Donohue, 'W.P. Dando's Improved Tableaux Vivants', p. 155.

developed the flying apparatus from the gridiron above the stage that allowed his wife, 'Mademoiselle Aenea', to dance the *'Mouche d'Or'* in thin air, as well as new lighting effects.

Like the *poses plastiques* in Leicester Square (see Chapter 5), paintings were 'realized' on the stage, with the lighting of the original works exactly reproduced. The figures, however, did not move and their apparent nudity was simulated by tight-fitting, flesh coloured body stockings. This made it easier to defend against opposition from the National Vigilance Association. Supporters noted the aesthetic quality of *tableaux vivants* and insisted this was art and not pornography. Everyone knew the models were not actually naked. Even Laura Ormiston Chant did not object as the *tableaux vivants* had artistic credentials. Victorians thus had complex attitudes to the nude. The campaigning journalist W.T. Stead argued that *poses plastiques* were indecent but only in so far as 'statues are indecent no more, no less'.[53] This kind of contained sexuality remained a feature of West End attractions.

The Palace continued to trade in the exotic. In 1908, the Canadian Maud Allen appeared in *The Vision of Salome*. Her dance of the seven veils (difficult to censor as the house was not regulated by the Lord Chamberlain) was hugely suggestive; her costume was brief and her body was exposed. The play with its roots in Oscar Wilde's drama expressed the spirit of decadence and liberation from Victorian prudery. As Judith Walkowitz argues, she had a cosmopolitan and bohemian allure which turned her into an object of fascination.[54]

The rise of oriental dancing on stage proved controversial. In 1911 the LCC forced the London Palladium to modify a dance titled 'The Dawn of Love' which featured Adam and Eve. It was danced by Nydia Nerigne, wearing very little clothing whilst the man playing Adam merely had a 'garland of leaves round his loins'. Not only was the oriental form of dancing sexually suggestive but it seemed to undermine the grace of classical forms of dance. The *Daily Chronicle* spoke to a 'well known professor of dancing' who opined, 'The dances of eastern women in the low haunts of Tunis and Rangoon and Cairo are not exactly the kind of thing that we would want to provide for the young men and women of English society...Dancing is melody in movement. This Eastern business is contortionism.'[55] The contests over the Empire and about oriental dancing represented the continuation of attempts at moral regulation that the West End had witnessed through its history. Moral reform was the flip side of the pleasure district. It served to reveal sexual anxieties and tensions. For all the conservatism of West End

---

[53] Stead was discussing the performance of La Milo at the London Pavilion in 1906. His remarks are quoted in David Huxley, 'Music Hall Art: La Milo, Nudity and the pose plastique, 1905–1915', *Early Popular Visual Culture*, 11 (2013), p. 234.

[54] Walkowitz, *Nights Out*, ch. 3.

[55] LCC Theatres Committee London Palladium, 1904–10: LCC/MIN/10/10, 847 (London Metropolitan Archives); *Daily Chronicle*, 16 November 1911, p. 1; *Stage*, 16 November 1911, p. 14.

entertainments, they possessed their disruptive elements as well, which challenged conventional morality.

The other form of spectacular variety show was represented by the London Hippodrome which opened in 1900. On the corner of the Charing Cross Road and Cranbourn Street (leading into Leicester Square), Frank Matcham designed an imposing redbrick concoction for entrepreneur Edward Moss who wanted to create a space that combined the circus, the music hall, and the variety show. It was built around a tank which contained 100,000 gallons of water. Elephants were led in (it was literally a hippodrome) and jumped into the tank. At the same time, it was an adaptable space, which could feature music hall and revue. Thus an evening in 1900 included the French horse, 'Mr Good Night', who entered fully dressed, wearing hat, coat, coloured shirt, trousers, and a handkerchief brandished in his coat pocket. He was so gifted that he got into bed. Also on the bill that evening was the comedian Little Tich, and Julius Seeth's act with twenty-one lions.[56]

Four years later, as we have seen, Oswald Stoll opened the London Coliseum on St Martin's Lane. It was designed to hold 2358 people. Stoll introduced a major innovation by offering four performances during the day with shows beginning at twelve, three, six, and nine. The twelve o'clock show was repeated at six and the three o'clock show was repeated at nine. To sustain this intensive schedule, Stoll employed 186 front of house staff and 178 backstage (including 110 scene shifters) (Fig. 12.7).[57]

Stoll saw his mission as improving the quality of music hall entertainment, meaning it had to be lavish and respectable; a theatre 'to which women and children may go in perfect freedom', as noted by his manager Arthur Croxton.[58] Stoll was catering to a public that was more educated after the Education Acts of 1870 and 1880, which made them more open to sophisticated light entertainment. There were musical spectacles representing Derby Day on stage and the recent assault on Port Arthur during the Russo-Japanese War, as well as Loie Fuller dancing and the Meister Glee Singers. The Coliseum was not initially successful and required a refit in 1907 (dropping the twelve o'clock show) before it took off. It featured many of the great variety performers of the day including singer Albert Chevalier ('Funny without being Vulgar'), comedian George Robey, and Bransby Williams doing his impersonations of Dickens characters. There were so many animals on stage that the Coliseum needed its own stables.[59]

---

[56] Era, 17 February 1900, p. 18.

[57] Felix Barker, The House that Stoll Built: The Story of the Coliseum Theatre (London: Frederick Muller, 1957), p. 19.

[58] Arthur Croxton, Crowded Nights—And Days: An Unconventional Pageant (London: Sampson Low, 1934), p. 157.

[59] Barker, The House that Stoll Built, p. 85.

THE LONDON COLISEUM

Fig. 12.7 The London Coliseum (Michael Diamond Collection)

The Coliseum's architect Frank Matcham also built the London Palladium which opened in 1910 as a variety house. It became one of the most enduring sites for light entertainment in London, featuring operetta, dancing girls, farces, and musical comedy. Its location close to the intersection of Regent Street and Oxford Street helped appeal to shoppers seeking diversion. The London Palladium's architecture was palatial with a palm court at the back of the auditorium where refreshments were served while a ladies' orchestra performed. It copied the Coliseum with a twice-nightly format.

The Alhambra, the Empire, the Palace Theatre of Varieties, the London Hippodrome, the London Coliseum, the London Palladium; these all embodied the populist palatial style. By the Edwardian period, the pleasure district was studded with stately mansions of fun; material expressions of the West End brand. Despite the existence of music halls elsewhere, they turned the West End into a major destination and drew in a heterogeneous audience with their cheerful vulgarity, sensuous lustre, and brassy self-importance. The spectacle was such that an audience would always leave feeling they had got their money's worth. The mansions signalled that the West End was a place designed for family entertainment with material that was suitable for children, eschewing the raffish image that the district had earlier in the nineteenth century. Suburban families would have been less likely to encounter lewd behaviour in the audience which was a risk in smaller halls elsewhere. On the one hand, West End variety houses represented huge feats of labour, with large numbers both on stage (front and back) but also in the front of house. On the other, what they offered was the opposite of Victorian earnestness. Variety contrasted with the greater focus on realism and naturalism that started to take over the Edwardian theatre in the form of, for example, the plays of George Bernard Shaw. Moreover, it offered the opposite of the deep absorption required to appreciate the plays of figures like Shaw.

Variety instead constructed its audience as people who would not only be open to different forms of entertainment but subject to diversion and distraction; much as the arcades did. We might compare the contrasting acts with the different floors of the department store. Both variety and department stores promised something for everyone. Variety theatre was the logical consequence of the growth of consumer society with the arousal of different forms of desire.

Transformations

The end of the century and the beginning of the next brought changes to light entertainment. On 21 February 1896, the Polytechnic on Upper Regent Street (which was devoted to showing off new scientific discoveries) presented the first short films which had been made by the Lumière brothers and exhibited in Paris just two months before. The short films were then shown by the Empire as part of its commitment to up-to-dateness in entertainment, forming part of the programme with other performances. The same month the Egyptian Hall showed R.W. Paul's Theatreograph. The cinema had arrived.

There were no purpose-built cinemas until 1906 when a building opened up in Oxford Street to exhibit *Hales's Tours and Scenes of the World*. It was not immediately obvious that cinema would become a more popular alternative to both the theatre and the music hall for the masses. Even in 1908, when Ralph Blumenfeld bumped into the actor Jimmy Welch, the latter could express his disdain for the 'kinematograph shows' in these terms:

> He does not think they can ever compete with the legitimate stage, and that in any case the music-hall has nothing to fear from moving pictures as a means of a full-programme entertainment. The music-hall, he says, will absorb the moving picture...[60]

But by this time even illustrious figures of the stage such as Sarah Bernhardt and Herbert Beerbohm Tree had turned to the cinema. The moving image changed the nature of popular entertainment, but cinemas, as they emerged in the early twentieth century, emulated the populist palatial style and opted for the kind of grandeur that had characterized the Alhambra and the Empire. The Egyptian Hall reopened as a cinema in December 1907, offering continuous performances and a Japanese tea room (where women dressed as geishas served refreshments). The *Era* reported that the 'performance will be of such a refined and wholesome character that ladies who happen to be shopping in the West End in the afternoon may with perfect safety betake themselves and their children to the new Egyptian Hall'.[61] In due course the Alhambra was knocked down and replaced by the Odeon Leicester Square in 1937 whilst the Empire ended its theatrical existence in 1927 with *Lady Be Good* featuring the young Fred Astaire. The site was purchased by Metro Goldwyn Mayer who turned it into a cinema the following year.

But there were other changes that transformed the kind of culture on which the West End depended. In 1911, Diaghilev's *Ballets Russes* performed at Covent Garden and exposed how old-fashioned West End ballet had become. The use of ballet as just one act of a variety bill seemed shallow when the Russian troupe demonstrated that ballet was a serious art form and not just a vehicle for men about town to ogle women. Dancers like Nijinsky and Anna Pavlova came from a different world. The splendour of the colourful costumes was dazzling. They were quickly asked back with Pavlova performing at the Palace Theatre of Varieties. The actress Elsa Lanchester was taken as a child to see Pavlova dance and later recorded 'I was never quite the same after that' (it launched her into the world of modern dance for a time).[62] The Great War ended the ballet world of Leicester Square.

Another new cultural form also arrived in London in 1911 that would be even more transformative. This was ragtime. One of the big hits of 1912 was *Hullo Ragtime!* at the Hippodrome. It heralded the development not only of jazz but

---

[60] Ralph D. Blumenfeld, *R.D.B.'s Diary, 1887–1914* (London: Heinemann, 1930), pp. 69, 226–7.
[61] *Era*, 14 December 1907, p. 26.
[62] Elsa Lanchester, *Elsa Lanchester Herself* (New York: St Martin's Press, 1983), p. 19.

also of a major shift in popular music from an emphasis on melody to a focus on rhythm. Ragtime was a translation of American black music for a white audience. It signified a shift away from Victorian manners and restraint and its arrival was therefore controversial. Whilst there was resistance to the American invasion, it reveals the way in which variety could shape English manners and sociability. Ragtime announced itself as new and defiantly modern. In the same year as *Hullo Ragtime!* George Edwardes's musical *The Sunshine Girl* at the Gaiety introduced the tango into Britain; it was followed by *Hullo, Tango!* at the Hippodrome in 1913.[63] Ragtime and the tango both in different ways promoted an emphasis on the body in its most sensuous form.

The West End absorbed exotic and modernist influences from Paris, Berlin, and Buenos Aires but it also became a vehicle for a major cultural force: Americanization. The leads in *Hullo Ragtime!* were recruited from New York vaudeville. Along with *Everybody's Doing It!* at the Empire and *Kill That Fly!* at the Alhambra, the show established revue as a popular form that would then start to dominate live entertainment and move on from music hall and variety. The revue proved a metropolitan form that thrived in the West End as it rejoiced in topicality with significant public figures being impersonated and mocked. The carefree revue format seemed to say that nothing was sacred. Revue thrived on proclaiming what was up-to-date and celebrating its own cosmopolitanism.[64]

The populist palatial style developed by entrepreneurs such as George Edwardes, Oswald Stoll, and Augustus Harris helped democratize pleasure in the West End. Its entertainments drew in a wider range of people but it was expressed in a conservative form; validating pleasure but not undermining the social order. West End light entertainment managed to integrate prestige and vulgarity.

By the outbreak of war in 1914, the West End was absorbing international influences on its stages which fed through into dance, into sheet music, and into records and gramophones. These porous new media in turn shaped print media, fashion, and the way people walked and spoke. Light entertainment had real cultural dynamism, even shaping artistic modernism. Artists and intellectuals in Britain and France, as the twentieth century beckoned, found themselves shaped by popular culture.[65]

The Alhambra, for example, influenced the avant-garde with its erotic allure. Arthur Symons later said that his most magical glimpse of the Alhambra was once, when he was outside, the doors were thrown open and he saw the curtain

---

[63] Kerstin Lange, 'The Argentine Tango: A Transatlantic Dance on the European stage', in Len Platt, Tobias Becker, and David Linton (eds), *Popular Musical Theatre in London and Berlin, 1890–1939* (Cambridge: Cambridge University Press, 2014), p. 155.

[64] Peter Bailey, '*Hullo Ragtime!*: West End Revue and the Americanisation of Popular Culture in pre-1914 London', in Platt, Becker, and Linton, *Popular Musical Theatre*, pp. 135–52.

[65] Jeffrey Weiss, *The Popular Culture of Modern Art: Picasso, Duchamp and Avant-gardism* (New Haven, CT: Yale University Press, 1994); Robin Walz, *Pulp Surrealism: Insolent Popular Culture in Early Twentieth Century Paris* (Berkeley: University of California Press, 2000).

calls 'in a sort of blue mist'. For Symons, it meant the 'charm of rouge of fragile cheeks' (the fact that made-up actresses resembled the painted ladies in the gallery and on the streets was part of the effect). It mattered that the Alhambra offered a world of pure pretence. Symons attended a rehearsal for the Alhambra pantomime, *Aladdin*, and was fascinated by the costumes of the dancers. The move from front of stage to backstage had an aesthetic impact on him, characteristic of the way modernism became fascinated by form:

> To watch a ballet from the wings is to lose all sense of proportion, all knowledge of the piece as a whole; but in return, it is fruitful in happy accidents, in momentary points of view, in chance felicities of light and shade and movement. It is almost to be in the performance oneself, and yet passive, a spectator, with the leisure to look about one. You see the reverse of the picture.

Symons's fascination with the disassembling of elements and the 'charm of the artificial' shows why intellectuals were fascinated by what they found at variety houses. For twentieth-century moderns, great art was always unfinished; the desirable form of art were necessarily a sketch, or, in the example Symons gave, a rehearsal. The ballet, he concluded, was 'a picture in movement' which is why it had the effect of a great painting, but one where 'the figures of the composition are real, and yet, by a very paradox of travesty, have a delightful, deliberate air of unreality'. The Alhambra appealed because it did not aspire to teach but merely to be beautiful.[66]

Light entertainment of the sort treated in this chapter suffers from not being taken seriously; neither high art nor vulgar popular culture. But what if we consider it as an integral part of social history? The revolving globe that adorned the London Coliseum and Gaiety Girl cheesecake expressed a metropolitan culture that was aspirational but sought to mediate between extremes. It was a world that was not bound by traditional forms of cultural authority and unembarrassed by its stark commercialism. Whilst it employed images of the exotic it was also shaped by a kind of London Englishness: neither northern nor southern but one intended to serve an imperial metropolis (see Chapter 16). In an age that saw polarization by class taking stark forms, light entertainment helped create an inoffensive middlebrow approach to pleasure. Apart from the prostitutes at the Empire, variety usually stayed the right side of respectability (avoiding the lewdness that existed even in West End music halls) whilst also acknowledging the sensuality that the public culture of the Victorians so often denied. The complaint of Laura Ormiston Chant's witness about the Empire dancer in 'La Frolique' placing her foot in a man's hand caught some of this; a pictorial emblem of sexual

---

[66] Arthur Symons, 'At the Alhambra', *Savoy*, 5 (1896), pp. 75–83.

intimacy. Light entertainment was the product of new conceptions of sexuality associated with decadence and then modernism. The Empire Theatre was thus as much an architect of modernity as Ibsen.

Building on our investigation of West End theatres, we see the construction of a larger utopian space that was imagined as 'show business'. The pleasure district was built on a confected, mass-produced form of glamour that was developed by print and pictorial media but could be found on its stages. Here was a world that could draw in all classes from the intelligentsia to workers seeking a treat. It thus suited a society that was democratizing, with many male workers getting the vote and the Woman Question taking new forms. Its sophistication also spoke to a society that was more educated and, courtesy of the developing media, aware of the world at large. Light entertainment may have been conservative but it did not mandate snobbery. It was not (as John Hollingshead would put it) 'stuck-up'.

The forms of light entertainment that developed in the later nineteenth century were not entirely new. Musical comedy, operetta, burlesque, and music hall ballet fed off the spaces that the West End provided and hailed spectators with formats that could express colour, joy, and wonder. Hollingshead was not wrong to employ the metaphor of the *soufflé* in describing the appeal of the Gaiety (perhaps acknowledging an inner emptiness at the heart of the entertainment?). Light entertainment was to the stage what the *soufflé* was to gastronomy. The pleasure district needs to be encountered, as we have seen, through its sensory dimensions: its visual delights, its smells, its tastes, its constructions of glamour. The social function of pleasure districts is to make the rest of life seem small by comparison.

PART FOUR
OUR HOSPITALITY

13

Eating Out

Pêche Melba

In 1879, the architect Thomas Verity delivered a paper at the Royal Institute of British Architects on 'The Modern Restaurant'. It had been, he noted, a common complaint that it was difficult to get a good meal in London. Food was a problem if you wanted a night out in the West End. Certainly, clubland London could offer fine dining but that only a served a small minority. Now, he was able to announce, that had all changed.[1]

This was a self-serving statement on the part of Verity as he employed the paper to promote his own building. Through 1873–4, he had been engaged by the caterers Spiers and Pond to create the Criterion complex on Piccadilly Circus; a grand restaurant (launched in 1873) linked to a theatre (which opened the following year). The Criterion became a signature destination in the West End, because of its French Renaissance facade, neo-Byzantine marble ceiling, and lustrous gold mosaics. In *A Study in Scarlet*, it is at the Criterion that Dr John Watson first hears the name 'Sherlock Holmes'.

In turn, it helped make Piccadilly Circus the centre of London nightlife. Amongst its multiple dining and banqueting rooms, the Criterion was famous for its American Bar, which pulled in the sporting set. Gourmet Nathaniel Newnham-Davis noted how the habitués of the Criterion all had 'a tinge of the racing man about them'; indeed, he observed some guests dash in from Kempton races still with their racing glasses slung over their shoulders. Among the men at the bar (famous for its American cocktails) were a 'sporting baronet, who takes an interest in yachting' and 'a dramatist, who has written more than one racing play, and no doubt finds the American Bar useful for his local colour'.[2] Gay men would meet there, perhaps drawn to its homosocial atmosphere.[3] Women (apart from barmaids) were banned from the bar as well as the room for masonic meetings. Other rooms, however, were open to women and the Criterion became a popular place for female shoppers coming up to town, not only because of the food but the elegance of its rest rooms. During 1909–10 the Actress's Franchise League,

---

[1] *Caterer and Hotel Proprietor's Gazette*, 4 March 1879, pp. 30–1.

[2] Nathaniel Newnham-Davis, *Dinners and Dining: Where and How to Dine in London* (London: Grant Richards, 1899), pp. 181, 182, 185.

[3] Matt Cook, *London and the Culture of Homosexuality, 1885–1914* (Cambridge: Cambridge University Press, 2003), p. 26.

London's West End: Creating the Pleasure District, 1800–1914. Rohan McWilliam, Oxford University Press (2020).
© Rohan McWilliam.
DOI: 10.1093/oso/9780198823414.001.0001

part of the Suffragettes, held meetings at the Criterion's Grand Hall. The Women's Social and Political Union also gathered there to greet released Suffragette prisoners in 1909 and in 1910.[4] This feminine presence was evidence of the way that the West End was changing.

The restaurant in its modern form was also relatively new. It epitomized the expanding urban culture of the nineteenth century. Eating out became integral to business deals and to political fixing but was also central to making of the middle-class world. In 1885, Pascoe's guide to London could claim 'There is probably now no capital in Europe that can show so many spacious and splendid restaurants as London.'[5] The West End became a site for emulation. For example, in the 1880s, the Paragon Theatre of Varieties on Mile End Road offered a saloon bar which featured 'all the comforts of a West-End Restaurant', evidence of the way in which the West End dominated the cultural imagination when it came to food.[6] It was not ever thus.

The next three chapters deal with restaurants, hotels, and shopping. They are connected in that they constitute an exploration of the way the West End produced different kinds of commercial hospitality. We are familiar with hospitality as a dimension of the domestic sphere but, I argue, we need to think about the deployment of the rhetoric of hospitality and welcome in social locations elsewhere. Restaurants, hotels, and shops helped cater for people's needs in contrasting ways. They celebrated luxury and status (accompanied by various forms of exclusion to remove undesirables). This in turn produced a rhetoric about the importance of hospitality and service. Workers, whether in the form of shopgirls, porters, theatre ushers, or waiters, were increasingly encouraged to treat customers as honoured guests and deploy performances of politeness and deference. This act of hospitality, I argue, involved the recreation of the domestic in a different form and drew on the rituals and discourse of domestic service. These institutions offered a counterpart to the forms of hospitality offered in clubland London but also to music halls (which, of course, served alcohol and food): *otium cum dignitate*. Pleasure districts function partly through a discourse of hospitality which makes them inviting but they also make decisions about who to include and exclude in the process of welcome.

Eating out was never just about the consumption of food. As the example of the Criterion shows, it was about the facilitation of social interaction. For that reason, restaurants took on symbolic dimensions based around class, status, and

---

[4] Elizabeth Crawford, 'WALKS/Suffrage Stories: Suffragettes and Tea Rooms: The Criterion Restaurant, Kate Frye, and the Actresses' Franchise League', Women and Her Sphere blog: https://womanandhersphere.com/2012/09/05/suffrage-stories-suffragettes-and-tea-rooms-the-criterion-restaurant-kate-frye-and-the-actresses-franchise-league/ (accessed 3 September 2018).

[5] Charles Eyre Pascoe, *London of To-Day: An Illustrated Handbook for the Season* (London: Sampson, Low, Marston, Searle and Rivington, 1885), p. 45.

[6] John Marriott, *Beyond the Tower: A History of East London* (London: Yale University Press, 2011), p. 197.

gender. They were as much forms of spectacle as the London Coliseum and a restaurant meal became an important ancillary to seeing a show. The West End developed fine dining establishments aimed at High Society, such as Romano's on the Strand, but this chapter demonstrates how the restaurant meal also became an important part of middle-class life from the mid-century onwards. We will explore this by looking at the food empire of Joseph Lyons and then the Gattis. Food was thus integral to the making of the pleasure district.

If there was a female dimension to the new West End, it should be said that the pleasure district reaffirmed masculine roles. In restaurants, the star chefs were usually male, despite cooking often being viewed as a female occupation. Thus the restaurant could pose as the inversion of the female-run domestic sphere; a place that people could recognize but which was different. Many waiters were male and the head waiter was always male. The West End restaurant helped create the figure of the gourmet (usually a man) but also the bon viveur whose insider knowledge and (more importantly) large income allowed him to sample the best cuisine available and to recognize the genius behind the culinary creations of figures such as Escoffier.

Food was linked to high culture, with the West End establishing equivalents to Delmonico's in New York. Being on familiar terms with the headwaiter was a mark of distinction and *savoir-faire*; so was knowing how much to tip. The use of French names for food was a nod to the sophistication of some guests but it could alienate or discriminate against others who had inferior palates or who simply could not make head nor tail of the menu. 'None of your d–d *à la's*' insisted a fox-hunting rural friend of Nathaniel Newnham-Davis whom he took out for dinner.[7] Knowledge of the wine list, a preening form of cultural capital, could also be a marker of distinction.

The cost of a meal went far beyond the price of the ingredients that went into it. High end restaurants made a point of dressing up a basic commodity (food) and constructing enticing environments in which it could be appreciated. The rituals surrounding food and drink are central to forms of sociability in all societies. Food may be a universal need but cultural attitudes to its preparation, cooking, and presentation vary. The West End became a point of entry for the cuisines of other countries to be appreciated in Britain. Relations with the continent opened London up to French, Italian, and German dishes. The empire led to the first Indian restaurants and indeed to curry being served at the Criterion.[8] Brenda Assael thus talks of 'gastro-cosmopolitanism', a feature of West End life as people encountered the cuisines of different nations.[9] Such openness to non-British

[7] Newnham-Davis, *Dinners and Dining*, pp. 28–9.
[8] Newnham-Davis, *Dinners and Dining*, ch. 22.
[9] Brenda Assael, *The London Restaurant, 1840–1914* (Oxford: Oxford University Press, 2018), ch. 5. See also Judith R. Walkowitz, *Nights Out: Life in Cosmopolitan London* (London: Yale University Press, 2012).

influences needs to be mapped onto other forms of West End cosmopolitanism; the love of Italian opera, the adoption of French fashion, the panoramas that opened up the globe. The cosmopolitan mode allowed pleasure districts to define sophisticated taste in terms of international influence.

In the West End, food was turned into a form of entertainment with a rich theatricality. Newnham-Davis compared Frascati's on Oxford Street to a panto-mime transformation scene with its elaborate use of gold and silver.[10] There was profuse use of glass and palm trees (a frequent symbol of luxury). Tables were separate and not shaped into booths as in the old chop-houses. Restaurants inter-sected with theatre in other ways. As we have seen, the Criterion was constructed as both theatre and restaurant. The Savoy was built as a theatre which then became a hotel and a leading restaurant. The Gaiety on the Strand was a theatre and restaurant (see Fig. 13.1). Her Majesty's Theatre was rebuilt in 1897 as part of a complex which included the Carlton Hotel with its spectacular restaurant. The pre- and post-theatre meal was a standard part of West End dining though there were complaints about the law which from the early 1870s forced restaurants to

Fig. 13.1 The Gaiety Theatre restaurant, early twentieth century (Westminster City Archives)

[10] Newnham-Davis, *Dinners and Dining*, p. 264.

close by 12.30 at night, limiting options for theatre-goers.[11] There are other linkages one can make between theatres and West End hospitality industries. Auguste Escoffier's most famous dish is arguably the Pêche Melba. This was invented when he was the chef of the Carlton Hotel restaurant and was intended to celebrate the diva Nellie Melba. Following her success at Covent Garden in *Lohengrin*, Escoffier presented her with a desert made up of peaches and ice cream on ice shaped in the form of a swan to evoke the opera.[12] The West End made these connections possible.

There was nothing new about eating and drinking out, which had long been part of the urban experience. In London it had taken the form of dining in inns and taverns. During the eighteenth century, the coffee house became an important site not only because coffee was so popular but because it was a place to find newspapers and engage in conversation about the events of the day.[13] The restaurant as an institution emerged in Paris in the later eighteenth century. The word 'restaurant' was derived from the French word for a soup or broth that was considered to have restorative powers. The places where one could eat this soup and other fine meals became increasingly luxurious, drawing in a wealthy clientele. In contrast to taverns, the use of separate tables allowed guests to be private in a public space. The figure of the waiter, the development of the menu, and the use of fixed prices were all novelties developed in Paris.[14]

London had sprouted taverns, coffeehouses, and chop-houses in the eighteenth century. It is not true to say that London did not have cafés on the continental model. However, London cafés never developed the kind of mystique that the café did in Paris, Vienna, and elsewhere, patronized as they were by intellectuals. Henry James noticed this gap after his time on the continent and put the English gentleman's disdain for cafés down to the fear of mixing with people from different stations in life.[15] The world of the coffee house in the West End became dissipated into gentleman's clubs, cigar divans (smoking rooms), pubs, and restaurants.[16]

Fine Dining

In the later nineteenth century, London began to establish restaurants aimed at the elite. These were places that were defined by the employment of a celebrity chef, who was often foreign, and international cuisine. They featured spectacular

[11] *Caterer and Hotel-Keeper's Gazette*, 15 March 1906, p. 116.

[12] Auguste Escoffier, *Memories of my Life* (New York: Van Nostrand Reinhold, 1997), p. 115.

[13] Jurgen Habermas, *The Structural Transformation of the Public Sphere: An Inquiry into a Category of Bourgeois Society* (Cambridge, MA: MIT Press, 1989); Brian Cowan, *The Social Life of Coffee: The Emergence of the British Coffeehouse* (New Haven, CT: Yale University Press, 2005).

[14] Rebecca Spang, *The Invention of the Restaurant: Paris and Modern Gastronomic Culture* (Cambridge, MA: Harvard University Press 2001); Rachel Rich, *Bourgeois Consumption: Food, Space and Identity in London and Paris, 1850–1914* (Manchester: Manchester University Press, 2011), ch. 4.

[15] Henry James, *English Hours* ed. Leon Edel (Oxford: Oxford University Press, 1981), p. 90.

[16] Markman Ellis, *The Coffee House: A Cultural History* (London: Weidenfeld and Nicolson, 2004), pp. 207–24.

surroundings and expected guests to observe a strict dress code. The latest in female fashions were paraded and small orchestras provided music. Many of these restaurants were located in grand hotels, such as the Savoy, but others such as Romano's on the Strand were independent. Moncrieff's guide to London in 1910 was cynical about this fine dining trend: 'most of their customers will be well content so long as the charges are high enough; and that, once a name is won for luxury and fashion, the snobbish sheep come flocking in to fatten beside the "best" society, that so willingly exhibits itself in a glow of electric light'.[17]

How did food establish itself as a major draw in the West End? One of the earliest high-end restaurants was Verrey's, established on Regent Street in 1825. It was one of the first French restaurants in London though the founder was Swiss.[18] The atmosphere was always select and drew on a clientele derived from the embassies (an important audience for West End pleasures). By the 1850s it had become a standard eatery for foreign aristocrats but was also much used by ladies who lunch; wealthy or titled women who had come to town to shop. Verry's was known to have excellent wine cellars; by the 1880s, one could obtain the '69 Lafite (*tirage du chateau*) and the '74 Pommery. A typical menu for dinner might include *Oeufs à la Russe* (made with real grey caviar), *consommé à l'okra, sole à la Dreglère, boudins à la Richelieu, tournedos à la Périgueux, pommes Anna, Beccassines, salade*, and *parfait au café*.[19] The elaborate French names were part of the performance.

Oscar Wilde's great haunt in the West End was the Café Royal, where he would lunch with Lord Alfred Douglas.[20] Here artists, bohemians, journalists, and politicians congregated. Whistler, Sir Arthur Sullivan, Max Beerbohm, Arthur Symons, Frank Harris, and George Augustus Sala would often come to drink, dine, and converse.[21] It was founded in 1865 by a French immigrant, Daniel Nicholas Thévenon, who used its Regent Street location as a draw, together with increasingly opulent interior design and the best cuisine. Revolutionary fervour and ultra-conservatism could be found here but it also became a place where the ideas of decadence and artistic modernism were explored, a reputation it enjoyed well into the twentieth century. Such establishments showed that restaurants retained some features of the eighteenth-century coffee house as centres of political discussion and argument.

Restaurants often had an exotic or orientalist quality. Romano's, on the Strand, much cherished by the stage community, was a French and Italian restaurant

---

[17] A.R. Hope Moncrieff, *London* (London: A. and C. Black: 1910), p. 98.

[18] *The Epicure's Almanac; Or, Calendar of Good Living* (London: Longman, Hurst, Rees, Orme and Brown, 1815), pp. 123, 133.

[19] Pascoe, *London of To-Day*, pp. 48–50.

[20] Guy Deghy and Keith Waterhouse, *Café Royal: Ninety Years of Bohemia* (London: Hutchinson, 1955).

[21] R.D. Blumenfeld, *R.D.B.'s Diary, 1887–1914* (London: Heinemann, 1930), pp. 88–9; see also Leslie Frewin (ed.), *Parnassus near Piccadilly: An Anthology* (London: Leslie Frewin, 1965).

(famous for its macaroni) whose decorations were meant to suggest the eastern Mediterranean with a contrasting Japanese room on the second floor.[22] It started as a small café and grew with its fame until it was able to charge high prices. It proved a hit with the sporting set and bohemian journalists from Fleet Street: 'the bar was full of racing men, coaching men, men from the Stock Exchange, and men about town of every type'.[23] For that reason, the restaurant achieved a mythological status because of the people one met there. These included journalists such as Shirley Brooks of *Punch* and a variety of contributors to the *Sporting Times* (always known as the *Pink 'Un*), as well as theatre people, soldiers, and, inevitably, the Prince of Wales, who was the consummate man about town. Conversation seems to have focused on the turf. Romano's was, in effect, an alternative to a gentleman's club. An example of the way it made journalists feel at home was the addition of a soup to the menu called *Crème Pink 'Un*. Hospitality was extended to women who were allowed to dine so it was not simply a location for masculine camaraderie. Gaiety Girls could often be found there. The Sisters Leamar, a music hall double act, sang a song with the line 'Romano's, Italiano, Paradise in the Strand'. Most of the music hall audience could not have afforded to go to Romano's but the song is evidence of the self-mythologizing quality of the West End, the transformation of sites of pleasure into landmarks.[24] It was destroyed in the Blitz.[25]

Far more spectacular than Romano's was the coming in 1896 of the Trocadero on Coventry Street at the top of the Haymarket. Formerly the Argyll Rooms dance hall and then a music hall, it was the creation of the Lyons food empire (of which more below). The enormous venue possessed the same kind of grandeur as the spectacular theatres of the period. The entrance was a big hall with a wide marble staircase leading up to the grand restaurant with gallery and orchestra. These were overlooked by a frieze depicting the legends of King Arthur and a ceiling adorned with paintings of clouds, figures, and flowers. There was also a large salon in the Louis XV style and downstairs a big grill room in Flemish style with smoking and billiard rooms en suite as well as a buffet. The wine cellars were extensive. Between 1895 and 1896, Lyons bought every single bottle of Chateau Belair St Emilion.[26] Dinner in the grand restaurant varied from 5s to 10/6. The downstairs grill offered a meal for 2/6 on a table d'hôte. The Trocadero was never intended to offer cheap meals but nor was it out of the reach of middle-class professionals. Such locations became the new temples of bourgeois life.

Whilst dominated by English and French cuisine, the West End also provided other kinds of food, some of which reflected Britain's imperial rule. The capital was full of soldiers and administrators who had served in India and developed a

---

[22] Newnham-Davis, *Dinners and Dining*, p. 87.

[23] John Bennion Booth, *Old Pink 'Un Days* (London: Grant Richards, 1924), p. 184.

[24] Booth, *Old Pink 'Un Days*, p. 184.

[25] Guy Deghy, *Paradise in the Strand: The Story of Romano's* (London: Richards Press, 1958).

[26] Peter Bird, *The First Food Empire: A History of J. Lyons and Co.* (London: Phillimore, 2000), p. 51.

taste for Indian cuisine. There were also many Indian nationals who were now in London and able to cook. Charles Stenbridge's Oriental Depot at 34 Leicester Square imported curry powder and Indian condiments whilst J. Halford of St Martin's Lane provided tinned curried fowl using herbs procured from India.[27] In 1906, Fateh Mohamed opened an Indian restaurant at 5a Stafford Street (off Old Bond Street); its location providing evidence that it was aimed at an upscale clientele. It included a Hindu chef who only made vegetarian dishes and a Muslim who presumably made everything else. The menu included Madras Curry, *Mooley Muchee* (Light Curry), *Jhalfuryjee* (Hot Lucknow curry); *Khorma* (Spiced Chicken or Mutton), and *Biryanee*.[28]

In the first half of the nineteenth century, women could not enter most West End restaurants. The theatre critic Clement Scott recalled that '[t]heir presence would have been considered fast, if not disreputable'.[29] Verrey's and Epitaux's on Pall Mall were among the few exceptions in allowing women to dine.[30] After 1850, the restaurant became a space that was increasingly open to women although even in 1925 Panton Street boasted a restaurant (with a 'Tom and Jerry' atmosphere) that continued to exclude women.[31]

Women often had to be escorted by men in restaurants but the Berkeley on Piccadilly, the Savoy, and Claridge's became known as hotels where women could dine (even without an escort) by 1900.[32] So was the more downmarket Gambrinus restaurant on Glasshouse Street by Piccadilly which served German and Dutch food. A female friend of Newnham Davis's told him 'We girls often go there by ourselves, for nobody says anything to us, and we haven't to dress up, and we are not stared at like we are in your real swell restaurants.'[33]

The culture of dining out was therefore becoming diffused through Victorian society. Food was integrated into the nature of the pleasure district; a space that could bring together different kinds of cuisine and therefore promise to satisfy all kinds of needs. Cosmopolitanism was, I argue, bound up with notions of commercial hospitality. Diners could expect a warm welcome provided they were prepared to pay, to dress well, and to exhibit a sense of sophisticated *savoir-faire*. Food therefore had its own theatricality and performative rituals including dressing up and knowing where to be seen.

[27] Advertisement in St Martin's Scrapbook Series: Leicester Square Vol. 1 part 2 p. 8 (Westminster City Archives); *Caterer and Hotel-Keeper's Gazette*, 5 April 1879, p. 46.

[28] *Caterer and Hotel Keeper's Gazette*, 15 February 1906, pp. 66–7.

[29] Clement Scott, *How They Dined Us in 1860 and How They Dine Us Now* (London: Trocadero, c.1900), p. 8.

[30] *London at Dinner: Where to Dine in 1858* (London: David and Charles, 1969 [1858]), p. 11. See also Blumenfeld, *R.D.B.'s Diary*, pp. 227–8.

[31] James Bone, *The London Perambulator* (London: Jonathan Cape, 1925), p. 104.

[32] Newnham-Davis, *Dinners and Dining*, p. 208.

[33] Newnham-Davis, *Dinners and Dining*, p. 354.

Food for the Many

The West End may have been the home of the high society restaurant but it also played a major role in providing cheap meals that offered some of the ambience of the more illustrious spaces. There was a food revolution led by the ABC chain, the Lyons tea shops, and Gatti's restaurants. Entrepreneurs like Spiers and Pond made a fortune through railway buffets as well as launching restaurants such as the Palsgrave on the Strand, which specialized in fast turnover and efficient, cheap service.[34] They served the many workers who toiled in the West End but also made a cheap night out possible for people arriving to enjoy an evening's entertainment.

The later nineteenth century saw the emergence of restaurant chains in London, such as Slaters, which commenced at 212 Piccadilly in 1894 and quickly developed through the West End, Victoria, and the City. It was possible to eat for under a shilling. With its clean and cheerful interiors and its advertising which emphasized its 'Ladies Retiring Room', Slaters made the act of eating out look cutting-edge.[35] This was important in the West End and the City as there were a large number of workers (most of whom did not live nearby) who needed cheap and quick meals. The Aereated Bread Company (ABC) opened its first tea shop in the Strand in the early 1860s. It was founded by Dr John Daughlish who developed a new way of baking bread without yeast and forcing carbon dioxide into the dough to aid fermentation. This was not only a cleaner process but was also cheaper, pushing prices down and leading to a proliferation of ABC tea-rooms around the globe. The ABC serving girls could be the object of mirth for their primness whilst also serving as objects of male desire.[36] An ABC teashop on Norfolk Street, off the Strand, was the setting for Baroness Orczy's 'Old Man in the Corner' armchair detective stories in 1908. He solved mysteries whilst seldom leaving the confines of the restaurant's marble hall.

The Lyons food empire also had its roots in the West End.[37] This started with two families (the Glucksteins and the Salmons), who had become a major force in tobacco retail. Despite this success, they doubted the future profitability of the tobacco market and began to diversify into a relatively new area: catering. Montague Gluckstein was appalled at the poor quality of the catering at the Royal Jubilee Exhibition in Manchester in 1887 and spotted an opening. Most other members of the family dismissed the idea of going into catering and would not let their name be used. He needed someone else who could run his proposed catering venture and alighted upon a distant cousin, Joseph Lyons. At the time Lyons

---

[34] Assael, *The London Restaurant*, p. 34.
[35] *Slater's Restaurants Illustrated*: London Collection Pamphlets Box 323: D.91.15 (Bishopsgate Institute).
[36] *Sketch*, 8 November 1893, p. 105.
[37] On Lyons, see Bird, *The First Food Empire*; Thomas Harding, *Legacy: One Family, A Cup of Tea and The Company that Took on the World* (London: Heinemann, 2019).

was running a market stall but this proved an inspired choice because he was a brilliant entrepreneur who grasped the possibilities of catering.

The Lyons company quickly won contracts and began catering for music halls, theatres, shooting galleries, and P.T. Barnum's show in Olympia. Joseph Lyons then in effect went into show business. Working with the great producer Imre Kiralfy, he staged water spectaculars such as *Venice in London* at Olympia in 1890. Lyons not only provided the catering but created a syndicate to purchase Olympia. He also acquired Cadby Hall in Hammersmith which became a huge factory that blended tea and supplied baked goods to all Lyons outlets as well as to others.

Maurice Gluckstein had also appreciated the popularity of Buszard's tea room on Oxford Street and saw another opportunity. The first Lyons tea room was opened at 213, Piccadilly in May 1894. It was attractively designed in the Louis XVI style and offered quality food for a cheap price. It was respectable and operated on temperance lines. The food was produced at Cadby Hall and was completely standardized. Tea, however, was freshly brewed for each customer so that it contrasted with the stewed sludge on offer elsewhere. Mutton pie was the favourite dish on the menu and it was only 7d.[38] There was also iced Bovril and soda, egg rissoles, and truffled foie gras sausage at 3d. Moreover, there was a greater choice of items than at comparable restaurants. People responded to the price and to the product. At the same time, Lyons eclairs (then a novelty) proved so successful that upscale patrons in carriages would turn up to put in orders for them whilst actors such as Ada Reeve were familiar sights in the Piccadilly branch.[39] By the following year, Lyons was able to open twelve new shops in London and they went on to become common sights throughout the country. Oxford Street would eventually have nine Lyons tea shops on it.[40]

In the 1890s customers were mainly men with women and children coming in on matinee days but it was to prove a distinctly female, family-friendly space (the provision of ladies lavatories was important).[41] The femininity of the tea-rooms was accentuated by the fact that Lyons opted to use waitresses rather than waiters. The waitress was not completely unknown before this but waiting tables had tended to be a male pursuit.[42] Lyons worked on the basis that there should be one waitress for every eight customers, making for efficient service. Waitresses were selected on the basis of looks and height (tall women were preferred). Nell Bacon, who rose from being a waitress in the first Piccadilly branch to becoming chief superintendent for all Lyons teashops, recalled that when she started in 1897, 'not one of us had a waist measuring more than 19 inches'. Waitresses originally wore a

---

[38] Bird, *The First Food Empire*, p. 40.
[39] Memories of Nell Bacon (Lyons archive): ACC/3527/231 (London Metropolitan Archives).
[40] Bird, *The First Food Empire*, p. 43.
[41] Memories of Nell Bacon (Lyons archive): ACC/3527/231 (London Metropolitan Archives).
[42] Assael, *The London Restaurant*, pp. 112–13.

high necked grey cashmere dress, extending down to the ankles, with an apron.[43] Bacon would go on to design the later 'Nippy' costume with a shorter skirt and lower collar with a cap. The dresses were originally made by a Paris costumier until Lyons took over manufacture. In 1912, waitresses were paid 7/6 weekly, making them the lowest paid workers for Lyons. Cashiers by contrast were paid 11/6 a week. All staff paid 1/6 per week for dinners to be provided for them.[44] The Lyons waitress offered a female form of welcome which may have been reassuring for families.

Migrants often play a major role in bringing innovation to the entertainment and food cultures of major cities, as a glance at American vaudeville and Times Square shows. The Glucksteins were Jewish immigrants from Prussia. This is also true of the Gatti family who were Swiss and shaped the West End, bringing food and entertainment to the many.

The paterfamilias of the Gatti family was Carlo Gatti, who was born in 1817 and hailed from the Blenio Valley in Ticino, the Italian-speaking part of Switzerland.[45] He came to London in 1847 where he set up a stall selling waffles in Battersea Fields. This was the beginning of a remarkable food empire. Within months of his arrival, he established a French café in the Great Hall of Hungerford Market. Businesses of this type were an innovation in this period. Symptomatic of the new West End, he created a café that was family-friendly, including the device of providing light music from a small string orchestra for diners. Five fiddlers knocked out standards from Rossini and various Italian hits.[46] He went on to open similar premises in Oxford Street, Whitechapel High Street, and the Edgware Road. His decision to buy more and more bays in Hungerford market was vindicated when it was purchased for the building of Charing Cross Station, leading to generous compensation.

Gatti became one of the first people to popularize ice cream for the masses. Ice cream recipes had been handed down in Italy through the gelato tradition but Gatti came on the scene when ice cream production was becoming speedier and less cumbersome. It therefore ceased to be a delicacy for the rich.[47] At street level ice cream was popularized by what were called 'Hokey Pokey Men'. Gatti's carts were a familiar sight on London streets. When Lord John Russell refused to receive a delegation of working men, it was suggested by a newspaper that his 'cool' behaviour might make him a rival to Gatti's, evidence of how far the firm had become a brand name in the ice cream business.[48] Gatti was a visionary

[43] Memories of Nell Bacon (Lyons archive): ACC/3527/231 (London Metropolitan Archives).
[44] Wages of staff 1912–1919: ACC/3527/187 (London Metropolitan Archives).
[45] ODNB (Carlo Gatti).
[46] Pascoe, London of To-day, p. 51; The Gattis obtained a music and dance licence in 1858: Era, 3 October 1858, p. 5.
[47] Laura B. Weiss, Ice Cream: A Global History (London: Reaktion Books, 2011).
[48] Lloyd's Weekly Newspaper, 2 August, 1863, p. 6.

because he recognized the importance of ice (and hence refrigeration) for the food industry of the future. To support this, he bought an ice well on the Regent's Canal and then developed a hugely successful business importing cheap ice from Norway.[49] His company lasted up till 1981.

In 1862 Carlo and Giovanni Gatti established Gatti's Palace of Varieties, a leading music hall cum restaurant in South London, run much of the time by Carlo's daughter Rosa. George Leybourne (better known as 'Champagne Charlie') played there. Four years later, Carlo Gatti established premises on Villiers Street underneath Charing Cross Station. It became a leading music hall known popularly, as Gatti's under the Arches (with restaurant and billiard saloon attached) and the start of a music hall syndicate.

The key figures in the next generation of Gattis were Carlo's nephews, Agostino and Stefano Gatti. In 1861, they acquired the Royal Adelaide Gallery on the Lowther Arcade, Strand, which became known as 'the most popular restaurant in London' with more diners than any other establishment.[50] Let us look more closely at the Strand restaurant (usually referred to as 'Gatti's'). The advertisement in Fig, 13.2 reveals it as an example of the populist palatial style. It was such a landmark that the Sketch could run a short story called 'The Man I met at Gatti's'.[51] When the Gattis took over the Gallery, they offered a café on the ground floor and a restaurant above. Gatti's restaurant, in its early days, was known to cater for clerks, foreign nationals, bohemians, political exiles, and soldiers taking out lady friends.[52] Above all, it became what one guidebook described as 'the best middle-class dining place in London'.[53] The restaurant offered elegant settings and live music which flattered the diners. Gatti's offered the semblance of high-end dining but at a cheap price. Significantly, the menu card printed the price of all dishes in contrast to some upmarket restaurants, but the food compared well in terms of quality and expense.[54]

Originally, Gatti's cuisine was entirely English but, from the 1880s, it began to offer continental (especially French) food, but very much alongside traditional English cooking. This included pre- and post-theatre dinners, a good example of the way different West End industries interacted with one another. In the early 1880s, the restaurant employed between 180 and 200 waiters, and about forty chefs. The waiters worked from eight in the morning till midnight. The chefs were paid but the waiters usually were not. They lived on tips but did receive free lodgings and food. Many waiters came from Ticino expecting to return home at some point.

[49]   Felicity Kinross, *Coffee and Ices: The Story of Carlo Gatti in London* (privately printed: 1991).
[50]   Pascoe, *London of To-day*, p. 51.
[51]   J. Holt Schooling, 'The Man I met at Gatti's', *Sketch*, 1 May 1895, p. 24.
[52]   Morley Roberts, 'Waiters and Restaurants', *Murray's Magazine*, 7 (1890), p. 543.
[53]   Pascoe, *London of To-day*, p. 51.
[54]   Newnham-Davis, *Dinners and Dining*, p. 114; Charles Eyre Pascoe, *London of To-day*, p. 51.

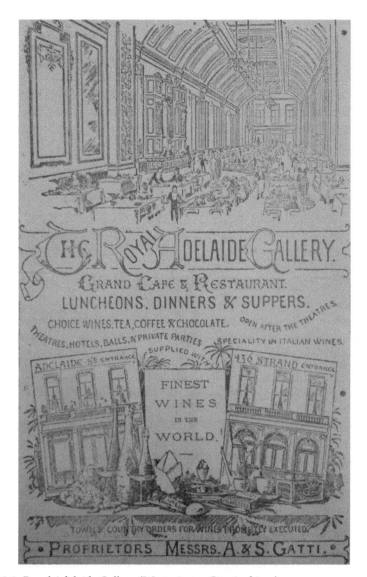

Fig. 13.2 Royal Adelaide Gallery (Westminster City Archives)

The Gatti brothers branched out into running promenade concerts and panto-mimes at the Covent Garden Theatre. They took over the Adelphi Theatre in 1879 and then, in 1892, the Vaudeville theatre close by. The Adelphi specialized in melodrama (in 1900 it did well with William Gilette's play *Secret Service*). The Vaudeville, by contrast, offered light comedy. As Peter Barber and Peter Jacomelli argue, the Gattis put on 'precisely the type of drama likely to appeal to the middle-class clientele of their café-restaurants'.[55] Indeed, one characteristic of a show at the Adelphi was that it had to end in time for the audience to catch a late meal at Gatti's.[56] One contemporary wrote of how the Gattis had become a household word 'in melodrama no less than in méringues'.[57]

Their impact was even more fundamental. The Gattis wanted the Adelphi to be provided with electricity which no power company would supply. They therefore created the Charing Cross and Strand Electricity Supply Corporation which ended up supplying electricity to much of the West End, the City, and Westminster. This in turn led the Gattis into local government. Agostino's son, John Maria Gatti, became mayor of Westminster in 1911 after serving as a Conservative representative for Charing Cross ward on Westminster City Council. He was also a founding member of the Society of West End Theatre Managers which he chaired through 1919–20. The electricity company survived until it was nationalized by the Labour Government after the Second World War and the Gatti family retained the freehold of the Adelphi Theatre until 1955.

Carlo Gatti described himself as a licensed victualler but he was clearly much more than that. He created a culture industry that linked food and drink to mass entertainment, a legacy built upon by his nephews and other members of the Gatti family. For that reason it made sense that they became key figures in the development of music hall. The Gattis offered innovation and change whilst being distinctly conservative in all senses.

With the example of the Gattis, we have described here a cultural field which links chocolates and ice cream to beer to billiards to music hall to cafeterias to melodramas to Rossini to electricity to musical comedy. This is the world that the West End made possible. This chapter has charted the ways in which food and its meanings were an integral part of the pleasure district, satisfying appetites in more ways than one. The restaurant developed new forms of sociability; its most upscale versions borrowing elements of London clubland. The spatial proximity to St James's with its clubs was important but the restaurant (for all the undeniable forms of exclusivity at places like Romano's) was a more open institution if only because of the presence of female diners. To that extent the restaurant was the product of women entering the public sphere in the later Victorian period.

Londoners had long eaten out, but the dining culture explored here was a distinctive development of the later nineteenth century and one in which the West End led the way. The examples of the Gattis's and the Lyons's food empires show the provision of dining experiences could become opportunities for entrepreneurialism. Restaurants also required a new approach to manners. Understanding the

---

[55] Peter Barber and Peter Jacomelli, *Continental Taste: Ticinese Emigrants and their Café-Restaurants in Britain, 1847–1987* (London: Camden History Society, 1997), p. 9.

[56] Nathaniel Newnham Davis, *The Gourmet's Guide to London* (New York: Brentano's, 1914), p. 231.

[57] (Mrs) E.T. Cook, *Highways and Byways in London* (London: Macmillan 1911), p. 290.

conventions of eating out (for example, tipping) became a social accomplishment in itself. Less sophisticated diners could find themselves confronted by forms of cutlery they were not always familiar with. Yet restaurants, even at the more popular level, were always about more than food. They offered a kind of popular fantasy, not least the release from domestic drudgery (someone else cooked and washed up). Frederick Willis recalled being taken to what he thinks was Gatti's as a child in 1893 and said 'The waiter looked after us like a mother.'[58] This kind of hospitality was not peculiar to the West End but it did mesh with the claims that the pleasure district made for itself. A meal could be turned into an aesthetic experience. The use of an orchestra in some eateries established the claims of an establishment to prestige and sophistication. West End restaurants were often spaces for music. Gatti's arguably assisted with the popularization of music far more than the St James's Hall on Piccadilly did and reached a wider audience. Dining out possessed a strongly theatrical dimension and a large part of this was due to the fact that it often took place in the pleasure district. A restaurant meal could be an end in itself or an accompaniment to an evening at a show, an extension of a business meeting or the inevitable preliminary to falling in love.

[58] Frederick Willis, *A Book of London Yesterdays* (London: Phoenix House, 1960), p. 59.

14

Grand Hotel

A Little World in Itself

In 1906, *The Caterer* noted: 'houses are letting badly, as many well-to-do people now stay at hotels, which is a cheaper and more convenient plan than keeping up an establishment…'.[1] Hotels in 1906 were not new, but the later nineteenth century witnessed a major innovation which shaped the West End: the Grand Hotel. This was part of a global trend with hotels becoming ever larger; monumental landmarks in the urban scene. The long antiseptic corridors of hotels with their anonymous doors on either side that looked exactly the same became a common sight. They enjoyed a surprisingly outsize role in the cultural imagination given that, for most people, they were mainly places in which to sleep; they frequently featured in novels, films, and detective stories.

Pondering the hotel lobbies of Weimar Germany, the great cultural theorist Siegfried Kracauer argued that the hotel was a modern version of a church, as the people who came there visited as guests. The difference was that in a church, people came to meet God and establish community whereas the hotel had no such meaning.[2] The large spaces devoted to the lobby had no real purpose, expressing the emptiness of modern culture. This study takes a different view. Lobbies were a statement about wealth and expansiveness, a rejection of cramped conditions. The large spaces offered by lobbies were an advertisement, linking the hotel to the other attractions of the pleasure district. They reflected the fact this was public space on private property; an invitation for the public to use the restaurant and other facilities even if they were not staying the night. It has also been pointed out by Vanessa Schwartz (writing in a Parisian context) that the lobby was a great place to people-spot and comprehend the urban pageant.[3] Its size was a physical manifestation of hospitality; an openness to diverse visitors from all over the globe who could stay the night, eat, and conduct business on the premises.

If the West End generated the cultural style we have called the populist palatial, the grand hotel with its rationale to look after the rich might be viewed as an example of the plutocratic palatial (indeed it was intended to feel like a palace).

[1] *Caterer and Hotel-Keeper's Gazette*, 15 May 1906, p. 185.
[2] Siegfried Kracauer, 'The Hotel Lobby', in his *The Mass Ornament: Weimar Essays* ed. Thomas Y. Levin (Cambridge, MA: Harvard University Press, 1995), pp. 173–85.
[3] Vanessa R. Schwartz, *Spectacular Realities: Early Mass Culture in fin-de-siècle Paris* (Berkeley, CA: University of California Press, 1998), p. 23.

London's West End: Creating the Pleasure District, 1800–1914. Rohan McWilliam, Oxford University Press (2020).
© Rohan McWilliam.
DOI: 10.1093/oso/9780198823414.001.0001

Like the restaurant, it was another form of hospitality industry that took shape in many places, but in the West End in particular. As we saw in the previous chapter, hotel restaurants like the Savoy were major sites for fine dining. Moreover, their architecture and uses connected with department stores, as both benefited from advances in technology (such as lifts) which allowed them to climb higher and add more floors.

We began our study of the nineteenth-century West End with the arcades which seemed to offer the magnetic appeal of being small towns in miniature. The grand hotel had a similar kind of attraction. The Hotel Cecil claimed it was 'a little world in itself located in the very centre of the hub of the richest capital of the world'.[4] Grand hotels were in effect a development of clubland London, with their exclusive atmosphere (and of course it was possible to stay at clubs). They offered fine dining, a place for the rich to mingle, and a range of hospitality services from laundering clothes to booking tickets for the latest show. Some can even be claimed as progenitors of the twentieth-century dance hall. The Savoy and Ritz became famous locations for dancing.[5]

Hotels catered to a world shaped by travel and the state of sojourn. One peculiarity of their appeal was that they endorsed an identity that marked the release from domestic ties if a traveller was away from home. Despite a strong emphasis on respectability, hotels always have retained associations with illicit sexuality: the love affair, the location for prostitution. They were places for social mixing in which men and women could be thrown together. They could also be places of anxiety in a different way. Might the hotel staff help themselves to valuables left in a bedroom? They also became badges of status. To stay at the Ritz or the Savoy meant something. At Oscar Wilde's committal, the judge was appalled to discover that sex between men might have taken place at the Savoy hotel (and gone unreported by a chambermaid): 'It is a state of things one shudders to contemplate in a first class hotel.'[6] The hotel had a dynamic effect on the culture and yet remains curiously under-studied as one of the institutions that have created modern metropolitan living.[7]

---

[4] *St Cecilia*, May 1896, p. 24.

[5] James Nott, *Going to the Palais: A Social and Cultural History of Dancing and Dance Halls in Britain, 1918–1960* (Oxford: Oxford University Press, 2015), pp. 13, 15.

[6] Matt Cook, *London and the Culture of Homosexuality, 1885–1914* (Cambridge: Cambridge University Press, 2003), p. 58.

[7] See Derek Taylor and David Bush, *The Golden Age of British Hotels* (London: Northwood, 1974); Elaine Denby, *Grand Hotels: Reality and Illusion* (London: Reaktion, 1998); A. K. Sandoval-Strausz, *Hotel: An American History* (New Haven, CT: Yale University Press, 2008); Molly Berger, *Hotel Dreams: Luxury, Technology, and Urban Ambition in America, 1829–1929* (Baltimore, MA: Johns Hopkins University Press, 2011); Alexandre Tessier, *Le Grand Hôtel: l'invention du luxe hôtelier, 1862–1972* (Rennes: Presses Universitaires de Rennes, 2012); Kevin J. James, A.K. Sandoval-Strausz, Daniel Maudlin, Maurizio Peleggi, Cédric Humair, and Molly W.Berger, 'The Hotel in History: Evolving Perspectives', *Journal of Tourism History*, 9 (2017), pp. 92–111; Sasha Hamlin, 'Grand Hotels: Cosmopolitan Caravansaries, Gastronomy, and Performance Spaces of Late-Nineteenth and Early-Twentieth Century London' (University of Cambridge, M.Phil. thesis, 2018).

The term 'hotel' is French in origin, like the word 'restaurant'. It originally meant a town mansion and the grand hotels of the later nineteenth century retained some of that meaning. The modern usage which refers to a place where people can stay began to be used in English from the mid-eighteenth century but did not really catch on until the early Victorian period when it was identified with a particular type of building. There was a major transition in West End life around mid-century. Hotels had previously occupied pre-existing structures often intended as homes; after 1850 they were increasingly purpose-built and modelled themselves on the palatial equivalents in New York and Paris.

The rise of the modern hotel reflected the movement of peoples; hence it was a statement about trade, commerce, cosmopolitanism, and (sometimes) empire. International tourism helped create it as steamships and railways made access easier and cheaper. London's status as heart of empire was a major draw. The expansion of hotels was also part of the social and economic Big Bang that was London in the mid-nineteenth century. Travellers both from outside and inside Britain required places to stay. West End hotels, as we will see, took different forms though they were particularly aimed at the rich and the middle classes. The great terminus stations in London were soon joined by major hotels catering for the huge number of people pouring into the metropolis. The Grosvenor Hotel was opened in 1862 by Victoria Station, a year after the station itself opened. It was built in the French Renaissance style and was one of the first hotels in London to have a 'rising room' (in other words, a lift).[8] Charing Cross Station was opened in 1864 and the following year the Charing Cross Hotel was opened. Hotels had become a major business. A sign of this was the creation of *The Caterer and Hotel Proprietor's Gazette* in 1878 which linked the restaurant, catering, and hotel trades together.

The hotel aimed to emulate the domestic and provide a home from home. Yet the atmosphere was really a transformation of the domestic: provisional, unsettled, a re-imagining of social space. As an institution, the hotel was the product of a society of strangers, where people did not find it uncomfortable to occupy a bed that had been occupied by an unknown person the night before (provided the sheets were changed).[9] It offered hospitality and a refuge from an unknown society outside. When staying at Morley's Hotel in Trafalgar Square, Henry James appreciated the fire in the coffee room and the 'hospitable mahogany' as well as the vast four-poster bed that the establishment provided.[10]

Grand hotels reflected the way in which the residential population of Mayfair was becoming less aristocratic; its grand mansions occupied by offices and

---

[8] Taylor and Bush, *The Golden Age of British Hotels*, pp. 31–2.

[9] James Vernon, *Distant Strangers: How Britain Became Modern* (Berkeley, CA: University of California Press, 2014).

[10] Henry James, *English Hours*, ed. Leon Edel (Oxford: Oxford University Press, 1981), p. 3.

embassies as the great families moved out. Some of the landed elite found that it was no longer necessary to maintain an expensive London address as they could stay at a leading hotel when in town. The Grand Hotel on Northumberland Avenue was particularly patronized by 'old country families' and leading manufacturers from the North.[11] The Metropole on the Thames Embankment attracted business people and some wealthy families used it as their home.[12]

The hotel as an institution was a familiar part of West End life by mid-century. In 1849 a guidebook explained: 'The stranger who comes to London for pleasure, and pleasure only, will find the best description of lodging in the West-end of London, in the streets issuing from Piccadilly.'[13] For people who were less well off, the options were less clear cut though there were boarding houses and cheap lodgings in Bayswater, Kensington, and Bloomsbury.

Origins

There was nothing new about the hotel. Inns and coaching establishments on major highways served a mobile population and became important landmarks, providing a bed for the night, refreshment, and stables for horses. At one level, the hotel emerged from establishments like the White Bear coaching inn on Piccadilly. Travellers in the early modern period would often find themselves thrown together, even to the extent of having to share a bed. The modern hotel differed from this in that it aspired to provide a room for each person, couple, or family. The Royal Clarence Hotel in Exeter, first built in 1769, is often viewed as Britain's first purpose-built hotel. Five years earlier, however, a Mrs Martin had opened a 'Gentleman's Hotel' in King Street, St James's Square. She claimed in the *London Evening Post* that her hotel was aimed at 'all Noblemen, Gentlemen, Foreigners and others, that they may be accommodated with genteel Lodgings for one Night, or as long as they think proper'. She also claimed that hers was 'the only Hotel in London'.[14]

Mayfair and St James's began to develop hotels in the later eighteenth century, aimed at the rich. These included Pulteneys at 105 Piccadilly (notable for its flushing toilets). Tsar Alexander I stayed there in 1814. When in town Walter Scott would stay at Longs, 16 New Bond Street, which was associated with the beau monde. Slightly more downmarket, Brunet's Hotel on Leicester Square catered for

[11] Nathaniel Newnham-Davis, *Diners and Dining: Where and How to Dine in London* (London: Grant Richards, 1901 [1899]), p. 301.

[12] Newnham-Davis, *Diners and Dining*, p. 303.

[13] Peter Cunningham, *A Handbook for London, Past and Present* (London: John Murray, 1849), Vol. 1, p. xvi.

[14] *London Evening Post*, 1–4 December 1764, p. 2. I am grateful to Peter Tyldesley for this reference.

army officers and diplomats.[15] Limmer's on Conduit Street was patronized by the sporting set and young army officers. It actually provided gentlemen with a secret passage so that they could escape onto New Bond Street if their creditors turned up.[16] Limmer himself had been the head waiter at New Exchange Coffee House in 365 Strand and became close to the Prince of Wales, later Prince Regent.[17] The largest hotel in the early nineteenth century was probably the Clarendon on New Bond Street. Its chef, Jacquier, had once cooked for Louis XVIII and helped establish the popularity of French cuisine in London.[18] By the early nineteenth century, it was considered legitimate that the nobility seek out hotels when they were on the move.

In 1812 Mivart's Hotel was established at Brook Street in Mayfair and built up a reputation by appealing to the best circles. Lord William Beauclerk (acting for the Prince of Wales) bought the lease of the building and gave James Edward Mivart the job of running it as a private hotel which could attract the aristocracy. It was possible to rent furnished apartments a month at a time and so was an alternative to maintaining an expensive town-house for some. Mivart's also benefited from the presence of embassies close by and was patronized by diplomats which allowed the hotel to expand into nearby buildings. Mivart retired in 1854 and the business was taken over by William Claridge and his wife who owned Coulson's hotel next door. Claridge is thought to have started life as a butler, which is not insignificant as the hospitality industry was an extension of the world of domestic service. The Claridges combined their buildings with Mivart's to create a grand hotel aimed at the wealthy. The atmosphere was deliberately private and discreet, set back from the main West End thoroughfares. In 1856, the hotel became known as Claridge's and secured its reputation in 1860 when the Empress Eugenie opted to use it on her visit to England. Queen Victoria was entertained there. Royal connections were important. Queen Emma of the Sandwich Islands and Leopold II of the Belgians also patronized Claridge's.[19] By the end of the century, Claridge's brought in an estimated £90,000 worth of business of which £30,000 was profit for Richard D'Oyly Carte who had bought the hotel in 1893.[20]

There were, however, hotels that catered for a slightly less illustrious clientele. Morley's Hotel was constructed on what would become Trafalgar Square in 1832 (see Fig. 14.1). As we have seen, Henry James stayed there. So did Sir Arthur

[15] The Epicure's Almanac; Or, Calendar of Good Living (London: Longman, Hurst, Rees, Orme and Brown, 1815), p. 152.

[16] Taylor and Bush, The Golden Age of British Hotels, p. 4; http://www.georgianindex.net/London/l_inns.html (accessed 17 September 2018); A.L. Humphreys, Crockford's; Or, The Goddess of Chance in St. James's Street, 1828–1844 (London: Hutchinson, 1953), p. 33.

[17] Charles Eyre Pascoe, London of To-Day: An Illustrated Handbook for the Season (London: Sampson, Low, Marston, Searle, and Rivington, 1885). p. 30.

[18] Jean Desebrock, The Book of Bond Street Old and New (London: Tallis, 1978), p. 80.

[19] ODNB (William Claridge).

[20] Memorandum to Directors of the Savoy Hotel, 4 May 1899: THM/73/8/15 (Victoria and Albert Museum Theatre and Performance Archives).

Fig. 14.1 Morley's Hotel (Westminster City Archives)

Conan Doyle and William F. ('Buffalo Bill') Cody. Covent Garden had the Tavistock (which only took men) and the Hummums; Osborne's was in the Adelphi whilst Hatchett's was in Piccadilly. Fricour's on St Martin's Lane and the Sablonière on Leicester Square both catered for foreigners.[21] The expanding number of hotels showed that there was an increasing number of people who needed them. As a technology of organizing people, the hotel had its rituals, starting with the register which had to be signed so that people could be kept track of and the bill made ready for departure. The closest figure to a host was the registrar who took the name of the guest and assigned a room. He had a policing function, keeping out undesirable people or figures who did not look as if they had the money to pay.

De Luxe

In 1880 it was noted that 'Until comparatively recently, London was perhaps the least well off of our large cities for really good hotels.'[22] The grand hotel in the

---

[21] Newspaper clipping in St Martin's Scrapbook Series: Leicester Square, Vol. 1 p. 39 (City of Westminster Archives).

[22] *Caterer and Hotel Proprietor's Gazette*, 5 June 1880, p. 104.

nineteenth century proved to be a global phenomenon. France and the United States in particular developed the models for luxurious establishments. The Grand Hotel in Paris was opened in 1862; an extension of the revamping of the city centre by Baron Haussmann. Like Claridge's, it became a signature destination for foreign royalty. In the world of the hotel, French solutions were often seen as the best solutions.

Hotels in the United States also provided an important model, especially as London from mid-century was increasingly populated by American visitors who had grown used to a certain level of comfort at home. In 1880 the *Caterer* commented on American hotels: 'Such magnificence is never to be seen in Europe, except perhaps in a few royal and imperial *salons* at Paris, Berlin, and Vienna, or a few wealthy mansions in Manchester and the Black Country.' It put this down to the fact that 'In America...the people are sovereign', meaning that the market responded to popular demand.[23] British visitors to the United States were shocked by the size and scale of American hotels. In 1861, George Augustus Sala claimed 'The American hotel is to an English hotel what an elephant is to a periwinkle.'[24] American skills at hospitality really shaped the hotel on an international scale, an early example of what a later generation would call 'Americanization'. By 1910, one guide to London offered the opinion, 'It is Transatlantic custom, I take it, that has chiefly made the demand for the luxurious accommodation affected by simple-minded republicans away from home...Wherever he goes, Uncle Sam is content with nothing but the best to be got...'.[25] We have already noted the presence of *de luxe* American bars in West End restaurants. The number of American millionaires who visited London meant that we should see the West End as an extension of the Gilded Age in the United States. This was the class that was analyzed by Thorstein Veblen in terms of its love of conspicuous consumption.[26]

The Strand, Trafalgar Square, and their environs became characterized by a concentration of hotels. Guests wanted to be in the centre of town, a short stroll from all West End attractions. The Grand Hotel opened on the corner of Trafalgar Square and Northumberland Avenue in 1881, offering suites of rooms together with arrangements for the servants of guests to eat their meals separately.[27] It was followed by the Metropole Hotel in 1883–5 and then the Hotel Victoria in 1887 (both on Northumberland Avenue). The Grand Hotel made a huge splash on its opening, looking as it did onto Nelson's Column. Its lobby and staircase were in the Italian style with grey and red marbling. Its reading room was lined with American walnut wood and fluted columns inspired by the Louis Seize style.

---

[23] *Caterer and Hotel Keeper's Gazette*, 1 October 1880, p. 160.

[24] Quoted in Sandoval-Strausz, *Hotel*, p. 121.

[25] A.R. Hope Moncrieff, *London* (London: A. and C. Black: 1910), p. 88.

[26] Thorstein Veblen, *The Theory of the Leisure Class: An Economic Study of Institutions* (London: Allen and Unwin, 1924).

[27] *The Grand Hotel, Trafalgar Square, London: Tariff* (London: Grand Hotel, 1888?).

Chippendale furniture was in abundance. There was a ladies' drawing room which adopted a domestic look. Lifts were available (built on the Waygood safety system), demonstrating how hotels needed to offer the latest in technology. The bedrooms were lined with pine. As was common, the restaurant was available for outsiders as well as guests (though guests could have the charge for meals put on their hotel bill). Another common use of the dining facilities at hotels like the Grand was for regimental dinners and wedding breakfasts. Facilities were available to provide haircuts or to obtain tickets for the opera and the theatre. There was also a telephone which was available in the gentleman's cloakroom (meaning that it was not available to women). The Grand therefore felt like a town in miniature.[28]

The Strand proved equally fertile territory for hotels. The Savoy Hotel was the inspiration of Richard d'Oyly Carte who had established the Savoy theatre in 1881 (see Fig. 14.2). The hotel very much vindicated D'Oyly Carte's vision and flair. On trips to the United States he had become aware of the superiority of American hotels and wanted something similar for London. The Palace Hotel in San Francisco was far in advance of its West End competitors. Just as his was the first

THE COURTYARD—RESTAURANT ENTRANCE

Fig. 14.2 The original courtyard at the Savoy: *Souvenir of Savoy Hotel* (London: Black and White Publishing Company, 1893) (British Library 10349.e.19, p. 11)

---

[28] *Caterer and Hotel Proprietor's Gazette*, 5 June 1880, pp. 104–5; *The Grand Hotel, Trafalgar Square*.

theatre to use electricity, his hotel was the first to be not only powered by electricity but to have an electric lift. Another side of D'Oyly Carte's vision was that he increased the number of bathrooms available to seventy. This was an innovation and an example of the grand hotel adapting to new standards of hygiene and comfort. Over at the Hotel Victoria on Northumberland Avenue, which catered for five hundred guests, there were just four bathrooms. Most people used a flat bath which could be found under their beds and which could be assembled and filled with cans of water. Notoriously, when the builder was told that the Savoy would have seventy bathrooms, he asked if the guests were amphibious.[29] A single bedroom cost 7s/6d whilst a double was 12s. Room service was available with speaking tubes in each room so that food and drinks could be easily ordered. For D'Oyly Carte, the Savoy had to be up to date and embody the new.

Its rooms (depending on where they were situated) provided splendid views of the Thames and the Houses of Parliament on one side or St Paul's on the other: the classic London landscapes. A suite at the Savoy consisted of a sitting room, one or more bedrooms, a private bathroom and a lavatory. The look of the early private sitting rooms at the Savoy replicated the tone of the middle-class drawing room. As a promotional booklet put it, each suite 'is thus a little home in itself' (see Fig. 14.3).[30]

To oversee his hotel, D'Oyly Carte chose César Ritz as hotelier, not least because he wanted its restaurant to rival Delmonico's in New York.[31] Ritz was Swiss by birth but learned the hotel trade in Paris, rising from the job of waiter at the Restaurant Voisin during the siege of Paris (where he managed to serve up elephant's trunk in sauce chausseur) before running the restaurant of the Grand Hôtel in Nice. He moved from location to location satisfying the demands of the nineteenth-century jet set who enjoyed new luxuries such as the Orient Express and the ocean liner. When Ritz was hired by D'Oyly Carte to run the Savoy (shortly after a disastrous opening), he in turn recruited key members of the staff at the Grand Hotel in Monte Carlo. A luxury hotel depended for its reputation on excellence in food. Auguste Escoffier was hired to create the kind of food that would satisfy the international elite. Escoffier had thirty-six sous-chefs under his command at the Savoy as well as other assistants. He streamlined the organization of the Savoy kitchen and insisted that cooking was an art. His gastronomic marvels included the *Soufflé aux ecrevisses à la Florentine*, the *Pêches à l'orientale* and the *Canard en chemise*.[32] Some of the really spectacular dinners could run to sixteen courses and cost £15.[33] When the wedding of the sister of the Duke of

---

[29] Stanley Jackson, *The Savoy: A Century of Taste* (London: Frederick Muller, 1989 [1964]), p. 20.

[30] *Souvenir of Savoy Hotel* (London: Black and White Publishing Company, 1893), p. 7.

[31] Luke Barr, *Ritz and Escoffier: The Hotelier, the Chef, and the Rise of the Leisure Class* (New York: Clarkson Potter, 2018), p. 16.

[32] *Souvenir of Savoy Hotel*, p. 18.   [33] Barr, *Ritz and Escoffier*, p. 84.

A PRIVATE SITTING-ROOM

Fig. 14.3 A private sitting room at the Savoy: *Souvenir of Savoy Hotel* (London: Black and White Publishing Company, 1893) (British Library 10349.e.19, p. 3)

Orléans to the Duke of Aosta took place at the Savoy, thirty-seven princes and princesses attended the ten-course banquet.[34] The presentation of the food mattered and the Savoy had to sell decadence. Whilst food from many countries was included on the menu, the dominant source of culinary imagination was French. As at many hotels, most of the waiters were foreign; the best floor waiters were thought to be German.[35] There was, however, a considerable level of performance. Turkish coffee was available from staff wearing national costume creating an orientalist effect (see Fig. 14.4).

Ritz reshaped the Savoy around his taste. Each guest was to have a valet. Ritz was allegedly the first to adopt the saying that the customer was always right.[36] Full evening dress was expected in his restaurant and prostitutes were kept out. Johann Strauss and his orchestra were engaged to play for diners in a grand dining room with a gold and red ceiling. High Society, Indian princes, and the greatest

---

[34] Auguste Escoffier, *Memories of my Life* (New York: Van Nostrand Reinhold, 1997), p. 91.
[35] Clarence Rook, *London Side-Lights* (London: Edward Arnold, 1908), pp. 234–5.
[36] Jackson, *The Savoy*, p. 26.

CAFÉ À LA TURQUE

Fig. 14.4 Café à la Turque: *Souvenir of Savoy Hotel* (London: Black and White Publishing Company, 1893) (British Library 10349.e.19, p. 12)

theatrical and operatic stars of the age would dine in all their finery. The presence of so many leading figures in one place generated its own air of excitement. The debt of D'Oyly Carte to Gilbert and Sullivan was not forgotten with dining rooms sporting names like the Pinafore Room, thus further endowing the hotel with a

HOTEL CECIL, LONDON,
FROM RIVER THAMES.

Fig. 14.5 Hotel Cecil (author collection)

playful theatricality. Escoffier provided elaborate menus that showed off his remarkable skills though an Indian cook was also employed. The Savoy dining room became such a landmark that a reproduction of it featured on stage in a farce called *To-Day* at the Comedy Theatre as early as 1891.[37] Ritz spent much of his time away, overseeing other hotels abroad, and built up his Ritz Hotel Development Company which would construct luxury hotels all over the world. The first of these was the Paris Ritz in 1898.[38] Ritz resigned from the Savoy after a dispute with the D'Oyly Cartes but moved on to the Carlton Hotel, taking Escoffier with him as well as significant parts of high society which reduced profits at the Savoy for a time.[39] He was replaced by other leading hoteliers from the continent who cemented the hotel's reputation.

But the Savoy was not the only major hotel on the Strand. It was joined in 1896 by the Hotel Cecil which offered 1000 rooms with a banqueting hall that could seat 1500, as well as an American bar and English buffet (see Fig. 14.5). Like other similar establishments it had its own masonic hall that could seat 300 (the Gaiety restaurant and the Waldorf also included masonic temples).[40] Freemasonry was an accepted part of the associational life of upper middle-class men. The southern block included tapestries that depicted historical scenes. Maples of Tottenham

---

[37] Michael R. Booth, *Theatre in the Victorian Age* (Cambridge: Cambridge University Press, 1991), p. 91.

[38] ODNB (César Ritz).   [39] Stanley Jackson, *The Savoy*, p. 38.

[40] Ernest Runtz, *Hostelries: Ancient and Modern* (London: Institute at 34 Russell Square, 1908), pp. 93–5.

Court Road provided the furniture though Chippendale seems to have also been much in evidence. The bedrooms followed contrasting styles: Louis XV and XVI, Empire, Georgian. Such an approach copied the style of European palaces whilst insisting on its modernity. It included an Indian floor, where the design was inspired by a reproduction of the Emperor Akbar's palace at Fatehpur Sikri. The smoking room was also Indian in style, meaning that the hotel acknowledged its connections to trans-national and imperial networks.[41]

The first manager was G.P. Bertini who had previously worked at Delmonico's and then the Criterion in London. The hotel needed eighty cooks, two hundred waiters, fifty chambermaids, as well as numerous porters, housemaids, and lift boys. Prices for rooms were kept down, starting from six shillings a night. Eighty people applied for rooms before the hotel even opened.[42] Rooms were designed with connecting doors so that they could function as larger suites if necessary. A publicity guide to the hotel was produced in German, evidence of its international appeal.[43] The hotel even spawned its own periodical, St Cecilia, noting that the latter had been the 'patron saint of musical and society festivities'.[44]

The Hotel Cecil was situated on the site of what had once been Salisbury House, home of the first Earl of Salisbury. Despite being a new hotel owned by a private company, the hotel emphasized the ancient lineage of the Cecil family after whom it was named. St Cecilia published a miniature biography of Robert Cecil, the first earl of Salisbury (1563–1612) whilst Robert Gascoyne-Cecil, third Marquess of Salisbury, was the current prime minister when the hotel was founded. Salisbury's cabinet would later be waggishly nicknamed the 'Hotel Cecil'. The Strand, St Cecilia noted, had once been the site of great aristocratic palaces.[45] The cultural project of the Hotel Cecil was to employ novelty (every bedroom had a phone) whilst adopting the ancient associations of nobility as well as empire.[46]

Its dining rooms were important meeting places for high society. The Royal Caledonian Ball was held there every year with about 2000 guests. The 5th Lancers and the 13th Hussars would dine regularly. In 1905, its Grand Hall (which could also function as a concert hall) hosted the dinner to welcome Viscount Milner back after his governorship of South Africa. Joseph Chamberlain was in the chair and other attendees included Lord Curzon and Field Marshall Lord Roberts. Altogether the hotel had eleven major dining halls.[47] If we look at the postcard of the hotel's Palm Court in Fig. 14.6, we see how the hotel offered a

[41] St Cecilia, May 1896, p. 15.
[42] Caterer and Hotel-Keeper's Gazette, 15 May 1896, pp. 230–1.
[43] Hotel Cecil, London (n.d.): London Collection Pamphlets Box 323: D.93.1. (Bishopsgate Institute).
[44] St Cecilia, May 1896, p. 24.   [45] St Cecilia, May 1896, pp. 3–8.
[46] St Cecilia, May 1896, p. 15.
[47] Hotel Cecil Banqueting Department (London: Hotel Cecil, 1911.), pp. 5–7: London Collection Pamphlets Box 323: D.91.15 (Bishopsgate Institute).

Fig. 14.6 Palm Court, Hotel Cecil (author collection)

place of luxury and high fashion: entrance to an idealized, pampered class where women wore the best hats at afternoon tea. The American plutocrat would feel at ease in such surroundings. The effect is a fantasia of refinement (note the small band playing on the balcony).

The West End hotel that César Ritz had least to do with was, ironically, the Ritz as, by the time of its opening in 1905, he had retired to Paris and was starting to disengage himself from business (though he did not die till 1918). The new hotel was designed by the architect Charles Mewès. The main entrance was placed in Arlington Street so that guests could avoid the heavy traffic in Piccadilly. Its interior was in the Louis Quatorze style and the ground floor devoted to high class shops. There were 250 bedrooms with sitting rooms. The Ritz became known for its fine dining rooms which made its reputation.[48]

The Ritz also signalled that Mayfair was increasingly being taken over by major hotels. The Coburg Hotel in Grosvenor Square (later renamed the Connaught) was described, when it opened in 1896, as 'in every respect like a wealthy man's private mansion'. The Connaught presented itself as a place for the aristocracy to stay. It made guests feel they were in 'a luxurious and refined home'. The manager of the hotel was Sir John Blundell Maple, son of the founder of the furniture makers on Tottenham Court Road. On either side of the Connaught's lobby were a smoking room and a morning room as well as a coffee room panelled with

---

[48] *Caterer and Hotel-Keeper's Gazette*, 15 January 1906, p. 23.

tapestries depicting hunting scenes. The first floor was made up of self-contained suites, decorated (as in other London hotels) in multiple styles: Louis XV, Louis XVI, Empire, Renaissance, Georgian.

The coming of the Ritz inspired the rebuilding of the Savoy in 1903 to see off the competition. The management run by Sir George Reeves Smith transformed the hotel. Its original entrance was via the Thames. The hotel opted to open out onto the Strand which was actually widened by agreement with Westminster City Council. Adjoining properties were purchased for demolition including Simpson's which was taken over by the Savoy. A new block of residential chambers (Savoy Court) was built whose tenants included Lillie Langtry. Two hundred new rooms were added with more bathrooms. The Savoy Grill was opened up to women (the romantic novelist Elinor Glyn could frequently be seen there). There was a further rebuilding in 1910 which added two new storeys and enlarged the rooms. Its dance hall was expanded into a major ballroom. The Savoy was particularly attractive for American visitors; so much so that an Anglo-American Club, the Pilgrims, was established with headquarters at the hotel. Its sister organization in New York was at the Waldorf-Astoria. This was not the only club set up: Winston Churchill and F.E. Smith helped set up the Other Club which was intended as a dining club to encourage cross-party dialogue among politicians whilst the Shikar Club was for big-game hunters.[49] Grand hotels thus became a real alternative to gentlemen's clubs.

Membership of the best circles meant acquaintance with the great West End hotels. They became places where aristocracy and new money could meet. With the use of electricity and lifts, they were forces for novelty and modernization. Yet they also borrowed from other aspects of West End life. Their size was part of the monumentalist built environment cultivated by the district. They were based on similar patterns of entrepreneurialism. Figures like D'Oyly Carte recognized that the West End was the hub of both culture and global finance.

The public spaces of hotels were central to the formation of the late Victorian elite even though the late Victorian aristocracy had entered its period of decline.[50] New money had no such problems. Hotels were less exclusive than clubland London and were now the real centre of fine dining. The Savoy and the Ritz were places where the plutocracy could meet in elegant surroundings which celebrated their wealth and endowed guests with a sense of importance. The balls and regimental dinners demonstrate how the grand hotel was vital in the construction of elite networks. The price of a room and, even more, the price of a meal at the Savoy were ways in which the elite performed its difference from the rest of society. Hotels were the palaces of the rich and an expression of their right to rule.

---

[49] Jackson, *The Savoy*, ch. 2.
[50] David Cannadine, *The Decline and Fall of the British Aristocracy* (London: Picador, 1992 [1990]).

15

Shopocracy

'What do you think is the main purpose of advertising?' he asked.
'First to sell goods, second to educate.'
'I should put it the other way round', he said.
Alfred H. Williams on being interviewed by Harry Gordon Selfridge.[1]

The Thick of the Sales

Henry James loved the Strand and its many emporia. In a wistful reminiscence, he reflected:

> I love the place to-day…It appeared to me to present phenomena, and to contain items of every kind, of an inexhaustible interest; in particular it struck me as desirable and even indispensable that I should purchase most of the articles in most of the shops. My eyes rest with a certain tenderness on the places where I resisted and on those where I succumbed. The fragrance of Mr. Rimmel's establishment is again in my nostrils: I see the slim young lady (I hear her pronunciation) who waited upon me there. Sacred to me to-day is the particular aroma of the hair-wash I bought from her…Memorable is a rush I made into a glover's at Charing Cross—the one you pass, going eastwards, just before you turn into the station…Keen within me was a sense of the importance of deflowering, of despoiling the shop.[2]

James's language with its playful sexual overtones and relish for the sensual aspects of shopping captures something of the retail world that emerged in the West End in the second half of the nineteenth century. The world of spectacular shopping (even if only in the form of window shopping) meant that the final cornerstone of the pleasure district was in place.

This chapter is about the deflowering of the West End shops that took place between 1850 and 1914. Evidence about individual shops is sparse but we can piece the evidence together to uncover the way the district shaped consumer

---

[1] Alfred H. Williams, *No Name on the Door: A Memoir of Gordon Selfridge* (London: W.H. Allen, 1956), p. 17.
[2] Henry James, *English Hours*, ed. Leon Edel (Oxford: Oxford University Press, 1981), p. 4.

London's West End: Creating the Pleasure District, 1800–1914. Rohan McWilliam, Oxford University Press (2020).
© Rohan McWilliam.
DOI: 10.1093/oso/9780198823414.001.0001

desires. Whilst the Great Exhibition of 1851 was probably only incidental to this process, it exploited glass, spectacle, and the display of goods. Many shops resembled emporia elsewhere but in the context of the pleasure district they became a form of education in taste, fashion, and status. They dramatized capitalist abundance but, we will see, within a frame shaped by orientalism and cosmopolitanism. This chapter examines, in particular, Liberty's and Selfridge's, whilst emphasizing that most West End purchases took place in smaller shops.

The presence of women behind the counter also confirmed West End shops as a realm that women could enter, as Erika Rappaport has shown in her classic work on shopping.[3] Thus Liberty's tearoom had a lavatory for women but not for men (evidence of the people they thought would be its customers).[4] The pleasure district was associated with fashion and hairstyles. Jean Stehr, for example, offered ladies' hairdressing at no. 235 Oxford Street in the 1890s. Department stores also increasingly offered hairdressing services where previously this was done at home.[5] As Gordon Selfridge put it, 'In my store, women can realize some of their dreams.'[6] The more prosaic truth is that Selfridge and his team constructed dreams for women (and men) but he captured something of the experience that drew thousands to his store. Shopping constituted an aspiration to a lifestyle. Selfridge's approach to running his store reflected the reality that female consumers were now an inescapable part of the urban scene. Shopping was a device that allowed women to become *flâneurs* in their own right, a role that had previously been largely masculine. The department store shared a rhetoric of comfort, hospitality, status, and respectability with other West End pleasures.

An account in 1902 claims the atmosphere of Oxford Street and Regent Street was transformed when the sales were on. The streets were packed with women who descended on the shops with dark green satin bags, strengthened by hold-all straps, who fought to get in the shops as they opened. The women created a tumult in which they 'elbowed and pushed and ejaculated at each other'.[7] This account of women shopping (probably written by a man but we do not know) interprets shopping in terms of mass hysteria, which had become a common way of representing female shoppers from the 1890s. It built on the tendency observable from mid-century onwards to argue that women had a susceptibility

---

[3] Erika Diane Rappaport, *Shopping for Pleasure: Women in the Making of London's West End* (Princeton, NJ: Princeton University Press, 2000).

[4] Alison Adburgham, *Liberty's: A Biography of a Shop* (London: George Allen and Unwin, 1975), p. 43.

[5] *Hotel*, December 1892, p. iv; Kim Smith, 'From Style to Place: The Emergence of the Ladies' Hair Salon in the Twentieth Century', in Geraldine Biddle-Perry and Sarah Cheang (eds), *Hair: Styling, Culture and Fashion* (Oxford: Berg, 2008), pp. 56–7.

[6] Williams, *No Name on the Door*, p. 96.

[7] *Draper*, 12 July 1902, p. 973. See Christopher P. Hosgood, 'Mrs Pooter's Purchase: Lower-Middle-Class Consumerism and the Sales, 1870–1914', in Alan J. Kidd and David Nicholls (eds), *Gender, Class and Consumerism: Middle-Class Identity in Britain, 1800–1940* (Manchester: Manchester University Press, 1999), pp. 146–63.

to 'kleptomania' and involved a construction of femininity in which women were imagined as susceptible to temptation; another 'female malady' like fainting, hysteria, and insanity. Shopping was medicalized.[8] When Mary-Anne Batholomew, wife of a West End tradesman, was arrested for stealing a packet of needles and two bottles of pomade (hair oil) from the Soho Bazaar in 1863, Mr Lewis for the defence said, 'The prisoner was well connected, and had no need to commit these petty pilferings; but it was one of those irresistible passions, for which she herself...could not account. The accused was labouring under a severe domestic affliction.' She was given three months hard labour.[9] Despite the condescension of some male observers, women shoppers were not subject to irrational hysteria or capable of manipulation. Bargain hunting, one could argue, had an intellectual dimension which came with knowing the right shops and the best time to look on the shelves for reduced stock. It required thought and even research (keeping a careful eye on newspaper advertisements, for example). In this new world of consumerism, fancy goods were no longer simply the preserve of the elite; now, more and more people could get them and, even better, not pay full price. Although some women shopped in a group, the key point is that women felt at liberty to come to town by themselves, unaccompanied. Decisions about what to wear involved a complex set of purchase decisions, involving notions of taste, respectability, fashion, and cost. The novelty of the latest styles of clothing meant that it was a way of situating oneself in relation to modernity.

Increasingly, the world of goods in the West End was opened up to workers (who now had small amounts of disposable income) but far more to the middle classes travelling in from the suburbs and from out of town. The pleasure district became a centre to equip the domestic interior with comfortable furniture that was a mark of status, with ornaments and art, with domestic appliances, and the objects that cluttered the middle-class home. Middle-class culture was also changing with the shift away from the strict Victorian focus on thrift. Credit was not seen as the undesirable thing it had often been, although indebtedness had been bound into social and economic relationships from at least the eighteenth century onwards.[10]

The draw of the West End was surprising as it had so much competition elsewhere and it was cheaper to shop locally. In 1907, a visitor from New York

[8] Christopher H. Hosgood, '"Doing the Shops" at Christmas: Women, Men and the Department Store in England, c.1880–1914', in Geoffrey Crossick and Serge Jaumain (eds), *Cathedrals of Consumption: The European Department Store, 1850–1939* (Aldershot: Ashgate, 1999), pp. 97–115; Patricia O'Brien, 'The Kleptomania Diagnosis: Bourgeois Women and Theft in late Nineteenth-Century France', *Journal of Social History*, 17 (1983), pp. 65–77; Elaine S. Abelson, *When Ladies Go a-Thieving: Middle-Class Shoplifters in the Victorian Department Store* (New York: Oxford University Press, 1989); Tammy C. Whitlock, *Crime, Gender and Consumer Culture* (Aldershot: Ashgate, 2005).

[9] *Daily News*, 26 March 1863, p. 7.

[10] Margot C. Finn, *The Character of Credit: Personal Debt in English Culture, 1740–1914* (Cambridge: Cambridge University Press, 2003).

commented in the *Evening News* in 1907, 'I have seen a great deal of shops in Brixton, Kilburn, Islington, Hampstead, Fulham, and other places, and they seem to me to be equal, in all things that matter, to the big West End shops.' A Wimbledon correspondent retorted that this was not an issue for her as she was just a short train ride from Victoria, after which, within minutes, she could be 'in the thick of the sales'. The pleasure district had the merit of being a location all Londoners could get to easily. Another correspondent wrote in to say: 'We prefer to take an excursion straight to the West End where we know where to go and can get exactly what we want rather than run the risks incurred in trying new and unexplored territory.' She felt the West End stood for quality. A Mrs E. Wilson of Crouch End probably spoke for many in acknowledging the merit of local stores but commenting: 'I delight, as every fashionable woman does, in taking a journey once every season to the West End, and thoroughly doing the sights.'[11] This illuminating use of the 'sights' explains the appeal of the West End: the sales promoting a bargain but one that was linked to a rich visual culture. There was also the satisfaction of moving from an advertisement in a newspaper to finding the advertised goods in a store. This was the city as a living exhibition in which advertising served as a kind of catalogue. The purchase of goods became a souvenir of the West End. There was a continuum between the desire for luxuries at Selfridge's and the musical comedies at Daly's. As Erica Rappaport argues, fashions first encountered on the West End stage could find their way into stores and eventually into a woman's wardrobe.[12]

The West End was therefore an exercise in consumer education. Men and women employed it to discover what to wear and what to adorn their homes with. They learned to develop an eye for a bargain but also for what was stylish and what would no doubt impress the neighbours. Shops helped make pleasure districts a laboratory of style and taste.

West End Shopping

Molly Hughes as a child in the 1870s walked down Bond Street with her mother who spotted a sailor hat in a window which would suit her daughter. When she went in to ask the price, she was told it was three guineas and 'nearly fell out of the shop'.[13] Her mother would have found the shops on Regent Street and Oxford Street slightly more affordable and accessible than Bond Street. No longer was West End shopping so dominated by the requirements of the elite as it was in the early nineteenth century (see Chapter 2).

---

[11] *Evening News*, 9 May 1907, p. 3; 10 May 1907, p. 1; 13 May 1907, p. 3. See also Rappaport, *Shopping for Pleasure*, p. 4.
[12] Rappaport, *Shopping for Pleasure*, p. 185.
[13] Molly Hughes, *A London Child of the 1870s* (London: Persephone, 2005 [1934]), p. 54.

The mid-Victorian period witnessed new developments in West End retail which we can express in the following way. In 1851, the year of the Great Exhibition, Marshall and Snelgrove (later part of Debenhams) extended its Vere Street draper's shop onto Oxford Street, offering, amongst other things, ladies' fashions. Five years later, a young man joined another department store on Oxford Street, as a buyer, specializing in silks and other items for ladies' dresses. He did sufficiently well that he was able to open his own drapery business at 132 Oxford Street in 1864. Initially, he concentrated on dress fabrics but then began to focus on household goods, providing furniture, and all sorts of decorations. He was John Lewis. In 1875, yet another young man, this time with experience of purchasing clothing and fabric from the Far East, set up a shop on Regent Street called East India House. He began to sell a look based on oriental fashions to middle-class women. He was Arthur Lasenby Liberty and his shop became Liberty's.

Shopping took place in independent shops, department stores, mail order houses, and what would come to be known as supermarkets. West End shops tended to open by 8.30 and would close at 6 or 7 pm (in the winter) and sometimes 8pm (in the summer). On Saturdays, shops would shut at 2 pm (and all day on Sundays) which meant that they were not open at a time when large numbers of workers were free to patronize them.[14]

The press and magazines also fed this culture of consumption which developed its key form of literature: the advertisement.[15] One function of advertising was to make consumers feel that a trip up to town was worth it. Shops became meeting places and possessed a strongly theatrical dimension. Not for nothing was Harry Gordon Selfridge a fan of the theatre. Department stores turned shopping into a form of performance as they were dressed like stage sets in order to attract custom and stoke up desire for goods that people did not always realize they wanted. They also sold theatre tickets which enhanced the connection with the stage.

The desire for the latest clothes helped make the West End a major part of the retail experience. Fashions, especially in women's dress, often started in Paris but would then show up in the West End and spread through the country. The West End seeped into people's desires. In the late Victorian period, Jeanette Marshall of Savile Row would regularly visit John Lewis or Liberty's to obtain trimmings and materials; her diary records that it was unusual for her not to make a purchase.[16]

Some of the patterns we observed in the early nineteenth century remained. Regent Street and the shops of Mayfair drew on aristocratic clientele. Frederick

---

[14] Christopher P. Hosgood, '"Mercantile Monasteries": Shops, Shop Assistants, and Shop Life in Late-Victorian and Edwardian Britain', *Journal of British Studies*, 38 (1999), p. 328.

[15] Lori Anne Loeb, *Consuming Angels: Advertising and Victorian Women* (New York: Oxford University Press, 1994).

[16] Zuzanna Shonfield, *The Precariously Privileged: A Professional Family in Victorian London* (Oxford: Oxford University Press, 1987), p. 44.

Willis, who worked in a Mayfair hat shop at the end of the century, remembered: 'Like the Ritz Hotel they were open to all, but also like the Ritz Hotel, the vulgar public never crossed the threshold—it was not done.'[17] This was an area that thrived on exclusivity. Willis recalled the continuing importance of patronizing the right kind of shop: 'No man of discrimination would dream of buying his hat at a big store...the really smart hatters were accommodated in small, old-fashioned shops which the ordinary citizen passed unnoticed.'[18]

The West End developed a range of goods and services that constructed the middle-class home. In the 1860s, for example, John Ward and Sons sold American easy chairs and bath chairs from 5–6 Leicester Square whilst the Tottenham Court Road was associated with the furniture trade. Hampton and Russell, off Leicester Square and next door to Burford's Panorama, sold furniture and carpets.[19] The West End existed to furnish the artistic home as curated by the middle class. This meant not only wallpaper, fabric, and furniture but also antiques and curiosities. Soho recommended itself with its huge number of antique shops but many department stores, such as Waring and Gillow on Oxford Street offered a large antiques section. Book hunting tended to be seen as a very male pursuit, but female collectors started to develop collections and purchase antiquarian volumes.[20]

The West End offered other retail attractions. It was the place to purchase musical instruments (a vital addition to the middle-class home). Cramer and Co. (founded in 1824) on Regent Street needed huge premises as it sold pianos. Customers could find a selection of some 300 pianos on the premises at all times. It also sold sheet music and tickets to the opera.[21] Photography was another draw. The London Stereoscopic and Photographic Company had a shop on Regent Street as well as in Cheapside (and in New York). Its Regent Street shop was particularly splendid. Pictures were taken and then developed at their premises in Kilburn where twenty-six men were needed to process all the photographs. It also offered photographs of many actors and celebrities.[22] When Prince Albert died, the photograph shops on Regent Street were surrounded by mourners wanting to purchase an image of the consort.[23] Music and photography became service industries of the middle-class lifestyle. So were allegedly trivial forms of consumption. The district was notorious for its confectioners who appear to have sold particularly well to female customers. These included Charbonnel and

[17] Frederick Willis, *A Book of London Yesterdays* (London: Phoenix House, 1960), pp. 133–4.

[18] Willis, *A Book of London Yesterdays*, pp. 133–4.

[19] Clipping in SC/PZ/WE/01 2201-1350 (London Metropolitan Archives).

[20] Heidi Egginton, 'Book Hunters and Book-huntresses: Gender and Cultures of Antiquarian Book Collecting in Britain, c.1880–1900', *Journal of Victorian Culture* 19 (2014), pp. 346–64.

[21] Henry Mayhew (ed.), *The Shops and Companies of London and the Trades and Manufactories of Great Britain* (London: Strand, 1865), pp. 87–8.

[22] Mayhew, *Shops*, pp. 93–5.

[23] Derek Hudson (ed.), *Munby: Man of Two Worlds* (London: Abacus, 1974), p. 111.

Walker at 173 New Bond St, Thompson's at 188 Regent Street, and Marshall's opposite Charing Cross Station.

Fashion, photographs, pianos, furniture, chocolates: the West End shaped the material culture of the Victorians, supplying it with objects that serviced aspirational lifestyles. By mid-century, the West End was drawing in a much larger middle-class public, even though many of the goods that could be purchased there were also available in shops elsewhere in London.

Clothing the Sexes

Arthur Munby noted the existence of what he called 'the hybrid fineladyism of Miss Swan & Edgar', the clothes shop that hovered over Piccadilly Circus.[24] What drew many people to West End shops were clothes, linen, and drapery. Swan & Edgar began selling drapery in an open market (it is not known where) before establishing their firm on Piccadilly in 1812. It came to enjoy a huge importance in the Victorian fashion world. Charles Worth, the dominant figure in French haute couture in the later nineteenth century, actually started as a draper working for Swan & Edgar. Another important emporium was Peter Robinson ('the birthplace of the blouse') which specialized in ladies' wear. Peter Robinson opened a linen draper's shop at 103 Oxford Street in 1833 which, like a number of such establishments, grew into a department store which employed 2000 workers.[25] The *Sketch*, trumpeting the merits of a black velvet woman's coat in 1895, was delighted to find it was available in the Regent Street branch of Peter Robinson, reinforcing the notion that the West End was the place to head to if one wanted to see what was in fashion and to own it.[26]

The West End was shaped by assumptions about gender. Oxford Street and Regent Street were female whilst, as Clarence Rook put it in 1908, the shops that stretched from Fleet Street to the Strand were 'the last outposts of masculinity. They were built for man, and they are man's preserve.'[27] The *Draper* considered the 'proper district' for female shoppers to 'pursue their sport' was Regent Street, Bond Street, Oxford Street, and Piccadilly.[28] Visiting Brandon's in Oxford Street to purchase a bonnet for his mistress, Hannah Cullwick, Munby found it a 'resplendent turkey carpeted drawing room, or suite of such...full of showy or tasteful female handiwork: many Mammas and daughters making purchases, and elegant young women in silks flitting about.'[29] The central section of Oxford Street

---

[24] Hudson, *Munby*, p. 35.   [25] Rappaport, *Shopping for Pleasure*, p. 150.
[26] *Sketch*, 16 October 1895, p. 677.
[27] Clarence Rook, *London Side-Lights* (London: Edward Arnold, 1908), p. 11.
[28] *Draper*, 12 July 1873, p. 374.   [29] Hudson, *Munby*, p. 86.

demonstrated the feminization of the West End as women came to shop or to look. Mayhew was not free of male condescension:

> Oxford Street is a good street for studying women 'doing' their shopping, because the emporiums, magasins, and establishments are close together, and the display in the windows is so enormous that the emotions amenable to the amiable sex are constantly aroused.

He did, however, evoke the way that husbands were visibly uncomfortable when shopping with their wives: 'he, hiding his face and trying to avoid recognition by looking as unlike himself as possible; all the while making feeble calculations as to how much he will be compelled to pay, and ready to explode with wrath at his "dearest life's" turning him into a public exhibition through her indiscreet loitering'.[30]

Aristocratic women continued to patronize the elite Mayfair firms for clothing. Redfern's female tailoring in Conduit Street, Mayfair, and New Bond Street became an international couture house with branches in a number of countries. John Redfern commenced with designing sporting clothing to wear at Cowes on the Isle of Wight and moved on to designing specially tailored clothes for women. If a fashionable woman was seen on a yacht, there was a good chance she was wearing a Redfern dress or suit. Redfern's new designs which included cloaks, jackets, mantles, and millinery were regularly promoted in *The Queen* magazine. It also enjoyed status through having branches in Paris and New York whilst musical comedies such as *An Artist's Model* included women stylishly dressed in Redfern attire. Redfern's designer Charles Poynter ran the Paris branch and brought new French influences into English fashion. The business also provided tailor-made dresses to Princess Alexandra. As Princess of Wales and as Queen, Alexandra was a major fashion icon for high society women although she also bought from West End stores like Swan & Edgar. For her coronation robe, the velvet was supplied by Marshall and Snelgrove.[31] Couture designs were quickly imitated at stores like Dickins and Jones which led to a downward diffusion of high fashion.[32]

There had long been a market for fashionable clothes but the beauty industry also took off in the later nineteenth century. For example, Eugene Rimmel, whom we have encountered before, built up an international reputation for his perfumery on Regent Street and the Strand (as well as shops in Paris and Nice). He introduced new kinds of vaporizers and pioneered the use of mascara.

---

[30] Mayhew, *Shops*, p. 86.

[31] Kate Strasdin, *Inside the Royal Wardrobe: A Dress History of Queen Alexandra* (London: Bloomsbury, 2017), pp. 9, 103–8, 131.

[32] Susan North, 'John Redfern and Sons, 1847 to 1892', *Costume*, 42 (2008), pp. 145–68; Susan North, 'Redfern Limited, 1892 to 1940', *Costume*, 43 (2009), pp. 85–108.

Men, as we have seen, had a more complex relationship with shopping. During the nineteenth century, it is often assumed that the bright colours of Georgian male clothing were abandoned. Victorian gentlemen were not meant to be interested in clothes. There was an emphasis on restraint with the dignified three-piece suit taking over in the nineteenth century and black or grey becoming the colours in which business was done. Male fashions, as Christopher Breward argues, emphasized neatness or plainness but broader sartorial tastes were in evidence. There was, for example, the ideal of the dandy which allowed for dramatic flourish: the dazzling button hole, the exuberant waistcoat. The swell and the masher were lower down the social scale but could pick up on some of these flourishes in his dress. Men shopped for clothes but opted for a subtle set of ideals of what constituted manly clothing.[33]

The fashion industry was transformed in the early Victorian years by the rise of ready to wear tailoring, bringing forms of mass production to the fashion industry. Moses and Son (later Moss Bros) was particularly associated with this development. It began with two shops in Covent Garden which sold second-hand clothes. Its branch on New Oxford Street became a major place to purchase or hire smart clothing at a cheap price. The interior was full of mirrors to make the shop look even larger and more impressive.[34] This allowed clothing styles associated with elite men to be mass produced and made affordable. One did not have to be rich to wear a checkered suit. The aspiration to be smart or to possess 'Sunday best' could be shared amongst a mass public.

The West End saw major developments in tailoring that were not confined to Savile Row. Gustave Jaeger caused a fashion revolution from the shop on Regent Street licensed in his name. Jaeger claimed that natural undyed wool was a healthy form of clothing and attacked the use of silk.[35] It became central to the demands for dress reform and sanitary clothing. His adherents included Oscar Wilde and George Bernard Shaw. Austin Reed developed a more democratic style of male clothing that was aspirational but non-elitist.[36] Whilst women continued to follow Parisian fashions, English male tailoring achieved a dominance over its French counterpart during the nineteenth century. Men were thus able to make discreet fashion choices including the vogue for checked trousers from the 1850s onwards (partly fuelled by the Victorian fascination with Walter Scott).[37]

[33] Christopher Breward, *The Hidden Consumer: Masculinities, Fashion and City Life, 1860–1914* (Manchester: Manchester University Press, 1999).

[34] Christopher Breward, Edwina Ehrman, and Caroline Evans, *The London Look: Fashion from Street to Catwalk* (London: Yale University Press, 2004), p. 45.

[35] Stella Mary Newton, *Health, Art and Reason: Dress Reformers of the Nineteenth Century* (London: John Murray, 1974).

[36] Breward, Ehrman and Evans, *The London Look*, p. 63.

[37] Brent Shannon, *The Cut of his Coat: Men, Dress, and Consumer Culture in Britain, 1860–1914* (Athens, OH: Ohio University Press, 2006), p. 7.

Luxurious clothing was an integral part of the modern dreamscape that the pleasure district developed. Whilst the female demand for fashionable clothes was more visible, the West End had an equally profound role in allowing men to subtly develop their sartorial appearance (often without seeming to do so). The streets of the West End were therefore about consumer education but they were also about the commodification of the male and female body and allowed for the emulation of different forms of dress by people lower down the social scale. This also alerts us to another function of pleasure districts. Fashions change all the time which means pleasure districts can never be fixed. The iconography that sustains them (from the theatrical poster to the dressed tailor's dummy in a shop window) is always in flux with new styles emerging all the time. Pleasure districts are never shaped by tradition but by perpetual novelty and challenges to established norms.

The Department Store

The 1894 Gaiety musical *The Shop Girl* set in the 'Royal Stores' commenced with a song that celebrated the department store:

> This noble institution of financial evolution
> Is the glory of our British trade.
> It's the wonder of our nation as a mighty aggregation
> of all subjects grown or made.[38]

After about 1850 the West End was shaped by the development of the department store: a wave of majestic buildings that captured the imagination and provided London with important landmarks. Regent Street and Oxford Street became dominated by these grand emporia whilst Harrods epitomized the development of Knightsbridge and Brompton as wealthy parts of London. The department store, like the arcade or the hotel, seemed to offer the thrill of a town within a town, bringing a variety of goods and services together. It also offered the convenience for customers of not having to negotiate different shops for different goods. Department stores spearheaded the shift away from credit (the usual way the aristocracy purchased goods) towards cash transactions whilst promising goods that could not be obtained elsewhere or simply an experience that could not be replicated easily.

We should, however, put its ascendancy in some perspective. In 1900, department stores were responsible for just 1.2–3 per cent of all retail sales in Britain as a whole. Even in 1920 the figure was only 9–11 per cent.[39] There were a number

---

[38] H.J.W. Dam, 'The Shop Girl', Act 1 (British Library ADD MS 53562B).
[39] James B. Jefferys, *Retail Trading in Britain, 1850–1950* (Cambridge: Cambridge University Press, 1954), p. 21.

of factors behind these low percentages (which are in any case based on data that needs to be handled with caution). They reflect low levels of disposable income and lack of transport. More profoundly, food occupied a much higher part of the household budget. Department stores did not sell food until later on (though Selfridge's opened a food hall in 1914). Many people did not shop in department stores but the latter did reflect the rise of the Victorian middle class.

If the department store appears to be a post-1850 phenomenon, there is a strong case for noting its points of continuity with earlier shops. Fortnum and Mason on Piccadilly dated back to 1707, offering a variety of different goods and services. The basis of Debenham's was a shop on Wigmore Street in 1778. We have seen how Harding, Howell, and Co. (established in Pall Mall in 1796) adopted a form of retail which anticipated the department store; so did the Pantheon on Oxford Street. Drapers shops like Swan & Edgar on Regent Street had been increasing in size and in terms of services since the beginning of the nineteenth century. The drapers Dickins and Smith was founded at the sign of the Golden Lion in Oxford Street. In 1835, it had become Dickins & Jones and moved to Regent Street. Shoolbred's opened on the Tottenham Court Road in 1817 as a draper's shop which moved from clothing into furniture and even children's toys. By the 1880s it had become an all-purpose department store. Heal's moved to the Tottenham Court Road in 1841 (having been founded in 1818) with Maple's opening a year later, making the street the ideal place to purchase furniture.

These developments were part of a global phenomenon. Most modern department stores were influenced by the creation of the Bon Marché in Paris; the redevelopment in 1852 of a drapery and fancy goods business that dated back to 1838. Aristide Boucicault transformed the enterprise creating a large scale department store. He re-sited the store on the Rue des Sèvres in 1869 and made it even larger three years later. The shop offered dry goods and fashionable clothes; there was a ready to wear department as well as beds, upholstery, jewellery, and japaneserie. It was based on a systematic design with a consistent approach to retail based on fixed prices and a mail order service. Boucicault's approach to retail was theatrical. The windows and interior displays needed to draw people in. Elsewhere, Marshall Field was established in Chicago in 1852, building slowly into a major department store. The same was true of Macy's, originally founded in 1858 in New York as a dry goods store, which expanded. Wherever they sprang up, department stores were a major force in shaping the middle class, providing them not only with goods and furniture but also a vision of a lifestyle.

In London the first modern purpose-built department store is usually taken to be Whiteley's in Bayswater. William Whiteley commenced work as a draper's assistant in Wakefield and came to London to make his fortune, saving enough money in 1863 to open a shop in Westbourne Grove selling ribbons. The location was fortuitous as Bayswater Station on the Metropolitan Line opened at the same time, reflecting the growth of middle-class suburbs in North London. Whiteley bought up adjoining properties so that he could offer all sorts of goods and called himself the 'Universal Provider'. As became common with large stores, he housed his huge staff in dormitories close by (the 'living in' system) and created a staff canteen so that they could be fed.[40]

The new West End department stores allowed customers to simply just look, though floor walkers existed who would sometimes sternly ask customers if they intended to make a purchase. The focus on just looking meant that they built on the kind of visual attractions that had been built up in theatre but also in fairgrounds, magic lantern shows, and optical extravaganzas. Customers developed a loyalty to particular shops just as they had a loyalty to certain theatres which they associated with a particular kind of show. Department stores were also sustained through a strong relationship with the popular press which was used for advertising purposes. They built their brands through advertising, posters, and through mail order which gave their business national status. These stores turned out to be extremely profitable. In 1902, Swan & Edgar made an annual profit of £33,324 0s 4d, Dickins & Jones made £74, 024, and Peter Robinson on Oxford Street made (once interest and dividends were accounted for) £91, 692 14s. 6d.[41] In 1911, Liberty's profits amounted to £59, 602.[42]

One of the major Oxford Street department stores was Marshall and Snelgrove which originally opened (as Marshall and Wilson) on Vere Street in 1838. It acquired premises on Oxford Street in 1851 and gained a reputation for stocking fashionable clothing. At the start of the Franco-Prussian war in 1870, a member of the firm went over to Lyons and managed to purchase huge quantities of silk at very low prices which helped strengthen the firm's profitability for many years, enabling the creation of a new building on Vere Street which was completed in 1875. The two buildings were under a single roof but one was aimed at elite customers whilst the other aimed at the less well off.[43] This made it a metaphor for the West End as a whole which continued to serve both the elite and the masses.

Marshall and Snelgrove developed strong relationships with customers. The diaries of Marion Sambourne show how customers could be demanding but this was part of the appeal of such stores: 'Sent back grey dress to Snelgrove, promised to send credit note.' She purchased a hat which her husband, the artist Linley Sambourne, did not like, and so returned it. Another diary entry records 'Changed jersey at Marshalls, fits so badly.' The possibility of returning goods (especially clothes) made firms like Marshall and Snelgrove feel reliable though Sambourne also began to enjoy shops that were closer to her Kensington home

[40] ODNB (William Whiteley); Linda Stratmann, *Whiteley's Folly: The Life and Death of a Salesman* (Stroud: Sutton, 2004).

[41] *Draper*, 15 March 1902, p. 363; 22 March 1902, p. 471; 29 March 1902, p. 510.

[42] Liberty's dividends 1912: 788/24/1 (Westminster City Archives).

[43] Alison Settle, *A Family of Shops* (Margate: Marshall and Snelgrove, 1951).

such as Barkers and Harvey Nichols. Her comment on Harrods was 'dirty place though cheap'.[44]

By 1886, Debenham & Freebody, then just north of Oxford Street, employed between 400 and 500 staff (in addition to toilers in the workroom). This number included a large number of boy apprentices. Junior assistants (aged from eighteen up to thirty-five) could earn between £20 and £80 a year, including board and lodging. Staff were entitled to a week's holiday during the year. The firm had no trouble attracting workers.[45] Shoolbred's on the Tottenham Court Road employed about 700 shop assistants.[46]

Liberty's, which opened on Regent Street in 1875, profited from the romance of bohemianism. Like so many department store owners, Arthur Lasenby Liberty commenced as a draper's assistant. In 1862, he secured a position at Farmer and Rogers' Great Shawl Emporium on the west side of Regent Street. Shawls were then the height of fashion for Victorian ladies. Liberty was struck by the paintings of the Pre-Raphaelites and saw that they offered a form of fantasy for women who could literally adorn themselves in its dreamlike images. Liberty cultivated the arts and crafts movement for new designs and images.[47] In 1888, *Woman's World* claimed that 'Liberty's is the chosen resort of the artistic shopper', where women could obtain colourful ribbons and silks which made them look like a painting come to life.[48]

Liberty was also taken by the goods at the Japanese section of the 1862 International exhibition. In May 1875, he opened his premises at 218a Regent Street. Despite only having half a shop (he soon took over the other half), it was named East India House. He was known for importing Japanese goods (assisted by the end on trade restrictions with Japan in 1868) but had the sense to also draw more widely on objects and clothes from the east including India, China, and Persia (see Figs 15.1 and 15.2) . Within five years the shop had developed into a department store, though one that was based in a set of buildings on Regent Street rather than under one roof (the present Tudorbethan building on Great Marlborough Street was built in 1924). There were rooms for purchasing furniture, silks, carpets, multiple kinds of fabric and embroidery as well as other goods. Stalls abounded with Indian necklaces with diamond shaped tablets, Egyptian bracelets of twisted chain work, silver Indian bracelets, Japanese bead necklaces, Turkish and Venetian beads, Indian pyjamas, and Fiji shells.

---

[44] Shirley Nicholson (ed.), *A Victorian Household: Based on the Diaries of Marion Sambourne* (London: Barrie and Jenkins, 1988), pp. 85–7.

[45] Report from the Select Committee on the Shop Hours Regulation Bill (1886), pp. 37–8.

[46] Report from the Select Committee on the Shop Hours Regulation Bill (1886), p. 93.

[47] Alison Adburgham, *Liberty's: A Biography of a Shop* (London: George Allen and Unwin, 1975), p. 17.

[48] Quoted in Newton, *Health, Art and Reason*, p. 120.

Mr. Liberty and his Co-Directors judging New Designs.

Fig. 15.1 Arthur Liberty choosing a new design (Westminster City Archives)

It was a site where the domestic and the global could meet in explicit and per-formed ways. Liberty's promised that it would offer (but adapt to modern needs) 'the beautiful Soft-clinging Draperies so much esteemed in ancient Greece'. At the same time they employed early Persian dyes.[49] For the opening of the short-lived Albert Palace in Battersea in 1885, Liberty's provided an Indian village and brought over skilled artisans from India to demonstrate their crafts as well as acrobats and dancing girls.[50]

West End consumption had long been geared up to importing goods from the empire. In the early 1820s, for example, Isaac Newton's shop at 14 Leicester Square promised customers Madras long cloths.[51] Liberty's was part of a longer history of selling fabrics derived from imperial and other exotic locations. Its 1883 cata-logue advertised its Nagpore silk in the following way:

> This Fabric is manufactured by hand in India from the finest Bengal Yarns. It is shipped to this country in the raw state, just as it comes from the looms, and is

---

[49] *Catalogue of Liberty's Art Fabrics* (1883) p. 1: 788/29/1 (Westminster City Archives).
[50] India Village Exhibition, Battersea: 788/23/1–4 (Westminster City Archives).
[51] Newspaper clipping in St Martin's Scrapbook Series: Leicester Square Vol. 1 part 1 p. 38 (Westminster City Archives).

Fig. 15.2 Liberty's Japanese furniture: Liberty's Collection (Westminster City Archives)

dyed by a permanent process specially for Liberty & CO. The irregularity of the weaving produces a play of colour rendering it unequalled for Art Drapery. The colours are reproductions of the finest examples of those of Ancient Art Work.[52]

Alternatively, it was possible to purchase Mandarin brocaded silk based on the robes of Chinese mandarins. The West End provided orientalism for the domestic sphere but the colours on view in a visit to Liberty's would have been spectacular; the touch of the fabrics enticing. Other late Victorian shops would have looked drab by comparison.

As the 1883 catalogue made clear, Liberty imported cloth from the east that was woven but undyed. He then developed techniques of dyeing in England. These became known as 'Liberty colours'.[53] In 1896, it offered a dinner gown

[52] *Catalogue of Liberty's Art Fabrics* (1883) p. 2: 788/29/1 (Westminster City Archives).
[53] 'The Growth of an Influence', *Art Journal*, February 1900, p. 48.

called the 'Elfrida', a green dress made of 'Liberty Bengal satin'.[54] Where William Morris despised mass production, Liberty happily employed machinery to produce more goods and reach a wide public. The silks produced by the shop were notorious for an irregular weave which was unmatched elsewhere. People went to Liberty's for fabrics rather than for made-up dresses which they did not offer. Liberty's provided a way of establishing a woman's taste and status.

There was always an aspect of fantasy about the Liberty's project, with its recycling of the imperial exotic at a time when people were taken with the empire on which the sun would never set. In the 1890s, however, it was also associated with the decorative style art nouveau, and its colour palette became central to late Victorian aestheticism. It even provided oak paneling for walls.[55] Liberty's promised to reshape the home and offered an aesthetic vision for the domestic interior.

Andrew Carnegie, who had made a fortune in steel in the United States, was not impressed by the shops of the West End. In 1900, he complained to Ralph Blumenfeld about his attempt to purchase some handkerchiefs and neckties in London.

> When he came out he said that London's shopping methods were all wrong. 'Just look at the jumble in the windows', he said, 'So much stuff that you cannot take it all in. And when you go into a shop they treat you most indifferently. You are scowled at if you ask for goods out of the ordinary, and you are made to feel uncomfortable if you do not buy. These shop people drive away more people than they attract. That's all wrong. I'd like to own a big draper's shop in Regent Street. I'd show 'em!' He recurred to this grievance throughout the hour that I was with him. 'What London wants', he said, 'is a good shaking up.'[56]

A 'good shaking up' is what the West End was about to get. Carnegie was really calling for the introduction of American methods of buying and selling. London's wealth and the opulence of the West End made it a natural fit for the American Harry Gordon Selfridge. His shop on Oxford Street would redefine department store shopping.

Selfridge built his reputation at Marshall Field in Chicago where he worked his way up from the day he was taken on as a clerk in 1879.[57] By 1886 he was manager of the retail department and helped turn the store into a powerhouse, one of the landmarks of Chicago. Here he proved a major innovator, introducing departments such as the bargain basement. He was also a deep student of retail methods and customer behaviour, travelling to Paris (where he took in the Bon Marché)

[54] *Lady*, 26 March 1896, pp. 411, 414.
[55] Liberty's Solid Oak Panelling: 788/36/1-10 (Westminster City Archives).
[56] R.D. Blumenfeld, *R.D.B's Diary, 1887–1914* (London: Heinemann, 1930), p. 119.
[57] ODNB (Harry Gordon Selfridge); Lindy Woodhead, *Shopping, Seduction and Mr. Selfridge* (London: Profile, 2012).

and London. Selfridge was a romantic about the shopping experience, which he saw in heavily theatrical terms. He was strongly influenced by P.T. Barnum's autobiography, *Struggles and Triumphs*, another rags-to-riches tale which trumpeted the values of show-business. His problem was that his boss Marshall Field would not make him a full partner; nor was he interested in Selfridge's proposal to build a branch of the store in London. Selfridge therefore decided to move to London and go into business for himself.

Arriving in the West End, he looked for the best site. A location on the Strand was a possibility but did not work out. He eventually settled on what was seen as the wrong side of Oxford Street. Selfridge, however, looked at the excellent underground connections which would make it easy for customers to go to and from his store. He computed that 12,000 buses a day passed his proposed site (and more on a Saturday).[58] The prosperous middle classes of West London could easily be brought in. The shop opened in 1909 and created a major sensation in the retail world. £36,000 in advertising was spent on promoting it.[59] For Selfridge it was alright for shoppers to just look, to come in with no intention to purchase anything. Just wandering around Selfridge's was meant to be a pleasurable experience. The shop became a major landmark though Selfridge failed in his long-running campaign to have the name of Bond Street tube station changed to 'Selfridge's'.

Over time, he made major innovations, placing perfume at the main entrance so that women could just pop in for that purpose. Scent had been expensive but the glycidic method allowed the shop to offer Selfridge's Lily of the Valley for 1/6d. He registered the way that young women were increasingly becoming interested in make- up and opened the first cosmetics department (previously part of the pharmacy) in 1910. The Selfridge's window displays were always spectacular, drawing customers down Oxford Street to see them. Selfridge's offered a children's department making it a positive environment for families. He continued to invest hugely in advertising, letting everyone know about his philosophy of shopping. The Selfridge's project recognized the power of the press, not just in providing advertising but also in the way a store was perceived. He told his advertising staff never to quarrel with a paper. As he put it, 'a newspaper can always have the last word'.[60]

The emphasis of Selfridge's was on clothing and home furnishings but there was far more to the store. He introduced a restaurant so that people could spend the whole day there. There were male and female lavatories. The atmosphere was similar to the grand hotels which were developing (the construction firm Waring-White built both Selfridge's and the Ritz). Conscious of the need to draw male shoppers in, he created a rifle range at the top of the store. The bargain basement

---

[58] Williams, *No Name on the Door*, p. 86.   [59] Williams, *No Name on the Door*, p. 86.
[60] Williams, *No Name on the Door*, p. 28.

was introduced in 1911 whilst the kitchen department offered demonstrations about cookery methods. Selfridge's was never gaudy and always respected cultivated taste. There were art exhibitions there right from the start and concerts later on. Selfridge was, however, the complete showman. When Louis Blériot succeeded in flying across the English channel in 1909, he was greeted by Harry Selfridge and shortly afterwards his aeroplane was displayed in the recently opened store shortly after it opened.

Selfridge's therefore brought flair to West End shopping, an example of the way Americanization was beginning to transform British culture. It was the product of the move to a society based on mass culture and consumerism. Selfridge should be seen as one of the key entrepreneurs such as Richard D'Oyly Carte and George Edwardes whose imagination turned the West End into a series of palaces of desire. With his understanding of the importance of communication (especially theatre, film, and design), he showed how the pleasure district might be a place of innovation for modern mass media.

West End retail was heavily dependent on female labour. With the feminization of the West End, it was thought that female shop assistants could draw in women customers as they understood their needs. Shopgirls in the 1870s received one-half to two-thirds of the pay of their male counterparts (though West End pay was higher than elsewhere).[61] They were expected to work long hours usually standing (with some shops issuing strict rules against sitting). It could be a punishing schedule. Workers had to be at the beck and call of employers. Most shop assistants in London tended to live above the shop or in special dormitories close by provided by employers.[62] The 'living in' system was also a way of ensuring that shopgirls were respectable. Even grand West End stores provided poor quality accommodation, with small bedrooms.[63] It was rare for shop workers to spend much time by themselves.

The necessity of housing shopgirls came about because they were troubling figures; unmarried young women in the city. In the popular imagination this meant that they were not too far away from the actress or the chorus girl; frivolous and preoccupied with urban pleasures. They could be ogled and sexualized.[64] Shopgirls were imagined in particular ways because they were in effect servants and therefore subject to orders and discipline. At the same time they were in a marginal position in terms of class relations; working-class people who could go

---

[61] Pamela Cox and Annabel Hobley, *Shopgirls: True Stories of Friendship, Triumph and Hardship from behind the Counter* (London: Cornerstone, 2014), p. 23; see also Pamela Cox, 'Shopgirls and Social Theory', *Revista Brasileira de História*, 37 (2017), pp. 243–71.

[62] Charles Booth, *Life and Labour of the People in London*, second series, Vol. 2 (London: Macmillan, 1889–1903), p. 84.

[63] Report and Special Report from the Select Committee on the Shop Hours Bill (1892), p. 52.

[64] Lise Shapiro Sanders, *Consuming Fantasies: Labor, Leisure and the London Shopgirl, 1880–1920* (Columbus, OH: Ohio State University Press, 2006).

between classes and would operate in a middle-class milieu (like the servants of West End mansions).

We can uncover some of the shopgirls's daily experience in a report by the barrister Thomas Suthurst (President of the Shop Hours Labour League) who interviewed shopworkers (male and female) about their experiences in 1884. 'Nellie G.' (who was working in a shop on Oxford Street) said her hours of work were meant to be 7.30 am–9 pm but too often the demands of her employer meant that it was 7 am–11 pm. On Saturdays she could sometimes be kept working till midnight. Her mealtimes were irregular. She complained:

> I was in very good health when I went into business four years ago, but now I am weak and almost worn out. All the assistants with whom I have come into contact have suffered more or less from the long hours and the standing. I have during my short experience known three deaths through consumption brought on by the overwork and constant standing. I should be satisfied with twelve hours a-day and a weekly half-holiday.

'Thomas B.', a grocer's assistant on the Strand, worked similar hours and complained about the effect of gas in the shop on his health. 'J.E.M.', who also worked on the Strand as a grocer's assistant claimed the long hours were in any case unnecessary. Few goods were sold in the evening. He put it down to 'old custom—always hard to break down, want of union amongst employers, and want of sympathy from the general public'.[65] There was a crisis of overwork, experienced not just in the West End but throughout the country as Suthurst's investigation revealed. Shop assistants worked seventy-five to ninety hours in a week.

The feminization of shop work meant that male shopworkers felt that their masculinity had been undercut by the petty tyranny of employers and the evident fact that a woman could do their tasks just as easily as they could.[66] Male shopworkers were the first to revolt against the living-in system which so compromised their independence. Debenhams abandoned the practice for men in 1907 though women were still expected to live in for some time after that. Selfridge's, however, never introduced the system even for women. The development of West End retail created new work opportunities for working-class or lower-middle class-women and men. At the same time it was responsible for a harsh form of work discipline. If the prices in the department stores were attractive (at least for middle-class consumers), they were made possible by the low pay and long hours of work that workers endured.

---

[65] Thomas Suthurst, *Death and Disease Behind the Counter* (London: Kegan, Paul, Trench, 1884), pp. 23, 161, 144.
[66] Christopher P. Hosgood, 'Mercantile Monasteries', p. 332.

The West End became central to middle-class lives after mid-century. If fashions emanated from Paris, it is nevertheless also true that West End shops were responsible for adorning the bodies of Victorians and Edwardians. The pleasure district, both in its shops and on the streets, was a guide to what to wear and the way to wear it. The West End was, in many ways, perceived as anti-domestic and yet its shops fed the domestic world. The later nineteenth century is associated with clutter in the middle-class home with its profusion of comfortable sofas, grandfather clocks, teapots, and *objets d'art*. These objects could be purchased in all sorts of places but many homes in London and elsewhere would have included goods and clothes obtained in the West End. Some West End shops were accessible to all; others far less so. They created an environment that traded on distraction. Yet if we are to understand the cultural work of pleasure districts, the key feature of West End shops was their role in creating a fantasy. The goods and clothes spoke to viewers about alternate selves and lives that could be lived once a delicious purchase was made. Many no doubt detested the process of shopping but it could also be a source of pleasure.

The West End with its consumerist fantasies may have seemed a long way from the travails of a nation facing economic decline, the challenges of the Labour movement, and the voices of women who were excluded from the system. In fact, as we shall now see, the West End was caught up in exactly the changes which were transforming Britain.

PART FIVE
HEART OF EMPIRE

16

The Other West End

'He's a Jolly Good Fellow'

Friday evening, 18 May 1900. Rumours had been spreading throughout the evening but until nine o'clock there was no official confirmation. At 9.20 Mansion House posted the news following a telegram from Reuters. Word spread from person to person and from cabman to van driver; it charged down Ludgate Hill in the shadow of St Paul's Cathedral and along Fleet Street. Could it really be true? The evening papers in turn quickly trumpeted the news. Within a few minutes the streets of central London were resounding to choruses of 'Rule Britannia' and a dramatic saturnalia of music and dancing took over the West End. Cyclists brandishing union jacks on long rods and men in carriages created an unruly percussion. The balconies above shops were filled with people waving anything they could get their hands on: flags, blankets, towels or 'various feminine garments which are usually displayed only on a clothes line'.

Joseph Lyons announced the news from the Trocadero restaurant's balcony on Piccadilly Circus; the smart set inside proved ecstatic. Charles Wyndham halted a performance of *Cyrano de Begerac* at the Wyndham's Theatre so that the audience could be informed. Mrs Patrick Campbell at the Royalty Theatre waited till the end of the first act of *Magda* to tell her admiring public. The orchestra then played 'Rule Britannia' and 'God Save the Queen' with the audience joining in. By eleven o'clock, Piccadilly Circus was a sea of union jacks and traffic could barely move for the chanting pedestrians in full reverie. Lights shone from the Criterion restaurant and rendered the 'walls all around alive with cheering and gesticulating figures'. A correspondent for the *Times* was assailed by an enthusiastic young man as he entered Regent Street: 'Is it true that Mafeking is relieved, sir?'[1]

The news was correct. For seven months, British soldiers in the South African town has been besieged by superior forces, a frustrating stalemate in the ongoing Boer War. Reports from journalists holed up with the garrison had leaked out and turned the British commanding officer, Colonel Robert Baden Powell, into a national hero, an emblem of British dogged determination. The man who would

---

[1] *Times* 19 May 1900, p. 12; Peter Bird, *The First Food Empire: A History of J. Lyons and Co.* (London: Phillimore, 2000), p. 51.

London's West End: Creating the Pleasure District, 1800–1914. Rohan McWilliam, Oxford University Press (2020).
© Rohan McWilliam.
DOI: 10.1093/oso/9780198823414.001.0001

use his fame to found the boy scouts maintained an attitude of calm until a force from Kimberly managed to break the siege. It was not the end of the war but it suggested that the British Empire could contain the revolt of the Boer republics. Far away on the thoroughfares of the West End a wave of unprecedented emotion was unleashed by this tale of British endurance against the odds.

A jubilant street party ensued, not only in London but throughout the country. The scenes in the West End were, however, heavily reported because it had been remade to function as the heart of empire. That night, at the Hippodrome in Leicester Square, Miss Lillian Lea sang a specially composed song to mark the occasion and enjoyed eight encores. As audiences issued from the theatres they stayed in town to celebrate the imperial adventure, creating a joyous street party: 'Ladies in evening dress were squeezed in the crowd, but only smiled happily.' Gentlemen in top hats and capes partied with working-class Londoners or cheered with the crowd from the balconies of their clubs.[2] Similar scenes were repeated throughout the next evening. Young boys marched together in the Strand beating time on empty biscuit tins. Italian and French restaurants in Soho happily displayed Union Jacks. The Hotel Metropole offered guests a Mafeking menu (coloured khaki) and with a portrait of the man already becoming known as 'B.P.'. Butchers marched down Piccadilly with pictures of Baden Powell on their backs. When the Colonel's family attended the Alhambra theatre that evening, the entire audience rose to its feet to sing the national anthem and 'He's a jolly good fellow'; it took a while for the programme to resume.[3] Mafeking Night was to become a regular anniversary thereafter. What made the celebrations in May 1900 linger in the memory was not just that allegedly straitlaced English people suddenly seemed able to abandon all decorum in public, but that the festivities were so spontaneous. The West End crowds embodied a conservative popular culture in which toff and cockney could unite around nation and empire.

This chapter shows how empire shaped the pleasure district but it also acts as a conclusion to this study. By 1900, the West End had come to embody the construction of a national consensus around aristocratic taste and middle-class virtues. We have seen the way this consensus was built up and etched into arcades and shops, into theatres and music halls, into Gatti's restaurant on the Strand and the Hotel Cecil. The crowd that spilled out onto Piccadilly Circus to celebrate Baden Powell's victory embodied a kind of liquid Toryism.

But, if we commence with one kind of crowd, evident in the Mafeking night pandemonium, we end with another; the unemployed who gathered to protest at their poverty and the women who challenged their exclusion from the franchise. The very conservatism of the West End made it a place that sparked resentment.

---

[2] *Times* 19 May 1900, p. 12; Shaw Desmond, *London Nights of Long Ago* (London: Duckworth, 1927), pp. 110–17.
[3] *Times* 21 May 1900, p. 12; *Illustrated London News*, 26 May 1900, p. 702.

To use a theatrical metaphor, we should not just look at the West End from the perspective of the front of house. I argue here that there was a backstage as well. The workers who have populated this book were not as deferential as they might seem. This chapter is a riposte to the others which have detailed the construction of a middle-class conservative consensus that the pleasure district expressed in spatial terms. The West End has in fact an overlooked history of political radicalism, which made it a natural location for protest. If the pleasure district was therefore a place of both imperialism and revolt in the later nineteenth and early twentieth centuries, then it was an echo of what was happening in the nation at large.

Empire and Nation

The West End was a place where the imperial and the domestic could meet. The emotional dimension to imperialism was hardwired into the West End. Empire suffused national life but the emotions it evoked were complex, mixing pride, opposition, and ambivalence.[4] Why did empire and nation cut so deep into the emotions of some (including presumably the people who celebrated the relief of Mafeking)? One explanation is that they were represented and imagined through sentimental mass entertainment. The heart of empire was as much located in Drury Lane as it was in the Colonial Office. As we saw in the case of the curiosities described in Chapter 5, the West End had a role in explaining the empire as well as constructing the exotic for a domestic audience. It provided the illusion that the imperial periphery had been drawn back to the centre through the vehicle of entertainment. In so doing, it built up a stronger sense of what British identity meant: the Romans of the modern world. The visual culture of the West End was in part an expression of British power; hence the classical frontage of the London Pavilion music hall on Piccadilly Circus.

Jonathan Schneer has memorably shown how empire was central to London's identity by 1900. He has, however, surprisingly little to say about the West End where empire was particularly visible.[5] The West End even possessed a music hall called the Empire (in Leicester Square). It was, as we saw in Chapter 11, another West End music hall that gave us the word 'jingoism'. There was therefore an explicit Tory dimension to West End entertainments. It became a stage for imperialist and royalist ceremonial.[6] For years after his death at Khartoum in 1885,

---

[4] John MacKenzie, *Propaganda and Empire: The Manipulation of British Public Opinion, 1880–1960* (Manchester: Manchester University Press, 1984); Bernard Porter, *The Absent-Minded Imperialists: Empire, Society and Culture in Britain* (Oxford: Oxford University Press, 2004).

[5] Jonathan Schneer, *London 1900: The Imperial Metropolis* (New Haven, CT: Yale University Press, 1999).

[6] David Cannadine, 'The Context, Performance and Meaning of Ritual: The British Monarchy and the "Invention of Tradition"', c.1820–1977', in Eric Hobsbawm and Terence Ranger (eds), *The Invention of Tradition* (Cambridge: Cambridge University Press, 1983), pp. 101–64; MacKenzie, *Propaganda*

wreaths were laid at the foot of the statue of General Gordon on Trafalgar Square.[7] There was also a crowd who paid their respects at the statue of Charles I on the anniversary of what they viewed as his martyrdom.[8]

Empire had long had associations with the West End. Burford's Panorama in Leicester Square frequently represented imperial scenes and in 1846 portrayed the Battle of Sobraon in the Punjab War as well as the British campaign to open up trade in China.[9] The West End stage, by and large, maintained a triumphalist approach to things imperial. For example, in 1886 the Drury Lane pantomime *Forty Thieves* included a procession showing off the territories of the British Empire.[10] When the Boer War broke out in 1899, the giant in the Drury Lane pantomime *Jack and the Beanstalk* was renamed 'Blunderboer' and sported a Kruger mask.[11] The 1892 Select Committee on Theatre pondered whether many people visited theatre in London because it was the capital of the empire, though it came to no fixed view on the subject.[12]

There was a strong continuity between empire, nation, and what audiences enjoyed on the stage. W.T. Moncrieff's *The Cataract of the Ganges*, first presented at Drury Lane in 1823, proved to be one of the most popular plays of the nineteenth century with its exotic scenes of Indian princes. Astley's over the river staged scenes of imperial spectacle as well as battles such as Waterloo. Although first performed in New York, Dion Boucicault's *Jessie Brown: or, the Relief of Lucknow* (Drury Lane, 1862) was a drama of the Indian Mutiny. At the Adelphi, William Terris played a series of swashbuckling nautical heroes (including *The Union Jack* in 1888), given authenticity by his time in the merchant navy. Visitors who took in Augustus Harris's 1885 imperialist spectacle, *Human Nature*, at Drury Lane would find General Gordon's rifle as well as other relics of that year's Sudan campaign in the theatre lobby.[13]

and Empire ch. 2; Felix Driver and David Gilbert (eds), *Imperial Cities: Landscape, Display and Identity* (Manchester: Manchester University Press, 1999).

[7] See, for example, *Black and White*, 6 February 1891, p. 21.

[8] Clipping in St Martin's Scrapbook Series: General Vol. 2 p. 14 (Westminster City Archives); *Daily News*, 31 January 1903, p. 12.

[9] Richard D. Altick, *The Shows of London* (Cambridge, MA: Belknap Press/Harvard University Press, 1978), p. 177.

[10] Robert Whelan, *The Other National Theatre: 350 Years of Shows in Drury Lane* (London: Jacob Tonson, 2013), p. 421.

[11] Michael Booth, 'Soldiers of the Queen: Drury Lane Imperialism', in Michael Hays and Anastasia Nikolopoulou (eds), *Melodrama: The Cultural Emergence of a Genre* (Basingstoke: Macmillan, 1996), pp. 9, 16.

[12] Report from the Select Committee on Theatres and Places of Entertainment (1892), p. 56.

[13] Marty Gould, *Nineteenth-Century Theatre and the Imperial Encounter* (London: Routledge, 2011), p. 22; see also Jeffrey Richards, 'Drury Lane Imperialism', in Peter Yeandle, Katherine Newey, and Jeffrey Richards (eds), *Politics, Performance and Popular Culture: Theatre and Society in Nineteenth-Century Britain* (Manchester: Manchester University Press, 2016), pp. 174–98.

In 1881, Drury Lane audiences could thrill to Augustus Harris's version of *The Armada*, which featured a spectacular battle at sea. Pride in the national achievement (defined in militarist and imperial terms) proved a way of attracting a mass audience. Harris's 1881 play, *Youth*, featured a scene of British soldiers under siege who are rescued in the nick of time from natives despite being prepared to die for the Union Jack. The production featured real Gatling guns. Such plays turned imperialism into a romance (literally so as they often feature the girl who has been left behind).

Freedom in 1883 was written by Harris and George Fawcett Rowe memorializing the British occupation of Egypt the previous year. The 'Freedom' of the title refers to the way the British were determined to bring progress by abolishing the slave trade. Its orientalist tone can be deduced from its opening line: 'Salaam Effendi! I seek the dwelling of Hassan, the sheik of the eunuchs.' The evil Araf Bey tells the British consul that Britain is only interested in the Nile as a gateway to the East. He is immediately told: 'We came to your cities as to a market, and with our inventions we bring you progress.' When freeing slaves on the high seas, the hero Ernest Gascoine, a sea captain, states proudly 'Look at the uniform I wear—look at the blue-jackets around me! If you have ever been to school you must have read that the broad seas are Britain's heritage—that there is hardly an inch of the blue waters where we have not carried their colours to indicate right. I am an Englishman and these are English tars.' The play was more prophetic than it knew. Gascoine is assisted in saving the heroine from the advances of Araf Bey by a wealthy American called Andrew Jackson Slingsby. The play celebrated the civilizing project not just of the British Empire but also of the Anglo-American world, well before Kipling told Americans to take up the 'white man's burden'.[14] The West End thus helped construct an image of empire based on orientalism and adventure that was a counterpart to the imperial fictions of H. Rider Haggard, Rudyard Kipling, and G.A. Henty. This convergence of imperialist storytelling subsequently led to such major Hollywood films celebrating empire as *Gunga Din*, *The Charge of the Light Brigade* (the Errol Flynn version) and *The Lives of a Bengal Lancer*.[15]

National identity shaped some of the entertainments on offer. For example, the 1893 pantomime at Drury Lane, *Robinson Crusoe*, included a scene of dubious relevance to the plot featuring a procession of all the Kings and Queens of England, starting with William the Conqueror and ending with Queen Victoria. One observer recalled 'the colour and splendour of it all stirred the patriotic emotions of everyone in the audience'.[16] The cultural politics of Toryism built on these emotional registers and feelings about the social order. When the Boer War broke

---

[14] George Fawcett Rowe and Augustus Harris, 'Freedom: A Drama in Four Acts' (1883), pp. 4, 17, 22 (British Library Add MS 53298).

[15] Jeffrey Richards, *Visions of Yesterday* (London: Routledge and Kegan Paul, 1973).

[16] Frederick Willis, *A Book of London Yesterdays* (London: Phoenix House, 1960), p. 63.

out, the actress Maud Tree (wife of Herbert Beerbohm Tree) took to the stage of the Palace Theatre of Varieties between October and December 1899 to recite Kipling's poem, 'The Absent Minded Beggar', which was specially composed to assist the war effort. Arthur Sullivan subsequently turned Kipling's poem into a song which played at the Alhambra.[17]

Empire and nation were important themes in West End ballet.[18] The 1892 ballet at the Empire, *Round the Town*, featured a tableau called 'The Daughters of the British Empire'.[19] Another Empire ballet, *The Girl I left Behind Me*, featured a young man who loses all his money at the turf but is redeemed when he enlists and wins the Victoria Cross in Burma.[20] During the 1897 Diamond Jubilee, Arthur Sullivan was hired by the Alhambra to create a patriotic ballet, *Victoria and Merrie England*, which included a scene with Robin Hood, a Restoration Christmas pageant, and a depiction of Victoria's coronation. On the first night, the coronation scene got three curtain calls, which was not normally permitted at the Alhambra. It ran for six months.[21] The 1889 ballet *Our Army and Navy* at the Alhambra played for almost a year. When the Boer War broke out, the Alhambra quickly mounted a ballet-cum-pageant entitled *Soldiers of the Queen*.

West End producers believed in doing their bit for empire. In 1879 the Gaiety Theatre put on an entertainment to support the families of soldiers who had fallen at Isandlwana in the Zulu War. The event was patronized by the Prince of Wales and included extracts from operettas as well as Henry Irving presenting the first act of Richard III. For the evening, a large number of West End theatres (including the Haymarket, the Princess's, the Adelphi, and the Vaudeville) provided sketches and drama.[22] Also for the 1897 Jubilee, Henry Irving put on a performance of the plays *Waterloo* and *The Bells* for the troops who had assembled from all over the world at the Chelsea Barracks. The troops were marched over to the Lyceum theatre for an event that was intended to symbolize imperial unity. In the audience were Indian princes and colonial premiers. It was so successful that the exercise was repeated for the celebrations of the Coronation of Edward VII in 1902. The Lyceum stage on the latter occasion was decked out in crimson and a huge Union Jack made up of a thousand coloured lights was hung over the dress circle. The audience included the Maharaja of Kohlapur, the Maharaja of Kooch

[17] Catherine Hindson, *London's West End Actresses and the Origins of Celebrity Charity, 1880–1920* (Iowa City, IO: University of Iowa Press, 2016), pp. 164–70.

[18] Jane Pritchard and Peter Yeandle, '"Executed with Remarkable Care and Artistic Feeling": Popular Imperialism and the Music Hall Ballet', in Yeandle, Newey, and Richards, *Politics, Performance and Popular Culture*, pp. 152–73.

[19] Ivor Guest, *Ballet in Leicester Square: The Alhambra and the Empire, 1860–1915* (London: Dance Books, 1992), p. 108.

[20] Guest, *Ballet in Leicester Square*, pp. 109–10.

[21] Guest, *Ballet in Leicester Square*, pp. 59–60.

[22] John Hollingshead, *Gaiety Chronicles* (London: Constable, 1898), pp. 356–9.

Bahar, and the Crown Prince of Siam.[23] There was nothing 'absent-minded' about the imperialism of the West End. It was a place where dreams of empire were manufactured. The culture of empire was built upon sentimental melodrama, music hall songs, and the romance of ballet. It explains why there was so much enthusiasm in the West End on Mafeking night. Such sentimental forms of entertainment contribute to understanding the emotional history of empire: the reasons why people of both sexes might feel a tear in the eye when singing the National Anthem or remembering the death of General Gordon. Imperialism for some meant conquest and plunder; for others, it meant adventure and sacrifice. British popular culture employed empire to lift the spirits. The Tory sensibility relishing status, nation, and empire, had etched its way into the fabric of the West End. Its hegemony was, however, never complete.

Radicalism

In political terms, the West End was contested territory. The very nature of the pleasure district meant that it became the source of dissatisfaction. It symbolized the elite, the bourgeoisie, and the status quo. It has thus been a problematic place for the political left. Yet I argue there was such a thing as a radical West End.

The left has always had an ambivalent relationship with the idea of pleasure itself (a contrast with the cultural conservatism which has pervaded this book). Simple fun, without ostensibly improving features, was a difficult issue for many early socialists and progressives. They feared it made the masses easy to manipulate and could serve as a distraction from inequality. The sexual content was a problem. Keir Hardie, the first Labour MP, regarded pubs, theatres, and music halls as degenerate.[24] Put crudely, the road to revolution did not start at the stage door of the Gaiety Theatre.

Its location in the centre of the city, however, made the West End a key space for radicals to meet in its pubs and public areas. The Strand and Covent Garden had long been key places in the construction of a radical underworld. Wych Street, off the Strand, was notorious for bookshops selling radical publications in the early nineteenth century, whilst the Crown and Anchor Tavern nearby was a major centre of political discussion (see Chapter 3). The Old Price riots at Covent Garden in 1809 showed how an elite institution could be employed to express dissent.

---

[23] Bram Stoker, *Personal Reminiscences of Henry Irving* (London: William Heinemann, 1907 [1906]), pp. 164, 212.
[24] Martin Pugh, *Speak for Britain!: A New History of the Labour Party* (London: Bodley Head, 2010), p. 58; see also Chris Waters, *British Socialists and the Politics of Popular Culture* (Manchester: Manchester University Press, 1990).

The West End was crammed into the eastern portion of the most radical constituency in the country: Westminster. Unusually, this was a constituency which enjoyed almost universal male suffrage before 1832 and was known for delivering radical MPs to Parliament.[25] The inhabitants of the West End in the early nineteenth century were often shopkeepers, skilled labourers, and the poor. The London Corresponding Society was founded by radical artisans at the Bell pub on Exeter Street, off the Strand, in 1792. Its response to the 'hardness of the times' was to demand parliamentary reform and its presence close by may explain why James Hadfield, the would-be assassin of George III, was asked if he was a member (see Chapter 1). The key figure in the organization was the shoemaker Thomas Hardy, who lived at no. 9 Piccadilly. He would later be arrested there on a charge of high treason.[26] When he was acquitted in 1794, supporters removed the horses from a carriage and drew him through the West End and back to his home with excited crowds cheering him all the way.[27] Hardy had been nurtured by a dissenting chapel in Crown Court, Covent Garden, a familiar location for nurturing oppositional thought.[28] It was artisans like Hardy and Francis Place who helped create the idea of 'Radical Westminster'. The constituency that contained the Houses of Parliament was notorious for MPs and demagogues like Francis Burdett who attacked 'old Corruption' and championed the liberties of the freeborn Englishman. Meanwhile, the followers of radical Thomas Spence, champion of land reform, met in a variety of pubs in Soho. The West End was thus a seedbed of radical thought and dissent. Westminster was even briefly represented briefly by the great liberal thinker John Stuart Mill (1865–8) though, by the later nineteenth century, its MPs were Tories.

Chartism was the great radical movement of the early Victorian period, which demanded democratic reform. Whilst its heartlands were in the north of England and in Wales, it came to establish a major presence in the life of the capital.[29] The Chartist convention headquarters was on the Tottenham Court Road, just off the West End. The Fraternal Democrats, who championed international revolutionary causes, had their regular monthly meeting in Drury Lane in 1848.[30] The outbreak of the French Revolution in 1848 produced rejoicing in Britain and hopes that something similar might take place. On 6 March that year, a major Chartist meeting was held in Trafalgar Square. It turned George W.M. Reynolds, the journalist and novelist, who addressed the crowd, into a popular hero when he championed the latest outbreak of revolution in France. The riot that followed was the

---

[25] Marc Baer, *The Rise and Fall of Radical Westminster, 1780–1890* (Basingstoke: Palgrave Macmillan, 2012).

[26] E.P. Thompson, *The Making of the English Working Class* (London: Penguin, 1968 [1963]), pp. 19–20.

[27] Thomas Hardy, *Memoir of Thomas Hardy* (London: James Ridgway, 1832), p. 54.

[28] Hardy, *Memoir of Thomas Hardy*, p. 5.

[29] David Goodway, *London Chartism, 1838–1848* (Cambridge: Cambridge University Press, 1982).

[30] Malcolm Chase, *Chartism: A New History* (Manchester: Manchester University Press, 2007), p. 294.

preliminary to the great Chartist demonstration on Kennington Common when it was feared revolution would break out. It also established that Trafalgar Square could function as a site for radical assembly and protest, as it provided open space for demonstrations close to the corridors of power in Westminster, to clubland London, but also to the theatres and shops of the rich.

What of the workers of the West End? At first glance, they might appear to be non-political figures who were not part of the rise of the labour movement. Yet in the later nineteenth century, many service workers (including those in the West End) became more militant because of poor wages and bad conditions at work. Waitresses at Lyons teashops, for example, worked a seventy-four hour week and lived on a 5 per cent commission and tips. In 1895, Joseph Lyons attempted to maximize profits by reducing the commission from 5 per cent to 2.5 per cent. This led to a strike at the Strand and Piccadilly teashops in which the leading trade unionist Tom Mann led a deputation demanding the restoration of the old system. Lyons had to respond by abolishing the commission system, introducing fixed salaries, and discouraging tipping.[31] In other words, waitresses behaved like other proletarians in the period and challenged conditions at work despite a role which emphasized service and hospitality.

Waiters were similarly exploited. Many were expected to live on tips rather than a proper wage. They found it difficult to eat regular meals (as they were working when everybody else ate), grabbing food at odd moments. If a diner did a runner and failed to pay, it was often the waiter who was expected to foot the bill.[32] They also needed energy and agility in an arduous job which is why they tended to be under forty-five. After that, they either became head waiters, returned to their country of origin, or moved into alternative employment.[33]

Waiters began to organize. Their success was limited but we do see the development of a political consciousness in their ranks. In 1898 the Amalgamated Waiters' Society of Great Britain petitioned the Theatre and Music Halls Committee of the London County Council requesting that licences be denied to all places of entertainment that did not 'pay the recognised trade union rate of wages' and approved conditions of work.[34] The request was rejected as it was not seen as within the committee's jurisdiction but it does demonstrate that waiters viewed themselves in political terms. The Amalgamated Waiters' Society approached the Conservative Home Secretary, Sir Mathew Ridley, for assistance but was rebuffed. It did, however, start to demand an hourly wage of one shilling for both waiters and waitresses, a ten-hour working day (as opposed to the

---

[31] Bird, *The First Food Empire*, p. 45.

[32] Brenda Assael, *The London Restaurant, 1840–1914* (Oxford: Oxford University Press, 2018), p. 89 (see ch. 3 for the social condition of waiters).

[33] C.H. d'E. Leppington, 'Work and Wages in Hotels and Restaurants', *Good Words* (1892), p. 756.

[34] Theatre and Music Halls Committee Agenda Papers, 15 June 1898, p. 9: LCC/MIN/706 (London Metropolitan Archives).

sixteen- to eighteen-hour working day some had to endure), and a six-day week. It saw its future through the promotion of Labour in Parliament.[35] The union noted how the dependence of waiters on tips often set one waiter against another, creating resentment and a sense of grievance. This in turn made them difficult to organize.[36] The union was, however, very small. Tipping was opposed by union leader Tom Mann in favour of a living wage but this was not the view of many waiters who supported the practice. Paul Vogel of the waiters' union complained that waiters were forced by managers to shave off their moustaches, an affront to their masculinity. Many trade unionists found it difficult to take the moustache issue seriously though the Café Monico, among other West End restaurants, gave in to this demand and allowed facial hair.[37] By 1900 waiters received a wage but it was only between two and four shillings a day.[38]

The growth of the labour movement and social reform created change for shopworkers. The Truck Act of 1896 led to the abolition of fines by many employers. In 1902, Jay's of Regent Street was fined by the inspector of factories and workshops for making young shopworkers do more overtime than they were allowed under the 1902 Factory Act.[39] The same year, the Amalgamated Union of Shop Assistants, Warehousemen, and Clerks held a demonstration in Trafalgar Square demanding a sixty-hour working week, the abolition of the living-in system, and fair remuneration. The union was pushing at an open door. The living-in system had begun to decline as firms started to get rid of it (women were expected to live at home or find their own lodgings). The Shops Acts of 1912 and 1913 mandated a maximum working week of sixty-four hours, including compulsory meal breaks. The effectiveness of this legislation was mixed but the conditions of work for the kind of service workers who sustained the West End (and elsewhere) had become a political issue.

Outcast London and Suffragettes

In the 1880s, the spectacle of the West End included not just theatres and grand buildings, it also featured increasing numbers of homeless, unemployed men who made poverty visible by sleeping rough in Covent Garden, Trafalgar Square, and on the steps of St Martin's in the Fields. There were soup kitchens in Ham Yard, Soho, and in Leicester Square (the latter kitchen opened in 1847 by the National

---

[35] *Waiter's Record*, February 1900, pp. 1–2.   [36] *Waiter's Record*, February 1900, p. 2.
[37] Rosalind Eyben, '"The Moustache Makes Him More of a Man": Waiters' Masculinity Struggles, 1890–1910', *History Workshop Journal*, 87 (2019), pp. 189–210.
[38] *Waiters' Record*, June 1900, p. 3.   [39] *Draper*, 3 May 1902, p. 667.

Philanthropic Association).[40] The West End was a different place for those who could not afford its multiple delights.

Poverty could no longer be disguised. St Giles remained a source of distress whilst Charles Booth's inquiry found much hardship in the back streets around Covent Garden and the Strand (alongside better-off workers), a situation made worse by the high rents of the area.[41] Booth found that many casual labourers had resorted to becoming 'sandwich men', walking the streets of the West End advertising products.[42] In 1885, Thomas Stevens a labourer, was found begging in Leicester Square at midnight with his wife, a baby, and two small children. He claimed that they had walked from Croydon the day before to see a man about some work and that a passer-by had innocently given him a penny. Stevens was given a month's hard labour by the Marlborough Street magistrate who claimed that he should not have had the children out at that time of night.[43]

The wealth of the West End would have felt like a rebuke to the poor. In a trivial but telling incident in 1886, one John Dawson was fined for using obscene language in New Bond Street, denouncing the 'aristocrats' and shouting that if he was not given bread he would break their windows.[44] The Social Democratic Federation, which began to trumpet the revolutionary new creed of socialism, drew attention to the spectacle of poverty amongst wealth. On 8 November 1886, along with the Fair Trade League (advocates of protectionism), it organized a demonstration in Trafalgar Square to highlight the plight of the unemployed. John Burns, the Labour leader (and later Liberal MP), reminded the crowd of the presence of the gentlemen's clubs close by on Pall Mall: 'What did the members of those clubs care for their...distress? Where were the Members of Parliament that day? They were sitting comfortably in their clubs, not caring a straw whether the public starved or not.'[45] When the demonstration agreed to move out of the square and proceed to Hyde Park they caught sight of a member of the Carlton Club showing what he thought of the hoi polloi by putting a finger up his nose. Worse, servant girls from the upper windows threw crusts of bread into the crowd.[46] A riot erupted through the streets of the West End and extended all the way up to Oxford Street with windows smashed. Peter Robinson's ladies' clothes

[40] Newspaper clippings in St Martin's Scrapbook Series: Leicester Square Vol. 1 part 2 pp. 18–21 (Westminster City Archives).

[41] Charles Booth, *Life and Labour of the People in London* (London: Macmillan, 1889–1903), First Series: Poverty Vol. 2, appendix, p. 1.

[42] Booth, *Life and Labour*, Third Series, Vol. 3, pp. 98–9.

[43] Newspaper clipping in St Martin's Scrapbook Series: Leicester Square Vol. 1, p. 49 (Westminster City Archives).

[44] Newspaper clipping in St Martin's Scrapbook Series: Leicester Square, Vol. 1, p. 50 (Westminster City Archives).

[45] Quoted in Rodney Mace, *Trafalgar Square: Emblem of Empire* (London: Lawrence and Wishart, 1976), p. 162.

[46] John Burns papers, Add MSS 46, 308 ff. 40–1 (British Library).

shop on Oxford Street suffered £40 worth of damage whilst Marshall and Snelgrove endured twice that amount of destruction to property. Clubland London (whose influence we have noted throughout this study) had become a provocation to the poor.

In the wake of the 1886 riots, the new Commissioner of Police, Sir Charles Warren, attempted to close the square to demonstrations. The Social Democratic Federation insisted that the Square belonged to the people and organized demonstrations from all over London attended by figures such as William Morris, Annie Besant, and John Burns. On what became known as Bloody Sunday (13 November 1887), the unemployed came into conflict with police fortified by detachments of grenadier guards. The Riot Act was read and there were fights in the Haymarket, St Martins Lane, and Trafalgar Square. About two hundred people were injured and several were killed, including the radical Alfred Linnell who was trampled under a police horse. For five years afterwards, demonstrations in Trafalgar Square were banned, a policy that had the support of many locals and shopowners. These episodes are familiar in the history of the making of late Victorian socialism. They take on new meaning, I argue, when we view them in spatial terms; as contesting the nature of the West End itself. The resentment against clubs, which were the networks of a ruling class (as we saw in Chapter 3), and against shops patronized by the middle classes, challenged territory based on the exclusion of the poor.

The West End then became a major centre of Suffragette activity. They held their first outdoor meeting in Trafalgar Square on 19 May 1906 when Sylvia Pankhurst appeared with Keir Hardie, and there was another major rally in the square on 11 October 1908 when an attempt was made to rush Parliament. The London Pavilion provided Suffragettes with a meeting place. From 1911 to 1913 the Women's Social and Political Union met there every Monday from two to five in the afternoon. Emmeline Pankhurst and her daughters addressed the meetings. The feminist Ruth Slate sold flowers for the Women's Freedom League in Piccadilly Circus.[47] The area became the subject of a major campaign on 1 March 1912 when Suffragettes began to smash the windows of West End shops.[48] The tactic was attractive because it was a way of making buildings vulnerable. The Pankhursts assembled large numbers of women who were prepared to make this disruptive protest in a concerted plan. Shops from the Strand all the way up to Oxford Street were damaged in the late afternoon and early evening. These included Burberry on the Haymarket, Edwards and Sons (jewellers) on Regent Street, and Walter Truefit (hairdressers) on New Bond Street. The Civil Service

[47] Tierl Thompson (ed.), *Dear Girl: The Diaries and Letters of Two Working Women* (London: The Women's Press, 1987), p. 150.

[48] Erika Diane Rappaport, *Shopping for Pleasure: Women in the Making of London's West End* (Princeton, NJ: Princeton University Press, 2000), pp. 215–22.

Co-Operative Stores on the Haymarket and the depots of the ABC and Lyons companies were attacked but the worst damage occurred on Regent Street, where shops from Swan & Edgar up to Liberty's were wrecked. Pavements were strewn with glass. The police made a large number of arrests forcing shop owners to board up their premises, another visible sign of what had happened. The windows of Number 10 Downing Street were also broken (whilst the destruction extended over to Kensington). Christabel Pankhurst told a journalist 'This is a demonstration simply to show that we are determined in our militant tactics to get the vote.'[49]

The owner of Liberty's told the *Evening News*, 'Women have regrettably turned against the shrines at which they usually worship.'[50] Suffragettes like Mary Richardson later insisted that 'It was not an attack upon West-End shopkeepers but upon the government through the medium of the insurance companies.'[51] It is difficult not to see this carefully rehearsed campaign as having a strong symbolic element, enhanced by the fact that West End shops were so close to the corridors of power. Women had turned against what was seen as their natural habitat. The episode suggests that women's attitudes towards these shops which were built around displays of female beauty and glamour were complex. One hundred and twenty-six women were brought to trial as part of the window-smashing campaign; of these seventy-six received hard labour. Joan Wilson (aged twenty-one) was given fourteen days for breaking a window at the Walk-over Show Company on the Strand, Mabel de Roxe was found guilty of attacking the Lyons restaurant among other venues on the Strand, and Emmeline Pankurst was sentenced to two months imprisonment for the incident at Downing Street.[52]

Suffragettes assembled on 4 March at the London Pavilion to show support for the militant actions against West End shops. Mrs Pethick-Lawrence in an address 'rejoiced when she looked at those broken windows.'[53] That same day there was another wave of window-smashing in the West End and the City, forcing the British Museum and Royal Academy to close to protect the exhibits. There was also a counter-reaction. Some 200 young men (believed to be medical students) smashed the windows of the Women's Press offices on the Charing Cross Road. The International Suffrage Shop, off the Strand, was also attacked.[54] On 11 March, representatives of large West End firms met at the Queen's Hall to discuss the crisis. Among the firms were D.H. Evans, Liberty's, Marshall & Snelgrove, Harrods, and Swan & Edgar. The meeting was assembled by William Boosey of Chappell's music publisher on New Bond Street. The government was urged to take firm action. A woman tried to add an amendment to the resolution, urging the

---

[49] *Times*, 2 March 1912, p. 8.
[50] Quoted in Lindy Woodhead, *Shopping, Seduction and Mr. Selfridge* (London: Profile, 2012), p. 122. Liberty employed similar language in a letter to the *Standard*: 4 March 1912, p. 11.
[51] Mary R. Richardson, *Laugh A Defiance* (London: George Weidenfeld and Nicolson, 1953), p. 39.
[52] *Times*, 4 March 1912, p. 4.   [53] *Times*, 5 March 1912, p. 6.
[54] *Times*, 5 March 1912, p. 8.

government to put a stop to disorder by giving women the vote. The Chairman refused to consider this as the meeting was not concerned with the reason for the grievance.[55] Selfridge's was not one of the stores at the meeting as it had championed the Suffragettes and its premises were not damaged (Harry Gordon Selfridge had even paid for the publication of the *Suffrage Annual Who's Who* which listed the details of important women who were ignored by the male-dominated *Who's Who*). The window-smashing campaign represented the inversion of what the West End was about. It was an assault on the culture of display and glamour which had been the stock in trade of the pleasure district. The revolt of both the unemployed and the Suffragettes need to be reclaimed as part of its history.

The Bloody Sunday riots and the Suffragette window-smashing campaign present a different spectacle from the scenes in the West End following the relief of Mafeking. The crowd that assembled that night in 1900 showed how the West End had become a place of collective enthusiasm amongst Londoners. Different classes could rub shoulders, drawn by the promises of the populist palatial. What happened on Bloody Sunday and in 1912 shows that the West End was also the source of hostility. The pleasure district allowed power in Britain to be questioned, because the elite existed in its most visible form there. What this shows is that the West End had become a place that, in a very particular way, foregrounded image and symbol; not just in its entertainments and its built environment but in its mythology. The West End was a space where the nation told stories about itself. Other such spaces existed (Whitehall took on this function, for example), but the pleasure district was a place that could speak of empire and the nation in conjunction with entertainment and consumerism. The revolt of the unemployed and the Suffragettes as they smashed shop windows was a deliberate disruption of the narratives on which the West End depended. The heart-warming sentiment of imperial melodrama at Drury Lane co-existed with the righteous anger of the poor and of socialists in Trafalgar Square.

If this book has largely been about the rich and the middle class, it is right that it ends with the dispossessed. If the excluded were a disruptive presence, it is right that they disrupt my book as well. Bloody Sunday suggests that the West End antagonized people because it was a place dedicated purely to the interests of consumption, in which the world of the producers who made the wealth celebrated in the West End was effaced. When we look at the various riots in the West End, we discover people who could see through the forms of fantasy in the district and who were antagonized by its pretensions. If I have emphasized the rhetoric of hospitality, the riots can be seen as being about people who recognize this as an imposture. They say boldly to West End shopkeepers and showpeople, 'You are

---

[55] *Times*, 12 March 1912, p. 6; HO 144_1193_220196 f. 155 (TNA).

not my friend.' At moments like this, the lack of authenticity in the pleasure district becomes clear. Yet, at the end of the day, it was not the radical crowd that created the West End; it was the crowd brought together by department store sales.

In the second half of the nineteenth century, this book has shown that the West End had come into its own as the world's leading pleasure district. The dynamic relationship between shops, department stores, arcades, theatres, cinemas, opera houses, concert halls, restaurants, pubs, exhibition sites, and spectacular buildings make it different from other parts of London. The West End invaded the popular imagination as a source of pleasure or, at least, as a place one read about in newspapers.

The function of pleasure districts is to place new styles, fashion, and forms of consumption and culture onto the public's agenda. The West End meant different things to different people and, as the examples in this chapter show, its cultural forms were not accepted uncritically. It stood for various forms of commercial hospitality but it was also about excluding the wrong sort of people or containing them. We should therefore not be surprised to find in the West End both conservatism and the carnivalesque. This book thus points to a strange paradox. The West End was conservative but it was also a transformative space (arguably the antithesis of conservatism). The essence of its glamour was that it opened up the possibility of alternate selves, achieved through clothes, objects, and style but also through the imagination. This was what the entrepreneurs who made the pleasure district tapped into. They created a space of fashion and fantasy. Pleasure was no longer to be the preserve of the leisure class, they proclaimed, but an integral part of metropolitan identities. By the time of the Gaiety Girl in the 1890s, these identities were increasingly sexualized. Images of beauty were employed to sell shows and other products. The West End was never totally respectable and, by the *fin de siècle*, it dripped sex appeal. For many, the area was a place of liberation because it expressed the joys of metropolitan living.

A history of the West End can never be simply a local history. It offers a way of understanding the story of modern Britain. New forms of culture industry rippled out from the one-mile radius around Piccadilly. As its entertainments toured the country and indeed the globe and as they were celebrated in print media from newspaper reviews to periodicals like the *Play Pictorial*, the centre of London increased in cultural importance. Moreover, shops such as Selfridge's and venues such as the Alhambra became icons to compare with the Tower of London; one had not seen London until one had been there.

The West End reconfirms the notion that social class was a determinant of experience; some people could afford West End entertainments and some could not. The door of the Ritz was not open to all. On the other hand, it also shows that notions of classes as in struggle and in conflict does not map onto to the fluidity of experience. In the West End discourse, people were constructed not as classes nor as citizens but as a patriotic people whose interests were best served by the wisdom of the patricians. The cultural experience offered by mass entertainment was a form of social glue.

The West End was, and remains, about marketing, buying, and selling. But that does not exhaust its meanings. It also offered its utopian moments, when one can glimpse a better life (or experience vicariously what the good life might feel like). There are the songs of courtship and love, the adoption of alternate identities, the conviviality of the family meal at Gatti's, the spring in the step induced by wearing one's sharpest clothes, the delight in transcendent art and ravishing music, the side-splitting laugh, the performance that is not so much acting as whirlwind. The West End made good on the promise of the city as a new way of living. It distributed arrows of desire on every street corner.

List of West End Theatres and some Music Venues, 1800–1914

Note: Some of the theatres in this list had a variety of different names or permutations of the same name in the period. I have gone for the one most familiar today. The list does not include pubs which were licensed for music.

Adelphi Theatre, Strand, 1806–
Aldwych Theatre, Aldwych, 1905–
Alhambra Theatre, Leicester Square, 1854–1936
Ambassador's Theatre, West Street, 1913–
Apollo Theatre, Shaftesbury Avenue, 1901–
Argyll Rooms, Great Windmill Street, *see* Trocadero
Argyll Rooms, Regent Street, 1820–30
Comedy Theatre, Panton Street, 1881–
Criterion Theatre, Piccadilly Circus, 1874–
Daly's Theatre, Cranbourn Street, Leicester Square, 1893–1937
Duke of York's Theatre, St Martin's Lane, 1892–
Empire Theatre, Leicester Square, 1884–1927
Evans's, late Joy's, Music and Supper Rooms, Covent Garden, *c.*1844–82
Exeter Hall, Strand, 1831–1907
Gaiety Theatre, Strand, 1868–1950 (on Aldwych from 1903)
Gallery of Illustration, Regent Street, 1856–73
Garrick Theatre, Charing Cross Road, 1889–
Gatti's Charing Cross Music Hall (now Charing Cross Theatre), Villiers Street, 1866–
Globe Theatre, Newcastle Street, Strand, 1868–1902
Globe Theatre, Shaftesbury Avenue, 1906–
Hanover Square Rooms, Hanover Square, 1774–1874
Her Majesty's Theatre, Haymarket, 1705–
Little Theatre, John Adam Street, 1910–41
London Coliseum, St Martin's Lane, 1904–
London Hippodrome, Cranbourn Street, Leicester Square, 1900–
London Palladium, Argyll Street, 1910–
London Pavilion, Piccadilly Circus, 1859–1934
Lyceum Theatre, Wellington Street, Strand, 1772–
Lyric Theatre, Shaftesbury Avenue, 1888–
Middlesex Music Hall, 1847–1919 (the Winter Garden Theatre 1919–65 and site of the present Gillian Lynne Theatre)
New Theatre (now the Noel Coward), St Martin's Lane, 1903–
Novelty Theatre, Great Queen Street, 1882–1941
Olympic Theatre, Wych Street, Strand, 1806–97
Opera Comique, Strand, 1870–99
Palace Theatre, Cambridge Circus, 1891–
Playhouse Theatre, Northumberland Avenue, 1882–
Prince of Wales's Theatre (later the Scala Theatre), Charlotte Street, 1772–1969

Prince of Wales's Theatre, Coventry Street, 1884–
Princess's Theatre, Oxford Street, 1840–1902
Queen's Hall, Upper Regent Street, 1893–1941
Queen's Theatre, Long Acre, Covent Garden (formerly the St Martin's Hall), 1867–79
Queen's Theatre (now the Sondheim Theatre), Shaftesbury Avenue, 1907–
Royal Strand Theatre, Strand, 1832–1905
Royalty Theatre, Dean Street, Soho, 1840–1938
Royalty Theatre, Kingsway, 1911–57 (now the site of the Peacock Theatre)
Royal Opera House, Covent Garden, 1732–
St James's Hall, Piccadilly, 1858–1905
St James's Theatre, King Street, 1835–1957
Shaftesbury Theatre (formerly the Prince's), Shaftesbury Avenue, 1911–
Shaftesbury Theatre, Shaftesbury Avenue, 1888–1941
Strand Musick Hall, Strand, 1864–66
Strand Theatre, Aldwych, 1905–
Terry's Theatre, Strand, 1887–1910
Theatre Royal, Drury Lane, 1663–
Theatre Royal, Haymarket, 1720–
Toole's Theatre, King William IV Street, 1869–95
Trocadero Music Hall, Piccadilly, 1882–95 (Argyll Rooms, 1846–82)
Vaudeville Theatre, Strand, 1870–
Wigmore Hall, Wigmore Street, 1901–
Wyndham's Theatre, Charing Cross Road, 1899–

Bibliography

Contents

Primary Sources
Manuscripts Sources
Printed Primary Sources
Articles in Contemporary Periodicals
Commentaries
Digital Primary Sources
Ephemera
Guides to London and West End locations
Letters, Memoirs, and Diaries
Newspapers and Periodicals
Novels, Plays, Songs, etc.
Parliamentary Papers

Secondary Sources

Books
Articles in Journals and Periodicals
PhD Theses
Websites and web-based publications
Encyclopedias, Dictionaries, etc.

Primary Sources

Manuscript Sources

University of Bristol Theatre Collection

BTC2011/0031: Robert Waters Gaiety Girls Collection.
EJE/1879: Daly's Theatre Programmes.
MM/REF/TH/GR/OXF/1: Oxford Music Hall.
MM/REF/TH/LO/ALH/1: Alhambra file (illustrations).
MM/REF/TH/LO/ALH/2: Alhambra file (special events).
MM/REF/TH/LO/ALH/3: Alhambra 1858–78 file.
MM/REF/TH/LO/DAL/2: 'A Gaiety Girl' souvenirs.
MM/REF/TH/LO/DAL/16: 'Merry Widow' file.
MM/2/TH/LO/DAL/1: Daly's Theatre file.
MM/2/TH/LO/DAL/4: 'An Artist's Model' ephemera.
MM/2/TH/LO/DAL/8: 'San Toy' and 'A Gaiety Girl' file.
MM/2/TH/LO/DAL/14: 'The Count of Luxembourg' file.
MM/2/TH/LO/PAV: London Pavilion History File.

MM/2/TH/LO/PAV/2: London Pavilion File.
MM/2/TH/LO/TRO: Trocadero and Toole's Theatre file.
PR/LALH/32 1887: Alhambra Theatre programmes.
TC/W/M/113: The George Edwardes Birthday Book.

British Library

Add MSS 46, 308: John Burns Papers.
Add MSS 27, 831: Francis Place Papers.
Evanion Collection.
Lord Chamberlain's Collection of Plays.

London Metropolitan Archives

B/MR/009: Ledger of Merry and Company, Saddlemakers, 4 St James's Street, 1885–99.
LMA/4467/A/03/001: Crosse and Blackwell Papers.
MBW/BA/37999: Alhambra Theatre of Varieties.
MJ/SP/1834/04/094: Middlesex/Clerkenwell Sessions.
MR/L/MD/0855: Petition from John Baldwin Buckstone.
MR/L/MD/858/01: Petition of the inhabitants of St Marylebone against Charles Morton's application for a music hall licence (1860).
MR/L/MD/858/04: Petition of Augustus Harris against Charles Morton's application for a music licence (1860).
MR/L/MD/860: Petition of the Churchwardens of St Martin in the Fields against the granting of a music license to the 'Windsor Castle', no. 27 Long Acre, kept by William McDonald (1860).
MR/L/MD/0877: Petition of A.F. Sharttner of the Windsor Castle, Long Acre, for a renewal of music licence (1858).
MR/L/MD/1403/03: Petition from the Alhambra Company against the renewal of the Empire Theatre's music and dance licence (1887).
MR/L/MD/1403/06: Plans of Empire Theatre.
SC/GL/SAR/003: Sargent, G.F.: Collection of Drawings of London Buildings.
SC/PZ/WE/01 1001–1100: Exterior of New Buildings: Westminster.
SC/PZ/WE/01 2201–1350: Leicester Square prints.
SC/SS/07/34 1–184: Westminster Streets.
London County Council Papers:
LCC/MIN/10, 705: Theatre and Music Halls Committee Agenda Papers 1889–92.
LCC/MIN/10, 711: Theatre and Music Halls Committee Minutes, 8 March 1887–4, Oct. 1889.
LCC/MIN/10, 712: Theatre and Music Halls Committee, 7 Oct. 1887–24 June 1890.
LCC/MIN/10, 768: LCC Theatre Committee Papers: Adelphi Theatre 1898–1906.
LCC/MIN/10, 801: LCC Theatre Committee Papers: Egyptian Hall, 1907–13.
LCC/MIN/10/10, 846: LCC Theatres Committee: London Pavilion, 1888–1903.
LCC/MIN/10/10, 847: LCC Theatres Committee London Palladium/London Pavilion, 1904–10.

Lyons Archives (London Metropolitan Archives)

ACC/3527/227: History of J. Lyons.
ACC/3527/231: Memories of Nell Bacon (London Metropolitan Archive).
ACC/3527/232: Trocadero.
ACC/3527/397: The Lyons Popular Café.

Old Bailey Sessions Papers Online

The National Archives (Kew, London)

CRES 26: Regent Street Papers.

CRES 35/2343: New Street (Regent Street) Bill, 1813/lists of Crown Property.

CRES 35/3267: Egyptian Hall.

H.O. 45/9511/17216: Police-Metropolitan: Efforts of Police to eradicate prostitution in Haymarket, 1869–85.

HO 107/1481/98: 1851 Census for the City of Westminster.

HO 119/4: Petition from patent theatres.

LC 1/70: Lord Chamberlain's Office.

MEPO 2/181: Metropolitan Police: Office of the Commissioner: Correspondence and Papers: Vagrants in Trafalgar Square.

MEPO 2/182: Metropolitan Police: Office of the Commissioner: Correspondence and Papers: Public Meetings and Riots 1886–8.

MEPO 2/1560: Suffragettes: Meetings at London Pavilion Music Hall.

Victoria and Albert Museum (Theatre Collection)

Richard D'Oyly Carte Papers

Henry Arthur Jones file.

Charles Wyndham file.

THM/LON/PAV: Royal Pavilion Theatre, Whitechapel file.

Royal Opera House, Covent Garden Archives

SC 1/1/15: Frederick Gye Diaries.

Westminster City Archives

0085/071: Indenture of Elizabeth Sander and Thomas Sisson, 19 November 1853.

0498/5–152: Benjamin Webster correspondence.

1197: Workbook of James Dean, draper, 23 Savile Row, 1839–40.

Liberty and Co. Papers

788/29/1: Catalogue of Liberty Art Fabrics (1883).

788/23/1–4: India Village Exhibition, Battersea.

788/24/1: Liberty's Dividends.

788/36/1–10: Handbook of sketches, *c*.1890.

Prints and Photographs Collection

St Anne's Westminster, Vestry Minutes.

St Martin-in-the Fields, Vestry Minutes.

Printed Primary Sources

Articles in Contemporary Periodicals

Booth, Michael R. (ed.), *Victorian Theatrical Trades: Articles from 'The Stage', 1883–1884* (London: Society for Theatre Research, 1981).

'Domestic Occurences', *Gentleman's Magazine*, Vol. 87 (Sept 1817), p. 272.

d'E. Leppington, C.H., 'The Gibeonites of the Stage: Work and Wages Behind the Scenes', *National Review*, Vol. 17 (1891), pp. 245–61.

d'E. Leppington, C.H., 'Work and Wages in Hotels and Restaurants', *Good Words* (1892), pp. 753–8.

'Dinner for 1000', *Pictorial Magazine*, 4 November 1899, pp. 397–400.

[Lewis, George Henry], 'The Opera in 1833–63', *Cornhill Magazine*, Vol. 8 (1863), pp. 295–307.

'Nimrod', 'The Anatomy of Gaming', *Fraser's Magazine*, Vol. 17 (1838), pp. 538–45.

'Perditus', 'Crockford and Crockford's', *Bentley's Miscellany* Vol. 17 (1845), pp. 142–55, 251–64.

Princip, Val C., 'A Chapter from a Painter's Reminiscences', *Magazine of Art*, new series, Vol. 2, (1904), pp. 281–6.

'Ralph Redivivus', 'The Lowther Arcade', *The Civil Engineer and Architect's Journal*, Vol. 2, (1839), pp. 83–4.

Roberts, Morley, 'Waiters and Restaurants', *Murray's Magazine*, Vol. 7 (1890), pp. 534–46.

'Rogues Walk', *Household Words*, Vol. 16 (1857) pp. 262–4.

[Sala, George Augustus], 'Arcadia', *Household Words*, Vol. 7 (1853), pp. 376–82.

Symons, Arthur, 'The Case of the Empire', *Saturday Review*, 10 Nov. 1894, pp. 501–2.

'The Street as Art-Galleries', *Magazine of Art*, Vol. 4 (1881), p. 299.

Wintle, W.J., 'Round the London Restaurants', *Windsor Magazine*, Vol. 4 (1896), pp. 445–50.

Commentaries

Acton, William, *Prostitution: Considered in its Moral, Social and Sanitary Aspects* (London: John Churchill, 1870).

Archer, William, *English Dramatists of To-Day* (London: Sampson Low, 1882).

Baudelaire, Charles, *The Painter of Modern Life* (London: Penguin, 2010 [1863]).

Bone, James, *The London Perambulator* (London: Jonathan Cape, 1925).

Booth, Charles, *Life and Labour of the People in London* (London: Macmillan, 1889–1903). 17 vols.

Borsa, Mario, *The English Stage of To-Day* (London: John Lane, 1908).

Bowdler, John, *Reform or Ruin Abridged; In which Each Man Learn the True State of Things at this Time* (London: John Hatchard, 1798).

Carlyle, Thomas, *Past and Present* (ed. Chris R. Vanden Bosche) (Berkeley, CA: University of California Press, 2005 [1843]).

Chant, Laura Ormiston, *Why We Attacked the Empire* (London: Horace, Marshall, and Son, 1895).

'A Constant Observer', *Sketches in Bedlam; Or, Characteristic Traits of Insanity* (London: Sherwood, Jones, and Co., 1823).

Dickens, Charles, *Reprinted Pieces: The Uncommercial Traveller and Other Stories* (London: Nonesuch Press, 1938 [1858]).

Dickens, Charles, *Night Walks* (London: Penguin, 2010).

Donne, William Bodham, *Essays on the Drama, and on Popular Amusements* (London: Tinsley Brothers, 1863).

Escott, T.H.S., *England: Its People, Polity, and Pursuits* (London: Cassell, 1879).

Filon, Augustin, *The English Stage* (New York: Kennikat Press, 1970 [1897]).

Garwood, John, *The Million-Peopled City; Or, One-Half of the People of London Made Known to the Other Half* (London: Wertheim and Macintosh, 1853).

Greenwood, James, *The Wilds of London* (London: Chatto and Windus, 1874).

Hobson, J.A., *The Psychology of Jingoism* (London: Grant Richards, 1901).

Hollingshead, John, *Ragged London in 1861* (London: Smith, Elder, 1861).

Hollingshead, John, *Rubbing the Gilt Off: A West End Book for all Readers* (London: John Camden Hotten, 1860).

James, Henry, *The Scenic Art: Notes on Acting and the Drama, 1872–1901* (London: Rupert Hart-Davis, 1949).

James, Henry, *English Hours*, ed. Leon Edel (Oxford: Oxford University Press, 1981).

Keynes, Geoffrey (ed.), *Hazlitt: Selected Essays* (London: Nonesuch Press, 1948).

Kracauer, Siegfried, *The Mass Ornament: Weimar Essays*, ed. Thomas Y. Levin (Cambridge, MA: Harvard University Press, 1995).

Lewes, George Henry, *On Actors and the Art of Acting* (Leipzig: Tauchnitz, 1875).

Maskelyne, John Nevil, *Modern Spiritualism* (London: Frederick Warne, 1876).

Nightingale, Joseph, *The Bazaar: Its Origin, Nature, and Objects Explained and Recommended as an Important Branch of Political Economy* (London: privately published, 1816).

Place, Francis, *A Brief Examination of the Dramatic Patents (extracted from the 'Monthly Magazine')* (London: Baylis and Leighton, 1834).

Runtz, Ernest, *Hostelries: Ancient and Modern* (London: Institute at 34 Russell Square, 1908).

Schlesinger, Max, *Saunterings In and About London* (London: Nathaniel Cooke, 1853).

Shepherd, Thomas, *Metropolitan Improvements in London* (London: Jones and Co., 1828).

Sims, George R. (ed.), *Living London* (London: Cassell, 1902–3) 3 vols.

Slater, Michael (ed.), *'The Amusements of the People' and Other Papers [Dickens' Journalism, Vol. 2]* (London: J.M. Dent, 1997).

Snow, John, *On the Mode of Communication of Cholera* (London: John Snow, 1855).

[Southey, Robert], *Letters from England: by Don Manuel Alvarez Espriella* (London: Longman, Hurst, Rees, Orme, and Brown, 1807]).

Suthurst, Thomas, *Death and Disease Behind the Counter* (London: Kegan, Paul, Trench, 1884).

Wyatt, Benjamin, *Observations on the Design for the Theatre Royal, Drury Lane* (London: J. Taylor, 1813).

Digital Primary Sources

London Low Life: Street Culture, Social Reform and the Victorian Underworld (Adam Matthew).

Ephemera

A Visit to the Bazaar (London: J. Harris, 1818).

The Bazaar, a Popular Song Arranged to a Popular Air (London: T. Holloway, c.1825).

A Collection of Handbills and Programmes of Exhibitions and Entertainments in Leicester Square, together with Admission Tickets; and of Advertisements of Tradesmen in Leicester Square. 1800–1870? (BL call mark: 1880.b.25).

Alhambra Theatre programme: 21 August 1899 (BL call mark: 1562/2).

Burford, *The Panorama Leicester Square. Tracts 1812–53* (BL call mark: 10349.T.15 (19–37).

Criterion Theatre Programmes, 1888–1958: BL call mark:11797 f.7.

The Grand Hotel, Trafalgar Square, London: Tariff (London: Grand Hotel, 1888?).

W. and F. Hamley, *Illustrated Catalogue of Conjuring Tricks etc* (London: W. and F. Hamley, c.1895).

Her Majesty's Theatre programmes, 1897–1900: BL call mark: 1874.b.4.

Maskelyne and Cooke, The Royal Illusionists and Anti-Spiritualists (London: Egyptian Hall, 1875?).

National Gallery of Practical Science, Blending Instruction with Amusement: Catalogue for 1833 (London: J. Homes, 1833).

The Nobby Songster: A Prime Selection as now Singing at Offleys, Cider Cellar: Coal Hole etc (London: W. West, 1842?).

Ruy Blas and the Blase Roue programme (London: Gaiety, 1889).

St Martin's Scrapbook Series (Westminster City Archive).

Sir Charles Wyndham (London: Payne-Jennings, 1919).

Some Foreign Press Opinions of 'David Garrick' (London: Criterion theatre, nd.).

Souvenir of Savoy Hotel (London: Black and White Publishing Company, 1893).

Souvenir of The Prisoner of Zenda (London: St. James's Theatre, 1896).

The Story of Old Soho: Picturesque Memories of mid-London (London: T. Pettit, 1893).

Guides to London and West End Locations

Blanchard, E. L., *Bradshaw's Guide through London and its Environs 1862* (London: W.J. Adams, 1861).

Boyle's Court Guide for 1812 (London: Eliza Boyle, 1812).

Burlington Arcade: Being a Discourse on Shopping for the Elite (London: Favill Press, 1925).

Cook, (Mrs) E.T., *Highways and Byways in London* (London: Macmillan 1911).

Cunningham, Peter, *A Handbook for London, Past and Present* (London: John Murray, 1849), 2 vols.

Doré, Gustave and Blanchard Jerrold, *London: A Pilgrimage* (London: n.p. 1872).

The Epicure's Almanac; Or, Calendar of Good Living (London: Longman, Hurst, Rees, Orme, and Brown, 1815).

Every Night Book: Or, Life after Dark (London: T. Richardson, 1827).

Fall, Marcus, *London Town: Sketches of London Life and Character* (London: Tinsley Brothers, 1880).

The Florence Restaurant Wholesale Wine List (n.d.) London Collection Pamphlets: Bishopsgate Institute: Box 323: D.91.15.

Grant, James, *The Great Metropolis* (London: Saunders and Otley, 1837).

Harris's List of Covent Garden Ladies: Or, Man of Pleasure's Kalendar for the Year 1788 (London: H. Ranger, 1788).

Hotel Cecil, London (n.d.): London Collection Pamphlets (Bishopsgate Institute) Box 323: D.93.1.

Hotel Cecil Banqueting Department (London: Hotel Cecil, 1911): London Collection Pamphlets: Bishopsgate Institute: Box 323: D.91.15.

Knight, Charles (ed.), *London* (London: Charles Knight, 1841–3) 6 vols.

Johnstone's London Commercial Guide and Street Directory (London: Barnard and Foley, 1817).

London at Dinner: Where to Dine in 1858 (London: David and Charles, 1969 [1858]).

London by Night: Or, the Bachelor's Facetious Guide to all the Ins and Outs of the Nightly Doings of the Metropolis (London: William Ward, 1859?).

Mayhew, Henry, *London Labour and the London Poor* (New York: Dover, 1968 [1861]).

Mayhew, Henry (ed.), *The Shops and Companies of London and the Trades and Manufactories of Great Britain* (London: Strand, 1865).

Miller, Thomas, *Picturesque Sketches of London* (London: National Illustrated Library, 1852).

Mitchell, Robert, *Plan and Views in Perspective* (London: Oriental Press, 1801).

Moncrieff, A.R. Hope, *London* (London: A. and C. Black, 1910).

The Monthly Mirror: Reflecting Men and Manners. With Strictures on their Epitome, the Stage (London: J. Wright, 1807).

The New Swell's Night Guide to the Bowers of Venus (London: J. Paul, 1846 [?]).

Newnham Davis, Nathaniel, *Dinners and Dining: Where and How to Dine in London* (London: Grant Richards, 1899).

Newnham Davis, Nathaniel, *The Gourmet's Guide to London* (New York: Brentano's, 1914).

[Nicoll, H.J. and D.], *A Visit to Regent Street, London* (London: Henry Vizetelley, 1856?).

Olivia's Shopping and How She Does It: A Prejudiced Guide (Stroud: Gunpowder Press, 2009 [1906]).

The Pall Mall Restaurant in the Haymarket: Its Historical Site, Early Associations and Present Popularity, 1713–1913 (London: Hudson and Kearns 1913).

Pascoe, Charles Eyre, *London of To-Day: An Illustrated Handbook for the Season* (London: Sampson, Low, Marston, Searle, and Rivington, 1885).

Pascoe, Charles Eyre, *London of To-Day: An Illustrated Handbook for the Season* (London: Sampson, Low, Marston, Searle, and Rivington, 1887).

The Pictorial Handbook of London (London: Henry G. Bohn, 1854).

Piggott and Co's National and Commercial Directory of Bedford, Cambridgeshire, Essex etc. (London: Piggott, 1839).

The Post Office London Directory (London: Frederick Kelly 1841).

The Post Office London Directory (London: Frederick Kelly 1851).

The Post Office London Directory (London: Kelly, 1886).

Private and Public Functions at the Empire Rooms, Trocadero Restaurant (n.d.): London Collection Pamphlets:Bishopsgate Institute: Box 323 D.93.1.

Rede, Leman Thomas, *The Road to the Stage* (London: J. Onwhyn, 1836).

Slater's Restaurants Illustrated (n.d.): London Collection Pamphlets: Bishopsgate Institute: Box 323: D.91.15.

Tallis, John, *London Street Views, 1838–40* (London: London Topographical Society, 2002).

The Tavistock Hotel, Covent Garden (London: Knight, Frank and Rutley, 1928): auction catalogue: London Collection Pamphlets: Bishopsgate Institute: Box 323: D.91.15.

Timbs, John, *Curiosities of London; Exhibiting the most Rare and Remarkable Objects of Interest in the Metropolis* (London: J.S. Virtue, 1867 [1855]).

Timbs, John, *Clubs and Club Life in London* (London: Chatto and Windus, 1908).

Yokel's Preceptor: Or, More Sprees in London! (London: H. Smith, 1855).

Letters, Memoirs, and Diaries

[Ablett, William], *Memoirs of an Old Draper* (London: Sampson Low, 1876).

Bamford, Francis and the Duke of Wellington (eds), *The Journal of Mrs Arbuthnot, 1820–1832* (London: Macmillan, 1950), 2 vols.

Bamford, Samuel, *Passages in the Life of a Radical* (Oxford: Oxford University Press, 1984 [1884]).

Bancroft, Squire and Marie Wilton, *On and Off the Stage* (London: Richard Bentley, 1888) 2 vols.

Barnes, J.H., *Forty Years On the Stage* (London: Chapman and Hall, 1914).

Beckson, Karl and John M. Munro (eds), *Arthur Symons: Selected Letters, 1880–1935*, (Basingstoke: Macmillan, 1989).

Beerbohm, Max (ed.), *Herbert Beerbohm Tree: Some Memories of Him and of His Art* (London: Hutchinson, 1920).

Bennett, Alfred Rosling, *London and Londoners in the Eighteen Fifties and Sixties* (London: T. Fisher Unwin, 1924).

Blackmore (Lieut.) John, *The London By Moonlight Mission: Being an Account of Midnight Cruises on the Streets of London during the Last Thirteen Years* (London: Robson and Avery, 1860).

Bloom, Ursula, *Victorian Vinaigrette* (London: Hutchinson, 1956).

Blumenfeld, R.D., *R.D.B.'s Diary, 1887–1914* (London: Heinemann, 1930).

Booker, Beryl Lee, *Yesterday's Child* (London: John Long, 1937).

Booth, John Bennion, *Old Pink 'Un Days* (London: Grant Richards, 1924).

Booth, John Bennion, *Sporting Times: The 'Pink 'Un World* (London: T. Werner Laurie, 1938).

Buchan, William, *John Buchan: A Memoir* (London: Buchan and Enright, 1982).

Burke, Thomas, *Nights in Town* (London: George Allen and Unwin, 1925 [1915]).

Burke, Thomas, *The Streets of London Through the Centuries* (London: B.T. Batsford, 1940).

Callow, Edward, *Old London Taverns: Historical, Descriptive and Reminiscent* (London: Downey, 1899).

Chambre, Major Alan, *Recollections of West-End Life; with Sketches of Society in Paris, India etc. etc.* (London: Hurst and Blackett, 1858).

Churchill, Winston, *My Early Life: A Roving Commission* (London: Fontana, 1972 [1930]).

Croxton, Arthur, *Crowded Nights—And Days: An Unconventional Pageant* (London: Sampson Low, 1934).

Desmond, Shaw, *London Nights of Long Ago* (London: Duckworth, 1927).

The Marquis de Vermont and Sir Charles Darnley, *London and Paris, or, Comparative Sketches* (London: Longman, Hurt, Rees, Orme, Brown, and Green, 1823).

Dostoevsky, Fyodor, *Winter Notes on Summer Impressions* (London: OneWorld Classics, 2008 [1863]) .

Escoffier, Auguste, *Memories of my Life* (New York: Van Nostrand Reinhold, 1997).

Evelyn, John, *The Diary of John Evelyn* (ed. E.S. de Beer) (Oxford: Clarendon Press, 1955).

Glover, James M., *Jimmy Glover, His Book* (London: Methuen, 1911).

Graham, Stephen, *London Nights: A Series of Studies and Sketches of London at Night* (London: Hurst and Blackett, 1925?).

Graham, Stephen, *Twice Round the London Clock and More London Nights* (London: Ernest Benn, 1933).

Hanley, Peter, *A Jubilee of Playgoing* (London: Tinkler, 1887).

Hardy, Thomas, *Memoir of Thomas Hardy* (London: James Ridgway, 1832).

Hawtrey, Charles, *The Truth at Last* (London: Butterworth, 1924).

Hayward, Arthur L., *The Days of Dickens: A Glance at Some Aspects of Early Victorian Life in London* (London: Routledge, 1926).

Hibbert, Henry George, *Fifty Years of a Londoner's Life* (London: Grant Richards, 1916).

Hollingshead, John, *Ragged London in 1861* (London: Everyman, 1986 [1861]).

Hollingshead, John, *My Lifetime* (London: Sampson Low, Marston, and Co., 1895) 2 vols.

Hollingshead, John, *Gaiety Chronicles* (London: Constable, 1898).

Hollingshead, John, *'Good Old Gaiety': An Historiette and Remembrance* (London: Gaiety Theatre Company, 1903).

Hudson, Derek (ed.), *Munby: Man of Two Worlds* (London: Abacus, 1974).

Hughes, Molly, *A London Child of the 1870s* (London: Persephone, 2005 [1934]).

Hughes, Molly, *A London Girl of the 1880s* (Oxford: Oxford University Press, 1978 [1946]).

Humphreys, Arthur L., *Piccadilly Bookmen: Memorials of the House of Hatchard* (London: Hatchards, 1893).

Hytner, Nicholas, *Balancing Acts: Behind the Scenes at the National Theatre* (London: Vintage, 2018).

Jerden, William, *The Autobiography of William Jerden* (London: Arthur Hall, Virtue and Co., 1852).

Johnson, Catharine B. (ed.), *William Bodham Donne and his Friends* (London: Methuen, 1905).

Jupp, James, *The Gaiety Stage Door: Thirty Years' Reminiscences of the Theatre* (London: Jonathan Cape, 1923).

Kirwan, Daniel, *Palace and Hovel; Or, Phases of London Life* (London: Aberlard-Schuman, 1963 [1870]).

Krout, Mary H., *A Looker-On in London* (London: B.F. Stevens and Brown, 1899).

Lanchester, Elsa, *Elsa Lanchester Herself* (New York: St Martin's Press, 1983).

Leverton, W.H. (with J.B. Booth), *Through the Box-office Window: Memories of Fifty Years at the Haymarket Theatre* (London: T. Werner Laurie, 1932).

Lumley, Benjamin, *Reminiscences of the Opera* (London: Hurst and Blackett, 1864).

Machray, Robert, *The Night Side of London* (London: John McQueen, 1902).

Masson, David, *Memories of London in the 'Forties* (Edinburgh: Blackwood, 1908).

Mathews, Mrs Anne, *Memoirs of Charles Mathews*, Comedian (London: Richard Bentley, 1839) 4 vols.

Moritz, Charles P.,*Travels, Chiefly on Foot, Through Several Parts of England, in 1782* (London: G.G. and J. Robinson, 1795).

Morley, Henry, *The Journal of a London Playgoer* (Leicester: Leicester University Press, 1974 [1886]).

Morton, W.H. and H. Chance Newton, *Sixty Years' Stage Service: Being a Record of the Life of Charles Morton, the Father of the Halls* (London: Gale and Polden, 1905).

Nevill, Ralph, *Fancies, Fashions and Fads* (London: Methuen, 1913).

Nevill, Ralph, *Mayfair and Montmartre* (London: Methuen, 1921).

Nevill, Ralph, *Night Life: London and Paris—Past and Present* (London: Cassell and Co., 1926).

Nevill, Ralph, *The Gay Victorians* (London: Nash and Grayson, 1930).

Newton, H. Chance, *Idols of the 'Halls': Being My Music Hall Memories* (London: Heath Cranston, 1928).

Nicholson, Renton, *Rogue's Progress: The Autobiography of 'Lord Chief Baron' Nicholson* (ed. John L. Bradley), (London: Longmans, 1965).

Nicholson, Shirley (ed.), *A Victorian Household: Based on the Diaries of Marion Sambourne* (London: Barrie and Jenkins, 1988).

Nowrojee, Jehangeer and Hirjeebhoy Merwanjee, *Journal of a Residence of Two Years and a half in Great Britain* (London: W.H. Allen, 1841).

Peel, Mrs Constance S., *Life's Enchanted Cup: An Autobiography* (London: John Lane, The Bodley Head, 1933).

Pepys, Samuel, *The Diary of Samuel Pepys* (ed. Robert Latham and William Matthews) (London: Bell and Hyman, 1970–83) 11 vols.

Robinson Planché, James, *Recollections and Reflections: A Professional Autobiography* (London: Sampson Low, 1901 [1872]).

Richardson, Mary R., *Laugh A Defiance* (London: George Weidenfeld and Nicolson, 1953).

Ritchie, J. Ewing, *The Night Side of London* (London: Tinsley Brothers, 1869 [1857]).

Ritchie, J. Ewing, *Days and Nights in London: Or, Studies in Black and Gray* (London: Tinsley Brothers, 1880).

la Roche, Sophie v., *Sophie in London, 1786: Being the Diary of Sophie v. la Roche* (ed. Clare Williams) (London: Jonathan Cape, 1933).

Rook, Clarence, *London Side-Lights* (London: Edward Arnold, 1908).

Sala, George Augustus, *Twice around the Clock; Or, the Hours of the Day and Night in London* (London: Leicester University Press, 1971 [1858]).

Sala, George Augustus, *Gaslight and Daylight, With Some London Scenes They Shine Upon* (London: Chapman and Hall, 1859).

Scott, Clement, *The Wheel of Life: A Few Memories and Recollections* (London: Lawrence Greening, 1897).

Scott, Clement, *The Drama of Yesterday and Today* (London: 1899) 2 vols.

Scott, Clement, *How They Dined Us in 1860 and How They Dine Us Now* (London: Trocadero, c.1900).

Scott, Margaret (Mrs Clement Scott), *Old Days in Bohemian London: Recollections of Clement Scott* (London: Hutchinson, 1919).

'One of the Old Brigade' [Donald Shaw], *London in the Sixties* (London: Everett, 1908).

Senelick, Laurence (ed.), *Tavern Singing in Early Victorian London: The Diaries of Charles Rice for 1840 and 1850* (London: Society for Theatre Research, 1997).

Sherwell, Arthur, *Life in West London: A Study and a Contrast* (London: Methuen, 1901 [third edition]).

Sims, George R., *My Life: Sixty Years' Recollections of Bohemian London* (London: Eveleigh Nash, 1917).

Slater, Michael (ed.), *The Dent Uniform Edition of Dickens' Journalism*, Vol. 1 (Columbus, OH: Ohio State University Press, 1994).

Smith [Lieut-Col.] Sir Henry, *From Constable to Commissioner: The Story of Sixty Years, Most of Them Misspent* (London: Chatto and Windus, 1910).

Soldene, Emily, *My Theatrical and Musical Recollections* (London: Downey, 1897).

Spencer, Walter T., *Forty Years in My Bookshop* (London: Constable, 1923).

Stoker, Bram, *Personal Reminiscences of Henry Irving* (London: William Heinemann, 1907 [1906]).

Terris, Ellaline, *Just a Little Bit of String* (London: Hutchinson, 1955).

Thale, Mary (ed.), *The Autobiography of Francis Place* (Cambridge: Cambridge University Press, 1972).

Thompson, Tierl (ed.), *Dear Girl: The Diaries and Letters of Two Working Women* (London: The Women's Press, 1987).

Trevelyan, George Otto (ed.), *The Life and Letters of Lord Macaulay* (London: Longman, 1908).

Vallès, Jules, *La rue à Londres* (Paris: G. Charpentier, 1884).

Ward, (Mrs) E.M., *Memories of Ninety Years* (London: Hutchinson, 1924).

Williams, Alfred H., *No Name on the Door: A Memoir of Gordon Selfridge*, (London: W.H. Allen, 1956).

Willis, Frederick, *101 Jubilee Road: A Book of London Yesterdays* (London: Phoenix House, 1948).

Willis, Frederick, *A Book of London Yesterdays* (London: Phoenix House, 1960).

Yates, Edmund, *Recollections and Experiences* (London: Richard Bentley, 1884) 2 vols.

Newspapers and Periodicals

Art Journal
Bell's Weekly Messenger
Black and White
The Builder

The Building News

The Caterer and Hotel Proprietor's Gazette (later *The Caterer and Hotel-Keeper's Gazette*)

The Courier

The Daily Chronicle

The Daily Chronicle and Clerkenwell News

The Daily Graphic

The Daily News

The Echo

The Entr'Acte

The Era

The Era Almanack

The Evening Mail

The Evening News

The Gentleman's Magazine

The Girl of the Period Miscellany

The Hampshire Advertiser

Hotel

The Illustrated London News

Illustrated Sporting and Dramatic News/Illustrated Sport and Theatrical News

Jackson's Oxford Journal

John Bull

The Lady

Licensed Victuallers' Mirror

London

London Evening Post

Lloyd's Illustrated London Newspaper

Lloyd's Weekly Newspaper

The Mirror of Literature, Amusement and Instruction

Modern Retailing

The Morning Chronicle

The Morning Herald and Daily Advertiser

The Morning Post

Music for All

The Musical World

The Musician and Music-Hall Times

Once A Week

The Pall Mall Gazette

The Penny Illustrated Paper and Illustrated Times

The Poor Man's Guardian

Punch, Or the London Charivari

The Queen: The Lady's Newspaper

The Repository of Arts, Literature, Commerce, Manufactures, Fashions and Politics

The Restaurant

Royal Cornwall Gazette, Falmouth Packet & Plymouth Journal

St Cecilia

Sam Sly, Or, The Town

The Savoy

The Sketch

The Sporting Times
The Stage
The Standard
The Star
The Theatrical Journal
The Theatrical Programme and Entr'Acte
The Times
The Vigilance Record
The Warehousemen and Drapers' Trade Journal; later The Warehouseman and Draper (later
    The Draper)
The Waiter's Record
The Westminster Budget

Novels, Plays, Songs, etc.

Byron, H.J., *Cyril's Success* (London: Samuel French, 1870).
Dam, H.J.W,.The Shop Girl (BL ADD MS 53562B).
Dickens, Charles, *The Pickwick Papers* (Oxford: Clarendon Press, 1986 [1836/7]).
Du Maurier, George, *Trilby* (London: Osgood, McIlvaine, 1895).
Du Maurier, George, *The Martian: A Novel* (London: Harper and Brothers, 1898).
Egan, Pierce, *Life in London* (London: Sherwood, 1821).
Forster, E.M., *Howards End* (London: Edward Arnold, 1956 [1910]).
Franceschina, John (ed.), *Sisters of Gore: Seven Gothic Melodramas by British Women,
    1790–1843* (New York: Garland, 1997).
Hunt, G.W., *True Blue for Ever!* (London: Hopwood and Crew, 1878?).
Hunt, G.W., *Waiting for the Signal* (London: Hopwood and Crew, 1878).
Hunt, G.W., *I Like a Little Toddle down Regent Street* (London: Hopwood and
    Crew, 1882).
McGlennon, Felix and T. Richards, *The Flower Our Hero Loved* (London: Hopwood and
    Crew, 1887).
Moncrieff, William T.,*Tom and Jerry: Or, Life in London* (London: W.T. Moncrieff, 1826).
Monros-Gaspar, Laura (ed.), *Victorian Classical Burlesques: A Critical Anthology* (London:
    Bloomsbury, 2015).
Orczy, Baroness, *The Old Man in the Corner* (London: Greening, 1909).
Parkin, Andrew (ed.), *Selected Plays by Dion Boucicault* (Gerrards Cross: Colin
    Smythe, 1987).
Reynolds, George W.M., *Robert Macaire in England* (London: Thomas Tegg, 1840).
Ripley, John (ed.), *Gilbert Parker and Herbert Beerbohm Tree stage 'The Seats of The Mighty'*
    (Toronto, Canada: Simon and Pierre, 1986).
Thackeray, William Makepeace, *The Newcomes* (London: Oxford University Press, 1908
    [1854]).
White, Percy, *The West End* (London: R.A. Everett, 1903).

Parliamentary Papers

Report from the Select Committee on Dramatic Literature (1832).
Report from the Select Committee on Theatrical Licenses and Regulations (1866).
Report from the Select Committee on the Shop Hours Regulation Bill (1886).
Report and Special Report from the Select Committee on the Shop Hours Bill (1892).
Report from the Select Committee on Theatres and Places of Entertainment (1892).

Secondary Sources

Books

Abelson, Elaine S., *When Ladies go a-thieving: Middle-Class Shoplifters in the Victorian Department Store* (New York: Oxford University Press, 1989).

Adburgham, Alison, *Liberty's: A Biography of a Shop* (London: George Allen and Unwin, 1975).

Adburgham, Alison, *Shops and Shopping, 1800–1914: Where, and in what Manner the Well-dressed Englishwoman Bought her Clothes* (London: Barrie and Jenkins, 1989 [1964]).

Adorno, Theodor and Max Horkheimer, *Dialectic of Enlightenment* (London: Verso, 1979 [1944]).

Altick, Richard D., *The Shows of London* (Cambridge, MA: Belknap Press/Harvard University Press, 1978).

Andersson, Peter K., *Streetlife in Late Victorian London: The Constable and the Crowd* (Basingstoke: Palgrave Macmillan, 2013).

Appadurai, Arjun (ed.), *The Social Life of Things: Commodities in Cultural Perspective* (Cambridge: Cambridge University Press, 1986).

Armstrong, Isobel, *Victorian Glassworlds: Glass Culture and the Imagination, 1830–1880* (Oxford: Oxford University Press, 2008).

Ashmore, Sonia, 'Liberty and Lifestyle: Shopping for Art and Luxury in Nineteenth-Century London', in David Hussey and Margaret Ponsonby (eds), *Buying for the Home: Shopping for the Domestic from the Seventeenth Century to the Present* (Aldershot: Ashgate, 2008), pp. 73–90.

Ashton, Rosemary, *142 Strand: A Radical Address in Victorian London* (London: Chatto and Windus, 2006).

Ashton, Rosemary, *Victorian Bloomsbury* (London: Yale University Press, 2012).

Askari, Kaveh, *Making Movies into Art: Picture Craft from the Magic Lantern to Early Hollywood* (London: British Film Institute, 2014).

Assael, Brenda, *The Circus and Victorian Society* (Charlottesville, VA: University of Virginia Press, 2005).

Assael, Brenda, *The London Restaurant, 1840–1914* (Oxford: Oxford University Press, 2018).

Auerbach, Nina, *Private Theatricals: The Lives of the Victorians* (Cambridge, MA: Harvard University Press, 1990).

Baer, Marc, *Theatre and Disorder in late Georgian London* (Oxford: Clarendon Press, 1992).

Baer, Marc, *The Rise and Fall of Radical Westminster, 1780–1890* (Basingstoke: Palgrave Macmillan, 2012).

Bailey, Peter, *Leisure and Class in Victorian England: Rational Recreation and the Contest for Control* (London: Routledge and Kegan Paul, 1978).

Bailey, Peter (ed.), *Music Hall: The Business of Pleasure* (Milton Keynes: Open University Press, 1986).

Bailey, Peter, '"Naughty but Nice": Musical Comedy and the Rhetoric of the Girl, 1892–1914', in Michael Booth and Joel Kaplan (eds), *The Edwardian Theatre: Essays on Performance and the Stage* (Cambridge: Cambridge University Press, 1996), pp. 36–60.

Bailey, Peter (ed.), *Popular Culture and Performance in the Victorian City* (Cambridge: Cambridge University Press, 1998).

Bailey, Peter, 'Entertainmentality: Liberalizing Modern Pleasure in the Victorian Leisure Industry', in Simon Gunn and James Vernon (eds), *The Peculiarities of Liberal Modernity in Imperial Britain* (Berkeley, CA: University of California Press, 2011), pp. 119–33.

Baker, Michael, *The Rise of the Victorian Actor* (London: Croom Helm, 1978).

Bakker, Gerben, *Entertainment Industrialised: The Emergence of the International Film Industry* (Cambridge: Cambridge University Press, 2008).

Baldwin, Peter C., *Domesticating the Street: The Reform of Public Space in Hartford, 1850–1930* (Columbus, OH: Ohio State University Press, 1999).

Baldwin, Peter C., *In the Watches of the Night: Life in the Nocturnal City, 1820–1930* (Chicago: University of Chicago Press, 2012).

Barber, Peter, *London: A History in Maps* (London: London Topographical Society/British Library, 2012).

Barker, Felix, *The House that Stoll Built: The Story of the Coliseum Theatre* (London: Frederick Muller, 1957).

Barker, Felix and Peter Jackson, *The Pleasures of London* (London: London Topographical Society, 2008).

Barr, Luke, *Ritz and Escoffier: The Hotelier, the Chef, and the Rise of the Leisure Class* (New York: Clarkson Potter, 2018).

Beaumont, Matthew, *Nightwalking: A Nocturnal History of London* (London: Verso, 2015).

Benjamin, Walter, *The Arcades Project* (trans. Howard Eiland and Kevin McLaughlin) (Cambridge, MA: Harvard University Press, 1999).

Bennett, Tony, *The Birth of the Museum* (London: Routledge, 1995).

Benson, John, *The Rise of Consumer Society in Britain, 1880–1980* (London: Longman, 1994).

Berg, Maxine, *Luxury and Pleasure in Eighteenth-Century Britain* (Oxford: Oxford University Press, 2005).

Berg, Maxine and Helen Clifford (eds), *Consumers and Luxury: Consumer Culture in Europe, 1650–1850* (Manchester: Manchester University Press, 1999).

Berger, Molly, *Hotel Dreams: Luxury, Technology, and Urban Ambition in America, 1829–1929* (Baltimore, MA: Johns Hopkins University Press, 2011).

Berman, Marshall, *All That is Solid Melts into Air: The Experience of Modernity* (London: Verso, 1982).

Bird, Peter, *The First Food Empire: A History of J. Lyons and Co.* (London: Phillimore, 2000).

Black, Barbara, *A Room of His Own: A Literary-Cultural Study of Victorian Clubland* (Athens, OH: Ohio University Press, 2013).

Blake, Peter, *George Augustus Sala and the Nineteenth-Century Periodical Press: The Personal Style of a Public Writer* (Farnham: Ashgate 2015).

Bland, Lucy, *Banishing the Beast: English Feminism and Sexual Morality, 1885–1914* (London: Penguin, 1995).

Bland, Lucy, *Modern Women on Trial: Sexual Transgression in the Age of the Flapper* (Manchester: Manchester University Press, 2013).

Bloom, Ursula, *Curtain Call for the Guv'nor: A Biography of George Edwardes* (London: Hutchinson, 1954).

Blyth, Henry, *Hell or Hazard; Or, William Crockford versus the Gentlemen of England* (London: Weidenfeld and Nicolson, 1969).

Boormann, Francis (with Jonathan Comber and Mark Latham), *St. Clement Danes, 1660–1900* (London: Victoria County History, 2018).

Booth, Michael R., *Victorian Spectacular Theatre, 1850–1910* (London: Routledge and Kegan Paul, 1981).

Booth, Michael R., *Theatre in the Victorian Age* (Cambridge: Cambridge University Press, 1991).

Booth, Michael R., 'Soldiers of the Queen: Drury Lane Imperialism', in Michael Hays and Anastasia Nikolopoulou (eds), *Melodrama: The Cultural Emergence of a Genre* (Basingstoke: Macmillan, 1996), pp. 3–20.

Booth, Michael R. and Joel H. Kaplan (eds), *The Edwardian Theatre: Essays on Performance and the Stage* (Cambridge: Cambridge University Press, 1996).

Borsay, Peter, *The English Urban Renaissance: Culture and Society in the Provincial Town, 1660–1770* (Oxford: Clarendon Press, 1989).

Borsay, Peter and Jan Hein Furnée (eds), *Leisure Cultures in Urban Europe, c. 1700–1870* (Manchester: Manchester University Press, 2016).

Boulton, Jeremy, 'The Poor among the Rich: Paupers and the Parish in the West End, 1600–1724', in Paul Griffiths and Mark S.R. Jenner (eds), *Londonopolis: Essays in the Cultural and Social History of Early Modern London* (Manchester: Manchester University Press, 2000), pp. 197–225.

Bourdieu, Pierre, *Distinction: A Social Critique of the Judgement of Taste* (London: Routledge and Kegan Paul, 2010 [1984]).

Brandon-Thomas, Jevan, *Charley's Aunt's Father: A Life of Brandon Thomas* (London: Douglas Saunders, 1955).

Bratton, Jacky S. (ed.), *Music Hall: Performance and Style* (Milton Keynes: Open University Press, 1986).

Bratton, Jacky S., Richard Allen Cave, Brendan Gregory, Heidi J. Holder, and Michael Pickering, *Acts of Supremacy: The British Empire and the Stage, 1790–1930* (Manchester: Manchester University Press, 1991).

Bratton, Jacky, *New Readings in Theatre History* (Cambridge: Cambridge University Press, 2003).

Bratton, Jacky, *The Making of the West End Stage: Marriage, Management and the Mapping of Gender in London, 1830–1870* (Cambridge: Cambridge University Press, 2011).

Breward, Christopher, *The Hidden Consumer: Masculinities, Fashion and City Life, 1860–1914* (Manchester: Manchester University Press, 1999).

Breward, Christopher, *Fashioning London: Clothing and the Modern Metropolis* (Oxford: Berg, 2004).

Breward, Christopher, Edwina Ehrman, and Caroline Evans, *The London Look: Fashion from Street to Catwalk* (London: Yale University Press, 2004).

Breward, Christopher and David Gilbert (eds), *Fashion's World Cities* (Oxford: Berg, 2006).

Brewer, John, *The Pleasures of the Imagination: English Culture in the Eighteenth Century* (London: Harper Collins, 2000).

Brewster, Ben and Lea Jacobs, *Theatre to Cinema: Stage Pictorialism and the Early Feature Film* (Oxford: Oxford University Press, 1998).

Briggs, Asa, *Victorian Cities* (London: Pelican, 1968 [1963]).

Briggs, Asa, *Victorian Things* (Stroud: Sutton, 2003 [1998]).

Briggs, Asa and John Callow, *Marx in London* (London: Lawrence and Wishart, 2008).

Briggs, Asa and Janet Lovegrove, *Victorian Music: A Social and Cultural History* (Brighton: Edward Everett Root, 2018).

Bristow, Edward J., *Vice and Vigilance: Purity Movements in Britain since 1700* (Dublin: Gill and Macmillan, 1977).

Brockett, Oscar G., Margaret Mitchell, and Linda Harberger, *Making the Scene: A History of Stage Design and Technology in Europe and the United States* (San Antonio, TX: University of Texas Press, 2010).

Bronner, Simon J. (ed.), *Consuming Visions: Accumulation and the Display of Goods* (New York: W.W. Norton, 1989).

Brooker, Jeremy, *The Temple of Minerva: Magic and the Magic Lantern at the Royal Polytechnic Institution, London, 1837–1901* (London: Magic Lantern Society, 2013).

Buckland, Theresa Jill, *Society Dancing: Fashionable Bodies in England, 1870–1920* (Basingstoke: Palgrave Macmillan, 2011).

Buse, Peter, Ken Hirschkop, Scott McCracken, Bertrand Taithe, *Benjamin's 'Arcades': An Unguided Tour* (Manchester: Manchester University Press, 2005).

Cannadine, David, *The Decline and Fall of the British Aristocracy* (London: Picador, 1992 [1990]).

Carlson, Marvin, *Places of Performance: The Semiotics of Theatre Architecture* (Ithaca, NY: Cornell University Press, 1989).

Carter, Alexandra, *Dance and Dancers in the Victorian and Edwardian Music Hall Ballet* (Aldershot: Ashgate, 2005).

Castle, Dennis, *Sensation Smith of Drury Lane* (London: Charles Skilton, 1984).

Certeau, Michel de, *The Practice of Everyday Life* (trans. Steven Rendall) (Berkeley, CA: University of California Press, 1988).

Chancellor, E. Beresford, *The Annals of the Strand: Topographical and Historical* (London: Chapman and Hall, 1912).

Chancellor, E. Beresford, *Wanderings in Piccadilly, Mayfair and Pall Mall* (London: Alton Rivers, 1908).

Charle, Christophe, *Théâtres en Capitales: Naissance de la societé du spectacle à Paris, Berlin, Londres et Vienne* (Paris: Albin Michel, 2008).

Charney, Leo and Vanessa R. Schwarz (eds), *Cinema and the Invention of Modern Life* (Berkeley, CA: University of California Press, 1995).

Chase, Malcolm, *Chartism: A New History* (Manchester: Manchester University Press, 2007).

Cherry, Deborah, *Beyond the Frame: Feminism and Visual Culture, Britain 1850–1900* (London: Routledge, 2000).

Clark, J.C.D., *English Society, 1688–1832: Ideology, Social Structure and Political Practice During the Ancient Regime* (Cambridge: Cambridge University Press, 1985).

Clark, Jessica P., 'Grooming Men: The Material World of the Nineteenth-Century Barbershop', in Hannah Greig, Jane Hamlett, and Leonie Hannan (eds), *Gender and Material Culture in Britain since 1600* (London: Palgrave Macmillan, 2016), pp. 104–19.

Clifford, Helen, *Silver in London: The Parker and Wakelin Partnership, 1760–1776* (New Haven and London: Yale University Press, 2004).

Cohen, Deborah, *Household Gods: The British and their Possessions* (New Haven and London: Yale University Press, 2006).

Coke, David and Alan Borg, *Vauxhall Gardens: A History* (New Haven and London: Yale University Press, 2011).

Colley, Linda, *Britons: Forging the Nation, 1707–1837* (London: Yale University Press, 1992).

Comment, Bernard, *The Panorama* (London: Reaktion, 1999).

Conlin, Jonathan, *The Nation's Mantlepiece: A History of the National Gallery* (London: Pallas Athene, 2006).

Conlin, Jonathan (ed.), *The Pleasure Garden, from Vauxhall to Coney Island* (Philadelphia: University of Pennsylvania Press, 2013).

Conlin, Jonathan, *Tales of Two Cities: Paris, London and the Birth of the Modern City* (London: Atlantic, 2013).

Cook, James W., *The Arts of Deception: Playing with Fraud in the Age of Barnum* (Cambridge, MA: Harvard University Press, 2001).

Cook, Matt, *London and the Culture of Homosexuality, 1885–1914* (Cambridge: Cambridge University Press, 2003).

Copeland, Edward, 'Jane Austen and the Consumer Revolution', in J. David Grey (ed.), *The Jane Austen Handbook* (London: Athlone Press, 1986), pp. 77–92.

Coveney, Michael and Peter Dazeley, *London Theatres* (London: Frances Lincoln, 2017).

Cowan, Brian, *The Social Life of Coffee: The Emergence of the British Coffeehouse* (New Haven, CT: Yale University Press, 2005).

Cowgill, Rachel, ' "Wise Men from the East": Mozart's Operas and their Advocates in Early Nineteenth Century London', in Christina Bashford and Leanne Langley (eds), *Music and British Culture, 1785–1914: Essays in Honour of Cyril Ehrlich* (Oxford: Oxford University Press, 2000), pp. 39–64.

Cox, Pamela and Annabel Hobley, *Shopgirls: True Stories of Friendship, Triumph and Hardship from behind the Counter* (London: Cornerstone, 2014).

Crais, Clifton and Pamela Scully, *Sara Baartman and the Hottentot Venus: A Ghost Story and a Biography* (Princeton, NJ: Princeton University Press, 2009).

Crossick, Geoffrey and Serge Jaumain (eds), *Cathedrals of Consumption: The European Department Store, 1850–1939* (Aldershot: Ashgate, 1999).

Curtis, Anthony (ed.), *The Rise and Fall of the Matinee Idol: Past Deities of Stage and Screen, their Roles, their Magic, and their Worshippers* (London: New English Library, 1976).

Dart, Gregory, *Metropolitan Art and Literature, 1810–1840: Cockney Adventures* (Cambridge: Cambridge University Press, 2012).

Davidoff, Leonore, *The Best Circles: Society, Etiquette and the Season* (London: Croom Helm, 1973).

Davidoff, Leonore, 'Class and Gender in Victorian England: The Case of Hannah Cullwick and A.J. Munby', in Davidoff, *Worlds Between: Historical Perspectives on Gender & Class* (London: Polity, 1995), pp. 103–50.

Davies, Rachel Bryant, *Troy, Carthage and the Victorians: The Drama of Classical Ruins in the Nineteenth-Century Imagination* (Cambridge: Cambridge University Press, 2018).

Davis, Jim and Victor Emeljanow, *Reflecting the Audience: London Theatregoing, 1840–1880* (Hatfield: University of Hertfordshire Press, 2001).

Davis, Tracy C., *Actresses as Working Women: Their Social Identity in Victorian Culture* (London: Routledge, 1991).

Davis, Tracy C., *The Economics of the British Stage, 1800–1914* (Cambridge: Cambridge University Press, 2000).

Davis, Tracy C. (ed.), *The Cambridge Companion to Performance Studies* (Cambridge: Cambridge University Press, 2008).

Davis, Tracy C. (ed.), *The Broadview Anthology of Nineteenth-Century British Performance* (Toronto: Broadview, 2012).

Davis, Tracy C. and Peter Holland (eds), *The Performing Century: Nineteenth-Century Theatre's History* (Basingstoke: Palgrave Macmillan, 2007).

Debord, Guy, *The Society of the Spectacle* (New York: Zone Books, 1995 [1967]) translated by Donald Nicholson-Smith.

Deghy, Guy, *Paradise in the Strand: The Story of Romano's* (London: Richards Press, 1958).

Deghy, Guy and Keith Waterhouse, *Café Royal: Ninety Years of Bohemia* (London: Hutchinson, 1955).

Denby, Elaine, *Grand Hotels: Reality and Illusion* (London: Reaktion, 1998).

Denisoff, Dennis, 'Small Change: The Consumerist Designs of the Nineteenth-Century Child', in Dennis Denisoff (ed.), *The Nineteenth-Century Child and Consumer Culture* (Aldershot: Ashgate, 2008), pp. 1–25.

Desebrock, Jean, *The Book of Bond Street Old and New* (London: Tallis, 1978).

DiBattista, Maria, *Fast-Talking Dames* (London: Yale University Press, 2001).

Donohue, Joseph W. (ed.), *The Theatrical Manager in England and America: Player of a Perilous Game* (Princeton, NJ: Princeton University Press, 1971).

Donohue, Joseph (ed.), *The Cambridge History of British Theatre*, vol. 2 1660–1895 (Cambridge: Cambridge University Press, 2004).

Donohue, Joseph, *Fantasies of Empire: The Empire Theatre of Varieties and the Licensing Controversy of 1894* (Iowa City, IA: University of Iowa Press, 2005).

D'Ormesson, Jean, *Grand Hotel: The Golden Age of Palace Hotels* (London: J.M. Dent, 1984).

Douglas, Mary and Baron Isherwood, *The World of Goods: Towards an Anthropology of Consumption* (London: Routledge, 1996 [1979]).

Driver, Felix and David Gilbert (eds), *Imperial Cities: Landscape, Display and Identity* (Manchester: Manchester University Press, 1999).

Durbach, Nadja, 'London, Capital of Exotic Exhibitions from 1830 to 1860', in Pascal Blanchard, Nicolas Bancel, Gilles Boëtsch, Eric Deroo, Sandrine Lemaire, and Charles Fosdick (eds), *Human Zoos: Science and Spectacle in the Age of Colonial Empires* (Liverpool: Liverpool University Press, 2008), pp. 81–8.

Durbach, Nadja, *Spectacle of Deformity: Freak Shows and Modern British Culture* (Berkeley, CA: University of California Press, 2010).

Dyer, Richard, *Light Entertainment* (London: BFI, 1973).

Dyer, Richard, *Only Entertainment* (London: Routledge, 2002 [1992]).

Dyhouse, Carol, *Glamour: Women, History, Feminism* (London: Zed Books, 2011).

Ehrlich, Cyril, *The Music Profession in Britain since the Eighteenth Century* (Oxford: Clarendon Press, 1985).

Ehrlich, Cyril, *The Piano: A History* (Oxford: Clarendon Press, 1990 [1986]).

Ehrman, Edwina et al. (eds), *London Eats Out: 500 Years of Capital Dining* (London: Museum of London, 1999).

Eisenberg, Christiane and Andreas Gestrich (eds), *Cultural Industries in Britain and Germany: Sport, Music and Entertainment from the Eighteenth to the Twentieth Century* (Augsburg: Wissner, 2012).

Elkin, Robert, *Queen's Hall, 1893–1941* (London: Rider, 1941).

Elkin, Robert, *The Old Concert Rooms of London* (London: Edward Arnold, 1955).

Ellis, Markman, *The Coffee House: A Cultural History* (London: Weidenfeld and Nicolson, 2004).

Ellmann, Richard, *Oscar Wilde* (New York: Knopf, 1988).

Eltis, Sos, *Acts of Desire: Women and Sex on Stage, 1800–1930* (Oxford: Oxford University Press, 2013).

Erenberg, Lewis A., *Steppin' Out: New York Nightlife and the Transformation of American Culture, 1890–1930* (Westport, CT: Greenwood Press, 1981).

Ewen, Shane, *What is Urban History?* (Cambridge: Polity, 2016).

Eyles, Allen and Keith Skone, *London's West End Cinemas* (Sutton: Keystone, 1991).

Farkas, Anna, *Women's Playwrighting and the Women's Movement, 1890–1918* (London: Routledge, 2019).

Faulk, Barry J., *Music Hall and Modernity: The Late Victorian Discovery of Popular Culture* (Athens, OH: Ohio University Press, 2004).

Fawkes, Richard, *Dion Boucicault: A Biography* (London: Quartet, 1979).

Finn, Margot C., *The Character of Credit: Personal Debt in English Culture, 1740–1914* (Cambridge: Cambridge University Press, 2003).

Flanders, Judith, *Consuming Passions: Leisure and Pleasure in Victorian Britain* (London: Harper Collins, 2006).

Fletcher, Pamela and Anne Helmreich (eds), *The Rise of the Modern Art Market in London, 1850–1939* (Manchester: Manchester University Press, 2011).

Flint, Kate, *The Transatlantic Indian, 1776–1930* (Princeton, NJ: Princeton University Press, 2009).

Forbes-Winslow, D., *Daly's: The Biography of a Theatre* (London: W.H. Allen, 1944).

Foulkes, Richard (ed.), *British Theatre in the 1890s: Essays on Drama and the Stage* (Cambridge: Cambridge University Press, 1992).

Fox, Celina, *Londoners* (London: Thames and Hudson, 1987).

Fox, Celina (ed.), *London-World City, 1800–1840* (London: Yale University Press, 1992).

Frewin, Leslie (ed.), *Parnassus near Piccadilly: An Anthology* (London: Leslie Frewin, 1965).

Garlick, Görel, *Charles John Phipps F.S.A.: Architect to the Victorian Theatre* (Cambridge: Entertainment Technology Press, 2016).

Gatrell, Vic, *City of Laughter: Sex and Satire in Eighteenth-Century London* (London: Atlantic, 2006).

Gatrell, Vic, *The First Bohemians: Life and Art in London's Golden Age* (London: Allen Lane, 2013).

Gay, Peter, *The Naked Heart: The Bourgeois Experience Victoria to Freud*, Vol. 4 (London: Fontana, 1998).

Geist, Johann Friedrich, *Arcades: The History of a Building Type* (Cambridge, MA: The MIT Press, 1983).

Gilbert, Pamela K,. *Cholera and Nation: Doctoring the Social Body in Victorian England* (New York: State University of New York, 2008).

Gilbert, Pamela, 'Sex and the Modern City: English Studies and the Spatial Turn', in Barney Warf and Santa Arias (eds), *The Spatial Turn: Interdisciplinary Perspectives* (London: Routledge, 2009), pp. 102–21.

Glasstone, Victor, *Victorian and Edwardian Theatres: An Architectural and Social Survey* (London: Thames and Hudson, 1975).

Glenn, Susan, *Female Spectacle: The Theatrical Roots of Modern Feminism* (Cambridge, MA: Harvard University Press, 2000).

Glinert, Ed, *West End Chronicles: 300 years of Glamour and Excess in the Heart of London* (London: Allen Lane, 2007).

Goodway, David, *London Chartism, 1838–1848* (Cambridge: Cambridge University Press, 1982).

Gould, Marty, *Nineteenth-Century Theatre and the Imperial Encounter* (London: Routledge, 2011).

Goulden, John, *Michael Costa: England's First Conductor: The Revolution in Musical Performance in England, 1830–1880* (Aldershot: Ashgate, 2015).

Greig, Hannah, *The Beau Monde: Fashionable Society in Georgian London* (Oxford: Oxford University Press, 2013).

Guest, Ivor, *The Romantic Ballet in England: Its Development, Fulfilment and Decline* (London Pitman, 1972 [1954]).

Guest, Ivor, *Ballet in Leicester Square: The Alhambra and the Empire, 1860–1915* (London: Dance Books, 1992).

Gundle, Stephen, *Glamour: A History* (Oxford: Oxford University Press, 2008).

Gundle, Stephen and Clino T. Castelli, *The Glamour System* (Basingstoke: Palgrave Macmillan, 2006).

Gunn, Simon, *The Public Culture of the Victorian Middle Class: Ritual and Authority in the English Industrial City, 1840–1914* (Manchester: Manchester University Press, 2008).

Gurney, Peter, *The Making of Consumer Culture in Modern Britain* (London: Bloomsbury, 2017).

Habermas, Jurgen, *The Structural Transformation of the Public Sphere: An Inquiry into a Category of Bourgeois Society* (Cambridge, MA: MIT Press, 1989).

Haddon, Archibald, *The Story of the Music Hall: From Cave of Harmony to Cabaret* (London: Fleetwood, 1935).

Hahn, H. Hazel, *Scenes of Parisian Modernity: Culture and Consumption in the Nineteenth Century* (Basingstoke: Palgrave Macmillan, 2009).

Hai, Catherine, *Fun Without Vulgarity: Victorian and Edwardian Popular Entertainment Posters* (London: Stationery Office, 1996).

Hall-Witt, Jennifer, *Fashionable Acts: Opera and Elite Culture in London, 1780–1880* (Durham, NH: University of New Hampshire Press, 2007).

Hamilton, James, *A Strange Business: Making Art and Money in Nineteenth-Century Britain* (London: Atlantic, 2014).

Hancock, Claire, *Paris et Londres au XIXe Siècle: Représentations dans les guides et récits de voyage* (Paris: CNRS, 2003).

Harding, Thomas, *Legacy: One Family, A Cup of Tea and the Company that Took on the World* (London: Heinemann, 2019).

Harvey, John, *Men in Black* (London: Reaktion, 1995).

Harvie, Jen, *Theatre and the City* (Basingstoke: Palgrave Macmillan, 2009).

Henderson, Mary C., *The City and the Theatre: New York Playhouses from Bowling Green to Times Square* (Clifton, NJ: James T. White, 1973).

Hessler, Martina and Clemens Zimmermann (eds), *Creative Urban Milieus: Historical Perspectives on Culture, Economy and the City* (Frankfurt: Campus Verlag, 2008).

Hewitt, Martin and Rachel Cowgill (eds), *Victorian Soundscapes Revisited* (Leeds: Leeds Trinity and All Saints, 2007).

Hindson, Catherine, *Female Performance Practice on the fin-de-siècle Popular Stages of London and Paris: Experiment and Advertisement* (Manchester; Manchester University Press, 2007).

Hindson, Catherine, *London's West End Actresses and the Origins of Celebrity Charity, 1880–1920* (Iowa City, IA: University of Iowa Press, 2016).

Hobsbawm, Eric and Terence Ranger (eds), *The Invention of Tradition* (Cambridge: Cambridge University Press, 1983).

Hobhouse, Hermione, *A History of Regent Street: A Mile of Style* (Chichester: Phillimore, 2008).

Hollingshead, John, *The Story of Leicester Square* (London: Simpkin, Marshall, Hamilton, Kent, and Co., 1892).

Holmes, Rachel, *The Hottentot Venus: The Life and Death of Saartjie Baartman: Born 1789—Buried 2002* (London: Bloomsbury, 2007).

Holroyd, Michael, *A Strange, Eventful History: The Dramatic Lives of Ellen Terry, Henry Irving and their Remarkable Families* (London: Chatto and Windus, 2008).

Homans, Jennifer, *Apollo's Angels: A History of Ballet* (London: Granta, 2010).

Horrall, Andrew, *Popular Culture in London, c.1890–1918: The Transformation of Entertainment* (Manchester: Manchester University Press, 2001).

Hosgood, Christopher H., '"Doing the Shops" at Christmas: Women, Men and the Department Store in England, c.1880–1914', in Geoffrey Crossick and Serge Jaumain (eds), *Cathedrals of Consumption: The European Department Store, 1850–1939* (Aldershot: Ashgate, 1999), pp. 97–115.

Houlbrook, Matt, *Queer London: Perils and Pleasures in the Sexual Metropolis, 1918–1957* (Chicago: University of Chicago Press, 2005).

Howarth, Stephen, *Henry Poole: Founders of Savile Row: The Making of a Legend* (Honiton: Bene Factum Publishing, 2003).

Huhtamo, Erkki, *Illusions in Motion: Media Archaeology of the Moving Panorama and Related Spectacles* (Cambridge, MA: MIT Press, 2013).

Humphreys, A.L., *Crockford's; Or, The Goddess of Chance in St. James's Street, 1828–1844* (London: Hutchinson, 1953).

Hunt, Tristram, *Building Jerusalem: The Rise and Fall of the Victorian City* (London: Phoenix, 2005 [2004].

Hyde, Ralph, *Panoramania! The Art and Entertainment of the 'All-Embracing' View* (London: Trefoil, 1988).

Hyman, Alan, *The Gaiety Years* (London: Cassell, 1975).

Hyman, Alan, *Sullivan and his Satellites: A Survey of English Operettas, 1860–1914* (London: Chappell, 1978).

Ibell, Paul, *Theatreland: A Journey Through the Heart of London's Theatre* (London: Continuum, 2009).

Jackson, Lee, *Palaces of Pleasure: Entertaining the Victorians* (London: Yale University Press, 2019).

Jackson, Stanley, *The Savoy: A Century of Taste* (London: Frederick Muller, 1989 [1964]).

Jakle, John A., *City Lights: Illuminating the American Night* (Baltimore, MA: Johns Hopkins University Press, 2001).

Jefferys, James B., *Retail Trading in Britain, 1850–1950* (Cambridge: Cambridge University Press, 1954).

Jeffries, Nigel with Lynn Blackmore and David Sorapure, *Crosse and Blackwell, 1830–1921: A British Food Manufacturer in London's West End* (London: Museum of London/ Crossrail, 2016).

Jenness, George A., *Maskelyne and Cooke: Egyptian Hall, London, 1873–1904* (London: George A. Jenness, 1967).

Jensen, Oscar Cox, David Kennerley, and Ian Newman (eds), *Charles Dibdin and Late Georgian Culture* (Oxford: Oxford University Press, 2018).

Johnson, James H., *Listening in Paris: A Cultural History* (Berkeley, CA: University of California Press, 1995).

Jones, Gareth Stedman, *Languages of Class: Studies in English Working-Class History* (Cambridge: Cambridge University Press, 1983).

Joyce, Patrick, *The Rule of Freedom: Liberalism and the Modern City* (London: Verso, 2003).

Kasson, John F., *Amusing the Million: Coney Island at the Turn of the Century* (New York: Hill and Wang, 1978).

Keire, Mara L,. *For Business & Pleasure: Red-Light Districts and the Regulation of Vice in the United States, 1890–1933* (Baltimore, MD: The Johns Hopkins University Press, 2010).

Kember, Joe, *Marketing Modernity: Victorian Popular Shows and Early Cinema* (Exeter: University of Exeter Press, 2009).

Kember, Joe, John Plunkett, and Jill A. Sullivan (eds), *Popular Exhibitions, Science and Showmanship, 1840–1910* (London: Pickering and Chatto, 2012).

Kern, Stephen, *The Culture of Time and Space, 1880–1918* (London: Weidenfeld and Nicolson, 1983).

Kift, Dagmar, *The Victorian Music Hall: Culture, Class and Conflict* (Cambridge: Cambridge University Press, 1996).

Kingsford, Charles Lethbridge, *The Early History of Piccadilly, Leicester Square, Soho & Their Neighbourhood* (Cambridge: Cambridge University Press, 1925).

Kinross, Felicity, *Coffee and Ices: The Story of Carlo Gatti in London* (London: privately printed: 1991).

Koslofsky, Craig, *Evening's Empire: A History of the Night in Early Modern Europe* (Cambridge: Cambridge University Press, 2011).

Kuchta, David, 'The Making of the Self-Made Man: Class, Clothing, and English Masculinity, 1688–1832', in Victoria de Grazia and Ellen Furlough (eds), *The Sex of Things: Gender and Consumption in Historical Perspective* (Berkeley: University of California Press, 1996), pp. 54–78.

Laite, Julia, *Common Prostitutes and Ordinary Citizens: Commercial Sex in London, 1885–1960* (Basingstoke: Palgrave Macmillan, 2012).

Lancaster, Bill, *The Department Store: A Social History* (Lancaster: Lancaster University Press, 1995).

Laver, James, *Hatchards of Piccadilly, 1797–1947* (London: Hatchards, 1947).

Leach, Robert, *An Illustrated History of British Theatre and Performance* (London: Routledge, 2019).

Levine, Lawrence, *Highbrow/Lowbrow: The Emergence of Cultural Hierarchy in America* (Cambridge, MA: Harvard University Press, 1988).

Lindfors, Bernth (ed.), *Africans on Stage: Studies in Ethnological Show Business* (Bloomington, IN: Indiana University Press, 1999).

Lindfors, Bernth, *Ira Aldridge: The Early Years, 1807–1833* (Rochester, NY: University of Rochester Press, 2011).

Lobel, Cindy R., *Urban Appetites: Food and Culture in Nineteenth-Century New York* (Chicago: University of Chicago Press, 2014).

Loeb, Lori Anne, *Consuming Angels: Advertising and Victorian Women* (New York: Oxford University Press, 1994).

Longstaffe-Gowan, Todd, *The London Square: Gardens in the Midst of Town* (New Haven and London: Yale University Press, 2012).

Lorente, Jesús Pedro and Clare Targett, 'Comparative Growth and Urban Distribution of the Population of Artists in Victorian London', in Peter Borsay, Gunther Hirschfelder, and Ruth-E. Mohrmann (eds), *New Directions in Urban History: Aspects of European Art, Health, Tourism and Leisure since the Enlightenment* (Berlin: Waxmann, 2000), pp. 65–86.

MacKeith, Margaret, *The History and Conservation of Shopping Arcades* (London: Mansell, 1986).

MacKenzie, John, *Propaganda and Empire: The Manipulation of British Public Opinion, 1880–1960* (Manchester: Manchester University Press, 1984).

MacMichael, J. Holden, *The Story of Charing Cross and its Immediate Neighbourhood* (London: Chatto and Windus, 1906).

MacQueen-Pope, W., *Carriages at Eleven: The Story of the Edwardian Theatre* (London: Hutchinson, 1947).

MacQueen-Pope, W., *Gaiety: Theatre of Enchantment* (London: W.H. Allen, 1949).

Mace, Rodney, *Trafalgar Square: Emblem of Empire* (London: Lawrence and Wishart, 1976).

Maloney, Paul, *The Britannia Panopticon Music Hall and Cosmopolitan Entertainment Culture* (Basingstoke: Palgrave Macmillan, 2016).

Mandler, Peter, 'From Almack's to Willis's: Aristocratic Women and Politics, 1815–1867', in Amanda Vickery (ed.), *Women, Privilege, and Power: British Politics, 1750 to the Present* (Stanford, CA: Stanford University Press, 2001), pp. 152–67.

Mandler, Peter, 'Art in a Cool Climate: The Cultural Policy of the British State in European Context, c.1780 to c.1850', in Tim Blanning and Hagen Schulze (eds), *Unity and Diversity in European Culture, c.1800* (Oxford: British Academy, 2006), pp. 101–19.

Marx, Peter W. (ed.), *A Cultural History of Theatre in the Age of Empire* (London: Bloomsbury, 2017).

Mayer, David (ed.), *Playing out the Empire: 'Ben Hur' and other Toga Plays and Films, 1883–1908* (Oxford: Clarendon Press, 1994).

Mayer, David, 'The Actress as Photographic Icon: From Early Photography to Early Film', in Maggie B. Gale and John Stokes (eds), *The Cambridge Companion to the Actress* (Cambridge: Cambridge University Press, 2007), pp. 74–94.

McCalman, Iain, *Radical Underworld: Prophets, Revolutionaries and Pornographers in London, 1795–1840* (Cambridge: Cambridge University Press, 1988).

McKellar, Elizabeth, *The Birth of Modern London: The Development and Design of the City, 1660–1720* (Manchester: Manchester University Press, 1999).

McKendrick, Neil, John Brewer, and J.H. Plumb, *The Birth of a Consumer Society: The Commercialisation of Eighteenth Century England* (London: Europa, 1982).

McKenna, Neil, *Fanny and Stella: The Young Men who shocked Victorian England* (London: Faber and Faber 2014).

McWilliam, Rohan, *The Tichborne Claimant: A Victorian Sensation* (London: Continuum, 2007).

McWilliam, Rohan, 'The Bazaars of London's West End in the Nineteenth Century', in Helen Kingstone and Kate Lister (eds), *Paraphernalia!: Victorian Objects* (London: Routledge, 2018), pp. 17–36.

Meisel, Martin, *Realizations: Narrative, Pictorial, and Theatrical Arts in Nineteenth-Century England* (Princeton, NJ: Princeton University Press, 1983).

Melman, Billie, *The Culture of History: English Uses of the Past, 1800–1953* (Oxford: Oxford University Press, 2006).

Milhous, Judith, Gabriella Dideriksen, and Robert D. Hume, *Italian Opera in Late Eighteenth-Century London* Vol. 1: *The King's Theatre, Haymarket, 1778–1791*; Vol. 2: The Pantheon Opera and its Aftermath, 1789–1795 (Oxford: Clarendon Press, 2000).

Miller, Michael B., *The Bon Marché: Bourgeois Culture and the Department Store, 1869–1920* (London: George Allen and Unwin, 1981).

Milne-Smith, Amy, *London Clubland: A Cultural History of Gender and Class in Late Victorian Britain* (London: Palgrave Macmillan, 2011).

Mitchell, Rosemary, *Picturing the Past: English History in Text and Image* (Oxford: Oxford University Press, 2000).

Moers, Ellen, *The Dandy: Brummell to Beerbohm* (London: Secker and Warburg, 1960).

Moody, Jane, *Illegitimate Theatre in London, 1770–1840* (Cambridge: Cambridge University Press, 2000).

Moore, Kemille, 'Feminisation and the Luxury of Visual Art in London's West End, 1860–1890', in Deborah Simonton, Marjo Kaartinen, and Anne Montenach (eds), *Luxury and Gender in European Towns, 1700–1914* (London: Routledge, 2014), pp. 74–96.

Morrison, Kathryn A., *English Shops and Shopping: An Architectural History* (New Haven and London: Yale University Press, 2003).

Mort, Frank, *Capital Affairs: London and the Making of the Permissive Society* (London: Yale University Press, 2010).

Mui, Hoh-Cheung and Lorna H. Mui, *Shops and Shopkeeping in Eighteenth-Century England* (Kingston: McGill-Queen's University Press, 1989).

Müller, Sven Oliver, 'Audience Behaviour in the Nineteenth Century', in Daniel Morat (ed.), *Sounds of Modern History: Auditory Cultures in 19th and 20th Century Europe* (New York: Berghahn, 2014), pp. 153–74.

Nasaw, David, 'Cities of Light, Landscapes of Pleasure', in David Ward and Oliver Zunz (eds), *The Landscape of Modernity: New York City, 1900–1940* (Baltimore: Johns Hopkins University Press, 1992), pp. 273–86.

Nasaw, David, *Going Out: The Rise and Fall of Public Amusements* (Cambridge, MA: Harvard University Press, 1993).

Nead, Lynda, *Victorian Babylon: People, Streets and Images in Nineteenth-Century London* (London: Yale University Press, 2000).

Nevett, T.R,. *Advertising in Britain: A History* (London: Heinemann, 1982).

Newey, Katherine, *Women's Theatre Writing in Victorian Britain* (Basingstoke: Palgrave Macmillan, 2005).

Newey, Katherine and Jeffrey Richards, *John Ruskin and the Victorian Theatre* (Basingstoke: Palgrave Macmillan, 2010).

Newton, Stella Mary, *Health, Art and Reason: Dress Reformers of the 19th Century* (London: John Murray, 1974).

Nord, Deborah Epstein, *Walking the Victorian Streets: Women, Representation and the City* (Ithaca, NY: Cornell University Press, 1995).

Nott, James J., *Music for the People: Popular Music and Dance in Interwar Britain* (Oxford: Oxford University Press, 2002).

Ogborn, Miles, *Spaces of Modernity: London's Geographies, 1680–1780* (New York: The Guilford Press, 1998).

Olsen, Donald J, *The Growth of Victorian London* (London: B.T. Batsford, 1976).

Otter, Chris, *The Victorian Eye: A Political History of Light and Vision in Britain, 1800–1910* (Chicago: University of Chicago Press, 2008).

Payen-Appenzeller, Pascal and Brice Payen, *Champs Elysées: The Story of the World's Most Beautiful Avenue* (Paris: Ledico, 2014).

Pearson, Hesketh, *Beerbohm Tree: His Life and Laughter* (London: Columbus Books, 1988 [1956]).

Peck, Linda Levy, *Consuming Splendour: Society and Culture in Seventeenth-Century England* (Cambridge: Cambridge University Press, 2005).

Peduzzi, Pino, *Pionieri ticinesi in Inghilterra: La Saga della Famiglia Gatti, 1780–1980* (Bellinzona, Switzerland: Edizioni Casagrande, 1985).

Pelling, Henry, *Winston Churchill* (London: Pan, 1977).

Pick, John, *The West End: Mismanagement and Snobbery* (London: Offord/City Arts, 1983).

Picker, John, *Victorian Soundscapes* (Oxford: Oxford University Press, 2003).

Piggott, Gillian, *Dickens and Benjamin: Moments of Revelation, Fragments of Modernity* (Farnham: Ashgate, 2012).

Pike, David L., *Metropolis on the Styx: The Underworlds of Modern Culture, 1800–2001* (Ithaca: Cornell University Press, 2007).

Platt, Len, *Musical Comedy on the West End Stage, 1890–1939* (Basingstoke: Palgrave Macmillan, 2004).

Platt, Len, Tobias Becker, and David Linton (eds), *Popular Musical Theatre in London and Berlin, 1890–1939* (Cambridge: Cambridge University Press, 2014).

Pollock, Della (ed.), *Exceptional Spaces: Essays in Performance and History* (Chapel Hill, NC: University of North Carolina Press, 1998).

Porter, Bernard, *The Absent-Minded Imperialists: Empire, Society and Culture in Britain* (Oxford: Oxford University Press, 2004).

Porter, Roy, *London: A Social History* (London: Penguin 1994).

Potter, Jonathan, *Discourses of Vision in Nineteenth-Century Britain: Seeing, Thinking, Writing* (Basingstoke: Palgrave Macmillan, 2018).

Potts, Alex, '*Eros* in Piccadilly Circus: Monument and Anti-monument', in David J. Getsy (ed.), *Sculpture and the Pursuit of a Modern Ideal in Britain, c.1880–1930* (Aldershot: Ashgate, 2004), pp. 105–39.

Price, Richard, *An Imperial War and the British Working Class: Working-Class Attitudes and Reactions to the Boer War, 1899–1902* (London: Routledge and Kegan Paul, 1972).

Pugh, Martin, *Speak for Britain!: A New History of the Labour Party* (London: Bodley Head, 2010).

Qureshi, Sadiah, *Peoples on Parade: Exhibitions, Empire, and Anthropology in Nineteenth-Century Britain* (Chicago: University of Chicago Press, 2011).

Rappaport, Erika Diane, *Shopping for Pleasure: Women in the Making of London's West End* (Princeton, NJ: Princeton University Press, 2000).

Rees, Terence, *Theatre Lighting in the Age of Gas* (Cambridge: Entertainment Technology Press, 1978).

Rendell, Jane, ' "Industrious Females" & "Professional Beauties", or, Fine Articles for Sale in the Burlington Arcade', in Iain Borden et al. (eds), *Strangely Familiar: Narratives of Architecture in the City* (London: Routledge, 1996), pp. 32–6.

Rendell, Jane, 'Subjective Space: A Feminist Architectural History of the Burlington Arcade', in Duncan McCorquodale, Sarah Wigglesworth, and Katerina Ruedi (eds), *Desiring Practices: Architecture, Gender and the Interdisciplinary* (London: Black Dog, 1997), pp. 216–33.

Rendell, Jane, 'Thresholds, Passage and Surfaces: Touching, Passing and Seeing in the Burlington Arcade', in Alex Coles (ed.) *The Optics of Walter Benjamin* (London: Black Dog, 1999), pp. 168–91.

Rendell, Jane, *The Pursuit of Pleasure: Gender, Space and Architecture in Regency London* (London: Athlone Press, 2002).

Rich, Rachel, *Bourgeois Consumption: Food, Space and Identity in London and Paris, 1850–1914* (Manchester: Manchester University Press, 2011).

Richards, Jeffrey, *Sir Henry Irving: A Victorian Actor and his World* (London: Hambledon, 2005).

Richards, Jeffrey, *The Ancient World on the Victorian and Edwardian Stage* (Basingstoke: Palgrave Macmillan, 2009).

Richards, Jeffrey, *The Golden Age of Pantomime: Slapstick, Spectacle and Subversion in Victorian England* (London: I.B. Tauris, 2014).

Richards, Thomas, *The Commodity Culture of Victorian England: Advertising and Spectacle, 1851–1914* (London: Verso, 1990).

Richardson, D.J., 'J. Lyons and Co. Ltd: Caterers and Food Manufacturers, 1894–1939', in Derek Oddy and Derek Miller (eds), *The Making of the Modern British Diet* (London: Croom Helm, 1976), pp. 161–72.

Roberts, W., *The Book-Hunter in London: Historical and other Studies of Collectors and Collecting* (London: Elliot Stock, 1895).

Rosenfeld, Sybil, *A Short History of Scene Design in Great Britain* (Oxford: Basil Blackwell, 1973).

Russell, Gillian, *The Theatres of War: Performance, Politics and Society, 1793–1815* (Oxford: Clarendon Press, 1995).

Sachs, Edwin O. and Ernest A.E. Woodrow (eds), *Modern Opera Houses and Theatres* (London: B.T. Batsford, 1896) 3 vols.

Sanders, Lise Shapiro, *Consuming Fantasies: Labor, Leisure and the London Shopgirl, 1880–1920* (Columbus, OH: Ohio State University Press, 2006).

Sanderson, Michael, *From Irving to Olivier: A Social History of the Acting Profession in England, 1880–1983* (London: Athlone Press, 1984).

Sandoval-Strausz, A.K., *Hotel: An American History* (New Haven, CT: Yale University Press, 2007).

Sassen, Saskia, *The Global City: New York, London, Tokyo* (Princeton, NJ: Princeton University Press, 1991).

Satz, Aura and Jon Wood (eds), *Articulate Objects: Voice, Sculpture and Performance* (Oxford: Peter Lang, 2009).

Schivelbusch, Wolfgang, *Disenchanted Night: The Industrialization of Light in the Nineteenth Century* (Oxford: Berg, 1988).

Schlör, Joachim, *Nights in the Big City: Paris, Berlin, London, 1840–1930* (London: Reaktion, 1998 [1991]).

Schneer, Jonathan, *London 1900: The Imperial Metropolis* (New Haven, CT: Yale University Press, 1999).

Schoch, Richard W., *Queen Victoria and the Theatre of her Age* (Basingstoke: Palgrave Macmillan, 2004).

Schorske, Carl E., *Fin-de-Siècle Vienna: Politics and Culture* (New York: Vintage Books, 1981).

Schwartz, Vanessa R., *Spectacular Realities: Early Mass Culture in fin-de-siècle Paris* (Berkeley, CA: University of California Press, 1998).

Seeley, Paul, *Richard D'Oyly Carte* (London: Routledge, 2019).

Sennett, Richard, *The Fall of Public Man* (New York: Norton 1992 [1974]).

Sennett, Richard, *Flesh and Stone: The Body and the City in Western Civilization* (London: Faber, 1994).

Settle, Alison, *A Family of Shops* (Margate: Marshall and Snelgrove, 1951).

Shannon, Brent, *The Cut of his Coat: Men, Dress, and Consumer Culture in Britain, 1860–1914* (Athens, OH: Ohio University Press, 2006).

Shannon, Mary, *Dickens, Reynolds, and Mayhew on Wellington Street: The Print Culture of a Victorian Street* (Farnham: Ashgate, 2015).

Sherwood, James, *Savile Row: The Master Tailors of British Bespoke* (London: Thames and Hudson, 2010).

Shonfield, Zuzanna, *The Precariously Privileged: A Professional Family in Victorian London* (Oxford: Oxford University Press, 1987).

Siegel, Jerrold, *Bohemian Paris: Culture, Politics and the Boundaries of Bourgeois Life, 1830–1930* (London: Viking, 1986).

Silva, João, 'Porosity and Modernity: Lisbon's Auditory Landscape from 1864 to 1908', in Ian Biddle and Kirsten Gibson (eds), *Cultural Histories of Noise, Sound and Listening in Europe, 1300–1918* (London: Routledge, 2017), pp. 235–51.

Simmel, Georg, *The Sociology of Georg Simmel* (ed. Kurt H. Wolff) (London: Free Press, 1950).

Snowman, Daniel, *The Gilded Stage: A Social History of Opera* (London: Atlantic, 2009).

Sontag, Susan, *Notes on Camp* (London: Penguin, 2018 [1966]).

Spang, Rebecca, *The Invention of the Restaurant: Paris and Modern Gastronomic Culture* (Cambridge, MA: Harvard University Press 2001).

Speiser, Peter, *Soho: The Heart of Bohemian London* (London: British Library, 2017).

Spiers, R.G., *Spiers and Pond: Restauraunteurs, Cricket Promoters and Hoteliers Extraordinaire* (Tring: R.G. Spiers, 2008).

Strasdin, Kate, *Inside the Royal Wardrobe: A Dress History of Queen Alexandra* (London: Bloomsbury, 2017).

Stuart, Charles Douglas and A.J. Park, *The Variety Stage: A History of the Music Halls from the Earliest Period to the Present Time* (London: T. Fisher Unwin, 1895).

Summers, Judith, *Soho: A History of London's Most Colourful Neighbourhood* (London: Bloomsbury 1989).

Summerson, John, *Georgian London* (New Haven and London: Yale University Press, 2003 [1945].

Summerson, John, *The Life and Work of John Nash, Architect* (London: George Allen and Unwin, 1980).

Tambling, Jeremy, *Going Astray: Dickens and London* (London: Pearson, 2009).

Taylor, Derek and David Bush, *The Golden Age of British Hotels* (London: Northwood, 1974).

Taylor, George, *Players and Performances in the Victorian Theatre* (Manchester: Manchester University Press, 1989).

Taylor, William R., *In Pursuit of Gotham: Culture and Commerce in New York* (New York: Oxford University Press, 1992).

Taylor, William R. (ed.), *Inventing Times Square: Commerce and Culture at the Crossroads of the World* (Baltimore, MD: Johns Hopkins University Press, 1996 [1991]).

Tessier, Alexandre, *Le Grand Hôtel: l'invention du luxe hôtelier, 1862–1972* (Rennes: Presses Universitaires de Rennes, 2012).

Thornbury, Walter and Edward Walford, *Old and New London* (London: Cassell, Petter and Galpin, 1879–1885), 6 vols.

Thorne, Robert, 'Places of Refreshment in the Nineteenth-Century City' in Anthony D. King (ed.), *Buildings and Society: Essays on the Social Development of the Built Environment* (London: Routledge and Kegan Paul, 1980), pp. 228–53.

Trewin, Wendy, *All on Stage: Charles Wyndham and the Alberys* (London: Harrap, 1980).

Tromp, Marlene (ed.), *Victorian Freaks: The Social Context of Freakery in Britain* (Columbus, OH: Ohio State University Press, 2008).

Tullett, William, *Smell in Eighteenth-Century England: A Social Sense* (Oxford: Oxford University Press, 2019).

Tyack, Geoffrey (ed.), *John Nash: Architect of the Picturesque* (Swindon: English Heritage, 2013).

Van den Beukel, Karlien, 'Arthur Symons's Night Life', in Veleria Tinler-Villani (ed.), *Babylon or New Jerusalem: Perceptions of the City in Literature* (Amsterdam: Rodopi, 2005), pp. 135–53.

Vardac, Alexander Nicholas, *Stage to Screen: Theatrical Method from Garrick to Griffin* (Cambridge, MA: Harvard University Press, 1949).

Veblen, Thorstein, *The Theory of the Leisure Class: An Economic Study of Institutions* (London: Allen and Unwin, 1924).

Vernon, James, *Distant Strangers: How Britain Became Modern* (Berkeley, CA: University of California Press, 2014).

Vincent, David, *I Hope I Don't Intrude: Privacy and its Dilemmas in Nineteenth-Century Britain* (Oxford: Oxford University Press, 2015).

Waddy, H.T., *The Devonshire Club—and 'Crockford's'* (London: Evelyn Nash, 1919).

Lynne Walker, 'Vistas of Pleasure: Women Consumers of Urban Space in the West End of London, 1850–1900' in Clarissa Campbell Orr (ed.), *Women in the Victorian Art World* (Manchester: Manchester University Press, 1995), pp. 70–85.

Walker, Richard, *Savile Row: An Illustrated History* (New York: Rizzoli, 1989).

Walkowitz, Judith R., *City of Dreadful Delight: Narratives of Sexual Danger in late-Victorian London* (London: Virago, 1992).

Walkowitz, Judith R., *Nights Out: Life in Cosmopolitan London* (London: Yale University Press, 2012).

Walsh, Claire, 'The Newness of the Department Store: A View from the Eighteenth Century', in Geoffrey Crossick and Serge Jaumain (eds), *Cathedrals of Consumption: The European Department Store, 1850–1939* (Aldershot: Ashgate, 1999), pp. 46–71.

Walsh, Claire, 'Social Meaning and Social Space in the Shopping Galleries of Early Modern London', in John Benson and Laura Ugolini (eds), *A Nation of Shopkeepers: Five Centuries of British Retailing* (London: I.B. Tauris, 2003), pp. 52–79.

Walsh, Claire, 'Shopping at First Hand? Mistresses, Servants and Shopping for the Household in Early-Modern England', in David Hussey and Margaret Ponsonby (eds), *Buying for the Home: Shopping for the Domestic from the Seventeenth Century to the Present* (Aldershot: Ashgate, 2008), pp. 13–26.

Walter, Marc (ed.), *Grand Hotel: The Golden Age of Palace Hotels: An Architectural and Social History* (London: Dent, 1984).

Waters, Chris, *British Socialists and the Politics of Popular Culture* (Manchester: Manchester University Press, 1990).

Waters, Hazel, *Racism on the Victoria Stage: Representation of Slavery and the Black Character* (Cambridge: Cambridge University Press, 2007).

Weber, William, *Music and the Middle Class: The Social Structure of Concert Life in London, Paris and Vienna between 1830 and 1848* (Aldershot: Ashgate, 2004 [1975]).

Weiss, Laura B., *Ice Cream: A Global History* (London: Reaktion Books, 2011).

Wharf, Barney and Santa Arias (eds), *The Spatial Turn: Interdisciplinary Perspectives* (London: Routledge, 2009).

Whelan, Robert, *The Other National Theatre: 350 Years of Shows in Drury Lane* (London: Jacob Tonson, 2013).

White, Jerry, *London in the Nineteenth Century: A Human Awful Wonder of God* (London: Vintage Books, 2008).

White, Jerry, *London in the Twentieth Century: A City and its People* (London: Vintage Books, 2008 [2001]).

White, Jerry, *London in the Eighteenth Century: A Great and Monstrous Thing* (London: Vintage, 2013 [2012]).

Whitlock, Tammy C., *Crime, Gender and Consumer Culture in Nineteenth-Century England* (Aldershot: Ashgate, 2005).

Williams, Carolyn (ed.), *The Cambridge Companion to English Melodrama* (Cambridge: Cambridge University Press, 2018).

Williams, Raymond, *The Long Revolution* (London: Pelican, 1971 [1961]).

Wilmore, David (ed.), *Edwin O. Sachs: Architect, Stagehand, Engineer and Fireman* (Summerbridge: Theatresearch, 1998).

Windscheffel, Alex, *Popular Conservatism in Imperial London, 1868–1906* (Woodbridge: Boydell Press/Royal Historical Society, 2007).

Winter, James, *London's Teeming Streets, 1830–1914* (London: Routledge, 1993).

Woodhead, Lindy, *Shopping, Seduction and Mr Selfridge* (London: Profile, 2012).

Woolf, John, *The Wonders: Lifting the Curtain on the Freak Show, Circus and Victorian Age* (London: Michael O'Mara, 2019)

Woolf, Janet and John Seed (eds), *The Culture of Capital: Art, Power and the Nineteenth-Century Middle Class* (Manchester: Manchester University Press, 1988).

Wroth, Warwick, *Cremorne and the Later London Gardens* (London: Elliot Stock, 1907).

Yeandle, Peter, Katherine Newey, and Jeffrey Richards (eds), *Politics, Performance and Popular Culture: Theatre and Society in Nineteenth-Century Britain* (Manchester: Manchester University Press, 2016).

Zieger, Susan, *The Mediated Mind: Affect, Ephemera, and Consumerism in the Nineteenth Century* (New York: Fordham University Press, 2018).

Ziter, Edward, *The Orient on the Victorian Stage* (Cambridge: Cambridge University Press, 2003).

Articles in Journals and Periodicals

Assael, Brenda, 'Art or Indecency?: *Tableaux Vivants* on the London Stage and the Failure of Late Victorian Moral Reform', *Journal of British Studies*, 45 (2006), pp. 744–58.

Assael, Brenda, 'Gastro-Cosmopolitanism and the Restaurant in Late Victorian and Edwardian London', *Historical Journal*, 56 (2013), pp. 681–706.

Assael, Brenda, 'On *Dinners and Diners* and Restaurant Culture in Late Nineteenth-Century London', BRANCH: http://www.branchcollective.org/?ps_articles=brenda-assael-on-dinners-and-diners-and-restaurant-culture-in-late-nineteenth-century-london (accessed 31 July 2018).

Atkins, P.J., 'How the West End was Won: The Struggle to Remove Street Barriers in Victorian London', *Journal of Historical Geography*, 19 (1993), pp. 265–77.

Atkins, P.J., 'The Spatial Configuration of Class Solidarity in London's West End, 1792–1939', *Urban History Year Book*, 17 (1990), pp. 36–65.

Atkinson, Juliette, 'William Jeffs, Victorian Bookseller and Publisher of French Literature', *The Library: The Transactions of the Bibliographical Society*, seventh series, 13 (2012), pp. 258–78.

Bailey, Peter, 'Theatres of Entertainment/Spaces of Modernity: Rethinking the British Popular Stage, 1890–1914', *Nineteenth Century Theatre*, 26 (1998), pp. 5–24.

Barker, Clive, 'The Chartists, Theatre, Reform, and Research', *Theatre Quarterly*, 1 (1971), pp. 3–10.

Berger, Molly W., 'The Magic of Fine Dining: Invisible Technology and the Hotel Kitchen', *Icon*, 1 (1995), pp. 106–19.

Berry, Helen, 'Polite Consumption: Shopping in Eighteenth-Century England', *Transactions of the Royal Historical Society*, 12 (2002), pp. 375–94.

Briggs, Jo, 'Gavarni at the Casino: Reflections of Class and Gender in the Visual Culture of 1848', *Victorian Studies,* 53 (2011), pp. 639–64.

Burden, Michael, 'Pots, Privies and WCs: Crapping at the Opera in London before 1830', *Cambridge Opera Journal*, 23 (2011), pp. 27–50.

Cheang, Sarah, 'Selling China: Class, Gender and Orientalism at the Department Store', *Journal of Design History*, 20 (2007), pp. 1–4.

Cherry, Deborah, 'Going Places: Women Artists in Central London in the Mid-19th Century', *London Journal*, 28 (2003), pp. 73–96.

Cox, Pamela, 'Shopgirls and Social Theory', *Revista Brasileira de História*, 37 (2017), pp. 243–71.

Crawford, Elizabeth, 'WALKS/Suffrage Stories: Suffragettes and Tea Rooms: The Criterion Restaurant, Kate Frye, and the Actresses' Franchise League', Women and Her Sphere blog: https://womanandhersphere.com/2012/09/05/suffrage-stories-suffragettes-and-tea-rooms-the-criterion-restaurant-kate-frye-and-the-actresses-franchise-league/ (accessed 3 September 2018).

Davis, Jim and Victor Emaljanow, '"Wistful Remembrancer": The Historiographical Problem of Macqueen-Popery', *New Theatre Quarterly*, 17 (2001) pp. 299–309.

Diamond, Michael, 'Theatre Posters and How They Bring the Past to Life', *Nineteenth Century Theatre & Film*, 39 (2012), pp. 60–77.

Dideriksen, Gabriella and Matthew Ringel, 'Frederick Gye and "The Dreadful Business of Opera Management"', *19th Century Music*, 19 (1995), pp. 3–30.

Dobraszczyk, Paul, 'Victorian Bazaars', https://ragpickinghistory.co.uk/2011/05/11/victorian-bazaars/ (accessed 3 May 2016).

Donohue, Joseph, 'W.P. Dando's Improved Tableaux Vivants at the Palace Theatre of Varieties, London', *Theatre Notebook*, 63 (2009), pp. 151–79.

Edwards, Clive, 'Tottenham Court Road: The Changing Fortunes of London's Furniture Street, 1850–1950', *London Journal*, 36 (2011), pp. 141–60.

Egginton, Heidi, 'Book Hunters and Book-huntresses: Gender and Cultures of Antiquarian Book Collecting in Britain, c.1880–1900', *Journal of Victorian Culture*, 19 (2014) pp. 346–64.

Emaljanow, Victor, 'The Events of June 1848: The Monte Cristo Riots and the Politics of Protest', *New Theatre Quarterly*, 19 (2003), pp. 23–32.

Eyben, Rosalind, '"The Moustache Makes Him More of a Man": Waiters' Masculinity Struggles, 1890–1910', *History Workshop Journal*, 87 (2019), pp. 189–210.

Featherstone, Simon, 'The Egyptian Hall and the Platform of Transatlantic Exchange: Charles Browne, P.T. Barnum, and Albert Smith', *Nineteenth-Century Prose*, 29 (2002), pp. 68–77.

Foucault, Michel, 'Of Other Spaces', *Diacritics*, 16 (1986), pp. 22–7.

Ganzel, Dewey, 'Patent Wrongs and Patent Theatres: Drama and the Law in the Early Nineteenth Century', *Proceedings of the Modern Language Association*, 76 (1961), pp. 384–96.

Helmreich, Anne, 'The Socio-Geography of Art Dealers and Commercial Galleries in Early Twentieth-Century London', in Helena Bonett, Ysanne Holt, Jennifer Mundy (eds), *The Camden Town Group in Context*, Tate Research Publication, May 2012, https://www.tate.org.uk/art/research-publications/camden-town-group/anne-helmreich-the-socio-geography-of-art-dealers-and-commercial-galleries-in-early-r1105658 (accessed 27 April 2018).

Hosgood, Christopher P., '"Mercantile Monasteries": Shops, Shop Assistants, and Shop Life in Late-Victorian and Edwardian Britain', *Journal of British Studies*, 38 (1999), pp. 322–52.

Howell, Philip, 'Sex and the City of Bachelors: Popular Masculinity and Public Space in Nineteenth-Century England and America', *Ecumene*, 8 (2001), pp. 20–50.

Hughes, Alan, 'The Lyceum Staff: A Victorian Theatrical Organization', *Theatre Notebook*, 28 (1974), pp. 11–17.

Huxley, David, 'Music Hall Art: La Milo, Nudity and the Pose Plastique, 1905–1915', *Early Popular Visual Culture*, 11 (2013), pp. 218–36.

James, Kevin J,. A.K. Sandoval-Strausz, Daniel Maudlin, Maurizio Peleggi, Cédric Humair, and Molly W. Berger, 'The Hotel in History: Evolving Perspectives', *Journal of Tourism History*, 9 (2017), pp. 92–111.

Jerram, Leif, 'Space: A Useless Category for Historical Analysis?', *History and Theory*, 52 (2013), pp. 400–19.

Johnson, Paul, 'Conspicuous Consumption and Working-Class Culture in Late-Victorian and Edwardian Britain', *Transactions of the Royal Historical Society*, fifth series, 38 (1988), pp. 27–42.

Kent, Christopher, 'The Idea of Bohemia in mid-Victorian England', *Queen's Quarterly*, 80 (1973), pp. 360–9.

Kent, Christopher, 'The Whittington Club: A Bohemian Experiment in Middle-Class Social Reform', *Victorian Studies*, 18 (1974), pp. 31–55.

Kumin, Beat and Cornelie Usborne, 'At Home and in the Workplace: A Historical Introduction to the "Spatial Turn"', *History and Theory*, 52 (2013), pp. 305–18.

Kwint, Marius, 'The Legitimization of the Circus in Late Georgian England', *Past and Present*, 174 (2002), pp. 72–115.

Langley, Leanne, 'A Place for Music: John Nash, Regent Street and the Philharmonic Society of London', *Electronic British Library Journal* (2013) article 12 pp. 1–48: https://www.bl.uk/eblj/2013articles/article12.html (accessed 31 July 2018).

Lysak, Krista, 'Goblin Markets: Victorian Women Shoppers at Liberty's Oriental Bazaar', *Nineteenth-Century Contexts*, 27 (2005), pp. 139–65.

Maguire, Hugh, 'The Victorian Theatre as a Home from Home', *Journal of Design History*, 13 (2000), pp. 107–21.

Maier, William M., 'Going on the Hoist: Women, Work and Shoplifting in London, c.1890–1940' *Journal of British Studies*, 50 (2011), pp. 410–33.

Mayer, David, ' "Quote the Words to Prompt the Attitudes": The Victorian Performer, the Photographer and the Photograph', *Theatre Survey*, 43 (2002), pp. 223–51.

McWilliam, Rohan, 'The Licensed Stare: Melodrama and the Culture of Spectacle', *Nineteenth Century Studies*, 13 (1999), pp. 153–75.

McWilliam, Rohan, 'Elsa Lanchester and Bohemian London in the early Twentieth Century', *Women's History Review*, 23 (2014), pp. 171–87.

McWilliam, Rohan, 'Man about Town: Victorian Night Life and the Haymarket Saturnalia, 1840–1880', *History*, 103 (2018), pp. 758–76.

McWilliam, Rohan, 'Fancy Repositories: The Arcades of London's West End in the Nineteenth Century', *London Journal*, 44 (2019), pp. 93–112.

Milne-Smith, Amy, 'A Flight to Domesticity? Making a Home in the Gentlemen's Clubs of London, 1880–1914', *Journal of British Studies* 45 (2006), pp. 796–818.

Nichols, Harold J., 'Ben Webster and Legitimate Drama at the Haymarket', *Theatre Journal*, 31 (1979), pp. 319–27.

North, Susan, 'John Redfern and Sons, 1847 to 1892', *Costume*, 42 (2008), pp. 145–68.

North, Susan, 'Redfern Limited, 1892 to 1940', *Costume*, 43 (2009), pp. 85–108.

Plunkett, John, 'Moving Panoramas, c.1800 to 1840: The Spaces of Nineteenth-Century Picture Going', *19* (online journal) no. 17 (2013): http://www.19.bbk.ac.uk/index.php/19/article/viewFile/674/934 (accessed 29 October 2014).

Rappaport, Erika, 'Art, Commerce, or Empire?: The Rebuilding of Regent Street, 1880–1927', *History Workshop Journal*, 53 (2002), pp. 95–117.

Rendell, Jane, 'Gendered Space: Encountering Anthropology, Architecture and Feminism in the Burlington Arcade', *Architectural Design*, 66 no. 11/12 (1996), pp. 60–3.

Rendell, Jane, 'The Clubs of St. James's: Places of Public Patriarchy—Exclusivity, Domesticity and Secrecy', *Journal of Architecture*, 4 (1999), pp. 167–89.

Robinson, Terry F., 'National Theatre in Transition: The London Patent Theatre Fires of 1808–1809 and the Old Price Riots', BRANCH: http://www.branchcollective.org/?ps_articles=terry-f-robinson-national-theatre-in-transition-the-london-patent-theatre-fires-of-1808-1809-and-the-old-price-riots (accessed 1 January 2018).

Schulz, David, 'The Architecture of Conspicuous Consumption: Property, Class, and Display at Herbert Beerbohm Tree's Her Majesty's Theatre', *Theatre Journal*, 51 (1999), pp. 231–50.

Schwartz, Vanessa R., 'Walter Benjamin for Historians', *American Historical Review*, 106 (2001), pp. 1721–43.

Senelick, Lawrence, 'Politics as Entertainment: Victorian Music Hall Songs', *Victorian Studies*, 19 (1975), pp. 149–80.

Starkey, Pat, ' "Temporary Relief for Specially Recommended or Selected Deserving Persons": The Mission of the House of Charity, Soho, 1846–1914', *Urban History*, 35 (2008), 96–115.

Suk, Lena Oak, ' "Only the Fragile Sex Admitted": The Women's Restaurant in 1920s Sao Paulo, Brazil', *Journal of Social History*, 51 (2018), pp. 592–620.

'The Story of the Strand', *Strand Magazine*, 1 (1891), pp. 4–13.

Taylor, Antony, 'Shakespeare and Radicalism: The Uses and Abuses of Shakespeare in Nineteenth-Century Popular Politics', *Historical Journal*, 45 (2002), pp. 357–79.

Theiding, Kara Olsen, 'Anxieties of Influence: British Responses to Art Nouveau, 1900–04', *Journal of Design History*, 19 (2006), pp. 215–31.

Valverde, Mariana, 'The Love of Finery: Fashion and the Fallen Woman in Nineteenth-Century Social Discourse', *Victorian Studies*, 32 (1989), pp. 168–88.

Walsh, Claire, 'Shop Design and the Display of Goods in Eighteenth-Century London', *Journal of Design History*, 8 (1995), pp. 157–76.

Whyte, William, 'How do Buildings Mean? Some Issues of Interpretation in the History of Architecture', *History and Theory*, 45 (2006), pp. 153–77.

Wilson, Keith, 'Music-Hall London: The Topography of Class Sentiment', *Victorian Literature and Culture*, 23 (1996), pp. 23–35.

Witchard, Anne, 'Bedgraggled Ballerinas on a Bus Back to Bow: The 'Fairy Business', *19: Interdisciplinary Studies in the Long Nineteenth Century* no. 13 (2011) http://19.bbk. ac.uk/index.php/19/article/view/618 (accessed 1 January 2019).

PhD Theses

Crowhurst, Andrew John, 'The Music Hall, 1885–1922: The Emergence of a National Entertainment Industry in Britain', University of Cambridge, D.Phil. thesis, 1991.

Dyer, Serena, 'Trained to Consume: Dress and the Female Consumer in England, 1720–1820', University of Warwick, D.Phil. thesis 2016.

Flinn, Laurel, 'Elegant Buildings and Pestilential Alleys: Space, Society, and Politics in London's West End, 1753–1873', Johns Hopkins University, PhD thesis, 2014.

Hamlin, Sasha, 'Grand Hotels: Cosmopolitan Caravansaries, Gastronomy, and Performance Spaces of Late-Nineteenth and Early-Twentieth Century London', University of Cambridge, M.Phil. thesis, 2018.

Innes, Eilidh, 'The Many Lives of John Hollingshead', PhD in progress, Anglia Ruskin University.

Legnini, Jessica H., 'Identity, Class and Emulation: American Blackface Minstrelsy and its British Audiences', University of Warwick, PhD thesis, 2011.

Maguire, Hugh Francis Bernard, 'C.J. Phipps (1835–97) and Nineteenth Century Theatre Architecture (1863–97)', University of London/Courtauld Institute of Art PhD thesis, 1990.

Robinson, Clare, 'Popular Theatre in Manchester', University of Birmingham PhD thesis, 2015.

Shannon, Mary L., 'Wellington Street, Strand: The Print Culture of a Victorian Street', Kings College London, PhD thesis 2012.

Wingrove, Louise, 'Reigniting the "Vital Spark" : Reimagining and Reclaiming the Repertoires, Career Development and Image Cultivation of Serio-comediennes Jenny Hill and Bessie Bellwood from 1870–1896', University of Bristol, D. Phil thesis, 2016.

Websites and Web-based Publications

Adelphi Theatre Project: http://www.umass.edu/AdelphiTheatreCalendar/m06d. htm#Label003

Arthur Lloyd: http://www.arthurlloyd.co.uk/

Concert Life Project: www.concertlifeproject.com.

Pub History: https://pubshistory.com/.

Pubology: https://pubology.co.uk/index.html.

Romantic London: http://www.romanticlondon.org/.

Encyclopedias, Dictionaries, etc.

Howard, Diana (ed.), *London Theatres and Music Halls, 1850–1950* (London: Library Association, 1970).

MacKeith, Margaret, *Shopping Arcades: A Gazeteer of Extant British Arcades* (London: Mansell, 1985).

Mander, Raymond and Joe Mitchenson, *The Theatres of London* (London: New English Library, 1975 [1961]).

Mander, Raymond and Joe Mitchenson, *Lost Theatres of London* (London; New English Library, 1976 [1968]).

Oxford Dictionary of National Biography (Oxford: Oxford University Press, 2004–).

Richardson, John, *The Annals of London: A Year-by-Year Record of a Thousand Years of History* (London: Cassell, 2000).

Sadie, Stanley (ed.), *The New Grove Dictionary of Music and Musicians* (London: Grove, 2001).

Survey of London (London: Athlone Press/Yale University Press, 1900–).

Tanitch, Robert, *London Stage in the Twentieth Century* (London: Haus, 2007).

Tanitch, Robert, *London Stage in the Nineteenth Century* (Lancaster: Carnegie, 2010).

Weinreb, Ben, Christopher Hibbert, Julia Keay, and John Keay (eds), *The London Encyclopedia* (Basingstoke: Macmillan Reference, 2010 [1983]).

Index

Ackerman, Rudolph (bookseller and publisher) 24

acting profession and acting styles 14, 64, 79–81, 168–71, 181–2 (*see* names of individual actors and actresses)

Actress's Franchise League 249–50

Adamowitz, Helena (ballerina) 234

Adcock, A. St John (writer) 190

Adcock, John (inventor) 98

Adelaide Gallery, Strand 98, 260

Adelaide, Queen (wife of William IV) 38

Adelphi Theatre, Strand 33, 55, 71, 72–5, 77, 78, 83, 156, 157, 159, 161–2, 164, 166, 168, 169, 171, 173, 261, 262, 304, 306

advertising 86, 108–9, 119, 122, 127, 166, 228, 282, 283, 290, 295, 311

Aereated Bread Company (ABC) restaurants 257, 313

After Dark (Boucicault) 168

agents 81, 145, 205–6

Agnew, Jean-Christophe (historian of American culture) 6

Albany (bachelor apartments), Piccadilly 42, 74

Albermarle Street, Piccadilly 23, 137

Albert, Prince 28, 92, 161, 284

Albert Hall 141, 149

Albion, Drury Lane (pub) 81

Aldridge, Ira (actor) 77

Aldwych 72, 112, 148, 222

Aldwych Theatre, Aldwych 182, 183, 184

Alexander, George (actor manager) 176, 180

Alexandra, Princess and Queen 216, 286

Alhambra Theatre, Leicester Square (variety house) 5, 10, 96–8, 108, 111, 122, 128, 129, 134, 163, 181, 202, 205, 216, 220, 221, 222, 231–5, 237, 241, 242, 243–4, 302, 306, 315

Alice in Wonderland (Carroll) 177

All the Year Round 148

Allen, Arabella (impersonator of Dickens characters) 211

Allen, Maud (exotic dancer) 238

Almack's (assembly rooms) 43–4, 48, 74

Alma-Tadema, Sir Lawrence (artist) 139, 173

Ambassadors Theatre, West Street 183

Altick, Richard (literary historian) 86, 87

Americanization and American influences 78, 100, 206, 230, 232, 243, 249, 270, 271, 275, 278, 294, 296

Anelay, Henry (artist) 147

animal performers 72, 75, 77, 78, 239

Anna Bolena (Donizetti) 47

Apollo Theatre, Shaftesbury Avenue 111

Arbuthnot, Harriet (diarist and Tory hostess) 73, 74

arcades 3, 5, 6, 22, 30–36, 39, 74, 98, 119, 120, 241, 265, 288, 302, 315

Arcadians, The (Monckton and Talbot) 230

Archer, William (theatre critic) 193, 194

Archbishop Tenison's School, Leicester Square 118

Argyll Rooms (concert hall on Regent Street) 29–30, 123

Argyll Rooms (dance hall on Great Windmill Street) 132–5, 236, 255

Ariel (Burnand) 125

aristocracy and upper classes 4, 5, 6, 14, 15, 16, 17–18, 22, 24, 27, 28, 33, 36, 39, 40, 41, 42, 43–8, 52, 62, 70, 71, 86, 108, 128, 132, 139, 143, 154, 157, 161, 162, 169, 170, 176, 177, 190, 192, 208, 222, 236, 266–7, 268, 277, 278, 286, 288, 302, 311

Arkwright's Wife (Taylor) 165

Armstrong, Isobel (literary critic) 37, 123

Arnold, Matthew (critic) 149

Arrah-na-Pogue (Boucicault) 169

art galleries 19, 21, 37–38, 93, 107, 109, 121, 128, 137, 138–40

artists and art works 37–38, 61, 90, 91–6, 137, 138–40, 149, 159

Artist's Model, An (Hall, Greenbank and Jones) 230, 286

Assael, Brenda (historian of popular culture) 251

Astaire, Fred 242

Astley, Philip (circus owner) 72, 77, 304

Athenaeum (club), Pall Mall 43

Athenaeum, The 148

audience and auditorium (theatres and music halls) 8, 9, 13, 14, 44–6, 68, 69, 72, 76, 102, 120, 122, 142, 154, 155–6, 159–67, 179, 182–3, 184–5, 187, 189–92, 196–7, 199, 202, 208, 209–10, 219, 223, 231–2, 236, 241 (*see also* front of house in theatres and programmes, theatre)
  boxes 13–14, 16, 44, 45–6, 68, 69, 72, 161, 183, 188, 196, 223
  dress and upper circle 5, 68, 159, 161, 164, 182–3, 197
  gallery 45, 68, 72, 156, 159, 161, 163, 164, 165, 172, 183, 184, 185, 196, 232
  pit 13, 14, 45–6, 68, 69, 72, 154, 156, 159, 161, 185, 196, 232
  stalls 44, 45, 154, 156, 159, 161, 163, 164, 165, 182, 183, 188, 193, 196
Austen, Jane 21, 40
automata 86, 100, 103
Avenue Theatre, Northumberland Avenue (later the Playhouse) 180
Ayrton, William (music critic and director) 46
Aztec Liliputians 94

Baartman, Sara (the 'Hottentot Venus') 84–5, 86, 87, 100, 103
back stage staff 187, 188
Bacon, Nell (waitress and later superintendent at Lyons tea shops) 127, 258–9
Baden Powell, Colonel Robert 301–2
Baer, Marc (historian) 69
Bagehot, Walter (political scientist) 147
Baillie, Joanna (playwright) 78
Bailey, Peter (historian of popular culture) 95–6, 202, 211, 212, 214, 222
Bainbridge's (Newcastle drapers and department store) 36
Baker, Robert (tailor) 15
Ballantine, Serjeant William (barrister) 54, 60
ballet 34, 41, 47–8, 62, 67, 76, 170, 188, 206, 220, 221, 231, 232, 233–7, 242, 244, 306
Ballets Russes 242
Balzac, Honoré de 34, 115
Bamford, Samuel (radical) 53
Bancroft, Squire (actor manager) 157, 163, 164, 183, 185 (*see also*, Wilton (later Bancroft) Marie)
Barber, Peter (historian of the Gatti family) 261–2
Barker, Harley Granville (playwright and critic) 194
Barker, Robert (promoter of panoramas) 20, 88–9, 92
Barnum, Phineas T. 86, 99, 221, 258, 295

Barrie, James Matthew (novelist and playwright) 177
Barry, Charles (architect) 39, 43
Barry, Edward (architect) 144
Batholomew, Mary-Anne (stole from the Soho Bazaar) 281
Baudelaire, Charles 6, 31, 42
bazaars 30, 37–39, 91, 98, 154
Bechstein Hall, *see* Wigmore Hall
Bedford, Duke of 121
Beerbohm, Max (critic and wit) 254
Beethoven, Ludwig van 141
Bell, Alexander Graham (inventor) 101
Bells, The (Lewis) 119, 306
Bell's Weekly Messenger 69
Bellini, Vincenzo (composer) 143
Ben-Hur (Young) 176, 187
Benjamin, Walter (cultural critic) 5–6, 8, 22, 30, 31, 42, 120, 135
Bennett, Tony (cultural critic) 87
Bentham, Jeremy (philosopher) 147
Bernhardt, Sarah 114, 215, 221, 242
Bertini, G.P. (hotelier) 276
Bertolini's restaurant, St Martin's Lane 61
Bertorelli's restaurant, Charlotte Street 163
Berwick Street (and market) 114, 115
Besant, Annie (reformer) 312
Bessone, Emma (ballerina) 234
Betley (Donizetti) 224
Beverley, William (theatre designer) 102
Bignell, Robert (wine merchant and owner of Argyll Rooms) 133
blackface performers 60, 77–8, 142–3, 206, 232
Blake, William 52
Blériot, Louis (aviator) 296
'Bloody Sunday' riots 312, 314
Bloomsbury 26, 62, 128, 149, 267
Blumenfeld, Ralph (American journalist in London) 192, 217, 242, 294
bohemianism 7, 10, 42, 61–2, 139, 149, 163, 169, 171, 179, 238, 254, 260, 291
Bonaparte, Napoleon 26, 75, 98, 99
Bonham's, Leicester Square (auctioneers) 20
bookshops and bookselling 23–24, 34, 92, 111, 148, 284, 307
Bon Marché, Paris 289, 294
Bond Street, Old and New 2, 16, 21, 23, 44, 49, 124, 138, 139, 190, 209, 256, 267, 268, 282, 285, 286, 295, 311, 312
Booth, Charles (social investigator) 112, 113–4, 311
Booth, Edwin (actor) 166
Borsay, Peter (urban historian) 2

Borsa, Mario (journalist and theatre critic) 176, 179, 189, 205
Bosjemans 100
Boucicault, Aristide (owner of Bon Marché) 289
Boucicault, Dion (playwright) 107, 153, 154, 156, 157, 167–69, 170, 304
Bouffes, Les (Offenbach) 145
Boulton, Ernest (cross-dresser) 134–5
Bourdieu, Pierre (sociologist) 137
Bowdler, John (moral reformer) 23
Bowles, Thomas Gibson (Conservative MP) 179
bowling alleys 44, 54–5, 206
Box and Cox (Morton) 169
boxes (in auditoriums): see audience and auditorium
boxing 44, 49, 50, 53, 69, 71
box office: see front of house staff
Braddon, Mary Elizabeth (novelist) 35, 167
Bratton, Jacky (theatre historian) 7, 76, 214
Brees, Samuel Charles (painter and champion of emigration) 94
Breward, Christopher (fashion historian) 7, 287
Brewer, John (historian) 18
Brewer Street, Soho 18
Britannia music hall, Glasgow 206
British Empire and imperialism 10, 39, 85, 89, 93, 100, 102, 176, 179, 198, 210, 215–8, 234, 235, 251, 255–6, 266, 276, 292, 294, 301–7, 314
British Museum 116, 149, 313
Brooks, Shirley (journalist and critic) 159, 255
Brook's, St James's Street (club) 50, 51
Brougham, Henry (reformer and legal expert) 54
Brown, Rose (cross-dresser) 135
Brummell, George Bryan 'Beau' 23, 42
Brunet's hotel, Leicester Square 267–8
Buckstone, John Baldwin (actor manager and playwright) 154, 157, 169, 171
Bullock, William (naturalist and founder of Egyptian Hall) 98
Bulwer-Lytton, Edward 80, 82, 183
Burdett, Sir Francis (radical MP) 52, 308
Burford, John (panoramas) 89–90
Burford, Robert (panoramas) 89–90, 284, 304
Burke, Edmund 23, 24
burletta 74, 76
burlesque 64, 72, 76–7, 80, 161, 176, 193, 221, 222, 224
Burlington Arcade 8, 22, 30, 32–36, 39, 74, 98, 119, 134, 172
Burlington House 32
Burlington Magazine 139

Burnand, Francis Cowley (playwright and comic writer) 125
Burns, John (labour leader and later MP) 311, 312
Burne-Jones, Sir Edward 173
Burton, Decimus (architect) 43
Burton, Richard (explorer and adventurer) 61
Byron, Lord George Gordon 23, 42, 64, 80
Byron, Henry James (playwright) 201

Café d'Italie, Old Compton Street 124
Café Monico, Shaftesbury Avenue 122, 310
Café Royal, Regent Street 254
Cambridge Circus 111, 219, 237
Campbell, Mrs. Patrick (actress) 129, 194, 301
Cannibal Club 61
Canning, George 24, 42
Carlisle Arms, Soho (pub) 61
Carlson, Marvin (theatreologist) 64
Carlton Club, Pall Mall 43, 311
Carlton hotel, Haymarket 184, 189, 194, 252, 253, 275
Carlyle, Thomas 43
Carmen (Bizet) 144
Carnegie, Andrew (industrialist) 294
Carroll, Lewis (Charles Dodgson) 177
Caryll, Ivan (composer) 226
Carte, Richard D'Oyly (agent, impresario and hotel owner) 125, 145, 180, 182, 219, 224, 237, 268, 271–5, 278, 296
Cash, Johnny (singer) 57
Casino, Strand (dance hall) 98
Caste (Robertson) 169
Catalani, Angelina (soprano) 69
Cataract of the Ganges, The (Moncrieff) 78, 304
Caterer and Hotel-Keeper's Gazette 264, 266, 270
Catherine Street, Covent Garden 147, 222
Catlin, George (painter) 100
Cavendish, Lord George 32
Cerito, Fanny (dancer) 47
Chadwick, Spencer (architect) 230
Chalk Line, The (Ware and M'Owen) 129, 191
Challis's hotel, Rupert Street 124
Chamberlain, Joseph 276
Chambre, Major Alan (social observer) 42, 51
Chant, Laura Ormiston (moral reformer) 236–7, 238, 244
Chapman, John (publisher and bookseller) 147
Chappell (music publisher) 141, 313
Charbonnel and Walker, New Bond Street (confectioners) 284–5
Charing Cross 23, 25, 30, 57, 111, 145, 203, 262, 279
Charing Cross Hospital 118

Charing Cross hotel, Charing Cross 266
Charing Cross Road vii, 111, 183, 239, 313
Charing Cross Station 110, 154, 259, 260, 266, 279, 285
Charley's Aunt (Thomas) 173, 176
Charles II 15, 18
Charles II Street, St James's 30
Charlotte, Queen, wife of George III 24, 88
Charlotte Street, Fitzrovia 139, 163
Charrington, Frederick (moral reformer) 235–6
Chartism 65, 82, 109, 148, 308–9
Chaucer, Geoffrey 55
Chelsea 62, 149
Chevalier, Albert (comedian) 211, 239
children and children's entertainment 39–40, 98, 102, 135, 188, 189, 239, 241, 295
Chilpéric (Hervé) 234
Chippendale, Thomas 17
cholera (1854) 116–7
Christie's, King Street (auctioneers) 139
Christy Minstrels, *see* Moore and Burgess Minstrels
Churchill, Winston 227, 237, 278
Cibber, Colley (actor and playwright) 13
Cider Cellars 41, 55–9
cinemas 2, 6, 97–8, 103, 241–2
circus 44, 63, 71, 72, 77, 231, 239
Clarendon hotel, New Bond Street 268
Claridge's hotel, Brook Street 256, 268, 270
Claridge, William (hotelier) 268
Clifford, Henry (barrister) 69
clothes and clothes shops, *see* fashion (clothing)
clubs and clubland 42–3, 50–1, 81, 87, 109, 148, 162–3, 249, 250, 253, 255, 262, 265, 278, 311, 312
Coal Hole, Strand (pub) 53–4, 56, 161
Cobb, James (librettist) 13
Cody, William F. ('Buffalo Bill') 269
coffee houses 18, 42, 253, 254, 268
Coffin, Hayden (actor) 230
Colette, Charles (singer) 217
Coliseum, *see* London Coliseum
Colleen Bawn, The (Boucicault) 168
Collier, Constance (actress) 130, 227, 228
Collins, Lottie (music hall artiste) 128, 211
Collins, Marie (comedian) 210–11
Collins, William Wilkie (novelist) 61, 132–3, 159, 167
Comedy Theatre, Panton Street 180, 181, 182, 275
concerts and concert halls 18, 19, 29–30, 107, 120, 138, 140–3, 315
Congreve, William 224
Connaught hotel, Grosvenor Square 277–8

Conquering Game, The 33
conservatism 4–5, 7, 10, 43, 75, 177–9, 194, 202, 215–6, 229, 302, 303, 305, 307, 315
Conservative Party 43
consumption and consumerism 4, 5, 6, 7, 17, 21–40, 103, 108, 241, 279–98, 314 (*see also* shops, shopping and retail)
Cook, Mrs. E.T. (observer of contemporary scene) 129, 178
Cooke, Thomas P. (actor) 171
Cook, Edward Dutton (theatre critic) 159
Cooke, George Alfred (stage magician) 102, 103, 138
Coppélia (ballet) 234
Count of Luxembourg, The (Hood, Ross and Lehár) 230
copyright 78, 82
'correct likeness' artists 140, 141
Corsican Brothers, The (Boucicault) 153, 154, 156, 167, 172, 176
Corsican Trap (stage effect) 153, 156, 168
cosmopolitanism 3–4, 7, 114, 117, 119, 238, 243, 252, 256, 266
cosmoramas 85, 91
Costa, Michael (conductor) 9, 46, 143, 144, 146
Country Wife, The (Wycherley) 68
Court Gazette, The 147
Court Theatre (later the Royal Court), Sloane Square 177, 193, 194
Covent Garden 1, 4, 14, 15, 18, 20, 21, 41, 46, 48–9, 52, 53, 55, 61, 62, 69, 81, 112, 121, 137, 138, 148, 204, 205, 269, 307, 308, 310, 311
Cramer and Co, Regent Street (musical instruments) 284
Cremorne Gardens (pleasure gardens) 44, 60
Crewe, Bertie (architect) 183
Crimean War 93, 96
Criterion restaurant, Piccadilly Circus 119, 122, 189, 249–50, 252, 301
Criterion Theatre, Piccadilly Circus 107, 110, 166, 178, 180, 189, 208, 223, 249
Crown and Anchor Tavern, Strand 52–3, 307
critics, theatre 3, 159, 192–3 (*see* names of individual theatre critics)
Crockford, William (casino owner) and St James's Club (Crockford's) 50–1
cross-dressing 53, 134–5, 176, 199
Crosse and Blackwell 113
Croxon, Arthur (theatre manager) 239
Cruikshank, George and Robert (illustrators) 49
Crystal Palace 141, 144
Cullwick, Hannah (servant and later wife of Arthur Munby) 165, 172, 285

Curzon, Lord George 276
Cyrano de Bergerac (Rostand) 301
Cyril's Success (Byron) 201

Daguerre, Louis (pioneer of photography) 90
Daily Chronicle, The 238
Daily News, The 159
Daily Telegraph, The 61, 146, 159, 193, 222, 236
Dallas, Eneas Sweetland (journalist) 115
Daly, Augustin (impresario) 230
Daly's Theatre, Cranbourn Street 180, 230, 282
Dame aux Camélias, La (Dumas *fils*) 160
Dance, Charles (playwright) 33
Dando, W.P. (stage designer and
    engineer) 237–8
dandyism 22, 42
Dare, Phyllis and Zena (Gaiety Girls) 227
Dart, Gregory (literary critic) 49
Darwin, Charles 171
D'Auban, John and Emma (dancers) 199
Daughlish, Dr. John (founder of ABC restaurant
    chain) 257
Davenant, Sir William (playwright and poet) 18
Davis, Jim (theatre historian) 160
Davis, Nathaniel Newnham (gourmet and *bon
    viveur*) 115, 124, 249, 251, 252, 256
Davy, Sir Humphrey (inventor) 137
Dean, James (gentleman's tailor) 24
Dean Street, Soho 114, 115, 116
Debenham and Freebody, Wigmore Street 289,
    291, 297
Debrett's bookshop, Piccadilly 24
De Montfort (Baillie) 78
Delmonico's restaurant, New York 251, 276
department stores 5, 7, 8, 36, 108, 109, 226, 241,
    280, 283, 288–97, 317 (*see also* names of
    individual department stores)
Desmond, Shaw (social observer) 197, 198
Diaghilev, Sergei (dance impresario) 242
Dibdin, Charles (musician and
    entertainer) 20, 75
Dickens, Charles 31, 49, 53, 55, 61, 78, 132, 146,
    147, 148, 159, 190, 239
Dickins and Jones, Regent Street (department
    store) 286, 288, 290
Didcott, Henry Jay (agent) 205
Dilara (ballet) 235
dioramas 85, 90–1, 96
Disney, Walt 177
Disraeli, Benjamin 42, 215, 216, 224
Doll's House, A (Ibsen) 193
Dombey and Daughter (Nicholson) 53
domestic service, *see* servants
    and domestic service

Don Giovanni (Mozart) 46
Donizetti, Gaetano 41, 46, 47, 224
Donne, William Bodham (Lord Chamberlain's
    examiner of plays) 160
Doré Gallery, New Bond Street 139
Dostoevsky, Fyodor 134
Doyle, Sir Arthur Conan 268–9
Douglas, Lord Alfred 235, 254
Dramatic Literary Property Act (1833) 82
Draper, The 285
dress circle, *see* audience and auditorium
Drury Lane 14, 59, 60, 81, 112, 118, 157, 214,
    308 *see also* Theatre Royal , Drury Lane
Ducrow, Andrew (showman) 77
Duggan, Marie (singer) 212
Duke of York's Theatre, St. Martin's
    Lane 177, 180
Dumas, Alexandre, the elder 34, 153
Dumas, Alexandre *fils* 160
Duncan, Mabel (Gaiety Girl) 228
Duval, Madame (*poses plastiques*) 94
dwarfs 92, 93
Dyer, Richard (critic) 221–2
Dyhouse, Carol (gender historian) 127

Earl, John (theatre historian) 199
East End 118, 160, 178, 204, 205, 213, 217
Echo, The 147
Economist, The 146, 147
Edward VII 25, 112, 161, 216, 223, 255, 306
Edwardes, George (theatre impresario) 8, 9, 221,
    222–30, 234, 243, 296
Ebbers, John (manager of the King's Theatre) 23
Egan, Pierce (novelist and journalist) 48–50, 52
Egyptian Hall, Piccadilly 8, 86, 98–102, 138,
    172, 241, 242
electricity and electrification of West
    End 124–4, 182, 208, 262, 270
Eliot, George (MaryAnn Evans) 34, 147, 159
Elliston, Robert (actor and theatre manager) 72
Elssler, Fanny (dancer) 47
Emaljanow, Victor (theatre historian) 160
Emden, Walter (architect) 183
Emerson, Ralph Waldo (philosopher) 147
Emery, Winifred (actress) 129
emigration 94
Emma, Queen of the Sandwich Islands/
    Hawaii 268
Empire, *see* British Empire and imperialism
Empire Theatre, Leicester Square 10, 19, 202,
    229, 230, 231, 234–7, 241, 242, 245,
    303, 306
Engels, Friedrich 116
English Constitution, The (Bagehot) 147

English Opera Company 72
Epitaux's restaurant, Pall Mall 256
Era, The 33, 133, 147, 162, 171, 242
Eros, Piccadilly Circus 107, 111
Escoffier, Auguste (chef) 251, 272–3, 275
Ethiopian Serenaders 78
Eugenie, Empress 268
Euphonia 100–1, 103
Euryanthe (Weber) 144
Evans, John (manager of Cider Cellars) 57
Evans, William Carpenter (manager of
      Evans's) 59
Evans's Late Joy's 59–61, 204
Evening News, The 282, 313
Everybody's Doing It! (Berlin) 243
Every Night Book, The 50
Examiner, The 148
Exeter Hall, Strand 141
exhibitions 5, 84–103

Faber, Professor (inventor of automata) 100–1
fancy goods and repositories 33–4, 36, 38, 39–40
Faraday, Michael (scientist) 98, 137
Farnon, Ellen (actress) 157
Farren, Nellie (actress) 125, 171, 224
fashion (clothing) 7, 9, 21, 24–25, 34, 109, 114,
      119, 127, 129, 227–8, 254, 282, 283, 285–8
      see also tailors and tailoring
Favorita, La (Donizetti) 46
Faucit, Helena (actress) 57, 157
Fawcett, Helen, *see* Faucit, Helena
Fawcett, John (playwright) 77
Fechter, Charles (actor) 156, 157
feminsation of West End: *see* women, female
      identity, feminisation and female
      consumers
Fidelio (Beethoven) 165
Fine Art Society, New Bond Street 139
fire (in theatres) 68, 71–2, 144, 181, 183, 232
Fitzrovia 139, 149
flâneur 6, 31, 42, 50, 86–7, 280
'flash' style 48–52, 57, 74, 133
Fleet Street 19, 23, 112, 124, 146, 148, 255,
      285, 301
Floradora (Hall and Stuart) 230
Florence, Henry L. (architect) 194
flower sellers 111
Flynn, Errol 305
Fortnum and Mason, Piccadilly 289
Forster, John (critic and biographer of
      Dickens) 148
Foucault, Michel 103
Fox, Charles James 23
Francatelli, Charles Elmé (chef) 51

Frankenstein (Shelley) 70, 101, 103
Franklin, Sir John (explorer) 96
Frascati's restaurant, Oxford Street 252
freak shows 98, 99
Freedom (Rowe and Harris) 305
freemasonry 275
French in West End (and French cultural
      influences) 16, 26, 28, 30, 32, 113, 114, 115,
      125, 160, 169, 184, 251, 252, 254, 255, 270,
      273 (*see also* Paris and Parisian style)
Fricour's hotel, St Martin's Lane 269
front on houses in theatres 8, 182, 184, 187, 235
      attendants/ushers 166, 197, 198, 250
      bars 182, 192, 204, 207–8, 231, 237
      booking, box office and ticketing 164, 182,
            190–1, 265, 271, 283
      refreshments 166–7
Froude, James Anthony (historian) 147
Fry, Roger (artist and critic) 140
Fuller, Loie (dancer) 239

Gaiety Girl, A (Hall, Greenbank and Jones) 225
Gaiety Girls 130, 221, 225–9, 244, 315
Gaiety Theatre and restaurant, Strand 112, 121,
      125, 131, 157, 161, 163, 180, 183, 193, 221,
      222–29, 245, 252, 275, 288, 306, 307
galleries, *see* art galleries
gambling 43, 50–2, 64, 74
Gambrinus restaurant, Glasshouse Street 256
Gavarni, Paul (illustrator) 147
Gardoni, Italo (opera singer) 46
Garrick Club 81
Garrick Theatre, Charing Cross Road 180
Garrick's Head hotel, Bow Street 53
Gatano, Joseph (giant) 92
Gatti family and food/entertainment
      empire 259–62
Gatti's restaurant, Strand 121, 260–2, 263,
      302, 316
Gatti's Under-The-Arches (music
      hall) 203–4, 260
Gatrell, Vic (social historian) 42, 61
Gay Lord Quex, The (Pinero) 179
Geisha, The (Hall, Greenbank and Jones) 230
Geist, Johann (architectural historian) 31
gender 6, 41, 109, 135, 285
Genée, Adeine (ballerina) 235
Geological Society, Burlington House 137
George I 111
George II 14
George III 13, 88, 92, 308
George IV 23, 26, 70, 268
George V 216, 230
German Theatre, Leicester Square 75

Ghosts (Ibsen) 193
Gilbert, Alfred (sculptor) 111
Gilbert, Sir John (artist) 147
Gilbert, Sir William S. (librettist) 145, 146, 166, 173, 224, 226, 274
Gilbey, W and A (wine merchants) 39
Gilchrist, Constance (Gaiety Girl) 227
Gill, Basil (actor) 197
Gillette, William (actor) 261
Giovanni in London (Moncrieff) 80
Giselle (ballet) 47
glamour 3, 9, 127–31, 135, 215, 227–8, 313, 315
glass 22, 24, 25, 31, 37
Gladstone, William 159, 177, 217
Glee Club 53
Globe Theatre, Newcastle Street 165, 173
Globe Theatre, Shaftesbury Avenue (now the Gielgud) 111, 183
Gloucester, Duke of (opera supporter) 46, 71
Gluckstein, Montague (tobacco retail and caterer) 257, 258, 259
Goulden, John (music historian) 143
Goupil Gallery, New Bond Street 139
Gordon, General Charles 303–4, 307
Gordon Riots (1780) 19
gothic 30, 70, 101, 103
Grahn, Lucile (dancer) 47
Grafton House, New Bond Street (fabric shop) 21
Grand Hotel, Northumberland Avenue 122, 267, 270–1
Grand Hotel, Paris 184, 270
Grant, Baron Albert (MP and philanthropist) 111–2
Grant, James (social observer) 9, 43, 44, 48, 51, 63, 72
Graydon, James (manager of Middlesex Music Hall) 205
Great Exhibition (1851) 92, 96, 97, 102, 144, 154, 280, 283
Great Globe, Leicester Square 96
Great Windmill Street, Soho 116
Greek Street, Soho 115, 116
Greenmore, John 'Paddy' 60
Grieve, family (set designers) 90, 224
Grimaldi, Joseph (comic actor) 76
Grisi, Carlotta 47
Grosvenor Gallery, New Bond Street 124
Grosvenor hotel, Victoria 266
Gundle, Stephen (cultural historian) 127
Gunn, Simon (urban historian) 107
Guy Domville (James) 191
Gye, Frederick (opera impresario) 143–5, 146

Hadfield, James (would-be assassin) 13–14, 308
Hagen, Gunther von (anatomist) 102
Haggard, H. Rider 235, 305
hairdressing 22, 34, 35, 39
Halford, J, St Martin's Lane (grocer) 256
Hall, Owen (librettist) 230
Hall-Witt, Jennifer (opera historian) 45
Hamer, Hetty (Gaiety Girl) 227
Hamilton, Kate (night house owner) 131–2
Hampton and Russell, Leicester Square (furniture) 284
Hanover Gallery, New Bond Street 139
Hanover Square 94, 117
Hanover Square Rooms 30
Hardie, James Keir (founder of the Labour Party) 307, 312
Harding, Howell and Co. (early department store) 36, 289
Hardy, Thomas (radical shoe maker) 308
harlequinade 76, 221
Harley Street, Mayfair 25
Harp, Drury Lane (pub) 81
Harris, Augustus the elder (impresario) 144
Harris, Augustus the younger (impresario) 145, 181, 219, 221, 234, 235, 237, 243, 304, 305
Harris, Frank (journalist and man about town) 254
Harrods, Knightsbridge 226, 288, 291, 313
Harvey, Sir John Martin (actor) 127
Hase, Paul (ladies's shoes) 35
Hatchard, John and Hatchard's bookshop 23–24
Hatchett's hotel, Piccadilly 269
Haydon, Benjamin (artist) 37
Haussmann, Baron Georges-Eugène 21, 270
Hawtrey, Charles (actor manager) 164, 181
Haymarket 2, 3, 15, 30, 37, 42, 44, 48, 88, 94, 107, 113, 131–4, 312, 313
Hazlitt, William 64, 79, 159
Hedda Gabler (Ibsen) 193
Hemyng, Bracebridge (novelist and journalist) 35
Henrietta Street, Covent Garden 54
Henry V (Shakespeare) 154
Henty, George Alfred (author of boys' fiction) 305
Her Majesty's Theatre, Haymarket (formerly the King's Theatre/Italian Opera House) 8, 23, 30, 37, 41, 44–8, 62, 65, 122, 143, 144, 164, 165, 173, 177, 180, 181, 184, 189, 190–1, 193, 194–8, 235, 252
Herman, Henry (playwright) 193
Hibbert, Henry (man about town) 159, 205, 214, 215, 227

Hill, Jenny (music hall entertainer) 8, 203, 211, 212–15, 224
Hippodrome, *see* London Hippodrome
HMS Pinafore (Gilbert and Sullivan) 145, 274
Hobson, John Atkinson (economist) 217
Holcroft, Thomas (playwright and radical) 70
Holland, Henry (architect) 14
Hollingshead, John (journalist and theatre manager) 100–1, 103, 116, 121, 125, 145, 157, 159, 163, 164, 165, 180, 193, 221–5, 245
Holloway, Mr (stage door keeper at the Globe) 188
Holywell Street, near Strand 57, 61, 148
homosexuality 134–5, 221, 235, 249
Hope, Drury Lane (pub) 59
Horocastle, Frederick (bookseller) 34
Horse and Dolphin, Soho (pub) 59
hospitality and hospitality industry 10, 250, 255, 256, 263, 264, 265, 266, 268, 280, 309, 314, 315
Hotel Cecil, Strand 189, 265, 275–7, 302
hotels 3, 10, 15, 43, 83, 107, 109, 110, 121, 180, 250, 254, 264–78, 288 (*see also* names of individual hotels)
Hotel Victoria, Northumberland Avenue 270, 271
'Hottentot Venus', *see* Baartman, Sara
Household Words 147–8
Howell, James and Co. (jewellers) 28
Hudson, Thomas (singer) 56
Hughes Molly (memoirist) 189, 282
Hugo, Victor 34
Huguenots, Les (Meyerbeer) 144
Hullo Ragtime! (Hirsch) 242
Hullo Tango! (Hirsch) 243
Human Nature (Harris and Pettitt) 304
Hummums hotel, Covent Garden 269
The Humourist (James Cobb) 13
Hunt, G.W. (song writer) 215–6
Hunt, Henry (radical) 53
Hunt and Roskell (jewellers) 23
Hyde Park 16, 42, 92, 311
Hytner, Nicholas (theatre director) 10

Ibsen, Henrik 64, 169, 173, 178–9, 193, 215, 245
Illustrated London News, The 48, 51, 86, 100, 146–7, 154
Illustrated Times, The 162
imperialism, *see* British Empire and imperialism
Importance of Being Earnest, The (Wilde) 176
India and Indian influences in West End 255–6, 276, 291, 292–4
International Working Men's Association 116
In Town (Ross and Tanner) 225–6

Irving, Henry (actor manager) 72, 119, 127, 157, 171, 173, 177, 180, 181, 187, 188, 190, 191, 192, 193, 205, 306
Isaacs, Lewis H. (architect) 194
Italian Opera Company 37
Italian Opera House, *see* Her Majesty's Theatre
Ivanhoe (Sullivan) 219

Jacobi, Georges (musical director) 233
Jacomelli, Peter (historian of the Gatti family) 261–2
Jaeger, Gustav, Regent Street (tailor) 287
James, Henry 8, 121, 156, 166, 169, 190, 253, 266, 268, 279
jazz 242–3
Jeffs, William (bookseller) 34
Jenoure, Aida (actress) 163–4
Jermyn Street, St James's 17, 132
Jerrold, Blanchard, journalist 56
Jerrold, Douglas, playwright and journalist 60
Jessie Brown; or, The Relief of Lucknow (Boucicault) 304
Jewish immigrants 115–6
Joel, Herr Von (yodeller) 56
Johnson, Dr Samuel 1
Johnson and Co. (hatters) 28
Jones, Henry Arthur (playwright) 179, 193
Jones, Inigo (architect) 15
Jones, Owen (architect) 141
Jones, Sidney (composer) 226
Jopling, Louise (artist) 138, 139
journalism and newspapers 61, 86, 146–8 , 149, 173, 255 (*see* names of individual newspapers)
Joyce, Patrick (social historian) 202
Judge, Jack (singer) 218
Judge and Jury Society 53–4
Julius, William (cross-dresser) 135
Jullien, Louis (conductor) 141, 143
Jupp, James (stage door keeper at the Gaiety) 188, 227

Kean, Charles (actor) 130, 149, 153, 154–5, 157, 171, 172, 176
Kean, Edmund (actor) 21, 64, 67, 68, 78, 79–80
Kean's Head, Drury Lane (pub) 81
Keeley, Mary Anne (actress) 57, 171
Kemble, John Philip (actor) 68–9, 79, 82
Kendal, Milne and Faulkener (Manchester department store) 36
Kensington (including South Kensington) 16, 149, 267
Kettner's restaurant, Soho 115
Killigrew, Thomas (courtier and dramatist) 18

Kill That Fly! (Grossmith) 243
Kilpack, Thomas (tobacconist) 54–5
King John (Shakespeare) 154
Kingsway 2, 112, 183
King Street, St James's 43, 54–5, 59, 81, 157, 267
King's Theatre, *see* Her Majesty's Theatre
Kipling, Rudyard 305, 306
Kiralfy, Imre (producer) 258
Kirwan, Daniel (social observer) 231
Kracauer, Siegfried (cultural critic) 228–9, 264
Krosso, Professor ('The Modern Hercules') 92

Lacon and Ollier (booking agents) 190
Lancaster, John (businessman and theatre
    owner) 180
Lady Audley's Secret (Braddon) 35
Lady of Lyons (Bulwer-Lytton) 80, 188
Lady Windermere's Fan (Wilde) 135
Landseer, Edwin 94
Langham Place Group 109
Langley, Leanne (music historian) 29
Lanner, Katti (choreographer) 235
Lardner, Dionysus (editor) 167
Lawrence, Katie (music hall entertainer) 203–4
Lanchester, Elsa (actress and bohemian) 242
Langtry, Lilly (actress and socialite) 129,
    178–9, 278
La Roche, Sophie von (German novelist) 24, 123
Laurent, Emile (conductor) 133
lavatories 109, 170–1, 185, 280, 295
Lawrence, Gerald (actor) 197
Lawson, Lionel (businessman and theatre
    owner) 180, 222
Layton & Shears (trader in cloth) 21
Lea, Lillian (singer) 302
Leah the Forsaken (Daly) 159
Leamar, Kate and Alice (music hall artistes) 255
Lee, Nelson (theatre manager) 155–6
Legnani, Pierina (ballerina) 234
Leicester Square 1, 5, 19, 51, 61, 75, 85, 86, 88,
    89, 91–8, 102, 107, 111–2, 113, 118, 172,
    218, 230–37, 239, 256, 304, 310, 311
Lemon, Mark (journalist) 148
Leno, Dan (music hall entertainer) 205, 211,
    216, 237
Leopold II of Belgium 268
Lever, Ashton (naturalist) 19
Leverton, Bill (box office manager) 190–1
Levey, Abraham (porter at gambling den) 51
Lewes, George Henry (philosopher and
    critic) 34, 46, 79–80, 147, 159
Lewis, John (department store owner) 283
Leybourne, George ('Champagne
    Charlie') 199, 260

Liberal Party 43
liberalism 147
Liberty Arthur Lasenby (draper) 283, 291–4
Liberty's (fashions and fabric) 8, 119, 124, 280,
    283, 290, 291–4, 313
Lidusdroph, Herr (Russian fleas) 94
Life in London (Pierce Egan) 48–9, 74
light, artificial 24, 30, 88, 119, 122, 123–5
light entertainment 10, 202, 211, 219–45
    (defined 221)
lighting, theatrical 88, 123–4
Limmer's hotel, Conduit Street 268
Lincoln, Abraham 169
Lind, Jenny (soprano) 143
Linell, Alfred (radical) 312
Linton, Eliza Lynn (journalist and novelist) 146
Linwood Gallery (Savile House) 93, 96
Liston, Harry (comedian) 199
Liszt, Franz 29
Little Tich (comedian) 239
Liverpool Street Station 110
Lloyd, Arthur (singer and comedian) 211
Lloyd, Marie (Matilda Wood) (music hall
    entertainer) 204, 205, 211
Lloyd's Weekly Newspaper 57
local government 17, 109 (*see also* London
    County Council; Metropolitan Board
    of Works)
Lohengrin (Wagner) 144
Loibl, Ernst (music hall owner) 206
London as capital city 3, 4, 15
London Assurance (Boucicault) 167
London Coliseum, St Martin's Lane 4, 10, 219,
    231, 239–41, 243, 251
London Corresponding Society 13, 52, 308
London County Council 109, 112, 181, 184,
    211–12, 235, 236, 237, 238, 309
London Hippodrome, Cranbourn Street 10,
    231, 239, 241, 242, 243, 302
London Labour and the London Poor
    (Mayhew) 146, 148
London Library, St James's Square 43
London Palladium (variety house), Argyll
    Street 10, 238, 240–1
London Pavilion, Piccadilly Circus (music
    hall) 102, 107, 122, 202, 203, 204, 206–16,
    220, 221, 303, 312, 313
London School of Economics 112
Longs hotel, New Bond Street 267
looking, act of 32, 34, 85–91, 103, 120, 122, 123,
    133–4, 146, 172, 290, 295
Lord Chamberlain 18, 67, 70, 72, 82, 83, 160,
    170, 176, 178, 181, 193, 194, 205, 238
Love for Love (Congreve) 224

lower middle class 110, 140, 297
Lowther Arcade (Strand) 39, 98, 227, 260
Lowther Bazaar (Strand) 91
Ludwig II of Bavaria 219
Lumière brothers (pioneers of cinema) 241
Lumley, Benjamin (opera impresario) 143
Lyceum Theatre, Wellington Street 21, 47, 71–2,
    80, 83, 119, 144, 156, 169, 173, 180, 183,
    185, 187, 188, 191, 306
Lyons, Joseph (food entrepreneur) and Lyons
    company 251, 255, 257–9, 262, 301,
    309, 313
Lyric Theatre, Shaftesbury Avenue 111, 180, 183

Macaulay, Thomas Babington (Lord) 39, 42, 155
Macaulay, Zachary (abolitionist and
    reformer) 84
Macbeth (Shakespeare) 69
MacDermott, Gilbert Hastings (singer) 211,
    212, 215–6, 218
Macready, William (actor) 57, 67, 80, 81,
    157, 159
McKellar, Elizabeth (historian) 15
Mafeking, relief of (Boer War) 301–2, 303,
    306, 314
Magazine of Art 128
Magda (Sudermann) 301
magic lantern shows 97–8, 103,124, 172, 290
magic (stage) and conjuring 98, 103, 172
Maid and the Magpie, The (Pocock) 71
Maiden Lane 8, 41, 55–60, 62, 162
Major Barbara (Shaw) 193
Mann, Tom (trade unionist) 309, 310
Maples furniture, Tottenham Court
    Road 275–6, 277, 289
Marks and Spencer, Oxford Street 39
Marshall, Jeanette (diarist) 283
Marshall and Snelgrove, Oxford Street
    (department store) 138, 283, 286, 290,
    312, 313
Marshall Field, Chicago (department store) 289,
    294, 295
Martin, John (painter) 98, 172
Marvell, Andrew 55
Marx, Karl 116
Maskelyne, John Nevil (stage magician) 102,
    103, 138
mass culture, concept of 8
Matcham, Frank (architect) 183, 219, 239, 240
Mathews, Charles, the elder (actor) 84, 86
Mathews, Charles James (actor) 80, 157
matinees in theatres 109, 154, 163–4
Mayhew, Henry (social investigator) 9, 23, 28,
    31, 34, 35, 114, 123, 146, 148

Mayfair 2, 16, 17, 18, 19, 22, 25, 26, 42, 70, 109,
    117, 137, 139, 143, 144, 157, 194, 266, 267,
    277, 283, 284, 286
Melba, Nellie (opera singer) 145
melodrama 3, 30, 70–1, 74, 76, 119, 165, 169,
    224, 261, 262, 307, 314
men and masculinity 6, 7, 9, 38, 41, 42–3, 49–50,
    55–62, 92, 94, 135, 190, 214, 226, 251, 285,
    286, 287–8, 295, 297, 310
Mendelssohn, Felix 29, 141
Merchant of London, The (Serle) 78
Merchant of Venice, The (Shakespeare) 79
Merry Widow, The (Lehar) 230
Metropole hotel, Whitehall Place (now the
    Corinthia) 267, 270, 302
Metropolitan Board of Works 109, 111, 181, 206
Metropolitan Music Hall, Edgware 203–4
Metropolitan Opera House, New York 219
Meyerbeer, Giacomo (composer) 144
Mewès, Charles (architect) 277
middle classes 4, 6, 7, 10, 17, 24, 40, 42, 45, 46–7,
    48, 53, 71, 72, 86, 87, 93, 98, 102, 107–8,
    109, 110, 112, 120, 121, 132, 135, 136, 141,
    147, 149, 154, 155, 159, 160, 161, 162, 163,
    169, 170, 171, 172, 178, 185, 190, 196, 206,
    213, 251, 260, 266, 272, 275, 281, 284, 285,
    289, 295, 297, 298, 302, 312, 314
    (*see also* lower middle class)
Middlesex Music Hall, Drury Lane (now the
    Gillian Lynne Theatre) 204, 205, 214
Mill, James (economist) 147
Mill, John Stuart (philosopher) 148, 308
Millais, John Everett 139
Milner, Alfred Viscount (imperial
    statesman) 276
minor (non-patent) theatres 70–5 (*see also*
    names of individual theatres)
Mintram, William (hairdresser) 35
Miserables, Les (Boublil and Schönberg) 168
Miss Saigon (Boublil and Schönberg) 168
Mivart, James Edward (hotelier) 268
    (*see* Claridge's hotel)
modernism 222, 244
modernity 6, 31, 32
Mogul Saloon, Drury Lane (became Middlesex
    Music Hall) 60
Mohamed, Fateh (restaurateur) 256
Monckton, Lionel (composer) 226
Moncrieff, William Thomas (playwright) 33, 67,
    74, 78, 80, 304
Money (Bulwer Lytton) 183
Montgomery, Walter (actor) 224
Morley's hotel, Trafalgar Square 266, 268
Moore, Albert (artist) 184–5

Moore, Decima (Gaiety Girl) 227
Moore and Burgess Minstrels 142
More, Sir Thomas 222
Morning Chronicle, The 146, 159, 199
Morning Post, The 94
Morris William (artist, poet, businessman and
    socialist) 140, 222, 294, 312
Mort, Frank (cultural historian) 7
Morton, Charles (music hall entrepreneur) 199,
    205, 237
Morton, John Madison (playwright) 169
Moses and Sons, ready-to-wear clothes (later
    Moss Bros) 287
Moss, Sir Edward (owner of Moss
    Empires) 219, 239
Mozart, Wolfgang Amadeus 18, 46
Mudie's (library) 39
Munby, Arthur (diarist) 9, 130–1, 132, 142,
    154–5, 165, 199–200, 285
Murray, John (publisher) 23
music 9, 44–8, 55–62, 71, 120, 140–46, 149, 159,
    173, 259, 263
music hall 10, 48, 52, 60, 62, 107, 120, 128, 131,
    172, 180, 191, 192, 199–218, 220, 234, 239,
    242, 245, 250, 255, 262, 302, 303, 307
    (*see also* variety theatre and names of
    individual music halls)
musical, stage 9, 230
musical comedy 222, 224–30, 240
Musical World, The 141, 205
Mysteries of London, The (Reynolds) 49, 148

Nana Shib (ballet) 233
Napoleon III 25, 34, 219
Napoleonic Wars 14
Nash, John (architect) 26–30, 39, 43, 108
Nash, Jolly John (music hall singer and
    comedian) 206
National Gallery, Trafalgar Square 39, 91,
    138, 187
National Gallery of Practical Science,
    Strand 98
National Theatre 10, 194
National Vigilance Association 236–7, 238
Neal Street, Covent Garden 112
Nelson, Horatio 89
Nerigne, Nydia (dancer) 238
New Exchange, Strand 15
New Gallery, Regent Street 140
New Oxford Street 112
New Strand Subscription Theatre, Strand 82
New Swell's Guide to the Bowers of Venus 35
New Theatre, St Martin's Lane (now the Noel
    Coward) 122, 177, 183

New York 3, 4, 125, 173, 176, 214, 219, 243,
    281, 286
New York Daily Tribune 116
Newman, Robert (musical impresario) 141
Newman Street 18, 139
Newton, Henry Chance (theatre critic) 213
Newton, Isaac, Leicester Square (Indian
    fabrics) 292
Nicholson, Renton (rake and satirist) 50,
    53–4, 57
nightlife 4, 15, 41, 44, 121, 123, 249
night houses 131–2
Nijinsky, Vaslav 242
Nobby Songster, The 57–9
Norman-Neruda, Wilma (violinist) 142
Northumberland Avenue, Westminster 110, 122
novel, the (as form) 30, 33, 35, 39, 42, 49, 86, 89,
    146, 149, 159, 173, 264
Novelty Theatre, Great Queen Street 180, 193
nudity and undress 54, 91, 94–6, 238

Obi: Or, Three Finger'd Jack (Fawcett) 77
Obscene Publications Act (1857) 148
obscenity 53, 55, 57–59, 83, 95, 148, 205, 211–12
Octoroon, The (Boucicault) 167
Odeon Leicester Square vii, 242
Offenbach, Jacques (composer) 145, 224
Offley's, Covent Garden (song and supper
    room) 54
Old Compton Street, Soho 5, 115, 124
Old Oak Chest, The (Scott) 74
Old Price (O.P.) riots 68–70, 83, 183, 307
Old Vic (*see* Royal Coburg Theatre)
Olympic Theatre, Wych Street 33, 49, 71, 72, 75,
    80, 83, 165
omnibus transport 110, 171
Only Way, The (Harvey and others) 127
opera (including light opera) 23, 30, 41, 42,
    44–8, 62, 67, 74, 80, 143–6, 199, 200, 221,
    222, 224, 231, 271, 315
Opera Comique, Strand 129
Orczy, Baroness Emma (novelist) 257
oriental dancing 238–9
Osborne's hotel, Adelphi 269
Our American Cousin (Taylor) 169–70
Our Army and Navy (ballet) 234
Our Miss Gibbs (Ross, Caryll and
    Monckton) 226
Overland Route, The (Taylor) 165
Oxenford, John (theatre critic and
    playwright) 159
Oxford Circus 28, 29, 154
Oxford Music Hall, Oxford Street 199–200,
    204, 215

Oxford Street 1, 2, 15, 18, 23, 24, 26, 28, 36, 37, 39, 91, 107, 109, 113, 118, 123, 124, 130, 139, 140, 154, 157, 240, 241, 258, 259, 280, 282, 283, 285, 286, 288, 289, 290, 294, 295, 311, 312

Paddington Station 110
Palace Theatre, Shaftesbury Avenue 111, 128, 217, 231, 237–8, 241, 242, 306
Palais Garnier, Paris 219
Pall Mall, St James's 30, 43. 123, 137, 140, 289, 311
Pall Mall Gazette 159
Palladino, Emma (ballerina) 234
Palsgrave restaurant, Strand 257
Pankhurst, Christabel 313
Pankhurst, Emmeline 312, 313
Pankhurst, Sylvia 312
panoramas 6, 30, 85, 86, 87–91, 94, 98, 103, 172, 304
Pantheon, Oxford Street 22, 36–39, 289
pantomimes 74, 76, 77, 101, 160, 163, 177, 205, 214, 221, 222, 304
Panton Street, Haymarket 50, 131–2, 206, 256
Paris (and Parisian style) 4, 5, 6, 15, 16, 21, 22, 26, 28, 30, 32, 34, 42, 47, 61, 80, 84, 90, 110, 121, 125, 129, 130, 135, 144, 145, 184, 219, 223, 241, 243, 253, 260, 264, 266, 270, 272, 275, 277, 283, 286, 287, 289, 294, 298
(see also French in West End)
Parker, Louis (playwright) 197–8
Park, Frederick (cross-dresser) 134–5
Pas de Quatre (ballet) 47
patent theatres 18, 65–70, 73, 80, 81–3, 157, 160, 180 (see also names of individual theatres)
Patti, Adelina (soprano) 144
Paul, Robert W (pioneer of film) 241
Pavlova, Anna (dancer) 242
Pearson, Hesketh (actor and biographer) 196
Peel, Sir Robert 54, 83
Penco, Rosina (soprano) 144
Penniket, Tom (saloon singer) 56
Peril (Sardou) 156
Perrot, Jules (choreographer) 48
Perry (hairdresser) 33
Pertoldi, Ermenia (ballerina) 233
Peter Pan (Barrie) 177
Pethick-Lawrence, Emmeline (Suffragette) 313
phantasmagoria 124
Phantom of the Opera, The (Lloyd Webber) 158
Phelps, Samuel (actor) 170
Philharmonic Society 29–30, 141, 142
Phipps, Charles (theatre architect) 183, 184, 194, 222, 230

photographs and photograph shops 34, 85, 90, 130–1, 284
Piccadilly 3, 15, 23, 32, 33, 36, 42, 84, 86, 87, 98, 102, 111, 123, 137, 141, 258, 267, 277, 285, 302, 308, 309
Piccadilly Circus (Regent Circus) 1, 28, 107, 108, 110, 111, 119, 123, 134, 191, 202, 206, 207, 208, 218, 223, 249, 285, 301, 302, 303, 312, 315
Pickwick Papers, The (Dickens) 55
Pigott, Edward Smith (Lord Chamberlain) 179
Piggott, Mostyn (journalist) 192
Pinero, Arthur Wing (playwright) 179
Pitt the younger, William 23
Piver, J.T. (perfumer) 28
Place, Francis (tailor and reformer) 25, 82, 308
Planché, James Robinson (playwright) 80, 96
Platt, Len (historian of popular culture) 226
Play Pictorial 130, 226, 315
playwright, profession of 78–9, 167–70
(see also names of individual playwrights)
pleasure district, its meanings defined and explored 1–10, 15, 23, 31, 41, 49, 64, 74, 86, 87, 96, 102, 103, 107, 118, 119–25, 135–6, 140, 143, 147, 157, 173, 217–8, 245, 250, 256, 263, 280, 281, 282, 288, 290, 298, 307, 314–6
police and policing 51–2, 112, 132, 133, 134, 148, 160
Poole, Henry (gentleman's tailor) 24, 28
Poole, Richard (pewter ware) 17
Poor of New York/Liverpool/London/Manchester, The (Boucicault) 167–8
populist palatial 4, 61, 200–2 (defined), 208, 218, 231, 241, 242, 243, 260, 264, 314
pornography 35, 53, 54, 57–9, 61, 130–136, 148, 238
poses plastiques (tableaux vivants or living statues) 57, 94–6, 102, 103, 128, 211, 234, 237, 238
posters 63, 122, 127, 128–9, 288, 290
Poynter, Charles (fashion designer) 286
poverty 112, 113–4, 116, 117, 118, 148, 302, 310–12
Pre-Raphaelite painters 140, 291
Prince's Theatre, Shaftesbury Avenue 164
Prince of Wales, see Edward VII
Prince of Wales's Theatre, Charlotte Street (formerly the Queen's Theatre) 156, 161, 163, 164, 169, 181
Prince of Wales's Theatre, Coventry Street 180, 183
Prince Regent, see George IV
Princess's Theatre, Oxford Street 47, 130, 153, 154, 155, 166, 168, 169, 172, 183, 193, 306
Prisoner of Zenda, The (Rose) 176

Private Secretary, The (Hawtrey) 164
private theatres 75
programmes, theatre 154, 165–6, 182, 189, 192, 197, 202–3, 208–10, 217
prostitution and sex work 2, 22, 29, 35, 41, 46, 49, 50, 60, 68, 75, 96, 113, 117, 123, 131–5, 148, 154, 199, 212, 217, 223, 231, 235–7, 244
pubs 4, 14, 44, 50, 52–60, 64, 80, 83, 107, 112, 120, 134, 149, 199, 205, 208, 214, 315
Pulteneys hotel, Piccadilly 267
Punch 54, 148, 159, 255
Puritani, I (Bellini) 143
Pygmalion (Shaw) 193
Pygopagis twins 99

Queen, The 286
Queen's Bazaar, Oxford Street 91
Queen's Hall, Upper Regent Street 141, 313
Queen's Head, by the Haymarket (pub) 44
Queen's Theatre, Charlotte Street, *see* Prince of Wales's Theatre
Queen's Theatre, Long Acre 183, 184, 185
Queen's Theatre, Shaftesbury Avenue 111, 183, 184
Quicksands, Or, The Pillars of Society (Ibsen) 193

radicalism, political 9, 52–3, 67, 114, 116, 148, 177, 303, 307–10
race and race theories 6, 7, 77–8, 84–5, 100, 167 (*see also* blackface performers)
Racing Times, The 147
Ragtime 242–3
railways 110, 168, 266
Rappaport, Erica D (social historian) 7, 280, 282
Ray, Gabrielle (Gaiety Girl) 227, 228
Rayner, (Lionel) Benjamin (actor) 82
Redfern, John, Conduit Street (ladies' fashion) 286
Reed, Austin (male tailoring) 287
Reed, Charles Cory (moral reformer) 212
Reeve, Ada (actress) 226, 258
Reeve, John (actor) 171
Reform Club, Pall Mall 43
Regent's Hall, Oxford Street 118
Regent's Park 26
Regent Street 1, 5, 21, 22, 24, 25–30, 32, 38, 39, 51, 74, 91, 97, 107, 108, 109, 110, 111, 113, 119, 123, 124, 132, 133, 138, 140, 141, 218, 240, 280, 282, 283, 284, 285, 286, 288, 289, 291, 294, 301, 310, 312, 313
religious worship 118
respectability 60, 61, 131, 211, 217, 223, 265, 280, 315

restaurants 2, 3, 10, 15, 19, 30, 83, 107, 109, 114–5, 120–1, 122, 124, 142, 166, 180, 207, 249–63, 264, 265, 266, 295, 302
Reszke, Jean de and Edouard de (opera singers) 145
Reynolds, George William MacArthur (novelist and journalist) 49, 148, 308
Reynolds's Newspaper 132, 133, 148
Richardson, Mary (Suffragette) 313
Rice, Thomas 'Daddy' (entertainer) 78
Richard III (Shakespeare) 82
Richelieu (Bulwer-Lytton) 80
Ridley, Sir Matthew (Home Secretary) 309
Rigoletto (Verdi) 144
Rimmel, Eugene, Strand (perfumier) 166, 279, 286
Ritchie, J. Ewing (journalist) 133
Ritz, César (hotelier) 124, 271–75
Ritz hotel, Piccadilly 265, 277, 278, 284, 295, 315
Roberts, David (artist) 90
Roberts, Field Marshall Lord Frederick 276
Robertson, Tom (playwright) 157, 169, 177, 193
Robey, George (comedian) 239
Robins, Elizabeth (actress) 193, 194
Robinson, Lou (scientific exhibitions) 211
Peter Robinson, Oxford Street (department store) 285, 290, 311–2
Romano's restaurant, Strand 205, 251, 254–5, 262
Romanticism 47, 64, 70, 79, 89, 103, 172
Rook, Clarence (journalist) 285
Rosa, Carl (impresario) 144
Ross, Adrian (lyricist) 226
Ross, W.G. (entertainer) 41, 56–7
Rossetti, Dante Gabriel (artist) 132
Rossini, Gioachino 92, 259, 262
Rothschild family 25
Royal Academy, Burlington House 49, 94, 138, 139, 313
Royal Astronomical Society, Burlington House 137
Royal Coburg Theatre (Old Vic) 71, 82, 90
Royal English Opera House, *see* Palace Theatre, Shaftesbury Avenue
Royal Harmonic Institution 29
Royal Institute of Painters in Watercolours, Piccadilly 140
Royal Institution, Albermarle Street 137
Royal Literary Fund 78
Royal Opera Arcade 30
Royal Opera House, Covent Garden (Bow Street) 18, 42, 47, 49, 65, 67, 68, 70, 75, 77, 80, 81–2, 83, 90, 141, 143–5, 146, 160, 161, 170, 180, 200, 219, 242, 261, 307

Royal Panopticon of Science and Art
    (*see* Alhambra Theatre)
Royal Polytechnic Institution, Regent Street 97,
    172, 241
Royal Society, Burlington House 137, 138
Royal Strand Theatre, Strand 134
Royal Variety Performance 217
Royalty Theatre, Dean Street 114, 145, 193, 301
Rule, Thomas (restaurant owner) 55
Rules (restaurant), Maiden Lane 4, 20, 55
Ruskin, John (art critic and social reformer) 89,
    121, 159
Russell, Lord John 259

Sablonière hotel, Leicester Square 269
Sacred Harmonic Society 141
Sadler's Wells Theatre 71, 204
St. Cecilia 276
St Giles 112, 114, 118, 311
St. Giles's Boys School 118
St. James's 2, 16, 17, 18, 30, 41, 42, 43, 44, 51, 62,
    81, 144, 162, 262, 267
St James's Hall, Piccadilly (concert hall) 138,
    141–3, 263
St James's Palace 16
St James's Square 30, 43
St James's Street 16, 42, 50, 91
St James's Theatre, King Street 135, 145, 157,
    176, 178, 180, 191
St Martin's-in-the-Fields 118, 310
St Martin's Lane, Bedfordbury 17, 18, 61, 183,
    219, 312
St Martin's School of Art, Long Acre 140
St Martin's Theatre, West Street 183
St Pancras Station 110
St Paul's Church, Covent Garden (the actor's
    church) 118
Saints and Sinners (Jones) 179
Sala, George Augustus, journalist and social
    observer 31, 33, 38, 60, 61, 254, 270
Salisbury, Marquis of 176, 177, 276
Salvation Army 118
Salvini, Tomasso (actor) 157
'Sam Hall' 41, 56–7
Sambourne, Linley and Marion 164–5, 290–1
Sand, George (novelist) 34
Sangalli, Rita (ballerina) 233
Sans Pareil Theatre (*see* Adelphi Theatre)
Sans Souci Theatre, Strand and Leicester
    Square 20, 75, 223
Santiago de los Santos (dwarf) 92
Santley, Charles (singer) 199
Saturday Review, The 236
Savile, Sir George 19

Savile House 19, 92–4, 102
Savile Row 24–25, 28, 283, 287
Savoy hotel, Strand 119, 182, 189, 265,
    271–5, 278
Savoy hotel restaurant 1, 124, 227, 254,
    256, 265, 278
Savoy Theatre, Strand 125, 138, 145, 166, 173,
    177, 180, 182, 183, 224, 226
Scarlet Pimpernel, The (Orczy) 177–8
scenery and design, stage 156, 167, 168, 176,
    183, 187, 188, 224
School for Scandal, The (Sheridan) 67, 167
Schneer, Jonathan (historian) 303
Schwartz, Vanessa R. (cultural historian) 6, 264
science 87, 96, 97, 98, 100, 102, 137
Scott, Clement (theatre critic) 159, 193, 256
Scott, Jane (actress and playwright) 64, 72–4
Scott, John (founder of the Adelphi
    Theatre) 72, 75
Scott, Sir Walter 64, 155, 267, 287
Secret Service (Gillette) 261
Select Committee on Dramatic Literature
    (1832) 82
Selfridge, Harry Gordon 279, 280, 283,
    294–6, 314
Selfridge's, Oxford Street (department store)
    124, 138, 280, 281, 289, 294–6, 297, 314, 315
sensory dimensions of West End 5, 119–26
Serle, Thomas (playwright) 78
sexuality 7, 95–6, 119, 123, 130–5, 178, 211–2,
    217, 233, 265
Shaftesbury Avenue 1, 3, 10, 107, 109, 111, 113,
    114, 115, 122, 183, 184, 206
Shaftesbury, Earl of (Anthony Ashley-Cooper)
    (philanthropist) 111
Shaftesbury Theatre (1888–1941), Shaftesbury
    Avenue 180, 183
Shaftesbury Theatre (1911-), *see* Prince's Theatre
Shakespeare, William 18, 67, 80, 111–12, 154–5,
    156, 157, 173, 177, 178, 180
Shannon, Mary (literary critic and
    historian) 147–8
Shaw, George Bernard 64, 169, 173, 177, 192,
    193–4, 197, 241, 287
Shelton Street, Covent Garden 112
Sheridan, Richard Brinsley (playwright, MP and
    theatre owner) 13, 23, 64, 67, 167
Sherwell, Arthur (social reformer) 117, 136
She Would and She Would Not (Cibber) 13
Shoolbred's, Tottenham Court Road (department
    store) 289, 291
shops, shopping and retail 3, 7–8, 10, 19, 21–40,
    69, 72, 92, 108, 110, 111, 122, 123, 124, 136,
    139, 148, 154, 226, 250, 279–98, 309, 312–3

shopgirls, *see* shop workers
Shop Girl, The (Dam and Ross) 221, 226, 288
shop workers 3, 35, 38, 250, 290, 291, 296–7
Sickert, Walter (artist) 200
Siddons, Sarah (actress) 64, 79
Simpsons, Tottenham Court Road (building contractors) 184
Simpson's in the Strand (cigar divan and restauarant) 54, 278
Sisson, Thomas (hairdresser) 22
Sketch, The 129, 216, 260, 285
Slate, Ruth (feminist) 312
Slaters restaurant chain 257
slavery 77, 84
Smirke, Robert (architect) 68
Smirke, Sidney (architect) 37
Smith, Albert (lecturer and mountaineer) 60, 101–2, 132
Smith, Edward (publican and theatre manager) 161, 163
Smith, Frederick Edwin (politician) 278
Smith, Sir George Reeves (hotelier) 276
Smith, Samuel (Liberal MP) 179
Smith, Walter (poster manufacturer) 128
smoking 54, 55, 60, 191–2
Snow, John (doctor) 117
Soane, Sir John (architect) 28
Social Democratic Federation 311, 312
Society (Robertson) 169
Society Butterfly, A (Buchanan and Murray) 129
Society of Antiquaries, Burlington House 53, 137
Society of Female Artists 139
Society of Painters in Water Colours, Pall Mall 140
Society of West End Theatre Managers 173, 262
Soho 3, 5, 7, 18, 26, 59, 61, 109, 111, 113–18, 284, 302, 308, 310
Soho Bazaar 30, 281
Soho Square 30, 113, 114
soldiers at West End entertainments 14, 42, 134, 188, 227, 231–2, 234, 237, 255, 271, 276, 306
Sonnhammer, Charles (music hall owner) 206
Sotheby's, on Wellington Street up to 1917 (auctioneers) 139
Sothern, Edward Askew (actor) 157, 170
Soyer, Alexis (leading chef) 43, 55–6
Spence, Thomas (land reformer) 308
Spiers and Pond (catering company) 249, 257
sporting gentlemen and sporting set 43, 50, 133, 249, 255, 268
Sporting Times (Pink 'Un) 255
Sprague, William George (theatre architect) 112, 183, 184

stage-door Johnnies 188
Standard, The 129, 191
Stanfield, Clarkson (panoramas) 90
stars and stardom 10, 46, 127, 129–30, 274
Star, The 203
Stead, William Thomas (campaigning journalist) 238
Stevens, Thomas (labourer) 311
Steer, Jean (ladies' hairdressing) 280
Stenbridge, Charles (food importer and salesman) 256
Stoker, Bram (novelist and theatre manager) 187, 188
Stoll, Sir Oswald (theatre and music hall owner) 219, 221, 239, 243
Strand, the 2, 15, 16, 19, 23, 24, 39, 52, 53, 55, 67, 71, 73, 75, 98, 107, 110, 112, 118, 124, 133, 137, 138, 146, 147, 148, 157, 161, 163, 173, 183, 222, 223, 257, 260, 270, 271, 285, 286, 295, 297, 302, 307, 308, 309, 311, 312, 313
Strand Theatre, Aldwych (now the Novello Theatre) 183
Strauss, Johann 273
Streets of London, The (Boucicault) 169
String of Pearls The (James Malcolm Rymer) 70
Stuart, Helena (comedian) 206
Studholme, Marie (Gaiety Girl) 130, 131, 227, 229
suburbs 5, 6, 50, 110, 121, 136, 170, 241
Suffolk Street, Haymarket 161
Suffolk Street Gallery, Suffolk Street 140
Suffragettes 249–50, 312–14
Sullivan, Sir Arthur 145, 146, 166, 169, 173, 219, 224, 226, 274, 306
Sunday Times, The 193
Sunshine Girl, The (Rubens) 243
Surrey Theatre, Blackfriars Road 71
Suthurst, Thomas (barrister) 297
Swallow Street, Piccadilly 26, 28
Swan and Edgar (drapers) 36, 110, 123, 285, 286, 289, 290, 313
Swanborough, Edwin (music hall owner) 208, 211, 212
Swans, The (ballet) 234
Swinburne, Algernon (poet) 61
Sylph of the Glen, The (ballet) 233
Sylphide, La (ballet) 47, 233
Sylvester, William Henry (photographer) 130
Symons, Arthur (poet) 203–4, 236, 243–4, 254

'Tableaux vivants' (*see poses plastiques*)
Taglioni, Marie (ballet dancer) 47–8
tailors and tailoring 23, 24–25, 115, 116
Tale of Mystery, A (Holcroft) 70

Tango (dance) 243
Tartuffe (Moliere) 21
'Ta-ra-ra-Boom-de-ay' (music hall song) 128
Tavistock hotel, Covent Garden 269
Taylor, Tom (playwright) 157, 165, 168, 169
tea shops 109, 139, 257, 258–9, 309
Tempest, Marie (actress) 230
Tennyson, Alfred Lord 177
Terris, William (actor) 304
Terry, Ellen (actress) 157, 190, 191, 215
Terry, Fred (actor) 177
Terry, Kate (actress) 156
Terry's Theatre, Strand 180, 181
Thackeray, William Makepeace (novelist) 42, 60, 148, 190
Theatre Regulation Act (1843) 83, 160
Theatre Royal, Covent Garden, *see* Royal Opera House
Theatre Royal, Drury Lane 13–14, 15, 18, 42, 47, 50, 65, 67, 68, 71, 72, 77, 78, 79, 80, 81–2, 83, 90, 95, 143, 147, 161, 163, 165, 166, 173, 176, 180, 181, 200, 219, 235, 303, 304, 305, 314
Theatre Royal, Haymarket 15, 30, 65, 76, 77, 81, 154, 161, 162, 166, 169, 181, 183, 185, 187, 190, 196, 306
Theatre, The 130
Theatres and theatre going 2, 3, 4, 5, 7, 13–14, 19, 21, 42, 48, 63–83, 89, 103, 107, 111, 114, 119, 122, 124, 127, 128, 131, 134, 146, 149, 153–98, 253, 255, 260, 302 , 309, 315
(*see also* audiences, first nights and names of individual theatres)
Theatrical Benevolent Society 81
Thénevon, Daniel Nicholas (founder of Café Royal) 254
Thespis (Gilbert and Sullivan) 145
Thomas, (Walter) Brandon (actor and playwright) 173, 176
Thoviste, Caroline (vendor of pornography) 130
'Thumb, Tom' (Charles Sherwood Stratton) 99
Ticket of Leave Man, The (Taylor) 168
Timbs, John (antiquarian) 37, 60
Times, The 159, 179, 301
Tivoli Theatre of Varieties, Strand 128, 204
Tom and Jerry (Moncrieff) 30, 35, 64, 74, 78
Tom Cribb's, Panton Street (pub) 50
Toole's Theatre, King William IV Street 173
Toryism, *see* conservatism
Tottenham Court Road 163, 181, 184, 235, 284
Tottenham Street Theatre 82
touring of plays 176
Town, The (newspaper) 53
tourism 3, 90, 91

toys 101, 114
toy theatres 156
Trafalgar Square 39, 270, 308–9, 310, 311, 312, 314
transport 17, 28
Travatore, Il (Verdi) 144, 206
Traviata, La (Verdi) 199
Traveller's Club, Pall Mall 43
Tree, Herbert Beerbohm (actor) 176, 177, 181, 189, 190, 192, 193, 194–8, 242, 306
Tree, Maud Beerbohm (actress) 129, 177, 306
Tree, Viola Beerbohm Tree (actress) 198
Trial by Jury (Gilbert and Sullivan) 145
Trilby (Potter) 176, 193, 204
Trocadero, Coventry Street (as music hall) 204, 217 (as restaurant) 255, 301
Trollope, Anthony 159
tube, *see* underground railway
Turner, Joseph Mallord William (painter) 55
Tussaud, Madame Marie (waxworks) 71, 99
Tynan, Kenneth (theatre critic) 193

Ude, Louis Eustache (chef) 51
Unity Club, Strand 61
underground railway 110
United Service Club 43

Valmore, Jenny (singer) 212
Vampire, The (Boucicault) 167
Vance, Alfred 'The Great' (singer) 199
Vandenhoff, John (actor) 76
variety theatre 202, 219–45
Vaudeville Theatre, Strand 161, 183, 185, 193, 261, 306
Vauxhall Gardens (pleasure gardens) 17, 30, 44, 143
Veblen, Thorstein (sociologist) 270
Verdi, Giuseppe (composer) 199
Verity, Frank (architect) 234
Verity, Thomas (architect) 183, 234, 249
Vermont, Marquis de (social observer) 46
Verrey's restaurant, Regent Street 166, 254, 256
Vestris, Auguste (ballet dancer) 80
Vestris, Eliza (actress) 33, 72, 73, 80, 171, 181
Victoria, Queen 24, 28, 55, 94, 144, 153, 161, 162, 268, 305, 306
Victoria Station 110, 154, 282
Villiers, Robert Edwin (music hall owner) 208, 211, 213
Vining, James (actor) 171
visual culture 86, 87–91, 103, 122–25, 127–8, 132, 172, 303
Vogel, Paul (waiters' union) 310

Voltaire (François-Marie Arouet) 55
Voysey Inheritance, The (Barker) 194

Wagner, Richard 144, 219
waiters and waitresses 212, 251, 258–9, 260,
    273, 309–10
Waldorf hotel, Aldwych 112, 275
Walhalla, Leicester Square 94–5
Walker, Lynne (social historian) 109
Walker, Romaine (interior decorator) 195
Walkowitz, Judith R. (cultural historian) 7, 238
Wallis, Ellen (actress) 180
Ward, John, Leicester Square (furniture) 284
Wardour Street, Soho 114
Ware, Samuel (architect) 32
Waring and Gilllow, Oxford Street (department
    store) 284
Warren, Sir Charle (Commissioner of
    Police) 312
Warton, Madame (Eliza Crow) 94–5
Waste (Barker) 194
Waterloo (Conan Doyle) 306
Watier's (club) 50
waxworks 71, 94
Weber, Carl Maria von (composer) 144
Weber, William (music historian) 140
Webster, Benjamin (actor manager) 161–2,
    164, 169
Wedgwood pottery 17
Welch, Jimmy (actor) 242
Wellington Street, Covent Garden 71, 147–8,
    206, 222
West Central Jewish Girls' Club, Soho 115
West End of London, defined 2, 42, 107, 146, 157
West End Synagogue 118
Weston, John (tailor) 23
White Bear Coaching Inn, Piccadilly 267
White's (gentleman's club) 42, 43, 51
Whiteley, William (department store
    owner) 289–90
Wilberforce, William 24
Wilde, Oscar 42, 64, 115, 123, 169, 173, 176,
    183, 200, 235, 238, 254, 265, 287
Wilhelm, C (stage designer) 235
William IV 38, 70
Williams, Bransby (actor) 239

Willis, Frederick (memoirist) 234, 263, 283–4
Wilson, Keith (literary critic) 217
Wilton (later Bancroft), Marie (actor
    manager) 157, 163, 164, 169, 185
Wimpole Street 25
Western Literary and Scientific Institution 96
Westminster Jews Free School 115
Westminster Review, The 147
White, George (American impresario) 221
Wigmore Hall, Wigmore Street 141
Wingrove, Louise (music hall historian) 213
Woman's World 291
women, female identity, feminisation and female
    consumers 7, 34–5, 36, 38, 39, 41, 43–4,
    45–6, 69, 80, 109, 123, 162, 166, 176, 185,
    192, 202–3, 208, 213, 214–5, 226, 227, 229,
    236–7, 242, 245, 249–50, 254, 256, 258, 278,
    280–1, 283, 285–6, 288, 294, 295,
    296–7, 302
Women's Social and Political Union 250, 312
Wood, Henry (conductor) 141
working classes 4, 46, 51, 52, 59, 65, 67, 68, 82,
    113–16, 119, 121, 148, 154, 160, 163, 164,
    165, 178, 180, 188, 204, 206, 213, 222, 283,
    297, 303, 309–10
World, The 159
Worth, Charles (fashion designer) 285
Wright and Ridgway, Piccadilly (bookshop) 23
Wyatt, Benjamin (architect) 51, 68
Wyatt, Philip (architect) 51
Wyatt, James (architect) 37
Wych Street, Covent Garden 57, 72, 112, 307
Wycherley, William 68
Wyld, James (MP) 96
Wyndham, Charles (actor manager) 180, 301
Wyndham's Theatre, Charing Cross Road 180,
    183, 191, 301

Yates, Edmund (journalist and novelist) 57, 102,
    159, 171
Yates, Frederick (actor manager) 161, 171
Yokel's Preceptor 132
Youth (Harris) 305

Zanettos (jugglers) 211
Ziegfield, Florenz (American impresario) 221